D0793621

Media Ownership and Concentration in America

Media Ownership and Concentration in America

Eli M. Noam

OXFORD
UNIVERSITY PRESS
2009

OXFORD
UNIVERSITY PRESS

Oxford University Press, Inc., publishes works that further
Oxford University's objective of excellence
in research, scholarship, and education.

Oxford   New York
Auckland   Cape Town   Dar es Salaam   Hong Kong   Karachi
Kuala Lumpur   Madrid   Melbourne   Mexico City   Nairobi
New Delhi   Shanghai   Taipei   Toronto

With offices in
Argentina   Austria   Brazil   Chile   Czech Republic   France   Greece
Guatemala   Hungary   Italy   Japan   Poland   Portugal   Singapore
South Korea   Switzerland   Thailand   Turkey   Ukraine   Vietnam

Copyright © 2009 by Oxford University Press Inc.

Published by Oxford University Press, Inc.
198 Madison Avenue, New York, New York 10016

www.oup.com

Oxford is a registered trademark of Oxford University Press

Library of Congress Cataloging-in-Publication Data
Noam, Eli M.
Media ownership and concentration in America / Eli M. Noam.
p.   cm.
Includes bibliographical references and index.
ISBN 978-0-19-518852-3
1. Mass media—Ownership—United States. 2. Telecommunication—
Ownership—United States. 3. Mass media—Economic aspects—United States.
4. Mass media—Political aspects—United States. I. Title.
P96.E252.U644 2007
302.230973—dc22   2007003546

9 8 7 6 5 4 3 2 1
Printed in the United States of America
on acid-free paper

For Nadine, Defender of Liberty

Acknowledgments

A project of this magnitude could not have been completed without the help, commitment, and labors of many research assistants, interns, and collaborators. They deserve many thanks. Several people stand out. Robert Freeman started thirteen years ago as a research assistant on an earlier version of the project and soon ended up drafting several of the survey sections. I would have been pleased to have completed the project jointly with him, but he moved on in 1997 to a career in law. He is owed many thanks for his contribution. Michael Turner, as a doctoral student in political science at Columbia, developed an early database and organized the information. The third essential person in this project, and the one deserving much credit for the data and graphs, has been Joost van Dreunen, doctoral student in communications at Columbia. Joost combined intelligence and tenacity with skill and judgment.

I also thank CITI's research managers over the period of this project—Ken Carter, Rosa Morales, Benjamin Bloom, and John Heywood.

On the publishing and editing side of this project, special thanks for their commitment and help go to James Cook, Suzanne Copenhagen, Sara Needles, John Rauschenberg, Christi Stanforth, and Jessica Ryan.

Given the sensitivity of the topic of media concentation, we have purposely avoided financial support by any firm or industry for the study; its origin was a small grant by the German government's Monopoly Commission for a report on trends in American media ownership. We are grateful for that impetus by Dr. Horst Greiffenberg and Professor Carl-Christian von Weizsäcker. We could draw on the Alfred P. Sloan Foundation as the major supporter of the Columbia Institute for Tele-Information (CITI), and thank Ralph Gomery and Frank Mayadas. Other general support of CITI, in small amounts and not specific to this project, comes from corporate affiliates, none of whom played any role in its content or process, and none of which is central to the mass media concentration debate (HBO is the exception, and its support is minor and not project related). Nor, it should be added, have I conducted any work for any of the firms, industries, or stakeholders subject to the analysis, invested in them, or worked for the FCC or Justice Department. I have, however, served as a Public Service Commissioner of New York State, which included responsibility for regulating the state's telecom and energy industries.

Of all the people deserving thanks, the deepest goes to my wife Nadine Strossen, for eighteen years National President of the American Civil Liberties Union, a leader in the struggle for free and diverse media, and my inspiration.

Contents

PART I

INTRODUCTION

Once upon a time there were the mass media, and they were wicked, of course, and there was a guilty party. Then there were the virtuous voices that accused the criminals. And Art (ah, what luck!) offered alternatives, for those who were not prisoners of the mass media.
Well, it's all over. We have to start again from the beginning, asking one another what's going on.

Umberto Eco

1

The Debate over Media Concentration and Ownership

ABOUT THIS BOOK

This book is a study of the American media and information sector over two decades—its change, its dynamics, and its concentration and ownership trends. Why this subject? A major debate has been unfolding in the United States and around the world over media concentration and its implications. In the policy arena this debate is often marked more by heat than by light. It is therefore the aim of this book to create a decent fact base, to interpret the data, and to analyze the underlying dynamics.

When it comes to media concentration, views are strong, theories abound, but numbers are scarce. To many media critics, the sky has been falling for decades. Others, often from free-market Washington policy think tanks or from the libertarian Internet community, believe that market and technological forces are overcoming all barriers, that we are in the midst of a flowering of media and information, and that there is no problem except for heavy-footed bureaucrats trampling those flowers. Media companies and other stakeholders deployed the arguments of both positions, depending on which side of a particular regulatory battle they were on. Advocacy groups sprang up. Academics became activists. The newspaper press chimed in, often opposing media concentration but seldom mentioning that local newspapers are perhaps the most concentrated news medium

of all. Commercial television rarely touched the topic beyond its immediate news aspects, thereby strengthening the arguments of its critics that self-interest colors its coverage.[1]

Part of the vehemence of the debate stems from the self-image of its advocates on both sides. Opponents of media concentration view themselves as engaged in a digital Thermopylae, a last line of defense against homogenized news controlled by five giant media conglomerates. They fear a situation for the United States like that of Italy, where Silvio Berlusconi used his media empire to achieve policy power and public office. In contrast, defenders of a deregulation of ownership restrictions see themselves as removing the shackles of the state. They argue that we are in the midst of a historic blossoming of information technology. Both sides project themselves as defenders of free speech, either protecting media from the heavy hand of government or, alternatively, protecting diversity from being choked off by communications empires. Both sides are to some extent correct. But both sides cannot concede the validity of the perspective of the other, which they view, respectively, as the grave diggers of democracy or as luddites with academic tenure.

Given all these perspectives and biases, how then should public policy be determined? At a minimum, it should be based on a solid factual base on the nature of the problem. It is one thing to disagree on the interpretation, whether a glass is half-full or half-empty, and what then to do about it. But it is quite another matter to disagree whether that glass is largely empty or full. It is therefore essential to proceed beyond a fixation on selective facts that are culled to suit respective policy preferences. Who is right? Are media becoming controlled by the few and closed to the many? Despite much conventional wisdom and anecdotes, the answer to this question is not an obvious "yes." And despite the hand-waving of free marketeers, the answer is not an obvious "no," either.

This then is the goal of this book: to answer the question of whether, where, and how American media are becoming more (or less) concentrated. Given the intensity of debate, it should be the role of academia to step back and help shed that light. This is the impetus for this book. Having heard political rhetoric and war stories for too long from both sides, I concluded that we needed a decent fact base as a foundation for policy making and further research. As the late Senator and Professor Daniel Patrick Moynihan was fond of saying, "you are entitled to your own opinion but not to your own facts."

To gather such a fact base is both exciting and tedious. As a regular columnist for the *Financial Times* (online edition), I can attest that writing opinion is much more fun than assembling an information-dense book covering 100 information industries over 25 years. But the subject is too important for shortcuts.

This is how the study proceeds: First, it discusses the dynamics of industries or industry clusters and provides a methodology (Chapters 1–3). It then provides market share data analysis and narration (Chapters 4–12) for each industry; calculates national, local, vertical and ownership concentration trends; and aggregates the data into increasingly larger segments and sectors (Chapters 12–16). It provides an explanatory model for long-term concentration trends, a new index for measuring local media concentration, and a concluding analysis (Chapters 17–20). I wish this could have been done more briefly but the topic requires thoroughness and consistency.

Why include so many industries? When people talk about media concentration, they tend to focus on a few examples, often picked based on their particular interest. Those fearing media concentration are likely to point to television. Those believing in the existence of media diversity are likely to emphasize the Internet. Those concerned with access to broadband networks will focus on telecom. Those worried about software applications will look at operating systems. At any given time, some media will concentrate while others diversify. The only meaningful way is not to pick and choose examples but to look across the broad sweep of media. Of course, specific problems should not be submerged in a big average, and we therefore also analyze and discuss the data for specific industries as well as for broader subcategories of industries.

Inevitably, different users of this book will focus on the industries they are most interested in and seek a greater granularity in its coverage. On the other hand, they will find the differentiation of industries outside their scope of interests to be excessive. Thus, for those involved in television content, there can be a world of difference between broadcast networks, cable channels, and syndicators. To those less involved, it's all just "TV programs." Similarly, for techies, there is a big difference between (and within) memory chips and microprocessors, whereas others might see them merely as variants of semiconductors.

Yet why go at all beyond mass media? Isn't the key issue the concentration of TV, newspapers, or cable TV? To many people, the focus is indeed the concentration of mass media. But to others the key concentration question is the dominance of Microsoft. To still others, it is the stranglehold of AT&T and its successor Bell companies over the network infrastructure. For decades, the regulatory battles in Washington over that control have been vastly more ferocious and tenacious than those regarding television. The importance one attaches to a partial segment of media and communications tends to be a reflection of one's interests, values, and professional sphere. To denigrate the importance of other segments of the information sector can be parochial. And it has no future. The underlying technologies of the information sector are growing closer. And their basic economics are becoming increasingly similar.

Even if the discussion of IT in this book or telecom sectors may be more detailed than necessary for readers primarily interested in mass media, they should recognize that for any intersectoral comparison to be meaningful the methodology and specificity must be similar. The only alternative to a full-scale analysis of IT, consumer media electronics, and telecom is not to have any cross-sectoral analysis at all.

The study was conducted without any pre-conception as to where the data would lead and without any attempt to prove a point or advocate a position. I did not reach final conclusions until the data for each industry had been collected, processed, analyzed, and aggregated. I had to revise several earlier preliminary conclusions.

As the study progressed, I was exhorted to also provide policy recommendations. I have resisted doing so here. For the present, the intermingling of normative policy analysis and positive data research would diminish the empirical contribution. Others have urged me to analyze the societal impacts of media concentration. This, too, is important, but it is not the question that this already long book addresses, and it is a topic that has already received much attention.

Another proposed dimension for potential expansion was to globalize it. But to do so would have blurred the focus of study. That said, the next step for this effort, already underway, is an international comparative effort based on expert partners in several countries. For now, only a brief section touches the subject.

What conclusion does the study reach? Because this is a long book, a preview is in order. There are numerous industry and sector-specific findings included in the various chapters. But several of the overarching findings will be briefly summarized here.

- Did concentration in the information sector rise in recent years? *No*, if the baseline year for comparison is 1984 or earlier. (The optimists are right.) *Yes*, if the baseline year is 1992. (The pessimists are right.) *No* again, if the baseline is 2001.
- We observe a U-shaped concentration trend pervading across the share of the information sector over the two decades. Of the 100 industries analyzed, we find the U-trend for 41%. It is a strong trend that cuts across numerous industries and characterizes three of the four subsectors of the information sector—IT, telecom, and the Internet.
- In distinct contrast, the mass media sector followed a rising S-shaped pattern, increasing in concentration slowly after 1988, rapidly from 1996 to 2001, and slowly thereafter. But its average concentration is at a much lower level than the rest of the information sector, and it is unconcentrated by the legal standards of the U.S. government's Antitrust Merger

Guidelines. This comparison does not imply that mass media concentration is low, since a strong case can be made for stricter concentration thresholds for mass media than for other industries. The average level of market concentration in the mass media is not in the range that would normally raise antitrust action if encountered in other industries. Hence, if one seeks a systematic deconcentration of media below the one prevailing, the general antitrust process is not likely to work.

- As concentration in mass media has steadily increased over the two decades, it has come closer to the concentration levels prevailing in the rest of the information sector. Whereas in 1984 mass media HHI concentration was only one quarter of that of the overall information sector, it was three quarters in 2005.
- Generally, the more electronic and "digital" a media subsector is, the more highly it seems to be concentrated, and the more it becomes subject to the more general economic dynamics of the information sector.
- Strong economies of scale, network effects, distance-insensitivity, and high complexity have led to a consolidation for the Internet itself as well as for many of its major applications. This pours cold water over the hope that the Internet will solve the media concentration problem. Key parts of this sector exhibits the same dynamics leading to concentration. If anything, its greater rate of change drives it there faster.
- There are only a handful of industries in the monopoly range (market share of over 60%). American information and media industries are not monopolies but more likely to be oligopolies. In the mass media industries, the average industry structure is a top firm of 23%, 3 firms of about 10%, and 5–10 smaller firms. But these are not necessarily the same firms across the various industries.
- The top five mass media firms accounted together for about 13% of the mass media sector in 1984. By 2005, their share had doubled to 26%. Even so, their aggregate share was much lower than that prevailing in many industries, and in the telecom and IT sectors, where the top five companies held an aggregate share of 61% and 43%.
- If we look solely at the electronic mass media, the top five firms' share was 42%, double

that of 1984. For the part of electronic mass media under the overall regulatory supervision of the FCC, the market share of the top five firms declined to 18% in 1992, then rose pronouncedly to 40% in 2001 and 42% in 2005.

- In the overall information sector, the smaller of the large firms increased in share, whereas the largest of firms saw it reduced.
- For all the talk of convergence, there is not much direct expansion by firms active in one traditional sector of the information sector (mass media, telecom, IT) directly into the others. The exception has been the Internet, which seems to be the ground on which other firms from the more traditional sectors meet and contest.
- The ownership by "insiders" (the major owners and founders, their families, and the top managers) declined significantly for most of the largest information sector firms. Even for mass media firms, where it is higher than in the rest of the information sector, it fell from 35% to 20%.
- At the same time, institutional ownership rose from 40% to 57% for the mass media sector and from 49% to 61% for the IT and telecom sector.
- Who then owns the media? The institutions with the largest equity positions in the major media companies include State Street Global Advisors ($68 billion), Barclays ($57 billion), Capital Research & Management ($47 billion), Fidelity Management & Research ($41 billion), Vanguard Group ($30 billion), and Wellington Management ($29 billion). Pension funds such as TIAA/CREF were also big investors.
- The largest institutional owners hold only a few percent (at most) of any single media company, but have stakes in many firms. Just twelve institutional investors own a quarter of the average top 25 mass media firms and 30% of the top IT and telecom companies. Thus, the view that the information companies are owned by a small group of media moguls is not an accurate one. A better description is one of a few dozen institutions owning many small slices of a very big pie.
- In the next chapter we present a simple model for the dynamics of the information sector. It is based on two variables, lower entry barriers, which induce a new entry, and growing

scale economies, which lead to a more concentrated market structure. Together, these two factors and their changes induce an upwardly trending oscillation trend.

The model and the observed forces in the information industries lead structurally to a two-tier media system, based on

1. Large integrator firms, assembling and bundling elements mostly produced by others, operating in an oligopolistic industry structure.
2. Numerous specialist firms surrounding the integrators in geographic and functional clusters and providing much of actual production and service elements. Some of these specialists may be quite large themselves and dominate their niche. But many of them are small and/or operate in competitive submarkets.

To summarize then, the concentration of the overall information sector has followed a U-shaped path, following dynamics that are explained in the theoretical model. It declined pronouncedly after 1984. It rose markedly after 1992, though to a level lower than where it used to be. And it declined again slightly after 2001. However, in mass media the trend was different. It increased fairly steadily over the period. But that concentration, although rising, is much lower than is often assumed. Yet this may be only a temporary consolation. Because of the economic dynamics of digital media this concentration is likely to increase further, though away from the conglomerate model that combines numerous media types. The media future is likely to be dominated by a few relatively focused integrator firms that put together elements provided by numerous smaller specialist firms.

Limited government rules on media ownership worked reasonably well originally when industries were simple and tools of control existed. But outside the ordered broadcast licensing scheme, the government's powers today are much more limited and becoming more so. If Google has significant market power, how should or could the search engine market be restructured? If a firm located in Korea is dominant in interactive games, what then is the U.S. government's remedy? Or, if Skype, the broadband telephony provider, becomes the vastly preferred voice telephony choice, how would one deal with that? And these are merely conceptual questions, to which are added those of politics, litigation, international trade, intellectual property rights, and international enforcement. It is always difficult for laws or regulations to modify fundamental transitions of industries. It is particularly difficult to do so where, as in the case of media, any regulation in a free society needs to be one of a light touch.

There is nothing new about this dilemma, as the next subchapter will discuss.

A LOST GOLDEN AGE?

Many people have worried, for many years, about the concentration of private power over the media. The fear is of a media mogul with a political agenda: a William Randolph Hearst who used his newspapers to help start a war, and who promoted himself for mayor, governor, and president. A Colonel Robert McCormick who ran a personal and political crusade against prep schoolmate Franklin D. Roosevelt and his New Deal and internationalism. Later, when television was controlled by three networks, all within ten blocks of each other in Manhattan, warning bells rang from the left and the right about control over hearts and minds, pocketbooks, and voting booths. And today, with electronic media becoming smart, powerful, and pervasive, with media mergers announced regularly, the same fear abounds more than ever: that in the end there will be only a handful of media companies remaining in the world and running the world.

Discussion of media concentration is not new. It has been part and parcel of historic discussion of media. The fewer choices, the greater their economic power. The fewer voices, the greater their political and idea power. Such fears go back in the United States to its early history, as can be seen in the following bird's eye overview of American media history.

In 1682, William Bradford, a printing apprentice, traveled to Pennsylvania with William Penn and received a printing monopoly. He was instructed by the ruling Quaker authority "not to print any thing but what shall have Lycense from ye Council."[2] In 1705 his son Andrew established a similar monopoly in New York.[3] (This was not an unusual arrangement. In politically turbulent seventeenth-century England, at various times only a single printer was licensed.)

In North America after the 1720s, print publications became more competitive. In Boston, newspapers grew in numbers to five in 1735.[4] Some consolidation took place in response. In 1741, probably the first media merger in North America took place, with the *Boston Gazette* consolidating with the *New England Weekly*.[5] In Philadelphia, the Bradfords' pro-establishment *Mercury* got Benjamin Franklin's more outspoken *Gazette* as competition. Franklin became the earliest American media mogul. As Walter Isaacson— journalist, biographer, and later CNN and Aspen Institute head—writes,

> Franklin's print shop had by [1748] grown into a successful, vertically integrated media conglomerate. He had a printing press, publishing house, newspaper, an almanac series, and partial control of the postal system. He also had built a network of profitable partnerships and franchises from Newport and New York to Charleston and Antigua. Money flowed in.[6]

Given Franklin's pioneering role in electricity, he undoubtedly would have moved into electronic media too, had he lived another fifty years to see them. The debate over the language of the First Amendment to the U.S. Constitution shows that from the beginning the press was seen as part of the institutions of political checks and balances, a counterforce to authority.[7] But in practice it was often a deployed tool rather than an independent voice. In the early days of the Republic, major political figures and parties routinely paid bribes and subsidies to assure favorable press support. Because most newspapers in the 1790s were advancing the conservative Federalist party's cause, Thomas Jefferson personally subsidized Republican-leaning papers such as the *National Gazette* and the Philadelphia *Aurora*.[8]

The power of the *Aurora* was heatedly denounced by the opposition. John Quincy Adams fulminated against the influence of its editor William Duane: "He had obtained by extortion almost the whole of the public printing."[9] And Treasury Secretary Albert Gallatin added: "[Duane was] possessed of an engine [the *Aurora*] which gives him irresistible control over public opinion."[10]

Circulation of newspapers rose as prices fell to a penny in 1833 under the leadership of New York's *Sun*, which sold 20,000 copies, among the world's largest. There were 10 other newspapers in New York that year,[11] an impressive number, but their combined circulation was only 6,500, giving them a meager market share relative to the *Sun*'s.[12]

Alexis de Tocqueville discerned the commercial nature of culture already apparent in America in 1835 and linked it to democracy: "Democracy not only infuses a taste for letters among the trading classes, but introduces a trading spirit into literature."[13]

As the nineteenth century progressed, barriers to entry for newspapers dropped as paper, typesetting, and printing advanced technologically, and as distribution improved with rails and roads. The number of literate Americans rose, and with it newspaper circulation. Many cities boasted multiple newspapers,[14] and most of them were locally owned. This was the golden age of newspapers. But even in the nineteenth century, American print media were much more concentrated than nostalgia suggests. In 1897, the nation's leading periodical, *Munsey's Magazine*, with its short stories and controversial artistic illustrations of "half-dressed women and undressed statuary," as contemporary critics alleged, had a circulation of 700,000, almost 40% of U.S. general magazine circulation.

Frank Munsey, the magazine's proprietor, acquired newspapers as well as detractors. His obituary by a Kansas publisher read: "Frank Munsey contributed to the journalism of his day the great talent of a meat packer, the morals of a moneychanger, and the manners of an undertaker. He and his kind have about succeeded in transforming a once noble profession into an 8 percent security. May he rest in trust."[15]

Print media also became concentrated geographically. U.S. postal data for 1878 shows that of mailed print publications, 32.1% originated in New York, with Chicago (7.9%), Boston (6.6%), Philadelphia (5.4%), and other cities far behind.[16]

The telegraph, first among electronic transmission media, quickly became monopolized by the Western Union company, financed by J. P. Morgan. Western Union became the world's largest private company. Although in 1851 there had been over 50 different telegraph companies in America, by 1866 almost all had either consolidated into Western Union or failed. Railroad financier Jay Gould bought the company in 1881, giving him a national telegraph monopoly as well as control over the Associated Press. The *New York Times*

opined anxiously that Gould would control "what has been the free press of America."[17]

And indeed, the Associated Press, using the telegraph, soon held a dominant position over wire service news and used its power. The AP's leader William Henry Smith was a close political friend of Republican presidential candidate Rutherford Hayes, and used his position to manipulate the outcome of the presidential election of 1876. Hayes had lost the popular vote to Democrat Samuel Tilden, but the results from several southern states were disputed. Western Union, allied to AP, leaked confidential Democratic cables to Smith, and the AP also tilted its news coverage. This enabled Hayes to outmaneuver Tilden in the Electoral College. Democrats, after being denied the White House, labeled the AP the "Hayesociated Press."[18] Decades later, AP's still-persistent power led to an important antitrust case in which the U.S. Supreme Court forced it to offer its service to other newspapers on a nondiscriminatory basis.[19]

In wireline telephony, which emerged later in the nineteenth century, AT&T became a national near-monopolist and soon the world's largest private company. To moderate its market power, it was treated in every state as a "common carrier" that could not discriminate on the basis of content or users. Its profits, service quality, and offerings became heavily regulated by state and federal governments. The company also became a regular target of antitrust challenges. After 1982, these challenges led to the breakup of AT&T.

In radio-telegraphy, the Marconi Company, founded by inventor Guglielmo Marconi at the turn of the twentieth century, held a patent monopoly for maritime communications. It refused to license or sell equipment, placing instead its employees as operators onboard ships owned by others. Marconi for a time refused to allow the operators to communicate with those stations that were using other firms' equipment.[20]

Even theater, a medium one would expect to be heavily local, became considerably concentrated in the nineteenth century, owing to changing transportation technology. A system of traveling companies emerged after 1870, replacing the traditional system of local repertory companies and entrepreneurs. These nomadic productions relied on well-known plays and stars, often from England. Most of the touring companies were owned by larger firms headquartered in New York. Around 250 companies toured the country, but after the 1890s two firms dominated this traveling theater business and the booking, owning, and leasing of theaters in important cities.[21] One of the firms, the Theatrical Syndicate, was founded in 1896 and dominated the industry until 1910 when it was joined by an early incarnation of the Shubert Organization. For a time there were between one and five Shubert theaters in each major city in the United States.[22]

As the twentieth century dawned, new technologies established new media and distribution. The film industry witnessed almost immediately an attempt to organize a wall-to-wall monopoly. The Motion Picture Patents Company, also organized by J. P. Morgan, brought together the interests of Edison, Pathé, Eastman Kodak, Vitagraph, and Biograph. The cartel, known as the "Edison Trust," pooled its patents, transacted only with distributors that paid high royalties, and with theaters that agreed to charge high prices and follow censorship rules. But the cartel was unable to suppress independent producers, which often originated in the vaudeville theater industry. These firms, which soon became "Hollywood," still dominate the film medium. Much of the early history of the film industry can be read through the antitrust cases dealing with its market power and practices. The book business, too, stabilized by the 1920s into a leadership of about a dozen major publishing houses, all but one located in New York.[23]

When broadcast radio emerged in the 1920s, its technology was first dominated by a single company, RCA, which was formed at the U.S. government's instigation by joining the major patent owners, Westinghouse, AT&T, and American Marconi. Although the local radio stations were mostly independently owned because of regulatory caps on ownership, the main broadcast content was delivered nationally by a handful of largely unregulated networks, with the local stations being the retailers rather than the creators. RCA's broadcasting arm, NBC, became dominant in content with its two radio networks, the red and the blue. An antitrust action forced it to divest one network, which became ABC.

Later, when television emerged, it replicated the radio's network system, and three companies (for a long time basically only two and a half, ABC being the runt of the litter), all located near each other in Manhattan, dominated an enormously influential medium.

Also in the late 1940s, a new type of information technology began to emerge—computers—that would soon enable new forms of communication. Almost immediately this industry became dominated by a single firm, IBM, leading to several federal antitrust attempts to break up the firm. In 1981, IBM introduced its PC microcomputer, but pressured by the antitrust lawsuit, it chose a pro-competitive "open" architecture, with the microprocessor and operating software supplied by Intel and Microsoft under nonexclusive terms. It thereby launched these two firms to their own market dominance, which in turn was followed by controversy, legal challenge, and activist opposition.

The purpose of this thumbnail of American media history is to provide a context to today's controversies. Media concentration is not a new phenomenon in America, though it sometimes seems, as has been said for sex, that each generation believes that it has discovered it. On the contrary, media concentration has a long and contentious history, commented upon and fought over at each stage in the country's past and often leading to governmental counter-efforts such as antitrust actions.

Of course, just because a problem is old does not make it less important. The opposite is often true. But the historic perspective may moderate some of the rhetoric of a looming crisis, a falling sky, and a lost golden age that pervades many of today's debates. The issue of media concentration has a long past and will have an even longer future. It is one of those fundamental issues of distribution of power and wealth that every generation needs to resolve.

TODAY'S DEBATE

Today the debate over media concentration continues. Recent years have witnessed the expansion of large media firms in the United States. This development has led to fears that American communications media are increasingly controlled by an ever-shrinking number of firms, and that those firms are capable of affecting public opinion, the national agenda, democracy itself, and global culture.

Other countries, too, are watching the U.S. debate closely, not only because of the global role of American communications firms, but also because U.S. tendencies are often early indicators for developments elsewhere. Media concentration is an issue around the world. The debate has become the information-age version of the industrial-age struggle over the control of the means of production. That issue is a central element of socialist theory and politics. It led, in some countries, to revolution, and in other countries to the socialization of key industries. The United Kingdom, for example, nationalized its heavy industry sector after World War II. The underlying notion was that private ownership of coal and steel companies could be leveraged into control over the economy as a whole and with it into control over the political system. With hindsight, such fear and the policies they engendered seem overblown. It points to the need for a careful analysis of facts and dynamics before launching policies.

What, then, are these facts about American media concentration?

The answer to the empirical question is not as obvious as many sincerely believe. First, although numerous mergers have taken place and have led to huge global media companies, the mass media and information sector have also grown rapidly, despite widespread price declines.

Second, in the past, different information industries were clearly separated from each other by law and technology. With digital convergence a much discussed tendency, firms have been crossing the lines that once divided the mass media, telecommunications, and computer industries. Cable TV companies are offering phone services; phone companies are entering video; software providers are creating multimedia platforms; and print publishers supply electronic information.

Third, the internationalization of economies and services means that well-established media firms from other countries have gained a presence in the United States.

Fourth, new media have been emerging, most notably the Internet, creating new distribution channels for new content providers.

Thus, although the fish in the pond have grown in size, the pond grew too, and there have been new fish and new and connected ponds. None of this contradicts trends of concentration. But it raises questions of fact.

This brings us to recent debates. A particularly rancorous political battle in Washington has been over the rules limiting media concentration. In 2003, Michael Powell, chairman of the Federal Communications Commission, narrowly pushed through his commission a set of rules that relaxed several restrictions on the limits on ownership of TV stations by a single company.[24] The Federal Communications Commission (FCC) is required to review its ownership rules every two years, in accordance with the 1996 Telecommunications Act. Fox Television Stations, Inc., a subsidiary of News Corp, challenged these rules in 2001, and a court struck them down in 2002 as basically without evidentiary support for its strictness.[25] But once it embarked on a revision, the Commission's appetite for change grew, and its new rules made it easier to own more TV stations and to combine them with newspapers. Unfortunately for Powell, the two FCC commissioners who by law must be from the other (in this case, Democratic) party, launched an aggressive public offensive against Powell's proposed rules.[26]

The result was a political firestorm in which the political right and left joined forces against free market advocates and major media companies. Three million letters were written to the FCC and Congress. It led to a lopsided Congressional vote of 400: 21 opposing parts of the FCC's relaxation of ownership restrictions. The White House, after some brave talk of a Presidential veto, retreated. At the same time, another federal court overturned the FCC's rules, this time basically because they were without evidentiary support for its relaxation[27] (the draft rules had also been modified to accommodate some specific concerns of commissioners and companies). Eventually, in December 2007, Powell's successor as FCC chairman, Kevin Martin, narrowly pushed through a cross-ownership relaxation for the top 20 markets, and the battle moved back to Congress and the courts.[28]

Having served as politically appointed New York State Commissioner of Public Services (by Democratic Governor Mario Cuomo) and on the President's Advisory Committee for Information Technology (by Republican President George W. Bush), and having testified regularly to congressional committees, I am not entirely naïve about the political process. But even with such perspective, the stridency of some advocates seemed out of the ordinary.

To one congresswoman, Rep. Lynn Woolsey (D-Calif.), the FCC's loosening of the ownership rules was an attempt to impose a centralized "Saddam-style information system in the United States."[29]

Another Congressman, Maurice Hinchey (D-N.Y.), charged that media ownership deregulation was part of "mind control" strategy by Republicans who were trying to "dumb down" the public.[30] Yet, media concentration trends do not follow party power.[31] The sharpest increases in concentration actually occurred in the years of the Democratic Clinton administration, as will be seen. And the most radical deconcentration action by the U.S. government was the AT&T breakup in 1982, during the conservative Reagan administration. Both are likely to have happened under administrations controlled by the opposing party, too.

Politically, the fight against the FCC was an odd bedfellowship. It activated the political left together with parts of the organized creative community such as the Writers Guild and the Screen Actors Guild, and activist groups such as the National Organization for Women.

But much of Washington's political muscle was provided from the right by the National Rifle Association and evangelical groups, who organized a writing campaign that resulted in hundreds or thousands of letters criticizing change in regulations. Although media reformers had Rupert Murdoch and his conservative "fair-and-balanced" Fox News Channel as their bête noire, the NRA had the liberal, anti-gun, and gay-tolerant TV networks in its cross-hairs. White supremacists chimed in,[32] as did the Green Party.[33]

The *Economist* editorialized: "Behind almost every argument about why the FCC endangers democracy lurks a grudge about content: it is too conservative; it is too liberal; it is too violent; it under-represents feminists, or the Catholic Church. Merely cataloging these conflicting grievances shows the impossibility of ever resolving them."[34]

One would think the difference among the anti-FCC allies to be irreconcilable. (And indeed, after the victory of this coalition, each of its major components largely avoided even acknowledging its odd bedfellow's participation, while taking most credit for itself.) But they also have common and legitimate needs; as political participants and activists they are major users of media, and media access and diversity is vital to them. Together, they created a politically impressive demonstration of the wide opposition, across the spectrum, to powerful media companies.

According to a survey by one of the advocates, the Consumer Federation of America, 70% of respondents believed that media firms were becoming too large, 58% believed that mergers do not result in better content and services, 50% that

higher prices are the result, and 36% that quality declines. Newspaper–TV mergers were considered bad for their community by 49%, and 55 to 75% believed them bad for the country.[35]

Opposition came also from the media business community itself. It included media moguls Ted Turner and Barry Diller, as well as medium-sized TV station groups. Some advertising agencies also weighted in, fearing higher advertising prices in a more concentrated media market.[36]

Conservative columnist William Safire, normally an old antiregulatory hand at the *New York Times*, manned the barricades for government rules on media ownership.[37] Some of it may have been lingering resentment about how his old boss Richard Nixon had been treated by "the media" over Vietnam and Watergate. Safire's counterpart on the *New York Times* op-ed page, the liberal economic commentator and 2008 Nobelist Paul Krugman, was in rare agreement.[38]

On the other side were ideological libertarians, economic free-marketeers, large media firms, and the investment banking community.[39] But they were no match to the forces of opposition.

MEDIA REFORM AS SOCIAL REFORM

The activism over media concentration is part of a much larger mobilization that has been taking place in opposition to ongoing trends in the information sector. It is similarly manifest in the "open source" movement that battles Microsoft; in the "copyleft" community that challenges companies such as Disney that benefit from expansion of restrictive copyrights; in the privacy protection advocacy against the use of personal information by marketers; in the peer-to-peer file sharing, which has moved beyond piracy to an ideology and has brought the music industry to its knees;[40] in the "unlicensed spectrum" initiatives that seek to undermine the exclusivity of access to airwaves of broadcasters and wireless providers;[41] and in the move for municipal and free wi-fi connectivity challenging the phone companies.

All of these developments have their particular reasons but also a common thread. They are manifestations of a wider conflict over the role of the private sector in the information society. As the information sector permeates society, society in turn permeates the information sector, with its internal and international conflicts.

Most observers are familiar with the various flash points but have not always connected the dots and recognized the emerging social movement. For years, information companies and governments have touted their sector as the key to the planet's economic and cultural future and the solution to many of its problems. No wonder that control over this sector is being contested by more than business competitors. And in that disputatious process, the role of academic research and analysis becomes especially important.

Part of the reason for the high pitch of the debate is that for many critics, media concentration has been an ink blot into which they project their hopes and fears.

Deconcentrated media provide a greater *source diversity* of content. That, by itself, is essential to democracy. The argument for deconcentration could stop right here and be persuasive. But it does not, because many people earnestly believe that other ills of society would be remedied by media deconcentration.

Whether it is violence, gender stereotyping, racism, offensive policy, materialism, hedonism, escapism, low political participation, lack of political debate, entrenched status quo, inequality, drug dependency, even obesity or bulimia—for all these and more, the media system is held partly responsible either as a contributing cause or as an absent remedy. In consequence, many critics expect simply too much from a reform of media. The size and power of large media companies are seen as the cause of much that is wrong with society. And since so many of society's ills are blamed on media, media reform becomes social reform.

Yet those hopes will be invariably dashed. Media deconcentration will increase source diversity and invigorate, hopefully, political debate, but it is no substitute or shortcut to resolving most problems of society, even indirectly. Even many media-specific problems will not be answered by deconcentration.

The reader should understand that observing these limitations is not being sanguine about present or future media concentration, nor is it a conclusion against a deconcentration policy, nor is it a disagreement with the desirability of many of the goals. But it is a warning against unrealistic expectations attached to such policy.

Localism

Despite the tide of globalism—or perhaps because of it—communal bonds of geography, ethnicity, or shared interests have become increasingly important to many people. Localism has always been a strong value in America. Some of this sentiment is genuine, as evidenced in Thornton Wilder's *Our Town* or Norman Rockwell's nostalgia for small-town America. Some of it is political cover for other goals, such as racial discrimination, historically couched in the language of states' rights. Some of it is a historically rooted philosophy of a diffusion of power. Localism has practical arguments on its side and enjoys wide political support. Everyone loves localism, including the author. The fact that its advocates are frequently inconsistent and result-oriented does not diminish the argument.[42] Yet the economic pressures against localism are strong and growing everywhere. Technological and economic revolutions have transformed industries into large national units. Food grocers, restaurants, hardware stores, and clothing shops have evolved into national chains. Similar dynamics have affected the media sector, too.

To many people, the ideal is a system of public-spirited, small, locally based media. It is an appealing vision. The closest examples in the private sector are family-owned small-town newspapers that sometimes operate with a certain "noblesse oblige," forgoing some profit for community-spirited coverage. Yet with the greatest of sympathy for such a system, one must also recognize its problems. Economically, it is based on the extraction of monopoly profits from local advertisers. Anybody who has placed a classified ad in a local newspaper can attest to that power. Politically, it provides major influence to the proprietors and their heirs; even when such power is used sparingly, its existence is clear to any survival-minded official. Nor is local proprietorship always likely to be used in ways to many a critic's liking. William Loeb, for decades the irascible and opiniated owner of the *Manchester Union Leader* newspaper, exerted extraordinary and often negative influence over the affairs of the small state of New Hampshire and over the outcome of the nation's earliest (and important) presidential primary.

Control over a local medium can breed an arrogance of power. Colonel Robert R. McCormick ran the family's *Chicago Tribune*, for a time the nation's largest paper, with high-handed arbitrariness. For example, McCormick banned for a while any mentioning of the state of Rhode Island from the newspaper (and had it blotted out on maps published in the paper), as retaliation for that state's legislature passing horse-racing legislation he opposed. McCormick also fiercely opposed President Franklin D. Roosevelt and the New Deal, allegedly nurturing a grudge over a romantic rivalry while both were prep-school students at Groton. (That, at least, was FDR's interpretation.)

Localism in ownership does not mean localism in content. Much of television programming is supplied by national networks to local stations. Similarly, programs picked by local stations are distantly produced for a national audience by syndicators. For network shows, a local TV station may select whether a national program will be carried or "preempted." This cuts both ways. In the 2000 presidential campaign, the NBC national network, to its discredit, pressured its local affiliate stations to carry a baseball playoff game instead of a presidential debate. But conversely, during the second Iraq war, some local affiliate stations switched from national network coverage of the war to popular regional college basketball games in which they held rights. And in the 1960s, local TV stations in the South preempted national programs that took a pro-integration perspective on social issues.

Thus, localism, although an important social and policy goal, should not be equated with being pro-news, pro-independent, or pro-public interest.

Commercialism

FCC Commissioner Jonathan Adelstein, as part of the debate, decried commercialism in media behavior as a "pernicious symptom of consolidation." But is the direction of causality he alleges correct? Critics often observe negative aspects of media, as well as trends of media concentration, and conclude that the former is born from the latter. But it is just as plausible that they are siblings, the twin result of the same fundamental force: profit orientation. Commercial firms, whether large or small, will operate in a profit-maximizing fashion, which generally include cost-cutting and audience maximization. Regardless of size, media firms may provide some public-interest activities as an investment in goodwill and credibility. They may at times move away from pure profit maximization in favor of social responsibility, but it must yet be shown that small media firms have more of that attitude. Some of the socially most benign firms were those with a near monopoly market position, and consequent high profits and lower cost pressures. Examples are AT&T, Xerox, and IBM in their period of dominance; or CBS, NBC, and ABC when they accounted for most of the TV audience; or local newspapers with near monopoly.

Conversely, small or medium-sized media firms can be irresponsible and profit-driven. Some medium-sized media companies have cut legal and ethical corners. For example, in 2005, Adelphia Cable's 80-year-old owner John Rigas was sentenced to 20 years in prison for skimming corporate money for personal investments and cooking the corporate books. In the same year the A. H. Belo newspaper chain acknowledged inflating circulation numbers, that is, cheating its advertisers. And Lord Conrad Black, the owner of the Hollinger International Group, was convicted in 2007 for looting the company for his own use, and sentenced to six and a half years in prison.

None of these companies is small, for sure, but they do not reach the size of the top firms. In the ranking of American media firms in 2001, Adelphia was number 15, Belo number 33, and Hollinger number 45. Both Adelphia and Belo have solid local roots.

Commercial pressures have led even nonconformist media to behave in the same anticompetitive spirit as established ones. The two leading chains of "alternative" papers have been *News Times Media* (11 papers, circulation 1.1 million) and *Village Voice Media* (seven papers, circulation 800,000). In 2002, the two companies contracted to close down their respective papers in Cleveland and Los Angeles, the *Cleveland Free Times* and the *Times Los Angeles,* so that they would not compete with the other company's paper in that city. It took the U.S. Justice Department's intervention to reverse this anticompetitive behavior, forcing the two publishing firms to pay a fine and to make some of their assets available to new entrants. The Justice Department stated: "Rather than letting the marketplace decide the winner, these companies chose to corrupt the competitive process by swapping markets, thereby guaranteeing each other a monopoly and denying consumers in Los Angeles and Cleveland the continued benefits of competition." And the *New York Times* wrote: "That [settlement] has left alternative news weeklies, which have generally chided government for its role in media consolidation, on the wrong end."

What ownership model might lead to a different conduct by a commercial media firm? Is it individual owners, institutional ownership, control by employee-managers, or nonprofit ownership? All exhibit problems. If individual owners are in control (whether Rupert Murdoch, Silvio Berlusconi, or William Paley), their personal power and empire-building tendencies are a problem.[43] And their heirs may well be the kind of dilettantes who helped doom feudalism.

Does the size of the firm make the difference? It is unclear why the dynamics of profit maximization would affect huge media firms more than small or medium-sized ones. Is a $10 billion company more interested in profits than a $1 million firm? One could argue this three ways. It is neither analytically nor empirically clear that profit orientation grows with size or share. Nor is it clear empirically that large firms are more profitable, or that such profitability, if it exists, is not based on economies of scale rather than on disregard for the newsroom.

Dennis Herrick, author on media management, critic of large media firms, and himself a local newspaper owner in Iowa, writes:

> As owner of a weekly newspaper, I bought another much smaller weekly in a town 12 miles away in 1987. I was able to make a profit on even a paper as small as it was because I could produce it entirely out of my larger paper's office with no increase in equipment, employees or overhead. I sold all of the smaller paper's equipment and stopped renting a building the smaller paper had been using. Then my existing staff took over all bookkeeping, ad sales, reporting and other functions. The smaller paper's only two full-time employees were the husband-and-wife owners. They left with the closing on the sale, of course, and there was no need to replace them. My own staff began producing both papers. Talk about economies of scale. A freelance writer who lived in the smaller town attacked my purchase in an article...lament[ing] the sale of his hometown weekly to an out-of-town owner....The writer even accusingly referred to my pip-squeak operation as "a chain."[44]

If we order newspaper chains by profitability, they rank, by circulation size, as number 1, 12, 5, 10, 22, 9, 21, 2, 6, 15, and 3.[45] No correlation is apparent. Studies by David Demers finds that "the corporate newspaper actually places less emphasis on profits than its entrepreneurial [i.e., family-owned] counterpart."[46] On the other hand, one study finds profits of 24% for publicly traded dailies—typically larger firms—versus 16% for

privately owned ones.[47] Benjamin Compaine and Gerald Stone reached similar conclusions.[48] The resolution of the profit issue is not within the scope of this book. The literature and the data are mentioned here only to alert the reader that the proposition that big media equals big profits is not as clear-cut as is often confidently believed.[49]

Even where an association of profits and size could be observed, it would not be clear in which direction the causality ran. Some firms are profitable because they are large. Other firms are large because they are profitable. And a more competitive media system does not mean less cost-cutting of the kind that affects news; quite possibly, it means the opposite.

Geneva Overholser, the respected editor of Gannett's *Des Moines Register* and ombudsman of the *Washington Post*, wrote: "Too often by far, being an editor in America today feels like holding up an avalanche of pressure to do away with this piece of excellence, that piece of quality, so as to squeeze out just a little bit more money."[50]

But the profit orientation of media is not a new problem, it goes back at least a century. Tension between journalism and commerce, between artists and bean-counters, between the creatives and the suits, between agents and principals, is endemic to all commercial media. Press historian Gerald Baldasty concludes that "By the late 19th century, the formula of the newspaper-as-business-first-and-foremost was firmly established."[51] In 1897, muckraker Lincoln Steffens wrote: "The magnitude of financial operations of the newspaper is turning journalism upside down. Big business was doing two things in general to journalism: it was completing the erection of the industrial institution upon what was once a personal organ; and it was buttressing and steadying the structure with financial conservatism."[52]

Jack Fuller, president of the *Chicago Tribune* (2001–2004) and a publishing business insider, observes: "The basic argument critical journalists make against the corporate form is that corporations have taken money out at a rate far higher than private owners did...but in the 1920s during the *Tribune*'s heyday under the proprietorship of Colonel Robert R. McCormick...the operating margin reached almost 29.8% in 1929, compared with 24.6% at its highest afterwards."[53] In 2005, not a bad year, it was 21.69%.

It therefore becomes necessary to postulate a change in the nature of capitalism to explain why media firms in the past were less aggressive in pursuing profits and efficiencies. That argument is usually that institutional ownership is more performance driven than was the direct shareholder ownership of the past. Institutional investors are profit oriented in financial terms, and their buy-sell decisions induce managers to act in a profit-oriented direction even without direct intervention. (This supposes that managers were not profit maximizers already.)

The pressures of fund managers on media managers for profits are often said to be a major factor in changing the nature of media behavior and quality. It forces cost-cutting that lowers quality, sensationalism to gain audiences, and a pandering to advertisers that reduces courage.[54]

But this causality is not clear at all. It requires us to believe that individual owners, especially large ones with a big and undiversified stake, care less about a firm's return than today's fractional beneficiaries of a mutual fund, in which a media firm is only a small component. The investor in such a fund seeks diversification, and reasonably assumes that some shares will perform better than others. Some fund managers will quickly sell a poorly performing stock. But other funds are in for the long haul. Still others invest in risky firms, for the upside potential. Still others prefer "pure plays" of specialized firms over conglomerates and will exert direct or indirect pressures for such firms to streamline themselves rather than grow. It is possible that such ownership exerts greater pressure than that of individuals. Again, the opposite case can also be made, that individuals with a large stake and exposure will keep management much more on its toes.

One comparison of publicly (i.e., stock-market-traded) and privately held newspapers shows that the count of full-time newsroom employees is 51.7 in publicly held dailies, versus 45.2 in privately (closely) held newspapers. This is a difference of 14.4% in favor of the investor-owned media. On the other hand, the latter are also larger in circulation, by 11.3%.[55] Thus, adjusted for size, the difference is negligible.

In most cases, hired managers run companies, and are increasingly independent from owners.[56] Critics have decried their profligacy and the lack of meaningful constraints on them. The Disney Company is an example. Management (Michael Eisner) was challenged in 2003 and 2004 by large shareholders, among other things, for squandering profit opportunities. The opposition was led by Roy Disney, Jr., the firm's then-largest shareholder, on the grounds that management had been wasteful and that profits were lower than before. Management prevailed—barely—but Eisner soon retired.

There seems to be no model of commercial ownership, control, or size that does not create problems of a priority of profit over public interest concern. The key factor for media behavior—aside from a few small family papers or radio stations run more as a vocation than a business—is a media firm's business orientation, not its size.

Some of the more perceptive among media critics have recognized that their beef is not really with media conglomerates as a form of business organization but more generally with private media and their commercial behavior. Robert McChesney, a leader of media reform, writes: "[E]ven competitive markets are problematic...media presents many unique attributes that undermine the suitability of market regulation" (i.e., market forces as a way to offset media company power).[57]

There are several major alternative models to commercial media. The first model is public media such as public broadcasting. In many countries national broadcast institutions exist, supported by some combination of tax, levies, or advertising. Such institutions, particularly in Europe and Japan, usually offer higher-quality content than commercial TV (although the difference is reduced with quality narrowcast cable TV channels).[58] They are a major way to diversify content. But public TV institutions that are nationally centralized have also been susceptible to politicization, and create enormous gatekeeper powers over the creative output of entire societies.[59]

A second alternative model is employee ownership, either directly by the employees of a media firm or through unions.[60] One medium-sized newspaper firm, the Community Newspaper Holdings Inc. (CNHI), is owned by Alabama's public-employee pension fund. In 2005, it was the thirteenth largest chain, with 91 newspapers and a daily circulation of about 1 million. The union's pension fund invested $2 billion in CNHI and controls the company. Yet even a union-controlled firm does not seem to behave in a manner more employee-friendly or less profit-oriented. In 1997, CNHI bought the *Niagara Gazette* from the nation's largest newspaper chain, Gannett. As reported in a rival newspaper, CNHI then reduced the number of reporters and editors by more than 50% over four years. Even so, the newspaper's financial performance was lagging, and it lost advertisers and reporters. By 2003, another round of firing cut a further 25% of the employees.

> Many were long-term employees, some having worked for the company for more than 30 years. "People were walking around crying." In his press release, [General Manager] Lowman said, "We remain committed to bringing local readers the very best community newspapers we can and delivering to our advertisers products, services, reach and results that are unequaled in our markets." The statement had many familiar with the struggling franchise laughing out loud. Few in the community thought the papers were committed to those things prior to the most recent round of firings.[61]

The point of this recitation is not to castigate a particular company or its owners, but rather to illustrate that a profit orientation to the exclusion of other factors is not the sole province of a commercial, Wall Street-driven firm. This Alabama public-employee pension fund works for its beneficiaries, the union's retirees, in preference to the press employees working in upstate New York for its investment assets.

A third model is one of private but nonprofit media. Some media are owned by religious organizations. Large newspapers owned in such a way are the *Christian Science Monitor* (Christian Scientists), the *Washington Times* (Reverend Moon's Unification Church), and the *Desert News* (Mormon church). Many media critics would not consider the last two as models for balance, even though they are not profit-driven.[62]

Other nonprofit media are owned by foundations or charitable trusts. Independent Newspapers, a medium-sized chain, is owned by a nonprofit holding company. Other examples are the *New London Day*, today's *Manchester Union Leader*, and the *St. Petersburg Times* (owned by the nonprofit Poynter Institute).[63] Usually, this model is based on bequests by an original owner to a foundation. Therefore, it is dependent on prior commercial ownership behavior. The *Manchester Union Leader,* as mentioned, was notorious for being the personal vehicle for its right-wing publisher, William Loeb III, and for his extreme views on race and communism. In other cases, the placing of media properties into a nonprofit entity does not greatly diminish the family

control. Germany's largest media firm, Bertelsmann, is owned by the Bertelsmann Foundation, which in turn is controlled by the Mohn family. Although the media firms' profits are used often in the public interest, the company's behavior is not perceptively less profit oriented or less expansionary than that of other firms. The firm, though owned by a nonprofit entity, has become Europe's largest media company, the United States' largest trade book publisher and, when it partnered with Sony, the world's largest music company. When a new CEO, Thomas Middelhoff, tried to steer the firm toward a public shareholder ownership model, he was ousted by the Mohn family partly because such an ownership model would have required greater public accountability.

A fourth alternative to commercial media ownership is community media, including the intriguing model of a "media commons" in which readers and other members of the public contribute to news coverage. The Korean *Ohmynews* and the *WikiNews* are examples. Community-based nonprofit media are most feasible for relatively low-cost media such as radio, periodicals, and Web sites. Their key obstacles are not legal barriers but weak financial support mechanisms and the incentives to produce content for national rather than local audiences. Once one goes beyond text or audio—as for example online sites, blogs, podcasts, or traditional college or community radio—and moves to video and multimedia, individualized contributions become technically and economically difficult and mostly national rather than local. An organized team production becomes necessary, with management and budgets. A related problem is the classic dynamic described as the "tragedy of the commons." Individual contributions with low validity and accuracy drive down the overall credibility of the rest. This requires a screening and editing system, that is, some management. And the selection of this management quickly becomes a quasi-political issue if the publication has any influence.

Thus, while pure commercialism in media is part of the problem, non-commercialism is only part of the solution.

Content Quality and Diversity

As Anthony Smith writes in *Goodbye Gutenberg*, "Quality is almost immune to investigative techniques of social science." There are troubling indicators, nonetheless.[64] Looking at outputs, a survey by the Project for Excellence in Journalism and the Pew Charitable Trusts of 4,000 major stories in the mass media shows that from 1979 to 1997, "soft" news grew from 15% to 43%. According to the Consumer Federation of America, despite the increase in the number of TV stations nationally, the number of local TV news operations has dropped by about 10% in recent years. But is the cause more concentration, or more competition?

Does size improve or reduce quality? Quite probably both outcomes happen. Acquisition by a larger chain debases some quality papers and improves some weak ones. Some profitable papers plow money into good journalism, thereby increasing reader loyalty and investing in the future; others do not. Some low-profit papers cannot afford quality; others are creative on a shoestring. Some media conglomerates cave in when pressure is applied to another part of the organization;[65] others have more strength to fight back.[66] The reader is referred to the voluminous literature on newspaper concentration.[67]

Another issue is the relation of bias to size or market share. Bias is much harder to define or measure than to feel. It is quite common that viewers feel the media perspective to be stacked against their point of view. Fox News, talk radio, Clear Channel, and Sinclair TV are the major offenders for the left, whereas conservatives feel marginalized by liberal "main-stream media" (MSM) such as CBS News, CNN, the *New York Times*, and PBS.

Several organizations are engaged in ferreting out bias.[68] Organizations such as Fairness and Accuracy in Reporting (FAIR), on the left, and Accuracy in Media (AIM), on the right, report their findings. Both find strong evidence for a media bias in favor of their political opponents.[69]

Much has been written about the relation between ownership and news bias,[70] and it is not the purpose of this study to add to this literature. Several theories are told about the character of political bias: large U.S. media firms seek government regulatory favors and hence pull their punches (example: the Iraq war). Or, they are powerful and unaccountable, and irresponsibly criticize the government, in difficult missions of national security (example: the Iraq war). Or, they are owned by rich white men who follow their class interest,[71] such as those of the Texas oil industry (example: the Iraq war). Or, media firms operate out of blue-state hotspots and reflect liberal values (example: the Iraq war). Or, they cater to Middle America and its patriotic values, because those are the audiences that advertisers seek (example: the Iraq war). Each of these contradictory stories has some truth. But how do they add up?

Probably the worst way to approach this question is by anecdote. At any given moment there are journalists, participants, creators, and artists who can tell a compelling story of bias, restriction, and failure of imagination. This is why both FAIR and AIM will never run out of valid material. But one needs to move beyond individual cases.

At any given moment, a huge number of creative projects and talents are competing with each other to be selected for funding, distribution, or jobs at media organizations. Statistically speaking, most projects would be turned down under any conceivable system, because of limited resources and limited attention relative to the continuously rising information productivity of society. It has been said that 90% of all scientists who ever lived, live today. The same is likely to be true for aspiring screenwriters, novelists, or directors. The result is inevitable disappointment for most participants. Such rejections can be rationalized as systemic, based on the control of media by a few firms. True, a different ownership system might lead to the approval of some previously rejected projects and artists, but at the expense of others who would be rejected. The overall number of productions or employment either would not change much in the aggregate or it might rise for some media, such as music, blogs, and home video, and drop for others, such as expensive special effects and animation. Subjective rejection of worthy projects is inherent to any media system.

There is substantial literature on content diversity, and it goes in several directions.[72] The historical evidence does not equate oligopoly with low content quality. In the heydays of newspaper competition in America, around 1900, irresponsible "yellow journalism" was at its peak. Conversely, when television was controlled by only three networks, it was less oriented to the stunts, violence, and vulgarity of later years. Internal network "Standards & Practices" offices exercised strong controls. Advertisers, having few alternatives, had to accept increasingly limited roles as broadcast TV matured. The three networks could lavish high advertising profits on flagship news operations, with authoritative anchormen providing a "that's the way it is" gravitas.

An early academic analysis by Peter Steiner concluded that a monopoly, perversely, might actually provide more content diversity.[73] The intuition is that concentrated media engage in counterprogramming instead of duplicating popular content formats, and therefore provide a greater diversity of content and serve wide audience constituencies. A more complex relation was analyzed by Bruce Owen and Steven Wildman.[74] On the empirical level, Robert Entman found no consistent relationship between competition and news diversity.[75] D. P. Lopes found that the music industry's content diversity was the same in 1969 as it was in 1990 despite considerably higher concentration.[76] Other empirical studies came to different conclusions.[77]

Regulatory and antitrust policies can diversify the ownership of private media somewhat, which address the distribution of media power. But whether it will result in a different media product is quite uncertain. For example, a regulatory rule that prohibits a TV network to show a TV show more than twice (the "Fin-Syn" rule, in force for many years) will not change the program characteristics of commercial TV. It will change the distribution of control and profits for TV products among different media companies, but not the content nature of the product itself.

Mara Einstein[78] of Queens College, in an empirical study of TV network program diversity, finds that "[d]iversity was at its peak in the late 1960s before the advent of financial interest and syndication rules and declined two years after its institution. Throughout the 1990s, [program] diversity has remained fairly constant, at a middle range but increased sharply in the most recent years" (p. 176).

Governmental media policy also provides conflicting incentives to content diversity. On the one hand, such diversity is extolled. But at the same time, the strong requirement of "free TV" leads to advertising-supported programs based on audience counts, which favors programs for mass audiences rather than for taste minorities.[79]

Do more voices mean more diversity? The FCC said yes. But the answer is less clear if one takes into account how loud some voices are. With numerous video and Internet avenues existing today, it is easier to speak but harder to be heard. To be heard requires higher volume, which typically means more resources. Thus, one cannot equate a greater number of content providers with greater diversity. The two may work in the same direction but need not. Those who equate the two commit an error of composition: just because it is easier and cheaper for me to reach an audience over the Internet does not mean that it's easier if everybody tries the same. It becomes much harder and more expensive to reliably get attention, necessitating greater marketing resources.

Let us conclude this skeptical tour of idealistic hopes.

Many people sincerely believe that many problems of media in society would be resolved by a deconcentration of media. But, to draw an analogy,[80] would a fragmentation of the supermarket chains A&P and Safeway into smaller chains reduce hunger? Occasionally, yes. Generally, no. A mom-and-pop grocery-based system will not create food or resources for the poor. A sporadic story about a charitable grocer who extends credit for a few weeks to long-time customers does not change that basic fact. Nor will a system of small grocery stores, each with limited shelf space, raise the diversity of food products over that of a mixed system of large chains, megastores, and specialty stores.[81]

Similarly, a more competitive commercial media structure will not be more redistributive in content terms but might be quite possibly less so. Redistribution, in media diversity terms, means the provision of content that the market does not generate. The creation of such content, just like creating food for the poor, requires more than the splitting up of large commercial media firms into medium and small-sized commercial ones. It requires the allocation of resources (including financial subsidies, electro-magnetic spectrum, and access rights). Structural media ownership rules, although helpful in encouraging source diversity, are no shortcut to the allocation of resources to support the creation of diverse content.

Where markets do not provide the desirable results, noneconomic social objectives must be accomplished through social policy and the allocation of public funds. For media, this means, in particular, public support mechanisms for noncommercial content and distribution. The notion that one could do so on the cheap, through ownership ceilings, is appealingly hopeful but certain to disappoint.

To repeat, this is not an argument against deconcentration, just against false expectations about what it can accomplish.

OVERVIEW OF PAST RESEARCH OF CONCENTRATION

The subject of media concentration has, of course, received much attention. Many authors postulate concentration trends as a given and focus on the implications. Others hold that whatever the market concentration might be, free markets and technology will take care of undue power, obviating the need to know details. There is nothing wrong with a nonempirical and principled analysis of issues of public policy. But it is also true that factual selectivity can be a labor-saving research method that also enables some of its practitioners, whether from the media left or the libertarian right to assume a posture of great rectitude.[82]

The two camps can be roughly characterized as media pessimists and media optimists. Media pessimists think of the sky as falling; media optimists see the dawn of a bright new day.

Let me first turn, skeptically, to the media pessimists, before turning, also skeptically, to the media optimists. If I spend more time on the former it is because more of them write books. Perhaps the most influential book on the subject has been Ben Bagdikian's periodically updated, frequently cited, regularly assigned, and provocatively titled work, *The Media Monopoly*.[83] Bagdikian is a Pulitzer Prize–winning journalist and former dean of the journalism school at the University of California, Berkeley. In other words, he deserves to be taken seriously, and he is.

For example, Dennis Herrick, otherwise a keen observer of the newspaper industry, analogizes him with no less than Gandhi. And he approvingly quotes the *St. Petersburg Times,* which calls Bagdikian's work "one of the most important critiques of the press ever written…the book that is still a must-read nearly two decades later in many colleges and universities….Its powering revelation of media consolidation has been vindicated since."[84]

Bagdikian writes that "by the 1980s, the majority of all major American media—newspapers, magazines, radio, television, books, and movies— were controlled by fifty giant corporations. These corporations were interlocked in common financial interest with other massive industries and with a few dominant international banks.…The fifty men and women who head these corporations would fit in a large room. They constitute a new Private Ministry of Information and Culture" (p. 54). Is Bagdikian right on the facts? Let us anticipate some of this book's findings: in 1984—to match Bagdikian's date—the top 25 U.S. mass media companies held 32.5% of the mass media market, and the next 25 companies held maybe another 5%,[85] together 37.5% for 50 companies, which is less than what a reasonable reader would associate

with Bagdikian's use of the words "majority" and "control." Of the top 25 companies hardly any firm held a share greater than 2% (RCA with 3.7%, ABC with 2.9%, and CBS and Warner with 2.4% and 2.3% respectively). Bagdikian continues: "In 1987, the fifty companies had shrunk to twenty-nine" (p. 21). Actually, in 1988, the top 29 mass media companies accounted for 35.6%, virtually unchanged from 1984, when the top 29 firms held 33.4%. By 2000, Bagdikian finds that the major media companies had been reduced to six: AOL Time Warner, Disney, Viacom, News Corporation, Bertelsmann, and General Electric: "these six have more annual media revenues than the next twenty firms combined" (p. 10). This is correct. The mass media share of these six firms was 26.6% of all of mass media (for an average share of 4.4%), while the remaining 20 companies added up to 25.8%, for an average share of 1.3%.

By 2004, Bagdikian's number had further dropped. In his newest book, *The New Media Monopoly,* he concluded: "Five global-dimension firms, operating with many of the characteristics of a cartel, own most of the newspapers, magazines, book publishers, motion picture studios, and radio and television stations in the United States."[86] These firms are Time Warner, Viacom, Disney, News Corp, and Bertelsmann.

He observes, remarkably considering such rival contenders as Hitler, Stalin, and Mao: "This gives each of the five corporations and their leaders more communications power than was exercised by any despot or dictatorship in history" (p. 3).

Bertelsmann is actually, by revenue, the number 13 media company in the United States. Comcast, unmentioned, is four times larger. Bertelsmann's German TV or book revenues are not particularly relevant to Bagdikian's U.S. analysis; but without including Bertelsmann in the top five list, he could not argue control over book publishing. If we will accept his lineup of companies and media industries, we find the following aggregate ownership of these five firms for his benchmark year of 2004: of newspapers (counting revenues, not number of dailies, thereby helping Bagdikian's case),[87] these five firms owned less than 1% (basically, the lagging *New York Post,* and after 2008, the *Wall Street Journal* added another 2.6%);[88] of magazines, 18.7%; of trade books and paperback books, 36.6%; of motion picture studios, 60.8%; of radio stations, 11.9%; of TV stations, 13.7%; of cable TV operators, 19.6%.[89]

The problem with Bagdikian is not his alarm-ism about media concentration or its extent—he makes good and thoughtful points. I, too, do not believe that economic efficiency should trump democratic concerns. But Bagdikian's numbers are tendentious.

Bagdikian is sloppy in service to a noble cause. His view is one of media Jeffersonianism, of sturdy media yeomen tilling the fields of democracy.

> There are 1,700 daily newspapers, 11,000 magazines, 9,000 radio and 1,000 television stations, 2,500 book publishers, and 7 movie studios. If each of these were operated by a dif-ferent owner there would be 25,000 individ-ual media voices in the country. Such a large number would almost guarantee a full spec-trum of political and social ideas distributed to the population. It would limit the concen-tration of power since each owner would share influence over the national mind with 24,999 owners....But there are not 25,000 different owners.[90]

Bagdikian's mantle has been assumed by Robert McChesney of the University of Illinois. McChesney has been an influential voice and activist. He is much more careful with his num-bers than Bagdikian. For example, he observes that there are thousands of media firms in the United States. The issue therefore is not simply counting voices but considering their significance. He correctly identifies an emerging three-tier sys-tem of American media. The first tier comprises seven "vertically integrated powerhouses—indeed vast conglomerates—with various combinations of film studios, TV networks, cable TV chan-nels, book publishing, newspapers, radio stations, music companies, TV channels, and the like." Examples are Time Warner or GE. Their revenues range from $15 to $40 billion. The second tier comprises 15 to 20 other firms such as Cox, the New York Times Company, Gannett, and Clear Channel, that is, firms that are strong in one or two areas. Their revenues are in the $3–10 bil-lion range, putting them in the top 700 or so U.S. firms. The third tier comprises thousands of other and much smaller media firms that "fill the nooks and crannies of the media system. Many survive because their markets—and profits—are too small to interest the giants."[91] McChesney's description is basically correct; but it does not sound like what Bagdikian calls a "media monopoly": maybe

27 big firms, some coming, some going, and thou-sands of small firms.

One can quibble with some of McChesney's data, but the question is to what purpose. McChesney makes economic points but his position is that economics do not matter anyway. Ultimately, the concentration argument for him is secondary and tactical. Even if markets functioned, McChesney writes forthrightly, as quoted before, "the problem with market regulation is not merely a matter of economic concentration—even competitive mar-kets are problematic. Perhaps we should not even expect the market to be the appropriate regulator for the media system, or many components of it, because media presents many unique attributes that undermine the suitability of market regulation."[92]

Nor is McChesney's problem that media com-panies do not serve some people's preferences. Echoing Jürgen Habermas, he argues: "Using mar-kets to regulate the production and distribution of ideas and culture is troubling. If one follows the logic of the 'marketplace of ideas' metaphor closely, it may well be that the rational thing for media firms to do is to produce exactly what the market shows a preference for, what everyone else is producing. Diversity may then be squashed."[93]

Bagdikian's more dramatic numbers have taken on a life of their own.[94] Celebrated film documen-tary maker Michael Moore picked the number five from Bagdikian and globalized it: "By the end of the millennium five men controlled the world's media."[95]

Lawrence Lessig, the noted Stanford law pro-fessor (and for a time my friendly co-columnist on new media at *Financial Times Online*), escalated the number: "Indeed, after the changes that the FCC announced in June 2003, most expect that within a few years, we will live in a world where just three companies control more than 85% of the media."[96] He adds: "Today, in most markets, the two largest broadcasters control 74% of that market's revenues" (pp. 162–163). But the actual market share in 2001 of the top two firms in local markets was 47.9%[97] (which does not yet account for the substantial viewership of cable satellite channels). This, of course, is still quite high, but much less than claimed. Lessig continues: "While the number of channels has increased dramatically, the ownership of those channels has narrowed to an even smaller few..." (p.165). Actually, the share of the top five firms in channel ownership, weighed by the revenues of these channels as a indicator of audiences, has declined from 86.7% in 1984 to 94.3% in 1996, 83.2% in 2001, and 79.4% in 2005. (If we only counted the number of channels rather than their revenues, these shares would be significantly smaller and further undermine Lessig's point.) For sure, 79% is a high and very troubling percentage. But Lessig alleges a trend opposite from the one observable, and hence a growing problem. From there, he reaches the conclusion: "This narrowing has an effect on what is produced. The product of such large and concentrated networks is increasingly homogenous. Increasingly safe. Increasingly sterile....This is not the communist party, though from the inside, it must feel a bit like the communist party. No one can question without risk of consequence—not necessarily banishment to Siberia, but punishment nonetheless. Independent, critical, different views are quashed. This is not the environment for democrats" (pp. 165–166).

Another analysis is that of Mark Cooper.[98] Cooper, a Washington consumer advocate, puts many of the academic researchers to shame with the effort he takes in ferreting out the data, and by providing also information that may undercut his case. Cooper's study, developed as part of litigation against FCC rules, covers broadcast television, cable TV, the newspaper industry, radio, and the Internet, and concludes that by "routine antitrust standards virtually all of the national and local media product markets are concentrated and most are highly concentrated" (p. 10). I discuss some of his work further below.[99]

I now turn to the views of the media optimists, who see an abundance of openness and diversity. Most of it is libertarian or free market in orientation.[100] (I ignore the self-interested advocacy documents of companies and trade associations.) From the economic press, *Washington Post* economics columnist Robert Samuelson wrote: "The idea that 'big media' has dangerously increased its control over our choices is absurd. Yet large parts of the public, including journalists and politicians, believe religiously in this myth. They confuse share with power."[101] Other media optimists include Bruce Owen, a Stanford economist and consultant who served in the White House's Office of Telecommunications Policy.[102] Perhaps the most comprehensive expression of the optimist view is Adam Thierer's book *Media Myths: Making Sense of the Debate over Media Ownership*.[103] Thierer, an economist with the Cato Institute in Washington,

D.C., dismisses media reformers: "[W]hat, then, explains the unusual passion they have exhibited during this debate?...It is the field of psychology, not law or economics, where the best explanation for such 'media madness' can be found" (p. 14). And he concludes: "To the extent that there was ever a 'Golden Age' of media in America, we are living in it today. The media sky has never been brighter and is getting brighter with each passing year. And this is most definitely not a case of looking for silver linings around the clouds; *there are no clouds*."

Thierer, however, is stronger in challenging his opponents' absence of data than in providing his own. What numbers he cites are those of others (including some by the author), with their strengths and weaknesses. Like his opponents, he "walks his cat" back from a conclusion to helpful facts. He therefore needs not confront the limits of a sanguine statement such as: "In such an age of abundance and hyper-choice, the question of who owns what or how much they own is utterly irrelevant" (p. 70).

As we can see, much of the literature on media concentration has been stronger in commitment than in empirical evidence. But there have been a few studies to the contrary.[104] Perhaps the most comprehensive data effort to date has been the volume *Who Owns the Media?*, edited by Benjamin Compaine, Sterling, Guback, and Noble in 1979.[105] A third edition appeared in 2000, this time with Compaine and Douglas Gomery as the authors.[106]

Compaine and Gomery, like Thierer, are media optimists.[107] They answer the question of who owns the media: "Thousands of large and small firms and organizations...controlled, directly and indirectly, by hundreds of thousands of stockholders, as well as by public opinion" (p. 578). They find market power in local newspapers and cable TV, as well as increased national concentration in cable TV, radio, TV stations, movie theaters, and booksellers. But their main conclusion, looking beyond these individual industries, is one of less concentration. "Looked at as a single industry, there can be little disagreement that there is more competition than ever among media players. The issue could be stopped with a single word, *Internet*. But it goes beyond this development" (p. 574).

Our own results are less optimistic for both the mass media sector and the Internet as a distribution system. Nor do we find, as Compaine and

Gomery do, that "the largest of the media companies are mere pixels in the economic tapestry." That vivid image underplays the issue.

For their overall conclusion on media concentration (as opposed to their studies of particular media industries), Compaine and Gomery use as a market definition one big media market. They aggregate one concentration index (the so-called HHI, to be discussed below) for the entire media sector by putting all of the top-50 media firms into that single market. The argument is that all media are contending voices, and thus rivals to each other as alternate options for audiences. They then find an HHI score of 268, slightly up from 205 in 1986. My own findings in this book, developed through step-by-step aggregations, show a weighted average HHI for the mass media sector of 1,165 for 2004, 1,084 for 2001, 693 for 1996, and 564 for 1984. These numbers are a good bit higher than Compaine-Gomery, and more rapidly rising. But that result is inherent in the different methodology. If instead we adopt the Compaine-Gomery methodology, calculating the share of the top 25 media companies in the entire mass media sector, we find an HHI number of 206 in 2005, which is closer to their number, even lower.

But such methodology gave critics an easy target. Edwin Baker, of the University of Pennsylvania responded: "[E]ven from a narrow, efficiency-oriented antitrust perspective, [Compaine] is wrong to identify the media as a whole as the relevant market...whether or not supplied by the same firm, content and its delivery are very different, non-substitutable products" (p .79).

There have also been empirical studies of particular firms, such as IBM,[108] AT&T,[109] Microsoft,[110] and the television networks.[111] The focus of these studies tends to be an account of dominant players in their subindustry. Some of these studies were the outgrowth of antitrust litigation.

Thus, the literature, while lively, would benefit from the addition of a systematic and data-based analysis.

INTERNATIONAL DIMENSIONS

Media concentration is not just an American issue. It is a subject of discussion around the world.[112] This book, however, does not deal with international comparisons, or with the global effects of U.S. media concentration. It already covers plenty of ground. The global themes are part of future

work. For now we will merely touch these issues to provide a context and perspective for the American debate.

I report the findings of others' research on Europe, and add the comparable American and Japanese numbers. These are at least useful as a global reality check which is sometimes needed.[113]

The numbers in table 1.1 show U.S. concentrations to be at the low end of the spectrum for eleven countries, among the world's most developed nations. National newspaper concentration is by far the lowest in the U.S., and the TV network concentration is almost the lowest, even disregarding the larger cable network audiences.[114] This should not be surprising, given the size of the U.S. domestic market and its ability to support more media products and services. A European Committee of Experts on Media Concentrations and Pluralism reported on the media ownership trends in several European countries (Council of Europe).[115] The trend in most European countries, it finds, has been one of high and increasing levels of media and cross-media concentration.[116] Several Eastern and Central European countries were observed to have increased diversity of media, but presumably this was relative to the bad old days.

In Germany, opposition to the newspaper power of the conservative Axel Springer slowed the general introduction of private TV in the early 1980s, but the country's major media firm became Bertelsmann, with strong stakes in book publishing, book clubs, magazines, Internet media, TV, film production, music, and printing, both in Germany and in other countries. Bertelsmann owns 24 TV stations and 14 radio stations in 10 countries.[117]

In Italy, Silvio Berlusconi's media firm Mediaset owns the three major private TV networks, an issue of continual controversy. His firm also owns Mondadori, Italy's largest book and magazine publishing group, and *Il Giornali*, the leading newspaper. Additional media holdings are multimedia, printing, and telephone directories.

In France, Vivendi (formerly a water utility) owns 100% of the Canal+ Group, the dominant French pay TV operator, having merged with number two provider TPS in 2005. It also owns 56% of the SFR Cegetal Group, the country's second largest telecom operator; Universal Music Group, the world's largest music group; the advertising group Havas; and the videogame giant Activision Blizzard.[118] Financial reverses forced it to sell most of its Hollywood film and TV production and

Table 1.1 Newspaper and TV Network Concentration: Europe, Japan, and the United States

	Circulation Share of the Top 3 Newspaper Companies (C3) in 2001[a]	TV Networks' HHI Concentration[b]
Finland	46	3,605
Netherlands	88	2,549
Sweden	85	2,834
United Kingdom	60	2,550
France	41	2,054
Ireland	66	2,347
Germany	35	3,140
Italy	43	4,081
Spain	53	2,207
Japan	45	2,116
United States	20	2,164

[a] Source for Europe: Albarran, Alan B., and Bozena I. Mierzejewska "Media Concentration in the U.S. and European Union: A Comparative Analysis," presented at 6th World Media Economics Conference, 2004. Source for Japan: *Japan Media Review*, accessed at http://www.japanmediareview.com/Japan/wiki/Shimbunwiki/
Source for U.S.: tables in this book.
[b] The HHI measure is explained in Chapter 3, and does not include cable and DBS channels. Source for United States: Tables in this book. Source for European TV: Alfonso Sánchez-Tabernero, "Competition between Public Service and Commercial Television Broadcasting in the European Market," presented at 6th World Media Economics Conference, HEC Montréal, Montréal, Canada, May 12–15, 2004. Source for Japan: InfoCom Research, Inc., Information and Communications in Japan 2006; NHK, Annual Report, 2006, by Kiyoshi Nakamura.

distribution unit, Universal, to GE in 2004, along with many of its Internet ventures. But it also expanded into one of the world's largest videogame developers. In its heyday, Vivendi controlled a far larger share of its national mass media sector than any American firm ever did.

In the United Kingdom, newspapers have been dominated by four companies since the 1950s.[119] Newspapers published outside these groups accounted since 1960 for only around 15% of the market.[120]

In Sweden, the Bonnier conglomerate, which accounts for about 25% of the country's newspaper circulation, bought a major stake in TV4, the second-largest TV broadcaster.[121] It also owns radio stations, book publishers, and magazines (including 18 in the U.S.).[122] Spanish telecommunications operator Telefonica acquired the innovative Dutch TV producer Endemol for $5.5 billion in 2000.

In Iceland, the nation's President Olafur Ragnar Grimsson vetoed in 2004 a law to restrict media ownership. It was the first-ever veto in the history of the country. One may note that in Iceland, it is the political right that favors media deconcentration, whereas the political left supports the concentrated status quo. Why? Because by far the largest retail and conservative media firm, the Baugur group, was supporting the left and had clashed with Prime Minister David Oddson over investigations of its accounting irregularities. (Baugur collapsed in 2009; its co-founder had been convicted in 2007.) This may give us an inkling that the positions on this issue are a bit less principled than their advocates on either side pretend them to be.

The EU countries with the greatest concentrations of press ownership in 2005 were small nations—Luxembourg and Ireland.[123] In Ireland, Tony O'Reilly owns 29% of Independent News & Media Group (INM), which holds more than 80% of the country's print media, as well as a large number of radio stations, cable operators, and newspapers internationally. O'Reilly chairs the Valentia consortium, which bought the fixed-line operations of the dominant incumbent telecommunications operator, Eircom, before flipping it to an Australian private equity fund.[124]

There are no Europe-wide media ownership rules. Each country has treated the issue separately, mostly with a deregulatory trend. The EU Commission has been cautious in entering this touchy area.[125] It did, however, issue a Green Paper, *Pluralism and Media Concentration in the Internal Market* (1992), which concluded that EU intervention in media ownership rules could be justified only if the proper functioning of the internal European market was at issue, but *not* in order to protect pluralism.[126] The European Parliament pushed for some Europe-wide approach but the problem was how to draft a uniform set of media ownership restrictions that would make sense for a small media market such as Slovakia, as well as a large one such as Germany.[127]

There are still, as a potent backup, the general anti-monopoly powers of the EU, and these have been applied regularly. The EU Commission rejected an agreement between British Telecom and SES, the Astra satellite operator, because it reduced competition and foreclosed entry. In the television advertising market, the exclusive agreement of the Luxembourg broadcaster CLT with its subsidiary for telemarketing on CLT channels was struck down because it blocked telemarketing competitors. Italian public broadcaster RAI's exclusive agreement to use its audience data was held to be discriminatory. The EU Commission also rejected a joint pay-TV venture of Deutsche Telekom, Bertelsmann, and Kirch. It challenged Microsoft, and forced it to open up to its competitors and application providers. A German public service broadcaster was stopped from abusing its dominant position by entering into exclusive agreements for films and sports. BSkyB had to divest itself of its 20% stake in the terrestrial British Digital Broadcasting.[128] In the music industry, the EU rejected in 2000 the merger attempts of the music firm EMI, first with Bertelsmann and then with Time Warner. It did, however, approve the 2004 merger of the music production units of Bertelsmann and Sony, allowing the "Big Five" to shrink to four. This change of heart, coming at the end of the tenure of an outgoing Commission, tried to distinguish that case from previous attempts at media mergers, but it was generally held to be based on a greater political and legal caution in applying its anti-monopoly powers.[129]

Moving beyond Europe, a government report in Australia in 2000 found that two firms (News Ltd. and John Fairfax Holdings) accounted for over 90% of the circulation of daily newspapers.[130] Both also have significant TV ownership holdings.[131] A new law came into force in 2007 which repealed many cross-ownership and foreign ownership rules and allowed any company to own a newspaper, two radio stations, and a TV station in the same market. The new law stimulated media mergers. It created a point system for regional media and required in each major market at least five voices or voice-groups.[132]

In Canada, government rules limited TV station ownership to one per market, but did not restrict cross-ownership with newspapers. There is therefore a good amount of broadcast-newspaper ownership. CTVglobemedia, which used to be jointly owned as Bell Globemedia by Bell Canada (68.5%) and the Woodbridge Company (31.5%) of the Thomson media interests, owns the largest private broadcast network CTV, which entails 24 affiliated network stations. It also owns 17 specialty TV stations, several independent stations, the *Globe and Mail*, Canada's national newspaper, and 35 radio stations.[133] CTVglobemedia was called Bell Globemedia until 2006, when Bell's ownership share dropped to 15% upon the acquisition of CHUM,[134] another major Canadian TV company. A second large media firm, CanWest Global, owns 15 television broadcast stations, a TV network, three radio stations, 32 newspapers, free papers, and an Internet news site. In addition, the company owns a 56% share of the Australian broadcast channel Network TEN, 70% of IWORKS, radio and TV stations in New Zealand and Australia, and 45% of TV3 in Ireland.[135] In 2007 it bought (with Goldman Sachs) the cable operator Alliance Atlantis with thirteen specialty channels.[136] Rogers Media is the largest cable company in Canada. It is also active in telecom and owns broadcast and cable channels, 44 radio stations, five cable stations, and magazines (Maclean's and others). In 2000 Quebecor Media bought Videotron, Quebec's largest cable company, the French language TV network TVA, and owns eight dailies and two other local newspapers. Astral Media owns 29 radio stations, and in 2007 bought 52 more from Standard Broadcasting, plus two TV stations. It also owns seventeen pay-TV channels. Osprey Media owns 21 dailies and 36 other newspapers; in 2001 it added 16 dailies and 12 other papers from Hallinger International, and in 2007 added 30 more newspapers (4 dailies) from Can West Global.

In Brazil, Globo is Brazil's leading TV network, with a 70% market share. Globo produces some 80% of its own programming and has good export success. The company is owned by the Marinho family and controls television operations in several countries.[137] Globo also owns the major Internet portal, globo.com, and operates satellite television channels in the United States, Mexico, Canada, Latin America, Europe, Japan, Africa, and Australia.[138]

In Mexico, the media company Grupo Televisa owns television, radio, and publishing.[139] It is Mexico's largest commercial TV broadcaster, with 260 local stations and four national networks, and a 40–60% market share. The company also has mobile phone interests in partnership with the dominant telecommunications group Telmex, and 60% of the Latin American satellite broadcaster Innova (SKY Latin America) with News Corp and Liberty Media.[140] In film, the most important studio is Estudios Churubusco: 95% of movies produced since 2000 in Mexico have been involved with the studio in some way.[141]

What this bird's-eye view of media concentration around the world shows is that it is a global, not just American issue, which suggests it is not the result of any particular administration's or government's policies, but most likely part of a broader dynamic.[142] The international trends will be the subject of future work by the author and collaborators.

This chapter has provided the setting for this book: its aim; the history of media concentration issues in America; today's debate and its combatants; goals and fears (localism, commercialism, quality, diversity, social reform); past research; and the international dimension. The next chapter will provide an analytical model for the dynamics of media concentration, followed by Chapter 3, on the methodology and data.

Notes

1. This is not a recent aberration. Newspapers, as the noted media critic A. J. Liebling commented acerbically fifty years ago, "cover themselves rarely and then only with awe."
2. This discussion of early media history was helped by Starr, Paul, *The Creation of the Media: Political Origins of Modern Communications.* New York: Basic Books, 2004.

3. Green, James N., "The Book Trade in the Middle Colonies, 1680–1720," in Hall, David, and Amory, Hugh, eds., *The Colonial Book in the Atlantic World.* New York: Cambridge University Press, 2000, p. 218.
4. The *Boston Gazette* printed 2,000 copies per issue, the *Massachusetts Spy*, 3,500. Clark, Charles, *The Public Prints, The Newspaper in Anglo-American Culture, 1665–1740.* Oxford University Press, 1994, pp. 123–140.
5. Emery, Edwin, and Michael Emery, *The Press and America: An Interpretative History of the Mass Media.* Englewood Cliffs: Prentice Hall, 1984, p. 39.
6. Isaacson, Walter, *Benjamin Franklin: An American Life.* New York: Simon & Schuster, 2003, p. 126. Franklin already knew how to reach his readers. "One reliable method, which had particular appeal to the rather raunchy young publisher was the time-honored truth that sex sells. Franklin's Gazette was spiced with little leering and titillating items." Walter, *Benjamin Franklin,* p. 68.
7. James Madison argued that the government had an affirmative obligation to protect a vigorous contention of ideas.
8. Pasley, Jeffrey L., *The Tyranny of Printers: Newspaper Politics in the Early American Republic.* Charlottesville: University Press of Virginia, 2001, pp. 60–104; Rosenfeld, Richard N., *American Aurora: A Democratic-Republican Returns.* New York: St. Martin's Press, 1997.
9. Pasley, *Tyranny of Printers,* p. 312. *Memoirs of John Quincy Adams,* 5:112, notes to pp. 295–299.
10. Albert Gallatin to John Badollet, Oct. 25 1805, *Gallatin Paper,* N.Y. Historical Society. In Pasley, *Tyranny of Printers.*
11. Starr, *Creation of the Media,* p. 131, and a source for some of the above.
12. In contrast to England and France, newspapers were not geographically concentrated in America. In 1820, there were 53 newspapers published in Massachusetts (including Maine) alone, originating in 23 separate towns. This meant greater localism, but possibly also greater local influence of a proprietor owning a town newspaper. Humphrey, Carol Sue, *This Popular Engine: The Role of New England Newspapers During the American Revolution.* Newark: University of Delaware Press, 1992; Brown, Richard D. "The Emergence of Urban Society in Rural Massachusetts, 1760–1820." *Journal of American History* 61, June 1974, 43.
13. Stone, John and Meunell, Stephen, eds., Alexis de Tocqueville, *On Democracy, Revolution, and Society* (1835). Chicago: University of Chicago press, 1982., p. 153.
14. Newspapers were much shorter, however, typically eight pages in length.
15. See Herrick, Dennis F., *Media Management in the Age of Giants.* Ames: Iowa State Press, 2003, p. 26.

16. Kielbowicz, Richard Burket, "Origins of Second-Class Mail Category and the Business of Policymaking,1863–1879." *JournalismMonographs*, No. 96:17, 1986. In Starr, *Creation of the Media*.

17. Klein, Maury, *The Life and Legend of Jay Gould*. Baltimore: John Hopkins University Press, 1986, p. 394.

18. Summers, Marl Wahlgreen, *The Press Gang: Newspapers and Politics, 1865–1878*. Chapel Hill: University of North Carolina Press, 1994, p. 303; Blondheim, Menahem *News over the Wires: The Telegraph and the Flow of Public Information in America, 1844–1897*. Cambridge: Harvard University Press, 1994, pp.177–184. In Starr, *Creation of the Media*.

19. U.S. Supreme Court. *Associated Press* v. *U.S.*, 326 U.S. 1 (1945).

20. Headrick, Daniel, *The Invisible Weapon: Telecommunications and International Politics. 1851–1945*. New York: Oxford University Press, 1991, pp. 117–120; Douglas, Susan J., *Inventing American Broadcasting 1899–1922*. Baltimore: Johns Hopkins University Press, 1987, pp. 64–80.

21. Poggi, Jack, *Theater in America: The Impact of Economic Forces, 1870–1967*. Ithaca: Cornell University Press, 1966.

22. Wikipedia, accessed December 30, 2005.

23. Random House, Simon and Schuster, McGraw-Hill, Macmillan, Grolier, Scott Foresman, Harcourt, Prentice-Hall, Harper and Row, Houghton Mifflin, Doubleday, and Little, Brown.

24. Federal Communications Commission, 2002 Biennial Regulatory Review. Review of the Commission's Broadcast Ownership Rules and Other Rules Adopted Pursuant to Section 202 of the Telecommunications Act of 1996, Report and Order and Notice of Proposed Rulemaking, FCC 03–127, July 2, 2003.

25. *Fox Television Stations, Inc.* v. *FCC*, 280 F.3d 1027, rehearing granted in part, 294 F.3d 123 (D.C.Cir. 2002). Available at http://www.fcc.gov/ogc/documents/opinions/2002/00–1222.html.

26. FCC *"Report and Order and Notice of Proposed Rulemaking"* June 2, 2003. FCC 03–127. Available at http://hraunfoss.fcc.gov/edocs_public/attachmatch/FCC-03-127A1.pdf.

27. *Prometheus Radio Project v. FCC*, (3rd Circuit Court of Appeals, June 24, 2004), http://www.ca3.uscourts.gov/opinarch/033388p.pdf.

28. In 2007, the FCC relaxed the 1975 cross-ownership restrictions for television or radio stations with a newspaper in the same market. In the largest 20 media markets, for such TV-newspaper cross-ownership, at least eight independent voices, including newspapers, would have to remain, and the TV stations could not be among the top four in the market. For radio-newspaper cross-ownership, no voice test was required. There was also the possibility of waivers to the restrictions in some other markets if at least seven hours of local news were

added by a station, or where either station or newspaper were in financial distress. The latter was defined by several economic yardsticks. The FCC vote was 3:2 along party lines, and shifted the fight to Congress, the courts, and a future FCC.

29. "Lawmakers Predict Revolt over Media Dictatorships." *Broadcasting & Cable*, July 23, 2003. http://www.broadcastingcable.com/index.asp?layout=articlePrint&articleID=CA313012.

30. Thierer, Adam D., quoted in Terry Lane, "Hinchey Pushes Fairness Doctrine Bill to CWA." *Communications Daily*, March 31, 2004, p. 9.

31. "Dean Vows to 'Break Up Giant Media Enterprises.'" *Drudge Report*, December 2, 2003. http://www.drudgereport.com/dean1.htm; McConnell, Bill, "Dean Threatens to Break Up Media Giants." *Broadcasting & Cable*, December 3, 2003. http://www.broadcastingcable.com/index.asp?layout=articlePrint&articleID=CA339546.

32. For the white supremacy perspective on media concentration, see Duke, David, *Jewish Supremacism*, 2003. See www.davidduke.com "My Awakening," ch. 19, "Who Runs the Media?"

33. www.gp.org/press/pr_05_30_d3.html.

34. "Media Madness," *Economist*, September 11,2003. http://www.economist.com/displayStory.cfm?Story_ID=2052042.

35. Consumer Federation of America. "New Survey Finds Americans Rely on Newspapers Much More than Other Media for Local News and Information: FCC Media Ownership Rules Based on Flawed Data." January 2004., Washington, D.C.

36. *Advertising Age*, Madison Avenue's bible, wrote that in 2003 the top six media firms' net U.S. revenues were larger than that of the next 51 media companies combined. (The actual share of the top six media firms in overall mass media revenues was 28.5% in 2005.)

37. Safire, William, "Localism's Last Stand." *New York Times*, June 17, 2003, p. A27.

38. Krugman, Paul, "In Media Res." *New York Times*, Nov. 29, 2002, p. A39.

39. See Knee, Jonathan, "Should We Fear Media Cross-Ownership." *Regulation*, Summer 2003, p. 17. http://www.cato.org/pubs/regulation/regv26n2/v26n2–3.pdf.

40. Noam, Eli and Lorenzo Pupillo, eds., *Peer- to-Peer Video: The Economics, Policy, and Culture of Today's New Mass Medium*." Springer, 2008.

41. Noam, Eli, "Spectrum Auction: Yesterday's Heresy, Today's Orthodoxy, Tomorrow's Anachronism. Taking the Next Step to Open Spectrum Access." *Journal of Law and Economics* 41, no. 2 (October 1998): 765–790.

42. See Noam, Eli. *Globalism and Localism in Telecommunications*. Elsevier, 1997; "Divergent Goals for the Deregulators." *New York Times*, editorial page article, August 6, 1981; "Opening Up Cable TV." *New York Times*, editorial page

article, March 19, 1981; "Ten Years After Bell Breakup: The Split-Up Worked. No It Didn't." *New York Times Viewpoint,* January 23, 1994; "The Airwaves as a Toll Road." *New York Times Viewpoint,* February 11, 1996.

43. When some media firms diverge from profit maximization to suit the wide values of their owners, the results might not be what critics envision. Sinclair Broadcasting, for example, a medium-sized company, has been quite outspoken in its conservative political preferences, even in the face of advertiser backlash, and has been widely castigated for it.

44. Herrick, Dennis F., *Media Management in the Age of Giants.* Ames: Iowa State Press, 2003, pp. 292–293.

45. See chapter 8 on Print and Publishing.

46. Demers, David, "Corporate News Structure and the Managerial Revolution." *Journal of Media Economics,* 2000.

47. Lacy, Stephen, and Alan Blanchard, "The Impact of Public Ownership, Profits, and Competition on Number of Newsroom Employees and Starting Salaries in Mid-Size Newspapers." *Journalism and Mass Communication Quarterly,* Winter 2003, 80:4, 949–968.

48. See Herrick, *Media Management in the Age of Giants,* p. 20; Compaine, Benjamin, "The Expanding Base of Media Competition." *Journal of Communication,* 35: 3, Summer, 1985.

49. In analyzing media profits one must use economically meaningful measures for profit. Operating margin—earnings relative to revenues—is not a good measure. Operating margin does not account for interest payments, depreciation, and tax. It is related to "EBITDA" (earnings before interest tax and depreciation). EBITDA figures are often used by firms to make themselves look good to investors. And they are used by their adversaries to show dramatic profits to audiences that do not understand the different profit measures.

A better measure is net profit margin—net profit relative to revenues. But that measure, too, has problems. A firm can be hugely profitable on low margins if it has a high volume of activity (turnover). For supermarket chains or stock brokerage houses this is the business model: low margins on high volumes, and potentially high total profits.

To economists, the more meaningful measures are return on assets (ROA) or return on shareholder equity (ROE). But these numbers, too, are not without problems, since they can be manipulated by the treatment of depreciation and are affected by the age of the assets and how they are carried on the books. Media firms' assets tend to be mostly intangibles—copyrights, contracts, goodwill, etc.—which lead to ROA measures that are not informative.

50. Herrick, *Media Management in the Age of Giants,* p. 13.

51. Baldasty, Gerald J., from Underwood, Doug,. *When MBAs Rule the Newsroom: How the Markets and Managers Are Reshaping Today's Media.* New York: Columbia University Press, 1993, pp. 42–43.

52. www.oneworldlowercase.com/plan/opening.htm.

53. Fuller, Jack, *New Values.* Chicago: University of Chicago Press, 1996, pp, 197–198; Herrick, *Media Management in the Age of Giants,* pp. 191, 198.

54. On the positive side, institutional shareholders were the ones who forced out Conrad Black from his control of Hollinger, with charges of financial malfeasance.

55. Herrick, *Media Management in the Age of Grants,* p. 220.

56. Berle, Adolph, and Means, Gardiner, *The Modern Corporation and Private Property.* New York: Macmillan, 1932.

57. McChesney, Robert W., *The Problem of the Media: U.S. Communication Politics in the 21st Century.* New York: Monthly Review Press, 2004, p. 175.

58. Noam, Eli, "Public Interest Programming in American Television," in Noam, Eli and Waltermann, Jens, eds., *Public Television in America.* Gütersloh: Bertelsmann Foundation Publishers, 1998, pp. 145–175.

59. Noam, Eli, *Television in Europe.* New York: Oxford University Press, 1992.

60. Herrick, *Media Management in the Age of Giants,* p. 206.

61. Hudson, Mike, "Gazette's Financial Woes Continue, Shaw Named 'Associate Publisher.'" *Niagara Falls Reporter,* July 8, 2003. Available at: http://niagarafallsreporter.com/gazettewoes.html.

62. Scherer, Michael, "The News in Mormon Country." *Columbia Journalism Review,* March-April, 2003.

63. Herrick, *Media Management in the Age of Giants,* p. 205.

64. Hickey, Neil, "Money Lust." *Columbia Journalism Review,* July-August 1998.

65. Viacom pulled a rerun of *South Park* mocking Scientology, allegedly because it offended its Paramount star, Tom Cruise.

66. CBS News against Sen. Joseph McCarthy.

67. See e.g., Coulson, D. C., "Impact of Ownership on Newspaper Quality." *Journalism Quarterly,* 1994; Coulson, D. C., and Anne Hansen, "The Louisville Courier-Journal's News Content After Purchase by Gannet." *Journalism and Mass Communications Quarterly,* 1995; Iosifides, Petros, "Diversity versus Concentration in the Deregulated Mass Media." *Journalism and Mass Communications Quarterly,* Spring 1999; Lacy, S., "A Model of Demand for News: Impact of

Competition on Newspaper Content." *Journalism Quarterly*, 1989; Wanta, W., and Johnson, T. J., "Content Changes in the St. Louis Post-Dispatch During Different Market Situations." *Journal of Media Economics*, 1994.

68. "Media bias comes in various dimensions, not just political. There is a *temporal* bias in favor of immediate news; a *visual* bias, especially for TV; a bias toward *bad news, conflict,* and *narratives;* a *commercial* bias toward advertisers; even *even-handedness* can be a bias, because it might give fringe groups a legitimacy that they do not merit. Sometimes something happens to be true, rather than just be a perspective. And then there is the bias of the creators or inputs, not their creation or output." Rhetorical.net, accessed January 3, 2006.

69. A proxy would be the political contributions of media firm employees and managers, which are public record. The public database of the Federal Election Commission allows calculations. For the election cycle of 2004, the employees and managers of major media companies made, on average, 69% of their $10.7 million in contributions to Democrats. This ranged from 5% at Sinclair to 100% at National Public Radio and the *New York Times*. Even News Corp's employees gave 69% to Democrats. The six largest firms made the bulk of donations, about 80%. On top of that, companies give through political action committees (PACs) and trade associations. For the 2008 election cycle, the major media companies and their employees contributed $47 million, 78% of which went to Democrats. This ranged from 1% at Salem, a religeous broadcast group and 20% Liberty Media, to 74% Disney, 77% News Corp., 81% Time Warner, 86% National Amusements (Viacom, CBS), and 93/100% for GE/NBC. At: http://www.opensecrets.org/industries.

70. Alger, Dean, *How Giant Corporations Dominate Mass Media, Distort Competition and Endanger Democracy*. Lanham, Md.: Rowman & Littlefield, 1998; ch. 6, *The Media and Politics*. New York: Harcourt Brace College, 2nd ed., 1996; Carter, Sue, Frederick Fico, and Joycelyn A. McCabe, "Partisan and Structural Balance in Local Television Election Coverage." *Journalism and Mass Communications Quarterly*, 79, 2002, p. 50; Edwards, E. S., and N. Chomsky, *Manufacturing Consent*. New York: Pantheon, 1988; Goldberg, Bernard, *Bias*. Washington, DC: Regnery, 2002; Glasser, Theodore L., David S. Allen, and S. Elizabeth Banks, "The Influence of Chain Ownership on News Play: A Case Study." *Journalism Quarterly*, 66, 1989; Levin, H. J., "Program Duplication, Diversity, and Effective Viewer Choices: Some Empirical Findings." *American Economic Review*, 1971; McManus, J., "How Objective Is Local Television News?" *Mass Communications Review*, 1991; Busterna, J. C., "Television Ownership Effects on

Programming and Idea Diversity: Baseline Data." *Journal of Media Economics*, 1988; Jatz, J., "Memo to Local News Directors." *Columbia Journalism Review*, 1990; McManus, J., "Local News: Not a Pretty Picture." *Columbia Journalism Review*, 1990; Snider, James H., and Benjamin I. Page, "Does Media Ownership Affect Media Stands? The Case of the Telecommunications Act of 1996." Paper delivered at the Annual Meeting of the Midwest Political Science Association, April 1997; Just, Marion, Rosalind Levine, and Kathleen Regan, "News for Sale: Half of Stations Report Sponsor Pressure on News Decision." *Columbia Journalism Review— Project for Excellence in Journalism*, November–December 2001, p. 2; Kim, Sei-Hill, Dietram A. Scheufele, and James Shanahan, "Think About It This Way: Attribute Agenda Setting Function of the Press and the Public's Evaluation of a Local Issue." *Journalism and Mass Communications Quarterly*, 79, 2002, p. 7.; Lacy, Stephen, and Todd F. Simon, "Competition in the Newspaper Industry," in *The Economics and Regulation of United States Newspapers*. Norwood, NJ: Ablex, 1999; Monroe E. Price, "Public Broadcasting and the Crisis of Corporate Governance," *Cardozo Arts & Entertainment*, 17, 1999; Soloski, John, "Economics and Management: The Real Influence of Newspaper Groups." Newspaper Research Journal, 1, 1979; Johnson, T. J., and W. Wanta, "Newspaper Circulation and Message Diversity in an Urban Market." *Mass Communications Review*, 1993; W. L. Bennet, *News, the Politics of Illusion*. New York: Longmans, 1988; Davie, W. R., and J. S. Lee, "Television News Technology: Do More Sources Mean Less Diversity." *Journal of Broadcasting and Electronic Media*, 1993, p. 455. A study of Germany shows a substantially negative coverage of the U.S. activity in Iraq in German television and press. The authors explain this not as a bias at all, but rather as an expression of the media following national consensus on international issues; Weiss, Maritz, and Hans Jurgen Weiss, "Indexing—A General Approach for Explaining Political Biases in War Coverage," in *Breakdown of Trans-Atlantic Dialogue? Political Tendencies in German Media Coverage of the Iraq War*. New York: International Communication Association, May 2005.

71. Jürgen Habermas: Media companies devoted to profit have turned the press into an agent of manipulation: "It became the gate through which privileged private interests invaded the public sphere." Habermas, Jürgen, *The Structural Transformation of the Public Sphere: An Inquiry into a Category of Bourgeois Society*. Cambridge: MIT Press, 1991, p. 185.

72. For example, S. Berry and J. Waldfogel measured the effect of concentration on product diversity in radio markets between 1993 and 1997. They find that reductions in the number of

owners actually led to increases in the number of formats; Berry, Steven, and Waldfogel, Joel, 2001, "Do Mergers Increase Product Variety? Evidence from Radio Broadcasting." *Quarterly Journal of Economics*, 116 (3), pp. 1009–10025. Other literature includes: Williams, George, Keith Brown, and Peter Alexander, "Media Ownership Working Group Radio Market Structure and Music Diversity." *Media Bureau Staff Research Paper,* Media Ownership Working Group, Federal Communications Commission, September 2002; Alexander, Peter, 1997, "Product Variety and Market Structure: A New Measure and Simple Test," *Journal of Economic Behavior and Organization,* 32, 207–214; Anderson, Simon, and Coate, Stephen, 2000, "Market Provision of Public Goods: The Case of Broadcasting." *NBER Working Paper No. W7513*; Beebe, Jack H., 1977. "Institutional Structure and Program Choices in Television Markets." *Quarterly Journal of Economics*, 91 (1), 15–37; Gabszewicz, J., Didier Laussel, and Nathalie Sonnac, 1999, "TV-Broadcasting Competition and Advertising." CORE Discussion Paper 2000/65.

73. Steiner, P. O., 1952, "Program Patterns and the Workability of Competition in Radio Broadcasting." *Quarterly Journal of Economics,* 66 (2), 194–223.

74. Owen, Bruce, Steven Wildman, *Video Economics.* Cambridge: Harvard University Press, 1992.

75. Entman, Robert, *Projections of Power: Framing News, Public Opinion, and U.S. Foreign Policy (Studies in Communication, Media, and Public Opinion).* Chicago: University of Chicago Press, 2003.

76. Lopes, D. P., "Innovation and Diversity in the Popular Music Industry, 1969 to 1990." *American Sociological Review,* 1992.

77. Berry, Steven, and Waldfogel, Joel, 2001. "Do Mergers Increase Product Variety? Evidence from Radio Broadcasting." *Quarterly Journal of Economics,* 116 (3), 1009–1025.

78. Einstein, Mara, *Media Diversity: Economics, Ownership, and the FCC.* Mahwah: Erlbaum, 2004.

79. Yoo, Christopher S., "Architectural Censorship and the FCC." *Regulation,* 28 (1), Spring 2005, p. 22.

80. Media managers and their critics do not agree on much, but they seem united in feeling denigrated by this analogy of food for thought and food for body and soul. Since almost any industry feels "different," the example is grating on purpose.

81. To confirm, visit the many small grocery stores in New York City, and suburban megastores.

82. The debate easily degenerates from one of facts and analysis to one of an author's motives or incentives. This, too, is a labor-saving methodology. My own independence has been questioned from the left, as an economist at an academic institution receiving corporate and other donations, and from

the right for my close association with the long-time national president of the American Civil Liberties Union, my wife.

83. Bagdikian, Ben, *The New Media Monopoly.* Boston: Beacon Press, 2004, p. 3.

84. Herrick, *Media Management in the Age of Grants*, p. 303.

85. Companies 20–25 held market shares of 0.7, 0.6, 0.5, 0.5, and 0.4. If we generously assume for companies 26–50 an average market share of 0.2, it would add up to 5%.

86. Bagdikian, *The New Media Monopoly*, p. 3.

87. Measuring market shares according to revenues rather than counting copies tends to give more weight to the largest market participants, since they usually can charge higher prices per copy or advertisement CPM (cost per thousand), *ceteris paribus*. Physical measures, furthermore, cannot be readily used for intermedia aggregation and averaging. A similar comment can be made for "attention intensity" or "attention time." If we counted instead the actual number of outlets or readers/audience, or similar indices, the largest of firms would show a somewhat smaller share. The use of revenues is hence normally a worst-case scenario in terms of concentration levels. (If there are exceptions to this, I will be glad to incorporate them.) Another type of weight, for news media, would be to look at value as a news source. This is briefly done in chapter 13, "National Horizontal Concentration," for illustrative purposes.

88. Acquisitions are not a one-way street. The Walt Disney Company sold its newspapers in 1997 to the Knight-Ridder chain (*Kansas City Star, Fort Worth Star-Telegram,* and two other papers) for $1.65 billion. On the other hand, in 2007, News Corp bought Dow Jones & Co., including its *Wall Street Journal.*

89. If we consider Viacom and CBS to be still under the same control, TV share becomes 20.6%.

90. Bagdikian, *The New Media Monopoly*, p. 3.

91. McChesney, Robert W. *The Problem of the Media: US Communication Politics in the 21st Century.* New York: Monthly Review Press, 2004, p. 183.

92. McChesney, *The Problem of the Media*, p. 175.

93. McChesney, *The Problem of the Media,* p. 189.

94. Bagdikian, *The New Media Monopoly;* Cooper, Mark, *Media Ownership and Democracy in the Digital Information Age.* Stanford: Center for Internet and Society, Stanford University Law School, 2003. http://cyberlaw.stanford.edu/blogs/cooper/archives/mediabooke.pdf; Sunstein, Cass, *Republic.com.* Princeton: Princeton University Press, 2001; Chester, Jeffrey, and Larson, Gary O., "A 12-Step Program for Media Democracy." *Nation,* July 23, 2002. http://www.thenation.com/doc.mhtml?i=20020805&s=larson20020723; Leanza, Cheryl, and Harold Feld, "More Than 'a Toaster

with Pictures': Defending Media Ownership Limits." *Communications Lawyer*, Fall 2003, pp. 12–22. http://www.mediaaccess.org/ToasterFINAL.pdf; Chomsky, Noam, *Media Control: The Spectacular Achievements of Propoganda*. New York: Seven Stories Press, 2nd ed., 2002.

95. Media reform quotes, at BetterWorld.net, http://betterworld.net/quotes/media-quotes.htm, accessed on December 28, 2007.

96. Lessig, Lawrence, *"Free Culture: How Big Media Uses Technology and the Law to Lock Down Culture and Control Creativity."* New York: Penguin, 2004.

97. Number is based on the aggregate C2 for the 30 local markets (see chapter 15, Local Media Concentration).

98. Cooper, *Media Ownership and Democracy in the Digital Information Age*, 2003.

99. Cooper's study on cable TV (video programming, multichannel video distribution, and high-speed Internet cable) finds in all three of its submarkets trends toward increasing media concentration and decreased competition. Another scholar who has ventured toward data issues in media concentration is Mark Crispin Miller. Miller published a series of articles in the *Nation*, in which he usefully mapped the ties that bind the major media outlets into large entertainment conglomerates. Miller, Mark Crispin, "Free Media." *Nation*, June 3, 1996, p. 9; "The Crushing Power of Big Publishing," *Nation*, March 17, 1997, p. 11; "Who Controls the Music?" *Nation*, August 25, 1997, p. 11.

100. It is not widespread in academia. One graduate student at another university wrote about me after what I hope was a balanced presentation: "Most interesting to me was the idea that there is even a school of thought that disagrees with the alarmist view towards media concentration."

101. Samuelson, Robert J., "The 'Big Media' Myth." *Washington Post*, August 6, 2003, p. A 17.

102. See, for example, Owen, Bruce, "Confusing Success with Access: Correctly Measuring Concentration of Ownership and Control in Mass Media and Online Services." *Stanford Law and Economics Online Working Paper No. 283*, May 2004.

103. Thierer, Adam D., *"Media Myths. Making Sense of the Debate Over Media Ownership."* Washington D.C.: Progress & Freedom Foundation, June 2005.

104. Earlier, Harvey Levin authored an empirical study of media concentration, measuring cross-ownership ties between broadcasters, publishers, and the film industry in the 1950s and before. Levin's thoughtful discussion remains relevant to this day. Levin, Harvey, *Fact and Fancy in Television Regulation: An Economic Study of Policy Alternatives*. New York: Russell Sage, 1980.

105. Compaine, Benjamin, Christopher Sterling, Thomas Guback, and J. Kendrick Noble, Jr., *Who Owns the Media?* White Plains: Knowledge Industry, 1979, 1982.

106. The books cover several major mass media industries. Trends of concentration are discussed mostly seriatim by medium. This was probably an outgrowth of the fact that the study's sections on different industries are divided among and credited separately to the coauthors. It is therefore not clear whether a chapter speaks for both of the book's authors. Compaine, Benjamin M., and Douglas Gomery, *Who Owns the Media? Competition and Concentration in the Mass Media Industry*, 3rd ed. Mahwah, NJ: Erlbaum, 2000.

107. Compaine and Gomery, *Who Owns the Media?*, 2000.

108. Delamarter, Richard T. *Big Blue: IBM's Use and Abuse of Power*. New York: Mead, 1986.

109. Brock, Gerald W., *The Telecommunications Industry*. Cambridge: Harvard University Press 1981; Crandall, Robert W., *After the Breakup: US Telecommunications in a More Competitive Era*, Washington, DC: Brookings Institution, 1991; Evans, David S., ed., *Breaking Up Bell*. New York: Elsevier, 1983; Temin, Peter, *The Fall of the Bell System*. New York: Cambridge University Press, 1987.

110. Bank, David, *Breaking Windows: How Bill Gates Fumbled the Future of Microsoft*. New York: Free Press, 2001.

111. Auletta, Ken, *Three Blind Mice: How the TV Networks Lost Their Way*. New York: Random House, 1991.

112. See, for example, Doyle, Gillian, *Media Ownership*, London: Sage, 2002.

113. Halimi, Serge (editorial board member of *Le Monde Diplomatique*), "United States: An Unfree Press." *Le Monde Diplomatique*, June 2003; "US Media Monopoly Dangers Raise More Concern. One US, One Market, One Media Mogul." *Guardian*, May 17, 2003.

114. One could argue that a few national newspapers provide more diversity than a system of numerous but locally monopolistic papers. But one would then lose localism, and would then have to accept the same argument for local TV stations, where it would militate against localism in favor of a few national networks.

115. Available at http://www.humanrights.coe.int/media/topics/pluralism/main.htm.

116. Doyle, Gillian. *Media Ownership. The Economics and Politics of Convergence and Concentration in the UK and European Media*. London: Sage, 2002, p. 142. Other studies include Sanchez-Taberno, A., *Media Concentration in Europe: Commercial Enterprise and the Public Interest*. Dusseldorf: European Institute for the Media, 1993; Sanchez-Taberno, A., and M. Carvajal, *Media Concentration in the European Market. New Trends and Challenges*. Pamplona: EUNSA,

2002; Iosifides, P. "Methods of Measuring Media Concentration." *Media Culture and Society*, Vol. 19, 1997, pp. 643–663; European Federation of Journalists, *European Media Ownership: Threats on the Landscape. A Survey of Who Owns What in Europe*. Brussels: EFJ, 2003; Albarran, Alan B., and Bozena I. Mierzejewska, "Media Concentration in the U.S. and European Union: A Comparative Analysis," paper presented at the 6th World Media Economics Conference, HEC Montreal, Canada, May 12–15, 2004; Meier, W. A., and Trappel, J. "Media Concentration and the Public Interest," in Mcquail, D., and K. Siune, eds., *Media Policy: Convergence, Concentration and Commerce*. London: Sage, 1998, pp. 38–59.

117. For further detail regarding media concentration in Germany see Kopper, Gerd. *Changing Media Markets in Germany and Strategic Options for the Newspaper Industry*. In Picard, Robert G. *Strategic Responses to Media Market Changes*. Jönköping: Jönköping International Business School Ltd, 2004, pp. 105–120.

118. http://www.vivendiuniversal.com/vu/en/group/default.cfm?idr=6.

119. Media concentration in UK is discussed in Collins, Richard. "Enter the Grecian Horse? Regulation of ics and Politics of Convergence and Concentration in the U.K. and European Media." *Journal of Cultural Economics* 27 (2003): 290–293 as well as in Doyle, Gillian, *Media Ownership*. London: Sage, 2002. "Media Ownership – The Economics and Politics of Convergence and Concentration in the U.K. and European Media." *Journal of Cultural Economics* 27 (2003): 290–293, as well as in Doyle, Gillian, *Media Ownership*. London: Sage, 2002. Hand, Chris. "Television Ownership in Britain and the Coming of ITV: What do the statistics show?" *Department of Media Arts, Royal Holloway University of London*, 2002; Tunstall, Jeremy. "The United Kingdom," in Kelly, Mary, ed. *The Media in Europe*. 3rd ed. London: Sage Publications Inc., 2004, pp. 262–273.

120. Sparks, C., "Concentration and Market Entry in the UK National Daily Press." *European Journal of Communication*, 10(2), C., 995.

121. Doyle, *Media Ownership*, 2002.

122. Swedish media ownership is covered in Hulten, Olof. "Sweden," in Kelly, Mary, ed. *The Media in Europe*. Sage Publications Inc. 2004, pp. 236–247; Rosengren, Karl Erik. "Sweden and its media scene – A bird's-eye view," in Rosengren, Karl Erik, ed. *Media Effects and Beyond*. 1st ed. London: Routledge, 1994, pp. 29–38.

123. Doyle, *Media Ownership*, 2002.

124. European Federation of Journalists. "*Media Power in Europe: the Big Picture of Ownership.*" Brussels: EFJ, 2005.

125. CEC, *Pluralism and Media Concentration in the Internal Market: An Assessment of the Need for Community Action*, COM (92) 480 Final. Brussels, December, 23, 1992, p. 99.

126. Doyle, Gillian, "From 'Pluralism' to 'Ownership': Europe's Emergent Policy on Media Concentrations Navigates the Doldrums." *Journal of Information, Law and Technology*, 1997 (3).

127. Humphreys, Peter, "Power and Control in the New Media." Paper presented at the ECPR workshop *New Media and Political Communication*, Bern, February, 27, 1997.

128. Gibbons, Thomas. "Concentration of Ownership and Control in Converging Media Industry." *Convergence in European TV Regulation*. London: Blackstone Press, 1999.

129. More information about media ownership in Europe can be found in Harcourt, Alison, "The Regulation of Media Markets in selected EU Accession States in Central and Eastern Europe." *European Law Journal* 9, no. 3 (2003): 316–340; Harcourt, Alison. "EU Media Ownership Regulation." *Journal of Common Market Studies* 36, no. 3 (1998): 369–389; Prehn, Ole, and Jauert, Per. "Ownership and Concentration in Local Radio Broadcasting in Scandinavia." *Nordicom Review* 1 (1996): 81–106; Shaver, Dan, and Shaver, Mary A. "Comparing Merger and Acquisition Activity in the U.S. and the European Union During the 1990s," presented at *5th World Media Conference*. The University of Central Florida, Turku, Finland, 2002; Süssenbacher, Daniela. "Foreign Ownership in SEE Region." *deScripto* 2 (2005): p. 11; Tılıç, Doğan. "Media Ownership Structure in Turkey." Ankara: Progressive Association, January 2000.

130. Broadcasting Inquiry Report, released on April 11, 2000 by Productivity Commission (the Australian government's principal review and advisory body on microeconomic policy and regulation).

131. Broadcasting Inquiry Report, April 11, 2000.

132. Other general international trends were recorded by Sylvia Chan-Olmsted, "Mergers, Acquisitions, and Convergence: The Strategic Alliances of Broadcasting, Cable Television, and Telephone Services." *Journal of Media Economics*, 11(3), 1998.

133. Source: company Web site http://www.ctv.ca.

134. For further detail regarding media concentration in Canada, see Keshen, Richard, and MacAskill, Kent. "I Told You So: Newspaper Ownership in Canada and the Kent Commission Twenty Years Later." *American Review of Canadian Studies* 30, no. 3 (2000): 315–325; Soderlund, Walter C., and Hildebrandt, Kai. *Canadian Newspaper Ownership in the Era of Convergence*. Edmonton: The University of Alberta Press, 2005; Winsock, Dwayne. "Netscapes of power: convergence, consolidation and power in the Canadian mediascape." *Media, Culture & Society* 24, no. 6 (2002): 795–819.

135. Source: company annual report.

136. For further detail regarding media concentration in Canada, and a comparison with Korea, see Wu, Irene. "Canada, South Korea,

Netherlands and Sweden: regulatory implications of the convergence of telecommunications, broadcasting and Internet services." *Telecommunications Policy* 28, no. 1 (2004): 79–96; Shin, Dong-Hee. "Convergence of telecommunications, media and information technology, and implications for regulation." *Journal of Policy, Regulation and Strategy for Telecommunications* 8, no. 1 (2006): 42–56.

137. Source: company annual report.

138. http://en.wikipedia.org/wiki/Globo accessed July 21, 2006.

139. Mexico's media concentration is discussed in Lozano, José-Carlos. "Foreign ownership of the media and telecommunications industries in Mexico." Presented at the Foreign Ownership Seminar. Tecnológico de Monterrey, Monterrey, Montreal, march 1, 2002; Renteria, Maria Elena Gutierrez. "Media Concentration in the Hispanic Market: A Case Study of TV Azteca vs. Televisa." *International Journal on Media Management* 9, no. 2 (2007): 70–76.

140. Source: http://en.wikipedia.org/wiki/TV_Globo accessed May 15, 2006.

141. http://en.wikipedia.org/wiki/Estudios_Churubusco accessed July 24, 2006. For more information regarding media concentration in emerging markets see (for the Arab world) Gher, Leo A., and Amin, Hussein Y. "New and Old Media Access and Ownership in the Arab World." *International Communication Gazette* 61, (1999): 59–88; (China) Esarey, Ashley. "Cornering the Market: State Strategies for Controlling China's Commercial Media." *Asian Perspective* 29, no. 4 (2005): 37–83; (India) Kohli, Vanita. *The Indian Media Business*. Sage Publications Pvt. Ltd, 2006; Sonwalker, Prasun. "'Murdochization' of the Indian press: from by-line to bottom line." *Media, Culture & Society* 24, no. 6 (2002): 821–834; (South Africa) Hodge, James. "Extending telecoms ownership in South Africa: Policy, Performance and future options." Working Paper 7, University of Cape Town, 2003; Tomaselli, Keyan G. "Ownership and control in the South African print media: Black Empowerment After Apartheid." *Ecquid Novi* 18, no. 1 (1997): 21–68.

142. More on global media concentration can be found in McChesney, Robert W., & Schiller, Dan. "Foundations for the Emerging Global Debate about Media Ownership and Regulation." Technology, Business and Society Programme Paper 11, United Nations Research Institute for Social Development, 2003; Murdock, Graham. "Concentration and Ownership in the era of privatization," in Marris, Paul, ed. *Media Studies*. 2nd ed. New York: NYU Press, 2000, 142–155; Woodhull, Nancy J., & Snyder, Robert W. *Media mergers*. New Brunswick, NJ: Transaction Publishers, 1998.

2

The Dynamics of Media Concentration: A Model

THE MODEL

Since World War II, the information sector in the United States has been evolving through three stages: first, the stage of *limited media*, then *multichannel media*, and, finally, *digital media*. In the lengthy stage of limited media, major segments of the information sector were dominated by large firms. In the early 1980s, the three TV networks—ABC, CBS, and NBC—collectively had 92% of nightly TV viewership; AT&T controlled 80% of local telephone service and almost 100% of the long distance market; IBM accounted for 77% of the computer market; six Hollywood studios produced most film content; six companies provided most music; a handful of influential newspapers and magazines led the news and its interpretation nationally; and most towns and cities had only a single newspaper.

This stage of limited media, so different from the image of a past golden age of open media, prevailed into the early 1980s, when it changed quite rapidly, at least in the electronic realm. As with many transitions, one cannot specify an exact date for the change. But if a particular date must be chosen, 1984 is arguably the best. That year had been synonymous with totalitarian control. Yet when the real 1984 arrived it was characterized by several mileposts that, in retrospect, marked an opening for new media. In 1984, AT&T's telecommunications monopoly was broken up; Congress deregulated the cable TV industry, which then mushroomed into the major distributor of the TV that Americans are actually watching; home video came into its own; and microcomputers emerged as consumer products.

The third stage, that of *digital media,* is characterized by the emergence of computer communications as a mass medium and is exemplified by the Internet. This transition was well under way in some industries, such as electronic publishing, by the early 1990s, and later in the decade it emerged in other industries such as music distribution and telecommunications services. By 2004, it was spreading to mass audience video, too. The key to this stage is digitalization: the transformation of voice, text, video, and data information into binary on-off signals, and their move toward common platforms of transmission, storage, processing, and display.

The key year for that transition was 1996. In technical terms, digitalization was making headway in the information technology (IT) world, and subsequently in telecommunications, through the 1980s and 1990s. It accelerated with the World Wide Web in 1990, and reached its public policy embodiment with the 1996 Telecommunication Act, which recast the regulation of most communication media. That law was both the result and the cause of the frenzy of investment, mergers, and start-ups known as the Internet bubble.

The first transition, from the stage of limited communications to multichannel communications, increased the types and numbers of content distributors, telecommunications networks, and computer options. The second shift into the digital era is arguably even more historic in character: the transition from individual communications capacity, measured in kilobit per second (i.e., the voice phone), to an individualized megabit capacity (broadband) and, soon, to a gigabit capacity (ultra-broadband). Megabit capacity existed before but only on a simultaneous mass audience ("synchronous") basis through TV broadcasting and cable TV that offered the same content to millions at the same time. Now, such capacity becomes available on an individualized basis, and the difference is like the transition from the shared transportation of a railroad train to the individualized transportation of the private automobile. It would be appropriate, therefore, to describe the era of limited media as the "kilobit stage," the era of multichannel media as the "megabit stage," and the era of digital media as the "emerging gigabit stage" except that such terminology has a technology-deterministic ring to it, so we will stay with the terms "limited," "multichannel," and "digital."

The purpose of this book is to investigate, inform, analyze, synthesize, and occasionally debunk. As mentioned earlier, what the world needs on the subject of media concentration is more facts, not more opinions. However, I have also come to some interpretations, which should be presented at least briefly here and more extensively in future work. When I started precursors to this study in the mid-1990s, media structure was opening almost everywhere from a limited to a more diverse one. Competition was emerging in telecommunications, and I was glad to play a role in the United States and elsewhere in policy reorientation, first as an academic and then also as a policymaker, as a public service commissioner for New York State. In television, the cable multichannel structure overcame the more limited broadcast model, with its handful of channels, although at a cost of creating another set of market power issues.[1] Microcomputers had reduced IBM's control over the IT sector. And the Internet was rapidly emerging as a worldwide platform for creativity and diversity. This led me to view the dynamics of the information sector as one of steady progression to greater openness and competitiveness. The combination of new technology, liberalized policy, and business and cultural entrepreneurship

would inexorably open and diversify media. This first hypothesis can be called Hypothesis I, the "destined to diversity" scenario.

In the initial stages of this project, the data for the 1980s and early 1990s supported this view. Eventually, however, the information sector did indeed experience greater concentration. The data show that 1996 was a major turning point for the information sector and an acceleration point for concentration in mass media, which had grown moderately after 1988. For the next several years, concentration rose for the information sector as a whole, though not to the level prevailing in 1984. And for the mass media sector it grew well above the levels of the 1980s. This suggested, as an alternative hypothesis, that media industries were concentrating to a different equilibrium, perhaps because of growing economies based on digital technology in distribution and production. This might be called Hypothesis II, the "doomed to concentration" scenario.

Government, usually with a bit of delay, allows market structure to move closer to the business/economic equilibrium. The political equilibrium can be somewhat different from the economic equilibrium in order to mitigate some of its impact and to factor in other societal values. But the distance between the two cannot be too large before economic forces find ways—technological, business, legal, and political—to get around the restrictions. Thus, the scenario of pro-business versus pro-people politics does not provide a good framework for this aspect of political economy.

Hypothesis II suggests that left to itself, media concentration could go to extreme levels. The logical line of defense therefore was to seek state intervention.

But this second hypothesis, in which technology and economics were creating a new equilibrium market structure, was challenged in turn by developments after the year 2001. The information sector went through unprecedented turmoil and decline—the dotcom bubble, the telecom bust, the music industry free-fall, the semiconductor glut, the newspaper erosion, and more. A few years later, after 2008, the severe economic recession repeated pressures on the sector. The impact of this boom and bust on concentration was in two opposing directions. On the one hand, the near-collapse of some markets leads some competitors to drop out and others to consolidate. On the other hand, with stock prices in free-fall, the previously available merger-currencies of appreciated stock evaporated. In the past a merger announcement often raised stock prices so that an acquisition might almost pay for itself. Now, the stock and credit markets soured on empire building and rewarded companies sticking to their traditional knitting.

This requires again a modification of the hypothesis. Whereas the media-pessimistic "condemned to concentration" scenario did not accommodate the early 1990s, the optimistic "destined to diversity" scenario did not match the 2000s events.

Proponents of the two hypotheses had no great problem in reconciling trends that ran counter to their view, discussing them simply as temporary aberrations. To the media pessimists, the 1984–1988 deconcentration (rarely acknowledged) was seen as merely a temporary realignment, a brief loss of control by superannuated market leaders before more dynamic companies took control. IBM was being replaced by Microsoft, RCA was being eclipsed by Viacom, and so forth. Similarly, the reversal or slowdown of the concentration trends after 2001 (if even noticed) could be seen as merely a hiatus, one of those crises of the capitalist economy whose function was to destabilize the industry toward further takeovers. At the same time, the media optimists who were proponents of the "destined to diversity" scenario exulted in the concentration trend of the late 1990s as evidence of the dynamism of capitalism and of an extraordinarily expansive period. Any new concentration would surely be counteracted by the same dynamism of innovation, investment, and competition.

There is some truth in both perspectives, which makes it difficult to discern the overall patterns, just as the motions of the planets are confounding in their combination.

Many observers of media concentration deeply care about the diversity of media as a foundation for democracy, about the quality of media content and its impact on children and the citizenry, and about the power of the few over the thoughts of the many. Others tend to see it in the personal terms of media moguls and empire builders and of pliant government officials doing their bidding instead of supporting the vitality of the marketplace of ideas. Often, people also dislike the politics of some of the owners and their media, and believe that their own political perspective would be more widespread but for those gatekeeper powers. Yet the prevalence of media and information concentration trends around the world, and across so many industries of the information sector, should alert us to the possibility that more fundamental forces are at work than Rupert Murdoch or Bill Gates. The industrial economy led to certain business structures, and so does the information age. And just as the problems of industrialism led to a political reaction, so do those of the information economy today.

There are different methodology approaches to look at concentration trends. While I use the economic one here, I readily acknowledge the validity of other methods, and the fact that civic dimensions merit priority. In analytical terms though, concentration of a sector and of industries has strong economic aspects that need to be explored, even if the impacts and implications go much further.

The overall trend of media concentration (and of many other developments in the media and information sector) is the composite of three separate dynamics that overlay each other. I will develop this model first. The three forces are:

1. The growth in *economies of scale* in information sector operations.
2. The lowering of *entry barriers.*
3. *Digital convergence.*

Together these forces result in certain concentration patterns. The first two lead to an oscillation of concentration, with an upward trend. The third factor leads the concentration trend of mass media to converge to that of the overall information sector.

First, economies of scale. Digital technology raised the ratio of fixed cost of investment and the variable costs of serving people. Incremental costs are very low relative to fixed costs in a digital environment, and the average costs therefore keep dropping with size. This translates into growing economies of scale. There is a relation between the equilibrium market structure (i.e., of market concentration) and the economies of scale of an industry. Where the latter are high, an industry is likely to consist of a few firms only. An example is the automobile industry. Where economies of scale are low, there will be many providers, such as in the case of auto repair shops. Electronic technology has changed scale economies. The incremental costs for operating a broadband network, of producing semiconductors or consumer electronic devices, of distributing software programs, video games, news, or music has declined. On the Internet, incremental costs of content are typically miniscule.

Information products and services are characterized by high fixed costs and low marginal costs. They are expensive to produce but cheap to reproduce and distribute. Technology keeps making reproduction and distribution cheaper, whereas the greater choosiness of users and the slower technical progress in information creation makes production often more expensive. These cost characteristics mean substantial economies of scale and incentives for each competitor to expand in order to gain them. A related kind of size benefit is "network effects." Users of networks (and often of content) benefit from the presence of other participants. They can reach more people and share in common experience with friends, colleagues and neighbors. This creates advantages to size on the demand side, too.

The second economic trend in many media and information industries is the lowering of entry barriers. Electronic technology, in particular, makes it easier to produce content—magazines, music recordings, film, and so forth. Wireless technology enables the entry of new networks and applications by smaller firms. IT hardware can be designed by smaller firms. The digital revolution has led to dropping hardware costs, exemplified by "Moore's Law," with its exponential cost declines in electronic components. Many products can be put together from off-the-shelf hardware and software components or they can be outsourced to specialists, thus making it unnecessary to develop many aspects of a product in-house.

One reason for lower barriers is a more rapid pace of innovation. This provides openings to new and nimble companies that can leapfrog slower established firms. Another reason is the liberalization of legal and governmental restrictions. Liberalization policies have made it easier for new participants to enter some industries than in the past, when monopoly franchises or limited spectrum allocations protected incumbents. Remnants of protections remain, but they are fewer than in the past. Similarly, there has been a lowering of trade barriers restricting international entry.

It is easy to confuse entry barriers with economies of scale. The two are related but different. It may be easier to enter the market than before in terms of up-front investment or legal restrictions, but that does not mean there is an absence of efficiencies associated with larger operations in production. It is easier to start a phone company, a magazine, or an independent film company than it used to be, but it is not necessarily easier to contest a larger firm. The technology or innovation that makes entry easier is also usually available to all, including to established firms, unless it is proprietary and rare.

This can be seen in figure 2.1, which presents two states of an industry. The figure shows the cost per unit of a product for each quantity produced. The barrier to entry is the distance on the vertical axis for the first unit of production. In State 1, this cost is A, whereas in State 2, this cost is lower, at B.

Economies of scale, in contrast, are reflected by the *slope* of the cost lines. That slope depends on the incremental costs of production. If the incremental costs are low, the slope is steep, as it is in the case in State 1. In contrast, State 2 has relatively small scale economies. (Of course, State 2 could also have low entry barriers as well as high economies of scale, exemplified by State 3. The figure merely illustrates the difference between the two concepts.)

Applied to the debate over media concentration, one can characterize, perhaps simplistically, those who believe in wide-open media—the media-optimists—as focusing on the entry barriers and concluding that entry has become easy and plentiful. They are correct. In contrast, media pessimists, when seeking economic explanations, observe the economies of scale to explain ever-growing media firms. They are correct, too.

It is necessary to look at both elements, entry barriers and scale economies. If one does so, a dynamic scenario unfolds. Scale economies and entry barriers can rise or decline independently of each other.

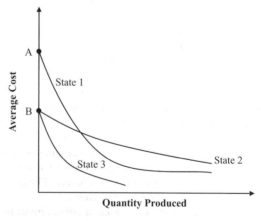

Figure 2.1 Economies of Scale and Entry Barriers

Table 2.1 Concentration Trend Impact of Scale Economies and Entry Barriers

		Scale Economies	
		Rising	**Declining**
Entry Barriers	**Rising**	Higher Concentration	Inverted-U Concentration Trend
	Declining	U-shaped Concentration Trend	Lower Concentration

Where they move in the same direction, the impact on concentration, if all other factors remain equal, is generally unambiguous. See table 2.1.

For example, if entry barriers drop while scale economies decline, there will be more firms contesting the market, while the optimal size of viable firms declines. Together, the two factors will lead to a lower market concentration. The opposite case occurs when both scale economies and entry barriers rise, in which case there will be fewer firms contesting and fewer firms surviving, that is, more concentration. The ambiguous situations are those in which the two factors move in opposite directions. When entry barriers rise while scale economies drop, the result is an initial decrease of contestants (higher concentration) but an eventual survival of more (lower concentration), resulting in an inverted U-shaped concentration trend. In contrast, where entry barriers drop while scale economies rise, the opposite is the case: there will be initially more contestants (lower concentration) but eventually fewer survivors (higher concentration). The trend is U-shaped. The trend of the two factors in recent decades has been just that—toward lower entry barriers and to higher scale economies. It is therefore not surprising to observe the U-shaped concentration pattern through many industries of the information sector.

To expand this discussion, let us assume that a stable industry, which has been based on certain economic characteristics, experiences a simultaneous change of lower entry barriers and higher scale economies. The adjustment to a new equilibrium takes several stages, which are depicted in figure 2.2.

Stage 1: *Competitive entry.* Lower entry barriers cause new participants to enter; the lower early costs enable them to compete. The concentration of the industry drops.

Stage 2: *Instability.* In a competitive environment, companies contest each other in prices

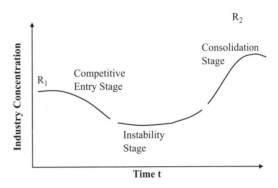

Figure 2.2 Cycles of Concentration

and features. The features lead to higher cost; but price competition is the main destabilizing factor. In competition, prices tend to be set at marginal cost (long term). For information products and services, this marginal cost is near zero. But at that level, prices are too low to cover the early (fixed) costs. If such prices persist, companies fail, industries are in crisis, and new entry slows. There are many recent examples for this in the information sector.

Stage 3: *Consolidation.* Eventually, some competitors fail, others consolidate, and the industry reconcentrates. Prices rise again and higher profits return. This attracts new entrants, and a new cycle begins.

This would describe a cyclical concentration trend of up-and-down. However, this is not quite the end of the story. Even within the cycles there can be a trend. This trend is based on the economies of scale. When these economies grow, they lead to relatively larger firms within an industry, that is, to a higher concentration level. This can be seen in figure 2.3. Figure 2.3 shows the oscillations in concentration that one could expect in an environment in which entry barriers steadily decline while economies of scale steadily rise.

Suppose one starts at an initial Point A. Entry barriers are fairly high, and scale economies are intermediate. This defines a highly concentrated industry. Now suppose that barriers drop while scale economies rise: the industry will go through the down-up trend described above, bottoming out at B, rising to C. In that range, competitive entry becomes viable again, and another cycle begins. Point C will be at a higher concentration if scale economies are rising. (It could be at C' (lower) if the impact of economies of scale is less than that of entry barriers, thus leading to an earlier competitive entry.)

On the one hand, the trend of scale economies raises the trend in the peaks of the cycles and hence the overall trends of concentration around which fluctuations take place. On the other hand, the trend of lower entry barriers leads to more frequent challenges to any equilibrium and to greater instability. It affects the timing of swings of the instability (frequency) and the magnitude of oscillation (amplitude). Entry barriers affect the *frequency* and *amplitude* of the changes in concentration, whereas economies of scale determine the axis around which they oscillate.[2]

The result is a concentration trend that is fluctuating but rising. If the economies of scale were to shift, maybe due to technology, the trend would reverse itself. This model can accommodate different combinations of scale economies and entry barriers.

The model can explain the tendencies of the media and information sector in recent years.

It can also explain different trends in major sub-sectors. In the past, mass media were distinct from telecom networks, consumer electronics, and computer hardware and software. Their economic characteristics were different and hence their industry structure differed. This is less true now. In an increasingly electronic and digital environment, mass media assume many of the technical elements of networks and technology industries, and with them also fundamental economic characteristics of the information sector generally—low marginal costs, high fixed costs, and falling entry barriers. Hence, the concentration trends of mass media converge with those of the rest of the information sector. This can be shown schematically in figure 2.4.

This convergence tendency suggests that the mass media sector, from a relatively low level of concentration, will move to a higher level that is more similar to that of the overall information sector. It will create a steeper axis for the oscillations of the sector, de-emphasizing the down-phases and strengthening the up-phases in the process of convergence.

IMPLICATIONS

What are some of the economic implications of these trends? Do they lead to larger media companies or to smaller ones? Based on our analysis, the answer has to be both. We expect the following characteristics in the emerging media and information sector:

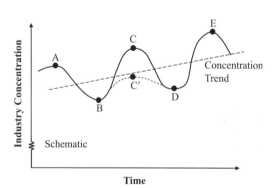

Figure 2.3 Concentration Trends, with Continuously Rising Scale Economies and Declining Entry Barriers

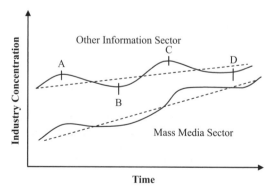

Figure 2.4 Convergence of Concentration of Overall Information Sector and Mass Media Sector

1. *Giants.* The trend of larger economies of scale leads to larger firms, both absolutely and relatively.
2. *Mavericks and Innovators.* The trend of lower entry barriers leads to more and smaller participants in the early stages of an innovation.
3. *Specialists.* Smaller firms can also benefit from economies of scale by finding a niche in which they can have a large share even if their size is moderate.

And this leads to:

4. *Vertical disintegration.* Specialization leads to a realignment of production and companies, from vertical firms that do a little of everything to horizontal firms that do everything of a little.
5. *Integration.* There will be a need, greater than before, to put together the elements created by the specialists, whether they are small or large. Thus, some firms will be *integrator* firms that combine the various modules of specialists into larger products and services. These firms are the key players in the emerging media and information landscape. Their integrator functions would be primarily in product and process management, quality supervision, financing, branding, marketing, and distribution. For the integrator function, too, scale economies exist. Integrator firms are likely to be the giants mentioned above, although some giants will be specialists and some integrators can be medium-sized.
6. *Bundling.* The logic of integration also leads to a bundling of several products and services within the same integrator. This should be distinguished from the traditional media conglomerates, which did much of everything in-house. In contrast, integrators create a destination and a brand, but in a pure case are not a producer themselves.
7. *Clustering.* The logic of specialization and integration leads to geographic clustering of related or complementary specialists. Hollywood or Silicon Valley are examples.

8. A *Hub-and-spoke* networked industry system. An integrator firm develops strong ties with favored specialist firms, which often become part of its orbit.
9. *Globalization.* The economic logic of economies of scale, the lower entry barriers to trade, and the "death of distance" to many informational activities leads to internationalized operations. In concept, this is not a one-way street. But in practice, it favors providers with scale economies, often with a large and early home base. However, specialists from other countries can fit into the hub-and-spoke system.
10. *Volatility.* This volatility was shown in the oscillations of figure 2.4.

If we put all these elements together, what kind of information industries do they suggest? The structure would be stratified into two major levels of firms:

- A few large integrator firms, with global operations, whose main function is to conceive the basic product, implement it through specialists, and distribute it to the world in branded bundles.
- Numerous specialist firms clustering around the integrators.

This is the emerging shape of media and information industries, left to themselves.

Notes

1. See Noam, Eli, "Towards an Integrated Communications Market." *Federal Communications Law Journal*, 34(2), Spring 1982, pp. 209–257; "The Political Economy of Cable Television Regulation," in *Proceedings from the Tenth Annual Telecommunications Policy Research Conference*, O. Gandy, et. al., eds. New York: Ablex Press, 1983, pp. 137–155; "Economies of Scale and Regulation in CATV," in *Analyzing the Impact of Regulatory Change in Public Utilities*, M. Crew, ed. Lexington, MA: Lexington Books, 1984, pp. 95–110.
2. Amplitude will depend on the change in entry barriers; frequency on the rate of change.

3

Seeking the Answers

THE INDUSTRIES INVESTIGATED, THE MARKETS DEFINED

The central research question for this book is: Has the American information sector become more concentrated? To provide an empirical answer, I consciously picked a methodology that is straightforward, simple, and transparent: the trend of two concentration indices used in American antitrust enforcement, the so-called Herfindahl-Hirschmann Index (HHI) and the 4-firm market share index, the C4. More complex metrics and models are possible—the data would readily support them—but use of one would then raise the question of how much the specification would affect the results.

This book looks at the market concentration trends for 100 separate information industries in America. Examples for such industries are broadcast TV, cable TV, film distribution, daily newspapers, Internet service providers, TV set makers, microcomputers, local phone service, and cellular mobile providers. For each of these industries, we tracked individual firms' revenues in the U.S. market and calculated their U.S. market shares in this particular industry. We used a wide variety of data sources, such as Securities and Exchange Commission (SEC) and FCC filings, Wall Street reports, news articles, consultants' studies, and so forth for a period of over 20 years. Sources are listed in the respective chapters. The effort was

extensive, and the resultant database is unprecedented in its scope.

The chapters of the second part of this book trace the historical development for each of these industries, with market shares and concentrations for the years after 1984 (and in some cases 1983).

I then summarize these results in the third part of the book. Chapters 13 through 16—National Horizontal Concentration, Vertical and Cross-Industry Concentration, Local Media Concentration, and The Ownership Structure of the American Information Sector—provide broad aggregations and trends. Horizontal concentration refers to market shares of industries. Vertical concentration deals with the ownership across related information industries, such as firms participating in film, music, and TV.

Local concentration refers to ownership shares in local markets, such as local newspapers and cable TV distribution. It is important to understand the difference between national and local media concentration. A newspaper company may own several local newspapers around the country that add up to a modest national market share among newspaper companies; but each of these papers may be the only local paper in its town, giving it substantial powers there over local news coverage and advertising prices. It is therefore necessary to look at both national and local concentrations, where distinct local media markets exist.

The chapter on the concentration of ownership (chapter 16) analyzes ownership categories as well as their changes over time.

The final section of the book (chapters 17–20) proposes a different concentration index for media and presents the findings and conclusions.

ANTITRUST FOR MEDIA?

In a central paradigm of the economics of classic industrial organization, the traditional SCP model, the *structure* of the market affects the *conduct* and hence the *performance* of these firms. Although economists have come to recognize the limitations of the SCP model, market structure has remained the key element of mainstream antitrust analysis. A market is defined, concentration is measured, various factors are considered, and conclusions are drawn.

But is such an approach appropriate for media?

Media are a central cultural and civic resource. Media policy is not primarily driven by considerations of economic efficiency. The economic equilibrium is not necessarily the social optimum. Yet there is also an economic dimension to the operation of commercial media firms, and it needs to be analyzed.

Media critics find themselves in a love-hate relation with antitrust. On the one hand, they believe that antitrust analysis and enforcement should be revitalized as a tool against media conglomerates. On the other hand, the same antitrust analysis and enforcement are seen as unworthy tools for media as the carriers and vessels of culture and political discourse. Antitrust analysis seems to apply the same methodology to media as it does to refrigerators.

Many free market adherents share the antipathy to antitrust, too, but from a different perspective. Some hold that the task for antitrust law is exclusively to protect against the economic impact of market powers and to ignore noneconomic considerations.[1] Others want markets to regulate themselves. But some media industries might have cost characteristics that make them "natural monopolies," such as local cable TV distributors. Even Milton Friedman conceded that in a natural monopoly situation a governmental role might be justified.

Bruce Owen, a free-marketeer, argues in favor of antitrust with no special considerations for media.[2] "Nothing about the media as business suggests that antitrust analysis is less appropriate for them than for other businesses, or that there is anything to be gained from inventing a media-specific approach."

Media critics disagree. They want to see media treated differently. But such a construction cuts both ways, not only toward stricter rules. Communication markets tend to be especially dynamic technologically, and courts might therefore give them more slack. Or, because they are, or might be, directly regulated by the FCC, antitrust enforcement might defer to that agency. Or, courts might extend to media an extra protection from governmental infringement because of the First Amendment.

A 2003 OECD (Organization for Economic Co-Operation and Development) report observes: "media mergers may present difficult trade-offs. In particular, competition authorities might be confronted with a merger having beneficial effects on one side of a media market while having harmful effects on the other; for example, advertising prices may go down but prices of content to consumers go up. Competition authorities might also have to deal with situations where content diversity declines but their general quality rises, with the result that content consumers with majoritarian tastes are better off while other consumers are worse off."[3]

Robert Pitofsky, a law professor and former high antitrust official as the chairman of the Federal Trade Commission, posits a pragmatic middle position. Pitofsky views the existing antitrust analysis, including the use of HHI measures, as adequate, provided it is merely the starting point for a more thoroughly contextual analysis. (This is actually true for every industry, which is why the thresholds are "guidelines" rather than a firm set of rules.)

The problem with discretion is that one person's review of all pertinent considerations is another person's invitation to abuse. Antitrust enforcement, being often a judgment call, has always been heavily affected by politics and ideology. Influential media companies might be treated with kid gloves. The change of enforcement attitude at the Justice Department toward Microsoft from the Clinton (strict) to the Bush administration (lenient) is an example. Earlier instances are direct presidential interventions, subtle but unmistaken, into information industry antitrust proceedings: Nixon in the case against ITT, Reagan in the FCC's Fin/Syn (financial interest and syndication rules) proceedings and in the case against AT&T.[4]

A special problem for the use of antitrust in media markets is that some of these markets have been only recently deregulated. Pitofsky writes: "The very fact an industrial sector was regulated suggests the possibility of some past market failure, or at least some competitive peculiarities..., and therefore calls for a special sensitivity in applying conventional antitrust rules."[5]

Edwin Baker of the University of Pennsylvania observes that "something resembling anti-trust standards that look solely at market power to raise prices above competitive levels has replaced previously invoked democratic concerns."[6] And indeed, the U.S. antitrust authorities have increasingly focused on economic harm, such as a given merger's impact on advertising rates in a local geographic market, whereas nonprice dimensions of harm could also be considered, such as the reduction of informational diversity. "To a consumer/citizen, such diversity will be more important than an impact on advertising."[7]

The focus therefore often moves from economic markets to the "marketplace of ideas," a concept going back at least to Supreme Court Justice Oliver Wendell Holmes.[8] As Walter Lippman observed, the strength of the free press was not that it was right every time but that it had a built-in self-correction.

For antitrust purposes, the pluralist "marketplace of ideas" approach would look on the impact of a merger on the diversity of viewpoints presented by media. Whereas under a strictly economic market test a merger of the makers of similar products would be more closely scrutinized than that of dissimilar products, under a "marketplace of ideas" policy it would be the opposite. Assume, for example, a city with two newspapers, both liberal in orientation, and a radio station with a conservative bent. Under the economic test, the merger of the two newspapers would be much more of a problem than that of one of the newspapers with the radio station. But under the "marketplace of ideas" approach, a merger of the two liberal papers would be more acceptable, since it preserves the diversity of points of view. The problem with this approach is how to define and measure "viewpoints." Such an exercise is also likely to run afoul of the test of content neutrality required by

courts on government action, based on the First Amendment.

An OECD report observes that countries adopt one of two main approaches for media merger reviews. The first is a "two-stage approach," in which the competition authority focuses only on economic welfare and the media regulator focuses on other factors, including pluralism. A merger that fails either review is blocked. This is the Canadian approach, and partly that of the United States insofar as the FCC also reviews media mergers, although not for viewpoint pluralism. The alternative is the "one-stage approach." Spain, Austria, the United Kingdom, and Ireland require the competition authority to directly consider pluralism in their merger reviews.[9]

However, the OECD report finds that "competition authorities are often reluctant to include pluralism considerations in merger reviews or even to advise concerning them. This reluctance is sometimes explained by referring to measurement difficulties, and a lack of synergy in terms of the expertise required to assess economic and pluralism effects" (p. 10).

This book does not use antitrust enforcement rules as a policy guide or analytical tool; it only uses its measuring system. To use the measurement methodology of antitrust measurement for media does not imply adoption of the same criteria for its conclusions. And that is a key point. Once markets are defined and their concentration measured, the next question is what the threshold for unacceptable concentration ought to be. Arguments can be made that the limits ought to be lower than for other industries. It should therefore be understood that this book's use of index tools of antitrust analysis, such as the HHI and C4 (to be explained below), does not imply an agreement with the proposition that the particular threshold measures of the U.S. Department of Justice (DOJ) should govern media structure. One can accept an index while holding that the thresholds for media concentration should be different than for other industries. But it should also be pointed out, for perspective, that almost any industry will claim, when challenged by an anti-trust case, that it is "different"—more essential, more fragile, more complex, more global, more open, more regulated, more naturally monopolistic, and so forth. Even so, I believe that the diversity of the media sector is indeed more important to society than, say, that of the airline industry, vital as the latter may be.

In consequence, I am proposing a different index later in this book (Chapter 18). One major distinguishing factor is the First Amendment's prohibition of the direct regulation of media conduct, which leaves the maintenance of a competitive industry structure as the main policy approach for dealing with abuses.

DEFINING MARKETS

In measuring concentration, the definition of markets tends to be the key question. The same fish may be small in a big pond but big in a small pond. Hence, the question of how to define a market is always fought over by lawyers and their expert witnesses.

The major question is whether different media are in the same market, that is, substitutes for each other and affecting each others' prices. In the case of newspapers, courts have usually held against including other media such as radio and TV in the relevant product market definition as functional substitutes.[10] But in motion picture antitrust cases, courts held that competition existed among first-run films and second-run theaters.

The test for a separate market is whether a product or service category is sufficiently different from another category, that it is no mere substitute. "Different" is both subjective and objective. Antitrust analysis applies economic tests of cross-elasticity: if raising the price for one product raises sales for another product more than minimally, they are in the same markets. This needs to be measured. For the 100 industries of our study, it would necessitate 10,000 econometric estimations of cross-elasticities, requiring data that is mostly unavailable. Even if one limited such analysis to industries that appear to be substitutes, it would still be a formidable task.

Investigating this question econometrically, Joel Waldfogel of the University of Pennsylvania, in a study for the FCC, looked at consumer substitution between several media. He finds that substitution exists between Internet and broadcast TV; between daily and weekly newspapers; between daily newspapers and broadcast TV news; between cable and daily newspapers; between radio and broadcast TV for news; and between the Internet and daily newspapers for news. He does not find

such substitution between weekly newspapers and broadcast TV, or between radio and either Internet or cable.[11]

But he also concludes that his study "cannot completely answer the question of whether substitution is sufficiently effective that all media should be considered substitutes for news and information purposes." And in any event, would we seriously consider the Internet and broadcast TV to be in the same market for antitrust purposes so that a single company could be permitted, under antitrust rules, to have 90% of the ISP business, because four TV networks exist and are supposed to be in the same market?

Another FCC study, by C. Anthony Bush, looks at the substitutability of local media for advertisers. The author concludes: "The elasticity of substitution is relatively small, and the elasticity of substitution between radio and television is not statistically different from zero."[12]

The question of market definitions is hence not an easy one to answer. Yet it is not as difficult as some make it out. Clearly, any lawyers worth their retainer fee who represent a defendant in an antitrust case or shepherd a merger through review will try to muddy the waters by showing that the market should be defined widely (if the merger is within the same industry) or narrowly (if the merger is with a firm in an adjoining industry). This has led to a cottage industry of expert witnesses, often followed by academic articles and books. But taken out of the litigation environment, defining media industries is usually not all that difficult. The industries often overlap, of course, but only partly. Radio is different from TV; daily newspapers are different from most magazines; microcomputers are different from mainframe computers; and so forth. The areas of overlap and their line-drawing questions should not obscure various media's differences in terms of history, identity, participating firms, practices, marketing, and image. In our study, only a few judgment calls had to be made; in particular, whether cable TV and Direct Broadcast Satellite (DBS) were separate markets or a single multichannel TV market (we resolved it by using, alternatively, *both* the separate and the joint market definitions).

The more straightforward method of selection is to identify industries as they have evolved, and as they are differentiated publicly. The U.S. Government's industry classification system is useful up to a point. The North American Industry

Classification System (NAICS) replaced the long-standing U.S. Standard Industrial Classification (SIC) system that had no Internet industries. NAICS classifications mostly track ours; they are sometimes too narrow ("drive-in theaters") and sometimes too broad ("book publishers"). We added our own judgment.

The stepwise aggregation of this study can accommodate wider market definitions quite easily. (It is harder to retrofit narrower definitions.) I will be happy to modify market definitions where a good case can be made. There is no hidden agenda lurking in the methodology or market definitions.

The study defines and tracks the major firms in 100 separate industries that together comprise the information sector. The geographical market definition is national, that is, the United States of America. A global market definition would be misleading, since a company could have a big share in America but not globally, or vice versa. This means that we exclude non-U.S. revenues of U.S. firms, and we include the U.S. market revenues of non-American firms. This approach, though laborious, seems more appropriate than letting the vast global income of companies such as IBM or Sony distort the U.S. picture.

In one chapter of this book we use a *local* definition of media instead of national definitions in order to assess the concentration trends for local media such as newspapers and radio stations.[13]

Listed in table 3.1 are the industries analyzed, as well as their broader categories. The broadest level, the information sector, comprises four *subsectors*, those of mass media, telecommunications, information technology (IT), and Internet. Each *subsector*, in turn, is composed of a number of narrower *industry segments*, such as film or computers, which in turn consist of *industries* such as TV production or microcomputers. In some cases, such as international telecommunications, several subindustries have already been aggregated.

This is a long list indeed, and it requires explanations.

It must be recognized that the more disaggregated the analysis, the higher the market shares and concentration. Thus, if one uses the methodology of the FCC or the one by Compaine and Gomery mentioned above, which are to consider all media forms as "voices" in one big overall "media market," one would get low concentration scores. This methodology is not wrong per se,

as long as the traditional DOJ benchmark scores for "highly concentrated," and so forth, are not applied to it. Lower benchmarks would be required if the market definition is expanded. Furthermore, the Compaine/Gomery and FCC approaches are useful for purposes of observing *trends*. Whatever the absolute measure of temperature, whether in degrees of Celsius, Fahrenheit, or Reamur, if the numbers are rising, it's getting hotter.

In analyzing 100 different industries we do not assume that they are all of equal importance. First and most obviously, some are much larger than others. In the averaging, this is accounted for by assigning different weights to industries according to their revenues. (Revenues may overstate aggregate concentration somewhat, since highly concentrated industries are likely to charge higher prices, and thus their relative weights rise. Hence, the finding of aggregated concentration is likely to be somewhat biased upward.)

Revenues, however, do not measure importance. Thus, to most people, newspapers are more important than video stores or software services, in a hard-to-define, harder-to-measure sense. Yet are they more important than search engines, which are becoming the gateway, organizers, prioritizers, and filers of society's information? Or are they less important than microprocessors, the building block of information technology? Value judgments would have to be made to assign different weights of "societal importance" to different media industries. Our data could accommodate alternate weighting schemes beyond dollars, but this was not the approach taken, because it would introduce greater subjectivity in the selection and assignment of the weight. But there is nothing in principle to preclude a broadening and modifying of the weight scheme. One alternative weighting system would be to consider the subjective importance given to a medium as a news source. This had been the approach taken by the FCC in its Diversity index (which used a survey of the importance of a medium as a news source), and the agency was roundly criticized for it—although more likely for tactical legal and for methodological reasons than for the concept itself. But the furor that the FCC's scheme of weights based on news importance unleashed suggests that it would be difficult to find an acceptable subjective system. Furthermore, such a news-based system would leave out entertainment media industries such as film or music, which are important in other ways, such as shaping values and culture.

Table 3.1 The Industries Analyzed

		Information Sector		
Mass Media		**IT**	**Telecommunications**	**Internet**

Mass Media	IT	Telecommunications	Internet
PRINT & PUBLISHING	*IT HARDWARE*	*TELECOM SERVICES*	Backbones
Daily Newspapers	**Media Consumer Electronics**	Local Service	Narrowband ISPs
Books	TV Sets	Long Distance	Broadband
Trade and Paperbacks	Home Video Equipment	Private Line/Business	Providers
Educational Books	Camcorders	**International**	Portals
Trade and Paperback	Set Top Boxes	International Voice	Browser Software
Other Books	DBS receivers	International Text	Internet Search
Book Retailing	CD and MP3	International Private	Engines
Book Stores	Audio Systems	Line	IP Telephony
Online Book Retailing	AM/FM Radios	**Wireless Service**	Media Players
Magazines	VCRs	Cellular/PCS	
Consumer and Trade	DVDs	Radio Dispatch	
Magazines	PVRs	Paging	
Academic Journals	**Semiconductors**		
Local Magazines	CISC Memory		
	RISC Microprocessors	*TELECOM*	
	Microprocessors	*EQUIPMENT*	
MUSIC	Microcontrollers	**Consumer Equipment**	
Performance Rights		Corded Handsets	
Music Publishing	**Computers**	Cordless Handsets	
Music Production & Distrib.	Supercomputers	Fax Machines	
Music Retailing	Mainframes	Mobile Handsets	
Music Stores	Midranges	PBXs	
Online Music Retailing	Workstations	**Network Equipment**	
Music Cable Channels	Microcomputers	Internetworking	
	PDAs	Equipment	
	Video Game	Routers	
FILM	Consoles	LAN Switches	
Film Production		Central Office	
Film Production & Distrib.	**Peripherals and Storage**	Switches	
TV Prime Time Production	**Storage Devices**	Multiplexers	
Retail Distribution	Disk Drives	Fiber Optical Cables	
Theater Exhibition	Hard Drives	Copper Wire & Coax	
Home Video Distribution	Optical Storage	Microwave Equipment	
Video Rental	**Printers**	Cellular Infrastructure	
	Copiers		
	Modems		
ELECTRONIC RETAIL	Cable Modems		
DISTRIBUTION	DSL Equipment		
Radio Stations			
TV Stations	*COMPUTER SOFTWARE*		
Cable TV Operators	**Operating Software**		
DBS Providers	**Network Operating Software**		
	Enterprise App. Software		
	Mainframe Software		
PROGRAMMING	**Consumer App. Software**		
NETWORKS	**Software Services**		
Radio Networks	**PC Entertainment Software**		
TV Networks	**Games Software**		
Syndication			
Cable TV Channels			
Pay TV Channels			

Our methodology also permits various segmentations and aggregations, for example according to "content" versus "distribution" or "electronic media" versus "traditional media" or "regulated media" versus "unregulated media," and so forth. And this was indeed done, along with a brief explanation of a new weighting system.

What industries should be included? Definitions of "media" or of the "information sector" vary. To some, the film industry is not part of the information sector, since its purpose is to entertain rather than to inform. But often it does both, as do novels or consumer magazines.

It is a fair question whether one should look at both news media and entertainment media. News and entertainment are regularly combined in the same medium. To many people, hard news carries the greater weight. To many others, the role of entertainment in shaping the long-term values and attitudes of society is more important than updates of bond prices. Even the definition of "news" is subjective and increasingly so.

Media critics often agree. Herbert Marcuse writes, "Can one really distinguish between the mass media as instruments of information and entertainment, and as agents of manipulation and indoctrination?"[14] Technologists have a more relaxed definition of "information;" it need not be useful, elevated, or novel. It is basically "organized data." Our working definition for the information sector is similarly broad. It includes the industries and firms that produce such organized data, *content*; those that provide the means of communicating it to others, *communications*; and those that create the instrumentalities for such production and communications, *media devices*.

It is important to understand that one cannot vary disaggregation levels from one sector to another. Once one decides to look at other segments of the information sector, such as telecommunications or IT, one must use the same general level of disaggregation that is applied to the mass media industries. If one takes instead a shortcut and looks at broad segments only, for example "computers," these sectors will appear to be less concentrated than when they are more disaggregated, such as "microcomputers" and "mainframes." Comparisons of broader sectors would then become less meaningful. Thus, even if the IT or telecom sectors may be more detailed for readers primarily interested in mass media, they

must still recognize that for any intersectoral comparison to be meaningful, the methodology, including the extent of disaggregation, must have roughly the same granularity. As mentioned above, the only alternative to a full-scale comparative analysis of IT, consumer media electronics, and telecom is not to have any cross-sectoral analysis at all.

There is another reason for including other parts of the information sector beyond classic mass media: The underlying technologies of the information sector are growing closer in the process of digital convergence. And their basic economics are increasingly similar: high fixed costs, low marginal cost, and distance insensitivity. Some similarity always existed, but the remaining differences have narrowed with digital convergence and will continue to do so. The content nature of newspapers is different from that of game software, or of music, or of PDA operating systems, as are the respective public policy concerns. But their basic economics and dynamics are increasingly similar.

One must therefore proceed beyond content mass media and also observe the parallel trends in telecommunications networks, the Internet, and information technology. They might help us understand the dynamics of concentration trends. The broader approach does not eliminate the narrower one. Results specific to mass media industries and to the broader mass information sector are both reported here.

This study therefore goes beyond "media" narrowly defined to encompass the "information" sector. The term "media" is imprecise and used in various ways. For some, it is limited to "content media" such as TV or magazines. But the term connotes not just content but the means of its delivery. A medium is a way to distribute content; it is not content per se. According to Merriam-Webster, a medium is "a channel or system of communication, information, or entertainment." Thus, a broadcast satellite is a medium, as is a wireline or wireless network. Internet instrumentalities are media, such as portals, ISPs, or backbones. Are the physical components of media part of the information sector? Yes. Without transmitters and receivers a radio station is an abstraction. Without PCs, routers, and servers there is no Internet. Where then does one draw the line? The criterion used in this study was to include industries that provide non-generic elements of the production and distribution of information. This means that the production of plain paper, or of electricity, education, or silicon wafers, is not included, since they are generic inputs. I include critical hardware industries that are fundamental to the information technology (IT) sector, such as computers, game hardware, and modems. Since electronic equipment draws on certain fundamental and complex elements such as software and microprocessors, these have also been included. I similarly include the distribution chain such as the retailing of books, home video, and music, since they parallel the distribution by electronics means.

Not included are certain content producers that often tend to be live and local: theater, dance, music performances, and sports. Even with these omissions, covering 100 information industries is an ambitious undertaking, far beyond anything done previously on the media concentration in the United States or any other country.

MEASURES OF CONCENTRATION

A number of indices for concentration exist, such as the Lorenz curve and the related Gini coefficient. The Gini coefficient is the ratio of the area under a Lorenz curve to a perfectly equal distribution. The Lorenz curve shows inequality by ranking parties according to their size (or income) and drawing the curve of the cumulative share. A perfectly equal market share for all firms would result in a Gini coefficient of zero. Whether there are 300 firms in the market or three, the coefficient would be the same as long as the firms were of equal size. Hence, the Gini coefficient is a measure of inequality among firms rather than of market concentration.

One could also construct definitions for media concentration that are more complex, incorporating, for example, variables such as the political leanings of the particular publication or channel, or their multiplier effects in influencing other media. For technology-oriented firms, one could count the patents; for network firms, one could count fiber-miles; and so on. The problem with such refinements of data and models is that they raise the question whether the results are robust or sensitive to the model's specification. As has been said, if one tortures the data enough it will confess to anything. Thus it seems least objectionable to use the standard, official U.S. antitrust concentration measure. And although this measure has its

problems, as will be amply noted, it has the advantage of not being *ad-hoc*. Improvements to the index can be made and are proposed at the end of this study. But for the empirical body of research, I did not wish to enter methodological disputes that would muddy the water. Generally speaking, the choice of an index is less important than its consistency over time, which enables inter-temporary trend analyses. Furthermore, a consistent measure permits the comparisons of concentration levels across different media industries.

One traditional antitrust way to measure concentration is to combine the market share of the top four firms ("C4 ratios") for an industry. A C4 ratio is defined by the aggregate total of market share percentage of the four largest companies within an industry. It is given by:

$$C4_j = \sum_i^4 S_{ij}$$

where S_i = firm i's market share of a given industry j and where firms are ordered by size of market share.

Thus, if the market shares of the top 14 firms are 40%, 30%, 10%, and 10%, with 10 other firms holding 1% each, the C4 index would be 90. However, the index has its limitation, because it cannot differentiate between markets heavily dominated by one firm and those in which four firms are of similar size. In the examples above, if the top firm acquired its three main competitors, the C4 would only rise by a few points of tiny firms (which would now be the #2, 3, and 4) to 93, even though the market is vastly more concentrated than before. For this reason, the Antitrust Division of the U.S. Department of Justice (DOJ) has been using a different index. The main index for concentration used by it has been the Herfindahl-Hirschman Index.[15] This widely used HHI concentration measure is equal to the sum of the squares of the market shares of all market participants:

$$HHI_j = \sum_{i=1}^f S_{ij}^2$$

where

f = number of firms participating in an industry,
S_{ij} = each firm i's market share in the industry j.

The HHI can range between zero—where the share of each firm is infinitely small—to 10,000, where a single firm accounts for 100% of the market. In the example above, the HHI would be HHI = $40^2 + 30^2 + 2 \times 10^2 + 10 \times 1^2 = 2{,}710$.

The DOJ's antitrust enforcement guidelines classify market concentration levels as follows:

HHI < 1,000	Unconcentrated market
1,000 < HHI < 1,800	Moderately concentrated market
1,800 < HHI	Highly concentrated market

If a proposed merger crosses the upper threshold, it would be seriously scrutinized.

In Europe, the EU Commission has defined "significant market power" (SMP) as its criterion in telecom regulation. Companies not possessing SMP are left unregulated, whereas those that possess it are subject to some restrictions and obligations. In its 1998 framework, the threshold for SMP was 25%. In 2002, a new framework moved telecom SMP in line with EU competition law, following the wording of "dominance" of Article 82 of the Rome Treaty. This raises the SMP threshold to about 40%, corresponding to an HHI of at least 1,600 and most likely to about 2,000 (assuming conservatively that the remaining 60% is shared by three firms with 10% and six firms with 5%). This is close to but somewhat more lenient a threshold for a highly concentrated market than the U.S. standard of 1,800.

The HHI has several drawbacks. To begin with, HHI measures are nonintuitive in their interpretation, in contrast to C4s, which can be easily grasped. For that reason, I will often use both the C4 index and the HHI to describe a market's concentration. This allows for a comparison of trends between the two measures. As it turns out, the trends tend to be quite similar.

To help evaluate an HHI figure one may want to keep in mind that an HHI below 1,000 would require at least 10 equal-sized market participants, and an HHI of 1,800 would have at least six equal-sized participants. A typical highly concentrated industry may have a market leader with 60%, a runner-up with 30%, and two niche players with 5% each, for an HHI of 4,550. A classic unconcentrated market might have 10

firms with 5%, 3 firms with 10%, and 20 firms with 1%. The HHI would be 570.

Where a single firm has 50% of the market, with several smaller firms also competing, the HHI is most likely to be around 3,000. Where two firms share the market equally, the HHI will be at 5,000. If the two firms share the market in a 2:1 ratio, the HHI would be still higher.

A monopoly does not, by American antitrust case history, require a firm to literally account for 100% of a market. Typically, government and courts have drawn the line at around 65% of a market, that is, an HHI of over 4,200 (depending on the size of minor firms). A "tight" oligopoly would include about three to five major firms, with an HHI of 2,000 or more.

The concentration trends of individual industries are important by themselves, but each industry experiences specific developments and transactions that create particular market structures. The concentration of newspapers and academic journals might rise, whereas that of magazines declines and that of books remains stable. To get the big picture then, it is important to look at trends for larger media categories, in this case that of "print publishing," which is a weighted aggregate of the several industries that comprise the print sector. Accordingly, we aggregate the individual industries along the dimensions of industry segments and broader sectoral categories. Such measures aggregate the various industries, with weights based on size in terms of revenues. The weighted average HHI is defined as

$$\text{HHI}_\text{w} = \sum_{j=1}^{n} \frac{m_j}{\sum m_j} \sum_{i=1}^{f} S_{ij}^2$$

where

j = an industry,
m_j = total revenue of an industry,
S_{ij} = firm i's market share of an industry j,
n = number of industries,
f = number of firms in an industry.

For example, suppose the HHI of industry A for a given year is 1,000 and the size of the industry is $10 billion, whereas the HHI for a second, industry B, is 2,000 and its size is $20 billion. The weighted average HHI of the two industries would be 1,666.

A similar approach to aggregations is also used for the industry-specific C4 indices. The weighted aggregate C4 is

$$C4_W = \sum_{j=1}^{n} \frac{m_j}{\sum m_j} \sum_{i=1}^{4} S_{ij}$$

where

j = an industry j within a larger segment,
m_j = total revenue of an industry j,
S_i = market share of firm in a given industry,
i = firm in an industry,
n = number of industries.

The aggregate concentration measures are likely to be skewed upward for several reasons. First, as already mentioned, highly concentrated industries are likely to charge higher prices (relative to cost) than competitive industries, thus increasing their weight in cross-industry aggregations.

Second, the exponential nature of the HHI index generates high numbers at the extreme. If a firm's market share increases from 80% to 90%—not a big difference in dominance—the HHI rises by 1,700. But if a firm's share rises from 20% to 30%, a more significant change, the HHI goes up by only 500.

But as it turns out, huge national market shares (larger than 50%) are rare, as will be seen.[16] In 2005, such shares were found for national markets only for the following industries and firms:

- Mainframe computers and their software: IBM
- PC operating systems software: Microsoft
- CISC microprocessors: Intel
- Music TV cable channels: Viacom
- Search engines: Google

In 2006, Google joined this exclusive club; its 2008 U.S. share for search engines, according to Nielsen, was 61.2%, 8.1% more than in the preceding year.

In addition to the more traditional measures of horizontal concentration, we also developed a series of indices to measure trends in vertical integration, with an eye toward providing a rough proxy of each firm's power in the overall information sector. The Participation Index (PI) score tallies a firm's presence in all relevant industries. The Sector Share Index (SSI) score sums the product of a firm's share in the information sector. The Company Power Index (CPI) score aggregate provides a firm's weighted HHI scales proxy for the ability to leverage strength in one or more industries into other industries. These measures, when considered together, enable us to identify and interpret broader concentration trends, both vertical and horizontal, in the information sector. They are described in greater detail in chapter 14.

We also define a Local Concentration Index (LCI) across a set of local media, weighted by their contribution to individuals' local information. This is discussed in chapter 15.

We also go beyond companies and look at their actual owners. We identify both institutional and individual owners and assess their shares in each major firm. We examined the largest owners of the media and communications companies and the "ownership concentration" of large firms.

After extensive use of the various forms of concentration indices, I have come to appreciate the robustness of both the HHI and C4 in tracking trends over time, when used in a consistent manner, and it is here that their primary usefulness lies. But I have experienced the limitations of each. I will therefore propose a Media Ownership Concentration and Diversity Index (MOCDI) later in this book.

Empirical Procedure

After the choice of industries and of the concentration index, the third step is to determine the period for investigation. We chose the 21-year period 1984–2005, sometimes expanded beyond where data were available, and occasionally also including 1983 for illustrative purposes. Why this period? To determine trends, one must cover several years. If the period is too short, observed change may be merely a temporary blip. But a period of many decades, and for numerous industries, creates insurmountable problems of data collection. Our analysis covers over two decades, a period that stretches the data availability of several industries.

The year 1984 was critical for the telecom sector, because of the historic divestiture of AT&T that took place on January 1, 1984. For cable TV, similarly, the year brought important legislation. The year 1984 is therefore a logical starting point, since an earlier initial date would lead to results distorted by changes brought about by law. At times, however, we peek before 1984 to the predivestiture markets as a way of making further comparisons, or to post-2005 developments such as the 2005 mergers SBC-AT&T, Verizon-MCI, and AT&T-Bell South.

For these two decades, we look at six data points, four years apart: 1984, 1988, 1992, 1996, 2001, and 2005 (and occasionally also 1983 or 2006/7).[17]

For each of these six years, and for each of these 100 industries, we collected the revenues for the firms active in that industry. To do so was a laborious process. Sometimes we could use an official source. But in many cases we had to use a combination of official and unofficial reporting, such as filings to the S.E.C., news stories, financial analysts' reports, and many other sources. Furthermore, companies are usually active in several industries, a situation that presented questions of allocation and required a variety of sources, personal interviews, and extrapolations from available data points.

Another problem was the allocation of revenues to the U.S. market business on a worldwide business basis. As mentioned, since this study looks at the concentration of information markets in the United States, the revenues of American firms from their international activities are not included. Conversely, revenues of non-U.S. firms in America are included. For example, IBM's presence in Japan is not relevant to this study, but Sony's activities in America are.

In a data effort of this magnitude, no doubt there will be some inaccuracies. It is in the nature of a wide coverage that experts on any particular segment will take issue with some detail. If at times an inaccuracy has crept in, a correction would be appreciated by the author. There is no intent to use numbers strategically to prove a preconceived position. This is a study whose overall findings came together only after years of data research. Given the number of firms and industries surveyed, it is difficult for any such error to affect the aggregates more than minimally, especially since such errors should be randomly distributed and offset each other. The large size and number of industries makes it unlikely that any particular firm's smaller or larger revenue in some year would have more than a minimal effect on the broader trends of industries and sectors.

Another issue is that there is some unavoidable double-counting, when firms buy inputs from others and resell them in the same form or in new combinations. Ideally, one would calculate and use the "value-added." This is fairly easy in some cases—for film distribution and film theaters, for example. But it is almost impossible to do for other interindustry relations, such as music firms and their deals with film producers, and vice versa.

Once the revenue figures were determined, they had to be translated into market shares. To do so we had to determine the size of the U.S. market, based both on firm data and other information sources. The bulk of the data represents companies' market shares based on revenue within a particular industry. In several instances it was more practical to calculate market shares based on subscriber numbers (such as for Internet Service Providers), shipped units (for computers and for consumer electronics), and so on.

The market share figures were then used to calculate the HHI and the C4 concentration indices for each year and for each industry and to find and map the concentration trends. Next, with the findings for each industry concentration over two decades in hand, I could aggregate the industries into broader subsectors, in successive steps, until a concentration measure is reached for the information sector as a whole. For example, radio was aggregated with TV broadcasting, cable, and satellite distribution into the category "electronic mass media distribution." This, in turn, is aggregated with the industries of "electronic mass media programming" (e.g., radio networks, TV networks, TV syndication, cable TV channels, and pay-TV channels) to obtain trends for the broader sector of "electronic mass media." This, in turn, is aggregated with the various subindustries of film (5 industries), print (10), and music (5) into trends for the "mass media." And this, in turn, is aggregated with the industries of telecommunication, IT, and Internet media to an overall information sector concentration trend.

This data effort was extensive and the subsequent use of the data by the author and his collaborators is likely, so that ground rules should be set for its reuse. Other researchers may freely cite this information or reproduce its tables with attribution. However, the large-scale use of the database, for example for econometric and similar quantitative research, requires a copyright waiver and the express permission of the author.

I have tried to keep the methodology stone-simple so as not to distract from the story itself or to raise the question whether the methodology was result-driven. Even so, to some it is already too technical. Such readers should simply remember that concentration for each media industry is being measured by a particular index used traditionally by the U.S. government, and that the concentrations of related industries is then being averaged, adjusting for industry size.

The data effort covered 100 industries, most of them for a period of over 20 years, and with typically 10 to 20 companies in each industry, some consolidating, some entering, and some leaving. Where the time series is shorter, it is either because the industry did not exist in 1984 (for example, Internet portals) or ceased operating (for instance, the telegraph industry).

A final word: the use of an index for media concentration does not imply that it should be the touchstone for what is essentially a societal and political question. But opposition to numbers-based measures cannot be selective and result-oriented. Often, people argue against a numbers-based approach if the numbers come out against them. True, principles require no numbers. But the actual translation of principles into policy, law, and regulation requires, unavoidably, some criteria, standards, and red lines, which usually require some quantification.

Notes

1. Nesvold, Peter, *Communication Breakdown: Developing an Antitrust Model for Multimedia Mergers and Acquisitions*. Accessed on Jan. 4, 2008, from http://www-vii-org/papers/peter.htm.

2. Owen, Bruce, "Confusing Success with Access: Correctly Measuring Concentration of Ownership and Control in Mass Media and Online Services," John M. Olin Program in Law and Economics, Working Paper 283, May 2004. Prepared for "Media Concentration and the Internet—Empirical, Business and Policy Research," a Symposium at the Columbia Institute for Tele-Information (CITI), Columbia Business School, April 15, 2004 (p. 9).

3. Organisation for Economic Co-Operation and Development, Directorate for Financial, Fiscal, and Enterprise Affairs Competition Committee, "Media Mergers." JT00149676. OECD.org. 19 September, 2003. Page 52. Accessed on January 4, 2008, from http://www.oecd.org/dataoecd/15/3/17372985.pdf.

4. "The politicization of antitrust is not just a matter of historical curiosity. Politics stalk many of the high-profile cases brought by President Clinton's trustbusters, including Primestar's planned purchase of a key satellite as well as the

mergers proposed between Staples and Office Depot, Worldcom and MCI, and Lockheed Martin and Northrop Grumman." Shughart II, William F., "The Government's War on Mergers: The Fatal Conceit of Antitrust Policy." *Policy Analysis*, No. 323, October 22, 1998.

5. Pitofsky, Robert, FTC chairman, "Competition Policy in Communications Industries: New Antitrust Approaches." Glasser Legal Works Seminar on Competitive Policy in Communications Industries: New Antitrust Approaches, March 10, 1997. Available at http://www.ftc.gov/speeches/pitofsky/newcomm.htm.

6. An example for a principles-rich but numbers-poor concern for the impact of media concentration: Baker, Edwin C. *Media Concentration and Democracy: Why Ownership Matters*, New York: Cambridge University Press, 2007. Also, see Baker, Edwin C., "Media Concentration: Giving Up on Democracy." Public Law and Legal Theory Research Paper Series, Research Paper No. 16, Fall 2002, University of Pennsylvania Law School.

7. Averitt, Neil W., and Robert H. Lande, "Consumer Choice: The Practical Reason for Both Antitrust and Consumer Protection Law," *Loyola Consumer Law Review* 44, 1998; Averitt, Neil W., and Robert H. Lande, "Consumer Sovereignty: A Unified Theory of Antitrust and Consumer Protection Law." *Antitrust Law Journal* 713, 1997.

8. Stucke, Maurice E., and Allan P. Grunes, "Antitrust and the Marketplace of Ideas." *Antitrust Law Journal*, Issue 1, Vol. 69, p. 249, 2001.

9. Organisation for Economic Co-Operation and Development, Directorate for Financial, Fiscal and Enterprise Affairs Competition Committee, "Media Mergers." JT00149676. OECD.org. 19 September, 2003. Page 10. Accessed on January 4, 2008, from http://www.oecd.org/dataoecd/15/3/17372985.pdf.

10. Nesvold, Peter. *Communication Breakdown: Developing an Antitrust Model for Multimedia Mergers and Acquisitions*. Accessed Jan. 4, 2008, from http://www-vii-org/papers/peter.htm.

11. Waldfogel, Joel. "Consumer Substitution among Media." Media Bureau Staff Research Paper, Media Ownership Working Group, Federal Communications Commission, September 2002.

12. Bush, C. Anthony. "On the Substitutability of Local Newspaper, Radio, and Television Advertising in Local Business Sales." Media Bureau Staff Research Paper, Media Ownership Working Group, Federal Communications Commission, September 2002.

13. The same operation can be both local and national. For example, a cable TV operator transacting with customers is in a local market. When it transacts with program channels for transmissions, it is in the national market.

14. Herbert Marcuse, *One-Dimensional Man: Studies in the Ideology of Advanced Industrial Society.* London: Routledge, 1964, p. 8.

15. The HHI is often known as "the Herfindahl."

16. Local markets are much more concentrated, e.g., for daily newspapers, cable TV, telecom, etc. This is discussed and empirically investigated in chapter 15.

17. The year 2001 was chosen because 2000 was the peak of a boom that distorts trends; 2000 overaccentuates the rise of 1996–2000 and the decline of 2000–2004.

PART II

MASS MEDIA

4

Electronic Mass Media: Retail Distribution

RADIO

We begin with the electronic mass media of distribution—radio, TV, cable, satellite.[1] These media consist of two major segments; there are *local retail media* and *national wholesale networks*. Retail media distribute content directly to audiences. Examples are local radio and TV stations and cable distribution systems. In contrast, wholesale networks bundle programs created by content producers and distribute them to retailers. Examples are radio and TV networks, cable channels, and program syndicators.

Radio Station Ownership

Radio, the oldest of electronic mass media, has long been a multiprovider-, multiformat-oriented medium. After an early amateur-based period, the first commercial station began transmitting in Pittsburgh in 1920. In 1984, 9,642 radio stations were on the air,[2] and in 2006[3] there were 13,748, with almost 50 stations in the largest metropolitan areas; 85% of these stations were commercial.

Radio has become the poster boy for media concentration. Most public discussions of media trends refer to the developments in radio and its lessons for public policy. Others point to the proliferation of audio media alternatives. Is radio, since 1906 the pioneer of all electronic mass media distribution, again at the forefront of creating a new media environment, either concentrated or diverse?

No U.S. media industry has changed more in ownership than local radio stations. Until the 1990s, concentration was extremely low because of the cap on station ownership imposed by the FCC. No group could own more than 7 AM and 7 FM stations, out of many thousands of stations. This was raised to 12 each in 1985, 18 each in 1992, and 20 each in 1994. After 1996, there were no national caps left at all.

By antitrust enforcement standards, the national radio broadcast industry was highly unconcentrated into the early 1990s. Table 4.1 demonstrates the changes in market concentration measured by *number of stations* owned. In 1984, the HHI was only 0.1. No other industry of the information sector (and perhaps of the entire economy) was then as nationally unconcentrated as radio stations. Earlier, in the Golden Age of radio, 1925–1945, radio content supply had been much more concentrated, with NBC and CBS dominating through their networks and leveraging that role to power over the numerous local affiliated stations. (More on this in chapter 5.) With regulatory relaxation, however, radio stations changed hands at a dizzying rate (figure 4.2). The number of stations sold between 1984 and 1996 was greater than the total number of stations operating in the United States. As ownership restrictions were relaxed, average station values rose from $1.2 million in 1984 to

$4.2 million in 1996, based on actual transactions (figure 4.1).

A major acquisition driver was a leveraged buyout firm, the Dallas-based Hicks Muse Tate and Furst, which recognized early the financial opportunity presented by the lowering of owner-ship caps. Capstar, one of its acquisition vehicles, bought about 250 stations in an 18-month period

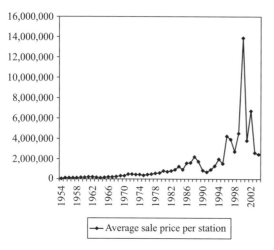

Figure 4.1 Average Sale Price per Station, 1954–2003

in 1996 and 1997. Several other radio companies emerged and bought a large number of stations: Jacor, Infinity, Chancellor, Citadel, Cumulus, and Clear Channel. Clear Channel became the indus-try leader. Concentration in station ownership increased. By 2004, the HHI by station ownership had risen to 98, a major increase from zero, but still quite unconcentrated under national antitrust guidelines. Even industry colossus Clear Channel, with its array of 1,184 stations in 2005, accounted for only 9.2% of stations. The next firms—Cumulus, Citadel/ABC, Viacom, and Hispanic—were in the 0.6–2.4% range. The number of stations increased by 6.8% from 1996 to 2007 to 10,956 commercial stations. But the number of owners declined from 5,133 to 3,121, a reduction by 39% according to the FCC.[4] Program format diversity did not change and was about 10 in metropolitan markets and 16 in the top 10 markets. Gross profitability of radio station companies was higher than the Standard & Poor's Index, but due to the high debt load, net profitability was actually lower, according to the FCC. Advertising rates rose substantially faster than inflation.[5]

Tables 4.1 and 4.2 show the trends in the own-ership of stations over the period 1984–2005.

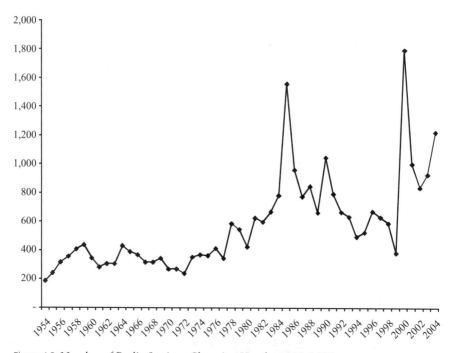

Figure 4.2 Number of Radio Stations Changing Hands, 1954–2004.

Source: Broadcasting and Cable Yearbook, 1991 and *2001* (New Providence, N.J.: Bowker), 1991, 2001.

Table 4.1 Radio Station Groups, by Number of Stations Owned

	1984	1988	1992	1996	2000	2001	2004	2005	2007
Clear Channel	12	14	20	86	1202	1231	1194	1190	1005
AM/FM					Clear				
Radio Equity Partners				19	Clear				
Jacor		10	11	95	Clear				
Evergreen	2	3	7	39	Clear				
Chancellor			14	51	Clear				
Capstar				275	Clear				
SFX			2	25	Clear				
Citadel				89	206	205	224	297	223
Disney/ABC				21	55	58	73	Citadel/ABC	
CapCities			21	Disney					
ABC	12	21							
		Cap Cities							
CBS	12				184	186	180	178	140
Viacom					Viacom			CBS	
Westinghouse (Group W)	11	14	14	79	Viacom				
Infinity	8	15	18	Westinghouse					
CBS	12	14	21	Westinghouse					
American Radio Systems				37	Viacom				
Cox	12	12	20	43	82	81	78	78	86
Entercom	1	2	2	7	95	104	106	103	111
Radio One				9	36	64	68	69	54
Emmis	5	7	12	11	23	21	25	25	25
Cumulus					227	243	304	303	336
Hispanic/Univision		2	4	54	47	52	70	70	61
All Others	9,567	10,347	10,858	11,194	10,560	10,687	10,610	10,610	11,002
Total Stations	9,642	10,461	11,024	12,134	12,717	12,932	12,932	12,932	13,046
C4	0.5	0.6	0.7	4.5	14.3	14.4	14.7	15.2	13.1
C8	0.8	1.0	1.3	6.4	16.5	16.8	17.2	17.7	15.5
HHI	0.1	0.1	0.2	8	99	100	98	99	72

Notes: Group station totals from company SEC filings. Station totals are pro forma from date of acquisition in order to properly reflect ownership changes.

Sources: Bear Stearns, *Radio Broadcasting*; *Radio Broadcasting: Fact Book*, April 2005; Journalism.org, *The State of the News Media 2006*, May 2006; *Broadcasting and Cable Yearbooks*, 1992, 1996, and 2000. Radio Advertising Bureau, *Radio Facts*, 1984, 1988, 1992. Westinghouse purchased CBS in 1996 and Group W's radio division was merged into CBS's existing radio group.

[a] In 2006 Disney merged its radio holdings into a joint company with Citadel, which became controlled by Citadel.

Table 4.2 Radio Station Market Shares, by Number of Stations Owned

	1984	1988	1992	1996	2000	2001	2004	2005	2007
Clear Channel	0.1	0.1	0.2	0.7	9.5	9.5	9.2	9.2	7.7
AM/FM					Clear				
Radio Equity Partners		0.0	0.0	0.2	Clear				
Jacor		0.1	0.1	0.8	Clear				
Evergreen	0.0	0.0	0.1	0.3	Clear				
Chancellor			0.1	0.4	Clear				
Capstar				2.3	Clear				
SFX				0.2	Clear				
Citadel			0.0	0.7	1.6	1.6	1.7	2.3	1.7
Disney/ABC				0.2	0.4	0.4	0.6	Citadel/ABC	
CapCities		0.2	0.2	Disney					
ABC	0.1	CapCities							
CBS				0.0	1.4	1.4	1.4	1.4	1.1
Viacom				0.7	Viacom			CBS	
Westinghouse (Group W)	0.1	0.1	0.1						
Infinity	0.1	0.1	0.2	Westinghouse					
CBS	0.1	0.1	0.2	Westinghouse					
American Radio Systems				0.3	Viacom				
Cox	0.1	0.1	0.2	0.4	0.6	0.6	0.6	0.6	0.7
Entercom	0.0	0.0	0.0	0.1	0.7	0.8	0.8	0.8	0.9
Radio One				0.1	0.3	0.5	0.5	0.5	0.4
Emmis	0.1	0.1	0.1	0.1	0.2	0.2	0.2	0.2	0.2
Cumulus					1.8	1.9	2.4	2.3	2.6
Hispanic		0.0	0.0	0.4	0.4	0.4	0.5	0.5	0.5
All Others	99.2	98.9	98.5	92.3	83.0	82.6	82.0	82.0	84.3
Total Stations	9,642	10,461	11,024	12,134	12,717	12,932	12,932	12,932	13,046
C4	0.5	0.6	0.7	4.5	14.3	14.4	14.7	15.2	13.1
C8	0.8	1.0	1.3	6.4	16.5	16.8	17.2	17.7	15.5
HHI	0.1	0.1	0.2	8	99	100	98	99	72

From 1992 to 2005 the market share of the top four firms, by stations owned, rose from less than 1% to 15.2%. This increase resulted largely from several expansions: Westinghouse's acquisition of CBS in 1995 and of Infinity in 1996 (for $4.3 billion), and its own acquisition by Viacom in 2000 for $49 billion; Chancellor's acquisition of Evergreen and SFX in 1997 and Capstar in 1998; and Clear Channel's acquisition of Jacor in 1998, of AMFM in 1999 for $23.5 billion, and of Chancellor in 2000.

In 2004, two firms dominated the industry, Clear Channel and CBS (previously Viacom's Infinity). Citadel joined in 2006 through its merger with Disney's ABC radio properties.

Of course, station count is only one dimension of ownership. Some stations are much larger than others in terms of audience reach and hence advertising revenues. This is provided in table 4.3.

Clear Channel was by far the largest radio group in revenues ($3.6 billion in 2004), and Viacom had $2.3 billion. The market was much more concentrated on a revenue basis than on a station's basis. The concentration figures show the HHI increasing from 20 in 1984 to 535 in 2004, a large increase in relative terms but a low number by DOJ's standards. The C4 more than quadrupled from 8.3% 1984 to 35.9% in 2005. The greatest changes came around 1996, when national station ownership caps were lifted entirely. Clear Channel and Viacom

Table 4.3 Radio Group Market Shares, by Revenues

	1984	1988	1992	1996	2000	2001	2004	2007
Clear Channel	0.3	0.5	1.0	2.8	12.4	18.7	18.9	17.2
Radio Equity Partners				0.4	Clear			
Jacor		0.9	0.8	1.9	Clear			
Evergreen			0.6	2.5	Clear			
Chancellor			0.1	2.1	Clear			
Capstar				2.1	Clear			
SFX			0.2	2.0	Clear			
Viacom					12.5	12.0	11.9	8.7
Westinghouse (Group W)	2.4	2.4	2.4	4.6	Viacom			
Infinity[a]	1.3	1.3	1.8	W'house				
CBS	2.1	2.0	2.5	W'house	Viacom			
American Radio Systems[b]				2.7	Viacom			
Citadel				0.2	0.4	1.8	4.6	3.0
Disney					3.4	2.2	2.3	Citadel
CapCities			2.4	2.4	Disney			
ABC	2.4	CapCities						
Cox	0.8	0.8	1.2	1.6	2.4	2.5	2.6	2.2
Entercom				0.4	1.9	1.9	2.6	2.3
Radio One			0.1	0.2	1.6	1.6	2.0	1.6
Emmis	0.9	0.9	0.9	0.8	1.6	1.5	1.6	1.6
Cumulus					1.2	1.4	1.7	1.6
Univision							1.8	2.1
Hispanic	0.0	0.0	0.2	0.6	1.3	1.4	Univision	
XM							1.1	5.0
Sirius							0.4	4.6
Other	96.6	94.0	90.1	75.4	65.8	60.1	52.3	50.0
Total U.S. Revenue ($ mil)	5,596	7,511	8,378	11,947	18,819	17,450	18,932	20,154
C4	8.3	8.1	9.0	13.6	29.6	35.4	38.0	35.4
C8	10.3	11.1	13.0	22.1	36.5	42.2	46.0	45.1
HHI	20	20	25	75	337	519	545	403

Notes: Revenues are post acquisition.

Sources: BIA Financial Network, company SEC filings, and Crain Communications. Data for 2004 from Bear Stearns "*Radio Broadcasting: Fact Book*," April 2005.

[a] The remaining public float of Infinity was merged into Viacom in February 2001 subsequent to Viacom's purchase of CBS in 2000, but it is shown here as a separate entity.
[b] American Radio Systems was created by a three-way merger in 1995.

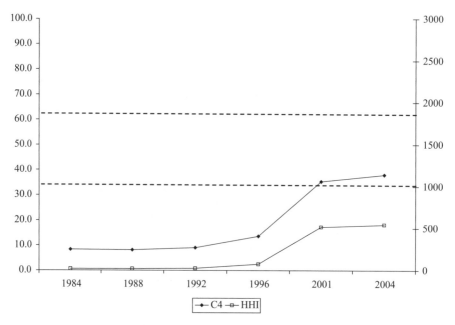

Figure 4.3 Radio Stations: Concentration

achieved market shares of 18.9% and 11.9%; Citadel had 4.6% through its acquisition/merger spinoff of Disney's radio stations. Cox, Entercom, and RadioOne were much smaller, with market shares between 2 and 3%. These trends are shown in figure 4.3, which illustrates the rise in concentration after 1996 (actually, 1995, when several major acquisitions anticipated the change in the law).

Although Clear Channel has been the largest group in both revenue and number of stations, it ranks low among the large groups in revenue per station, with $3 million per station per year. Viacom earned, in contrast, $11.8 million in revenue per radio station, and Cox ($6.2 million) and Disney ($6.2 million) also had much higher numbers. Clear Channel's stations were often in second- and third-tier markets, whereas Viacom's were top stations in top markets. But since competition tended to be weaker in smaller markets, profit margins there might well be higher.

In 1984, Clear Channel's predecessor firm was barely a player with only 0.3% market share, compared to Westinghouse, CBS, and ABC with 2.0% to 2.3% each. In 2004, these ratios were reversed, with Clear Channel having nine times the share of Disney (ABC). But Clear Channel, and radio station concentration with it, may have peaked. In 2007, Clear Channel agreed to be acquired for $19.5 billion by the private equity firm Bain Capital and Thomas H. Lee. To finance the deal,

the buyers would sell off 450 stations. Many aspects of these transactions ran into trouble as the financial markets soured on large and highly leveraged radio companies. Citadel, similarly, was delisted in 2009 by the New York Stock Exchange when its share prices plummeted.

Local Radio Markets

The local nature of most radio advertising and news programming makes local ownership concentration a greater concern than national concentration. For that reason, the FCC (and Congress) did not remove limits on local ownership entirely, even when it did so for national ceilings. In 1992, the FCC relaxed its "Duopoly Rule" (a misnomer for the policy of limiting a firm's station ownership to two stations per market) to allow any single company in a local market to own up to two radio stations per "service," that is, four stations (AM and FM are considered different services, for anachronistic reasons). The same entity could also own a noncontrolling share of two additional stations per service if they were owned by ethnic minorities or small-business firms. The Telecommunications Act of 1996 again doubled the local limit on station ownership up to eight (although no more than five per service) in markets with 45 or more commercial radio stations, which at the time consisted of New York, Los Angeles, and Chicago. For smaller markets the rules were stricter. In markets with 30 to 44 commercial radio stations, the ceiling was eight stations, but a firm could not own more than four per service. In markets with 15 to 29 commercial radio stations, the ownership ceiling was six, and in markets with fourteen or fewer commercial stations, the ceiling was five, which had to add up to less than 50% of local radio revenues.[6] In 2003, some inconsistencies were rectified by the FCC in a way that slightly tightened these limits. As a result of this loosening of local ownership ceilings, companies began to own clusters of local stations. In content terms, they could segment the audience. Radio was becoming a multichannel medium, albeit with a much reduced number of owners.

The number of stations grew strongly. 4,106 new stations were licensed from 1984 to 2006. Table 4.4 illustrates the increase in the number of radio stations from 1983 through 2006. It has remained stable in large markets where the available licenses were mostly already assigned. But there has been a relatively high increase in small but growing sunbelt markets exemplified by Amarillo, Texas, where the number of stations doubled from 1983 to 1998.

The number of stations is not the whole story. A company that owns the allowed maximum of eight stations in a market with 45 stations holds less than 18% of stations in purely numerical terms but usually accounts for a considerably higher share of advertising revenues. The acquisition of Infinity by Westinghouse/CBS in 1996 gave Westinghouse/CBS control of 44% of the Philadelphia radio revenues, and at least 30% of radio revenues in New York, Chicago, Boston, Dallas, and Detroit.[7] Other groups that gained large shares of the revenue in specific markets through 1996 mergers include Jacor (with 53% of Cincinnati), American Radio Systems (66.4% of Rochester, New York),

Triathlon Broadcasting (with 48.5% of Lincoln, Nebraska), and Patterson Broadcasting (with 48.6% of Honolulu).[8]

The increased pace of merger activity after the passage of the Telecom Act of 1996 forced the U.S. Department of Justice to take a position on how much market control by any one group it would allow. Previously, there was no set threshold, because FCC rules limited concentration. Through its negotiations with Jacor and American Radio Systems on their proposed acquisitions at the time, the Justice Department gave unofficial guidance that it would tolerate a 40% to 50% local market revenue control by a single firm. Approval of major radio mergers was conditioned on the groups' agreements to divest enough stations to bring their share of radio advertising revenues in individual markets down to 40% to 50%. This is a very high threshold.

Also, it excludes joint sales agreements.[9] Broadcasting groups can achieve higher shares of local advertising markets through joint sales agreements (JSAs), joint operating agreements (JOAs) or local marketing agreements (LMAs).[10] These arrangements allow stations to achieve greater economies of scale in the sale of advertising time by allowing supposed competitors to sell advertising time in a joint way. This creates opportunities for oligopolistic pricing. At one point, government investigated JSAs as a form of illegal price-fixing. It then permitted them on a case-by-case basis.

Table 4.5 shows local radio concentration trends, based on an analysis of 30 local markets (small, medium, and large). Local concentration in 2006 was significantly higher than it was in 1984. The weighed average share of the top firm in a market (C1) grew from about 20% in 1984 to almost 34% in 2006, and for the top four firms from 52.6% to 84.4%. An FCC report in 2007 also found a C4 of about 84%

Table 4.4 Number of Radio Stations in Selected Markets

	1983	1987	1991	1994	1998	2001	2006
New York	45	44	44	45	44	45	43
Los Angeles	47	46	45	46	46	44	44
Chicago	48	50	48	48	46	44	45
San Francisco	35	37	41	39	39	38	38
Cleveland	28	27	28	27	26	25	24
Richmond	20	21	23	26	26	27	25
Amarillo	13	18	21	25	26	24	25

Source: Broadcasting and Cable Yearbook, 2006. New Providence, N.J.: Bowker.

Table 4.5 Local Radio Concentration[a]

	1984	1988	1992	1996	2002	2006[b]
	C1 Concentration					
C1 Large Cities	14.1	14.6	14.4	32.3	34.3	29.9
C1 Medium Cities	22.3	22.2	25.0	34.8	37.8	37.5
C1 Small Cities	25.6	24	23.5	35.6	31.8	34.6
Weighted Average	19.9	19.7	20.3	34	34.7	33.6
	C4 Concentration					
C4 Large Cities	43	42.2	45.8	67.7	80.3	78.8
C4 Medium Cities	57.2	62.6	68.0	88.8	91.8	87.1
C4 Small Cities	61.4	60.5	64.6	77.4	82.1	87.3
Weighted Average	52.6	53.8	58.1	77.1	84.4	83.8
	HHI Concentration					
HHI Large Cities	592	756	816	1,733	2,139	1,989
HHI Medium Cities	1,094	1,298	1,572	2,457	2,798	2,569
HHI Small Cities	1,263	1,238	1,333	2,173	2,330	2,537
Weighted Average	939	1,062	1,200	2,085	2,400	2,326
	Avg. Annual Rev. per Household					
Rev. Large Cities	41	55	62	92	144	200
Rev. Medium Cities	32	41	46	63	90	120
Rev. Small Cities	26	33	41	57	72	82

[a]Local radio revenues and market shares are based on *Duncan's Radio Market Guide*; 1985, 1989, 1994, 1997, and 2002 editions, respectively. Copyright © James H. Duncan, Jr. Local market concentration was established using the *Broadcasting and Cable Yearbook* (1984, 1988, 1992, 1996, and 2001, respectively), published by R.R. Bowker, New Providence, N.J.
[b]2006 data based on Arbitron market ratings.

for markets 1–10, of 90% in markets 50–100, and of 92% beyond market 100. The HHI index rose from a level that is fairly unconcentrated by DOJ standards (939) to a highly concentrated 2,326 in 2006. Even in large cities, the index rose steeply to 1,989. These are large increases, and it is not much of a comfort that radio is still among the least concentrated of local media. As we will see below in the chapter on local concentration, such concentration in 2006 was much higher for wire line (HHI = 4,993), multichannel TV (6,629), local magazines (6,547), and newspapers (7,676). Looking at three sizes of markets (large, medium, and small cities), we observe what we find for other media, too: although the large markets are the least concentrated, as one would expect, the small markets have actually a somewhat lower concentration than the medium-sized ones. The explanation must be that in small markets, audiences also listen more to stations from adjacent cities, whereas audiences in medium-sized cities, given that there are more directly local choices, listen more to their own local stations.

An FCC econometric study looked at the impact of local radio concentration on advertising prices.[11] The findings were that local radio consolidation modestly raised advertising prices. A full doubling of the HHI market concentration was associated with local advertising prices that were higher by 3% to 4%. Such a small increase suggests a highly elastic demand for local advertising. Given the high levels of local radio concentration (HHI of 2,326) and the absence of strong alternative media for drive-time advertising access, such small percentage is lower than expected. (Our figures show, on average, an increase of the local HHI by a factor of about 2.5, and of 3.5 in the large cities.) But even if the FCC's finding is accepted, it would still signify an added cost of $650 million annually for local advertisers.

The FCC study also finds that large radio firm size led to lower prices for regional and national advertisers, perhaps, it speculates, due to advantageous economies that are passed on as lower prices. This is less persuasive. One would expect these economies and resultant lower transaction costs to make radio a more desirable vehicle for advertisers, and hence raise willingness to pay, while reducing the number of suppliers competing for regional and national coverage and hence strengthening their bargaining power.

Alternative Audio Media

The FCC estimated in 2004 that there were about 800 million radio sets in use in the United States.[12] Seventy-seven percent of Americans listened to radio daily, and 96% tuned in at least once a week.[13] In 2005, the average American over 12 years of age listened to the radio an average of 19.5 hours per week.[15] In 1995, 38% of adults relied on radio for their daily morning news (37% relied on TV, and 20% on newspapers).[16] Factors in radio's continued popularity include its mobility, localism (79% of radio advertising revenues are local), low cost, convenience, and limited attention requirement.

But should one only look at classic broadcast radio? What about its new rivals? Two such alternatives have been offshoots of video delivery media: cable radio and satellite radio. Three other options are Internet-delivered: online distribution of broadcast stations, nonbroadcast music Web sites, and "pod-casting" by individuals. Broadcast alternatives are lower power FM stations and digital radio ("HD-Radio").

Cable radio was launched in 1990 by two firms. One was Digital Cable Radio, a joint venture among General Instrument, International Cablecasting, and Digital Radio Labs. A second was America's Music Choice, backed by the music companies EMI and Sony. Cable radio networks reach into millions of homes. But as an unbundled service, cable's lack of portability and the availability of free alternatives has caused penetration to remain low—between 2% and 4%—on an a la carte basis. Actual penetration is higher when the channels are bundled into the basic or enhanced basic digital cable offering, but actual utilization is not high.

Beginning in 1994, radio was also distributed over satellites, with 30 channels available to subscribers of DirecTV. Reception was not mobile, however. This was alleviated by specialized satellite-based digital radio. In 1997, the FCC licensed two companies, Sirius and XM Satellite Radio. Service began in 2002.[14] The subscription prices

were about $10 per month for 100-plus radio channels. Upscale car manufacturers included the receivers in their offerings. The average price for the satellite radio receivers was $200 and falling. With about 200 million registered private motor vehicles, 110 million daily commuters, 17 million new cars every year, and 30 million new car stereos each year, the business plan aimed to persuade 4 million new car buyers each year. In 2006, XM had 8 million subscribers and Sirius had 6 million, and was growing faster. Starting from nowhere in 2002, the two companies were by 2006, respectively, the number 3 and 5 radio companies by revenues, mostly from subscriptions. In 2008, the two companies merged into Sirius XM Radio and began joint operations, broadcasting a joint channel lineup on both satellite platforms. Despite cost reductions and price increases, the merged company hovered near Chapter 11 bankruptcy in 2009.

Still other radio alternatives are low-power (community) radios, which have limited audiences, and digital "HD-Radio" broadcasting, a terrestrial service that has yet to take off with audiences since it requires new receivers.

Broadcasting over the internet is another alternative, offered by radio companies, satellite radio providers as well as specialized netcasters and podcasters.[17] In 2008, Arbitron reported that the weekly audience for the six major online radio services (CBS, Clear Channel, Live 365, RL Select, TargetSpot, Yahoo, and Total RL) was 7.5 million people. This may account for half of online music channels. Comparing this number with weekly audience figure for radio as reported by the Radio Advertising Bureau (230 million[18]), we can estimate that online radio accounted for around 6–7% of the radio audience in 2008 by number of people, and less in the crucial drive time.

In the aggregate, the alternative real-time distribution media have not yet greatly reduced the audiences of broadcast radio. Recorded media such as MP3 have been more of a competitive issue for traditional music companies than for live radio, because they do not provide news, weather, or act as an effective outlet for advertisers. From 1998 to 2007, the average share of listeners per quarter hour in the population has dropped from 16.3% to 14.0%, a moderate decline of 14%, in share. Radio has a huge legacy structure in place; it is reasonably diverse, cheap, convenient, ubiquitous, and mobile. It is losing audience niches, but its overall market still remains quite large. For now, it looks as though the first of the analog electronic mass media will remain the last analog one, too.

BROADCAST TELEVISION

Unlike broadcast radio, which usually had enough stations to function as a multichannel medium, at least in terms of capacity, broadcast TV was historically a limited-channel medium. This limitation, one should note, was one of government: the sparse allocation of frequencies created a locally oligopolistic market structure. The transformation of TV from a limited over-the-air medium to a multichannel medium occurred with the expanding capacity and penetration of cable and direct broadcast satellites (DBS) and with the beginning of digital broadcast TV with its multicast potential.

Thus, though broadcast television stations have been increasing in number, their total viewership steadily declined: audience shares fell from 88.3% of TV audiences in 1984 to 49% in 2008, while the share for cable networks and pay cable increased from 11.7% to 51% in the same period.[19] The audience share of network affiliate stations for the original major networks (ABC, CBS, and NBC) shrunk from 64.2% in 1984 to 34.1% in 2005. On top of that, the actual viewing of local TV stations by most households is of signals transmitted over cable and not over the air.

National Group Ownership

The number of TV stations in operation (1,784 in 2006),[20] while considerable, is much smaller than the number of radio stations. The TV industry has always been more concentrated, even under similar FCC ownership ceiling rules. In the mid-1980s, 80% of the stations in the top 100 markets were owned by multiple-station firms.[21] But there were many such TV chains, since ownership was capped by regulation, as it was for radio. These caps at first limited ownership to 7 stations, and then to 12 stations (14 if the extra stations were controlled by racial minorities or small businesses). Later, a cap was adopted which did not limit the number of stations but rather their total national audience "reach" (the potential audience, not the actual one). Initially the cap limited group ownership to a reach of 25% of the national audience, or 30% if two of the stations were owned by small or minority-controlled businesses.

The rationale for national ownership caps was harder to articulate in a multi- channel media environment than for local caps. As cable television and satellite TV increased in penetration and channel capacity, the distributors of video programs could bypass TV stations altogether in accessing viewers on a nationwide scale. The largest of station groups therefore lobbied to remove the caps on their ownership of local TV outlets. Smaller station groups, on the other hand, argued in favor of restrictions on national reach. They feared, in particular, the loss of bargaining power if the national TV network companies would gain local distribution to most American households without having to rely on independently owned local affiliates. This issue split the broadcast industry and reduced its lobbying effectiveness before Congress. The 1996 Telecommunications Act loosened national restrictions. It raised the limits on the absolute number of TV stations which an entity might own; raised the cap on national audience reach to 35%; and eliminated the prohibition on local ownership of more than one TV station by a single entity within the same television market, as long as there were at least eight separately owned stations within each market, and if both stations were not in the top four by audience share. But this was not the end of the story.

The major station group firms (which also owned the four major TV networks) pushed for the rules to be eliminated entirely. In 1999, when Viacom acquired CBS, and again in 2000, when News Corp acquired Chris-Craft, both acquirers were betting that they would not be forced to divest stations from these transactions even though they exceeded the national ownership limits. And indeed, neither firm was denied completion of its respective mergers by the Justice Department or the FCC. The FCC gave Viacom one year to comply with its 35% attribution cap, which meant it would have to divest stations. Instead, Viacom sued the FCC in 2001 and won its case on the grounds that the FCC caps were "arbitrary and capricious." The court ordered the FCC to provide evidence for a particular ownership rule. The FCC, after reviewing its rules at length, issued new ones in 2003.

There were several changes. The most controversial ones raised the national reach ceiling still further, from 35% to 45%. The FCC also modified cross-ownership and duopoly ownership limits.[22] A single group was allowed ownership over two television stations in a local market if there would be at least five separately-owned stations remaining, down from the previous limit of eight. This allowed such duopolies in 162 out of 210 markets. The FCC also loosened cross-ownership restrictions by eliminating the newspaper-broad-cast cross-ownership ban and the television-radio cross-ownership ban in markets with nine or more TV stations. All this unleashed a huge contro-versy. Critics argued that small, local media would be gobbled up by large media conglomerates, thereby detrimentally affecting the information flow in local communities. The FCC was forced to retreat, and the limit on the national reach was set by Congress at 39%. Meanwhile, a federal appeals court struck down the FCC's whole set of rules (*Prometheus Radio Project vs. FCC.*, 2004). The FCC, divided and defeated, responded to this barrage of criticism and embarked on an investi-gation "to evaluate how broadcasters are serving their local communities," by creating a Localism Task Force. (For a further discussion of the rules, see the chapter on Local Concentration.) This was followed, in December of 2007, by FCC chairman Kevin Martin narrowly pushing through cross-ownership relaxations for the top 20 markets.[23]

One practical question has been how to define "ownership." Suppose a firm owns a station in partnership with others? Or suppose it is a minority investor in numerous stations? So-called "attribution" rules have evolved to deal with dif-ferent ownership structures. This was not a the-oretical issue. As national TV groups sought to expand their reach, they looked continually for ways to skirt the 35% cap. If they could not own more stations directly, they would make invest-ments in others in the form of debt or preferred shares or enter into cooperations such as joint sales agreements. In response, the FCC insti-tuted a cap on the amount of combined debt and equity one TV group could hold in another, (33% of a firm's total balance sheet), before the other firm would be counted in the ownership ceiling calculations.

The FCC's attribution rules are based on the nature of a group's percentage ownership as well as the indirect ownership and financial support in the form of investments. Under the FCC's rules, an "attributable" interest generally includes, as men-tioned, equity and debt interests which together exceed 33% of a licensee's total assets; or, if the interest holder supplies more than 15% of total weekly programming; or, if it is a same-market media entity, whether TV, radio, cable or newspa-per; or, if it holds more than of 5% voting stock, or 20% or greater of voting stock, if the holder is a qualified passive investor; or, if it holds any equity interest in a limited liability company or limited

partnership, unless properly insulated from man-agement activities; or, if it shares officers and directors. A station may own up to 49% of another with no additional attribution if that company also has a "single majority" shareholder who controls a majority of the voting rights.

NBC's investment in Paxson Communications illustrates this concept. In 1999, NBC invested $415 million in Paxson in the form of convert-ible preferred shares and a series of warrants and options which would have allowed NBC to eventually take control of the company, should the FCC lift the national ownership cap. In the meantime, however, NBC acquired no additional attribution for the Paxson stations because it did not actually control Paxson or own any equity interest in the company as long as the convert-ible preferred shares remained unconverted. NBC's investment equaled approximately 25% of Paxson's combined debt and equity, well below the 33% cap. NBC and Paxson went on to set up a series of JSAs and programming agreements, all in anticipation of a change in the national attribu-tion rules, at which time NBC would have exer-cised its warrants and options and take control of the company.

The FCC also discounted the numbers in several ways when it measured the "reach" of a station. Some types of stations (UHF stations, low-power TV stations, and stations owned by a racial minor-ity) received discounts, when their market reach was calculated. A UHF station was attributed only half of a market's size, due to its weaker signal and lesser attractiveness to audiences. For example, a VHF station operating in New York would receive attribution of 6.8%, but a UHF station in the same city would be attributed only 3.4%.

This method of allocating attribution explains why a station group such as Paxson Communi-cations could have a reach that was nearly twice as high as its FCC reach; most of its stations were UHF and therefore were only attributed at half the actual market size. This distinction was a central part of Paxson's strategy in building a national presence. Paxson bought up UHF sta-tions cheaply across the United States and then used the cable must-carry rules to build the larg-est station group in the country. As can be seen in table 4.6, Paxson's actual reach was 65% of U.S. homes, but it received substantial discounts, as did Sinclair, Univision, and Entravision. That table also shows that Viacom/CBS and Fox, without the discounts, would exceed the Congressional limits.

Table 4.6 Top TV Groups by Station Ownership

	Stations Owned 2003	Stations Owned 2007	U.S. Homes (%) 2003	FCC "Reach" 2003	FCC "Reach" 2007
Sinclair	61	55	22.61	13.46	12.34
Paxson/ION	58	53	64.73	32.36	31.86
Univision	37	37	42.87	22.34	22.97
Viacom/CBS	35	27	44.78	38.92	35.65
Fox	35	27	44.55	37.72	31.36
NBC/GE	29	25	38.30	33.56	31.41
Entravision	27		19.14	10.09	
Tribune	26	23	40.21	30.02	27.53
Trinity	22	34	31.29	15.67	17.89
ABC	10	19	23.72	23.48	23.17
Gannett		21			
Raycom	–	35	–	–	9.38
Local TV LLC	–	17	–	–	9.92
Hearst/Argyle	–	27	–	–	15.28
Belo	–	21	–	–	13.47
Cox	–	15	–	–	10.24

Source: FCC, "2002 Biennial Regulatory Review: Review of the Commission's Broadcast Ownership Rules and Other Rules Adopted Pursuant to Section 202 of the Telecommunications Act of 1996." Washington, D.C.: Federal Communications Committee, FCC03–127, June 2, 2003. (The report subsequent to the 2002 Biennial Review was not yet available as of January of 2009. However, *Broadcasting & Cable* published the FCC's reach numbers, June 8, 2008.)

Table 4.7 Top TV Groups Market Share by Revenues

	1984	1988	1992	1996	2000	2001	2004	2006
News Corp (Fox)			2.3	2.9	6.3	7.2	9.1	9.1
Chris-Craft	0.6	1.7	2.4	2.1	2.0	Fox		
CBS (prev. Viacom)					6.2	6.2	6.9	6.9
Group W[a]	3.3	2.9	3.3	3.9	Viacom			
CBS	3.3	2.6	3.2	Westinghouse				
NBC	3.2	4.1	3.7	4.8	5.4	5.7	6.8	6.8
Tribune	2.4	2.8	3.2	4.1	4.9	5.3	4.9	4.9
Disney				5.3	4.3	4.3	4.6	4.6
CapCities		5.3	4.9	Disney				
ABC	4.6	CapCities						
Gannett	3.3	2.5	2.4	3.1	3.1	3.1	3.2	3.2
Hearst-Argyle[b]		0.1	0.2	0.4	2.9	3.0	2.9	2.9
Belo	1.5	1.2	1.3	1.6	2.7	2.8	2.7	2.7
Saban Ent.								2.5
Univision		0.2	0.6	0.9	1.6	1.6	2.5	Saban
Paxson				0.1	0.8	0.9	0.4	0.4
All Others	77.7	76.5	72.4	70.7	60.0	59.9	56.0	56.0
Total U.S. Rev. (mil $)[c]	10,572	14,417	15,630	20,747	25,806	21,479	25,613	25,613
C4	14.5	15.1	15.2	18.2	22.8	24.4	27.7	27.7
C8	22.3	23.3	25.5	27.9	35.7	37.6	41.0	41.0
HHI	73	80	88	110	182	199	253	253

Sources: Station group revenues are from company SEC filings and from "Special Report: Top 25 TV Groups," *Broadcasting and Cable*, p. 48. April 8, 2002. Data for 2004 is from Bear Stearns, *Television Broadcasting: Broadcast Television Fact Book*, December, 2004. Data for 2006 uses 2004 numbers, with only the effect of the Saban acquisition shown.

[a] From Westinghouse, 1993. Revenue for that year split 5/2 for TV/radio.
[b] Pre-1996 revenues are Argyle TV (spun off as IPO after 1997 merger with Hearst TV).
[c] Revenues consist of local and national spot television advertising expenditure. Source: Bear Stearns *Radio Broadcasting: Fact Book*, p. 214–215.

They, plus NBC and Tribune, have a discounted reach of near or above the statutory 39%.

Because almost all broadcast revenues come from advertisers, and advertisers pay for audiences, revenue is a good proxy for audience share (table 4.7).[24] Three of the top four TV station groups by revenues are owned by the firms that operate the big-four TV networks. The highest growth was for the Fox station group that was started only in 1988. Paxson (since 2007 ION Television) and Sinclair, also relative newcomers, owned the largest number of stations and operated in most of the top 50 markets, but were ranked low by revenues, because most of their stations operate in the UHF band with smaller audiences,[25] low-budget programming, and frequently paid-for programming (infomercials).

From 1984 through 1988, revenue concentration in the national station group market remained at a steady, fairly low level, with the top eight firms accounting for less than 20%, because of the rules preventing any firm from owning more than 12 stations and reaching more than 25% of TV audiences. These audiences were then split with the other stations in those markets. Thus, if a firm reached 25% of TV households and had to contend with four other equally popular stations in each market, it would account for about 5% (i.e., 0.25×0.2) of the national audience. In the 1990s, major TV broadcasting firms lost viewers to cable competition but increased their audience reach via station acquisitions, made possible by the loosening of restrictions on station ownership. They got a larger slice of a smaller pie.

As shown in table 4.7, the combined revenue share of the top eight TV station groups in the TV station market increased from 22.3% in 1984 to 41% in 2006, and the HHI increased approximately three-fold, from a very low 73 in 1984 to a still low 253 in 2005. (Those numbers could be lower if we looked at the shares of total stations instead of revenues.) The greatest concentration changes came after 1992, with the HHI for the station revenue market increasing from 88 to 253 in 2004. The C4 increased from 15.1% to 27.7%. Of the Big Four station groups, Fox increased its market share the most, from 2.3% in 1992 to 7.2% in 2001 and 9.1% in 2006, owing to two significant acquisitions: New World and Chris-Craft. CBS's market share increased from 3.2% to 6.9% over the same period, largely due to its combination with Westinghouse in 1995 (which acquired it) and later by its acquisition by Viacom in 2000. ABC, however, lost market share since 1992 because it did not acquire any new stations. Although the concentration indices have clearly gone up since 1984, they are not high by DOJ standards: a C4 of 27.7% of the market and an HHI of 253. These low but rising

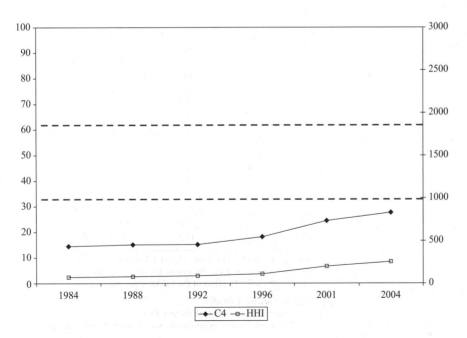

Figure 4.4 TV Stations: Concentration

Table 4.8 Local TV Station Concentration

	1984	1988	1992	1996	2002	2006
C1 Concentration						
C1 Large Cities	29.1	27.9	23.6	24.5	18.4	24.1
C1 Medium Cities	37.1	32.6	30.0	28.7	27.7	31.4
C1 Small Cities	35.9	36.3	32.9	32.3	31.2	37.6
Weighted Average	33.5	31.8	28.2	28.0	24.9	30.2
C4 Concentration						
C4 Large Cities	84.5	80.1	72.5	73.3	61.8	62.0
C4 Medium Cities	95.1	90.9	87.6	88.0	78.0	77.1
C4 Small Cities	91.4	91.4	90.1	89.0	85.2	84.5
Weighted Average	89.8	86.7	82.2	82.4	73.5	73.1
HHI Concentration						
HHI Large Cities	2,108	1,910	1,581	1,594	1,256	1,361
HHI Medium Cities	2,756	2,437	2,212	2,179	1,859	1,930
HHI Small Cities	2,634	2,595	2,384	2,306	2,207	2,619
Weighted Average	2,460	2,269	2,006	1,979	1,714	1,895
Avg. Annual Rev. per Household						
Advertising Rev. Large Cities	111	146	158	200	258	264
Rev. Medium Cities	80	104	110	134	167	165
Rev. Small Cities	47	59	67	82	102	104

Notes: Local television revenues are based on *Duncan's Radio Market Guide*; 1985, 1989, 1994, 1997, and 2002 editions, respectively. Copyright © James H. Duncan, Jr. Concentration values C4 and HHI have been calculated using Nielsen TV Shares. Data used were for July, except in 1996 when the Olympic games held in Atlanta increased NBC's market share for that period. In consequence, for 1996 the November period was used.

figures can be seen in figure 4.4. No single company accounts for more than 10% of the market.

Local Television Markets

Few issues in media policy are more contentious than the control over local television. Has this ownership become more concentrated on the local level? This question is different from the one about overall ownership of local stations, another major bone of contention, which has been discussed above. The findings are provided in table 4.8, and are discussed more thoroughly in chapter 15.

Local concentration of TV has declined over the two decades under study, from a C4 of 90% in 1984 to 73.1% in 2006 (62% in large markets). For the market leader, the share dropped on average from 33% to 25% in 2001 but then climbed back to 30% in 2006 (24% in large markets). The HHI declined from 2,460 to 1,714, then rose to 1,895 in 2006. This is due, numerically, to:

1. A somewhat large number of local TV stations, and
2. A lessened audience share of the top three (and later four) stations affiliated with the major national TV networks, relative to other stations. These erosions would be larger if the major station audience shares were taken among *all* channels, including cable channels. In that case, the four-network affiliates decline collectively by still another 50%, to about 25%. (However, this would understate concentration of local TV news, which is mostly produced by local TV stations rather than cable channels.) The relative decline of broadcasting station audience is captured in their revenue figures.

As we shall see in Chapter 15, the level of local TV station concentration is the lowest among all of the eight local mass media we analyze (figure 15.1). Although most cities must be content with one newspaper and one local magazine (if at all), there are likely to be half a dozen or more TV stations. Radio used to be less concentrated than TV but more recently has overtaken it, with a much greater disparity among companies' market shares. Cable TV has generated some local channels, but their availability and audiences are still small.

Low Power Television (LPTV)

Starting in the early 1980s, the FCC sought to raise station diversity by licensing another category of TV station, low power TV (LPTV) stations. These stations are subject to various restrictions, and their licensing had been opposed by the established broadcasters.

The number of such stations increased rapidly, rising from 600 in 1989 to 800 in 1990; 1,782 in 1995; 2,212 in 2001;[26] and almost 3,550 in 2005.[27] LPTV stations are limited to 10 watts for VHF stations and 1 kilowatt for UHF stations. Thus, LPTV signal footprints are tiny, ranging from 5 to 20 miles, as compared to 65 miles for a full power VHF station.[28] The FCC's goals for LPTV were to provide new outlets for local programming and increasing minority ownership. However, in 1995, only 13% of LPTV stations were owned by minorities, mostly Native Americans on reservations,[29] and this share dropped to 3.5% by 2000.[30]

Summary of TV Broadcasting Concentration

There has been an increase in national TV broadcast station concentration. The top four firms' national share rose from 14.5% in 1984 to 27.7% in 2004. There has also been a slight reduction of concentration on the *local* level for TV broadcasting (the top four firms' share declined from 89.8% to 73.5%), not counting the reduced share of broadcast TV in overall TV viewing. If we factored this in, local TV C4 shares would drop to 43% in 2002[31] and 38% in 2005.

However, the aggregate audience share of all broadcast TV stations in those two decades declined greatly, from 87.8% down to 48.7%.[32] (This also includes viewing of local TV stations that are retransmitted over cable or DBS.) We can calculate the approximate magnitude of the larger slice of the smaller TV pie (table 4.7). The top four station groups "owned" in 1984 12.7% of the national TV primetime audience. In 2004, they accounted for 13.5% of the same audiences.

Thus, the audience share of top-four TV station groups increased in a minor way (and was likely headed down in the future) where the entertainment role of TV is concerned. That share has grown, however, for local TV news, since cable channels are no real substitute. For that dimension, local concentration has risen.

CABLE TV DISTRIBUTION

Cable's multichannel transmission capacity let it develop beyond its initial role as a "community antenna" (CATV) retransmission medium to become the gateway and distribution medium for many new programming channels. The number of actual channels available per year for an average coaxial cable system increased steadily at a rate of about 1.6 channels per year. The channel number for the average cable subscriber in 2008 was 74.

A standard TV channel requires 6 MHz. Cable companies invested $60 billion since 1996 to upgrade their facilities.[33] When cable distribution plants are fully fiber-based (with capacity in the Terabit range) and fully digitalized, they will technically be able to offer many thousands of regular downstream channels, plus ultra-broadband Internet and voice telephony.[34] And this is not even close to the limit of the technology.

Local Concentration

Cable TV companies are rarely subject to competition from other cable operators within the same franchise area.[35] For a long time, there was no effective competition by other multichannel distribution media. This began to change with the entry of high-power digital DBS after 1994. Technological innovation in cable TV was more rapid in new markets where competition for the franchise existed and slower in already existing franchises.[36] Videocassettes and big-dish receivers of low-power satellite receivers were only a partial substitute. Although localities, after court decisions, could not offer exclusive cable franchises, they generally did not favor multiple entrants in their areas. Thus most cable systems had de facto local exclusivity for channels not available via regular broadcast channels. In 1993, the FCC studied 420 cable-served communities. It found that "overbuilds" (the industry's term for direct cable competition) existed in only 9% of communities. And in only 3% of communities were at least some homes given a choice between two multichannel delivery systems.[37] In 2002, the number had dropped to less than 3%.

The FCC study linked the existence of local cable monopolies with higher cable rates. It found that the existence of "effective competition" (defined as existing in communities with less than 30% cable penetration) reduced the per-channel cost of cable service by 10%.[38] The study was reported as part of the congressionally mandated rollback of cable rates. Its methodology was disputed because its sample included few large systems.[39]

Direct broadcast satellites emerged as alternatives, first among home-dish owners who tuned into free satellite feeds. In time, signals were scrambled, and offered for pay by DBS providers. Their share gradually increased to about 15% nationally, and more in rural areas. Cable and DBS are, however, not perfect substitutes. DBS carries few local TV stations and no local public access and governmental channels. Cable's interactivity enables it also to be a platform for broadband internet and telephony, although these features were not factors before 2000. On the other hand, DBS operations are

normally better suited than cable Multiple Systems Operators (MSOs) for national advertising, for reaching thin but nationally substantial audiences, and for reaching rural, low-density areas.

Other potential cable competitors are

1. Multichannel multipoint distribution system (MMDS, or "wireless cable"). Uses terrestrial line-of-sight microwave broadcasting to distribute programs to homes and hotels. However, MMDS has never proved successful.
2. Digital terrestrial broadcasting. In 1996, the FCC initiated a transition from analog to digital TV broadcast transmissions by awarding each existing TV station a second channel, with the older analog channel to be returned in 2006 (subsequently extended to 2009). The new channel's main purpose was to move to high-definition broadband quality. But it also enables multicasting, in which a station can simultaneously broadcast four or more programs (depending on compression and the nature of the program). This will create terrestrial multichannel broadcasters.

Table 4.9 Concentration measures for Local Multichannel TV

	1984	1988	1992	1996	2002	2006
C1 Concentration						
C1 Large Cities	97.6	96.1	95.7	94.6	78.9	84.3
C1 Medium Cities	95.9	93.3	92.6	90.6	76.5	78.1
C1 Small Cities	95.9	93.3	92.6	90.6	77.8	77.8
Weighted Average	96.6	94.5	93.9	92.2	77.8	80.5
C4 Concentration						
C4 Large Cities	100	100	100	98.9	99.3	99.4
C4 Medium Cities	100	100	100	97.9	99.3	99.6
C4 Small Cities	100	100	100	97.8	99.5	99.6
Weighted Average	100	100	100	98.3	99.4	99.5
HHI Concentration						
HHI Large Cities	9,539	9,264	9,179	8,962	6,454	7,090
HHI Medium Cities	9,213	8,755	8,605	8,238	6,101	6,322
HHI Small Cities	9,211	8,752	8,602	8,234	6,302	6,313
Weighted Average	9,344	8,960	8,836	8,529	6,300	6,629
Avg. Annual Rev. per Householdp						
Rev. Large Cities	100	132	205	298	456	467
Rev. Medium Cities	118	132	200	269	446	442
Rev. Small Cities	97	107	151	215	383	438

Sources: Television and Cable Factbook: 1983, 1989, 1993, 1997, and 2002, respectively. Warner Communications and News Telecom and Media Intelligence. The Cable TV Financial Databook-2000. Paul Kagan Associates. Data for 2006 based on Television & Cable Factbook Online, Warren Communications, 2007. www.warren-news.com/factbook.htm.

3. Internet TV. Of great potential, this transmission type enables individualized and interactive video.[40] In 2006, several of the major TV firms began to use broadband as a platform for some of their programs, both directly and through intermediate aggregators.

4. Telecom TV. As telecom operators upgraded their networks with fiber, they increasingly offered a menu of cable-style TV channels. Most active was Verizon with its FiOS video service which had, by the end of 2008, about 2 million subscribers.

Local market concentration trends for multichannel TV service (cable and DBS) can be seen in Table 4.9. The data are for 30 American cities. Details are provided in Chapter 15.

Concentration for multichannel distribution is very high but declining; the market share of cable declined especially after 1996 (from 97% to 78%, HHI from 9,344 to a still high 6,300). But if the market definition would be only "cable TV," market share would be 100% almost everywhere. The inclusion of DBS lowers the percentage by about 22%.

Since 1984, the size of the cable industry has grown to the point that it is by far the largest of local mass media. Cable has more competition than it used to have in local multichannel distribution. But this segment is still heavily concentrated, and its importance (size) as a medium has grown enormously.

Cable Pricing

The Cable Communications Policy Act of 1984 deregulated much of cable. It protected cable operators in the franchise renewal process from local governments, and prohibited these authorities from regulating cable prices where effective competition existed. Effective competition was then defined as any cable system that operated where there were at least three over-the-air broadcast signals. Because this was the case almost everywhere, rate regulation was effectively abolished. Over 97% of all cable systems in the nation were therefore deregulated when this provision took effect at the end of 1986.[41] Rates therefore could rise, and they did.

In 1988, the General Accounting Office (GAO) attributed almost half of these increases to the existence of market power in local cable markets and the rest to increases in costs.[42] Congress responded by passing (over President George H. W.

Bush's veto, the only time a veto was overridden during his entire administration) the 1992 Cable Television Consumer Protection and Competition Act. The groups lobbying for this legislation, a coalition of consumers and TV broadcasters, were successful in persuading enough Republicans to join in overturning the presidential veto.

The 1992 Cable Act reestablished rate regulation over the basic service tier for those areas where it was not subject to effective competition.[43] The FCC delegated municipalities the responsibility for setting and monitoring rates (following FCC benchmarks). Rates for nonbasic cable programming services such as pay-TV could be rolled back to 1992 levels if the FCC found them to be "unreasonable."[44]

In setting price guidelines, the FCC did not analyze actual costs or establish a fair rate of return for cable systems. Instead, it looked at the average per-channel costs in those cable markets with effective competition and used them as a benchmark.

It then established an initial 10% mandatory rate decrease for cable operations that had no effective competition. A 7% reduction followed. By 1995, the rate cuts totaled, according to the FCC, approximately $3.5 billion.[45]

But the policy was short-lived. After Republicans gained control over Congress in 1994, the regulatory pendulum swung back toward deregulation. The Telecommunications Act of 1996 deregulated the rates of small cable systems and provided for complete deregulation of nonbasic tier rates in 1999. Yet the issue kept bubbling up.

National Cable Concentration

National cable concentration has risen considerably from the days of the cable boom of the 1970s and 1980s, when hundreds of companies were contesting for franchises, and when the largest of them, TCI, accounted for only 5.4%. In 2006, in contrast, the market leader Comcast held about 32%, and Time Warner Cable (after 2009 independent of Time Warner) had 20%. Three other firms (Cox, Charter, and Cablevision) were far behind. Similar findings are obtained for market shares by subscribers rather than revenues (HHI: 1984, 234; 2006, 1,521). (Figure 4.5)

The national C4, as applied to revenues, increased from 20.7% in 1984 to 43.5% in 1996 and to 68.1% in 2005. The national HHI rose from 162 to 1,568.

Table 4.10 Cable MSO Market Shares by Revenues

	1984	1988	1992	1996	2000	2001	2002	2005	2007
Comcast	1.0	3.0	3.4	5.9	11.5	12.8	30.9	31.8	37.8
Jones Intercable	0.1	0.4	0.6	1.1	Comcast				
Lenfest	0.9	0.8	0.9	1.4	Comcast				
Storer (50% interest)		KKR	1.5	1.6	Comcast				
AT&T Broadband					23.0	23.0	Comcast		
MediaOne				10.3	AT&T				
Continental Cablevision	3.1	5.8	5.3	MediaOne					
TCI	5.4	12.7	15.7	13.5	AT&T				
Viacom Cable	2.3	2.5	1.9	1.7	TCI				
Storer (50%)		1.8	1.5	1.6	TCI				
Heritage	1.5	TCI							
Storer Communications	4.2	KKR	TCI						
Time Warner[a]				13.8	11.8	12.0	12.2	19.6	20.5
American TV and Comms. & Warner Comms.	4.4	6.1	9.9	TWE					
Newhouse (BrightHouse)	1.7	1.8	2.4	TWE				2.8	3.2
Westinghouse	6.0	TWE							
Adelphia		1.2	1.4	1.5	7.1	6.8	6.8	TW/Comcast	
Century	0.9	1.2	1.5	1.3	Adelphia				
Charter					8.0	8.5	8.5	8.2	8.0
Marcus Cable			2.1	1.6	Charter				
Bresnan		0.3	0.4	0.9	0.5	Charter			
Falcon	0.1	0.2	0.2	0.8	Charter				
Cox Communications	4.9	3.7	3.1	5.3	8.6	8.7	8.7	8.6	8.3
Times Mirror	3.0	2.5	2.1	Cox Communications					
TCA Group	0.3	0.5	0.7	0.9	Cox Communications				
Cablevision Systems	1.4	3.7	2.7	1.0	2.0	1.7	1.7	4.0	4.8
Mediacom					0.8	1.3	1.3	2.0	2.0
Insight					1.2	1.5	1.5	1.7	1.0
CableOne	1.4	1.1	0.8	0.8	0.9	0.8	0.8	0.9	1.0
All Others	57.2	50.9	42.0	33.5	24.7	22.9	24.8	20.0	16.4
Total U.S. Revenue ($ mil)	8,331	13,409	21,079	27,706	40,855	43,518	49,427	62,267	75,206
C4	20.7	28.3	34.3	43.5	54.8	56.5	60.3	68.1	74.6
C8	33.3	39.9	44.6	53.6	73.1	75.0	73.2	79.1	83.6
HHI	162	292	430	565	994	1,038	1,316	1,568	2,282

Notes: Revenues from Kagan Research, LLC. *Broadband Cable Financial Databook,* 2004, as found on http://www.ncta.com/Docs/PageContent.cfm?pageID=309. Starting 1996, 20% of TW's market share has been allocated to MediaOne. Data for 2005 includes the Adelphia acquisition by TW and Comcast. TW maintains an ownership state in Bright House after the earlier partnership with Advance Newhouse dissolved in 2003. Also from NCTA.com, and company reports of subscriber numbers. Revenues are cable TV only, excluding internet and telephony revenues.
[a] Time Warner cable was spun off Time Warner in 2009.

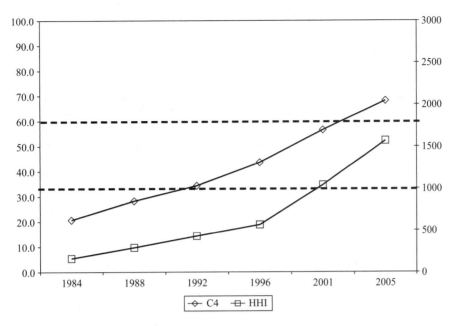

Figure 4.5 Cable TV Providers

The most notable transactions contributing to these concentration changes were AT&T's acquisitions of the number one cable firm TCI in 1999 and of the number three firm Media One in 2000, catapulting AT&T from a nonparticipant in cable in 1996 to the largest cable MSO in 2000. But AT&T failed to integrate these acquisitions into its existing telecom business as planned, and it was forced to sell its cable business to Comcast, making the latter the largest firm in the industry in both revenue and subscribers. Time Warner and Comcast also unwound their entwining Time Warner Entertainment (TWE) partnership, which held Time Warner Cable, among other assets.

After 1993, the FCC set limits of 30% for national cable ownership, and of 40% for channel occupancy by the MSO's own channels. Under Democratic Chairman Kennard this ceiling was changed in 1999 by a change in the calculation method. The relevant percentage became that of actual subscribers as a share of overall multichannel video programming subscribers, not just of cable subscribers. In practical terms, this new formula raised the ceiling from 30% of cable subscribers to 36.7% at the time, and to still more as DBS grew. These rules were struck down in 2001 by the DC appellate court.[46] The court found that the limits unduly burdened cable operators' First Amendment rights, that evidence and rationale

submitted by the FCC did not meet standards of review, and that the FCC did not react sufficiently to market changes since the 1992 Act.

DIRECT BROADCAST SATELLITES

In 2007, DBS, known also as DTH (direct to home), had a penetration rate of 25.2% of all households.[47]

In 1984, there were no commercial DBS providers, although individual households could receive the feeds aimed at TV companies and broadcast stations by using low-C-band satellite receivers. Meaningful growth in DBS came in the mid-1990s after national program providers such as HBO began to scramble their satellite signals, which in turn enabled a market for national packages of satellite channels. Pay-DBS then became more widespread, especially in rural areas not passed by cable. By 2006, the industry consisted primarily of two major commercial DBS providers—EchoStar (renamed Dish Network Corp.) and DirecTV. DirecTV was owned by Hughes Electronics, a satellite manufacturer and operator. Hughes was acquired by the car maker General Motors, which subsequently wanted to unload its media and electronic activities. Negotiation with Rupert Murdoch faltered over the price. EchoStar then tried to acquire its competitor DirecTV in 2002 but was blocked by the Justice Department. DirecTV was then acquired in 2003 by Murdoch's News Corp, for a much lower price. In 2003 Rainbow DBS, owned by Cablevision, entered the market with a service named Voom but was sold to EchoStar in 2005, after internal disputes within Cablevision's Dolan family. Voom had only 26,000 subscribers. DirecTV did not stay long with Murdoch. In 2006, Murdoch swapped control to cable TV pioneer John Malone, in return for Malone's share in News Corp, which had become a threat.

The DBS industry is a highly concentrated duopoly with an HHI of 4,593 in 2005 as applied to revenue. This represents a major increase over the 1996 HHI of 2,337. This significant level of concentration is not surprising considering the high barriers to entry in terms of capital and marketing investment required to launch DBS services. Of course, the question is whether the relevant market definition is DBS or all "multichannel video delivery" media. Although cable TV and DBS are often both available, in many areas they are not.

When the Justice Department blocked the proposed $11.2 billion merger between DirecTV and EchoStar, it argued that it would reduce competition from three companies—the two satellite providers and a cable MSO in most populated areas—to just two, whereas in rural areas not served by cable it would eliminate competition altogether. The satellite companies countered that the deal would promote a stronger competitor against the local cable providers, especially since the latter were increasingly concentrating (as demonstrated by the Comcast acquisition of AT&T's cable operations).

News Corp tried to stop the merger, because it had tried to acquire DirecTV and would try to do so again. The company organized legal and political opposition, garnering support from a coalition of Christian conservative leaders who filed a petition arguing that the merger would curtail the access of religious broadcasters.[48] Some consumer groups that usually opposed media mergers were supportive in this case, believing that a stronger competitor against cable was needed.

Figure 4.6 shows the concentration trend for DBS. Since meaningful market shares start only in 1994, the figure has only limited informational value before that year. It shows the increase in concentration after the acquisition by DirecTV of the third market participant PrimeStar and the decline of backyard satellite direct reception due to the scrambling of signals. These factors moved the industry from a de facto four-option structure to a duopoly, with News Corp and EchoStar holding 55% and 44%, respectively, in 2006.

Table 4.11 DBS Providers (Market Shares by Subscribers)

	1984	1988	1992	1996	2000	2001	2002	2004	2007
News Corp/Liberty Media[a]								56.1	58.2
(DirecTV/Hughes Electronics)				27.0	57.1	55.2	55.6	Liberty	
TCI Satellite Entertainment/ Tempo/PrimeStar			50	18.2	DirecTV				
US Satellite Broadcasting Corp				23.0	DirecTV				
EchoStar/DishNW				4.2	31.5	37.1	38.7	36.5	41.8
Rainbow (Cablevision)[b]							2.0	EchoStar	
Pegasus				0.5	4.2	3.2	2.2	2.9	
Satellite Direct Viewers	100	100	50.0	27.1	7.2	4.5	3.5	2.5	
Total U.S. Revenue ($ mil)			5	1,293	7,628	10,748	12,047	15,350	26,600
C2/3/4			100.0	95.3	100.0	100.0	100.0	98.0	100.0
HHI			5,000	2,342	4,322	4,454	4,606	4,498	5,142

Source: Company revenues from SEC filings.

[a] In 2006, Liberty Media acquired control over DirecTV.
[b] Rainbow was sold to EchoStar in 2005.

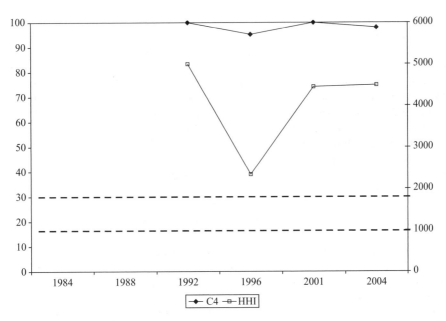

Figure 4.6 DBS Providers

CONCLUSION

We are now in a position to calculate overall trends for the electronic mass media distribution sector, defined as the retail-level means of electronic content distribution—radio stations, TV stations, and the multichannel systems of cable on DBS.[49]

First, the subsector has grown strongly since 1984. In 2004 dollars, the total revenues more than doubled from about $50 billion to $111 billion.

Second, national concentration, as defined by the C4 index, rose for radio stations by 332% and for TV stations by 81%, and it declined for multichannel providers by 175%. If cable and DBS were treated as separate industries, cable would stay near 100% for the top firm (C1) concentration, and DBS would be near 100% for C2 concentration, higher than in 1996.

Third, the average weighted concentration changed from unconcentrated (by DOJ standards) to moderately concentrated. This major shift occurred after 1996. This was influenced by two factors: first, the heavy increase in revenue of the markets for DBS and cable TV operators in combination with the high (even though declining) concentration in those industries both separately or combined; and second, the increase in concentration of national radio and TV station markets.

Thus, the weighted average concentration in the mass media retail distribution sector rose strongly after 1984. Using the C4 index as the base, it increased from a weighted average of 13.6 to one of 72.7%. (These are not the same four firms in all the industries, however.) The increase in concentration was gradual at first, but after 1996 it rose more rapidly and shifted from unconcentrated to moderately concentrated (by DOJ standards) in 2004.

Fourth, there is less overlap among the four electronic video distribution platforms than is often assumed. With one exception, no firm that is in the top four of one platform is also in the top four of another platform. The exception is CBS, which is number two in both radio and TV stations. Disney is not a top four firm in any of the distribution platforms. Altogether, 15 firms are in the top four of one of the four platforms. In 1984, there were only seven firms in the top three platforms. There was an identity of top firms for radio and TV. Not anymore. Thus, the distribution platforms actually became more specialized among firm clusters, at least at the top ranks.

A summarizing set of tables (tables 4.12, 4.13) and a figure (figure 4.7) show the shares of companies in a pooled video retail distribution market. The first set treats TV stations, cable MSOs, and DBS as basically interchangeable and in the same

Table 4.12 Pooled Electronic Video Retail Distribution ($ Million) (TV Stations, Cable MSOs, and DBS)

	1984	1988	1992	1996	2001	2005/6
Comcast	83	402	717	1,635	5,570	18,317
Jones Intercable	8	54	127	305	Comcast	
Lenfest Communications	75	107	190	388	Comcast	
Storer (50% interest)		KRR	316	443	Comcast	
AT&T					10,009	Comcast
MediaOne				2,854	AT&T	
Continental Cablevision	258	778	1,117	MediaOne		
TCI	450	1,703	3,309	3,740	AT&T	
Viacom Cable	192	335	401	471	TCI	
TCI Entertainment/Tempo/			5	417		
Primestar						
US Satellite B'casting Corp				192		
Storer (50% interest)		241	316	443	TCI	
Heritage	125	TCI				
Storer Communications	350	KKR	TCI/Comcast			
Time Warner			2,087	3,823	5,222	11,290
American TV & Warner Comms.	367	818	TW			
Westinghouse Cable	500	AOL TW				
Adelphia		161	295	416	2,959	TW/Comcast
Century	75	161	316	360	Adelphia	
Newhouse Broadcasting/Bright	142	241	506	TWE		1,843
House						
Cox Communications	408	496	653	1,468	3,786	4,954
Times Mirror	250	335	443	Cox		
TCA Group	25	67	148	249	Cox	
Charter				360	3,699	4,723
Marcus Cable			443	443	Charter	
Bresnan		40	84	249	Charter	
Falcon	83	27	42	222	Charter	
Cablevision Systems	117	496	569	277	740	2,304
News Corp			358	601	1,550	2,330
Direct TV/Liberty			3	349	News	1,744
					Corp	(Liberty)
Chris-Craft	66	250	377	446	New Corp	
CBS (prev. Viacom)					1,338	1,760
Group W	345	420	519	809	Cox	
CBS	353	382	503	Westinghouse		
GE/NBC	335	590	585	1,000	1,233	1,743
Tribune	259	400	500	861	1,130	1,250
Disney				1,100	920	1,171
CapCities		770	767	Disney		
ABC	482	CapCities				
Mediacom					566	1,152
Insight				55	653	979
Gannett	353	367	371	641	662	821
Hearst-Argyle		10	27	73	642	753
Belo	163	178	201	333	598	679
Saban Ent.						644
Univision		28	100	193	335	Saban
CableOne	117	148	169	222	48	518
Paxson Comunications				15	200	111
EchoStar/Dish NW				54	641	1,527
All Others	13,048	17,821	20,155	23,956	24,445	25,871
Total U.S. Revenue ($ mil)	19,028	27,826	36,715	49,746	66,305	83,213

Note: Includes TV stations, cable MSOs, and DBS providers.

Table 4.13 Pooled Electronic Video Retail Distribution (%) (TV Stations, cable HSOs, and DBS)

	1984	1988	1992	1996	2001	2005/6
Comcast	0.4	1.4	2.0	3.3	8.4	22.0
Jones Intercable	0.0	0.2	0.3	0.6	Comcast	
Lenfest Communications	0.4	0.4	0.5	0.8	Comcast	
Storer (50% interest)		KRR	0.9	0.9	Comcast	
					15.0	
AT&T						Comcast
MediaOne				5.7	AT&T	
Continental	1.4	2.8	3.0	MediaOne		
Cablevision						
TCI	2.4	6.1	9.0	7.5	AT&T	
Viacom Cable	1.0	1.2	1.1	0.9	TCI	
TCI Entertainment/			0.0	0.8		
Tempo/ Primestar						
US Satellite B'casting				0.4		
Corp						
Storer (50% interest)		0.9	0.9	0.9	TCI	
Heritage	0.7	TCI				
Storer Communications	1.8	KKR	TCI/Comcast			
Time Warner			5.7	7.7	7.8	13.6
American TV & Warner	1.9	2.9	TW			
Comms.						
Westinghouse Cable	2.6	AOL TW				
Adelphia		0.6	0.8	0.8	4.4	TW/Comcast
Century	0.4	0.6	0.9	0.7	Adelphia	
Newhouse Broadcasting/	0.7	0.9	1.4	TW		2.2
Bright House						
Cox Communications	2.1	1.8	1.8	3.0	5.7	6.0
Times Mirror	1.3	1.2	1.2	Cox		
TCA Group	0.1	0.2	0.4	0.5	Cox	
Charter				0.7	5.6	5.7
Marcus Cable			1.2	0.9	Charter	
Bresnan		0.1	0.2	0.5	Charter	
Falcon	0.4	0.1	0.1	0.4	Charter	
Cablevision Systems	0.6	1.8	1.6	0.6	1.1	2.8
News Corp			1.0	1.2	2.3	2.8[a]
DirectTV/Liberty				0.7	News Corp	1.8
Chris-Craft	0.3	0.9	1.0	0.9	News Corp	
CBS (prev. Viacom)					2.0	2.1
Group W	1.8	1.5	1.4	1.6		
CBS	1.9	1.4	1.4	Westinghouse		
GE/NBC	1.8	2.1	1.6	2.0	1.9	2.1
Tribune	1.4	1.4	1.4	1.7	1.7	1.5
Disney				2.2	1.4	1.4
CapCities		2.8	2.1	Disney		
ABC	2.5	CapCities				
Mediacom					0.8	1.4
Insight				0.1	1.0	1.2
Gannett	1.9	1.3	1.0	1.3	1.0	1.0
Hearst-Argyle		0.0	0.1	0.1	1.0	0.9
Belo	0.9	0.6	0.5	0.7	0.9	0.8
Saban Ent.						0.8
Univision		0.1	0.3	0.4	0.5	Saban
CableOne	0.6	0.5	0.5	0.4	0.5	0.6
Paxson Communications					0.3	0.1
EchoStar/Dish NW				0.1	0.8	1.1
All Others	68.6	64.0	54.9	48.2	36.7	30.1
Total U.S. Revenue ($ mil)	19,028	27,826	36,715	49,746	66,305	83,213
C4	9.7	14.6	19.8	24.2	36.9	47.2
HHI	54	89	158	197	464	777

Note: Includes TV stations, cable MSOs, and DBS providers.

[a] In 2007, News Corp sold DirecTV to Liberty Media.

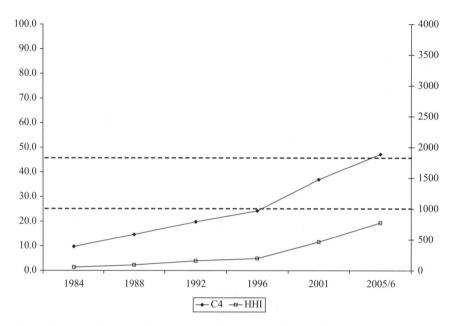

Figure 4.7 Pooled Electronic Video Retail Distribution (Without Home Video)

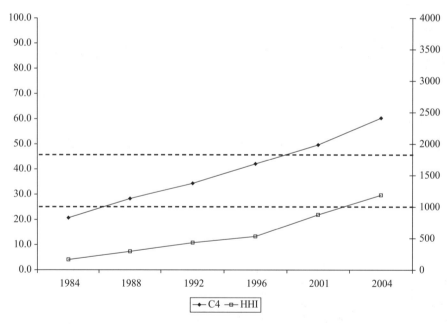

Figure 4.8 Multichannel Video (Cable and DBS)

product market, and calculates revenues and share in the pooled market. Concentration increased from a minuscule HHI of 54 to a still low 777. The four-firm concentration ratio rose from 9.7% to 47.2%. The largest four firms in 2005 were Comcast (22.0%), Time Warner (13.6%), Cox (6.0%), and Charter (5.7%). These are all cable MSOs, and they dwarf the local distribution role of the traditional major TV companies CBS (2.1%), Disney/ABC (1.4%), and GE/NBC (2.1%). These network firms have remained at about the same level of market shares they had in 1984.

Table 4.14 MultiChannel (Cable and DBS)

	1984	1988	1992	1996	2001	2005/6
			Cable TV Operators			
Comcast	1.0	3.0	3.4	5.7	10.4	25.2
Jones Intercable	0.1	0.4	0.6	1.1	Comcast	
Lenfest Communications	0.9	0.8	0.9	1.4	Comcast	
Storer (50% interest)		KRR	1.5	1.5	Comcast	
AT&T Broadband					18.6	Comcast
MediaOne				10.0	AT&T	
Continental Cablevision	3.1	5.8	5.3	MediaOne		
TCI	5.4	12.7	15.7	13.1	AT&T	
Viacom Cable	2.3	2.5	1.9	1.6	TCI	
Storer (50% interest)		1.8	1.5	1.5	TCI	
Heritage	1.5	TCI				
Storer Communications	4.2	KRR	TCI/Comcast			
Time Warner			9.9	13.3	9.7	15.5
American TV and Comms. & Warner Comms.	4.4	6.1	TW	TW		
Newhouse Broadcasting/Bright House	1.7	1.8	2.4			2.5
Westinghouse	6.0	AOL TW				
Charter				1.3	6.9	6.5
Marcus Cable		0.3	2.1	1.5	Charter	
Bresnan		0.2	0.4	0.9	Charter	
Falcon	0.1	1.2	0.2	0.8	Charter	
Adelphia		1.2	1.4	1.4	5.5	TW/Comcast
Century	0.9		1.5	1.3	Adelphia	
Cox Communications	4.9	3.7	3.1	5.1	7.1	6.8
Times Mirror	3.0	2.5	2.1	Cox	Cox	
TCA Group	0.3	0.5	0.7	0.9		
Cablevision Systems	1.4	3.7	2.7	1.0	1.4	3.2
Mediacom					1.0	1.6
Insight				0.2	1.2	1.4
CableOne	1.4	1.1	0.8	0.8	0.7	0.7

Continued

Table 4.14 (*Continued*)

	1984	1988	1992	1996	2001	2005/6
				DBS Providers		
News Corp (DirecTV/Hughes Electronics/Liberty)				1.2	11.0	11.9[a]
TCI Satellite Entertainment/Tempo/PrimeStar				0.8	DirecTV	
US Satellite Broadcasting Corp				1.0	DirecTV	
EchoStar (DISH)				0.2	7.4	7.7
Pegasus					0.6	0.6
Rainbow (Cablevision)						0.4
All Others	57.2	50.9	42.0	32.4	9.5	15.9
Total U.S. Revenue ($ mil)	8,331	13,409	21,081	28,649	53,788	72,566
C4	20.7	28.3	34.3	42.1	49.7	60.3
HHI	162	292	430	532	876	1,189

Note: Includes cable MSOs and DBS providers.

[a] In 2007, News Corp sold DirecTV to Liberty Media.

The final table (table 4.14) and figure (figure 4.8) show a pooled multichannel distribution market (of cable MSOs and DBS), illustrating national concentration measure if the two delivery systems are considered to be in the same market. Both the HHI and the C4 measures increased considerably, but to a level still below the U.S. Justice Department's threshold.

Notes

1. Bob Freeman contributed helpfully to this chapter's historic narratives. The Internet is discussed separately in chapter 12.

2. Station totals. *Broadcasting and Cable Yearbooks, 1992, 1996,* and *2000.* New Providence, NJ: R. R. Bowker; Radio Advertising Bureau, *Radio Facts,* 1984, 1988, 1992.

3. FCC Broadcast Station Totals Index. http://www.fcc.gov, accessed May 2006.

4. Williams, George. FCC Report, *Review of the Radio Industry, 2007,* Washington, DC, 2007.

5. Williams, George. FCC Report, *Review of the Radio Industry, 2007,* Washington, DC, 2007.

6. Pike & Fischer, *The Telecommunications Act of 1996: Law and Legislative History.* Bethesda, MD: Pike & Fischer, Inc., 1996, p. 27.

7. Petrozello, Donna, and Elizabeth Rathbun, "Mega-deal Rocks Radio." *Broadcasting and Cable,* June 24, 1996, p. 6.

8. Rathbun, Elizabeth A., "Justice Caps Radio Ownership." *Broadcasting and Cable,* August 12, 1996, p. 9.

9. Rathbun, Elizabeth A., "Justice Caps Radio Ownership," p .9; "U.S. Agrees to Merger of Westinghouse and Infinity." *New York Times,* November 13, 1996, p. D4.

10. JSAs allow radio stations to sell advertising time to competing stations, in addition to its own stations. LMAs are time brokerage agreements that allow stations to transfer the rights to sell advertising time and to provide some programming. Holland, Bill, "Justice Dept. Investigates Post-Telecom Act Radio Mergers." *Billboard,* November 2, 1996.

11. Roberts, Scott, Jane Frenette, and Dione Stearns, "A *Comparison of Media Outlets and Owners for Ten Selected Markets: 1960, 1980, 2000.*" Media Bureau, FCC, October 2002.

12. Shriver, Jube, "Satellite Radio Aiming High." latimes.com. February 4, 2002. http://www.latimes.com

13. "Digital Audio Broadcasting Systems and Their Impact on the Terrestrial Radio Broadcast Service." FCC, May 2004.

14. *News Generation* http://www.newsgeneration.com/radio_resources/info.htm, June 2001.

15. Radio Advertising Bureau. *2006 RAB Radio Marketing Guide and Factbook,* 2006, Washington, DC.

16. Bartlett, David, "News Radio: More Than Masters of Disaster," in Pease, Edward C., and Everette E. Dennis, eds., *Radio: The Forgotten Medium.* New Brunswick, NJ: Transaction, 1995, pp. 31–41.

17. For earlier data, see also Arbitron/Edison Media Research. *The Value of Internet Broadcast Advertising,* 2004. For 2008 data, see www.arbitron.com/onlineradio/home, accessed December 2008.

18. Radio Advertising Bureau. *Radio Facts: Radio Weekly Reach,* 2008. For still lower 2007 figures, see www.rab.com/public/pr, accessed December 2008.

19. Dempsey, John, "Cable TV Hits Record Numbers," Variety, July 2007.

20. *Broadcasting and Cable Yearbook 2006.* New Providence, NJ: R. R. Bowker, 2006.

21. Auletta, Ken, *Three Blind Mice: How the TV Networks Lost Their Way.* New York: Random House, 1991, p.86.

22. FCC, "2002 Biennial Regulatory Review: Review of the Commission's Broadcast Ownership Rules and Other Rules Adopted Pursuant to Section 202 of the Telecommunications Act of 1996." Washington, DC: Federal Communications Committee, FCC 3-127, June 2, 2003.

23. In 2007, the FCC relaxed the 1975 cross-ownership restrictions for television or radio stations with a newspaper in the same market. In the largest 20 media markets, for such TV-newspaper cross-ownership, at least eight independent voices, including newspapers, would have to remain, and the TV stations could not be among the top four in the market. For radio-newspaper cross-ownership, no voice test was required. There existed the possibility of waivers to the restrictions in some other markets, if at least seven hours of local news were added by a station, or where either station or newspaper were in financial distress. The latter was defined by several economic yardsticks. The FCC vote was 3:2 along party lines, and shifted the fight to Congress, the courts, and a future FCC.

24. The largest owners tend to own the most popular stations in the largest markets, and revenues are not quite proportional to number of stations owned.

25. BIA Publications, Deutsche Bank as cited in Deutsche Bank Alex Brown, "Broadcasting Industry," January 22, 2001, p. 70.

26. FCC, "Broadcast Station Totals," FY 2001 http://www.fcc.gov/Bureaus/Mass_Media/News_Releases/2001/nrmm0112.txt.

27. "Low-power Broadcasting." *Wikipedia* http://en.wikipedia.org/wiki/LPTV.

28. "Low-Power TV Survey Notes Progress, Goal." *Electronic Media*, April 3, 1989.

29. "Take It to the Banks." *Communications Daily*, January 26, 1996, p. 2.

30. "Changes, Challenges, and Charting New Courses:MinorityCommercialBroadcastOwnership in the United States," National Telecommunications and Information Administration, December 2000, Washington, DC.

31. Broadcast television had 59% viewership in 2001.

32. Bear Stearns, "Broadcast Television Factbook." May 2005, p. 163.

33. NCTA, *Cable and Telecommunications Industry Overview 2002*, p. 1, from Kagan World Media, *Broadband and Cable Financial Databook*, 2001.

34. Bear Stearns, "Cable TV and Broadband," May 1, 2001, p. 31.

35. Noam, Eli M. ed., *Video Media Competition: Regulation, Economy, and Technology*, 1st ed. New York: Columbia University Press, 1985.

36. Noam, Eli M., "Cable Productivity Likely to Slow." *Cable TV and New Media*, March, 1986, p. 8.

37. FCC, *In re* Implementation of Sections of the Cable Television Consumer Protection and Competition Act of 1992: Rate Regulation, *Survey Results and Technical Appendix to Report and Order and Further Notice of Proposed Rulemaking*, 8 FCC Rcd. 5631, app. e, 1993.

38. Ibid.

39. Besen, Stanley M., and John R. Woodbury, "Rate Regulation, Effective Competition, and the 1992 Cable Act." *Hastings Communications and Entertainment Law Journal*, 17:1, Fall 1994, pp. 203–224.

40. Noam, Eli M., Jo Groebel, and Darcy Gerbarg, eds., *Internet Television*, 1st ed. London: Erlbaum, 2004.

41. Allard, Nicholas W., *Reinventing Rate Regulation*, 46 Fed. Com. L.J. 63, 83, December, 1993, Washington, DC.

42. 138 Cong. Rec. S413, S425, daily ed. Jan. 27, 1992. (Statements from Senators Danforth and Gore, citing an Aug. 1991 Justice Dept. study, *Market Power and Price Increases for Basic Cable Service Since Deregulation*.)

43. Effective competition now existed only if cable had less than 30% penetration, an unaffiliated multichannel distributor offered comparable programming to 50% of households, or 15% of households subscribed to other multichannel distributors.

44. A grandfather clause allowed pre July-1990 franchise agreements to continue for the remainder of the agreement.

45. "Appeals Court OKS Regulation of Rates for Cable Television." *News and Record*, June 7, 1995, p. A3.

46. *Time Warner Entertainment* vs. *FCC*, 94–1035 DC Cir. 2001.

47. "Rules and Regulations: Broadcast Services; Radio Stations, Television Stations." *Federal Information and News Dispatch*, 2001; and UBS Warburg, "The Cable Sector: A Primer," p. 13, June 6, 2001; "DVR Is Fastest Growing Home Technology." *Research Alert*, 23(6): 10, March 18, 2005; "FCC: Cable Losing Ground to Satellite TV Services." *Online Reporter*, 12, February 26, 2005; "GM Town in Flux." *Broadcasting and Cable*, 133(48): 25, December 1, 2003. www.multichannel.com/article/CA6425963, accessed December 2008.

48. Labaton, Stephen, "Justice Dept. Staff Said to Be Opposing Satellite TV Merger." *New York Times*, September 24, 2002, section A1, p. 1.

49. Narrowband and broadband Internet are discussed in chapter 12.

5

Program Networks

Given the relative cheapness of electronic and physical distribution, it is usually more cost effective to produce a program centrally and distribute it widely rather than for each retail outlet to produce its own content. Therefore networks and syndicators emerged which acquire programming or produce it themselves. They package that content and distribute it to retail outlets such as broadcast stations, cable network operators, and satellite distribution systems. These retail outlets were discussed in the previous section. This section is about content networks.

RADIO PROGRAM NETWORKS

Commercial Radio Programming Sources

Commercial radio has long been a multichannel medium that narrow-casts to audience submarkets. Table 5.1 displays the popularity of different formats commonly used.

The popularity of formats has been fairly stable but not static. News/talk and Spanish formats rose, "easy listening" (Muzak) evaporated, Top 40 dropped and revived. The top format, news/talk (incl. in Spanish), was carried by over 1,000 stations in 1996, a number that almost doubled to 1,849 stations in 2008.[1]

Radio content distribution used to be dominated by a small number of radio networks run by major companies. But by the 1960s they were a mere shadow of their pre-TV golden age of the 1930s and 1940s. Over 75% of radio programming is not provided (i.e., packaged) by networks but by syndicators or by the local stations themselves. The radio network industry, including syndicators, is quite small relative to the radio broadcast station industry, with only $1 billion of revenues in 2005 in comparison to the $19 billion revenues of radio stations.

National networking debuted in 1926 with the NBC Radio Network, founded by the Radio Corporation of America (RCA), a new but major manufacturer of radio equipment formed by GE, AT&T, and Westinghouse. By 1927 the company was carrying regular national broadcasts on its two networks, labeled "Blue" and "Red." Radio became a major source for news, theater, and entertainment and soon reached a huge and loyal audience. Other emerging major radio networks were the Columbia Broadcasting System (CBS) and Mutual. NBC was forced by the government to divest itself of its Blue networks, which became ABC. With the advent of TV, radio lost much of its role in news reporting, theatrical entertainment, and features. Music became the main staple, and that could be programmed fairly easily by local stations' disk jockeys, adding local flavor and

Table 5.1 Audience Share of Radio Programming Formats (Percentage of Total Radio Audience)

Format	1989	1992	1996	2000	2003	2008
News/Talk	11	14	17	16	17	13.9
Adult Contemporary	17	18	15	15	14	7.2
Country	9	13	11	9	9	13.5
R&B/ Urban	8	9	11	8	9	17.5
Oldies	6	6	6	8	7	2.6
Album Rock	9	10	8	9	9	2.1
Top 40	16	11	7	7	11	5.6
Spanish	3	4	6	7	8	7.9
Modern Rock	1	1	4	5	2	1.9
Classic Rock	4	4	4	4	4	4.5
Adult Standards	3	4	4	3	2	11.5
Jazz	2	1	3	3	3	2.2
Religious	2	2	2	2	3	4.8
Classical	2	2	2	2	1	2.0
Easy Listening	7	2	1	1	1	0.2

Sources: Arbitron National Format Rating Data; *Radio Advertising Bureau, Radio Marketing Guide & Fact Book for Advertisers 2001–2002 Edition*; Arbitron American Radio Trends, Fall 2001, *Arbitron American Listening Trends Report*, April 2002; *Arbitron American Radio Listening Trends Report*, July 2006.

advertising patter to nationally produced music. Radio networking declined.

By 1984, the radio program network industry had diversified to eight major firms but consolidated to six by 1986: ABC, Westwood One (including the former Mutual network), NBC networks, CBS, Unistar (formerly RKO), and American Urban Radio. NBC sold its radio networks to Westwood One in 1987 after being itself acquired by GE in 1985. The industry further consolidated to four firms in 1994 when Westwood One acquired Unistar. Westwood One was particularly successful at diversifying its programming lineup for younger audiences. ABC sold most of its radio networks and stations (except for ESPN) in 2006/2007 to the radio company Citadel Broadcasting (owned by the private equity firm Forstmann Little & Company) for about $1.5 billion. A new entrant, Premiere, has 18.5% of the market. Premiere is owned by the largest radio station group—Clear Channel—and provides programs to its own stations and others. It syndicates 70 radio programs to over 5,000 radio affiliations.

ABC's radio networking market share fluctuated between 34–25% over the period 1984–2005, generally declining. By contrast, Westwood One doubled its market share since 1984 (as NBC) through acquisition, and it accounted in 2004–2005 for 37% of radio network revenues. CBS's market share (based on its news program orientation) dropped significantly from 14% in 1984 to 6% in 2004, even as it became linked with

Westinghouse and then Viacom before being spun off as CBS again. It had close operating and ownership relations with Westwood One. In 2007 the two firms agreed to go their separate ways, and control over Westwood was acquired by the private equity firm Gores Group. While there are several dozen radio network companies, the radio networking market has always been concentrated, with HHI measure of 1,378 in 1984 (see figure 5.1) and increasing to 2,584 in 2001. With the entrance of several new firms in 2004, the overall HHI declined slightly to 2,253.

Public Radio

Public nonprofit radio has traditionally been a financially weak part of the American media landscape. There are a good number of such stations, often beloved by their audiences, but there are no strong national station groups. There are 2,471 public, nonprofit radio stations in America, not a small number.[2] But they are underfunded and often with low transmission power. They are sometimes owned by private nonprofit organizations or by state bodies such as state universities.[3] There are two major public media networks. Public Radio International (PRI) was founded in 1983 and distributes about 400 hours of weekly programming to 726 affiliated radio stations, which are heard by 15 million listeners.[4] National Public Radio (NPR) is a membership organization of 780 radio stations. NPR has been a strong news source through its

Table 5.2 Radio Network Market Shares (by Revenues)

	1984	1988	1992	1996	2001	2005/6
Westwood One[a]	4.1	20.9	26.8	29.4	33.0	30.9
Mutual	3.2	Westwood				
NBC	12.7	Westwood				
Unistar			4.0	Westwood		
United	3.1	Unistar				
TransStar	2.1	Unistar				
Citadel						20.2
Disney[b]				34.4	27.1	Citadel
CapCities		32.7	33.2	Disney		
ABC	28.4	CapCities				
Satellite Music Network	4.1	ABC				
Premiere (Clear Channel)		0.5	6.6	11.8	15.6	17.0
CBS/Westinghouse/CBS/Viacom/CBS[c]	14.4	14.4	12.7	9.7	6.7	5.5
American Urban Radio	3.1	2.9	2.9	4.1	3.1	3.4
Salem					2.1	3.2
CNN (Time Warner)				1.0	3.3	3.1
NPR	2.0	2.2	2.4	2.5	2.5	2.6
PRI			1.0	1.5	1.9	2.6
Dial-Global Communications						2.5
Jones MediaAmerica						1.3
Crystal						0.8
Others	24.8	26.4	10.4	5.5	6.9	6.9
Total U.S. Revenue (mil $)	388	382	377	465	919	1,081
C4	64.9	70.9	79.3	85.4	82.4	73.6
HHI	1,380	1,728	2,055	2,309	2,141	1,736

Sources: "Broadcasting's Exclusive 'Big-Three' Financial Breakdown," Broadcasting & Cable, May 1, 1989; "Big Year for Big 4," Broadcasting & Cable, March 3, 1997. Data for 2005 using Arbitron RADAR audience shares to calculate relative growth percentages from "Arbitron Releases Radar® 84 March 2005 Radio Network Ratings" and "Arbitron Releases RADAR® 79 December 2003 Radio Network Ratings." Available at http://www.arbitron.com/national_radio/home.htm.

[a] Westwood One, an independent company, was operated for a number of years by CBS, and provided sales and marketing support for the CBS Radio Network. In 2007 the two firms agreed to separate their activities.

[b] After 2006 Disney sold its radio interests to Citadel Broadcasting.

[c] CBS was acquired by Westinghouse in 1995, which renamed itself CBS. Viacom acquired Westinghouse/CBS in 1999. Radio stations and networks were spun off in 2006 as CBS again. Revenues from Bear Stearns *"Radio Broadcasting Fact Book,"* April 2005, p. 222. Market shares for CNN extrapolated from 2005 audience shares.

Morning Edition and *All Things Considered* programs. It produces and distributes over 120 hours weekly of original programming and reaches an audience of more than 26 million. Both NPR and PRI are supported by membership dues, programming fees, corporate sponsorships, foundation grants, and so forth. One to 2% of their budget comes directly from the federal government, and some more indirectly, through member stations.

Adding up commercial and nonprofit radio networks in terms of revenues and audiences, we obtain the market shares in Table 5.2 and Figure 5.1.

Syndicated programming, in which only a few programs are distributed instead of a full program lineup, and not necessarily in real time, earned revenues of $125–$200 million in 1996.[5] It is an efficient programming source for radio stations. Nationally popular syndicated radio programs, often controversial like those of Howard Stern, Rush Limbaugh, and Dr. Laura Schlessinger, boosted ratings and attracted local and national advertisers.

There are several distribution platforms for radio networks: telecom wireline, satellite, cable, Internet, and cellphones. Satellite radio reaches listeners directly and requires specific equipment and a subscription. There were two major American satellite radio providers: Sirius and XM, which merged in 2008, with still separate satellite constellations but shared content channels. In 2009, Sirius XM had about 20 million subscribers. Much of their programming consists of their own

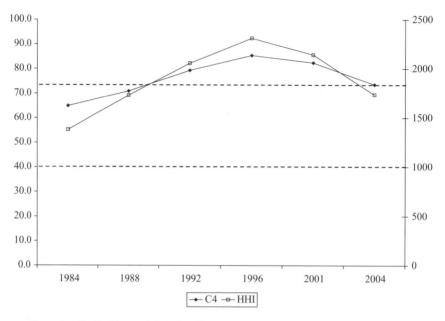

Figure 5.1 Radio Network Market Concentration

channels; other channels are those of networks and syndicators.

Cable radio consists primarily of three main providers: Digital Cable Radio (DCR) (now Music Choice), Digital Music Express (DMX), and Cable Radio Network (CRN). Cable radio is often included in digital cable packages to homes and is also used for office background music.

Internet radio works through the streaming of audio information through the Internet and allows radio stations a wide geographic reach. Many Internet radio stations are offered by terrestrial radio stations. Others are provided by regular radio networks. Clear Channel provides online content corresponding to its 1,200 terrestrial radio stations through its Clear Channel Internet Group. Infinity launched KYOURADIO, an Internet radio channel that derives its content exclusively from podcasts contributed by its listeners. CBS Radio has a strong online presence. Many Internet radio channels are entirely separate from actual broadcasters. Popular Internet radio networks, a fast-changing cast, include Live365, RL Select, Target Spot, Yahoo/LaunchCast, and Total RL Radio.

TV PROGRAM PROVISION

Broadcast TV Networks

TV Broadcast networks deliver a prime-time schedule of programs to a relatively stable group of affiliated stations. Syndicators, in contrast, sell individual programs to a shifting cast of stations. In the 1980s, the emergence of multichannel television disrupted the traditional world of the (then) three major commercial networks, causing them to lose their bearing and, soon, their ownership. The lifting of the regulation that limited the integration of conduit and content (the FCC's financial interest and syndication rules, discussed below) spurred the major Hollywood program production companies to form or acquire national networks.

The 1980s changed the TV network industry. CBS was acquired by Loews, a medium-sized conglomerate. ABC was bought by Capital Cities, a medium-sized TV station group. And NBC, with its parent RCA, was bought by giant conglomerate GE. These near-simultaneous changes in network ownership in 1985–1986 passed control of the networks from the broadcasting industry's founder-owners to more conventional corporate management. The new owners sold off many of the networks' non-TV holdings and expanded their TV-related holdings.

The new owners were also more cost conscious than their predecessors. In its first year of control, notoriously frugal Capital Cities cut ABC's costs by $100 million by firing 1,600 people from ABC-owned TV stations. GE cut 300 positions at NBC[6] in the first year, and CBS reduced the total number of employees by 9%.

The downsizing had an impact most visibly on the networks' news departments. Whereas the earlier owners viewed their news departments as prestigious symbols of public service commitment (and sources of political and regulatory influence), the new owners viewed them more as cost items. A logical strategy would have been to more fully exploit the news resources by expanding coverage beyond the traditional 25 minutes a day of evening news to a 24-hour format. But this would have required accommodations with the cable industry (to gain carriage), which had a stake in its own CNN channel (owned by Ted Turner but subsequently controlled by the cable firms TCI, Time Warner, Turner, and Comcast). Also, the networks' news operations were locked into a cost structure that precluded a bare-bones operation like that of the early CNN.

A second wave of ownership changes began 10 years later, in 1995. A precipitating factor was the FCC's removal of the Financial Interest and Syndication Rules (Fin Syn), which had limited the major networks' involvement in program production and syndication. The lifting of these rules allowed the networks to vertically integrate upstream into production, but also allowed major content producers (the Hollywood film studios) to do the same, that is, to vertically integrate downstream into TV distribution networks. A new stage of merger transactions resulted, reflecting the shift of the bottleneck from distribution to the program production side. Content was becoming king.

Westinghouse Electric Corporation, owner of the Group W radio and TV station group, purchased CBS in 1995–1996 from Loews, then sold or spun off its own nonmedia holdings[7] such as electric generator equipment, and adopted the name CBS for itself. Viacom (itself spun off by CBS in 1973 to comply with the Fin Syn rules) bought CBS in 1999. In 2001, it also bought Infinity Broadcasting, a major radio company. Viacom also acquired UPN (United Paramount Network), a fledgling and struggling new network, which had been established in 1995 as a joint venture between Paramount and Chris-Craft Industries. Viacom, Paramount's parent company, bought out Chris-Craft's share in 2000. In 2005, Viacom split itself into two parts by spinning off a new CBS, which includes the TV network.

Also in 1996, Disney bought Capital Cities/ABC for $19 billion, creating what was briefly the world's largest media company, until the merger of Time Warner and Turner later that year.

In the past, high-entry barriers had thwarted the creation of new TV networks. This changed with the first new entrant into broadcast TV network, Rupert Murdoch's Fox, owned by the Fox Entertainment Company. Network. Its deep pockets enabled Fox to absorb early losses ($80 million in 1988 alone).[8] Because Fox provided less than 15 hours per week of prime-time programming, it was not subject to FCC rules that prohibited broadcast networks from producing their own entertainment programs, a restriction aimed at the Big Three. Fox, vertically integrated with the film production firm Twentieth Century Fox, thus had an advantage over the incumbent networks.[9] Fox's competition forced the major networks to pay an additional $250 million to their own affiliates to secure their loyalty and pay higher prices for programs such as sports nights; it also reduced their audiences.

Cable TV's rise helped additional TV networks gain a foothold, partly via UHF stations. Most UHF stations had insufficient power to transmit clear, over-the-air signals to large audiences and were located inconveniently on the dial. Cable expanded the reach of UHF stations through "must carry" distribution that was equal in quality to those given to VHF stations. This allowed these stations to become viable network affiliates,[10] and led to the weakening of the WB and UPN networks, affiliated with the major studio owners Time Warner and Viacom, respectively. But the two newcomers were lingering and in 2006 decided to merge into the CW Channel—C for CBS; W for Warner Bros. Undaunted, Fox started in 2006 another new national TV network, MyNetworkTV (MNT). There was also PAX TV, created in 1998 by Paxon Communications and reaching 89% of the U.S. television households. Most of Paxon's stations were UHF outlets accessible primarily through cable. NBC owned 50% (in the form of warrants and stock) of the company. But in 2003, NBC and Paxon ended their relationship. Paxon moved away from its "family-friendly" format and instead served as a national distribution outlet for independent producers and syndicators. It changed the network's name to ION Media Networks.

Other new TV networks are those serving the rapidly growing Spanish language market. Of those, Univision is the largest, with the top Spanish-language prime time hits. In Los

Angeles and Miami, Univision even beats all of the English-language networks. In 2003, the FCC approved Univision's purchase of HBC (Hispanic Broadcasting Corporation) for $3.2 billion. Univision became the number one Spanish-language TV and cable network, radio broadcaster, Latin music company, and even the most visited Spanish language online destination in the United States. Its overall 2006 revenues were about $2 billion. In 2006, Univision was involved in disputes with its main program supplier, the Mexican media giant Televisa. It put itself up for sale, and was acquired for $12.7 billion by a private equity group headed by the media entrepreneur Haim Saban. The number two Spanish-language provider was Telemundo, acquired in 2001–2002 by NBC/General Electric. After the acquisition, Telemundo began producing its own content. It focuses more on Hispanics of Cuban, Puerto Rican, and other Latin American descent whereas Univision largely targets Mexican-Americans. Other Spanish language commercial broadcast TV networks are TeleFutura and Azteca America.

There are also a variety of broadcast networks for shopping programs (Shop at Home, HSN, etc.) and religious networks (TBN, CTN, Cornerstone, Daystar, Eternal World).

The public broadcasting system in America (in contrast to Western Europe, Canada, Japan, and other countries) has been traditionally underfunded and overfragmented, just as discussed above for public radio. Programs are produced or acquired by hundreds of individual stations. There is a national distribution through the Public Broadcasting Service (PBS), a network owned and operated by 348 public television stations. The major program producers are the five flagship stations in New York, Boston, Washington, Los Angeles, and Pittsburgh. The Corporation for Public Broadcasting (CPB) is the federal organization that finances program creation for the major stations as well as those of the public radio networks. PBS's revenue in 2007 was $624 million, most of which (47%) was station payments for program services. The network also receives federal grants (24%) and royalties and license fees (14%) and derives some income from educational product sales (12%).

In 1991, 60% of households could receive two or more separate public TV stations; in some metropolitan areas that number was higher still, thus in effect creating rivalry for the same audiences and funders. Contributions by business and private donors were flat after adjusting for inflation. As some commercial theme channels progressed also in quality, such as Discovery, the History Channel, Ovation, Bravo, and so forth, public TV's audience stagnated at 2.8%. It faced competition for viewers of cultural and educational programming from quality cable channels. Furthermore, the entry of these cable networks as buyers of quality programs also drove up program acquisition costs for public broadcasting, which previously had an unchallenged relation with producers such as the BBC. Indeed, the BBC itself entered the U.S. market with its own channel.

Table 5.3 illustrates the shares of the national audience accounted for by various network types.

The dominance of the overall TV viewer market by the original three major broadcast networks declined considerably, from 64% in 1984 to 40% in 1996 to 29% in 2004 (and to 36% if Fox, the fourth major network, is added). But they remain by far the largest providers. Public TV's

Table 5.3 TV Network Total Day Shares: 1984–2004

Comparative Primetime Shares (%)	1984	1988	1992	1996	2001	2004	2007
Original TV Networks' Affiliates (ABC, CBS, NBC)	64.2	56.6	49.9	40.4	31.5	29.4	25.7
Fox Affiliates	–	–	8.8	9.2	8.3	6.4	6.4
Other TV Network Affiliates and Independents	20.8	21.7	10.1	11.0	9.3	10.1	9.5
Public TV	2.8	2.8	3.7	2.8	2.8	2.8	2.0
Pay Cable	5.7	6.6	4.6	5.5	5.6	5.5	4.8
Cable Networks	6.6	12.3	22.9	31.2	42.6	45.9	50.4

Source: Bear Stearns, Television Broadcasting: *Broadcast Television Fact Book,* May, 2005, p. 163. Nielsen TV Ratings, 2007. Shares have been recalculated to percentages.

programming added diversity but its audience share hovered below 3%. Increased cable and satellite penetration sharply raised cable networks' overall viewing market share from 12.3% (both basic and pay cable) in 1984 to 36.7% in 1996 to 51.4% in 2004 and still rising. However, since this market share was divided among as many as 531 national programming networks in 2005[11] (plus a variety of local claimants to carriage by cable), the individual share of each such channel remained small.

Table 5.4 TV Broadcast Network Market Shares (% audience)

	1984	1988	1992	1996	2001	2005/6	2007
Viacom				27.7	29.7	31.7	28.3
CBS	35.2	27.9	29.1	20.9	23.0	24.9	
UPN[a]				5.8	6.8	6.8	
GE (NBC, Telemundo)	29.2	33.3	25.9	25.5	21.4	21.6	19.6
News Corp (Fox, MNT)		8.1	16.9	15.9	16.5	18.0	21.7
Disney (ABC)	33.7	28.5	25.7	23.1	22.4	17.5	21.7
Time Warner (WB)[a]				5.2	6.8	7.1	6.5
PBS	2.0	2.1	2.3	2.2	2.4	2.7	2.0
Univision (Saban)	–	–	–	0.4	0.8	1.5	2.0
Paxson (ION)				0.1	0.7	0.3	0.2
Total U.S. Revenue (mil $)	8,318	9,320	10,149	13,081	14,300	16,713	16,677
C4	100.0	97.9	97.7	92.2	90.0	88.8	91.3
HHI	3,228	2,775	2,474	2,234	2,168	2,159	2,177

Notes: Table based on data in Bear Stearns, "Television Broadcasting: Broadcast Television Fact Book," May, 2005. Market shares calculated from total day shares (p. 163), ratings for prime time broadcast season (p. 156), and annual advertising expenditures (p. 134). Revenue for Viacom consists of combined revenue for CBS and UPN. Total not included in overall market revenue; GE controls 32% of Paxson. Revenue for Galavision (Univision) estimated based the ratio of its share compared to that of PBS and Paxson. 2007 data from Bear Stearns, "Television Broadcast Factbook," January 2008.

[a] UPN and WB were merged in 2006 into The CW, jointly owned by Time Warner and CBS.

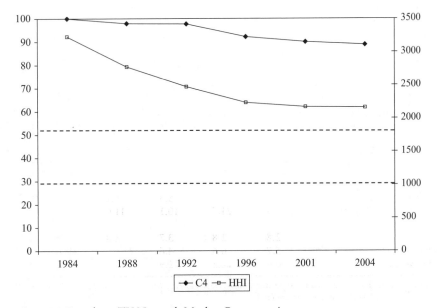

Figure 5.2 Broadcast TV Network Market Concentration

The broadcast TV network industry has always been highly concentrated. This can be seen in table 5.4 and figure 5.2.

Until the late 1980s there were only three commercial networks, plus the public PBS. Concentration was consequently relatively high, with an HHI above 3,000 in 1984. With the introduction of new broadcast networks by Fox, Time Warner, and Viacom, and with the emergence of Hispanic networks, the number of broadcast TV networks increased to ten, and the HHI dropped to 2,159. Note that this is merely competition within and among broadcast TV networks, not with cable TV networks. That form of competition will be discussed below.

Television Program Syndicators

The major TV networks also lost market share to program syndicators. Syndicated programming is aired by all commercial TV stations, partly due to the FCC's Prime Time Access Rule (1975) that limits network-provided programming to 3 hours of the 4 hour evening period.[12] Although the FCC hoped that this would encourage more locally produced programming, most stations filled the remaining prime time hour with national programs distributed by syndicators. Those programs were primarily re-runs, talk shows, and game shows.

An additional limitation on the major networks was the FCC's financial interest and syndication rules (Fin-Syn), in place since 1970, which prevented the three major TV networks from acquiring interests in non-network program producers. This aimed at preventing the major networks from leveraging their power in distribution to production, for example, by requiring program producers to cede them either a financial interest or syndication rights to the programs they aired.[13] The FCC removed Fin Syn in 1995, arguing that the proliferation of cable and DBS had reduced the broadcasters' market power over program producers.

With Fin-Syn gone, the program syndication market moved from unconcentrated (HHI < 1,000) in the 1980s to moderately concentrated (1,000 < HHI < 1,800) in the 1990s. As shown in table 5.5 and figure 5.3, the combined share of the top four syndicators doubled from 30.2% in 1984 to 60.7% in 1994.

After the 1980s, several mergers increased concentration. The HHI rose from a low 345 in

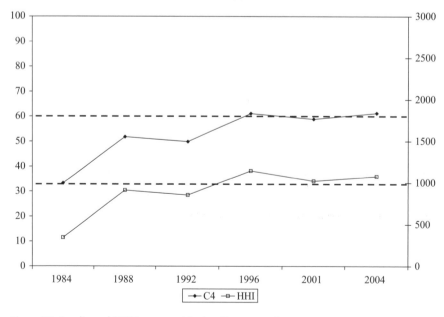

Figure 5.3 Syndicated TV Programs Market Concentration

1984 to an intermediate 1,278 in 2004, and then declined a bit. One set of consolidations focused on Time Warner. In 1985, Telepictures (the number eight syndicator) and Lorimar (number 24) merged to form Lorimar-Telepictures (number two). It was acquired in 1989 by Warner Communications (number five).[14] Time Warner also bought Turner.

A second set of mergers centered on Columbia Pictures. In 1987, Coca-Cola consolidated its 42% share of Tri-Star Pictures with its 1985 acquisitions of Columbia (syndicator number three) and Embassy (number five) to form Columbia Pictures Television, which it sold it to Sony in 1989.[15]

Disney (Buena Vista) bought ABC and its syndication arm. Viacom bought King World, the

Table 5.5 TV Syndication Market (Market Shares by Revenues)

	1984	1988	1992	1996	2000	2001	2004/5
Viacom /CBS[a]	2.5	6.7	7.4	15.2	23.9	20.6	19.4
CBS			2.1	5.6	Viacom		
King World			14.8	18.4	CBS		
Paramount/G&W	3.8	11.6	17.6	Viacom			
Spelling Entrt.	4.8	5	7.6	Viacom			
Worldvision				Spelling			
Republic Pictures	0.1	0.5	1.3				
Time Warner			6.2	7.2	9.7	9.3	10.8
Lorimar Telepic.		20.5	Time Warner				
Telepictures	3.5						
Lorimar	9.9						
Turner	0.4	8.3	7.1	Time Warner			
New Line	0.2	0.5	1.3	Time Warner			
News Corp–20th Century Fox				10.4	15	13.5	15.8
Disney (Buena Vista)	10.8	11.4	9.9	11.5	15.5	13.9	15.2
Gannett							
Multimedia	1.9	2.7	3.8				
Sony			2.9	3.3	4.5	4.3	5.1
Columbia P. E.		3.3	Sony				
Columbia		CPE					
Embassy		CPE					
TriStar	3.1	CPE					
Vivendi Universal				8.4	11.3	10.9	8.9
MCA	7.8	8.3	Matsushita	Seagram	Vivendi		
Others	51.2	21.2	20.1	20	20.1	27.5	24.8
Total U.S. Rev. ($ mil)	420	901	1,370	2,218	3,108	3,102	3,674
C4	33.3	51.8	49.9	61.1	65.7	58.9	61.2
C8	46.2	75.1	74.4	85.1			
HHI	345	911	854	1,145	1,278	1,024	1,079

Notes: Companies' 10K reports are used as the basis for the table. For years where individual syndication revenues were unavailable, extrapolations from adjoining year have been used. The growth rate for the period 2000–2001 is based on revenue figures from Bear Stearns, "Television Broadcasting: Broadcast Television Fact Book," May, 2005, pp.132–134. "Viacom betaalt voor CBS ruim 75 miljard," NRC Handelsblad, September 8, 1999. http://www.nrc.nl/W2/Nieuws/1999/09/08/Med/03.html

[a] After 2006, Viacom's TV syndication was part of the spun-off new CBS.

major independent syndicator during the 1990s. Universal absorbed PolyGram's syndication division as a result of Seagrams purchase of the company's TV and music holdings, and eventually became part of General Electric's NBC. As a result of these changes, although the syndication industry is not especially concentrated horizontally, it is heavily integrated vertically with the major studio distribution companies and with the TV networks owned by them. This meant less competition than before between syndicators and networks.

CABLE TV PROGRAM NETWORKS

Unlike over-the-air commercial TV networks which are supported mostly by advertisers, cable and direct broadcast satellite channels (DBS) are also funded by viewer subscriptions. Subscriber payments enable pay cable programming networks to capture, indirectly, at least part of the viewer's willingness-to-pay for themselves. In over-the-air broadcasting, a program's revenues are determined by its value as a vehicle to advertisers and by competitive alternatives. Usually, however, a program's value to viewers exceeds the price that advertisers are willing to pay for their attention.[16] Thus, economically, broadcast viewers benefit from a significant "consumer surplus" by receiving a program for free (or rather, for the value of their time subjected to advertising messages), for which they often would have been willing to pay at least a small amount, though this means higher prices. Capturing this consumer surplus is the economic foundation of content expansion. It changed program offerings by making higher production budgets available, or at least by offsetting their shrinkage due to fragmented audiences. It enabled niche viewer segments to receive programming that could not be supported by advertisers alone.[17]

These economic factors, coupled with the greater channel capacity of cable and satellite, have also enabled the emergence of many narrowcasting channels, numbering by industry count today more than 1,000 distinct topics and submarkets.[18] Each year, over 50 new channels or program services are launched.[19] Their initial hurdle was to gain carriage on a sufficient number of local cable distribution systems and hence obtain access to potential viewers.

The vertical integration of cable content networks with cable distribution declined over time

in pure numbers. According to the FCC, whereas it encompassed 39.5% of channels in 1996, it was 35% in 2001,[20] and 21.8% in 2005.[21] However this does not take audience size into account. For that, we look table Table 5.6. Vertically integrated (MSO and cable channel) companies in 2004 accounted for 27% of the cable channels market (vs. 35% in 1996), virtually all of it by Time Warner. Time Warner management was under pressure by insurgent shareholders to sell or spin off the cable MSO division, since that would, they claimed, "unlock value."

In time, cable channels developed source diversity. Until 1996, Turner's CNN and CNN Headline News were the only 24-hour general news channels. After 1996, both News Corp and NBC (in a partnership with Microsoft) launched competing 24-hour cable news channels (MSNBC, CNBC, and Fox News). Bloomberg provided a financial news channel, and local 24-hour news channels exist in several of the larger markets.

Greater competition among channels led to both higher and lower quality in programs. Congress responded to the greater sensationalism and explicitness in content by including in the Telecommunications Act of 1996 a requirement that all new TV sets include a "V-chip," enabling parents to prevent reception of programming based on ratings that broadcasters have "voluntarily" instituted, based on inclusion of violent or sexual content. The law also required cable operators and other multichannel distributors to fully scramble all programs on channels providing primarily adult type programming.

Market Shares of Cable Programming Networks

Table 5.6 and figure 5.4 show the market shares of the major basic (nonpay) cable network firms as measured by the share of total cable revenues received by each.

Total revenues for cable programming hugely increased from $2.5 billion in 1984 to $39 billion in 2006. About half of this increase came from rapid growth in ad spending on cable networks, from a trivial $5.5 million in 1984 to $16.4 billion in 2004.[22] Affiliate revenue (the fees charged to cable MSOs by the programmers for the right to show the channel) grew greatly, from approximately $2 billion in 1984 to $15 billion in 2004. During this period, cable subscribers increased by approximately 96%. Thus, both advertising and affiliate revenue grew much faster than cable penetration. Affiliate revenue payments, which are mostly passed on to subscribers, were $5.5 billion higher than from a mere proportionate increase of subscribership, at a level of about $80 extra per cable household per year. This was partly based on the market power of "must have" channels such as ESPN and MTV, and partly due to the larger number of channels provided as part of a subscription package. (As mentioned previously, the average channel capacity rose at a rate about 1.4 channels per year.)

In 1984, there were few basic cable channel providers, primarily TBS and CNN (Turner), MTV (later acquired by Viacom), and ESPN (acquired later by Disney). Industry concentrations fluctuated. As new channels were rolled out, concentration levels decreased. By 1992 new providers began to make their presence felt, especially Discovery, Liberty, and NBC. Concentration rose again after 1996 with Time Warner's purchase of Turner Broadcasting Systems, making it by far the largest firm with 33% of the market, more than double that

of Disney, its nearest competitor. Concentration levels decreased subsequently with the emergence of Fox, the continued success of Discovery, and the entry of others. By 2004, the HHI for this industry almost reached unconcentrated levels, at HHI = 1,079. The number of national cable channels in operation increased from 87 in 1992 to 287 in 2001[23] and to 531 in 2005.[24]

Because the major cable network companies usually own multiple channels, concentration trends for programming networks must be examined by firm, not by channel. In 1984, cable TV was still in its infancy with four firms controlling 66.4% (62.4% by just three firms) of the relatively small, cable-only programming market. As cable penetration increased, the supply for new programming grew, and concentration levels fell significantly, with the top four firms' share dropping to a still considerable 53.2% by 1992. More firms entered, such as Discovery Networks and Liberty Media, but the major firms also launched new channels and acquired competitors and concentration rose again. Time Warner's acquisition of Turner raised the combined share of the top four firms still further

Table 5.6 Cable TV Programming (Market Shares by Revenues)

Cable TV Group	1984	1988	1992	1996	2000	2001	2004/5	2007
Time Warner			5.1	33.0	28.6	26.1	23.5	18.2
TBS	26.9	25.0	23.1	TW				
Viacom	13.8	15.1	13.8	10.9	16.6	16.1	15.8	15.9
Disney	21.8	11.1	11.1	13.2	14.8	14.3	15.7	16.4
Discovery Networks		0.2	3.0	4.3	4.3	5.3	6.4	10.3
News Corp				0.2	5.3	5.4	6.3	7.5
NBC Universal (Vivendi/GE)			1.0	2.3	2.6	2.9	7.0	15.3
USA Networks	4.0	4.0	4.0	4.6	4.6	4.1	Vivendi/GE	
Liberty Media			2.1	1.5	3.1	3.2	4.8	1.6
Cablevision Systems				3.3	2.0	2.2	2.8	2.8
Rainbow					Cablevision			
Comcast					0.2	0.4	0.7	
All Others	33.6	44.6	36.7	26.7	18.2	20.4	17.6	14.8
Total U.S. Revenue (mil $)	2,466	4,261	6,504	10,906	20,205	22,917	26,879	
C4	66.4	55.2	53.2	61.7	65.3	61.9	62.1	65.8
HHI	1,403	992	906	1,443	1,400	1,244	1,214	1,260

Sources: Company data from Company SEC filings and *Broadcasting and Cable*. Affiliate fee estimates from Veronis Suhler, Communications Industry Forecast, 2000, 1992, 1989. Cable ad revenues from Cable TV Advertising Bureau and Paul Kagan & Associates. Data for 2004 based on Hoover's company profiles. Other data from: http://www.cmcsk.com/phoenix.zhtml?c=118591&p=irol-newsArticle&ID=636294&highlight=. In some cases, especially in the early years of cable, some channels were jointly owned by several cable MSOs. In analyzing reviewers and market share, we allocated according to the ownership shares of each partner. 2007 data from "Television Broadcasting FactBook," Bear stearns, Jan. 2008.

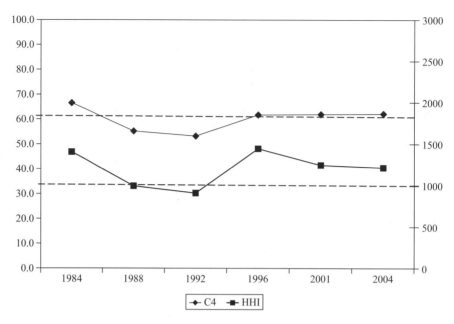

Figure 5.4 Cable TV Channel Market Concentration

to 61.7% by 1996 and 67.1% in 2004. The HHI of the cable TV programming industry was intermediate. After 1996 it declined somewhat to about 1,200. Several of the top cable programmers were vertically combined with integrated cable MSOs (Time Warner Cable; TCI through Liberty until its sale to AT&T and then to Comcast; and Viacom until 1996), which created a gatekeeping power and affected the market access of competitors. Comcast and Cablevision also hold stakes in cable TV networks, but they are fairly small. The vertical integration of cable MSOs and cable channels declined since 1996, from 37.8% to 26.5% in 2004 (mostly Time Warner) of cable channel revenues.

Although no single cable programming network has consistently attracted even a 2% share of the overall TV viewing audience, cable programming networks have amassed significant shares of certain submarkets. For example, in the Saturday morning children's programming submarket, Viacom's Nickelodeon has become competitive with the broadcast networks.

Table 5.7 presents cable channels owned by the major media firms.

Pay-cable networks compete in a market somewhat different from that of basic-cable networks, as they target paying subscribers for premium entertainment available at additional cost over the basic monthly rate. The pay-cable market in the 1980s became heavily dominated by Time

Warner's HBO. The top four firms' market share in the pay-cable market increased from 37% in 1984 to 53% by 1996 and to 74% by 2004. Time Warner's share increased from 24% in 1984 to 42% in 2004. In terms of HHI, concentration levels rose by 190%, from 738 in 1984 to 1,489 in 1996 and a highly concentrated 2,282 in 2004. Viacom's Showtime (part of CBS after the 2005 Viacom split) and TMC were at 16.6%, and Liberty's Starz and Encore rose to 15.9%. Other pay-TV services were being rolled out. But the advantage of HBO in accessing premium content and producing innovative new programs gave it a strong market position. Even so, digital cable Video-On-Demand (VOD), often controlled by the cable MSOs, was eating into the HBO market. The substantial remainder went to regional sports channels, offered for premium access to professional sports events of local teams (see Table 5.8 and Figure 5.5).

PROGRAM NETWORKS COMBINED

We can now calculate a weighted average concentration of the electronic programming networks (Figure 5.6). The trend line is influenced primarily by TV Networks and Cable TV Channels, since these two industries represent 80% of the aggregate sector.

Table 5.7 Cable Channels by Owner (2005)

Time Warner	Viacom	Disney	Discovery Networks	News Corp	NBC Universal
Boomerang	BET	A&E networks (37.5%)	Animal Planet	Fox College Sports	Bravo
Cartoon Network	CMT	ABC Family	Civilisation	Fox Movie Channel	CNBC
CNN	Comedy Central	Biography Channel	Discovery	Fox Sports Network	MSNBC
CNN Headline News	Flix	Classic Sports	Health	Fox Reality	Sci Fi
Court TV	LOGO	Disney Channel	The Learning Channel	Fox News	Shop NBC
HBO Networks	The Movie Channel	ESPN Channels	Military Channel	FSN	Telemundo
Local News Networks	MHD	The History Channel	Science Channel	Fuel	Sleuth
Nascar	MTV	Lifetime (50%)	Travel Channel	FX	USA
Road Runner	N	SoapNet		National Geographic	Weather Channel
TBS	Nick at Nite	Toon Disney		Speed	
TNT	Nickelodeon			Sky Channel	
Turner Classic Movies	Noggin				
	Showtime				
	Spike TV				
	Sundance				
	TV Land				
	VH1				

Sources: "Who Owns What," *Columbia Journalism Review* www.cjr.org, and company website for updates.

Table 5.8 Pay-TV Market (Market Shares by Revenues)

Company	1984	1988	1992	1996	2000	2001	2004/5
Viacom CBS	13.2	12.3	11.2	12.7	16.2	16.4	16.6
Showtime	*(11.0)*	*(10.3)*	*(8.4)*	*(9.8)*	*(12.2)*	*(12.3)*	*(12.4)*
Flix				*(1.3)*	*(1.6)*	*(1.6)*	*(1.6)*
The Movie Channel	*(2.1)*	*(2.0)*	*(2.8)*	*(1.6)*	*(2.4)*	*(2.5)*	*(2.5)*
Time Warner	23.8	25.0	28.1	36.2	39.4	40.7	41.9
HBO	*(16.4)*	*(17.3)*	*(19.4)*	*(25.0)*	*(28.0)*	*(29.2)*	*(30.0)*
Cinemax	*(7.3)*	*(7.7)*	*(8.7)*	*(11.2)*	*(11.4)*	*(11.5)*	*(11.9)*
Liberty Media			3.1	4.2	13.6	14.7	15.9
Starz!				*(1.4)*	*(5.6)*	*(6.1)*	*(6.6)*
Encore			*(3.1)*	*(2.8)*	*(7.9)*	*(8.6)*	*(9.3)*
Others	63.1	62.7	57.7	47.0	30.8	28.2	25.7
Total Premium TV Industry Rev. ($mil)	3,410	4,491	5,140	4,757	5,408	5,873	6,402
C4	36.9	37.3	42.3	53.0	69.2	71.8	74.3
HHI	738	776	924	1,489	1,999	2,143	2,282

Sources: Company revenues for 1996, 2000, and 2001 from Morgan Stanley. "An Analysis of Premium Television," April 9, 2001. 1984–1992 company revenues were calculated by using subscriber numbers and revenues reported in SEC filings. Total industry revenues are from NTCA. Assumed same growth for 2001–2004 as 2000–2001.

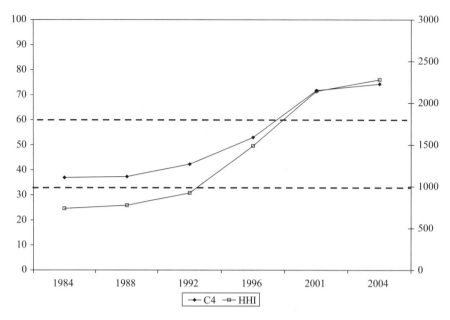

Figure 5.5 Pay TV Channel Market Concentration

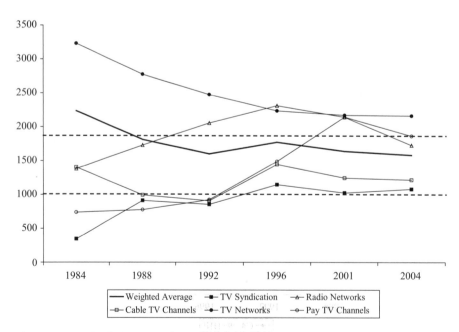

Figure 5.6 Weighted Average of Market Concentrations in TV and Radio Network Industries (HHI)

Weighted average concentration zigzags; it declines after 1984 and again after 1996. Mergers between 1992 and 1996 raised the aggregate HHI to a peak close to the highly concentrated level by DOJ standards (1,771 in 1996).

After 1996, the category "Cable TV Channels," which has a moderate concentration on a national level, grew significantly in volume and drove down overall network concentration to more moderate overall levels. After various ups and downs, concentration is almost identical in 2004 to 1984. Thus, the data does not support the notion of increasing concentration for electronic program networks after 1984, although it supports that thesis for the period 1992–1996.

If we differentiate video (TV, cable, syndication) from audio (radio), we find a fairly pronounced decline for video program networks and a strong rise, then fall, of radio network concentration.

We also analyze the data somewhat differently by assuming that all of the video programming networks participate in the same market, competing for the same audience. To that end, we combine the data for TV broadcast networks, cable networks, pay-TV and TV syndication networks into one big market and calculate the market shares, by revenues, of the major firms and their concentration. We thus obtain tables 5.9 and 5.10 and figure 5.7.

Presented this way, the data show a strong rise in concentration in the period 1992–1996, and a flattening thereafter. Since average concentration in the separate video network markets declined in the period after 1996 (figure 5.6), the conclusion is that it was vertical integration across the four types of provision that raised overall concentration for video provision after 1996, even as several submarkets became more competitive within themselves.

OVERALL ELECTRONIC MASS MEDIA: RETAIL DISTRIBUTION AND NETWORKS

We can now summarize some of the findings for the entire electronic mass media sector—both distribution and networks.

Radio   Because radio is often used as an example for media concentration trends, it needs to be discussed at greater length. In about one decade, from

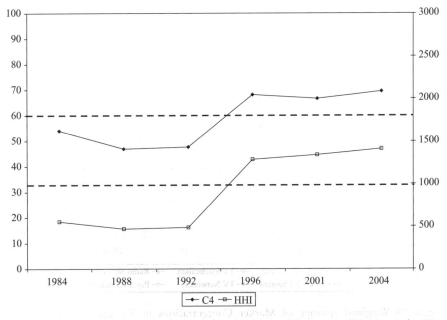

Figure 5.7 Market Concentration for Pooled Video Network Industries (TV Networks, TV Syndicators, Cable Channels, Pay-TV)

Table 5.9 Combined Video Network Industries (Revenues): (TV Broadcast Networks, TV Syndication, Cable Channels, Pay-TV)

Mil $	1984	1988	1992	1996	2001	2005	2006
Viacom[b]	843	1,356	1,725	6,161	9,643	11,312	5,200
CBS	2,930	2,602	2,955	Viacom			6,200
UPN							*(1,135)*
King World	80	280	503	663			
Paramount			600	Viacom			
Spelling Ent.	100	120	258	Viacom			
Republic	3	13	45	Viacom			
Time Warner	810	1,122	1,776	5,326	8,715	9,296	
Turner	672	820	1,745	Time Warner			
WB				*(684)*	*(966)*	*(1,187)*	
Lorimar Telepic		494	Time Warner				
Telepictures	73						
Lorimar	206						
NewLine Cinema	4	12	45	Time Warner			
GE/RCA/NBC	2,425	3,107	2,770	4,430	5,161	8,084	
MCA	163	200	Matsushita	Seagram			
USA	99	170	260	502	931	NBC	
News Corp		757	1,713	2,472	4,076	5,329	
Disney/ABC	3,376	3,222	3,466	4,677	6,865	7,688	
Discovery Networks		9	194	473	1,223	1,717	
Liberty Media			157	199	863	964	
Cablevision				360	501	750	
PBS	163	194	236	285	348	445	
Sony			97	119	154	199	
Columbia Pic		79	Sony				
TriStar	64	Sony					
Gannett Multimedia	40	66	129	Gannett			
Paxson Communication				10	103	56	
Univision (Saban)				57	116	250	
TeleFutura						Univision	
Comcast					100	200	
Others	6,317	8,954	8,925	5,137	5,751	4,389	
Total U.S. Rev. ($mil)	11,976	17,466	19,328	27,381	41,449	48,937	

Sources: Tables in this book for the 4 industries.

[a] Viacom and CBS split in 2006, but remained under the same board chairman, Sumner Redstone.

Table 5.10 Combined Video Network Industries (Market Shares): (TV Broadcast Networks, TV Syndication, Cable Channels, Pay-TV)

	1984	1988	1992	1996	2001	2005	2006
Viacom[a]	7.0	7.8	8.9	22.5	23.3	23.1	10.6
CBS	24.5	14.9	15.3				12.6
UPN							(2.3)
King World	0.7	1.6	2.6	2.4			
Paramount			3.1	Viacom			
Spelling Ent.	0.8	0.7	1.3	Viacom			
Republic		0.1	0.2	Viacom			
Time Warner	6.8	6.4	9.2	19.5	21.0	19.0	19.0
Turner	5.6	4.7	9.0	Time Warner			
WB				(2.5)	(2.3)	(2.4)	(2.4)
Lorimar		2.8	Time				
Telepic			Warner				
Telepictures	0.6						
Lorimar	1.7						
New Line	0.0	0.1	0.2	Time			
Cinema				Warner			
GE/RCA/NBC	20.2	17.8	14.3	16.2	12.5	16.5	16.5
MCA	1.4	1.1	Matsushita	Seagram			
USA	0.8	1.0	1.3	1.8	2.2	NBC	
News Corp		4.3	8.9	9.0	9.8	10.9	10.9
Disney/ABC	28.2	18.4	17.9	17.1	16.6	15.7	9.9
Discovery		0.7	1.0	1.7	3.0	3.5	3.5
Networks							
Liberty Media			0.8	0.7	2.1	2.0	2.0
Cablevision				1.3	1.2	1.5	1.5
PBS	1.4	1.1	1.2	1.0	0.8	0.9	0.9
Sony			0.5	0.4	0.4	0.4	0.4
Columbia Pic.		0.5	Sony				
TriStar	0.5	Sony					
Gannett							
Multimedia	0.3	0.4	0.7	Gannett			
Paxson					0.2	0.1	0.1
Univision (Saban)				0.2	0.3	0.5	0.5
Comcast					0.2	0.4	0.4
Others	52.7	51.3	28.9	16.4	13.9	9.0	9.0
Total U.S.							
Rev. ($mil)	11,976	17,466	19,328	27,381	41,449	48,937	
C4	79.9	58.9	56.7	75.2	73.3	74.3	63.8
HHI	1,939	1,036	1,109	1,535	1,529	1,553	1,290

Source: Gale Broadcasting & Publishing Directory, 1990, 1996, and 2001 edition respectively. 2006 uses 2005 figures with structural changes of 2006.

[a] Viacom and CBS split in 2006, but remained under the same board chairman, Sumner Redstone.

1992 to 2001, the market share of the top four firms increased from 9.0 to 38%. The national level of radio concentration was less dramatic than its rapid rate of change, coupled with local concentration.

Local radio concentration rose significantly. The weighed average share of the top firm in a market (C1) grew from about 20 to 35%, and for the top four firms from 53 to 84% (those are not necessarily the same four firms in each case); and the local HHI index rose from a fairly unconcentrated 939 to a highly concentrated 2,400.

These are large increases. But they reach levels that are actually not high relative to other mass media industries. Previously, the radio industry—about 12,000 stations—had been regulated to be atomistic, probably more than any single other industry with national characteristics, media or otherwise. The step-wise abolition of most of these restrictions, coupled with strong economies of scale, then led to the concentration trends toward a level that in any other media industry would not be unusual. What is different for radio is that two companies (Clear Channel and Viacom/CBS) were so much larger than the rest (18.9%, 11.9%, respectively). A distant third player emerged after the Citadel/ABC radio merger with 4.6%. On the local level, the four-firm concentration rose from 19.9 to 34.7%. This is a hefty increase, but one should compare it with daily newspapers, cable TV, and multichannel TV generally, which are all significantly more concentrated locally. What is happening to radio structurally is that it is becoming a multichannel medium like cable TV before it, with a company offering multiple formats instead of only one. This has some positive aspects (greater content diversification) and some negative ones (higher market power, lower source diversity). What is being lost? Localism. More stations than before are controlled from a central headquarters, along the model of many European public radio institutions. But one should not glorify the past as some kind of lost golden age. Local stations' music and news were mostly national, either nationally produced or nationally networked.

What has been reduced is the bargaining strength of the music companies relative to the radio stations. Music companies always had to finagle their way into airplay, which was the most effective way to promote their music products. But

now, three radio station groups have some real gatekeeping power over the kind of music is played over the air.[26]

In contrast to the past, there is much less vertical integration between radio stations and radio networks and none with major music production. None of the major four music firms owns a radio station group as a distribution vehicle. This situation contrasts with the past, when CBS and RCA owned both, and it contrasts with that in film and TV production, which is highly vertically integrated with TV stations, networks, program production, and some theaters.

Radio networking, too, increased in concentration to a domination by three firms, Citadel (after the acquisition of Disney's radio operations in 2006), Westwood One, and Premiere (Clear Channel). However, the industry as a whole greatly declined in importance since the golden days of radio. It has become quite small at about $1 billion of revenues compared to radio stations, which account for almost $19 billion.

To conclude: radio station groups have greatly increased their concentration nationally from their atomistic past, and local concentration has also increased substantially. For radio networking, concentration increased. But there is no vertical integration with the content production of its main input, music. Looking at the whole picture, concentration has risen substantially. But to describe it, as Robert McChesney does, as the "most concentrated and centralized medium in the U.S." is an exaggeration.

Television   The combined revenue share of the top four TV station groups in the TV station market nearly doubled, to 27.7% in 2005. But in comparison to most media industries, this is low. (HHI = 253 in 2005.) Furthermore, viewership of content delivered by TV stations, groups (whether over-the-air or via cable and satellite) fell to one half. In other words, the owners of the major TV station groups now have a larger slice of a smaller pie. If we choose the broader definition than broadcast TV and include all of "video channel retail distribution" (local TV stations, cable TV operators, DBS, and video scores), concentration numbers are moderate, showing an HHI of 1,733 in 2005, largely because of cable TV distribution.

We can also anticipate here some of the findings on local concentration provided in Chapter 15. The *local* concentration of broadcast TV declined over the two-decade period. For the market leader, the share of broadcast TV viewers dropped on average from 34 to 25% (18% in large markets). This reduction resulted partly from a somewhat larger number of local TV stations, and partly from the lessened audience share of the top three (and later four) stations affiliated with the major national TV networks, relative to other broadcast stations. Here, too, these erosions would be much larger if the audience shares of the major stations were taken among *all* channels viewed, including those of cable and DBS. If we do that, as would make sense for entertainment programming, the share of the top four stations declined collectively by still another 50%, to 36.5% in 2001–2002 from over 70% in 1984. But this would not take into account their share in local TV news, where cable and DBS play only a minor role beyond retransmission.

Local TV station concentration is the lowest among all of the five local mass media. Although most cities must be content with one newspaper and one local magazine (if at all), there are likely to be half a dozen or more TV stations. Radio used to be less concentrated than TV but more recently has overtaken it, and has a much greater disparity among companies' local market shares.

The major TV networks have lost considerable market power over the last two decades. Cable networks have collectively taken 51.4% of the total U.S. television audience in 2004.[27] According to the FCC's 2003 report, the average American household receives seven broadcast TV networks and an average of 102 channels per home. There were over 500 satellite-delivered national cable channels (though some may not be active). There were also at least 85 regional nonbroadcast channels, including 31 for sports and 32 for local and regional news. The original three TV networks' share of all TV viewing, according to the FCC, was only 24.9% in 2002, or about one-third of what it used to be; with Fox added, the top four networks' share becomes 35.8%,[28] or 37.8%[29] according to Wall Street analysts or 32.1% by our data for 2007. Either way, it is less than 10% per major network.

But this may be a bit simplistic. First, GE, News Corp., and CBS also have interests in other broadcast networks (Telemundo; MNT, and CW). This adds another 5%. Second, the four major TV network firms also own many of the cable satellite channels. If we look at the latter, our data (table 5.6) show that the top four broadcasting companies have 44.8% of the cable channel market. (If we add to this number the share of Time Warner, which is not one of the top four TV networks but a distant fifth, the share of these five firms in cable channels becomes 68.3%. This is very high, though not quite the 85% figure regularly mentioned, and lower in 2005 than in 2000.) To return to the concentration in TV program networking: if we define the network market to include broadcasting and cable channels, then the share (by revenues) of the original Big Three network firms (ABC, CBS, NBC), which used to be 72.9% in 1984, declined by 2006 to 39.0% for their four successor firms Disney, CBS, and GE. If we add a fourth firm—News Corp, with the fourth TV network, Fox, which did not exist in 1984—this number rises to 49.9%. If we add a fifth firm, Time Warner, which has a strong position in cable networks, the top five share rises to 68.9%. And if we add a sixth firm, Viacom, the combined share is 79.5%. This is a high number, and it is not much of a consolation that the combined share for six firms is not much higher than what three firms used to have. But in 2006, the HHI concentration index was much lower (1290) than in 1984, when it stood at 1939.

The concentration trend in TV station ownership has received high visibility. Why? First, because it is true, even if the claims tend to be exaggerated. Second, because there is a general discomfort in accepting TV as simply another industry. Former FCC chairman Mark Fowler's view that TV was merely a "toaster with pictures" has rarely been accepted. Third, because local stations held by medium-sized groups and single-station owners fear a reduction of their bargaining strength with the major content networks. As these networks create larger footprints of their owned and operated "O&O" stations, they depend less on affiliates that need to be mollified and financially supported. Affiliate power, in concept, is a positive expression of localism, but reality is often more complex. Affiliates also oppose any competition to their local audience. For a long time, this prevented the national networks from creating cable TV channels, such as all-news or sports channels, because this would have undermined the local stations.

The third reason for the attention given to the TV station ownership issue was misunderstanding about the FCC's proposed rules, which expanded the ceiling to 45% of any firm's reach. "Reach" is not synonymous with "audience" or "number of stations." With the audience market share of a network-owned station typically 20% of local broadcast TV station audiences, and with broadcast station viewership (over-the-air and by cable) down to about 40% of all TV viewing, a 45% reach translated to a national market share of about 9% of TV station audiences and 3.6% of overall audiences. Nor does station ownership change much of the actual reach of the network programs, which are about 100%. Whether these programs are delivered through O&O stations or affiliates makes little difference to viewers. (The non-"clearance" by an affiliate of a networks program, based on local circumstances, is rare, and would also be often exercised by O&O station managers, based on similar considerations of audience maximization.)

Perhaps more importantly, cable TV has become the major delivery platform for additional video channels. It is the quintessential multichannel medium. And here, its role in terms of diversity is dual. On the one hand, it enabled an enormous increase in the number of channels and their diversity. Whereas a typical viewer in 1964 could get about five channels and in 1979 less than seven, in 2004 the number was, according to the FCC, on average 103. 645 different channels were offered in 2008, according to the National Cable Television Industry Association.

But the other side of that coin is the ability of cable distribution networks to choose most of the channels that they carry. The channel capacity, even while growing, has always been lower than the number of channels offered. And cable, for a long time, was the only (and today still the primary) means for a nonbroadcast channel provider to reach the audience. This provides some local and (for the bigger MSOs) national gatekeeping power.[30]

Notes

1. Arbitron, *Radio Today: How America Listens to Radio, 2005, 2008 Edition.* Available at http://www.arbitron.com.
2. http://en.wikipedia.org/wiki/Media_economics.
3. http://en.wikipedia.org/wiki/College_radio#United_States; http://en.wikipedia.org/wiki/Public_radio.
4. Arbitron, Nationwide/Act 1 Systems. "Persons 12+ in DMA, Mon–Sun 24 hours based on station broadcast schedules."
5. Petrozello, Donna, "Syndication Faces Boom Times: Radio Syndication," *Broadcasting and Cable*, Washington D.C., 127, June 9, 1997, p. 22.
6. Auletta, Ken, *Three Blind Mice; How the TV Networks Lost Their Way.* New York: Random House, 1991.
7. "Westinghouse Said to Be Planning Asset Sale." *New York Times,* March 22, 1995, p. D2.
8. Sterling, Christopher, and John Kittross, *Stay Tuned: A Concise History of American Broadcasting,* 2nd ed. Belmont, CA: Wadsworth, 1990.
9. Thomas, Laurie, and Barry R. Litman, "Fox Broadcasting Company, Why Now? An Economic Study of the Rise of the Fourth Broadcast Network." *Journal of Broadcasting and Electronic Media,* 35(1), 1991, pp. 139–157.
10. Goolsbee, Austan. "Vertical Integration and the Market for Broadcast and Cable Television Programming." *Federal Communications Commission.* FCC.gov. Study No. 9, MB Docket No. 06–121. April, 2007. FCC.gov. Pp. 36. Last accessed on January 4, 2008, from http://hraunfoss.fcc.gov/edocs_public/attachmatch/DA-07–3470A10.pdf.
11. In 2004, there were 388 channels. Goolsbee, Austan. "Vertical Integration and the Market for Broadcast and Cable Television Programming." *Federal Communications Commission.* FCC.gov. Study No. 9, MB Docket No. 06–121. April, 2007. FCC.gov. Pp. 36. Last accessed on January 4, 2008, from http://hraunfoss.fcc.gov/edocs_public/attachmatch/DA-07–3470A10.pdf.
12. Prime Time Access Rule, 50 F.C.C. 2nd 829, 32 R.R. 2nd 697 (1975).
13. These rules applied only to broadcast networks that provided more than 15 hours a week of prime-time shows.
14. Chan-Olmsted, Sylvia M. "A Structural Analysis of Market Competition in the U.S. TV Syndication Industry, 1981–1990." *Journal of Media Economics,* Fall 1991, pp. 9–28.
15. Chan-Olmsted, Sylvia M. "A Structural Analysis of Market Competition in the U.S. TV Syndication Industry, 1981–1990." *Journal of Media Economics,* Fall 1991, pp. 9–28.
16. Avrahami, Ram, "Attention and Cost of Time in Mass Communication Systems," Ph.D. dissertation. Communications Program, Columbia University, 2008.
17. Noam, Eli M., *Television in Europe.* New York: Oxford University Press, 1991.
18. Numbers from NCTA count. The FCC count for 2004 is 339. The subject matters include the following: adult shopping; antiques; audience participation; autos; BBC world news; bingo; blacks; black shopping; books; business; buying homes; careers; catalogs; celebrity shopping;

cinema listings; classic arts; classic sporting events; collecting; computers; cowboys; crime; cultural arts; dating; deaf, and disabled; ecology; elderly; enrichment; environment; fashion; Filipinos; fitness; gambling; game shows; gardening; generation X; golf; gospel music; healing; health; history; hobbies; holistic health; how to; human development; independent films; infomercials; inspiration; interactive talk; international business; international news; Irish; jazz Las Vegas; lectures; lottery; military; museums; mothering; multicultural; new age; outdoors; performing arts; pets; public policy; recovery; relationships; romance; self-help; science; sewing; shopping; short movies; singles; soap operas; Spanish; Spanish movies; Spanish news; Spanish shopping; Spanish sports; talk; technology; video games; and women's sports.

19. NTCA, *Cable Developments*, 2002, 26(1), pp. 151–170. See also www.NCTA.com/cableprograms.

20. FCC, Annual Assessment of the Status of Competition in the Market for the Delivery of Video Programming, FCC 01–389. Available at http://hraunfoss.fcc.gov/edocs_public/attachments/FCC-01–389A1.pdf.

21. Goolsbee, Austan. "Vertical Integration and the Market for Broadcast and Cable Television Programming." (Federal Communications Comission Study No. 9, April, 2007; MB Docket No. 06–121). FCC.gov, Page 36. Accessed on January 4, 2008, from http://hraunfoss.fcc.gov/edocs_public/attachmatch/DA-07-3470A10.pdf.

22. Bear Stearns, *Television Broadcasting: Broadcast Television Fact Book*, May, 2005.

23. NTCA, *Cable and Telecommunications Industry Overview*, 2002, p. 10, from FCC, "Eighth Annual Report on the Status of Video Competition," January 2002.

24. Number for 2006 is defined as "National Video Programming Services/Networks (June 2005)" by the NCTA. Available at http://www.ncta.com/ContentView.aspx?contentId=54. And the NCTA count is over 1000 and 339 by the FCC.

25. The case of "shock-jock" Howard Stern, whose syndicated program was dropped by Clear Channel, illustrates such a problem. Stern bounced back profitably to satellite radio provider Sirius, but other radio performers have fewer alternatives.

26. Beyond anecdotes, the systematic evidence has not established a reduction in music industry content diversity. One study, by Joel Waldfogel of the University of Pennsylvania and Steven Berry of the FCC, measured the effect of concentration on product diversity in radio markets between 1993 and 1997. They find that the reductions in the number of owners (that is, source diversity) led to increases in the number of formats, that is, of content diversity (Berry and Waldfogel, 2001). Waldfogel, Joel, "Consumer Substitution among Media." *Media Bureau Staff Research Paper.* Media Ownership Working Group, Federal Communications Commission, September 2002.

27. Bear Stearns, *Broadcast Television Fact Book*, May 2005, p. 163.

28. FCC, In the Matter of Broadcast Ownership Rules, Cross-Ownership of Broadcast Stations and Newspapers, MM Docket 01–235, July 2, 2003, p. 15.

29. Bear Stearns, *Broadcast Television Fact Book*, May 2005, p. 163.

30. If we use a market definition more lenient than "cable TV," namely that of "multichannel video distribution," (that is, including DBS, the emerging telecom-delivered TV and Internet-boxed TV), a definition used by the FCC and the DOJ, we find that the local concentration for multichannel distribution is very high but declining, with the market share of local cable operators declining, especially after 1996, as a result of DBS. The share of the top firms (that is, of the cable operators) dropped from 97% to a still very high 78%.

6

Film

Six Hollywood studio companies have historically dominated the production, financing, distribution, and exhibition of motion pictures. This handful of firms, all located in the Los Angeles area, has exercised an extraordinary control over the film medium of the U.S. and the entire world. But while this market structure has persisted for an extraordinary ninety years or so, it has been far from placid. In 1949, the U.S. government forced the major firms to divest their theater chains. In the 1950s and 1960s, weakened by the emergence of television and the shrinking of theater attendance, most studios were acquired by general business conglomerates, and in a later round by media firms. They became holdings in the portfolio of entertainment assets of communications companies, both American and foreign. Vertical integration increased again as these companies diversified their distribution into TV network ownerships and returned to theater ownership. The major film companies themselves became primarily distribution and financing firms that supported and bundled the production of semi-independent production companies.

FILM PRODUCTION

Theatrical Film Concentration Trends

The film industry has long been an oligopoly.[1] Commercial motion pictures began in 1894–1895 with the Lumière brothers' Cinématographe, and Edison's peepshow, kinetoscope. To gain control over the burgeoning market, the Edison Manufacturing Company and its main competitors formed the Motion Picture Patents Company (MPPC) in 1908. The MPPC (known as the Edison Trust), collaborating with George Eastman and the financier J. P. Morgan, controlled distribution, technology, and exhibition. In 1915 it was held to violate federal antitrust law, but its monopoly had already been undercut by upstart entrepreneurs originating in urban vaudeville theater entertainment. These men owned no major patents but possessed a keen sense of mass audience tastes. They formed the nucleus of the emerging movie industry. Soon, they moved their operation from New York to California, whose courts were less favorable to Edison and J. P. Morgan. After World War I, this industry cluster became the preeminent center of the world's film production.

The period 1930–1948 was the golden age of Hollywood. TV had not yet emerged. Eight major studio firms dominated film production and distribution: Warner Bros., Twentieth Century Fox, Paramount Pictures, Universal, Walt Disney, Columbia, Metro Goldwyn Mayer (MGM), and Radio-Keith-Orpheum (RKO). The first six of these studios were still at the top in 2009. Warner Bros. became part of Time Warner. Paramount Pictures eventually was acquired by Sumner Redstone's Viacom. Twentieth Century Fox became part of

Rupert Murdoch's News Corporation. Universal was bought by Seagram in 1997 from the Japanese Matsushita and sold for $34 billion to the French media firm Vivendi, which resold most of it in 2004 to General Electric. UA Columbia, together with the smaller studio TriStar, were acquired in the 1990s by the Japanese consumer electronics firm Sony as part of its expansion into content. Sony also acquired in 2005 most of what was left of MGM, in a partnership with Comcast and private equity funds. The Walt Disney Company, founded in 1923 for animation, greatly expanded in the 1980s and 1990s and bought the TV network ABC. RKO disappeared in 1957. In the 1990s, a new studio—DreamWorks SKG—was formed but its live-action production was absorbed, for a time, by Viacom's Paramount Pictures in 2005.

Television's emergence after World War II severely depressed the film industry. Almost simultaneously, it was forced to divest its film theaters. Collectively, it lost control of its traditional distribution system[2] and was grasping unsuccessfully for a new one, at first fighting the television medium tooth-and-nail before becoming its major supplier of content. By the 1960s, the major studios had become acquisition targets as a result of a combination of depressed stock prices and attractive assets (strategically located real estate and film libraries for TV). In 1962, Lew Wasserman's Music Corporation of America (MCA) acquired Universal Pictures; Charles Bludhorn's Gulf & Western conglomerate purchased Paramount; and another conglomerate, TransAmerica, acquired United Artists. In 1968, still another conglomerate, Steve Ross's Kinney National Services, a parking lot and funeral parlor firm, acquired Warner Brothers/Seven Arts and renamed itself Warner Communications, Inc.

A major transformation of distribution channels began in 1972, when Time, Inc. started Home Box Office (HBO), a satellite-delivered pay cable service that distributed movies, sports, and special events. This greatly increased the demand for programming, as HBO and its rivals had to fill thousands of hours annually. It also meant that movie "season tickets" could be sold for television, thereby altering the business model of the TV and film industry. Once again, the control-minded Hollywood studios at first fought the new distribution medium. Their effort to establish their own joint pay TV channel was promptly held to violate antitrust law.[3] A still more powerful form of distribution emerged with videocassette recorders (VCRs), and the film industry fought it all the way to the U.S. Supreme

Court, but lost.[4] By 1990, 70% of U.S. households owned VCRs, and they represented by far the largest income stream for Hollywood, which had tried to suppress the new technology. Video-on-demand emerged in the late 1990s. And broadband Internet delivery of films started in the following decade.

Table 6.1 shows the change in the composition of film industry revenues between 1990 and 2005.

As total film industry revenues more than tripled, the share of domestic box office sales shrank to 11% of revenues. In 1980 they were 29.7%. In the same period, the home video market's share of overall industry revenues grew from zero in 1980 to almost one half (30% for domestic and 20% for international home video).

The substantial growth in ancillary revenues has made the studios increasingly driven by blockbusters. The first weekend box office as a percentage of total domestic box office rose from 19% at the beginning of the 1990s to 26% by the end of it, reflecting marketing strategies of wide release with a large initial promotion effort.

A second wave of mergers and acquisitions began in 1981, when MGM bought United Artists to form MGM/UA Communications and was acquired by Ted Turner in 1986; in 1982, Coca-Cola purchased Columbia Pictures; and in 1988, Metromedia acquired Orion. The mergers now assumed an international flavor. In 1985, News Corp (Australia, United Kingdom) acquired Twentieth Century Fox; Sony (Japan) bought Columbia Pictures and TriStar for $3 billion; Pathé (France) purchased MGM/UA and Canon; and Matsushita (Japan) acquired MCA and its Universal Studios.[5] Also in 1989, Warner Communications merged with Time, Inc. Time's cable TV properties included Home Box Office, Cinemax, Black Entertainment Television, part (and later full) ownership of Turner Broadcasting, and control of the second-largest multiple cable system operator (MSO). Of great importance in these mergers was the increasing value of the major studios' film libraries, which could now be exploited through cable TV programming.[6] Table 6.2 estimates the number of non-silent theatrical films in the libraries of the major studio firms.

The demand for high-quality films also led to the re-emergence of "art-house" companies associated with the studios. Disney purchased Miramax; Sony and Fox started Sony Classics and Fox Searchlight, respectively. They also bought several of the independent television production firms that had emerged in the 1970s: Time Warner acquired

Table 6.1 Sources of Film Industry Revenue (%), 1990–2005

	1990	1992	1994	1996	1998	2000	2001	2003	2004	2005
Dom. Theatrical	16.9	15.8	14.9	12.4	12.9	12.9	13.5	11.9	11.5	11.0
Intl. Theatrical	16.0	12.3	13.3	12.7	13.5	11.3	10.3	9.6	9.1	8.7
Domestic Home Video	19.0	22.9	24.9	25.5	25	24	25.5	29.1	29.9	30.5
Intl. Home Video	17.7	19.3	18.5	18.4	16.3	16.3	16.8	19.1	19.5	19.8
Domestic Pay TV	4.9	4.2	4.2	3.9	4.1	4.0	4.1	3.5	3.6	3.4
Dom. PPV/ DBS/VOD	0.2	0.4	0.6	0.8	0.9	0.9	1.0	1.2	1.3	1.5
Domestic Basic Cable	1.9	1.9	1.5	3.0	3.9	4.8	4.4	4.6	4.6	4.5
Dom. Broadcast	1.3	1.2	1.2	2.2	2.1	2	1.8	1.6	1.5	1.4
Dom. TV Syndication	5.5	3.5	2.6	1.3	0.5	0.5	0.4	0.4	0.3	0.3
Dom. Hotel/ Airline	0.2	0.2	0.2	0.2	0.2	0.2	0.2	0.2	0.2	0.2
Intl. Pay TV	2.4	3.5	3.6	4.8	5.5	6.1	6.4	5.2	5.0	5.0
Intl. Network TV, Syndication	7.1	7.2	6.5	7.2	7.3	8.8	7.5	6.5	6.3	6.2
Intl. PPV/ Hotel/Airline				0.1	0.2	0.3	0.3	0.3	0.4	0.5
Dom. Merchandise Licensing	2.9	3.1	3.2	2.9	2.8	2.8	2.8	2.7	2.6	2.5
Intl. Merchandise Licensing	3.8	4.3	4.8	4.6	4.8	5	4.9	4.3	4.1	4.4
Total U.S. Distributor Revenue (mil $)	13,532	14,912	18,402	24,093	27,289	31,107	32,412	41,314	45,038	49,121

Source: Kagan World Media, *Yearly Trends in Domestic Box Office*, various years.

Lorimar-Telepictures; Columbia/Sony bought Embassy; Paramount/Viacom bought Spelling; Disney acquired Witt/Thomas/Harris; News Corp purchased New World Communications and Stephen J. Cannell; and Turner acquired New Line and Castle Rock.

The major force driving the ownership changes of the 1990s was the belief that vertical and horizontal integration were necessary to ensure continued access of film production to video distribution platforms. All the major producers were vertically and horizontally integrated with content distribution firms. Each had the capability to produce, distribute, and market movies to video, broadcast, and theatrical outlets around the world.

Film Production and Distribution

Movie distributors' function is to support a film reaching theaters and other retail delivery platforms. After film production and editing are complete, exhibition prints are created and distributed, and expensive marketing campaigns are generated.

Full vertical integration became the normal industry structure in the 1930s. The Hollywood production studios controlled large segments of the distribution and exhibition markets. By the late 1940s, just when competition from television began to lower ticket sales, the studios were forced by a 1948 Supreme Court decision to separate from their theater ownership.[7] However, the

Table 6.2 Film Library Ownership, 2000 and 2005

Company	2000	2005
Warner Bros. (TW) (incl. New Line, and pre-1987 MGM)	4,500	6,600
Universal (incl. pre-48 Paramount) (GE)	4,000	5,000
Columbia/TriStar (Sony)	2,400	8,000
MGM (incl. Orion)	4,400	Sony
Twentieth Century Fox (News Corp)	2,000	3,260
Disney	600	1,121
Paramount (Viacom)	1,000	1,100

Source: Vogel, Harold, "Film Comment." *Entertainment Industry Economics*, 2001, 4th ed, p. 58. Data for 2005 from J.P. Morgan, *"Media & Entertainment: Home Video 2005,"* April 18, 2005. North American Equity Research, p. 20, Table 9, "No. of Films Released on DVD Through Jan. 7, 2005."

Supreme Court allowed the vertical integration of production and distribution to remain.

The major studio-distributors often arrange for production financing, in addition to coordinating the distribution and promotion of independent film productions. Without a deal with one of these major studio-distributors, it is difficult for an independent producer to finance a film and to distribute it nationally. Smaller and regional independent distribution companies are not able to provide financing on the same level as the major studios and therefore are limited in their ability to compete for distribution rights. Even when a large distributor does not provide financing, the independent producer generally needs its commitment in order to raise financing elsewhere. Large distributors also have the advantages of an experienced staff and the long-term, personal connections with individual theater chains that assure the successful, nationwide (and possibly international) release of a film.

Distributors can be expected to favor films produced by their own studios. However, as with any form of vertical integration, discrimination by a distributor in favor of one's own films is practical only as long as that product is not inferior. Ultimately, the market power of distributors rests on their access to attractive content, not vice versa.

In practice, it is impossible to separate distribution and production revenues, because the functions, not to mention the accounting, are

intertwined. Between 1970 and 2004, the top six firms accounted for about 80% of the market of film distribution; the top four firms accounted for about 60%. The firms' market shares fluctuated with box office success. Twentieth Century Fox seesawed from a high of 19.5% in 1970 to a low of 8.7% in 1987 to 11.7% in 2004. Disney dropped to a 4.8% market share in 1978 but grew to 21% in 1996.

Figure 6.1 and table 6.3 show the concentration trend of film distribution. This market has been fairly concentrated, with the top four firms consistently accounting for nearly two-thirds of the market and the six major studio producers-distributors accounting for about 80%. (See the C6 line.) "Mini-majors" such as MGM and DreamWorks SKG have been absorbed into the six-firm structure. But since no firm accounts for more than 20%, the HHI concentration is flat and in the 1,100–1,300 range, well inside the moderate level by DOJ standards.

TV Programs and Telefilms

Through the mid-1950s, Hollywood's major studios largely ignored television. Because early television programs were produced on shoestring budgets and were often broadcasted live, they lacked the technical polish of Hollywood films. The major studios believed that television's popularity would wane with its novelty, and then tried to contain TV. Actors or directors who dared to work for TV were blacklisted by the studios. This attitude was self-defeating. Just at that time, the studios had lost all of their movie theaters due to antitrust action, and were thus free to use any distribution medium or sequence—theaters, TV, and later cable and home video. But old ways of thinking prevailed.

Soon, economics prevailed over pride, and the major studios began selling or licensing TV rights to their libraries of old films. In the mid-1960s, Hollywood studios tried to enter television program production in full force. Before TV, power over content had made film companies dominant. But now, market power was in mass distribution, that is, in the hands of the program networks. Networks began to demand syndication rights and shares of shows' profits in return for providing nationwide distribution. The share of network TV programs in which the

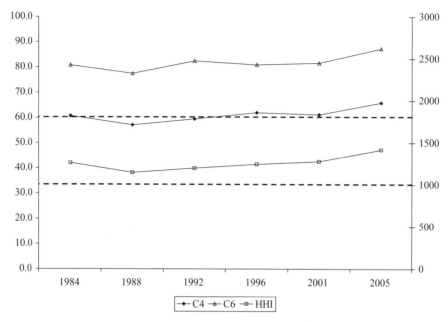

Figure 6.1 Film Production and Distribution (1984–2004): Concentration Trends

networks did not have a direct financial interest dropped from 35.6% in 1957 to 3.8% in 1968.[8] Therefore, the Hollywood film industry went to Washington and succeeded in getting the U.S. government involved. The FCC introduced its financial interest and syndication rules (the Fin/Syn rules), which strictly prohibited broadcast television networks from producing, or acquiring interests in firms that produced their programming, or in the programs themselves, beyond the rights to two showings. (They could still produce some of their own programming, such as soap operas, news, and sports.)

As a result, the TV production market included many independent producers (e.g., Spelling, MTM, Lorimar, Quinn Martin, and Tandem), and market concentration was lower than in the film industry. Lower, but not low. By the mid-1980s, nine firms of roughly equal TV production levels produced about three-quarters of TV programming.

Television networks again became more heavily involved in program production after the FCC's 1995 repeal of its financial interest and syndication rules.

Table 6.4 and figure 6.2 show the concentration trends in the prime time TV production market. In the 1970s and 1980s, small firms, because of the regulations in place, produced more programs for the major networks. With changes in regulation in the mid-1990s, the Big Three networks soon began to produce more of the shows they broadcasted. More significantly, these Hollywood studios bought two of the three major networks, started a fourth, and added two minor networks. Thus, major Hollywood studios remained the largest TV producers. Lorimar was acquired by Time Warner in 1992. Its competitors Viacom, Disney, and News Corp all increased their shares through acquisitions in the late 1990s. Viacom acquired a string of companies and grew from 9 to 20% in 2002–2003. These acquisitions caused the concentration index to breach the threshold of moderate concentration in 2003. The C4 increased from 37.0% to 67.0% in the same period. The remainder of the market was divided among a handful of relatively small companies. The overall revenue in this industry grew from $2.2 billion in 1984 to $6.8 billion in 2003.

The smaller producers are fragmented and dependent on the graces of the major networks, their own competitors in production. On the other hand, the major production companies also provide programs for rival networks, for whose business they compete. These figures should be interpreted

Table 6.3 Film Production/Distribution (Market Share, Box Office %)

	1970	1974	1978	1982	1984	1988	1990	1992	1994	1996	2000	2001	2004	2006
Time Warner (Warner Bros./Warner Comm.)	5.3	23.2	13.2	10.0	11.0	12.7	13.1	14.7	16.2	15.7	11.9	21.4	17.7	17.7
NewLine						2.7	4.4	5.4	6.4	5.3	6.3	TW		
Disney (incl. Miramax)	9.1	7.0	4.8	7.0	9.8	14.5	15.5	17.5	19.5	21.0	19.1	17.8	16.6	16.6
Sony							Sony						16.8	16.8
Columbia/TriStar	19.4	7.0	11.6	10.0	10.3	11.8	13.9	11.7	9.5	10.6	8.8	10.3		
TriStar						Columbia								
MGM/UA/Pathe	3.4	N/A	N/A	11.0	8.3	3.7	2.8	2.8	2.8	5.1	1.3	5.3	Sony	
News Corp							News Corp							
Fox	19.5	10.9	13.4	14.0	11.9	10.2	13.1	11.3	9.4	12.6	9.7	10.2	11.7	14.8
Viacom/Paramount[a]									Viacom					
Paramount/G&W	11.8	10.0	23.8	14.0	16.3	18.1	14.9	14.6	14.2	12.7	11.7	10.6	6.8	9.8
DreamWorks SKG											10.3	4.8	9.9	9.8
GE													GE	
Vivendi Universal											Vivendi			
Seagram										Seagram				
Matsushita								Matsushita						
Universal/MCA	13.1	18.6	16.8	30.0	21.6	10.3	13.1	12.9	12.6	8.4	14.5	11.4	9.8	9.8
Orion/Metromedia						8.8	5.6							
Others	18.4	23.3	16.4	4.0	10.9	7.3	3.6	9.3	9.4	8.6	6.5	8.2	5.7	2.8
Total U.S. Revenue ($ mil)	1,430	1,910	2,644	3,453	4,031	4,458	5,022	4,871	5,396	5,912	7,661	8,413	9,406	9,407
C4	63.8	62.7	67.2	69.0	60.7	57.1	57.4	59.5	62.5	62.0	57.2	61.2	62.8	65.9
C6	78.2	76.7	83.6	89.0	80.8	77.5	83.6	82.5	81.4	81.0	77.2	81.7	82.5	87.4
HHI	1,190	1,201	1,360	1,662	1,262	1,146	1,229	1,198	1,231	1,245	1,171	1,278	1,248	1,419

Source: Entertainment Data Inc. as listed in *Screen Digest*, Feb. 1, 1997; Wasko, Janet, *Movies and Money: Financing the American Film Industry*, Ablex Publishing Corporation, 1982, p. 152. Domestic market shares (percentage of U.S. and Canadian rentals) compiled from *Variety*, Jan. 15, 1975; Feb. 11, 1977; and Jan. 18, 1979. Leisure Time, *Standard and Poor Industry Surveys*, 1983, 1992, 1996, 2001, 2004, 2007.

[a] Viacom's Paramount bought DreamWorks SKG for $1.6 billion in 2006, then sold the DreamWorks film library to private investors for $900 million. DreamWorks Animation remains a separate independent production company, distributed by Paramount.

Table 6.4 TV Shows for Network Prime Time (Market Shares Based on Program Hours)

Producer	1970	1975	1980	1984	1988	1992	1996	2001	2004/5
News Corp						2.7	4.4	11.6	18.7
20th Century Fox	9.2	2.5	3.8	8.0	4.6	News Corp			
Cannell			0.6	7.0	4.9	0.2	Fox		
New World					5.2	1.7	Fox		
Disney	1.9	2.5	2.9	3.0	4.3	9.8	9.5	14.1	18.7
ABC					1.8	4.1	Disney		
Viacom			0.3	1.3	5.4	3.8	8.9	14.7	14.6
Spelling	2.3	4.2	8.4	8.4	2.7	0.6	Viacom		
Quinn Martin		10.3	2.8	Spelling			Viacom		
Paramount	6.4	6.9	7.4	7.0	5.4	6.3	Viacom		
CBS	1.9	2.5	1.1	n/a	1.0	7.8	12.2	Viacom	
Time Warner (Warner Bros.)	1.9	4.5	5.4	8.9	10.0	22.3	23.3	16.9	10.4
Lorimar		3.6	8.3	7.6	9.8	TW			
GE	1.8	2.5	5.2	0.5	0.7	1.5	6.1	8.3	10.4
Vivendi (Universal/MCA)	14.4	22.4	14.8	8.6	12.8	13.5	10.0	5.5	GE
Endemol								4.0	8.3
Sony					8.1	4.7	7.8	6.2	4.2
Columbia	6.0	7.3	6.2	11.1	Sony				
Embassy			2.5	4.8	Sony				
Tandem (Lear)		5.2	3.2	Embassy					
MGM	4.5	2.4	2.9	2.0	2.4	2.5	2.4	2.4	Sony
MTM		5.0	6.8	8.0	2.8				
Alan Landsburg			1.6	3.8	2.0				
Witt-Thomas			1.8	1.1	2.3	2.5	3.3	3.0	2.0
Filmways/Orion	4.4	n/a	1.3	2.2	1.8				
Bochco						2.8	4.4		
Carsey Werner				0.6	2.3	5.3	2.2	2.0	2.0
Other	56.4	23.2	20.0	24.1	30.5	26.4	19.4	37.1	14.6
Total U.S. Revenue ($mil)	696	1,056	1,602	2,236	3,122	4,358	6,083	6,430	6,776
C4	36.0	46.9	38.9	37.0	40.7	53.4	55.0	57.2	62.4
C6	44.9	57.1	51.9	53.0	51.5	65.0	71.7	71.7	81.1
C8	49.1	65.8	62.5	67.6	61.6	73.8	82.2	81.2	87.3
HHI	428	842	619	681	618	991	1,119	1,005	1,223

Source: Viacom acquired Paramount in 1994, Spelling Entertainment in 1995, and CBS in 1999; Sony bought Columbia and Embassy in 1989; Time Warner acquired Lorimar in 1989; Vivendi acquired Seagram (Universal's parent company) in 2004; film and TV operations were sold to an entity that is 80% owned by GE's NBC; News Corp acquired 20th Century Fox in 1985; Fox acquired New World and Stephen Cannell Productions in 1994; Disney acquired ABC in 1995. TV production revenues were estimated using $1.9 million for ½ hr of programming a prime-time show for 30 weeks of the year and $0.95 million for the remaining 22 weeks with 56 hours of prime time television per week , for all major networks, with 8% increase in cost per year after 1996.

carefully, therefore. What the numbers show is that after 1996, the six major Hollywood studios have collectively dominated television production. The major change was vertical integration. By 2004, the six major producers, except for Sony, owned TV broadcast networks, the traditional three plus two to three new ones. This reduced market access for independents as well as for rival network companies. In 2004, ABC chose nine Disney programs out of thirteen regular series, whereas Fox picked seven of its own series out of ten. CBS was less

vertically integrated (three series), and NBC had not yet implemented its post-Universal merger programming decisions.

MOVIE THEATERS

In 1945, the five largest motion picture production firms (Paramount, Warner Bros., MGM, Twentieth Century Fox, and RKO) had ownership stakes in 17% of U.S. theaters.[9] Paramount owned 1,236

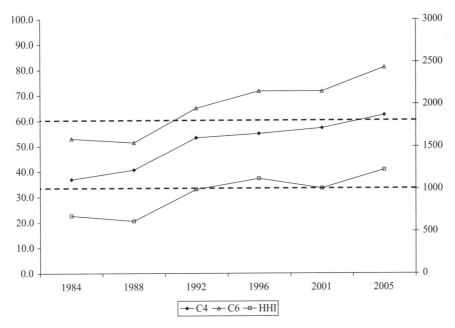

Figure 6.2 Prime-Time TV Production (1984–2004): Concentration Trends

theaters in 49 cities; Fox had 423 theaters in 177 cities; Warner 306 theaters in 155 cities; RKO 150 theaters in 66 cities; and MGM 17 theaters in 14 cities. In the cities with populations above 100,000, over 70% of the first-run theaters were affiliated with one of the five major producers.[10] The major film producers/distributors competed against each other in only 27% of these cities.

The major film producers engaged in the following practices, according to the findings of the courts: pooling agreements; price-fixing; mandated runs (successive showings of a feature film in a given area); and clearances (stipulating the time that must elapse between runs of a feature film within a particular area or in specified theaters.)[11] Consequently, the government brought an antitrust case against the major studios, which led the Supreme Court to cut the vertical integration structure of distribution and exhibition in its 1948 *Paramount* decision.[12] All this helped independent producers and distributors.

But just at that time, the importance of theatrical exhibition suffered greatly with emergence of TV. Ticket sales fell from 4.7 billion in 1946 to less than one billion in 1970 despite growing population and income. Due to rising ticket prices, box office revenues declined more slowly, dropping from $1.7 billion in 1946 to $1.4 billion in 1966, then rising to $9.4 billion in 2004, as shown in

table 6.5. In real terms, however, box office revenues fell by 65% from 1946 to 1965 and stayed at that level into the end of the 1990s, despite substantial population increase.

In the 1990s, theatrical attendance gradually increased, and then stagnated. Special-effects-intensive films and improved facilities enabled film theaters to remain viable as providers of affordable out-of-home entertainment. Theatrical distribution was still a film's main marketing event, linked to press coverage, word-of-mouth, and awards, all of which affected subsequent nontheatrical distribution. Thus, a film's box office success in its initial domestic theatrical run remained an essential industry measure.

In 1985, the U.S. government, friendly to film producers under the administration of an ex-Hollywood actor and Screen Actors' Guild (union) head, President Ronald Reagan, allowed the studios to return to theatrical exhibition. Twenty-four states passed laws to prevent abuses. Sony, Universal, Paramount, and Warner Bros. (Time Warner) reentered exhibition, after 40 years of forced absence. By 1987, these four studios had acquired 8% of total screens. But it was not a one-directional acquisition. In 1987, Sumner Redstone's National Amusements theater chain gained control of Viacom, and then of the Hollywood studio Paramount.

Table 6.5 Movie Ticket Sales and Amount Spent on Movie Admissions (1946–2005)

Year	Tickets Sold (mil)	Box Office Rev. ($mil)	In 2005 dollars ($mil)
1946	4,700	1,700	17,457
1965	1,032	1,042	6,208
1970	921	1,429	7,199
1975	1,033	2,115	7,922
1980	1,022	2,749	6,982
1985	1,056	3,749	6,653
1990	1,189	5,020	7,466
1995	1,263	5,490	6,830
2000	1,421	7,670	8,518
2002	1,630	9,520	10,162
2003	1,570	9,490	9,970
2004	1,505	9,530	9,787
2005	1,400	8,990	8,990
2006	1,395	9,138	8,920
2007	1,409	9,629	9,140

Source: Encyclopedia of Exhibition, National Association of Theater Owners, Hollywood, 1995, pp. 136–38. Figures for 1996 and 1946 "tickets sold" data from McCormick, Lynde, "What's Happening to Hollywood?" *The Christian Science Monitor*, December 12, 1980, p. B4, [http://boxofficemojo.com]. Data for 1966 "tickets sold" from Dretzka, Gary, "Hollywood Hits an All-time High With Its '96 Ticket Sales," *Chicago Tribune*, March 5, 1997, Sec: Business, p. 1. The National Association of Theater Owners, Statistics http://www.holly-wood.com/nato/s_stats1.html. Figures for 2001 from "2001 Economic Review," Motion Picture Association of America http://www.mpaa.org/useconomicreview. Data for 2002–2007 for tickets sold and box office revenue from the Motion Picture Association, U.S. Theatrical Market: Statistics http://www.mpaa.org/useconomicreview

Warner and Paramount became partners in 1986 in Mann Cinemas (later renamed CinAmerica) until 1997, when they sold out to WestStar Holdings. MCA (Universal's parent) purchased 40% of Cineplex Odeon. In 1998 Sony Corporation's Loews Theaters merged with Cineplex Odeon (with Universal the largest shareholder) to create Loews Cineplex Entertainment Corporation (LCE). Sony owned 51%, and Universal owned 26%. In 2006, Marquee Holdings, the parent of AMC Entertainment, merged with LCE.[13] AMC, controlled by J. P. Morgan affiliates, owns 60% of the new company, and LCE interests (now consisting of the private equity investor groups Bain, Carlyle, Apollo, and Spectrum Equity) had the remaining 40%. The merger combined worldwide AMC's 229 theaters and 3,546 screens with LCE's 221 theaters and 2,218 screens.

As with theater attendance, the total number of U.S. cinema screens, after peaking in the late 1940s (18,600 in 1948), declined to 12,600 in 1963 (figure 6.3). But it then bounced back significantly with the construction of suburban shopping mall cinemas and their multiplexes (multiple screen cinemas) in the 1980s and 1990s, as well as the splitting up of large auditoriums into several smaller ones. New construction was also fueled by the emergence of large chain operators with economies of scale and access to capital markets. Between 1980 and 2000 the number of screens more than doubled to over 35,153. Attendance, however, grew by less than half that amount. Often, new screens were added by dividing a large (and half-empty) auditorium into several small ones. With ticket prices rising during this same period, overall revenues kept up for a while, until overcapacity started to exact its toll.

By 2000, movie theater seats were on average only 12% filled. Bankruptcy was declared by the chains General Cinema, Carmike, Cinemark, Loews, United Artists, and Edwards Cinemas, plus smaller chains. This enabled the companies to reorganize and to renegotiate their leases. Edwards as well as Hoyts (an Australian company) sold out to Regal. Regal then owned altogether 600 theaters and 6,100 screens. AMC, after the Loews merger in 2006, had almost 5,900 screens in thirteen countries. These two theater firms each controlled twice the number of screens than the next tier of firms, which included Cinemark with 3,000 and Carmike with 2,300. The third tier are the chains National Amusements (Viacom) with 1,200, Century Theaters with 900, and Marcus with 500.

Figure 6.4 shows the growth of chains in theater ownership. The share of screens owned by the top eight firms more than doubled from 1977 to 1997. Nonetheless, the theater industry remained nationally relatively unconcentrated by DOJ standards throughout this period, with the combined share of the top four firms at about 45% in 2006 (table 6.6).

Industry concentration grew, especially after 1996. Regal's acquisitions increased concentration as the company almost quadrupled its share to 16.6% between 1996 and 2001. The purchases by AMC similarly increased concentration. Total industry revenue grew from $3.1 billion in 1984

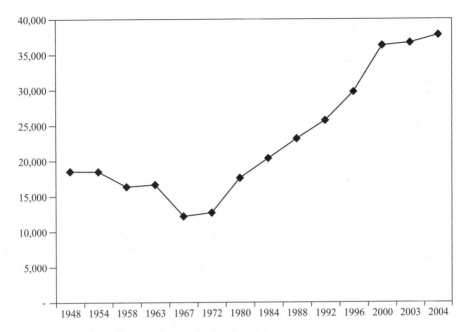

Figure 6.3 Number of Movie Screens in the United States.

Source: National Association of Theater Owners, "Statistics: Number of U.S. Movie Screens." Available at http://www.natoonline.org/statisticsscreens.htm.

to $9 billion in 2005, but the increase was less than inflation and population growth. Since 1984, the concentration trend in this industry has been moderately upward after considerable decline by the forced divestitures of 1946, with an HHI value hovering in the 200–500 range. In 1985, Hollywood studios were permitted again to enter theatrical exhibition. They all did—Universal, Sony, Viacom, Warner, and Paramount. Yet by 2007, all had left the market with the exception of Viacom, whose theatrical holdings were perhaps colored by the business history of Sumner Redstone. Even he, however, was forced to sell off most of his theaters in 2009 to repay debt. Thus, even in the absence of government regulation, a once notorious vertical integration did not reestablish itself.

HOME VIDEO

Wholesale Content Distribution

As VCR penetration increased in the 1980s (to over 70% of U.S. homes by 1990 and 93% by 2000), home video sales and rentals became the largest source of revenue for the major studios and distributors. After 2000, the number of DVD players increased tremendously as prices declined and viewing choices increased. Personal video recorders (PVRs), based on computer hard-drives, increased in penetration, too. The market for home video sales and rentals for VHS and DVD reached $9.5 billion in 2000 and $24.1 billion in 2004.[14]

The percentage of film studio revenue generated from home video (including both domestic and international) increased from 7% in 1980 to 38% in 2000 and 50.3% in 2004.[15] These data even understate the contribution of home video to the distributors. Whereas the distributors often share part of theatrical revenues with major stars and directors, only part of home video revenue flows into this pot.[16] Hence, contributions of home video to the firms' bottom line tend to be higher than the revenue distribution would suggest. An exact breakdown is not easy, given the opaque nature of Hollywood accounting. But since the practice is industrywide, it does not distort market shares, assuming equally skillful accountants among firms.

Table 6.6 Movie Theater Chains (% of Screens)

Circuit	1980	1984	1988	1990	1992	1996	2000	2001	2004	2006
Regal Entertainment					1.7	4.3	12.3	16.6	16.9	19.4
United Artists	5.0	8.7	11.6	10.5	9.5	7.4	5.1	Regal		
Commonwealth	2.0			MGM/ Universal						
Act III Theaters				KKR/ Regal						
Edwards Cinemas	1.0	1.0	1.2	1.4	1.6	1.8	2.0	Regal		
Hoyts							2.7	2.6	2.6	Regal
AMC Entertainment (Marquee)	3.5	5.2	6.5	6.9	6.9	6.6	7.5	9.4	9.2	13.3
General Cinema	5.2	5.7	6.0	6.3	5.5	3.9	2.9			
Loews Cineplex (Sony & Universal)							7.5	6.1	4.1	AMC
Sony					7.2	5.8	3.2	Loews Cineplex		
Loews	0.8	2.1	3.1	3.6	3.6	3.2	Loews Cineplex			
Plitt	3.0	4.9	6.4	Cineplex						
Cinemark USA			1.0	2.1	2.7	3.4	6.1	6.4	6.5	6.5
Carmike		2.6	3.0	5.6	6.9	8.5	7.8	6.6	6.2	6.2
Nat'l Amusement/ Viacom	2.2	2.5	2.7	2.8	2.5	1.7	3.0	3.1	3.1	3.1
Century Theatres	1.0	1.2	1.4	1.6	1.8	2.0	2.0	2.0	2.4	2.6
Marcus Theatres Corp	1.0	1.0	1.0	1.0	1.0	1.0	1.1	1.1	1.2	1.3
WestStar (Warner/ Paramount)			1.4	1.5	1.5	1.3	0.5	0.5	0.5	0.5
Mann/ Cinamerica	1.5	1.5	WestStar							
Others	73.8	63.7	54.7	49.4	49.1	51.6	39.5	45.5	47.5	51.1
Total U.S. Revenue (mil $)	2,201	3,116	4,460	5,020	4,870	5,910	7,670	8,410	9,530	9,530
C4	16.7	24.5	30.4	30.9	29.1	26.8	35.1	39.0	38.7	45.4
HHI	88	182	286	315	288	249	422	509	490	653
Total Number of U.S. Screens	17,590	20,360	23,129	23,814	25,214	29,731	36,280	35,173	35,995	37,740

Source: National Association of Theater Owners http://www.natoonline.org for screens. Shares for Century and Marcus from corporate Web sites; 2004 estimated. Data for 2006 are 2004 shares to show the effect of AMC's and Regal's acquisitions Cineplex.

The home entertainment markets changed dramatically with the introduction of digital video (or versatile) disc (DVD) in 1995. DVD included additional features, such as interchangeable PC and television formats, superior picture quality, multiple language tracks, and digital surround sound. Because the four major competing developers (Sony, Philips, Toshiba, and Time Warner) were able to compromise on a single technology, a destructive format war similar to the conflict between the VHS and Beta standards—or later between next generation Blu-Ray and HD-DVD—was avoided.

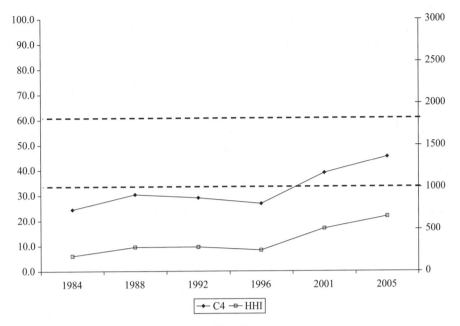

Figure 6.4 Movie Theaters: Concentration Trend

The penetration of TV households by DVD hardware grew at a rapid pace after 1997.[17] Table 6.7 charts the growth and market shares of video sales and rentals from 1978 through 2001.

The companies that have dominated the home video market have been the traditional Hollywood distributors. In 2004, the top four firms accounted for 66% of home distribution video revenues (figure 6.5).

The home video distribution business, like film distribution, generally consists primarily of six major companies, none of which dominates. Overall concentration is in the moderate range, by DOJ standards. Market shares fluctuate with the success of blockbusters. Disney entered the video market slowly in the early 1980s but rose to be one of the top two firms, along with Time Warner, with 2004 shares of about 20%. Of independent firms, only Vestron, IVE, Orion, Good Times, and Family Home Entertainment briefly attained market shares at or above 5%.

The concentration trend for this industry shows a zigzag pattern, with HHI values varying from 1,048 in 1984 to 702 in 1988, back up to 1,779 around 1996, and down again to 1,443 in 2003. This is mainly the result of the unstable market shares of the larger companies, driven by the

success of a few films. Time Warner increased its home video share significantly in the late 1980s with the acquisition of several smaller companies. Industry concentration peaked in 1997 when Walt Disney and Time Warner together accounted for over 50%. Since then their major competitors have gained market share.

Home Video Retailing

The video retail business has gone through major phases. The early industry structure was unconcentrated. Small retailers bought cassettes at a fairly high fixed price and rented them out. In time, the industry changed to one of the largest national chains. They also introduced revenue sharing with the big Hollywood distributors, which allowed lower fixed costs and multiple copies of the same title. This gave advantages to larger stores and chains, because they could attract customers with multiple copies of new releases. The industry became concentrated.

By far the largest of these large video rental chains is Blockbuster. The company began in Texas in 1985 and soon grew to 6,000 stores in 1997 and 8,700 stores in 2004. The firm accounts for more than half of the entire market. Hollywood

Table 6.7 Home Video Distribution (Market Share by Revenues)

Company	1982	1984	1986	1988	1990	1992	1995	1996	1997	2000	2001	2003	2004
Walt Disney	2.3	7.2	12.1	13.6	15.1	22.3	27.0	27.0	28.6	24.9	18.2	19.0	20.1
Time Warner Home Video	8.0	7.6	7.2	13.8	20.4	10.3	14.1	20.4	22.9	20.6	20.0	20.0	20.3
MGM/UA Home Video	8.5	8.2	7.9	Time Warner						2.5	4.1		
Karl Lorimar Home Video	2.7	8.2	13.7	Time Warner									
Thorn-EMI/Cannon	1.9	3.4	4.9	Time Warner									
News Corp				News Corp									
Fox Video										9.7	10.3	12.0	10.3
CBS-Fox Video	23.2	20.3	17.4	12.3	7.1	12.4	11.5	12.3	11.9	Fox			
GE/Universal/MCA Distribution	16.5	11.0	5.5	6.4	7.2	9.5	9.0	9.3	9.5	14.5	16.8	17.0	13.9
Viacom							Viacom						
Paramount/G&W	17.1	13.3	9.5	8.7	7.8	11.3	6.2	5.6	5.6	6.6	8.7	8.0	8.9
Sony					Sony								
RCA/Columbia	11.7	8.2	4.8	3.8		14.7	6.8	8.4	11.9	8.9	11.3	13.0	11.6
Dreamworks													4.6
Artisan (Live)									Artisan	3.2	2.7	4.0 Lions Gate	3.9
Family Home Ent.				6.8	13.1	LIVE			Artisan				
Vestron	5.6	3.8	2.0	1.1	0.2	LIVE							
GoodTimes							6.4	5.6	5.6				
Others	2.5	8.5	14.5		26.3	19.5	19.0	11.4	4.0	9.1	7.9	7.0	6.0
Total U.S. Revenue ($ mil)	500	1014	1,528	2,773	4,018	4,616	6,520	6,530	6,560	8,146	9,504	18,515	18,515
C4	68.5	52.8	52.7	48.3	56.4	60.7	61.6	69.0	75.3	69.7	66.3	69.0	66.0
HHI	1,424	1,048	923	702	987	1,191	1,267	1,516	1,779	1,488	1,347	1,443	1,398

Sources: 2000: VSDA VidTrac and Adams Media Research data as cited in *Video Business Magazine*, Year-End Report, Jan. 15, 2001. Market-share data based on video/DVD purchases. Universal 2000 market share includes DreamWorks. Data for 2001 from "U.S. Top Nine Motion Picture Distributors Ranked by Home Video Sales in Dollars and Percent Sales Market Share for 2001, with Sales and Market Share Breakdown for VHS Tape Cassettes and Digital Video Disks," *Video Business Magazine*. Revenue is 48% of the retail dollar amount listed in the table: $19.8 billion. 2003 market shares from "Consumers Electronic Daily," Nov. 30, 2004. Time Warner's 1990 share includes 5.3% from MGM/UA; its 1995 share includes 3.0% from MGM/UA, 0.7% from New Line, and 0.8% from HBO. Warner's 1996 share includes New Line's 3.1%, HBO's 0.9%, and MGM/UA's 4.6%. Warner's 1997 includes 3.0% from New Line, 0.9% from HBO, as well as 4.0% from MGM/UA. Warner acquired New Line Home Video when it merged with Turner Broadcasting System in 1995. Scala, Betsy, "Warner Claims Right to Sell Orion Product," *Video Business*, Nov. 3, 1997, p. 4. Warner acquired Lorimar in 1988. Thorn/EMI combined with Cannon and HBO Home Video in 1986. Warner acquired HBO Home Video when it merged with Time Inc. in 1989. Artisan was acquired by Lions Gate in 2003. Family Home Entertainment is the family and education division of Artisan's Home Entertainment division. LIVE Entertainment, Inc. acquired Vestron Inc. in 1991. LIVE Entertainment was reorganized as Artisan Entertainment in 1997. www.artisanent.com/company/com_index.html. 2000–2003 revenues are from Alexander & Associates, New York www.alexassoc.com. 1995, 1996 and 1997 revenues are from "Perspectives on the Filmed Entertainment Industry 2000," *The Seidler Company Equity Research*. Estimates for 1986 and 1990 are from using 41% of the U.S. film sales and rental to end users. The end user estimate is from *Perspectives on the Filmed Entertainment Industry 2000*, The Seidler Company Equity Research.

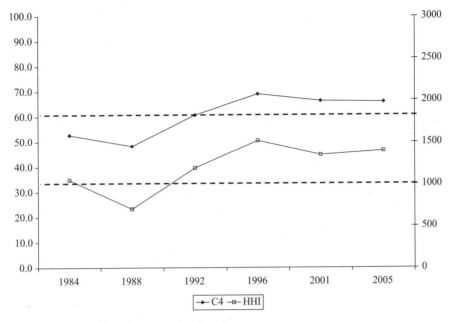

Figure 6.5 Home Video: Concentration Trend

Entertainment holds another 22%.[18] In 2005, Movie Gallery acquired the company after a fierce bidding war with Blockbuster, for $1.2 billion. The rest of the market is highly unconcentrated among supermarkets, independent video chains, and mom-and-pop stores.

HHI concentration grew from zero in 1985 to 3,346 in 2004. The C4 was 12 times as high in 2001–2002 as in 1988. The overall revenue grew from $2.9 billion in 1985 to $9.6 billion in 2001–2002 but declined to $8.2 billion in 2003 as sales (as opposed to rentals) increased and as video-on-demand (VOD) and cable channels increased (table 6.8; figure 6.6).

By 1998, Netflix started a highly efficient system of online ordering combined with mail distribution. By 2006, Netflix had 4.9 million subscribers[19] and about 8% of the U.S. rental market share.[20] This new style of distribution, the increasing popularity of VOD and PVRs, and the entry of Internet-based video distribution depressed the bricks-and-morter retail stores. With the handwriting on the wall, Viacom tried unsuccessfully to sell Blockbuster and in 2005 spun it off to its shareholders. Blockbuster was performing poorly, closing stores, losing money, starting its own mail order service, and acquiring the streaming service Movie Link. All to no avail.

SUMMARY

Prime-time TV production underwent great turmoil. Concentration rose in the wake of the abolition of the Fin-Syn restriction and TV networks' in-house production, and the mergers and acquisitions that united production and networking. The top five firms, including Time Warner, reached a share of 72.8%. Before the abolition of the rules, the three TV network firms accounted for only 3.5%.

Concentration in movie theater ownership increased, with the largest four firms accounting for 17% in 1984 and 45% in 2005. (Regal and AMC are by far the biggest.) It is much lower, however, than it had been in the "golden age" of film when the major studio firms owned thousands of theaters (17% of total screens, but 70%

Table 6.8 Video Retail Rental (Market Share by Revenues)

	1985	1988	1992	1996	1997	1998	2001	2004	2007
Blockbuster								53.2	50.2
Viacom				25.7	35.7	37.9	45.2	Blockbuster	
Blockbuster	0.2	5.2	14.1	Viacom					
Movie Gallery			0.3	2.8	3.0	2.6	3.3	21.8	27.9
Video Update				0.1	1.1	1.6	2.1	Movie G.	
Hollywood Entertainment			0.1	3.3	5.6	7.4	11.9	Movie G.	
Netflix							0.9	6.2	10.9
Family Video				0.2	0.6	0.9	1.4	1.6	1.8
Other	99.8	94.8	85.5	67.9	54.0	49.6	35.2	17.2	8.2
Total U.S. Revenues ($ mil)	2,900	5,460	7,260	7,710	7,380	8,100	9,551	8,200	8,200
C4	0.2	5.2	14.5	32.0	45.4	49.6	62.5	82.8	90.8
HHI	0	27	199	679	1,319	1,499	2,201	3,346	3,419

Sources: "Perspectives on the Filmed Entertainment Industry 2000,"*The Seidler Company Equity Research;* "Perspectives on the Filmed Entertainment Industry 1996," *Cruttenden Roth,* October 1996. Blockbuster Entertainment Inc. 10-k SEC Filing. Dealerscope. July 1986. p. 30. "Executive Summary." *Video Store Magazine,* April 28, 2002; "Top Chains Increased Rental Share." *Video Business Magazine,* 1998; "Equity Research: Blockbuster Inc." *Solomon Smith Barney,* September 9, 1999; "Equity Research: Viacom." *Dean Witter,* February 20, 1996; *Video Store Magazine,* December 5, 1996, p. 5. Data for 2004 based on company SEC filings, revenues from 2007 company. Hoover's www.hoovers.com National 2007 revenues Zeidler, Sue, "Convenience is Golden in Video Rental Market," Reuters, Feb. 28, 2008.

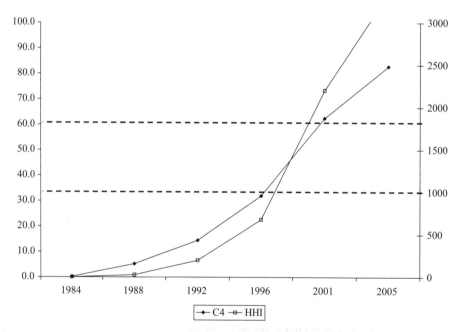

Figure 6.6 Video Rental: Concentration Trend

of first-run theaters, often without competing with each other in many cities.) The restrictions on vertical ownership were dropped after 1999. Several of the Hollywood firms entered, but eventually only Viacom was left indirectly through Sumner Redstone's vehicle National Amusements.

The film industry has always been an antitrust headache for government. Six Los Angeles

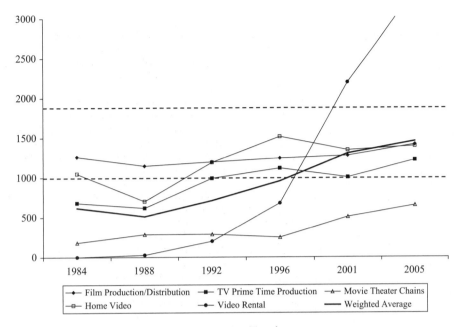

Figure 6.7 Film Sector Industries: Concentration Trends

area-based studios have long dominated film production, distribution, and often exhibition. The
key film production/distribution sector lost a bit in
HHI up to 2004 but remains a concentrated industry with six ("Hollywood") studios accounting for
over 87% of the market, up from 78% in 1984.

Figure 6.7 shows the average trends for the entire
film sector across all of the segments discussed
above. After 1984, the HHI more than doubled
from 619 in 1984 to 1,460 in 2004. The top eight
firm shares (really just six firms) trended similarly.

Vertical integration was reestablished after the
main distributors were permitted to reenter exhibition in the mid-1980s. Such entry did not work out
well. But in the 1990s, these firms were also read-
mitted into TV networking and strongly extended
operations in that direction.

Independents failed to capture or hold significant market share. The independents are important, however, in actual production, under the
umbrella of distribution and financing by the six
major firms.

Video rental has the largest concentration owing
to Blockbuster's market share, with an HHI of
3,419. Movie theater chains saw an increase in
concentration but only to a modest level of 653 in
2006.

Thus, in 2008, the six major firms collectively
retained market power over the mass markets for
theatrical film. Their ownership was varied: Japanese
(Sony); American-French (Vivendi Universal); U.S./
Australian/U.K. (Fox/News Corp); and American
(Time Warner, Disney, and Viacom-Paramount).
All were located in close proximity to each other in
the Los Angeles area.

The weighted average concentration of all segments of the film industry increased considerably
from 619 to 1,301; but it remained well below the definition of high concentration of the U.S. Department
of Justice. Only the video rental industry is above
the threshold, and its role is challenged by video-
on-demand and soon Internet TV.

The nature of increase in concentration
becomes clearer when we subdivide the five industries into two separate categories: (a) film and TV
production and wholesale distribution, and (b)
retail distribution. Figure 6.8 shows a relatively
stable and low concentration for production and
wholesale distribution; the HHI increases from
765 to 961 in the period 1984–2004. In contrast,
the retail distribution increased considerably in
concentration, from 272 to 1,629; it reached its
highest concentration in 2001, with an HHI of
1,808.

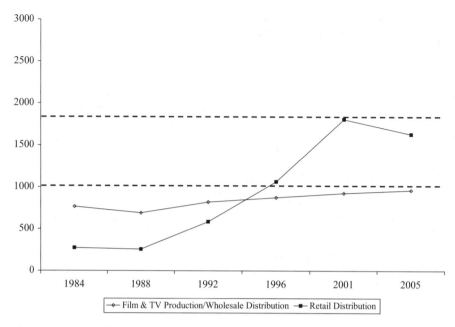

Figure 6.8 Film Production and Retail Distribution: Concentration Trend (HHI)

But both of these trends must be interpreted with caution. On the one hand, the film production industry is a tight community in which market shares understate the oligopolistic tendencies. On the other hand, retail distribution by theaters and video stores are only two ways for video producers to reach viewers. They compete with broadcast and cable TV, pay-TV, VOD, PPV (pay-per-view), and, in the near future, Internet-based film distribution.

Will the Internet change film industry concentration? In the past, improvements in distribution methods have not threatened the production sector in the long term, only the distributor. Although the Hollywood production and distribution industry has historically opposed almost any new delivery technology—broadcast television, pay-TV, VCRs—it ended up benefiting from them. The Internet, with its "long tail" of specialized content production, is not likely to reduce the importance of well-produced, high-budget, popular entertainment with special effects and famous stars.

Notes

1. Rob Freeman contributed much to the historical survey.

2. *United States* v. *Paramount Pictures*, 66 F. Supp. 323 (S.D.N.Y. 1946), aff'd in part and rev'd in part 334 U.S. 131 (1948).

3. *U.S.* v. *Columbia Pictures Industries, Inc., 507 F. Supp. 412 (S.D. N.Y. 1980).* ("The Premiere Case") Four major Hollywood studios set up a pay-TV channel, Premiere, to show films at least nine months before they were offered to other film pay channels such as Home Box Office (HBO). The Department of Justice blocked the project as "anti-competitive behavior which was tantamount to price-fixing and boycotting." An appellate court ruled that this temporary withholding of inventory could be considered a class group boycott.

4. *Sony Corporation of America* v. *Universal City Studios, Inc. 464 U.S. 417 (1984).* ("The Betamax Case") The Supreme Court ruled in favor of Sony—at the time only a hardware device company—that the creation of individual copies of TV programs for time-shifting did not constitute copyright infringement and that home video recording devices would also not be an infringement.

5. Steinbock, Dan, *Triumph and Erosion in the American Media and Entertainment Industries*, Westport: Quorum Books, 1995, p. 19.

6. Balio, Tino, ed., *The American Film Industry*, Madison: University of Wisconsin Press, 1976, p. 330.

7. Squire, Jason, ed., *The Movie Business Book*, New York: Fireside, 1992, p. 283.

8. In the Matter of Amendment of Part 73 of the Commission's Rules and Regulations with

respect to Competition and Responsibility in Network Television Broadcasting, 23 F.C.C. 2d 382, 388–393 (1970).

9. *United States* v. *Paramount Pictures,* 66 F. Supp. 323 (S.D.N.Y. 1946), aff'd in part and rev'd in part 334 U.S. 131 (1948).

10. Ibid.

11. Ibid.

12. Balio, Tino, ed., *The American Film Industry,* p. 317.

13. Sources: 2006 AMC Annual Report. http://www.investor.amctheatres.com/EdgarDetail.cfm?CompanyID=AEN&CIK=722077&FID=1047469–06-8942&SID=06-00 and Department of Justice, "Loews Theatres and Cineplex Odeon Corporation agree to condition of allowing merger to proceed," April, 16, 1998.

14. Wang, Spencer, John Blackledge, and Aaron Chew. *Media & Entertainment: Home Video 2005,* J.P. Morgan. North America Equity Research, New York: April 18, 2005, figure 3, p. 5.

15. Hellman, Heikki, and Martti Soramaki, "Competition and Content in the US Video Market."

Journal of Media Economics, 2000, pp. 29–47. VCR penetration statistic based on CEA data cited in "Consumer Electronics," Bear Stearns, April 17, 2001, p. 33.

16. Epstein, Edward Jay. *The Big Picture: The New Logic of Money and Power in Hollywood,* New York: Random House, 2005.

17. J. P. Morgan, *Media & Entertainment,* figure 3, p. 5.

18. According to Hoover's Business Information, in 2004 Hollywood Entertainment Corporation made $1,782 million in revenues, making it the second largest video chain before it was purchased by Movie Gallery in 2005.

19. "Wal-Mart and other online services such as GreenCine and CaféDVD made up the remaining 4%." Source: Netherby, Jennifer, *VideoBusiness.com,* "Blockbuster Nips Netflix Market Share," March 3, 2005. Available at http://www.videobusiness.com/index.asp?layout=articleFilename&articleID=9978&catID=1.

20. Zietchik, Steven, "Netflix Adds Its Own Pix to Mix," *Variety,* March 5, 2006.

7

Music

The music[1] industry is relatively small in size but large in cultural presence. It consists of those creating music (artists and composers), those creating or enforcing rights in music (publishers and performing rights licensing organizations), those producing recordings (labels), and those in the marketing of music (distributors). Because there are many labels and only a few distributors, the issue of ownership concentration arises primarily on the distribution level, where four companies dominate.

THE MUSIC INDUSTRY

Following a variety of automated mechanical piano devices, Thomas Edison invented electronic music recording in 1877. This was improved by Emile Berliner's discs and platters in 1897.[2] A vigorous recorded music industry emerged. Two companies predominated after the 1920s: Columbia (founded by Alexander Graham Bell, and acquired by CBS in 1938) and Victor (owned by RCA, the leading radio manufacturer and network provider). Decca and Capitol entered the market in the 1930s.[3] These four labels produced 75% of the records listed on Billboard's top sellers chart[4] between 1948 and 1955.

In the late 1950s, small independent labels made inroads by marketing emerging musical forms such as Rock & Roll and Rhythm & Blues that were being ignored by the major labels. As a result, by 1958 the four major labels' market share declined to 36%.[5]

In the late 1950s and the 1960s, the record industry entered a high-growth phase as post-WWII baby boomers entered their teenage years. Performers such as Elvis Presley, the Beatles, the Beach Boys, and the Rolling Stones achieved unprecedented levels of sales. The growth of the record industry continued unabated until 1978. Factors in the subsequent decline included smaller teen cohorts, piracy, and home recording devices.

The industry was revived through new distribution media. Warner Bros. and American Express started Music Television (MTV), the first music-based cable TV programming network. It provided record companies with a marketing alternative to radio stations. The second major boost was the compact disc (CD), introduced in 1983 by Philips and Sony. The improved fidelity and convenience offered by the laser-based CD storage technology motivated people to repurchase music they already owned on older formats. After 1986, CDs produced greater revenue and profit per unit sold than LPs. At the same time, the industry consolidated, leading the U.S. government to charge the companies with setting noncompetitive high prices. In 2000, the FTC reached settlements with the companies under which they discontinued certain marketing practices.

Double-digit annual growth continued until the mid-1990s, when another slump hit. Recordable

Table 7.1 Music Publishers (Market Shares by Revenue)

	1984	1988	1989	1991	1992	1993	1995	1996	1998	2000	2001	2002	2004
EMI	7.8	10.9	13.9	17.0	18.0	19.0	20.5	20.7	20.9	21.0	19.0	21.0	20.5
Warner Music (TW til 2004)	7.0	22.7	23.4	20.0	19.0	18.0	16.7	16.9	17.0	17.3	16.0	18.0	17.6[a]
Chappell	18.0	Warner											
UMG (Vivendi)									11.6	11.0 Vivendi	14.0	10.0	10.2
Seagram (UMG)	6.7	7.5	8.3	9.0	10.0	11.0	12.3	12.0					
PolyGram	4.9	6.1	7.2	4.0	6.5	9.0	Seagram						
MCA (Universal)	2.0	2.7	3.4	3.0	5.8	8.5	12.1	Seagram					
BMG (Bertelsmann)	5.0	6.0	7.0	9.0	10.7	12.3	10.0	11.4	12.7	13.0	8.0	6.0	6.4[b]
Sony			Sony	9.7	9.6	9.5	10.1	9.9	9.6	10.4	8.0	6.5	6.9
CBS	3.0	3.0	3.0										
Other	48.6	44.2	33.8	28.3	20.5	12.7	18.3	29.3	28.2	27.3	35.0	38.5	38.5
Total U.S. Revenue ($ mil)	523	641	758	913	1,007	1,100	1,329	1,462	1,595	1,816	1,939	1,215	1,314
C4	39.5	47.1	52.8	55.7	57.7	60.3	61.6	60.8	62.2	62.3	57.0	55.5	55.1
C5	44.5	53.1	59.8	64.7	67.3	69.8	71.7	70.7	71.8	72.7	65.0	61.5	61.5
HHI	541	778	931	970	1,066	1,201	1,199	1,081	1,114	1,138	941	943	920

Sources: "Top Publishers." *Music Week*, March 5, 1994, p. S59; "EMI Pulls Ahead in Publishing." *Music Week*, February 3, 1996, p. 1. *Marketshare Reporter*, 2000, p. 214; *Los Angeles Times*; from *Soundscan*, Dec. 31, 1998, p. C5; Informa U K Ltd., *Music & Copyright*, Jan. 1, 2003; market shares were calculated based on publishing revenues. Data for 2004 were based on company music division and global growth percentages. *Sources:* "Global Revenues of Music Publishers Rose 5% in 2004 to $ 3.6bn, Following a 3% Rise in 2003," *Music & Copyright*, March 2, 2005. CBS shares for 1984 and 1988 were estimated from 1982 figures.

a Spun off by TW in 2004.
b In 2007, UMG bought BMG's parts of the music publishing business.

CDs and the file-sharing of compressed music (MP3) off the Internet increased listening but reduced sales. After 1999, sales dropped fairly steadily worldwide, from 1,160 million units in 1999 to 814 million in 2004 to 749 million in 2005, of which 327 million were in the U.S. The decline in both units and revenues in 2005 alone was over 5%, accelerating in 2006–7 to negative 17.5% in terms of physical units, and 20.5% in terms of sales.[6] These trends led to further mergers as the industry tried to reestablish control.

LICENSING RIGHTS

Intellectual property rights are a key element in the music business. Music publishers and performance rights licensing organizations deal with those rights.

Music Publishers

Music publishing originated in the publishing of sheet music in the sixteenth century. Later, such publishers provided licenses to record labels. The term encompasses all firms with copyrights to license. In 2004, the music publishing industry was a $1.3 billion industry. Although technically there are tens of thousands of U.S. music publishers, most are merely self-publishers (composers who hold their own copyrights). Music publishing was dominated by the publishing affiliates of the major record distributors: EMI (CEMA, U.K.), Warner Chappell (Warner Music), BMG (Bertelsmann, Germany), Universal (owned by Vivendi, France), and Sony (Japan). But the vertical integration diminished somewhat after 2004. Just as horizontal concentration increased, Warner Music was sold by Time Warner to an independent investor group led by Edgar Bronfman. Soon thereafter, Sony and BMG merged in distribution and production, although to obtain interim regulatory approval, they had to keep their music publishing operations separate. In 2006, after Bertelsmann bought back the 25% of its shares owned by Groupe Bruxelles Lambert for $5.8 billion, it put its music publishing unit up for sale, and it was acquired in 2007 by Vivendi's Universal. In 2008, Sony bought out Bertelsmann and became sole owner of Sony BMG. In 2006, EMI and Warner Music made rival bids to buy control of each other, including their music publishing operations. Here, too, it was likely that an approval of any deal would be accompanied with a separation from music publishing. The market shares of the major firms are provided in table 7.1 and the concentration trends in figure 7.1.

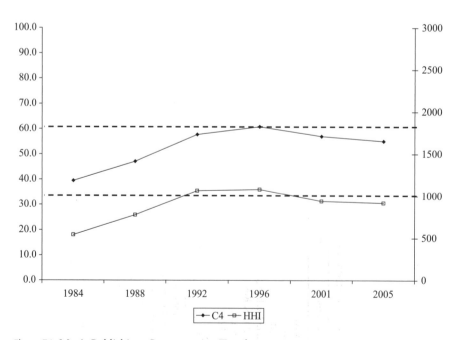

Figure 7.1 Music Publishing: Concentration Trend

Table 7.2 Performance Rights Licensing Organizations Market Share (Based on Fees Collected)

Organization	1963	1975	1984	1988	1989	1992	1994	1996	1998	2000	2001	2002	2003	2004	2007
ASCAP	70.4	59.9	65.5	66.2	66.4	59.4	54.5	52.3	50.2	49.2	49.7	47.2	44.3	41.5	42.7
BMI	27.8	38.0	32.3	29.2	28.5	35.5	40.4	40.7	42.0	42.7	41.5	42.6	44.0	41.8	43.6
SESAC	1.9	2.1	2.2	4.6	5.0	5.2	5.2	6.9	7.8	8.1	8.8	10.2	11.5	10.8	3.7
Sound Exchange													0.2	6.0	10.0
Total U.S. Rev. ($ mil)	54	141	319	414	438	640	775	921	1,012	1,171	1,301	1,346	1,425	1,537	1,402
C2	98.1	97.9	97.8	95.4	95.0	94.8	94.8	93.1	92.2	91.9	91.2	89.8	88.5	87.2	86.3
C3	100.0	100.0	100.0	100.0	100.0	100.0	100.0	100.0	100.0	100.0	100.0	100.0	99.8	94.0	96.3
HHI	5,727	5,034	5,340	5,256	5,254	4,810	4,623	4,445	4,344	4,309	4,273	4,148	4,048	3,855	3,838

Sources: Shemel, Sidney, and Krasilovsky, M. William, *This Business of Music.* New York: Billboard, 1977; Shemel and Krasilovsky, *This Business of Music;* 7th ed., 1995. Figures for 1984 were supplied by SESAC and ASCAP (estimated for BMI). MBI World Report, *U.S. Music Market,* 2000, pp.149, 320–321; Data for 1998 are from Hoovers Company Capsules, company estimates, "Hoover's Masterlist of Major U.S. Companies," 2000 www.hoovers.com; SESAC and BMI decline to report their figures. Data for 2002 are from *The New York Times,* Jan. 26, 2004, p. 6. Revenue figures for 1996 to 2002 are from Informa Publishing Group, *Music & Copyright,* May 28, 2003. Data for 1992 are extrapolations from 1989 and 1994 figures. 2004 data from Informa Publishing Group, *Music & Copyright,* Sept. 1, 2004. 2007 data for ASCAP, BMI from company webpages; SESAC data from yahoo! Finance. Sound Exchange revenue data from p2pnet.net/story/15658.

EMI is the largest of the music publishers. It owns, controls, or administers over one million copyrights. EMI's growth around 1980 was a result of its acquisition of SBK Entertainment World. Warner Music, the second largest publisher, raised its market share through its 1987 acquisition of Chappell, one of the oldest of music publishers. Overall, concentration of music publishing grew steadily in the late 1980s and declined a bit after 1993. It would have increased had the European Commission gone along with the proposed acquisitions of EMI by Warner Music or by Bertelsmann, or with a merger of BMG's and Sony's music publishing divisions. In 2007 EMI was acquired by the private equity firm Terra Firma, and a merger attempt with another music company was expected after restructuring and cost cutting. No single firm is dominant; the top firms have much of the market, but other firms collectively have a good share too. This industry is, therefore, by the standards of the Department of Justice, considered unconcentrated, if only barely so, and mostly because some mergers were blocked by Brussels.

Performing Rights Organizations

Performing rights organizations (PROs) collect royalties for performances of songs and distribute royalties to composers and writers. Two organizations, the American Society of Composers, Artists, and Performers (ASCAP) and Broadcast Music, Inc. (BMI), accounted for 87% of this industry (table 7.2) in 2003, modestly down from 98% in 1963.[7] The performance rights licensing market remains highly concentrated (HHI > 1,800). A third player is the for-profit SESAC, whose name originally stood for "Society of European Stage Authors and Composers," going back to 1930 when it was founded to serve European composers not adequately represented in America.[8] Sound Exchange was created in 2003 to help recording companies and artists to collect royalties.

These organizations reduce transaction costs by allowing a single negotiation for a library of songs to replace negotiations for each song. They also act as a collective bargaining agent for songwriters and publishers, preventing them from competing with one another for exposure by undercutting one another with licensing fees.

The U.S. government brought an antitrust lawsuit challenging the practice of blanket licenses. As a result individual song licenses were also made available.

Figure 7.2 shows the market size and concentration trends of this industry.

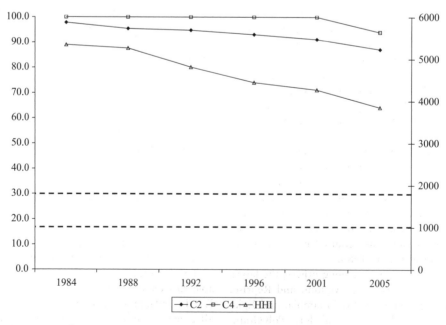

Figure 7.2 Performance Rights Organizations: Concentration Trend

Despite a 20% drop in market share since 1963, ASCAP has remained the market leader for performing rights licenses. However, the two top organizations have become more equal in size, and the HHI declined from 5,256 in 1984 to 3,855 in 2004.

It is not surprising to observe market power in this line of business, since that is its main raison d'être: to negotiate with distributors by exercising collective action. Such bargaining would be undercut by competition and fragmentation of existing ASCAP/BMI representation, and even the existing duopoly is already a reduction of such power.

MUSIC PRODUCTION AND DISTRIBUTION

Record labels sign up artists, finance the recording, and coordinate the manufacturing of albums, which distributors then ship to retail outlets around the United States and the world. Because even hit records have a short shelf life, a fast and efficient distribution is crucial.

Originally, all of the major labels used independent distributors. In the 1960s, they created international distribution networks to ensure that a record would be widely available in stores when it received its initial radio exposure.

From 1975 to 1980, the number of distributors with top 10 hits decreased from 21 to 9.[9] This increase in concentration was the result of both bankruptcies (Capricorn Records) and buy-outs of all of the large independent labels by major distributors (CBS acquired Chrysalis, Capitol bought United Artists, MCA acquired ABC and Motown, RCA acquired Arista and began distributing A&M).[10]

The vertical integration of the music industry proceeded with the consolidation of labels into a handful of music groups. Capitol (along with Angel, Chrysalis, Virgin, SBK, Manhattan, and Blue Note) became part of the English CEMA (owned by EMI); and RCA Victor (including Ariola and Arista) was acquired by the German BMG (Bertelsmann) in 1986.

Warner Music owns, among others, the labels Warner, Elektra, Atlantic, Asylum, and Reprise; Sony owns the labels CBS, Columbia, and Epic; Universal Vivendi holds Polydor, PolyGram, Island, Motown, MCA, A&M, Mercury, and Geffen; Bertelsmann owns RCA and Arista; and EMI has Capitol, Chrysalis, and Virgin, among many others.

In the mid-1990s, the largest surviving "indie" distributors were Independent National Distributors Inc. (INDI, owned by Alliance Entertainment), which then went bankrupt.[11] RED (still called an independent) was acquired by Sony in 1994. Thus, most independent labels relied on the major labels (their competitors) for national and international distribution. The Internet finally changed this dependency.

As a result of consolidation, six vertically integrated music groups came to dominate the music industry of the 1980s: CBS, WEA (Time Warner), PolyGram, MCA, Capitol (CEMA), and RCA. Vivendi evolved from the French electric and water utility holding firm Compagnie Generale des Eaux, which moved into media. It owned the mobile wireless firm SFR, the European pay-TV giant Canal Plus, and the advertising and publishing firm Havas. It then bought Seagrams for $34 billion, mostly in stock, and thereby acquired Universal Pictures and the Universal Music Group, the world's largest.[12]

By 2004, the market further consolidated into only four firms: Sony BMG, Warner Music, Universal (Vivendi), and EMI. EMI had earlier entered into unsuccessful merger agreements, first with Time Warner, then with Bertelsmann, but was blocked in both cases by the antimonopoly agencies. In 2004, Time Warner spun off its music group and sold it to a group of investors led by Edgar Bronfman, whose family had owned Seagram, and who had played a leading role in the several rounds of Universal deals, for $2.6 billion. Sony Music Group and BMG merged in 2004 after obtaining approval by European and American authorities. In 2008, Sony bought out Bertelsmann and renamed the music company Sony Music Entertainment. Also in 2006, EMI and Warner Music were trying to buy control of each other, which would have reduced the number of major firms to three. In 2007, control of EMI was acquired by the private equity fund Terra Firma. Vivendi, for its part, had been rumored for years to be seeking a buyer for UMG, the main remainder of its ill-starred acquisition of Universal.

The handful of major distributors have been able to exercise market power (figure 7.3, table 7.3). In 1995, music retailers filed an antitrust suit, alleging price fixing in the form of an industrywide wholesale CD price hike, even though production

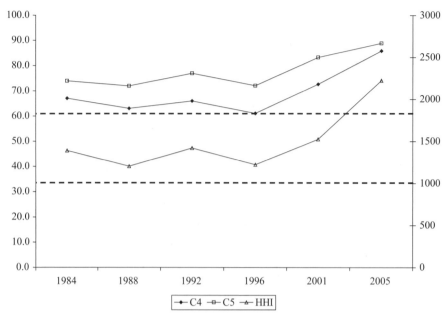

Figure 7.3 Music Distribution: Concentration Trend

costs had dropped and sales volume had increased. An investigation by the Federal Trade Commission estimated that U.S. consumers may have paid an extra $480 million because of illegal advertising practices affecting CD prices. Settlements were reached in 2000, prohibiting the companies from conditioning promotional funds to the advertised prices of their retail customers. The five companies also paid $67.4 million as compensation.

In 2004, the remaining four major music distributors accounted for 85 % of the market,[13] with an HHI of 2,224. In 1984, these numbers had been considerably lower, at 67% and 1,389, respectively. The merger and acquisition by Sony of BMG's distribution raised the new firm to 31% of the market and moved overall concentration into the highly concentrated range. Small distributors included MGM, Infinity, Redeye, and Presser.

Among the sublabels, market share tends to shift rapidly, rising and falling with the hit records of their major stars. To reduce fluctuations, the large firms diversify among their multiple labels and within each label. But the main sources of instability to the industry are the fundamental economics of the music industry: high fixed costs and low marginal costs, enabling easy copying and distribution. In a truly competitive environment, prices would drop; yet in actuality they are

significantly above marginal costs. This could be sustained through oligopoly. But an oligopoly is unlikely to be able to control and contain the new electronic distribution options.

MUSIC RETAILING

Records are sold in several ways: by specialized music retailers (both small independents and larger chains), by multiproduct retailers, by record clubs that are owned by the major label distributors, by online music retailers, and by downloading from Web site providers (table 7.4). Another method of distribution is file-sharing, in which participants download music from each other, usually without authorization by the copyright holder.

Mass merchandise retailers sell music recordings at a substantial discount compared to specialized music retailers. They may price some CDs at a loss to attract customers into their stores. These retailers more than doubled their market share (table 7.5). They are fragmented, however, among the thousands of supermarket chains, department stores, convenience stores, and consumer electronics retail chains.

The trend to music sales by large general retailers such as Costco or Best Buy had negative

Table 7.3 Music Distribution U.S. (Market Share by Revenues)

Distributor	1984	1988	1992	1994	1996	2000	2001	2002	2003	2004	2008
Universal (UMG)[a] Vivendi	7.0	9.0	11.0	11.0	14.0	26.8	26.4	28.9	30.0	31.1	35.1
Seagram/MCA					Seagram	Vivendi					
Polygram	7.0	9.0	13.0	13.0	11.0						
Sony[b]			17.0	15.0	11.0	15.2	15.7	15.7	13.0	31.0	22.8
CBS	25.0	18.0	Sony								
BMG (Bertelsmann)		16.0	11.0	13.0	13.0	16.3	14.7	14.8	18.0	Sony BMG[b]	
RCA Records	16.0	BMG (Bertelsmann)									
WMG (Time Warner)[c]	19.0	19.0	24.0	21.0	21.1	15.6	15.9	15.9	15.0	14.2	21.1
EMI	7.0	10.0	12.0	11.0	13.0	9.7	10.6	8.4	9.0	9.6	8.3
Other	19.0	19.0	12.0	16.0	16.9	16.4	16.7	16.3	15.0	14.1	12.6
Total U.S. Rev. ($ mil)	4,109	5,697	7,468	9,987	10,425	12,705	12,389	11,549	11,449	11,350	10,100
C4	67.0	63.0	66.0	62.0	61.1	73.9	72.7	75.3	76.0	85.9	87.3
C5	74.0	72.0	77.0	73.0	72.1	83.6	83.3	83.7	85.0		
HHI	1,389	1,203	1,420	1,246	1,221	1,552	1,525	1,624	1,699	2,224	2,226

Sources: *Billboard*, January 26, 2002; *Billboard Magazine*, January 16, 1999, p. 1, 82; *Billboard Magazine*, January 20, 2000, p. 70, *Marketshare Reporter*, 1995, p. 245; *Marketshare Reporter*, 1998, p. 210; *Los Angeles Times*, May 13, 1994; *USA Today*, November 27, 1996 from Soundscan. Total U.S. music distribution market size for 1984–2001 was estimated by multiplying retail sales by a factor of 80.1% and then adding that number to the sales that were sold directly to the consumer by the distributor (i.e., record clubs). The 80.1% factor was estimated by approximating the CD mark-up for U.S. retailers of EMI records in 2001. The 80.1% factor estimate was validated on page 21 of Krasilovsky, M. William, and Sidney Shemel, *This Business of Music, The Definitive Guide to the Music Industry*, Billboard Books, 2000; www.riaa.org, "2001 Year End Statistics"; Morgan Stanley, *Global Music Outlook*, January 25, 2002; and Bear Stearns, *EMI-Initiating Coverage*, September 4, 2002. Data for 1996 was from BPI Communications, Inc., *Billboard*, Jan. 24, 1998; data for 2000 was from BPI Communications, Inc., *Billboard*, Jan. 26, 2002; data for 2001 and 2002 was from Informa UK Ltd., *Music & Copyright*, Jan. 22, 2003; data for 2003 was from *Daily Variety*, Jan. 2, 2004; revenue numbers for 1998–2003 was from www.riaa.com, "Year End Statistics 2003", 2008 numbers Nielsen Soundscan, www.infacts.biz.music.

[a] UMG was owned from 1990 to 1995 by Matsushita which kept a 20% ownership share from 1995 to 2006.

[b] In 2008, Sony acquired Bertelsmann's 50% share in Sony BMG.

[c] WMG was sold in 2004 to an investor group led by Edgar Bronfman Jr. for $2.6 billion and subsequently was taken public.

Table 7.4 Record Sales By Outlet Type (%): 1987–2003

	1987	1992	1996	2000	2001	2002	2003	2004	2005	2007
Record Stores	65.0	60.0	49.9	42.4	42.5	36.8	33.2	32.5	39.4	31.1
Mass Merch. Retailers	22.0	24.9	31.5	40.8	42.4	50.7	52.8	53.8	32	29.7
Record Clubs	10.0	11.4	14.3	7.6	6.1	4	4.1	4.4	8.5	12.6
Other/Mail	3.0	3.2	2.9	2.4	3.0	2.0	1.5	1.7	2.4	1.7
Concert								1.6	2.7	1.5
Online				3.2	2.9	3.4	5	5.9	8.2	10.9
Digital Download									6.0	12.0
Total U.S. Rev. ($ mil)	6,058	7,941	12,534	14,323	13,741	12,614	11,854	12,338	12,270	10,322

Sources: www.riaa.org, Consumer Profiles, 2001, 2005, 2007. Category "Online" does not include online music clubs or digital downloads. Collected by Hart Research and Taylor Research.

Table 7.5 Music Retailing (Market Shares by Revenues)

Retailer	1984	1987	1988	1992	1994	1996	1998	2000	2001	2004/5	2007
Trans World Entertainment	2.4	2.0	2.6	5.0	4.5	4.0	4.2	7.5	7.7	11.6	
Warehouse Entert.	2.4	3.0	3.0	3.0	3.0	2.0	3.0	4.1	4.0	TWE	TWE
Musicland[a]	7.0	8.0	8.7	11.3	12.3	15.0	13.5	12.6	14.0	15.4	
Circuit City[b]			0.4	2.0	2.3	3.0	3.4	4.4	6.2	6.4	
MTS/Tower Records[c]	3.6	3.7	3.8	4.0	4.2	4.7	4.6	4.5	5.0	5.4	
Apple (iTunes)										2.8	9.8
Amazon.com							0.4	0.5	1.5	1.9	6.7
CDnow/BMG						0.1	1.0	1.0	0.9	1.0	
Hastings Entertainment				0.7	0.7	0.9		1.1	1.2	1.3	
CD Warehouse			0.1			0.1	0.1	0.2	0.2	0.2	
Wal-Mart											15.8
Best Buy											13.8
Target											6.6
Other	83.7	82.4	80.6	73.2	72.2	69.4	68.9	63.1	59.3	56.8	47.3
Total U.S. Revenue ($ mil)	4,370	6,058	6,435	7,941	10,619	10,758	12,165	12,705	12,389	11,053	
C4	15.4	16.7	18.0	23.3	24.0	26.7	25.7	29.0	32.9	38.8	46.1
C5	16.3	17.6	18.9	25.3	26.3	28.7	28.7	33.1	36.9	41.6	52.7
HHI	74	92	106	183	204	278	244	275	339	456	625

Sources: Market shares were calculated based on music retailers' revenues. Revenues were obtained from Dow Jones Interactive Financial Profiles, Hoovers.com Company Financial Reports. 2001 market share for Amazon was estimated by subtracting U.S. Book revenue from U.S. Book, Music and DVD Revenue. Total U.S. online market share for 2001 was 2.9%. Data for total revenue for 1996–2001 were obtained from www.riaa.org, "2001 Year End Statistics." 1992 and 1994 total revenue was calculated by multiplying "Total Value" by 88% (1996 Retail Value/Total Value), www.riaa.org, "2001 Year End Statistics." Numbers for 2003 were obtained from *Star Tribune*, Aug. 9, 2004, p. 4D, PR Newswire Association, Inc., Feb. 26, 2004 (JT). Apple share data: 4% of music was digital download in early 2005, of which 70% was accounted for by iTunes.com, "iTunes new 3rd largest music retailer in U.S.," June 22, 2007.

a Musicland, owner of Sam Goody, was acquired by Sun Capital Partners in 2004. If filed for bankruptcy in 2006 and was acquired by Trans World Entertainment.

b Circuit City filed for bankruptcy in 2008 and went out of business.

c Bankrupties in 2004 and 2006, and liquidation.

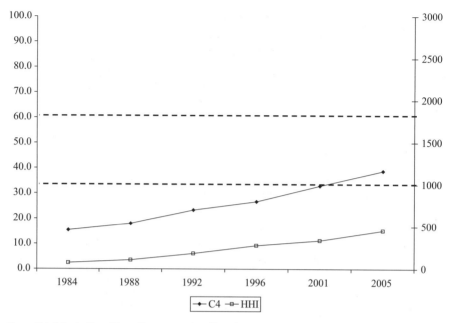

Figure 7.4 Music Retailing: Concentration Trend

implications for the music industry. A much smaller selection of albums is kept in such stores, with only a few older "back list" titles. This works in favor of the well-known performers and against new artists. It also reduces the ability of music companies to take unproven and risky acts, since their hit albums are being heavily discounted and do not contribute the same level of profits that could offset losses from other recordings.

Record clubs owned by major label distributors sell at a lower price by reducing distribution stages and by locking in buyers. Columbia started a record club in 1955, followed by Capitol and RCA in 1958.[14] In 1971, the Federal Trade Commission settled an antitrust suit against Columbia with a consent decree requiring record clubs (and others by implication) to carry products by artists from other labels. In the 1980s, the two major record clubs owned by RCA and Columbia were acquired by BMG and Sony (with Time Warner). Record clubs' combined share slid significantly from 15% in 1994 to 4.4% in 2004, as it became easier for consumers to shop for music in nonmerchandising outlets or online. They rose again to 12.6 in 2007.

Dedicated music stores lost market share in the 1990s. Among retailers, concentration is low but growing. In 2003, Musicland Group (Musicland,

Sam Goody, Discount Records), owned by the retailer Best Buy since 2000, was the largest with about $1.8 billion in revenues and 15% of retail sales. Musicland was acquired by Sun Capital Partners in 2004, filed for bankruptcy, and was acquired by second-place TransWorld Entertainment (F.Y.E., Record Town, The Wall, Coconuts). TWE also purchased Camelot Music in 1999.[15] Blockbuster sold its unprofitable music retailer, Blockbuster Music, to Warehouse Entertainment in 1998. Tower Records went bankrupt in 2006. Circuit City filed for bankruptcy in 2008 and shut down. As these changes were taking place, concentration rose from a tiny HHI of 74 in 1984 to a still low 447 in 2003–2004 (Figure 7.4).

Online sales accounted for 0.3% in 1997 (the first year in which these data were tracked) and increased with the emergence of sites such as CDNow and Amazon.com, which acquired CD Now in 2001. In addition, retail chains such as Tower Records, and smaller independently owned retailers, initiated online sales operations. But actual online music sales of physical recordings accounted for only 2.4% of all music sales in 2001 and 10.9% in 2007.

Electronic music distribution rose, however, with the use of MP3 (MPEG Audio Layer–3), a digital recording standard that allows music to be

Table 7.6 Music Cable Channels (Market Shares by Revenues)

Network	1984	1988	1992	1996	2000	2001	2004
Viacom	0	53.7	50.4	38.6	70.6	85.0	84.1
MTV		*(40.3)*	*(38.8)*	*(30.5)*	*(40.8)*	*(45.6)*	*(45.5)*
VH1		*(13.4)*	*(11.6)*	*(8.1)*	*(12.8)*	*(14.5)*	*(14.5)*
BET			7.0	10.5	*(17.0)*/Via	*(19.7)*	*(19.6)*
CMT						*(5.2)*	*(4.3)*
Spike							*(0.2)*
CBS/W					17.0	Viacom	
Gaylord (TNN)	26.9	31.3	34.6	35.9	CBS		
CMT	5.3	Gaylord					
Warner Comm.	90.3						
MTV	58.1	Viacom					
Jones Media							1.0
Gospel Music Channel							0.2
Other	9.7	15.0	8.0	15.0	12.4	15.0	14.7
Total U.S. Rev ($ mil)	113	211	388	698	1,350	1,260	1,470
C2	85.0	85.0	85.0	74.5	87.6	85.0	85.1
HHI	4,127	3,864	3,737	3,746	5,173	7,225	7,073

Sources: "MTV Fourth Quarter Revenues," *PR Newswire*, February 5, 1985. Viacom Inc., 10K SEC Filing, December 31, 1989. Gaylord Entertainment Company, 10K SEC Filing, December 31, 1992. Viacom Inc., 10K SEC Filing, December 31, 1992. Gaylord Entertainment Company, 10K SEC Filing. Viacom Inc., 10K SEC Filing, December 31, 1996. "The Advertising Report," *Morgan Stanley Dean Witter*, August 15, 1997. 2000 and 2001 data from Nielsen Media Research. Market share for 2004 for Spike TV (Viacom) and Gospel Music Channel are estimates based on subscriber numbers.

easily compressed in digital format so that it can be uploaded onto a computer or a network. MP3 (and other compression protocols) makes digital audio computer files relatively small while maintaining a fairly high audio quality. MP3 makes it easier to transmit near-CD quality music via the Internet; it also makes piracy easier. Napster, a service allowing Internet users to search and download music for free, built up a huge base of registered participants (over 72 million). The music industry went to court to shut down Napster, and in 2001 a U.S. court ordered the company to remove copyrighted music files. However, other sites took up the same function. Of these, KaZaa, Gnutella, Grokster, and e-donkey were the largest. In 2005, the U.S. Supreme Court held against Grokster in a case brought by the music industry.

Under pressure by file-sharing, the five major companies created their own download sites for pay. Pressplay was owned by Vivendi and Sony. Musicnet and Rhapsody were owned by RealNetworks, TW, Bertelsmann, and EMI. But they did not seem to put much energy into this new

form of distribution. Things changed, however, when the computer firm Apple introduced the music player iPod and the download site iTunes. Apple created iTunes as a supplement for its hardware iPod player, which became a huge success. iTunes had generated a cumulative 6 billion downloads by Christmas of 2008.[16] On Christmas Day 2007 alone, 20 million songs were downloaded. Digital downloads accounted for 12% of music sales in 2007, of which iTunes accounted for 70%. Apple thus accounted for 8% of music sales in 2007. In 2009 Apple became the largest music retailer, pulling ahead of Wal-Mart. The next largest music retailers were BestBuy, Amazon.com, and Target. The collapse of specialized music retaile chains was nearly complete.

Music Distribution Through Cable

Cable TV became a new medium for music exposure in 1981, with Warner's introduction (with American Express) of the 24-hour Music Television (MTV) cable programming network.

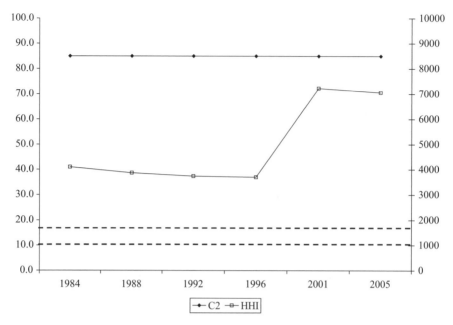

Figure 7.5 Music Cable Channels: Concentration Trend

MTV offered mainstream rock, pop, and rap music. Warner Amex later also introduced Video Hits One (VH-1), aimed at a somewhat older audience. Viacom acquired both of these channels in 1985. Other music TV channels include The Nashville Network (TNN), Country Music Television (CMT), and Black Entertainment Television (BET). Table 7.6 presents shares of the music cable revenues for each of these programming networks (see also figure 7.5).

By dominating cable-TV-packaged music channels, Viacom is an important gatekeeper, even if it is not a music distributor like TW or Vivendi. To combat Viacom's market power, the major music distributors briefly considered forming a joint venture to operate a music TV channel to compete with MTV, until antitrust concerns led them to abandon this plan.[18]

The distribution of music over cable TV (cable radio) was one attempt by music companies such as Sony and TW to bypass radio's (and Viacom's) gate-keeping. In consequence, they bought stakes in Digital Cable Radio, a firm started by General Instrument in conjunction with four major TV companies. Other distributors are CRN, Music Choice, DMX, and Muzak. The latter two merged

in 2007. However, none of them achieved significant listener shares due to the availability of free alternatives and the lack of portability.

CONCLUSION

The weighted average concentration of the music industry has grown. The industry itself grew from $9.4 billion in 1984 to $29.3 billion in 2001, but the overall revenue then declined to $26.8 billion in 2004. In the process, music publishing, performance rights, distribution, retailing, and music channels have all become more concentrated, and highly so. The weighted average sectoral results (figure 7.6) show a borderline moderate concentration, but with a steady increase, especially after 1996. Industry concentration is actually higher than the numbers suggest, insofar as the major four firms are also dominant internationally. Thus, there is no real likelihood of competition from major new entrants from abroad.

Music production and wholesale distribution have historically been concentrated, showing a fairly steady HHI trend line from 1,553 in 1984 to 1,871 in 2004. Music retailing, however, shows a

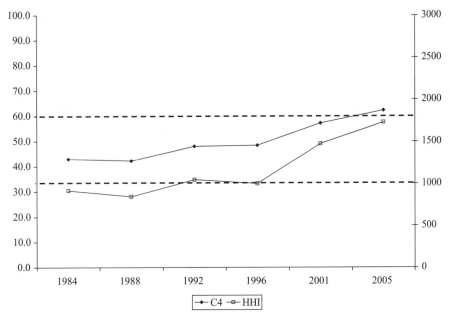

Figure 7.6 Music Industry: Weighted Average Concentration

far more dramatic increase from an HHI of 216 to 1,541 in the same period.

The music industry is characterized by the fundamental fact that its cost structure forces it to charge a price significantly higher than incremental costs. This is partly due to the high cost and high failure rate in selecting and creating artists, songs, and recordings. But partly it is based on an accumulated high cost structure and mode of operations. At the same time, incremental costs of copying and distribution are low and easy. This creates a fundamentally unstable situation. It also creates enormous incentives for companies to engage in oligopolistic price setting, and hence to a small number of firms. The alternative and secondary strategy is to differentiate artists and their music in such a way as to reduce buyers' price elasticity. But to do so requires expensive marketing whose returns tend to be uncertain and short-lived. Market structure protection (that is, concentration) is hence the major strategy. Periodically, new independent labels emerge that catch new music trends. They tend to be acquired by the major label distributors who desire to stabilize the market and acquire new talent assets. Also periodically, new technologies threaten to destabilize the market. To combat technology threats and eventually integrate them, a unified industry front is usually created, with strong dimensions of litigation and lobbying for legislative and regulatory protection. Yet for all these efforts, the music industry was in disarray, searching for new business models and industry structures.

Notes

1. Robert Freeman contributed significantly to the historical and early institutional narrative of this section and its early data.
2. Gooding, Wayne, "On the Record." *Financial Post (Toronto)*, July 1, 1997.
3. Vogel, Harold, *Entertainment Industry Economics*. Cambridge: Cambridge University Press, 1994; Denisoff, R. Serge, *Solid Gold*. New Brunswick, NJ: Transaction, 1975.
4. Denisoff, R. Serge, *Tarnished Gold: The Record Industry Revisited*. New Brunswick, NJ: Transaction, 1986.
5. Denisoff, *Tarnished Gold*.
6. "2005 U.S. Manufacturers' Unit Shipments and Value Chart," *Recording Industry Association of America* http://www.riaa.com. Same source for 2007.
7. Vogel, *Entertainment Industry Economics*.
8. Source: www.sesac.com.
9. Rothenbuhler, Eric W., and John W. Dimmick, "Popular Music: Concentration and Diversity in the Industry, 1974–1980." *Journal of Communication*, Winter 1982, pp. 143–149.
10. Denisoff, *Tarnished Gold*.

11. Brush, Michael, "In Music Retailing; Different Drummers." *New York Times*, July 27, 1997, Money & Business section, p. 5.

12. The music efforts of Hollywood mini-studio DreamWorks SKG were led by David Geffen, the "G" in SKG. However, this part of the operation was sold in 2003 to UMG.

13. "With Mergers Behind It, UMG Looks Ahead." *Billboard,* December 25, 1999, p. 78.

14. Vogel, *Entertainment Industry Economics.*

15. "Trans World Entertainment Corp: Net Income Increases 58%, Meeting Analyst's Estimate." *Wall Street Journal*, August 12, 1999.

16. www.apple.com.

17. Borland, Jim, "iTunes Outsells Traditional Music Stores." *CNET News.com*, November 21, 2005.

18. Tobenkin, David, "Cable: More Than Just MTV." *Broadcasting and Cable*, September 2, 1996, p. 37.

8

Print and Publishing

NEWSPAPERS

Industry Structure

Newspaper publishing in British North America began in Boston in 1690 when Benjamin Harris published the first (and only) issue of *Publick Occurrences, Both Foreign and Domestick*. After British authorities shut it down, no further attempt was made to publish a paper until 1704. The number of newspapers grew rapidly, and subsequently played an important role in the period of the American Revolution and the creation of the nation and its institutions. In the nineteenth century, growth was fueled by technical innovations such as the rotary press, cheap wood-pulp paper, Linotype typesetting machines, as well as the growth of population and literary rates.

Newspapers proliferated; many turned to sensationalist "yellow journalism" to attract readers. William Randolph Hearst's *Journal* challenged in the 1890s Joseph Pulitzer's *World* in New York, and the papers began to concoct stories, employ bold typefaces, and offer racier content.[1] Quality papers also emerged and often sustained themselves, even with small circulations, because the cost structure was low for editorial and production work. The decades before World War I comprised the most competitive era of American newspapers.

The emergence of radio and then television broadcasting was a major factor in a stagnation of newspaper circulation after World War II. Whereas the total circulation of newspapers grew 31% during the news-intensive 1940s, it only grew 9% during the 1950s and 5.5% during the 1960s, slower than the population. The number of daily newspapers dropped from a peak of 2,042 in 1920 to 1,611 in 1990, 1,533 in 1995, and 1,437 in 2006.[2] Circulation declined from 62.8 million in 1985 to 55 million in 2003 and to 52 million in 2006.[3]

The expense of faster presses and typesetting machines, news gathering and editorial costs, as well as the demands on the part of advertisers for larger circulations, created economies of scale and became the force behind chain ownership that replaced most independent, locally owned newspapers; 15% of all dailies were owned in 1930 by newspaper groups, 32% in 1960, 65% in 1980, and 69% in 2002.[4] In 1997 alone, 162 daily newspapers were sold out of 1,509.[5]

Although the average newspaper circulation is small by mass media standards (84% of U.S. newspapers have a daily circulation of less than 50,000), collectively they have a decent (albeit steadily declining) penetration. In 1970, 78% of the adult population read a daily paper; by 2005, this number had dropped to 51.6%.[6] Circulation declined both absolutely (after 1986) and on a per capita basis (figure 8.1).

Newspapers compete in two geographic markets: local/regional and national. In contrast to many other countries, and partly due to the size

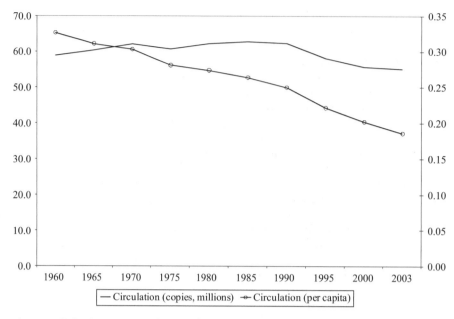

Figure 8.1 U.S. Newspaper Daily Circulation: Absolute and Per Capita

and diversity of America, national newspapers did not exist in the United States until recently. Only a few newspapers are distributed nationally, namely, *USA Today*, the *Wall Street Journal*, the *New York Times*, and the small and church-subsidized *Christian Science Monitor* (discontinued as a print publication in 2008). For the most part, the market for newspapers continues to be largely local.

As do many media, newspapers compete in two product markets: they sell information to readers and audiences to advertisers. Unlike broadcasters, newspapers have two sources of revenue: circulation and advertising.[7] Circulation revenues have grown at an average rate of 2.5% per year since 1985, although the total daily circulation of U.S. newspapers has been gradually declining since the mid 1980s. Advertising takes up 50 to 60% of the space in an average U.S. newspaper. In the 1990s, advertising revenues increased at a rate of about 5% per year to $48.7 billion in 2000, and then declined (partly as a result of the general economic slump) to $44.9 billion in 2003 and $46.7 billion in 2006. The decline in advertising revenues can also be attributed to competition from other media such as television and, more recently, the Internet, causing newspapers' share of the overall media advertising to drop from 27.4% in 1981 to 18.0% in 2007.[8] Advertising revenues draw from three primary sources—national accounts,

local retail accounts, and classified advertising. The composition of advertising revenues changed significantly since 1950. Traditionally, around 50% of receipts were from local business accounts, whereas national and classified ads each accounted for roughly 25%. However, national advertising declined while classified advertising increased. In 2006, classified ads accounted for 36.5% ($17 billion), national ads for only 16.1% ($7.5 billion), and local business ads for an also lower but still substantial 47.4% ($22.1 billion).[9] This trend can be largely attributed to the proliferation of large retail chains, which advertise relatively less per sales dollar than their medium-sized local counterparts. With national advertising comprising only 16%, newspapers have become primarily a local advertising medium—a vulnerable position to be in if alternative local platforms emerged, such as online electronic media, or when advertising declined, as it did in the economic recession after 2008.

Yet in spite of the vulnerability of the newspaper industry as a whole, the largest newspaper companies remained highly profitable through the 1990s. This good health, however, was not distributed equally throughout the industry. The leading local newspapers were profitable, but the second or third place papers generally performed poorly, if they still exist.

Thus, a major long-term trend has been the decline of competitive newspaper markets. In most U.S. cities, newspapers operate in a near-monopolistic market structure. In 2000, only 20 American cities were served by two or more separately owned, competing dailies.[10] (However, they tended to be in the most populous of metropolitan areas, such as New York, Chicago, Boston, and Washington.) In 2009, second newspapers closed down in Seattle, Denver, and San Francisco. Newspapers also reduced competition by combining their advertising sales, printing, and delivery capacities with neighboring papers. For instance, the *New York Times*, *New York Post*, and *Chicago Tribune* provide delivery services for competitor papers. In Los Angeles, the Knight-Ridder and Times-Mirror companies pooled national advertising sales efforts. Competitors could collaborate in such a way because of the explicit exemptions from the antitrust laws provided by the Newspaper Preservation Act of 1970. In addition, many large newspaper publishers started to seek interactive and electronic alternatives for delivering information.

National Market Concentration

The newspaper industry has become increasingly concentrated through the formation and expansion of newspaper chains. Because chains can offer advertisers coverage of an entire geographic region in a single transaction and can spread overhead costs among several papers, economics favor chains over individual papers.

The number of dailies owned by chains increased steadily after the early 1900s. In the period 1910–1930, the number of dailies owned by chains increased five-fold, from 62 to 311, 15% of all daily newspapers.[11] From 1930 to 1960, the number of newspaper chains grew to 109 and the number of chain newspaper titles rose to 560, comprising 32% of all daily newspapers.[12] By 1986, this percentage had doubled again to 70% of all dailies. By 2000, 77% of all daily newspapers were owned by 119 chains (table 8.1). The number of unique owners dropped from 422 in 2002 to 389 in 2005. Locally owned newspapers declined slightly from 469 in 2002 (32.4%) to 444 in 2005 (30.7%). Almost 70% of newspapers (by title, not circulation) are owned by an out-of-town company.[13]

The 10 largest chains owned 18% of newspapers in 2000 and 40% of the market by circulation.[14] The circulation share of the largest chains was fairly stable, 39.4% of the daily newspaper circulation for the 10 largest chains in 1984, 39.9% in 2000, and 37.8% in 2003.

Between 1985 and 1995, 460 newspaper companies of all sizes changed ownership.[15] Newspaper chains increasingly organized themselves as regional clusters through purchase and swapping. As of 2003, there were about 125 regional clusters with more than 400 dailies and many more weeklies.[16] Local papers thus became de facto regional papers, though typically with the local name remaining, plus some local content. The previous acquisition strategy of nationally scattered chains declined.

The logic of consolidation is powerful. As mentioned already in chapter 1, author and newspaper owner Dennis Herrick writes: "As owner of a weekly newspaper [a small operation in Iowa], I bought another much smaller weekly in a town 12 miles away in 1987. I was able to make a profit on a paper as small as it was because I could produce it entirely out of my large paper's office with no

Table 8.1 Trends in National Daily Newspaper Ownership

	1920	1940	1960	1986	1996	2000	2005
Newspaper Chains	31	60	109	127	129	119	
Chain Newspapers	153	319	560	1,158	1,146	1,134	
Average Dailies per Chain	4.9	5.3	5.1	9.1	8.9	9.5	
Independent Newspapers	1,889	1,559	1,203	499	377	346	
Total Dailies (%)	92.5	83.0	68.2	30.1	24.8	23.4	
Newspaper Owners	1,920	1,619	1,312	626	506	465	389

Sources: 1920–1986 data from Busterna, John C., "Trends in Daily Newspaper Ownership," *Journalism Quarterly,* 65, 833–838, Winter 1988. 1996 data from Campaine, Benjamin, ed., *Who Owns the Media?* 2000, p. 12. 2000 data from *Editor and Publisher International Yearbook,* 2001.

increase in equipment, employees or overhead.... A freelance writer who lived in the smaller town attacked my purchase in an article...lament[ing] the sale of his hometown weekly to an out-of-town owner.... The writer even accusingly referred to my pip-squeak operation as 'a chain' ".[17]

Table 8.2 provides revenue and national circulation market share figures for the largest newspaper chains. The C4 and C8 figures reveal a relatively level trend in market concentration of the largest newspaper chains based on both circulation and revenues, at about one quarter and one third, respectively. In 2003 the national HHI based on circulation shares was 200, relatively low.

The concentration trends for newspapers are shown in figure 8.2. National concentration has been fairly low, with moderate increases. The market shares of the biggest firms are modest nationally. Gannett, the biggest firm, holds a market share of about 10%, followed by McClatchy (acquirer of 20 of the 32 Knight-Ridder papers in 2006)[18] and the Tribune Company (which had bought Times-Mirror in 2000), with 4–5% each. In 2007, the *Wall Street Journal* and its parent company Dow Jones & Co. were bought by Rupert Murdoch's News Corp for

$5 billion. Moving into the newspaper business was an unusual move for one of the top media firms. In this case, the strong national and global brand of the *Wall Street Journal* content provided a great potential for expansion into other forms of distribution (cable business channels and websites). In contrast, the Tribune Company filed for bankruptcy in 2008. (To avoid that, it had sold its profitable Newsday to MSO Cablevision, thereby cable reducing competition in advertising in Long Island, New York. The HHI values show an increase from 155 in 1984 to 208 in 2001 and 191 in 2006. The C4 stayed around 22% over that same period.

However, the national market share is only one dimension of power. Some newspapers, such as the *New York Times* and the *Wall Street Journal*, hold much more influence than their firms' circulation shares (3.0% and 1.0%, respectively) suggest. Still more significant is that a firm's market share will be small nationally but very high locally.

Local Market Concentration

In contrast to its low national concentration, local concentration in the newspaper market is the

Table 8.2 Daily Newspapers (Market Shares by Circulation)

	1984	1988	1992	1996	2000	2001	2004	2006	2007
Gannett	7.6	8.6	9.5	10.5	11.0	10.3	9.9	10.2	8.9
McClatchy					2.0	1.8	1.9	4.4	3.3
Knight Ridder	5.8	6.2	6.5	6.9	5.8	5.2	4.6	McClatchy	
Tribune[a]	4.3	3.6	2.9	2.2	5.5	4.8	4.2	4.3	4.4
Times Mirror	4.0	4	4.1	4.1	Tribune				
Advance					4.4	3.8	3.6	3.7	3.0
Dow Jones[b]/ (News Corp)	3.5	3.7	3.9	4.1	3.6	3.0	3.4	3.5	5.3
New York Times Co.	2.8	3.2	3.6	4.0	3.6	3.2	2.9	3.0	3.0
Media News	0	0.8	1.7	2.5	2.7	2.2	2.6	2.6	2.5
Hearst	1.6	1.8	2.1	2.3	2.5	2.3	2.2	2.3	2.4
Cox	1.9	1.9	2.0	2.0	1.8	1.6	1.5	1.5	1.5
Washington Post	1.8	1.8	1.7	1.6	1.6	1.1	1.0	1.0	1.3
Other	66.7	66.2	63.7	59.8	55.5	60.6	62.2	63.6	64.4
Total U.S. Rev. ($ mil)	25,170	32,280	30,639	38,075	48,670	44,305	46,700	45,690	44,289
C4	21.7	22.5	24.0	25.6	26.7	24.2	22.3	22.5	21.9
HHI	155	176	200	230	254	208	189	191	172

Sources: Herrick, Dennis F. *Media Management in the Age of Giants.* Ames: Iowa State Press, 2003, pp. 292–293. Data for 1984–2000. Data for 2000 to 2004 from "The state of the news media, 2006." *The Project for Excellence in Journalism.* Journalism.org. Last accessed on 8 Jan. 2008 at http://www.stateofthenewsmedia.com/2006/contact.asp. Data for 2006 are used to show the effect of the McClatchy/Knight Ridder merger in 2006, using web site http://www.mcclatchy.com/news/2006/story/7528982p-7440749c.html. 2007 revenue from IBISworld.com; circulation figures from The Audit Bureau of Circulation, 2007–8.

[a] In 2007, the Tribune Co. was taken private by real estate investor Sam Zell. In 2008, the company declared chapter 11 bankruptcy.
[b] In 2007, Dow Jones & Co. was acquired by News Corp.

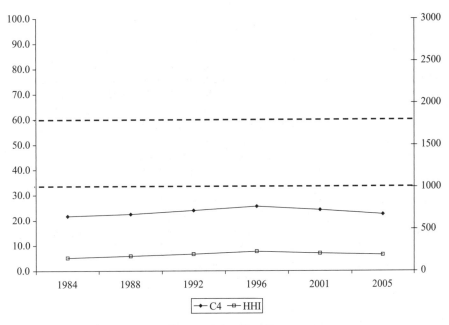

Figure 8.2 National Newspapers: Concentration Trends

highest among local media, even higher than for cable TV and local telephony. For over a century, the percentage of U.S. cities with only one daily newspaper in circulation has steadily increased, rising from 39% in 1889 to 43% in 1910, 87% in 1940, 92% in 1986, 94% in 1994, and 97% in 2000. From 1960 to 2000, the percentage of cities with competing (separately owned) dailies dropped from 4.2% to 1.4%.[19] To maintain some form of local inter-media competition, for many years law and regulation precluded newspaper companies from owning TV stations in the same areas as their newspapers (with old transactions being "grandfathered").

Supposedly to encourage local news competition, Congress enacted the Newspaper Preservation Act of 1970 (NPA), which permitted joint operating agreements (JOA) by exempting newspapers from some aspects of antitrust laws.[20] Two newspapers with different owners thus could combine business operations to create an advertising pool while maintaining competitive editorial departments. These JOAs are subject to Justice Department approvals and conditions. But even outside of such official JOAs, newspapers often collaborate in operations through unofficial "sharing" arrangements.

In some cases, this sharing has reached the newsroom. In 2002, the New York Times Company's *Sarasota Herald Tribune* agreed to share stories with Media General's three Tampa news properties, as well as a TV channel, a Web site, and the local cable news channel SNN.

The NPA generated much controversy while being largely unsuccessful in protecting smaller newspapers. One reason was that newspapers also have major scale economies in newsgathering, not only in advertising sales, production, and circulation, where JOAs can be effective. Due to the high and fixed editorial costs to create the first copy of a newspaper, average editorial cost declines sharply with circulation.[21] This gives advantage to the largest paper over others. At the same time, advertising revenues per copy increase with circulation, because advertisers tend to seek the largest available readership in order to reduce transaction costs.[22]

A second, smaller newspaper is therefore at a disadvantage unless it can draw on fiercely loyal readers and advertisers who do not consider the larger paper a substitute. The political perspective of a paper can be such a differentiating factor, especially where a society is polarized.

Table 8.3 contains data on the circulation and competition in daily newspaper markets.

The number of cities with two or more daily papers declined steadily, from 579 in 1920 to 124 in 1986 to 91 in 1994 to 49 in 2000–2001. Competitive markets fell from 552 cities with competing dailies in 1920 to just 20 in 2000.

Table 8.3 Trends in Local Daily Newspaper Ownership

	1920	1940	1960	1986	1994	1998	2000/1
Total Dailies	2,042	1,878	1,763	1,657	1,548	1,489	1,480
Cities with One Daily	716	1,092	1,222	1,389	1,457	1,440	1,431
Percentage of Total	55.3%	76.6%	83.6%	91.8%	94.1%	96.7%	96.7%
Cities with Two or More Dailies	579	334	239	124	91	49	49
Percentage of Total	44.7%	23.4%	16.4%	8.2%	5.9%	3.3%	3.3%
Cities with Jointly Owned/ Operated Dailies	27	153	178	96	62	30	29
Total Noncompetitive	743	1,245	1,400	1,485	1,519	1,470	1,460
Percentage of Total	57.4%	87.3%	95.8%	98.1%	98.1%	98.7%	98.6%
Cities with Competing Dailies	552	181	61	28	33	19	20
Percentage of Total	42.6%	12.7%	4.2%	1.9%	2.1%	1.3%	1.4%

Sources: Data for 1920–1986 from Busterna, John C., "Trends in Daily Newspaper Ownership," *Journalism Quarterly*, 65, 833–838, Winter 1988. Circulation and Total Dailies figures for 1994 through 2000 are from Newspaper Association of America at www.naa.org/info, 2001. Jointly Owned and Competitive data for 1998 to 2000 are from *Editor and Publisher International Yearbook*, 1999, 2000, 2001.

Table 8.4 Average number of Daily Papers Available per City, by Size Category of City

	1980	1985	1990	1995	2000
1,000,001 or more	5.17	3.75	3.13	3.50	3.00
500,000 to 1,000,000	3.13	2.53	2.27	1.81	1.40
100,000 to 500,000	1.51	1.55	1.22	1.07	0.93
50,000 to 100,000	0.92	0.75	0.63	0.61	0.60
25,000 to 50,000	0.59	0.55	0.54	0.46	0.41
Less than 25,000	0.05	0.05	0.05	0.04	0.04

By 1990, less than 1% of U.S. newspapers faced competition from a newspaper published in the same city.[23] Of course, the percentage of people with a choice between competitive dailies is higher, since large metropolitan areas are more likely to support more than one newspaper, as table 8.4 reveals. Examples were New York, Los Angeles, Chicago, Seattle, Washington, Boston, San Francisco, and Denver. (In 2009, the latter three lost their second newspaper). There is also greater choice in university towns. In about 75 towns the college paper functions as a second daily newspaper.[24]

Table 8.4 shows that the city population needed to generally assure a single paper in the year 2000 was above 100,000, whereas in 1980 it was 50,000. Multiple papers on average require a population of more than one million, whereas it was half a million in 1980. In about half of the cities whose size is between half a million and a million there are two papers. For all city sizes, the average number of newspapers has declined. (Several city populations increased, which may account for some of the numbers.) Concentration measured at the county level—which may include a city daily and several smaller suburban papers—is somewhat less bleak, although it shows a similar trend.

The local newspaper concentration trends can be seen in table 8.5 and also in figure 15.1 in chapter 15, where they are explained in greater detail. We analyze 30 local media markets.

Concentration is highest for medium-sized markets, which have between 0.5 and 1.4 million households (table 8.5). In such markets concentration is almost total (a C1 of 97.5%). It is almost as high in small cities (C1 = 97.3%). If it is slightly lower, it is because readers in small cities such as Lancaster, Pennsylvania, Green Bay, Wisconsin, or Fort Collins, Colorado, are more likely to buy a paper from a bigger, nearby city such as Philadelphia, Milwaukee, or Denver than

Table 8.5 Newspaper Local Concentration

	1984	1988	1992	1996	2002	2006
	C1 Concentration					
C1 Large Cities	60.1	59.4	58.9	64	64.6	62.0
C1 Medium Cities	93.3	93.6	97.3	97.4	97.6	97.5
C1 Small Cities	94.8	94.9	95.0	95.2	94.4	97.3
Weighted Average	80.3	80.2	81.1	83.3	83.4	83.1
	C4 Concentration					
C4 Large Cities	98.3	97.4	95.9	96.3	96.4	96.1
C4 Medium Cities	100	100	100	100	100	100
C4 Small Cities	100	100	99.6	99.8	100	100
Weighted Average	99.3	99	98.2	98.4	98.6	98.4
	HHI Concentration					
HHI Large Cities	5,047	5,081	4,996	5,571	5,562	5,464
HHI Medium Cities	9,064	9,083	9,588	9,602	9,629	9,622
HHI Small Cities	8,267	8,271	8,280	8,311	8,325	8,670
Weighted Average	7,219	7,239	7,367	7,612	7,621	7,676
	Avg. Annual Rev. per Household					
Rev. Large Cities	125	163	160	184	220	213
Rev. Medium Cities	93	119	114	130	148	147
Rev. Small Cities	56	68	68	88	92	98

Sources: Local newspaper revenues are based on *Duncan's Radio Market Guide*, 1985, 1989, 1994, 1997, and 2002 editions, Gale Broadcasting & Publishing Directory, annual editions.

readers in medium-sized markets tend to do. In the largest of cities, second papers often exist, and the C1 is lower but still high, at 62.0%.

The local concentration of newspapers increased in the past two decades as secondary papers fell by the wayside. The C1 concentration grew from 80.3% to 83.4% for the market leaders, and the HHI grew from 7,219 to 7,676. (Later in the volume we find that by 2002, local newspapers had become the most concentrated of all local content and distribution media.)

Newspapers are arguably the most important of local media when it comes to local news and public affairs. TV and radio rarely allocate more than a few seconds to a story and are reluctant to stick out their necks and alienate audience segments. Newspapers are also the main outlet for local advertising. The high local concentration of the newspaper medium is hence a particular problem in terms of its political gatekeeper role and economic power.

It is not within the scope of this study to determine the impact of newspaper concentration on newspaper quality. One study finds that larger newspaper chains tend to include shorter news stories

and devote a smaller percentage of their pages to news and editorials.[25] But another study finds that group-owned newspapers have fewer square inches of copy per reporter, a finding that implies that reporters have more time to write an article. Group papers were found to have more editorial and op-ed space devoted to the city in which they are located.[26] Many newsrooms are likely to be squeezed by new and more cost-conscious owners, but other news operations might benefit from greater resources, specific expertise, and economies of scale.

Conclusions

There has been a great deal of fear about the demise of the newspaper industry. The trend toward local market monopoly, the ascendance of newspaper groups, the shrinking circulations of newspapers, and the emergence of the Internet as a news source have raised alarms about the future vitality of newspapers. The outlook is mixed. Although the health of many papers, especially in single-newspaper markets, has been strong, and those of some chains of such papers is still better, most papers are vulnerable to circulation and advertising losses and shifts to other media and platforms. Newspaper firms have responded by consolidating and using technology to streamline production and distribution processes and by cutting editorial costs. Major newspapers have branded content, which can be "repurposed" in new electronic ways to enhance revenues and compete for consumer attention and advertiser support.

Often, cost cutting is attributed to profit-oriented owners, especially high-turnover investors. Yet cost pressures in newspaper operations are neither new nor purely based on the greed of rich corporations. Many newspapers—even good ones, such as the *New York Herald Tribune*—have closed; others have an uncertain future, with dwindling readership especially among the young, declining use as local advertising vehicles, and the emergence of online and free news.

Quite possibly, the cost cutting at local newspapers is a symptom of a steady but slow shift from local to national newspapers such as the *Wall Street Journal*, the *New York Times*, and *USA Today*, with local editions. A national market model for newspapers exists in the United Kingdom, France, Italy, and Japan, for example. If this is the trend, one should expect national tabloid-style newspapers to emerge, as well as some with more pronounced right- or left-wing perspectives. In other words, there would be fewer papers but with a wider spectrum of news perspectives. The future scenario for newspapers is discussed in chapter 19.

If traditional or new-style newspapers are struggling, why then is blogging flourishing? Beyond the sociological, cultural, and political explanations there are economic ones. Blogs are low cost. They are based on voluntarism, and they add positive externalities of sharing and community. Blogs tend to favor opinion and analysis (cheap) over shoe-leather reporting (expensive). Blogs have been based on a speech model, not a profit model. But in the future, they will require more work and a more sustained effort. And that means an organization with expenses, revenue requirements, operating models, and scale economics.

BOOKS

History

The technological origins of book publishing go back to Chinese and Korean inventions of the thirteenth century and to fifteenth-century Germany with Johannes Gutenberg and the movable type printing press. Gutenberg's interest in printing arose from his fascination with mechanical reproduction. The basic idea behind the movable type was fairly simple, but its practical implementation—finding effective inks, fashioning and designing the best typefaces, selecting the right paper, and finding the proper means of applying ink to paper—turned out to be a tedious development process.

Even from today's perspective, Gutenberg's first printing project was highly ambitious. His Bible, completed in 1455, had 1,280 large pages, a total of more than three million letters, and many elaborate illustrations. Considering that it was the first real book ever printed, the quality was amazingly good.

Gutenberg was much less successful as an entrepreneur than as an inventor, and his printing technology moved rapidly beyond his control. By 1500, 270 European cities had printing shops that collectively issued 40,000 different titles and 10 million volumes. Printers proliferated especially in Northern Italy and the Netherlands. In some European cities there were over 30 print shops. Many of these early printers functioned as publishers by securing manuscripts.

Printing in North America began with the arrival of the English colonists. Puritans wishing to escape English censorship began publishing their religious texts in the New World. Presses required government licenses and were primarily used by colonial and church authorities. Later, the U.S. Constitution of 1788 provided copyrights as part of Section I of the enumerated powers of the Union.[27] The first national copyright law was enacted in 1791, protecting American publishers domestically but not those of other countries.

Driven by technological innovations in printing, transportation, and communications, the U.S. book publishing industry grew significantly during the nineteenth century. Publishing houses established themselves in Boston, Philadelphia, Chicago, and particularly in New York, many of which still exist today.

The industry grew further after World War II as a result of the rise in college attendance and educational levels generally. A new influx of capital into the industry contributed to its structural change from a system of more family-run operations and closely held corporations to one dominated by about a dozen companies, many of whom traded in the stock market and are part of large media companies. In addition, there are thousands of small publishers with minute market shares.

Book Industry Structure

Many of the largest publishing companies in the United States were founded in the late nineteenth century. For publishing, as for the rest of the American economy, this was a period of rapid growth and concentration. Ownership in the early book industry was diffuse. The technological improvement of production and distribution processes in the late 1800s and early 1900s led to the formation of two industry powers, the United States Book Co. and the American Book Co. The United States Book Co. went bankrupt in 1893 owing to competition with cheap book publishers[28] and was later succeeded by the American

Publishers Corporation, until it, too, reached a similar fate in 1904.[29]

In the 1960s, several large media firms acquired publishing companies: RCA bought Random House; CBS took over Holt, Rinehart & Winston; ITT acquired Bobbs-Merrill; and Harcourt Brace Jovanovich bought Academic Press. In the late 1970s, CBS also acquired Fawcett, and Time purchased Little, Brown. An increasing number of mergers involved foreign firms seeking access to content businesses and distribution channels in the United States. Some of the largest transactions in the 1980s and beyond are shown in table 8.6.

In spite of these large deals, the market remained relatively unconcentrated through the 1980s with a C8 at 30.5% and HHI of 139 in 1984 (see table 8.10). The concentration level rose after 1992 to 42.3% in 2004. But these are not especially high numbers. The HHI index, correspondingly,

Table 8.6 Major U.S. Publishing Transactions Since 1984

Buyer	Acquired Publisher	Year	Price ($ mil)
Viacom/Paramount[a]	Simon & Schuster[b]	1975	$10
	Prentice Hall	1984	$710
	Macmillan	1993	$553
News Corp (US/Australia/UK)	Harper and Row[c]	1987	$293
	William Collins[d]	1989	$717
	Scott, Foresman	1989	$407
	Hearst Book Group[e]	1999	$180
Hachette (France)	Grolier	1988	$462.2
Pearson (United Kingdom)	Penguin	1971	N/A
	Viking	1975	$12
	Addison Wesley	1988	$283
	HarperCollins Educational	1996	$580
	Putnam Berkley	1996	$336
	Simon & Schuster (Professional)[f]	1998	$4,600
	Dorling Kindersley[g]	1998	$466
	Harcourt Education Assessment	2007	$950
Bertelsmann (Germany)	Bantam[h]	1977/1981	N/A
	Doubleday Dell	1986	$475
	Random House[i]	1998	$1,500
	Books on Tape	2001	N/A
Harcourt General	Mosby	1998	$415
Maxwell (United Kingdom)	MacMillan	1988	$2,640
Reed Elsevier/Thomson	Pergamon Press	1992	N/A
	Harcourt General	2001	$4,500
Scholastic Inc.	Grolier (Lagardère)	2000	$400
McGraw Hill	Tribune Education[j]	2000	$635
J. Wiley & Sons, Inc.	Hungry Minds	2001	$185
Vivendi Universal	Houghton Mifflin	2001	$2,200[k]

Table 8.6 (*Continued*)

Buyer	Acquired Publisher	Year	Price ($ mil)
Thomas H. Lee; Blackstone	Houghton Mifflin	2002	N/A
Riverdeep[o]	Houghton Mifflin	2006	$3
	Harcourt Education – Trade Greenwood-Heinemann (from Reed Elsevier)	2007	$4,000
Holtzbrinck Publishers[l]	Henry Holt and Company	1985	N/A
	Farrar, Straus, and Giroux	1994	N/A
	Macmillan Group[m]	1995	$350
	Roaring Brook Press	2004	N/A
Inter Media Partners	Thomas Nelson	2006	$473
Ripplewood/DHW	Time Life Inc.[n]	2004	N/A
Lagardèrè/Hachette/Grand Central Books	Time Warner Book Group (incl. Little, Brown)	2006	$538
Ripplewood/DHW	Reader's Digest	2007	$2,400
Cengage (Thomson Learning)	Houghton Mifflin College	2007	$750

Sources: Source for 2004 data: Jeanette Clinkunbroomer, ed., *Print Industry Insider,* Vol. 2, No. 15, August 4, 2004. Source for other data: Donald, William, and James Peters, "Standard and Poor's Indsutry Surveys: Publishing." March 9, 2006 http://umi.compustat.com/cgi-mi-doc/docserver.cgi?keytype=INDSUR&keyval=PUB&doctype=IS&docformat=pdf&date=200603&ie=.pdf.

[a] Simon & Schuster acquired Prentice Hall for $10 million. Paramount acquired Simon & Schuster in 1975. Viacom acquired Paramount in 1994.

[b] Annual Report, Gulf & Western Industries Inc., July 31, 1975.

[c] News Corp acquired Harper & Row and then merged it with William Collins to form HarperCollins in 1990.

[d] News Corp acquired 40% of William Collins in 1981. It completed the full acquisition in 1989.

[e] "News Corp Agrees to Buy Two Publishers." *New York Times,* May 18, 1999.

[f] Pearson acquired the educational and professional divisions of Simon & Schuster from Viacom.

[g] Caslon Analytics at http://www.caslon.com.au/mediaprofiles/pearson.htm, 2001.

[h] Bertelsmann acquired 51% of Bantam in 1977. It completed the full acquisition in 1981.

i Bertelsmann acquired Random House from Advanced Publications in 1998.

[j] Tribune Education includes Everyday Learning/Creative Publications, NTC/Contemporary Publishing Group, and Wright Group http://investor.mcgraw-hill.com/ireye, 2000.

[k] The transaction included the assumption of $500 million in debt.

[l] Holtzbrinck Publishers, "Who We Are" http://www.holtzbrinckus.com/about/about_who.asp.

[m] Thompson, John B. "*Books in the Digital Age*. Cambridge, U.K.: Polity Press, 2005.

[n] The acquisition of Time Life, Inc. included books, music, and DVDs. Direct Holdings worldwide is a partnership of Ripplewood Holdings and Zelnick Media.

[o] Riverdeep merged the companies into Honghton Mifflin Harcourt in 2007.

remained below 400. At the same time, the number of publishing companies climbed from 936 in 1963 to over 2,000 by 1980 and well over 3,000 in 2000, driven by the expanding number of specialty and niche publications.

Mergers and acquisitions of book publishers by media conglomerates aimed to achieve synergies such as cross-promotion of movies and books, and to capitalize on the global marketing span of their communications company parents. However, such integration can also create negative synergies. For instance, Rupert Murdoch blocked his publishing firm HarperCollins from publishing a promising book by the former British Hong Kong governor, Chris Patten, because it might have jeopardized his companies' satellite TV involvement with China.[30]

Table 8.7 shows the percentage of global revenues from worldwide book publishing in the major media and entertainment companies. Of the five major U.S. media companies, it is around 5% for CBS/Viacom and News Corp; it is negligible for Time Warner, GE, and Disney. Even for Bertelsmann, traditionally a print publisher, books accounted for only 10% of revenue.

The number of new titles published each year is one indicator of industry performance. That number remained relatively stable between 1910 and 1950, at around 10,000 per year. Output of new titles began to increase enormously after 1950, reaching over 51,000 by 1994, over 122,000 in 2000, and 175,000 in 2004.[31]

A partial explanation for the increase in new book titles comes from the emergence of new

Table 8.7 Book Publishing as a Percentage of Total Revenues of Major Media Companies
($U.S. Million, 2005)

	Book Revenues	Global Revenues	Revenue from Book Sales (%)
Bertelsmann	$ 2,293	$22,806	10.1
News Corp	$1,325	$23,859	5.6
CBS/Viacom	$763	$14,536	5.2
TimeWarner	$353	$43,652	0.8

Notes: Total revenue from 2004–2005 from operations in trade and paperback and "other books" for each company.

Table 8.8 Publishing Industry (Revenues and Shares of Book Market Segments

	1958	1976	1983	1993	1995	1997	1999	2000	2002	2004
Trade	12.7	13.7	19.8	28.0	29.6	27.2	25.6	26.5	26.3	26.2
Mass Paper	5.7	9.9	12.5	7.7	7.9	7.1	5.8	6.5	6.6	6.4
Religious	4.0	4.1	4.8	5.0	5.5	5.6	5.1	5.0	4.8	4.8
Professional	10.0	13.4	15.5	18.6	20.6	20.7	19.6	20.8	19.5	19.3
University Press	0.7	1.3	1.0	1.6	1.8	1.8	1.7	1.6	1.7	1.7
Primary Text	20.7	15.1	13.6	13.3	13.1	14.8	13.0	15.7	15.5	15.2
College Text	8.8	13.5	14.3	14.0	12.4	13.3	13.0	13.1	14.8	15.7
Subscription Ref.	24.7	6.8	4.3	3.4	3.6	3.7	3.3	3.3	3.0	3.0
Book Clubs	10.5	8.2	7.4	4.0	5.5	5.7	5.2	5.2	5.6	5.6
Other	2.2	14.0	3.8	4.4	0.0	0.1	2.3	2.2	2.3	0.0
Total U.S. Rev. ($ mil)	929	3,603	8,259	17,354	18,811	20,056	22,486	24,137	26,336	27,056

Sources: Data for 1993–1997 from Greco, Albert. Data for 1997 to 2003 from Association of American Publishers, Industry Statistics at www.publishers.org. Morgan Stanley Equity Research North America, *The Publishing Handbook, December 2003*, December 3, 2003.

channels of mass distribution of books: chains, superstores, and online retailing. This change made book purchasing easier and more convenient. Further, inexpensive hardware and software lowered the barriers to entry in the publishing industry, ushering in a wave of small, independent, and self-published titles.[32] And the U.S. population grew and educational levels increased. Total revenues rose from $3.6 billion in 1976 to $18.8 billion in 1995 to $27 billion in 2004 (see table 8.8).[33]

The greatest growth occurred in trade books (consumer-oriented books typically stocked by general bookstores) and professional books. Trade book sales grew from 12.7% of total book sales in 1958 to almost 30% in 1995, despite increasing TV viewership, but declined a bit thereafter. Professional publications doubled from 10% of book sales in 1958 to 19.3% in 2003 because of

growth in library acquisitions and in information-rich occupations. The share of professional books, too, has been stagnant since 1993.

The book publishing industry evolved into a three-tier industry consisting of a small group of large publishers, a second group of medium-sized houses, and thousands of small publishers. But in comparison to other media industries the combination of the top four firms is moderate: 31.3% in 2004. Tables 8.9 and 8.10 and figure 8.3 contain total book revenues and market share information of the major publishers.

Bertelsmann (Random House) is the largest trade book publisher (general audience books typically sold in bookstores). Its principal imprints include Alfred A. Knopf, Anchor, Ballantine, Bantam, Crown, Delacorte, Dell, Doubleday, Fawcett, Fodor's, Pantheon, and Random House.

Table 8.9 Book Publishing (Revenues, $ Million)

Million $	1984	1988	1992	1996	2001	2004	2006/7[d]
Pearson (Penguin/ Addison)	288	433	861	1,864	1,726[a]	1,588	1,308
McGraw Hill	464	576	600	999	1,393	1,826	2,225
Bertelsmann (Bantam Doubleday)	338	595	661	699	1,658	1,456	2,587
Random House	409	667	804	959	Bertelsmann		
Scholastic	210	209	353	655	1,284	1,617	216
Grolier	59	Hachette			Scholastic		
Reed Elsevier	121	115	129	150	467	1,100	1,025
News Corp (Harper Collins)		205	313	642	918	832	1,782
Holtzbrinck[b]				200	400	812	661
Viacom				863	766	669	1,293
Simon & Schuster	520	728	1,010	Viacom			
Reader's Digest/ (Ripplewood)	172	234	336	357	365	362	325
Lagardère/Hachette[c]		39	46	75	29	353	848
Time/Warner	64	115	136	200	312	Lagardère/ Ripplewood	
Other	5,614	8,890	12,104	11,969	13,794	15,526	10,730
Total U.S. Rev. ($ mil)	8,259	12,807	17,354	19,434	25,237	27,056	25,000

Sources: Figures represent all book sales, including trade, educational, and professional. Dessauer, John, "Book Industry Trends," Book Industry Study Group, 1980. Wharton, Bob, "Book Industry Trends," Book Industry Study Group, 2000. Company figures are from Simba Information, "Profit Margins Up for Leading Consumer Publishers in Fiscal 2000," *Book Publishing Report*, August 28, 2000. Simba Information, "Book Revenues Grew 3.9% for 20 Largest US Consumer Publishers in 1999," *Book Publishing Report*, June 26, 2000. Simba Information, "Big Winners and Losers as Publishers' Profitability Varied in 2000," *Book Publishing Report*, April 30, 2001. Simba Information, "Revenues of 20 Largest Consumer Book Publishers Rise in 1997," *Book Publishing Report*, August 3, 1998. Greco, Albert, "Market Concentration Levels in the U.S. Consumer Book Industry: 1995–1996," in *Journal of Cultural Economics*, 24, 321–336, 2000. Greco, Albert, "The Impact of Horizontal Mergers and Acquisitions on Corporate Concentration in the U.S. Book Publishing Industry: 1989–1994," *The Journal of Media Economics*, 12(3), 165–180. Additional data are from company annual reports and SEC filings.

[a] The average of 2000 and 2004 figures.
[b] Holtzbrinck data point for 2001 extrapolated. Ipsos Research, 2005.
[c] In 2006, Time Warner sold the Time Warner Book Group to French publisher Hachette Livre, of the Lagardère group.
[d] 2006/7 revenues derived from Table 8.10.

But it has no presence in the large educational and professional book markets. Scholastic became one of the world's leading children's book publishers, capturing 5.2% of the overall book market in 2004. Pearson and McGraw-Hill are major participants in the educational, professional, and textbook markets. Pearson acquired the Putnam Berkley Group in 1996 from Seagram and parts of Simon & Schuster in 1997. Viacom (and subsequently CBS) owned, among others, the Free Press, Pocket Books, Scribner's, Simon & Schuster.

News Corp owns and HarperCollins and its numerous imprints such as Avon. The German book publishing group Holtzbrinck entered the U.S. market in 1985. Its holdings include U.S. publishers Bedford/St. Martin's, Henry Holt, Farrar, Straus and Giroux, and Macmillan. Thomson sold its in 2008 educational publishing to the private equity from Apax, which renamed it Cengage. It then bought the financial information firm Reuters (for $18.3 billion), renamed it Thomson Reuters. It was owned 53% by the Canadian Wood-bridge family.

Educational publishing is a fairly concentrated sector of the overall publishing industry because the publication of a textbook entails a long-term investment in marketing, text preparation,

Table 8.10 U.S. Book Publishing (Market Shares by Revenues)

	1984	1988	1992	1996	2001	2004	2006/7
Pearson (Penguin/Addison)	3.5	3.4	5.0	9.6	6.8	5.9	5.2
McGraw Hill	5.6	4.5	3.5	5.1	5.5	8.9	8.9[a]
Bertelsmann (Bantam Doubleday)	4.1	4.6	3.8	3.6	6.6	5.4	10.4
Random House	4.9	5.2	4.6	4.9	Bertelsmann		
Scholastic	2.5	1.6	2.0	3.4	5.1	6.0	0.9
Grolier	0.7	Hachette			Scholastic		
Reed Elsevier	1.5	0.9	0.7	0.8	1.9	4.1	4.1[a]
News Corp (Harper Collins)		1.6	1.8	3.3	3.6	3.1	7.1
Holtzbrinck					1.5	3.0	2.6
Viacom				4.4	3.0	2.5	5.2
Simon & Schuster	6.3	5.7	5.8	Viacom			
Reader's Digest (Ripplewood)	2.1	1.8	1.9	1.8	1.4	1.3	1.3[a]
Lagardère/Hachette		0.3	0.3	0.4	0.2	1.3	3.4
Time/Warner	0.8	0.9	0.8	1.0	1.2	Lagardère/ Ripplewood	
Other	68.0	69.4	69.7	61.6	62.0	57.4	50.9[b]
Total U.S. Rev. ($ mil)	8,259	12,807	17,354	19,434	25,237	27,056	25,000
C4	21.0	20.0	19.2	24.1	24.0	26.2	31.6
C8	30.5	28.5	28.5	36.2	34.0	38.8	47.1
HHI	139	123	119	203	180	225	337

Notes: Based on the preceding table. Data for 2007 from Book Publishing news.blogspot.com, "Arbor Books Helps Authors Rejected by Top Publishers," sept. 23, 2007.

[a] 2006/7 data estimated from 2004 figures

[b] Data for 'other' assumes its market share corresponds to that of the past decade.

materials, and research. Unlike other segments of the industry, such as trade books and mass paperbacks, educational publishing has high entry barriers for new companies because only those with strong finances and marketing organizations can afford these investments. Significant concentration exists in the educational sector, increased by Pearson's 1997 purchase of Simon & Schuster's educational division.

Pearson is the world's largest educational book publisher (Addison Wesley, Longman, Prentice Hall, Scott Foresman, Harcourt Education, and others) with titles in 27 languages in 55 countries. It is also a major publisher of children's books (Putnam, Futton, Dial) and of general books (Penguin). It also owns the *Financial Times*, half of *The Economist*, and business magazines in several major countries. Its particular strength is in educational books for K–12, college texts, and professional books (Scott Foresman, Prentice Hall, Addison Wesley, Longman, and Allyn & Bacon). It

is also the largest private educational testing company in America (40 million standardized tests) and a large provider of teacher and administrator travel programs and software. Pearson trains the teachers who use Pearson textbooks to prepare their students for Pearson tests.

In 2001, Reed Elsevier purchased Harcourt General, and Harcourt's higher education and corporate training businesses were sold to Thomson Education in order to ease antitrust concerns.[34] In 2007, it sold Harcourt to Pearson and to Riverdeep Houghton Mifflin. Reed Elsevier owns Academic Press, Holt, Rinehart & Winston, Butterworths, Lexis-Nexis, Matthew Bender, and others.

Four companies account for most textbooks—Pearson, Cengage, McGraw-Hill, and Reed Elsevier (table 8.11). This small group of firms had a share of 88.2% in 2006, up from 57.8% in 1984 (figure 8.4). Facing this tight group is a strong buyer power. In almost half of states,

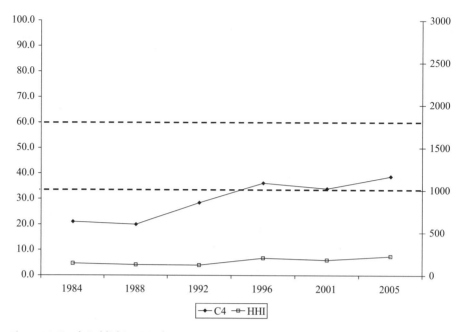

Figure 8.3 Book Publishing Market Concentration (U.S.)

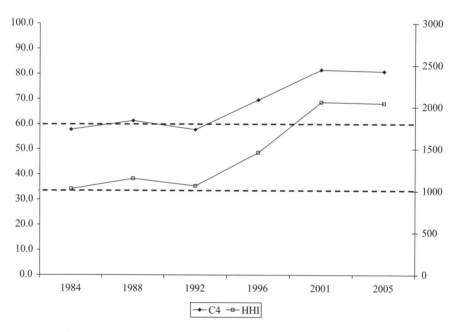

Figure 8.4 Educational Book Publishing: Concentration Trends

official textbook committees select the books acceptable for local school districts' choice. Three states account for a big share of such purchases— California, Texas, and Florida—and must be catered to in terms of content, thus resulting in pressure. Having to please these disparate states leads publishers to create texts with inoffensive blandness.

Table 8.11 Educational Books (Market Shares by Revenues)

	1980	1984	1988	1992	1996	1997[a]	2001	2004
Thomson Learning[b] (Cengage)	6.1	7.5	8.8	8.4	8.8	8.4	19.8	18.4
Houghton Mifflin[g]	8.8	9.5	10.2	10.9	9.3	10.0	8.8	7.6
Reed Elsevier	6.1	4.9	3.8	3.1	2.8	2.5	6.1[c]	7.9
Harcourt[d]	15.5	17.3	19.0	14.4	11.2	10.5	Reed Elsevier	
McGraw-Hill	18.7	18.8	19.0	18.0	18.6	17.2	18.2	20.7
Tribune Education	3.2	3.0	2.7	2.5	2.4	2.7	McGraw	
Scholastic	3.7	1.6	1.3	1.1	1.4	2.4	4.0	3.7
Grolier[e]/Lagardère	2.4	2.1	1.7	1.3	1.4	1.1	Scholastic	
Pearson Education[f]	5.5	6.2	6.8	13.3	22.3	21.4	34.7	33.8
Viacom					17.5	19.2	Pearson	
Simon & Schuster	12.0	12.2	13.2	12.0	Viacom			
Other	18.0	17.1	13.5	15.0	4.3	4.6	8.3	7.8
Total U.S. Revenue ($ mil)	1,904	2,469	3,034	4,165	5,373	6,534	7,652	8,820
C4	55.0	57.8	61.3	57.7	69.6	68.3	81.6	80.9
HHI	946	1,024	1,148	1,061	1,458	1,424	2,061	2,046

Sources: Figures from Dessauer, John, "Book Industry Trends," Book Industry Study Group, 1980. Wharton, Bob, "Book Industry Trends," Book Industry Study Group, 2000. Individual company figures are from annual reports, all converted to U.S. $ and derived from Hoover's Company Profiles. Total revenue 1997 and 2001 estimated based on a 8% annual growth.

[a] Carvajal, Doreen, "A Pot of Gold for Publishers of Textbooks." *New York Times,* May 26, 1998.

[b] In 2001, Thomson bought the higher education and corporate training businesses of Harcourt General from Reed Elsevier. In 2008 Thomson Learning was sold to the private equity partnership Apax, and renamed Cengage.

[c] Reed Elsevier sold the higher education and corporate training operations to Thomson Corporation in order to ease antitrust concerns.

[d] Reed Elsevier bought Harcourt in 2001 and sold some of its businesses (such as its higher education and corporate training operations) to Thomson in 2001 and 2007. It sold parts of Harcourt and Greenwood-Heinemann to Riverdeep in 2007 for $4 bil.

[e] Sold by Lagardère/Hachette (owner since 1988) to Scholastic in 2000 for $400 million.

[f] Based on Hoover's company profile. Assumes that 50% of total sales are in the United States, of which 62% is earned by Pearson. Viacom sold the educational division of Simon & Schuster to Pearson in 1998.

[g] Houghton Mifflin was acquired for $2.2 billion (including the assumption of $500 million in debt) by Vivendi Universal. In 2001 the company was sold to two investment firms: Thomas H. Lee and Bain. In 2006, it was acquired by Riverdeep for $3.36 bil., and its College Division sold to Cengage (Thomson Learning) for $750 mil.

Trade and paperback books are arguably the most influential segment of books. It has historically been a fairly unconcentrated segment, even though dominated by about a dozen publishers centered in New York. Several acquisitions, many by international media conglomerates, increased concentration somewhat. Table 8.12 shows concentration trends. Bertelsmann (of Germany) was the biggest trade paperback publisher in 2004 with a market share of about 16%. Following were Scholastic with a 12% market share, News Corp (originally Australia) and Pearson (United Kingdom), each with around 9%, and Viacom (7.0%).

The combined C4 rose from 29.4% in 1978 to 37.7% in 1984 to 40.2% in 1996 to 46.1% in 2004, mostly due to the mergers and acquisitions of the late 1990s. The concentration trends are shown in figure 8.5, showing a low concentration (2004 HHI of 693) with a fairly flat trend (a bit up after 1996, flat after 2001).[35]

Book Distribution

Books are distributed to consumers through a variety of channels: specialized and general retailers, college book stores, directly to the consumer (book clubs and mail order), and online services. They are beginning to be distributed electronically rather than physically, as electronic text or audio recordings. Table 8.13 provides the market shares of the major book distribution channels from 1980 to 2004.

The 1960s saw the emergence of large bookstore chains, which by the 1990s achieved dominance. The combined market share of the four largest retailers increased from 7% in 1963 to 11% in 1972, 25.7% in 1987, and 53% in 2004. The two largest retailers, Barnes & Noble and Borders, accounted for half of all retail book sales. Table 8.14 provides sales revenue data for bookstore chains.

Table 8.12 Trade and Paperback Book Publishing (Market Shares by Revenues)

Company	1978	1980	1984	1988	1992	1996	2001	2004	2007
Bertelsmann (incl. Bantam)	5.0	7.3	12.0	14.5	11.2	8.0	16.5	16.1	13.2
Random House	8.0	9.5	12.7	16.5	13.6	13.4	Bertelsmann		
Doubleday	2.2	2.5	3.2	Bertelsmann					
Scholastic	8.2	7.2	5.3	4.2	5.2	8.1	11.3	12.0	4.1
News Corp (Harper Collins)	6.2	5.9	5.3	5.0	5.3	9.0	10.2	9.2	10.2
Hearst	1.9	2.1	2.7	3.0	2.6	2.2	News Corp		
Pearson (Penguin USA)	1.3	2.3	4.2	5.6	5.2	9.3	10.6	8.8	10.6
Putnam (MCA/Seagram)	2.2	2.8	4.1	4.8	4.1	Pearson			
Viacom (Simon & Schuster)						8.6	4.2	7.4	7.6
Simon and Schuster	4.1	5.0	6.8	8.1	8.0	Viacom			
Holtzbrinck							2.9	3.0	2.4
Torstar (Harlequin)							5.7	6.0	
Reader's Digest/ (Ripplewood)	7.0	6.7	6.1	5.7	5.7	5.0	4.0	3.5	
Hachette Book/Lagerdère								3.9	5.4
Time Warner/Little Brown	2.2	2.3	2.4	2.5	2.3	2.8	3.6	Hachette	
Other	51.8	46.3	35.0	30.1	36.8	33.5	31.0	30.1	34.9
Total U.S. Revenue ($ mil)	1,720	2,106	3,217	4,043	5,914	7,159	8,657	9,044	9,577
C4	29.4	30.8	37.7	44.8	38.5	40.2	48.6	46.1	41.6
HHI	280	330	505	692	518	588	704	693	531

Sources: Data for 1995 from "The Media Nation: Publishing," *The Nation,* March 17, 1997, pp. 23–26. Data for other years are from company reports. Total revenues represent figures for trade and mass market paperbacks from Dessauer, John, "Book Industry Trends," Book Industry Study Group, 1980. Wharton, Bob, "Book Industry Trends," Book Industry Study Group, 2000. Trade book sales data for Reader's Digest and Scholastic for 1978 1987 are estimated from their historical average of 11.7% and 64.9% of total revenues, respectively. Some firm revenues are extrapolated for several intermediate years. 2007 data from Greco, Albert N., "The Market Demand for Books in the U.S. 2006–2011," Nov. 2008.

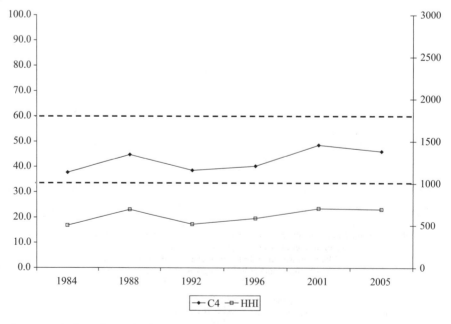

Figure 8.5 Trade and Paperback Book Publishing: Concentration Trends

Table 8.13 Sales by Distribution Channels ($ Millions)

		1980	1985	1989	1995	1997	1999	2000	2004
General Retail	$	1,682	3,621	4,401	6,523	6,868	7,873	7,801	8,682
	%	6	13	15.8	23.4	24.6	28.2	28	30.4
Online Retail	$					892	1,600	1,872	2,786
	%					4.5	6.9	7.8	9.8
College Stores	$	1,012	1,800	2,206	2,904	3,323	3,843	3,985	4,571
	%	3.6	6.5	7.9	10.4	11.9	13.8	14.3	16.0
Libraries	$	541	778	1,206	1,710	1,828	2,094	2,175	2,410
	%	1.9	2.8	4.3	6.1	6.6	7.5	7.8	8.4
Schools	$	1,158	1,638	2,192	2,770	3,314	3,781	4,218	5,159
	%	4.2	5.9	7.9	9.9	11.9	13.6	15.1	18.1
Direct	$	1,769	3,361	2,489	3,103	3,350	3,618	3,788	4,691
	%	6.3	12.1	8.9	11.1	12	13	13.6	16.4
Other	$	58	112	167	219	214	245	238	263
	%	0.2	0.4	0.6	0.8	0.8	0.9	0.9	0.9
Total (million $)		6,220	11,309	12,661	17,230	19,789	23,053	24,078	28,562

Sources: Data represent publishers' net sales. Dessauer, John, "Book Industry Trends," Book Industry Study Group, 1980. Wharton, Bob, "Book Industry Trends," Book Industry Study Group, 2000–2003. Data for 2004 from estimates by BISG, except for online retail, which are derived from table 8.14.

Table 8.14 Book Retailing (Market Shares by Revenues)

	1985	1987	1988	1992	1996	1997	1999	2000	2001	2004
Barnes and Noble	3.9	7.8	8.3	11.9	16.4	18.3	19.3	23.2	24.4	20.6
Borders[a]	8.1	14.8	14.6	14.3	15.4	15.4	21.4	21.2	19.8	16.5
Bookspan	5.1	9.3	9.2	9.0	9.7	9.7	13.5	14.5	16.2	13.5
Wal-Mart						2.0	4.0	6.0	7.0	7.5
Amazon									2.0	7.4
Costco						1.0	1.7	3.5	4.0	3.8
Books-a-Million			0.2	1.1	2.0	2.2	2.9	2.7	2.7	4.1
Crown	1.4	2.9	2.9	3.0	2.6	2.3	1.3	1.2	Books-a-Million	
Target							1.2	1.8	2.0	1.9
Lauriat's	0.5	0.6	0.6	0.5	0.8	0.9				
Other	81.0	64.6	64.2	60.2	53.1	48.2	34.7	25.9	21.9	20.0
Total U.S. Revenue ($ mil)	5,163	5,300	5,900	8,433	11,767	13,634	15,500	17,170	17,239	19,412
C4	18.5	34.8	35.0	38.2	44.1	45.7	58.2	64.9	67.4	58.1
HHI	109	376	376	438	612	682	1,043	1,258	1,330	1,025

Sources: Data for 1987 and 1991 (and all data on Lauriat's) are from Hoover's Company Profile Database, 1996. Data for 1994 and 1996–1997 (except Lauriat's) are from American Booksellers Association and Corporate Reports. Other sources Knowledge Industry Publications, White Plains, N.Y., 1978, pp.121–144. Dessauer, John, *Book Industry Trends,* Book Industry Study Group, Annual. Data for 1999 are from *Publishers Weekly,* New York; March 27, 2000; data for 2000 are from *Publishers Weekly,* New York; March 25, 2001. Data for total sales are from U.S. Retail Trade Surveys (inclusive of all "Book Store" SIC codes) and "Plunkett's Retail Industry Almanac," Plunkett Research, Ltd., 2001. Data for 2003 and 2004 are based on company revenues and Ipsos Book Trends. http://www.booksamillioninc.com/cgi-bin/news/general?ID=9851050727; http://www.fonerbooks.com/book-sale.htm

[a] In 1984, Kmart Corp. purchased Waldenbooks, and in 1992 it acquired Borders and formed the Borders-Walden Group. In 1995, the Borders-Walden Group was sold off again and renamed Borders Group, Inc.

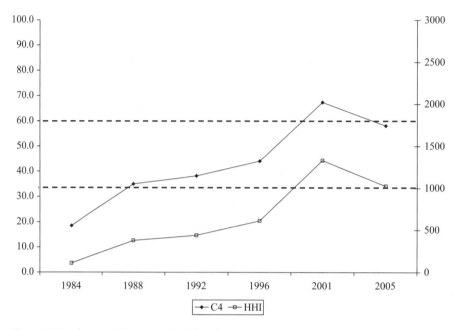

Figure 8.6 Bookstores: Concentration Trends

The bookstore retailing market increased significantly in concentration. Although in 1984 the mom-and-pop structure of the industry resulted in an HHI with a low value of 109, by 2004 it had become moderately concentrated with an HHI of 1,330. It declined a bit with the rise of online retailing (Amazon.com) and book sales by large general merchandisers (Wal-Mart and Costco) to 1048 in 2004, from a 3-firm structure in 2001 to a 5-firm structure in 2004 (figure 8.6).

Large chains have several advantages, including centralized buying, larger selection, bigger advertising budgets, better inventory and ordering systems, and the creation of community. Companies such as Barnes & Noble, and Borders/Waldenbooks have introduced "superstores" that encourage long visits and large purchases. They offer amenities such as coffee bars and reading areas, and events such as author appearances. The superstores offer selections of 50,000 to 175,000 titles, far greater than the 20,000 carried by the typical chain or independent bookseller. Barnes & Noble also entered book publishing itself through "house brands" of classics and of how-to books. About 4% of Barnes & Noble book sales are of its own published titles.

A different strategy is used by the general retailers such as Wal-Mart and Costco, which offer a limited selection at sharply discounted prices. Their market share, too, has risen significantly.

Perhaps most important, the increasing buying power of the bookstore chains has enabled them to negotiate substantial discounts from publishers. In 1996, the American Booksellers Association sued five large trade book publishers, accusing them of discriminatory pricing. Most of the publishers settled the suit and agreed to revise their pricing policies. Similarly, when in 1998 Barnes & Noble bought Ingram, the largest American book wholesale distributor, for $600 million, independent book retailers protested against the resultant reduction in their competitiveness, and the deal was dropped.

The role of small independent bookstores in the future may be to provide specialized "boutiques" with expert staff rather than to compete with the book chains' supermarket approach, the general retailers' traffic, and the online retailers convenience features.

Online Book Retailing

The face of the bookselling market changed significantly after 1995 as a result of the launch of Amazon.com, the first major electronic book retailer. Amazon provides a huge selection of books, often at lower prices than the traditional bookstores, and leads the online book retailing market. A number of rival online services followed, notably Barnesandnoble.com, and for a time Borders.com. These traditional "brick & mortar" book retailers remained a distant second to Amazon, however. Table 8.15 shows the online book retail market share and figure 8.7 shows the concentration trend for the online retail book industry. Strictly speaking, however, the online book retailers are not a separate market.

Since the late 1990s, Amazon.com has consistently been the market pioneer and leader in online book retailing, with a 53.5% share of the market in 1998, increasing to 77.1% in 2004.

Table 8.15 Online Book Retailing (Market Share by Revenues)

	1998	1999	2000	2001	2004	2007
Amazon.com	53.5	65.0	72.6	69.8	77.1	72.4
Borders.com[a]	0.4	1.1	1.4	Amazon		
BarnesandNoble.com	5.6	12.1	17.1	18.7	11.4	9.6
Fatbrain.com	0.7	1.3	BarnesandNoble.com			
eHarlequin				3.6	7.2	6.4
Other	39.8	20.5	8.8	11.5	11.5[b]	11.5
Total U.S. Revenue ($ mil)	1,100	1,600	1,872	1,875	2,786	3,530
C4	60.2	79.5	91.1	88.5	88.5	88.5
HHI	2,894	4,374	5,565	5,222	6,074	5,510

Sources: Individual company revenue data from SEC filings and company annual reports. Overall market data from Cross, Margaret, "Borders' online Traffic Is Borderline Disastrous," *Internet Retailer*, July, 1999, p. 12. Data for 2001 are extrapolated from "Amazon.com, Inc," Lehman Brothers, April 29, 2002 and Association of American Publishers. Market shares: Hoover's Company Profiles. Data for 2007 from "The New Media Record," July 8, 2008; http://newmediarecord.com/?p=5.

[a] After a 7 years partnership with Amazon.com, Borders.com returned in 2008 to the online sale of books.
[b] We assume "other" market share remaining at same level.

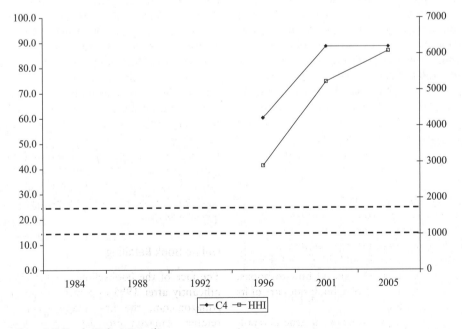

Figure 8.7 Book Online Retailing

Barnesandnoble.com remained a distant second, with just 11.4% of the market in 2004. In 2001, Amazon.com and Barnesandnoble.com acquired Borders.com and Fatbrain.com, respectively. The HHI in the online book retailing market, if looked at separately from other book retailing, increased from 2,894 in 1998 to 6,074 in 2003/2004, and the top two firms accounted for 89% (figure 8.7).

Conclusions

Book publishing developed in several stages. Changes in technology led to the separation of publishing and printing operations and created the modern industry structure in which several large publishers, mostly New York–based, competed with thousands of other smaller publishing houses. Concentration increased in the 1970s but to still low levels. The benefits of integration of publishing with entertainment and communications companies such as tie-ins, promotional channels, and the potential to benefit from video distribution, have proven elusive. Most concentrated is the educational textbook segment, which is dominated by three to four firms.

What has changed more than book publishers has been their distribution. Book retailing changed substantially with the growth of chains, superstores, and online retailing. The largest retailers possess advantages of resources, management, and volume. Concentration in retail distribution hence increased substantially. The use of the Internet helped increase overall sales of books, but it is also likely to lead to further concentration in book retailing, with an industry structure of these large chains, one online retailer, and maybe two general merchandisers.

MAGAZINES

History

The history of the American magazine goes back to 1741. Andrew Bradford issued the *American Magazine, or a Monthly View of the Political State of the British Colonies*, and Benjamin Franklin first published the *General Magazine and Historical Chronicle* three days later. The rival publications both originated in Philadelphia. Throughout the 1700s and 1800s, magazines were generally small and short-lived publications with circulations of 3,000 or fewer, targeted mainly at

educated readers. In the late 1800s, Congress provided for the low-cost (that is, subsidized) mailing of periodicals, and national magazines emerged. This provided manufacturers of consumer products with an effective national advertisement platform, the only one in existence. Because of these developments, magazine circulation rose. In 1895, *Munsey's Magazine* achieved a circulation of 500,000.[36] The growth in advertising revenues could sustain lower cover prices, which in turn yielded higher circulation figures.[37] Eventually, radio took away some of the national advertising. But this was nothing in comparison to the impact of TV, which largely replaced magazines as a vehicle for national mass advertising.

General-audience magazines such as *Life*, *Look*, and the *Saturday Evening Post* shut down entirely. Several major publishing firms and publications closed or merged. Major magazine publishers, such as Curtis and Crowell-Collier were absorbed by their competitors. The magazines that survived usually catered to specialized interests or to new preoccupations of the general audience.

Because of the economies of scale, early in the twentieth century the magazine industry as a whole experienced a relatively rapid increase in the levels of concentration. By the early 1920s, the industry was dominated by a few large publishers.[38] Despite the ever-increasing diversity of magazines, the post–World War II period also witnessed the formation of large magazine clusters, chiefly through mergers and acquisitions, which turned the magazine business into the complex pattern of enterprises that it still is today.[39]

Industry Structure

The magazine industry has traditionally been competitive, with fairly low entry barriers. In the period between 1954 and 1980, the number of periodicals doubled. In 1991 alone, there were 553 start-ups. From 1995 to 2005 there was an average of 17,726 magazine titles being published.[40] Figure 8.8 details the steady growth in the total number of titles compared to consumer-only magazines.

Between 1974 and 1984, magazine advertising revenues tripled in nominal terms from $1.4 billion to $4.7 billion.[41] They doubled in each of the next decades to $8.5 billion in 1994[42] and $18.3 billion in 2003.[43] This growth can be explained primarily by higher advertising rates (200% rise between

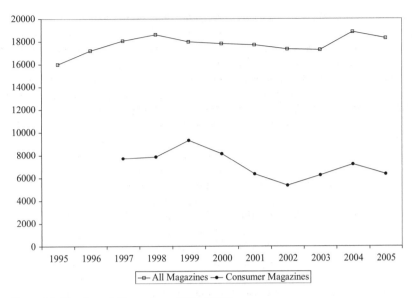

Figure 8.8 Number of Magazines, 1995–2005

1984 and 1998). The ratio of advertising to editorial pages since 1970 has been about 50%.[44] The share of magazine advertising in overall media advertising expenditures dropped from about 8% in 1950 to 5.5 % in 1984 to 5% in 2002.

The loss of advertising share led the magazine industry to develop new approaches. New periodicals have been increasingly directed to specialized audiences, thus enabling higher advertising CPMs and cover prices. Between the 1970s and 1990s, the magazine industry's subscription circulation revenues rose in importance from a third to approximately half of all magazine related revenues (advertising, newsstand sales, and circulation).[45]

The Internet added a new dimension to magazine publishing. It threatened advertising revenues, audience attention, and author commitment. Many magazines established their own Web sites, 1,750 in 1998 alone.[46] Some of these sites provide genuine content, sometimes free, sometimes on a subscription basis. There are also pure online magazines ("e-zines," or "webzines"), such as Salon or Slate; although it is interesting that some of these have subsequently added print versions, too.

Most online magazines include repurposed articles published in the print version, or variations thereof. Many also offer additional features, such as reader commentary sections, interaction with the magazine's writers or editorial staff, additional background information, audio and video clips, and archives. The extent to which consumers will switch from the print editions to online editions

remains to be seen. In 1996, the e-news "electronic newsstand" Web site listed over 2,000 e-magazines and webzines. By 2000, the Net.Journal Directory had already nearly 70,000 listings for more than 18,000 journal and newspaper titles, immediately viewable in full text, on hundreds of both free and fee-based Web sites. Barriers to entry in electronic publishing are low, but finding the revenue sources to support such publishing has proved difficult. The share of online magazines in overall magazine revenue is still small.

Concentration Trends

Group ownership of magazines offers several advantages. Better terms for printing and distribution can be negotiated. Advertising space and subscriptions can be marketed together, especially if the titles have some cross-appeal. There are fewer benefits on the editorial side, where separate staffs are usually required. But the advantages of scale cannot be very large beyond some point, because the periodical publishing industry has historically shown relatively less concentration of ownership than many other media industries. The C4 and HHI figures show that this market is unconcentrated, though less so over time.

The 1980s and 1990s constituted a period of heavy merger-and-acquisition activity. Between 1984 and 2001, at least 18 magazine groups were acquired by other media companies, not always with success.[47] Examples are Walt Disney Co.'s acquisition of Capital Cities/ABC's Fairchild Publications in 1995, subsequently sold to Advance (which also owns Condé Nast), and News Corps 1988 purchase of Triangle Publications and its *TV Guide*, also subsequently sold off. Table 8.16 details some of the largest mergers and acquisitions.

During the 1980s, foreign companies became active in the acquisition of U.S. magazines. The number of foreign companies with operations in the U.S. increased from one or two in the late 1970s to 20 or more in the late 1980s. In 1997 alone, four out of the 10 largest magazine deals involved a non-U.S. buyer. Major foreign owners of U.S. magazines and periodicals are Hachette, Bertelsmann, Reed Elsevier, and Holtzbrinck (table 8.16).

Table 8.16 Major Magazine Mergers and Acquisitions

Buyer	Merger/Acquisition	Price (in $ million)	Year
Advance	Condé Nast		1959
Gruner + Jahr (Bertelsmann, Germany)	Parent's Magazine		1978
Time Inc.	American Express Magazine Group	N/A	1984
CBS	Ziff-Davis consumer magazine	$363	1985
Holtzbrinck (Germany)	Scientific American	$53	1986
Diamandis	CBS Inc.'s magazine group	$680	1987
Hachette (France)	Diamandis Communications	$712	1988
Gruner + Jahr (Bertelsmann, Germany)	New York Times's Women's magazines		
News Corp	Triangle Publications	$3,000	1988
Elsevier (Netherlands)	Springer Publishing	$100	1988
Edgell (UK)	HBJ General Magazine Group	$334	1987
Walt Disney Co.	ABC's Fairchild Publications		1995
Reed Elsevier (Netherlands)	Disney's Chilton Business Group	$447	1997
Thomson Corp.	West Publishing Co.	$3,400	
Primedia	Cowles Business Media		1998
Primedia	Miramar Communications		1998
Advance/Condé Nast	Disney's Fairchild Publications	$650	1999
Gemstar[a]	News Corp (TV Guide)		1999
Time Warner	Times Mirror magazines	$475	2000
Advance Publications	New York Times Co. golfing magazines	$435	2001
Reader's Digest	Reiman Publications	$760	2002
Holtzbrinck (Germany)	Roaring Book Press		2004
Network Communications	Colorado Homes & Lifestyles and six other interior design magazines	$20	2005
Morningstar	Gruner + Jahr (Bertelsmann): Fast Company & Inc.	$35	2005
Meredith	Gruner + Jahr (Bertelsmann): Family Circle, Parents, Child, and Fitness.	$350	2005
Paste Magazine	Tracks Magazine	N/a	2005
InterMedia Partners	Primedia (20 magazines)		2006
Weider	Primedia (10 magazines)		2006
Ripplewood Holdings	Reader's Digest (14 magazines)	$2,400	2006
Advance Publications	Paul Allen (Sporting News)		2006
Clarity Partners/Modern Luxury	Shamrock (9 magazines)	~$300	2007
Bonnier	Time Inc. (18 magazines)	$200	2007
CanWest	New Republic		2007
Burkle (Source Interlink)	Primedia (78 magazines)	$1,200	2007
Macrovision	Gemstar	$2,800	2008
Open Gate Capital	TV Guide	$1.–	2008

Sources: Hoovers Company Records. "Advance Publications" http://proquest.umi.com/pqdweb?index=2&did=168171311&SrchMode=1&sid=4&Fmt=3&VInst=PROD&VType=PQD&RQT=309&VName=PQD&TS=1150835720&clientId=15403. "Mergers & Acquisitions". *Magazine Publishers of America.* 2006. Last accessed on 7 January 2008 at http://www.magazine.org/finance_and_operations/finance_operations_trends_and_magazine_handbook/15340.cfm.

[a] Gemstar owned 41% by News Corp

Table 8.17 and figure 8.9 show the concentration trends of the magazine industry from 1984 to 2004. Time Inc. has been the largest magazine company in the United States for a long time and steadily increased in market share throughout that period, reaching 14.3% of the total market in 2004. In 2007 it sold 18 magazines. Hearst, Advance (Newhouse), and Primedia market shares were in the 5–10% range. In 2007, Premedia sold 78 magazines to Source Interlink. The HHI values of market concentration were low but rising, growing from 146 in 1984 to 355 in 2001 to 347 in 2004.

Individual Magazines

The major concentration issue involves that of the parent companies. Another is that of the individual magazine titles. Here, the dominance of a few major magazine titles declined significantly between 1960 and 1981. Although in 1920 the five largest publications accounted for 56% of total magazine advertising revenues, by 1960, the four largest magazines accounted for only 20%, and by 1981, 15.5%. This share rose to 21.2% in 1992 and then declined to 14.9% in 2004. The share of the eight largest magazines was 25.8% in 2000 and 24.8% in 2004. There

Table 8.17 Magazine Publishers (Market Share by Revenue)

Company	1984	1988	1992	1996	2001	2004	2006
Time Warner[a]	9.0	9.3	9.8	11.1	14.0	14.3	13.3
Advance[b]		3.9	4.3	4.7	5.7	7.0	13.2
Hearst	2.2	3.2	5.2	5.2	6.1	6.0	8.2
Primedia[c]			0.9	2.5	4.5	3.4	Source Inter link
Reader's Digest[d]	1.3	3.1	3.4	3.3	2.2	2.6	
Meredith Corp[e]	2.3	2.6	2.6	2.3	2.1	2.6	2.4
Gruner & Jahr (Bertelsmann)[f]			3.0	3.0	2.7	2.5	
Thomson	3.8	3.2	3.8	3.8	2.5	2.5	Source Media
International Data Group	0.9	1.7	1.8	2.9	3.8	2.4	2.4
McGraw-Hill	2.1	2.2	2.2	1.9	2.7	2.1	3.1
Reed Elsevier		1.0	3.6	5.2	3.2	1.9	2.2
Ziff-Davis	0.5	1.2	1.5	2.0	1.6	0.9	
Lagardère/Hachette Filipacchi[g]			1.0	1.6	1.8	1.6	1.6[j]
Macrovision/Gemstar TV Guide[h]					2.0	1.9	
News Corp			0.7	0.9	Gemstar		
Triangle Publications	4.0	News Corp					
Others	70.1	63.7	53.6	47.5	45.1	49.1	50.6
Total U.S. Rev. ($ mil)[i]	8,191	11,681	14,284	21,498	29,479	31,611	
C4	21.0	19.7	23.1	26.3	30.2	30.7	38.2
C8	28.9	30.3	35.8	40.0	43.4	40.9	49.4
HHI	146	157	220	276	355	347	463

Sources: Revenues include advertising, subscriptions, and newsstand sales. *Sources:* "100 Leading Media Companies, 2000," at http://www.adage.com/page.cms?pageId=533; "100 Leading Media Companies, 1995," at http://www.adage.com/page.cms?pageId=871; company annual reports and SEC filings. Total market data are from "U.S. Industrial Outlook" for corresponding years. *TV Guide* was until 1988, when it was purchased by News Corp. Data for 2003 from "100 Leading Media Companies, 2003," owned by Triangle AdAge, August 2004. 2006 data from Seybold online, "Magazine Publishers," May 17, 2007. 2006 revenue from AdAge, "Top 25 Magazine Companies," 2007.

[a] Time Inc. sold 18 magazines to Bonnier in 2007.
[b] Advance bought Condé Nast in 1959 and Fairchild (from Disney) in 1999.
[c] Primedia, owned by the investment firm KKR, sold most of its magazines to Source Interlink in 2007.
[d] The Reader's Digest Association was acquired in 2006 by Ripplewood Holdings.
[e] Meredith Corp acquired in 2005 Bertelsmann's US women magazines.
[f] Bertelsmann sold its US magazines in 2005 to Meredith, Morningstar, and Diamandis.
[g] Lagardère controlled Hachette since 1981 and acquired Diamandis (formerly CBS Magazines) in 1988.
[h] In 1999, News Corp sold *TV Guide* to Gemstar, of which it owned 41%. Gemstar was sold in 2008 to Macrovision.
[i] Total revenue for each year of the U.S. magazine industry was estimated by adding advertising to estimated magazines sales revenues. The estimated advertising data source is Publishers Information Bureau. Sunday supplements are excluded from "magazines."
[j] 2006 revenue for Lagardère estimated from 2004 data.

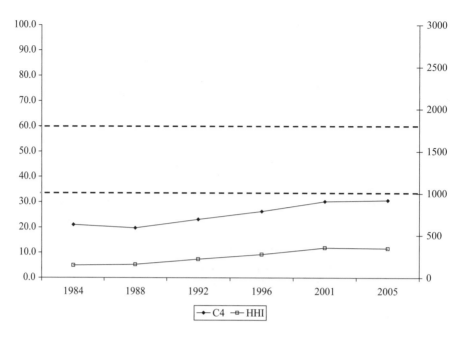

Figure 8.9 Magazine Publishing: Concentration Trend

was a high level of turnover among the top publications. Only three out of the top 10 magazines in 1960 were still among the top 10 in 1981, and although three out of the top five in 1981 remained among the top five in 2000, only one magazine among these, *Time*, even existed in 1961.

In 1997, the ten largest consumer magazines had a combined circulation and advertising revenue of $6.8 billion, which represented some 26% of the $25.8 billion total revenue of the top 300 magazines (table 8.18). In 1998, according to the industry's official Audit Bureau of Circulations, the 90 consumer magazines with a circulation of one million or more represented approximately 64% of total per issue circulation. In 2003 the top 88 magazines had circulations of greater than one million and their share was 66.4%.[48]

Similarly, with respect to circulation, the concentration of the top magazines increased from a C4 of 17.2% in 1984 to 17.8% in 1994, and then declined to 13.5% in 2000 (table 8.19). Of this, the bulk came from *Modern Maturity*, the membership magazine of the senior citizen organization AARP, which was riding favorable demographics. The share of the eight largest magazines declined from 25.3% to 19.1% between 1984 and 2000 but rose slightly in 2004 to 19.4%. However, unlike the market shares based on revenue, the five top magazines based on circulation shares remained the same between 1987 and 1997.

To conclude: in terms of the HHI and C4, the overall concentration of major magazine titles' market share, based on circulation (figure 8.10), has slightly and steadily decreased after 1987 and is quite low.

Academic Journals

Originally, academic journals were only published by learned societies and scientific associations, and commercial publishers played a relatively minor role. In the 1960s and 1970s, however, changes in the academic journal environment emerged: university enrollments and federal funding increased, and the pressure on faculty to publish and earn research support through grants grew as universities and faculty competed for status and prestige. As a result, the quantity of research grew beyond the capacity of the existing noncommercial scholarly publishing system, and commercial publishers stepped in to absorb an increasing share of academic journal publication. Further, the emergence of a core set of prestigious journals caught the attention of commercial publishers: these journals would have to be purchased by every research library worldwide, thereby creating a captive, constant, and price-inelastic customer base, and an unlimited supply of eager and free authors. Scholarly information therefore quickly became a valuable resource for commercial publishers.[49]

Table 8.18 Top Consumer Magazines (Market Share by Advertising Revenue)

	1981	1987	1991	1994	1997	2000	2004	2007
People	2.1	5.4	5.3	4.8	4.6	4.1	4.1	3.5
Time	4.3	5.8	5.0	4.4	4.2	3.7	3.6	1.9
Sports Illustrated	2.5	5.6	4.9	4.5	4.3	3.7	3.6	2.5
Better Homes & Gardens	1.9	2.5	2.4	2.6	3.0	2.7	3.6	3.2
Parade	2.8	3.5	5.9	5.6	4.1	3.3	3.3	2.5
Newsweek	3.5	4.2	3.5	3.3	3.2	2.5	2.3	1.6
Good Housekeeping	2.1	2.3	2.5	2.6	1.7	1.6	2.2	1.9
TV Guide[a]	4.9	5.9	4.3	4.6	3.2	2.5	2.1	0.8
Business Week	2.6	3.9	3.4	2.7	2.6	3.2	1.8	1.0
US News & World Report	1.7	1.9	2.6	2.6	1.9	1.3	1.1	1.0
C4	15.5	22.7	21.2	19.5	17.2	14.8	14.9	11.7
C8	24.8	36.9	34.9	32.5	29.1	25.8	24.8	18.1
HHI	91	190	174	153	116	90	86	47
Total U.S. Ad Rev. ($ mil)	$4,931	$5,626	$6,538	$8,505	$12,755	$17,665	$18,347	

Sources: Advertising Age, Standard & Poor's Industry Surveys, company reports. Market shares for 2004 were calculated using the Magazine Handbook 2004–2005 from www.magazine.org and "the 100 Leading Media Companies," August 2004, from AdAge. Magazine Publishers of America, www.magazine.org/advertising/revenue/by_mag_title_ytd/24510.aspx.

[a] TV Guide plummeted in circulation and ad revenues and was sold in 2008 for $1 to OpenGate Capital.

Table 8.19 U.S. Magazines (Market Shares based on Circulation)

	1984	1987	1994	2000	2004	2008
Modern Maturity/AARP The Magazine	0.3	4.7	6.4	5.5	6.4	6.3
Reader's Digest	5.8	4.8	4.5	3.3	2.9	2.7
TVGuide	5.5	5.1	4.2	2.6	2.6	0.9
Better Homes & Gardens	2.6	2.4	2.2	2.0	2.2	2.4
National Geographic	3.3	3.1	2.7	2.1	1.6	2.0
Good Housekeeping	1.7	1.5	1.5	1.2	1.3	1.2
Family Circle	2.3	1.8	1.5	1.3	1.2	1.0
Ladies' Home Journal	1.6	1.5	1.5	1.1	1.2	1.0
Woman's Day	2.1	1.6	1.4	1.1	1.2	1.0
Time	1.5	1.4	1.2	1.1	1.1	0.9
People	0.1	0.1	1.0	0.9	1.0	1.0
Sports Illustrated	0.9	0.9	1.0	0.8	0.9	0.9
Newsweek	1.0	0.9	1.0	0.8	0.9	0.7
McCall's	2.0	1.6	1.4	1.1	0.0	0.0
C4	17.2	17.7	17.8	13.5	14.1	13.5
C8	25.3	25.1	24.5	19.1	19.4	17.8
HHI	105	103	106	66	73	66
Total U.S. Circulation (000s)			363,566	378,919	352,601	377,515

Sources: Advertising Age, Magazine Publishers of America (MPA). Data for 2004 from *Media Week*, 15 (12), 38, March 21, 2005 (ISSN: 1055–176X). Circulation data for 2008 from Audit Bureau of Circulation, http://abca$3. accessabc.com/ecirc/magform.asp

The distribution of scholarly information has thus become a large and profitable industry. Though profits for scholarly journals are difficult to isolate, the margins for commercial scholarly publishers reportedly range up to 40%, far higher than the median for general publishing overall, which is around 5%.[50] This is a direct result of the uniqueness of scholarly publishing. Journal publishers' first-copy costs are relatively low because researchers create and contribute content for free in order to advance scientific knowledge, as well as their careers. They often even pay a submission fee for having the paper reviewed and a page charge for the actual production. Further, essentially the same group of scholars, more or less, also reviews the submissions, providing low-cost editorial functions.

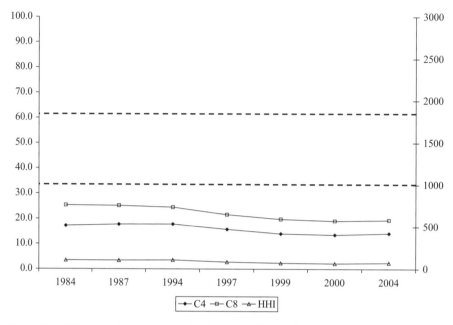

Figure 8.10 U.S. Magazine Concentration Based on Circulation

However, the average circulation of academic journals is low and shrinking as the number of journals has increased, which means that costs have to be recouped from a few hundred subscribers.

Concentration in the academic journal sector rose in the 1990s as a result of significant merger activity. British publisher Robert Maxwell, who had assembled Pergamon Press as one of the first major commercial scholarly publishing companies, was in financial distress and sold these publications in 1991 to Reed Elsevier. In 1996, the Thomson Corporation bought West Publishing, and then later sold its academic journals to Wolters Kluwer, which later bought Plenum Publishing in 1998. Also in 1998, Reed Elsevier, the number one company, tried to merge with Wolters Kluwer, the number two, but the deal was vetoed by antitrust regulators.[51] Reed Elsevier, however, won approval in 2001 to buy Harcourt General.

Market share data are difficult to define or measure in this segment. Publishers do not make their sales or circulation data freely available, and analysts must therefore estimate academic journal sales on the basis of published accounts.[52] There are also a very large number of small publishers of academic journals—learned societies, university presses, research institutes, and so forth—a situation that increases the difficulty of data collection. According to a 2001 report by Britain's Competition Commission, two commercial publishers (Reed Elsevier and Wolters Kluwer) published more than 500 journals. Seven other companies published 100 journals or more, and six others published at least 50 academic journals each. Small publishers, however, account for over three-fourths of all publishers, with 1,600 publishers producing only one journal each.[53]

As a result, the academic journal industry is less concentrated than generally thought, once one includes all publishers and not only the top commercial group (table 8.20). With 211 identified commercial publishers and thousands of noncommercial publishers in this sector, the top four publishers account for 26% of the market, with Reed Elsevier holding about 18%.[54] Overall concentrations (both C4 and HHI) have increased over the last two decades (figure 8.11) from a C4 of 18% to 26% and from an HHI of 110 to 343. But it must be understood that most journals do not compete with the plethora of other journals from numerous fields and subspecialties; at best, they compete with a small number of publications in the same specialty. Also, among the major five commercial publishers, two account for 84.2%.

Table 8.20 Academic Journals (Market Shares by Revenues)

Company	1984	1988	1992	1996	1998	2001	2004
Reed Elsevier	8.0	7.5	8.5	11.0	12.0	16.2	17.6
Pergamon Press		0.5	0.5	Reed Elsevier			
Harcourt General	5.0	6.0	6.5	6.0	6.0	Reed Elsevier	
(STM division)							
Times-Mirror	3.0	4.5	5.5	4.3	Harcourt		
Wolters Kluwer	2.0	3.0	4.5	5.0	6.0	6.0	5.4
Plenum Publishing	1.0	1.0	1.0	1.0	Wolters Kluwer		
Waverly	1.0	1.0	1.0	1.0	Wolters Kluwer		
Bertelsmann	1.0	1.0	1.0	1.0	2.0	2.0	1.8
Springer-Verlag	1.0	1.0	1.0	1.0	Bertelsmann		
J. Wiley & Sons	2.0	2.5	3.0	3.0	3.0	3.0	1.6
Blackwell		0.5	1.0	1.0	1.0	1.0	0.9
Others	76.0	71.5	66.6	65.7	70.0	71.8	72.7
Total U.S. Market	2,247	2,782	3,317	5,237	5,745	6,506	7,368
Total U.S. Rev. ($ mil)							
C4	18.0	21.0	25.0	26.3	27.0	27.2	26.4
HHI	110	132	179	215	230	312	347

Notes: Not all companies provide segregated revenue figures for scholarly publications. Some companies' academic journal revenues are estimated based on a percentage of overall net sales, as provided in Brendan Wyly's report: Wiley 47% of sales, Plenum 63%, Wolters Kluwer 14%, Bertelsmann 3%, and Reed Elsevier 17%. Data for 1997 are from Wyly, Brendan, "Competition in Scholarly Publishing? What Publisher Profits Reveal." The Association of Research Libraries. [http://www.arl.org/newsltr/200/wyly.html. 1998 data from Hipps, Kaylyn]. "Update on Scholarly Publisher Profits." *ARL Bimonthly Report*, 207 http://www.arl.org/newsltr/207/pubprofits.html. Other underlying revenue data are from annual reports and SEC filings. Total market revenues are from "Industry Trends, Size and Players in the STM Market." *Information About Information Briefing, Outsell, Inc.* 3(18), August 22, 2000. Springer-Verlag data are calculated at 3.1% of total worldwide revenues. All foreign currencies are converted to U.S.$ at the appropriate exchange rate for that year-end, and global revenues are adjusted to reflect the U.S. market only, with the U.S. share estimated as 59% based on Reed Elsevier's known share. Data for 2004 are estimated based on company revenues.

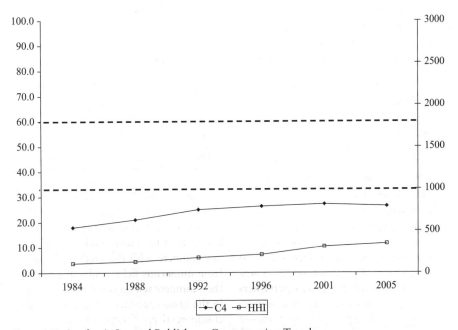

Figure 8.11 Academic Journal Publishers: Concentration Trends

Thus, the index measures understate actual concentration.

Local Magazines and Periodicals

This medium is somewhat hard to define. (For more details, see chapter 15.) Local periodicals include only those of general readership; special-audience local publications are not considered. The market share of the top magazine is quite high in top markets, overwhelming in medium markets, and nonexistent in small markets. Regional magazines have a bit less market power. There are also some hybrids, such as the *New Yorker*. (Only its New York City circulation is counted below as a local magazine.)

Table 8.21 shows, as one would expect, that local periodicals exist mostly in large cities only. The concentration of local periodicals slightly declines from a high HHI of 7,321 to a still-high 6,859 in 2001–2002.

Conclusions

Because of low entry barriers and the increasing prevalence of specialized publications, magazines have long been one of the least concentrated segments of the information industry, seen as a whole. In the era of multichannel media, magazines became increasingly specialized as a way to compete with the electronic mass media for advertisers. In the 1990s, new printing and distribution technology enabled magazine publishers to take a further step in this direction by creating customized editorial or regional sections for insertion into general interest magazines. The technological abilities to cheaply produce magazines, in either print or online form, have stimulated the growth in this sector. This growth, in turn, has led to the overall low concentration, in U.S. government terms, that typifies this market. However, the many specialty markets would show a much higher concentration.

Table 8.21 City Magazines and Publications (Local Concentration)

Magazines	1984	1988	1992	1996	2002	2006
	C1 Concentration					
C1 Large Cities	55.2	54.1	51.0	48.0	46.8	42.3
C1 Medium Cities	88.9	88.9	94.5	100	92.5	91.6
C1 Small Cities	70.2	68.1	68.5	68.9	69.5	89.6
Weighted Average	70	69	69.6	70.3	67.6	71.1
	C4 Concentration					
C4 Large Cities	98.9	98.4	98.0	97.7	97.4	98.0
C4 Medium Cities	100	100	100	100	100	100
C4 Small Cities	100	100	100	100	100	100
Weighted Average	99.6	99.3	99.2	99.1	98.9	99.2
	HHI Concentration					
HHI Large Cities	4,344	4,036	3,851	3,665	3,546	3,291
HHI Medium Cities	9,505	9,505	9,753	10,000	9,063	8,944
HHI Small Cities	9,145	9,125	9,131	9,137	9,143	8,533
Weighted Average	7,321	7,191	7,196	7,201	6,859	6,547
	Avg. Annual Rev. per Household					
Rev. Large Cities	34	38	40	43	48	50
Rev. Medium Cities	2	3	3	3	10	9
Rev. Small Cities	3	3	4	5	8	6

Sources: Gale Broadcasting & Publishing Directory, 1990, 1996, 2001 and 2007 editions.

Notes

1. Piers, Brendon. *The Life and Death of the Press Barons,* New York: Atheneum, 1983, pp. 100–101.
2. Journalism.org. "The State of the News Media 2006: An Annual Report on American Journalism." Number of Daily Newspapers. http://www.stateofthemedia.org/2006/chartland.asp?id=169&ct=line&dir=&sort=&col1_box=1&col2_box=1&col3_box=1&col4_box=1. "Total Paid Circulation." Newspaper Association of America. Naa.org. 2007. Accessed on January 4, 2007, from http://www.naa.org/TrendsandNumbers/Total-Paid-Circulation.aspx.
3. Newspaper Association of America. 2003. http://www.naa.org/info/facts04/circulation-daily.html.
4. Journalism.org. "The State of the News Media 2004: An Annual Report on American Journalism." Newspaper Ownership http://www.stateofthenewsmedia.org/chartland.asp?id=205&ct=pie&dir=&sort=&col2_box=1.
5. Hickey, Neil. "Money Lust." Columbia Journalism Review, July/August 1998. Part 5 of 6 http://archives.cjr.org/year/98/4/moneylust5.asp.
6. Newspaper Association of America. Daily Readership Trends: By Total Population. (1988–2005). http://www.naa.org/marketscope/pdfs/Daily_National_Top50_1998-2005.pdf.
7. Donald, William, and James Peters. "Standard and Poor's Industry Surveys: Publishing," March 9, 2006.
8. Newspaper Association of America. "2004 Facts About Newspapers: U.S. Advertising Expenditures—All Media" http://www.naa.org/info/facts04/expenditures-allmedia.html. "TNS Media Intelligence Reports U.S. Advertising Expenditures Decreased 0.3 Percent in First Quarter 2007." TNS Media Intelligence, June 5, 2007. Last accessed on 7 January 2008 at http://www.tns-mi.com/news/06052007.htm.
9. Newspaper Association of America. "2004 Facts About Newspapers. U.S. Daily Newspaper Advertising Expenditures." http://www.naa.org/info/facts04/expenditures-advertising.html. "Advertising Expenditures." Newspaper Association of America. NAA.org. June, 2006. Accessed on 4 January 2008 at http://www.naa.org/TrendsandNumbers/Advertising-Expenditures.aspx.
10. *Editor & Publisher International Yearbook 2001: The Encyclopedia of the Newspaper Industry.*
11. Busterna, J. C. "Trends in Daily Newspaper Ownership." *Journalism Quarterly,* Winter 1988, pp. 831–838.
12. Busterna, J. C. "Trends in Daily Newspaper Ownership." *Journalism Quarterly,* Winter 1988, pp. 831–838.
13. Duwadi, Kiran, Scott Roberts, and Andrew Wise. "Media Ownership Study Two: Ownership Structure and Robustness of Media." Fcc.gov. Last accessed on 8 Jan. 2008 at http://hraunfoss.fcc.gov/edocs_public/attachmatch/DA-07–3470A3.pdf.
14. Donald, William H. "Publishing: Industry Profile." *Standard & Poor's Industry Surveys,* May 3, 2001.
15. Morton, John. "Farewell to More Family Dynasties." *American Journalism Review,* October 1995, p. 68.
16. Herrick, Dennis F. *Media Management in the Age of Giants,* Ames: Iowa State University Press, 2003.
17. Herrick. *Media Management in the Age of Giants,"* pp. 292–293.
18. McClatchy bought all 32 Knight-Ridder papers and kept 20, including the *Miami Herald* and the *Charlotte Observer,* but sold the *Philadelphia Inquirer* and the *San Jose Mercury News.*
19. Busterna, J. "Trends," pp.831–838; 1994 figure from Newspaper Association of America.
20. Lacy, Stephen, and Todd F. Simon. *The Economics and Regulation of United States Newspapers,* New Jersey: Ablex, 1993, p. 10.
21. Rosse, James N. "The Evolution of One Newspaper Cities," Federal Trade Commission, *Proceedings of the Symposium on Media Concentration,* vol. 2. Washington, D.C.: Government Printing Office, 1979, pp. 429–471.
22. Gustaffson, K. E. "The Circulation Spiral and the Principle of Household Coverage." *Scandinavian Economic History Review,* 1978, 26, pp. 1–14.
23. Dertouzous, J. N, and W. B. Trautman. "Economic Effects of Media Concentration: Estimates from a Model of the Newspaper Firm." *Journal of Industrial Economics,* 39, September 1990, p. 1.
24. Herrick. *Media Management in the Age of Giants,* p. 311.
25. Lacy, Stephen. "Effects of Group Ownership on Daily Newspaper Content." *Journal of Media Economics,* Spring 1991, pp. 38, 43. Source: Litman, Barry R., and Janet Bridges, "An Economic Analysis of Daily Newspaper Performance." *Newspaper Research Journal,* 7, Spring 1986, pp. 9–26.
26. Lacy. "Effects of Group Ownership on Daily Newspaper Content," p. 40.
27. Noble Jr. Kendrick. "Book Publishing," in *Who Owns the Media?* Compaine, Benjamin, ed. New York: Knowledge Industry Publications, 1982.
28. Shove, Raymond Howard. *Cheap Book Production in the United States, 1870 to 1891.* Urbana: University of Illinois Library, 1937, pp. 98–105. Available at http://sdrc.lib.uiowa.edu/lucile/publishers/lovelljw/shove.htm.

29. Kurian, George Thomas. *The Directory of American Book Publishing: From Founding Fathers to Today's Conglomerates*, New York: Simon & Schuster, 1975.

30. Gurdon, Hugo. "American Critics Join in Attacks on 'Censorship': Hugo Gurdon Reports on the Growing Sense of Outrage at the Events at HarperCollins." *Daily Telegraph*, March 5, 1998.

31. *Bowker Annual 2004*, p. 508. The numbers for 2004 are Bowker's early estimates. Bowker, the source for these numbers, changed its cataloguing system in 1999, which resulted in a steep increase in the number of published titles.

32. U.S. Department of Commerce. "U.S. Industry & Trade Outlook 2000." New York: McGraw-Hill, 2000, pp. 25–73.

33. Revenue numbers excluded "standardized tests" as income.

34. Milliot, Jim. "From Harcourt to Reed to Thomson," *Publishers Weekly*, July 23, 2001, p. 18.

35. These numbers are slightly higher than those of Greco's for the period 1989–1994. Greco, Albert N. "The Impact of Horizontal Mergers and Acquisitions on Corporate Concentration in the U.S. Book Publishing Industry, 1989–1994." *Journal of Media Economics*, 12(3), pp. 172–173.

36. Recall the unfavorable comments about Frank Munsey quoted in chapter 1.

37. Tebbel, John, and Mary Ellen Zuckerman. *The Magazine in America, 1741–1990*. New York: Oxford University Press, 1991, pp. 140–141.

38. Part of the previous information on the history of the American magazine is based on Compaine, Benjamin, "Magazines," in *Who Owns the Media?* Compaine, Benjamin, ed. New York: Knowledge Industry Publications, 1982.

39. Tebbel, John, and Mary Ellen Zuckerman. *The Magazine in America 1741–1990*. New York: Oxford University Press, 1991, pp. 243–265.

40. *The Magazine Handbook 2006/2007*. http://www.magazine.org/content/Files/MPAHandbook06.pdf.

41. Publishers Information Bureau (PIB). Standard & Poor's Industry Surveys 1975–1984.

42. Publishers Information Bureau (PIB). Standard & Poor's Industry Surveys 1985–1995.

43. Magazine Publishers of America. The Magazine Handbook @ www.magazine.org, p. 34. This information is based on surveys by the Publishers Information Bureau, which tallies data from about 220 magazines and whose statistics are representative , not comprehensive.

44. Magazine Publishers of America. The Magazine Handbook @ www.magazine.org, p. 9.

45. Donaton, Scott. "Circulation Is Key Issue for 1990s." *Advertising Age*, October 15, 1995, p. 16.

46. Magazine Publisher's Association. FCB Media Report.: Questioning the Magazine Niche Myth. 1998.

47. Endicott, Craig, "The Advertising Age 100." *Advertising Age*, August 14, 1995. See also table 8.16.

48. The Magazine Handbook: A Comprehensive Guide for Advertisers, Advertising Agencies and Consumer Magazine Marketers, 2004/2005. MPA www.magazine.org.

49. Guedon, Jean-Claude. "Beyond Core Journals and Licenses: The Paths to Reform Scientific Publishing." *ARL Bimonthly Report* 218, October 2001.

50. "Scholars Under Siege," available at http://www.createchange.org/librarians/issues/silent.html.

51. Kirkpatrick, David. "Mergers Keep Pushing Up Journal Costs." *New York Times*, Nov. 3, 2000, p. C1.

52. Wyly, Brendan. "Competition in Scholarly Publishing? What Publisher Profits Reveal." The Association of Research Libraries. http://www.arl.org/newsltr/200/wyly.html.

53. "Reed Elsevier and Harcourt General, Inc: A Report on the Proposed Merger." Competition Commission [U.K.], July 2001. http://www.competition-commission.org.uk/reports/457reed.htm.

54. "Outsell Releases Annual Report on the $13.9 Billion STM Information Content Market." Burlingame, CA: Outsell, Inc. Nov. 19, 2001.

PART III

INFORMATION TECHNOLOGY

9

Consumer Electronics Media Devices

Part III deals, as part of the larger information sector, with the consumer electronics industry: the devices consumers use to receive, record, amplify, and display media information. Without them, electronic media would not exist. Together with content production and distribution systems, media devices form a triangle of media industries. They are the subject of this chapter.[1]

HISTORY

Consumer media electronics are everywhere (tables 9.1 and 9.2).

Although the consumer media electronics sector is novelty driven, it is not new. Thomas Edison was a pioneer. His contributions included the phonograph, the motion picture system, a microphone for the telephone, and in particular, electric power distribution, which enabled many subsequent applications. Beyond these inventions, Edison also pioneered the concept of the professional, ongoing research and development (R&D) laboratory to advance electronic devices.

After World War I, American consumer electronics firms became world leaders. General Electric (GE), Westinghouse, AT&T, and American Marconi, with U.S. government prodding, created the Radio Corporation of America (RCA) to compete with the British Marconi Company.[2] RCA, under its strong-willed leader, David Sarnoff,

soon weaned itself from its founding companies. By 1922, there were over 200 smaller U.S. radio set manufacturers. RCA, however, drove many of these firms out of business.

The Japanese Success

In the second half of the twentieth century, the consumer electronic sector became dominated by Japanese firms.[3] Partly as a result of supportive government policies, and partly due to an emerging extraordinary strength in R&D, manufacturing, and marketing, a vibrant industry emerged based on several large and diversified firms. By 1968, these firms dominated the U.S. radio market. Their success set the model for subsequent Japanese entry into other branches of the U.S. consumer electronics market. By 1974, not a single U.S. manufacturer of consumer radios, tape recorders, or monochrome television sets was left, and hardly any color TV production. American-owned firms were either put out of business or bought out by foreign firms, often mostly for the value of their brand names.

In the 1990s, Japan began to fall victim to its own success as the appreciation of the yen and increased labor cost reduced the price advantages of Japanese exports. One factor was the convergence of consumer electronics with computer and multimedia industries. This tempted American computer maker Apple to enter consumer electronics

Table 9.1 U.S. Household Penetration of Consumer Electronics (%)

Product	1984	1988	1992	2001	2005	2007
VCR Players	11	57	61	90	91	87
TV Sets	97	97	98	98	98	98
Cordless Phones				78	88	85
DVD Players				15	81	85
Answering Machines	4	19	45	74	75	
Computers	15	25	33	56	73	81
Cellular Phones				52	71	78
Car CD Players				28	49	62
Portable CD Players		6	20	26	47	
Video Game Consoles	25	28	30	15	42	
DBS Equipment			2	16	25	
MP3 Players				N/A	15	76
Digital Cameras					57	67
Camcorders				39		62

Sources: Numbers for 1984, 1988, and 1992 from a graph in Schement, Jorge Reina. "Wiring the Castle: Demography, Technology and the Transformation of the American Home." 6 June 2006. <http://web.mit.edu/comm-forum/forums/Schement%20MIT%20 2006.pdf>. Data for 2004/2005 are 2005 where available.
Sources: Deutsche Bank, "Specialty Hardlines," June 2001, Alex Brown, Inc., San Francisco, p. 26; Bear Stearns, "Consumer Electronics," April 17, 2001, p. 33. Steve Koenig, "CE Ownership," *Dealerscope,* June 2004, 46(6), 24. Steve Koenig, "U.S. Households Boast More CE Gear Than Ever," Dealerscope, June 2005, 47(6), 24.

Table 9.2 Adoption Rates of Selected Technologies by Consumers

New Product or Technology	Number of Years to 50% Penetration
Electricity	60
Telephone	70
Radio	9
B&W Television	8–9
Color Television	15
Cable Television	39
VCR	10
World Wide Web	7

Source: Bear Stearns, "*Consumer Electronics*," April 17, 2001, p. 32.

after 2000. The U.S. consumer electronics market became less concentrated. Table 9.3 shows the market shares of the major consumer electronics firms in the U.S. market from 1984 through 2004.[4]

In the 1980s, Sony, Matsushita, and Philips captured market share from RCA and Zenith. Overall concentration first increased but then declined in the 1990s as a result of the successful entrance of Korean firms (Samsung and LG Electronics) and the emergence of low-cost start-up firms from China.

Consumer media electronics comprise distinct submarkets. Between 1984 and 2001, the size of the overall U.S. consumer electronics market, narrowly defined to exclude home office, grew from $16 billion to $63 billion though they still constitute the largest submarket of the consumer electronic industry. TV sets declined from 49% of consumer electronics sales in 1984 to 19% in 2001. Home audio equipment declined from 12% to 7%. New product categories such as camcorders, home satellite receivers, and DVD players became important.

Television Sets

The first public demonstration of television occurred in 1926 in London, by John Logie Baird. The first large-scale television service was offered in Berlin, Germany, for the 1936 Olympics and by the BBC in the same year. Television service in the United States began in 1939, though stations had been licensed earlier. World War II halted the advancement of television but it picked up promptly afterward. Between 1948 and 1958, the number of American households with televisions grew from less than one million to 42 million.[5] Color television sets were slow to catch on—*Time* magazine declared them the "greatest industrial flop of 1956"—but steadily replaced the monochrome TV set.

Most American television makers were acquired by foreign companies. In 1974 alone, Matsushita (Japan) took over Motorola's color

Table 9.3 U.S. Consumer Electronics (Overall Market Shares by Revenues)

	1984	1988	1992	1996	2001	2004
Sony	7.1	10.5	15.8	17.2	22.1	21.0
Matsushita/Panasonic[a]	9.1	12.3	8.0	8.7	7.0	9.8
Sanyo	1.7	1.4	1.2	1.3	3.1	4.8
Philips[b]	8.8	11.9	7.7	8.4	6.7	9.5
LG Industries	1.7	5.1	5.0	4.9	6.3	8.9
Zenith Electronics	6.6	2.8	0.0	0.0	LG	
Toshiba	0.6	1.4	3.3	2.9	2.9	3.1
Thomson/TCL/Audiovox[c]	0.2	13.6	13.3	14.0	7.0	3.9
RCA	10.9	Thomson				
Tandy/RadioShack[d]	6.1	7.4	8.1	6.8	3.7	2.8
Samsung	0.3	1.2	0.9	1.0	1.1	2.7
Emerson[e]	0.0	1.9	1.5	1.3	0.7	0.5
Sharp	0.0	1.9	1.5	2.0	1.9	1.7
Hitachi	0.6	0.9	1.2	1.3	1.9	1.7
Others	46.6	27.7	32.6	30.3	35.7	29.5
Total U.S. Revenue ($ million)	18,167	21,571	26,053	30,756	32,284	33,888
C4	35.8	48.4	45.1	48.2	42.8	49.2
HHI	414	692	659	726	712	776

Notes: Market shares are calculated from revenues of the industries, discussed in this chapter, and by using geographic revenue distribution from Hoover's Company Profiles. Certain numbers were estimated or extrapolated. Total revenue is based on CITI research.

Sources: Hoover's Company Profiles; eBrain Market Research, *Electronic Market Share Data Book,* 1985, 1989, 1993, 1997, 2001, and 2002.

[a] In 2008, a Matsushita renamed itself Panasonic, and acquired Sanyo.
[b] Many of Philips' products are made by Funai of Japan.
[c] After 2004, Thomson transferred its TV business to the Chinese firm TCL; in 2007, it sold most remaining non-European operations to Audiovox, an American Company.
[d] RadioShack Corp. sells many products manufactured for it as proprietary brands.
[e] Emerson has become primarily a brand licensed to Funai (Japan), Sablian (China), and for a time, Daewoo (Koea).

television division; Sanyo (Japan) bought Warwick Electronics, Sears' television supplier; and Philips (Netherlands) acquired Magnavox.[6] In 1996, a chapter in U.S. manufacturing history came to a close when the Korean firm LG Electronics acquired 55% of the near-bankrupt Zenith. Only the brand names of American companies live on: the GE and RCA names survive through Thomson and TCL, Emerson's through Daewoo and then Funai, and the Zenith brand through LG. Table 9.4 shows the U.S. market shares of color TV manufacturers (by manufacturer, not brand names).

In 2004, the market leaders were Matsushita, Sony, and Sanyo, each with about 12–15% of the market. They were followed by a second tier comprised of Thomson, Toshiba, Samsung, Sharp, and LG Electronics, each with about 5–10%. As the number of major firms increased, the HHI decreased from 1,108 in 1984 to 982 in 2004. Overall, the HHI has been fairly flat, declining in the 1980s, rising again in the 1990s, and declining again after 2000.

Unit sales dropped from 26.5 million in 1994 to 24 million in 1996 to 18.8 million in 2005, thus indicating market saturation.[7] Prices of the traditional and bulky cathode ray tube (CRT) sets plummeted. But sales of digital flat and large screen monitors raised revenues again as their prices declined and consumers upgraded. These screens require complex and costly manufacture, and even some of the largest Japanese manufacturers used screens made by the Korean firms Samsung and LG, or those of the Japanese Sharp. Hence, the market shares in the consumer market understate the underlying production shares of those three firms.

Home Video Equipment

The recording of video on magnetic tape was not feasible technically until 1959, when Ampex increased the relative speed of tape to recording head by mounting the tape heads on a rapidly spinning cylinder. Ampex and Sony marketed the first videotape recorders using this technology in 1961.[8]

Table 9.4 TV Set (Market Shares by Revenues)

	1984	1986	1988	1990	1992	1994	1996	2001	2004	
Matsushita/ Panasonic (Japan)	8.0	7.0	8.0	7.0	7.0	7.0	7.0	15.5	15.5	
JVC (Japan)						2.0	3.5	Matsushita		
Sanyo (Japan)	9.0	8.0	7.0	6.0	5.0	5.0	6.0	12.0	12.0	
Sony (Japan)	7.0	6.0	7.0	7.0	7.0	7.0	8.0	14.1	14.6	
Toshiba (Japan)	1.0	2.0	3.0	4.0	5.0	5.0	5.0	6.0	11.1	
Samsung (S. Korea)	1.0	2.0	2.0	2.0	2.0	2.0	3.0	3.6	9.9	
Philips (Netherlands)	7.0	5.0	6.0	8.0	9.0	12.0	13.0	17.0	8.5	
Thomson (France)			22.0	24.0	21.0	22.0	23.0	15.0	8.4	
GE (US)	8.0	27.0	Thomson							
RCA (US)	20.0	GE								
Sylvania (US)	4.0	4.0	3.0	3.0	2.0	Siemens				
Sharp (Japan)	2	3.0	4.0	5.0	6.0	6.0	5.0	4.9	6.0	
LG (S. Korea)	1.0	2.0	2.0	2.0	2.0	2.0	2.0	2.5	5.2	
Zenith (US)	19.0	16.0	13.0	12.0	10.0	10.0	12.0	LG		
Daewoo (S. Korea)						1.0	1.0			
Emerson (US)		2.0	3.0	4.0	4.0	4.0	3.0	1.0	1.0	
Hitachi (Japan)	2	3.0	3.0	3.0	2.0	2.0	2.0	1.0	1.0	
Mitsubishi (Japan)	2.0	3.0	4.0	4.0	3.0	3.0	3.0	1.0	1.0	
Mont. Ward (US)	3.0	3.0	3.0	2.0	2.0	2.0	1.0	Bankrupt		
Other	6.0	7.0	10.0	7.0	13.0	8.0	2.5	5.4	14.8	
Total U.S. Rev. ($ mil)	5,500	5,900	6,300	6,972	7,352	7,600	7,947	8,174	8,400	10
C4	56.0	58.0	50.0	51.0	47.0	51.0	56.0	61.6	53.2	
HHI	1,108	1,227	936	1,021	851	958	1,090	1,180	1,028	1

Notes: GE bought RCA in 1986 and merged the company into its consumer electronics business, keeping the RCA brand. Two years
GE sold its consumer electronics business to Thomson. After 2004, Thomas transferred TV operations to TCL (China) Emerson and P
branded TV sets are made by Funai.

Sources: Hoover's company profiles; 2004 data for Sony, Toshiba, Thomson, and Sylvania are from *New York Times*, Jan. 17th, 2004,
2004 market share for Samsung from http://www.eet.com/news/latest/showArticle.jhtml?articleID=169400408. *Business News Publishing*
Special Report from TableBase, April 2001, "2000–2001 Market Share Reports by Category." *TWICE* (This Week In Consumer Electro
January 8, 2002. 2008 data from The NPD Group Company reports; and TWICE (This Week In Consumer Electronics), July 21, 2008.

^A 2008 market shares for Emerson, Philips and Thomson extrapolated.

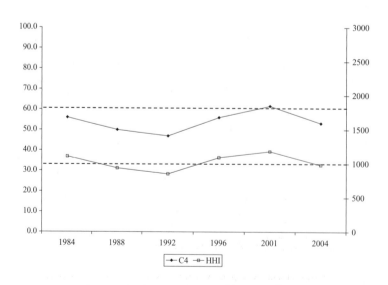

Figure 9.1 Television Sets: Concentration Trend

Because of their high price, recorders were mostly professional devices until the late 1970s. In 1975, Sony opened up the home market by introducing an affordable videocassette recorder (VCR), the Betamax. In 1977, Matsushita introduced a noncompatible format, the Video Home System (VHS), that doubled recording time.[9] Philips followed suit with its V2000. Although Beta had a superior picture quality, VHS ultimately emerged as the industry's consumer standard. Matsushita gained market leadership (27.5% in 2004), followed by Sony with 20%. Smaller providers included Philips, Thomson, and Sanyo. The VCR industry was highly competitive. The HHI was 1,194 in 1984, then dropped to 588 by 1996. The market volume, however, fell enormously from its high-flying days in the early 1980s. By 2001, the VCR market was saturated. Some suppliers left the U.S. market and the HHI rose by 2004 to a still moderate 1,329 (table 9.5, figure 9.2).

The DVD optical disc player format, an upgrade of CD optical storage technology, rapidly replaced VCR players. Each of two layers of one side of a DVD can store 4.5 gigabytes of data for a total of 18 gigabytes, compared to 700 megabytes of data for a CD. DVDs also transfer data faster. This enables 500 lines of resolution (twice that of VHS), multiple soundtracks, and additional material to be stored on a single disc.

DVDs quickly grew in penetration. A cumulative 18.5 million DVD players were sold in their first four years in the U.S. (1997–2001). Most of the suppliers were the traditional CE firms. But one newcomer, Apex, designed a low-cost player, had it manufactured in China, and successfully marketed these products to large consumer electronic retail chains. Apex gained over 15% of market share by units, although on only 7% of revenue.[10] It passed Sony in market share by units. Cyberhome, a German company, specialized in portable DVD players (table 9.6, figure 9.3).

Table 9.5 Video Cassettee Recorders (Market Shares by Revenues)

	1984	1988	1992	1996	2001	2004/5
Sony (Japan)	6.5	2.0	5.0	5.0	15.5	20.0
Matsushita (Panasonic, Quasar) (Japan)	24.0	13.2	14.5	8.0	20.5	27.5
JVC				6.0	7.0	Matsushita
Sanyo (Japan)	15.6	11.0	7.6	6.0	5.0	4.3
Philips (Magnavox, Sylvania) (Netherlands)	4.0	4.0	9.0	10.0	11.5	7.1
Thomson (GE, RCA) (France)		15.6	15.3	16.0	5.5	4.5
GE (U.S.)	16.0	Thomson				
RCA (U.S.)	5.0	GE				
Toshiba (Japan)	1.5	4.0	2.8	3.0	4.0	5.3
Symphonic/Funai (Japan)			2.0	3.0	4.0	5.3
Sharp (Japan)	3.5	7.5	5.8	4.0	4.5	4.5
Samsung (Korea)		2.5	2.5	4.0	2.5	1.6
Mitsubishi (Japan)	2.0	4.2	2.5	2.4	2.2	2.0
Hitachi (Japan)	3.8	2.0	2.4	3.0	1.0	0.3
Montgomery Ward (U.S.)	1.5	2.0	2.4	1.5	Bankruptcy	
LG (Korea)		4.2	3.0	2.0	Discontinued	
Daewoo (Korea)						0.5
Other	16.6	27.8	25.2	26.1	16.8	17.0
Total U.S. Rev. ($ mil)	3,585	2,905	2,947	2,767	1,058	757
C4	62.1	47.3	46.4	40.0	54.5	59.9
HHI	1,194	680	687	588	961	1,329

Notes: Assumes 55% growth per year between 1980 and 1984. Data for 2004 are extrapolated from growth percentages for the previous period.

Sources: Nielsen Media Research, "Nearly 84% of TV households now have VCRs," *Video Week,* February 10, 1997; "U.S. Video Cassette Recorder Manufacturer Shipments in Units for 1996 and 2001, with Top 12 Manufacturers Ranked by Percent Shipment Share," *Appliance Manufacturer,* Special Report: 2002 Market Profile, 50 (4), 1(4), April 2002. Manufacturer-shipment units given are for U.S.

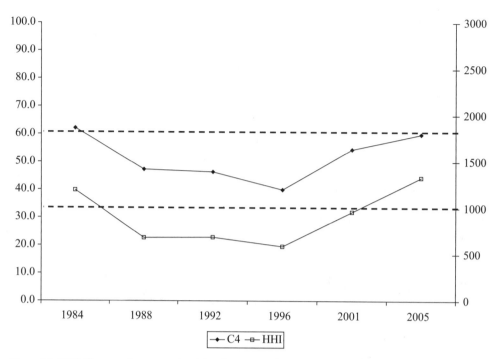

Figure 9.2 VCR Players: Concentration Trend

Table 9.6 DVD Players (Market Shares by Revenues)

	1997	1999	2000	2001	2004
Sony	29.0	28.1	25.5	21.3	11.9
Toshiba	20.0	14.5	10.7	7.9	7.8
Apex			4.1	7.3	7.3
Samsung		2.0	4.4	4.4	6.6
Philips/Magnavox		5.0	5.5	6.4	6.4
Thomson	8.0	8.3	8.7	5.5	5.5
Matsushita/Panasonic	14.0	17.0	12.0	12.7	5.1
JVC		2.3	2.5	Matsushita	
Cyberhome[a]					4.3
Pioneer		6.9	4.5	3.6	3.6
GE			4.1	3.4	3.4
Other	29.0	15.9	18.0	27.5	27.9
Total U.S. Rev (mil $)	171	1,099	1,713	2,697	1,800
C4	71.0	67.9	56.9	49.2	41.5
HHI	1,501	1,440	1,094	846	631

Source: New York Times, January 17, 2004, p. C7.

[a] Cyberhome, a German Company, produces a small-sized, portable DVD player successful in the United States through large retailess such as Wal Mart *NewYork Times,* January 17, 2005, p. C7, from NPD Group/NPD Techworld.

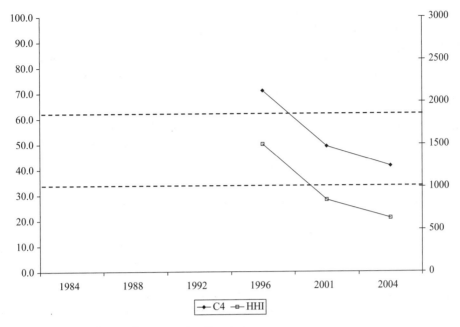

Figure 9.3 DVD Players: Concentration Trend

Conventional analog DVD players, too, soon moved onto the endangered list as high-definition optical discs using blue-light lasers were developed with still higher storage density. However, there was no industry agreement on standards. Two standards battled for supremacy, greatly delaying introduction: Blu-ray DVD by Sony, Philips, Hitachi, Panasonic, Pioneer, Sharp, Dell, HP, and Thomson. On the other side was the rival HD-DVD technology supported by Toshiba, NEC, Sanyo, RCA, Intel, and Microsoft. Support among content distributors was split.[11] But when Warner Bros. dropped HD-DVD in 2008, the battle was over and Toshiba conceded defeat. The market thereupon grew rapidly, while traditional DVD players could be bought for only $25.

In 2001, a new type of home video equipment emerged—the personal digital video recorder (PVR or DVR). A DVR is essentially a hard-disk drive connected to the television set that enables users to record, store, and time-shift favorite television shows. The first entrants were TiVo and ReplayTV, with Microsoft following. To avoid the commodization of a pure hardware device, these firms bundled the device with a subscription service for TV program listing.[12] They were using hardware manufactured by consumer electronics firms. Soon, DVRs were integrated into cable and satellite set-top boxes. They also became a standalone storage device without the service element (table 9.7).

Table 9.7 Digital Video Recorders (Market Shares by Revenues)

	2000	2001	2004
Philips	25.6	47.9	50.0
Sony	53.5	24.4	20.0
Matsushita/Panasonic		11.0	12.0
Thomson/RCA	20.8	10.1	10.0
Other	0.2	6.6	8.0
Total U.S. Rev. ($ mil)	44	54	65
C4	99.9	93.4	92.0
HHI	3,950	3,113	3,144

Sources: Revenues from *2002 CE STATS—Statistical Survey and Report, Dealer Scope,* Market share from "2000–2001. Market Share Reports by Category," *TWICE,* January 8, 2002. Revenue for 2004 is from *Electronic Market Data Book 2002,* eBrain Market Research, p. 12; Market share data for 2003/2004 estimated.

Camcorders

Camcorders combine the functions of a video camera and a videocassette recorder in a portable package. The popularity of camcorders in American households has steadily risen, from 26% in 1997 to 39% in 2001/2 and 62%.[13]

Several analog formats emerged for camcorders: Beta, VHS, VHS-C, and 8mm/HI8. In the late 1990s, digital formats were released for consumers. The most prevalent formats are Sony's Digital-8 format and the miniDV.

The market concentrated in the 1990s; C4 rose from 68% in 1990 to 83.4% in 1996 to 90% in 2001, with Sony leading at 55.6% and Matsushita's brands at 20.8%. After 2004, Sony's share dropped somewhat and the HHI concentration measure declined to a still-high 2,902 (table 9.8, figure 9.4).

Cable TV Consumer Equipment

Set-top boxes (STPs) connect to a television set for purposes of receiving cable television service. "Addressable" converters permit control of a subscriber's cable television services from a central

Table 9.8 Camcorder (Market Shares by Shipments)

	1984	1988	1992	1995	1996	2000	2001	2004
Sony	8.4	12.0	25.0	26.0	30.6	49.2	48.9	46.0
Matsushita/	24.0	22.9	23.0	30.0	29.1	25.5	27.3	26.8
Panasonic								
JVC					1.7	8.6	Matsushita	
Quasar						0.6	Matsushita	
Sanyo	5.0	9.0	7.0	3.0	2.4			
Canon	2.0	1.4	6.0	3.0	3.3	4.3	10.9	10.6
Samsung							0.9	10.5
Sharp	2.5	3.0	7.0	8.0	7.8	7.0	6.0	3.0
Thomson	22.0	17.5	13.0	19.0	15.9	3.4	3.3	2.0
Hitachi	4.2	4.0	3.0	3.0	2.5	0.5	0.4	0.4
Philips	6.0	6.5	4.0	4.0	3.2			
Others	25.9	23.7	12.0	4.0	3.5	0.9	2.3	0.7
Total U.S. Rev. ($ mil)	1,000	1,972	1,841	2,084	2,235	2,838	2,200	2,002
C4	60.4	61.4	68.0	83.0	83.4	90.3	93.1	93.9
HHI	1,219	1,125	1,482	2,044	2,134	3,225	3,303	3,070

Sources: Electronic Market Data Book 2002, eBrain Market Research, p. 12; *Dealerscope,* "2001 CE Stats," August 2001, p. 4.; 2001/2002 market shares are from *New York Times,* December 16, 2002, p. C18, from Gartner Dataquest. 2004 market shares are from *New York Times,* January 17, 2005, p. C7, from NPD Group/NPD Techworld.

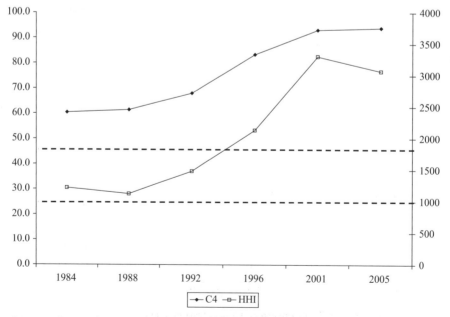

Figure 9.4 Camcorders: Concentration Trend

head end computer. This enables cable operators to charge access to those services without requiring access to the subscriber's premises. The marketing for STPs is not to consumers but to the decreasing number of cable operators who therefore exercise considerable monopsony power. Efforts by the FCC to enable consumers to select and buy STPs in the consumer electronics market have been resisted for years by the cable TV industry (table 9.9, figure 9.5).

Most set-top cable converters produced today for the U.S. market are digital and are part of infrastructure upgrades by the cable providers to compete better with DBS (satellite) and to offer new

Table 9.9 Set-Top Cable Converters (Market Share by Shipments)

	1984	1986	1988	1992	1996	2001	2004/5
Motorola[a]						43.4	38.3
General Instrument	36.0	38.0	44.0	56.0	50.0	Motorola	
Cisco/Scientific Atlanta[b]	28.0	26.0	24.0	22.0	28.0	27.2	34.0
Pace						7.7	6.4
Pioneer (Sharp)[c]	11.0	11.0	11.0	10.0	9.0	6.8	6.4
Panasonic/Matsushita		4.0	4.0				
Others	25.0	21.0	17.0	12.0	13.0	15.0	15.0
Total U.S. Rev. ($ mil)	1,200	1,006	996	985	1,195	1,450	1,610
C2	64.0	64.0	68.0	78.0	78.0	70.5	72.3
C4	79.0	79.0	83.0	86.0	93.0	85.0	85.0
HHI	2,000	2,257	2,649	3,720	3,365	2,724	2,700

Sources: Paul Kagan Associates, 1986 market revenue data. Warburg Dillion Reed, Telecom/Cable Equipment, Sept. 1, 1998. CS First Boston, General Instrument Equity Research Report, February 8, 1996. Prudential Financial: Scientific Atlanta Company Report, June 25, 2001. Data for 2003/2004 from "Demand for Cable Set-Top Boxes Remains Flat; Scientific-Atlanta Is Exception to Trend," *BroadcastEngineering*, Oct 13, 2003; "10.87 Mln Cable Set Top Boxes Sold in 2004," *ZDNet*, Nov. 23, 2004, available at http://blogs.zdnet.com/ITFacts/index.php?id=P2071.

[a] In 2000, Motorola bought General Instrument.
[b] Cisco purchased Scientific Atlanta in 2005 for $6.9 billion http://newsroom.cisco.com/dlls/2006/hd_022706.html.
[c] Sharp bought Pioneer in 2007.

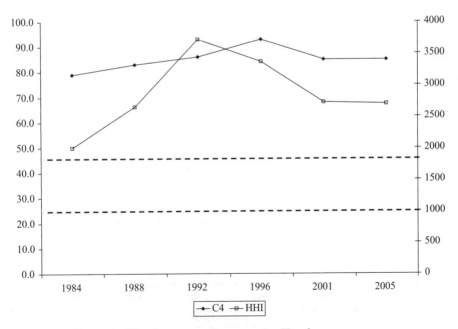

Figure 9.5 Cable TV Set-Top Converters: Concentration Trend

services such as high-speed Internet and telephony. This digitalization provided an opportunity for new entrants to challenge Cisco/Scientific-Atlanta and Motorola/General Instrument, the two dominant suppliers of analog set-top boxes.

Satellite Receivers

Direct-broadcast satellite television broadcasting became a viable alternative to already established cable television in the mid-1990s. The market driver was the emergence of high-power digital Ku-band broadcast satellites which can be received with a smaller and cheaper antenna than the older, low-power C-band satellite signals. In 2008, DirecTV had 20.1 million, and EchoStar had 13.8 million subscribers.[14]

The two major DBS service providers formed alliances with equipment manufacturers, often through outsourcing or rebranding. Thomson has the largest share among equipment manufacturers because it produces (under the RCA brand) much of the receiving equipment used by customers of DirecTV, the leading DBS service provider. Soon,

Hughes, owner of DirecTV, began to manufacture equipment and bundled it with its service. Similarly, EchoStar began distributing its own equipment. Under an outsourcing contract, Motorola gained market share, too, and became the number four supplier. But it is a tough market for third-party DTH equipment manufacturers. Thus, the market for DTH equipment in the United States is highly concentrated (table 9.10, figure 9.6).[15]

CD and MP3 Players

In 1983, Sony and Philips jointly introduced the compact disc (CD), a 5-inch diameter optical medium for high-fidelity, noise-free digital audio storage. The CD revitalized the recorded music and audio electronics industries. The CD player market has remained highly concentrated, with Sony producing 48% of all units sold in 2004, followed by RCA (Thomson) at 12% and Matsushita at 12% (table 9.11, figure 9.7).

Sony also pioneered the portable audio player with the release of its popular Walkman in 1979. Although the audiocassette had been around since

Table 9.10 DBS Equipment (Market Share by Shipments)

	1984	1988	1992	1995	1996	1999	2001	2004
News Corp								27.2
Hughes (DirectTV)	30.0	28.5	26.9	25.7	25.0	22.0	24.2	News Corp
Thomson (RCA)	5.0	17.8	30.6	32.2	31.8	28.3	22.4	22.5
EchoStar (Dish NET)					8.0	14.9	20.6	17.7
Motorola					16.0	14.6	16.3	16.3
General Instrument	20.0	24.6	28.0	31.4	Motorola			
Sony	5.0	5.4	6.0	6.6	6.8	6.4	3.0	3.0
Philips (Magnavox)						1.0	0.9	0.9
Matsushita JVC (Panasonic)						1.4	1.2	1.2
Samsung						0.1	0.2	0.2
Hitachi						0.1	0.1	0.1
Tandy (Radio Shack)	10.0	6.7	4.8	2.2	1.4	0.2	0.1	0.1
Others	30.0	17.0	3.7	1.9	11.0	11.0	11.0	11.0
Total U.S. Rev. ($ mil)	185	331	379	1,265	1,111	957	921	564
C2	50.0	53.1	58.6	63.6	56.8	50.4	46.7	49.6
C4	65.0	77.6	91.5	95.9	80.8	79.9	83.6	83.6
HHI	1,450	1,808	2,503	2,732	2,004	1,768	1,792	1,830

Notes: In 1985 General Motors acquired Hughes Space Electronics. GM then spun it off in 1997. News Corp acquired a 34% stake in DirecTV in 2003. Source: Frost & Sullivan, Mountain View, California, 1997, http://www.frost.com/prod/catlg.nsf/vwServices-BySector. Note: Revenue for 2004 is proportionate to growth in subscribership, as found in Broadcasting & Cable, 134(37), 1, September 13, 2004. News Corp sold its control in DirecTV to Liberty Media in 2007.

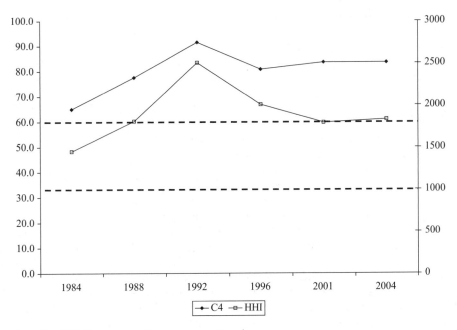

Figure 9.6 DBS Equipment: Concentration Trend

Table 9.11 CD Players Manufacturer (Market Share by Shipments)

	1984	1988	1990	1992	1995	1996	2001	2004
Sony	30.0	30.0	30.0	30.0	30.0	32.1	40.6	47.8
RCA (Thomson)		2.4	4.0	4.0	4.0	3.8	7.0	12.4
Matsushita (Panasonic) Technics	10.0	10.7	11.0	11.0	11.0	11.1	11.4	11.5
Yamaha		1.2	2.0	3.5	5.0	4.0	5.1	6.1
Philips (Magnavox)	20.0	8.6	7.0	5.0	3.0	2.8	2.2	5.2
Kenwood	5.0	5.0	5.0	6.5	8.0	7.0	5.5	3.3
JVC		3.6	6.0	7.0	8.0	7.0	2.3	3.2
Onkyo		1.2	2.0	3.0	4.0	3.0	2.7	2.4
Teac		1.2	2.0	1.8	1.6	1.6	1.3	1.1
Sharp	5.0	5.7	6.0	3.0				
Pioneer	10.0	10.0	10.0	11.5	13.0	11.0	6.7	4.6
Others	20.0	20.4	15	13.7	12.4	16.6	15.3	2.4
Total U.S. Rev. ($ mil)	200	430	661	2,597	4,532	4,667	4,802	4,887
C2	50.0	40.7	41.0	41.5	43.0	43.2	52.0	60.2
C4	70.0	59.3	58.0	59.5	62.0	61.2	65.7	77.8
HHI	1,550	1,269	1,295	1,319	1,387	1,422	1,947	2,684

Sources: Orlan, Amy. "The Tables are Turning for Compact Disc." *HFD: The Weekly Home Furnishings Newspaper,* April 2, 1984, p. 60; Market share data from *Appliance Magazine,* editorial staff; *U.S. Consumer Electronics Industry Today,* Consumer Electronics Manufacturers Association, 1998, p. 30; 1990 revenue is estimated from 1991 revenue, *U.S. Consumer Electronics Industry Today,* Consumer Electronics Manufacturers Association, 1995; 1984 revenue is from *Merchandising Monthly,* January 1985, p. 46; 1988 market share numbers are extrapolated from 1984–1990 numbers. In 2007 Sharp acquired Pioneer.

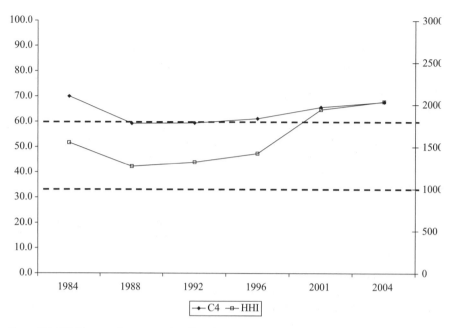

Figure 9.7 CD Players: Concentration Trend

1963, when Philips developed it, audiocassettes did not surpass the vinyl LP in sales until 1983 with the success of the Walkman and car stereos.[16] Sony's dominance continued, and its 2006 market share was almost four times than that of the next competitor. But the market as a whole declined with the advent of portable alternatives with better sound quality.

Audio continues to be a dynamic area, and new products have emerged, most notably the

Table 9.12 MP3 Player (Market Shares by Shipments)

	2000	2001	2002	2003	2004	2005	2006
Apple		2.3	15.7	15.0	58.6	65	75.6
HP[a]						5	9.7
Sandisk						4.7	
iRiver			5.3	5.4	6.2	4.6	
Creative Labs	12.2	6.4	14.2	13.9	3.2	3.2	4.3
Samsung	1.0	3.8	4.8	4.9		3.0	2.5
Rio	31.6	21.7	14.6	13.6	7.1		
RCA (Thomson)	5.1	6.3	7.3	6.8			
Digital-Way			1.6	1.7	4.4		
BenQ			7.8	7.6			
Archos			4.1	3.6			
Sony	16.3	18.3	1.1	1.1			1.9
Intel	3.0	0.6					
Compaq	8.2	1.5					
Iomega	1.0	1.6					
D-Link Systems	4.1	2.3					
Others	17.5	35.2	23.5	26.4	20.5	10.7	6.0
Total U.S. Rev. ($ mil)	80	100	484	997	2,053	4,230	5,400
C4	68.3	52.7	52.3	50.1	76.3	86.3	92.1
HHI	1,534	917	847	777	3,552	5,509	5,838

Source: Dealerscope, August 2005, Dealerscope Annual Statistical Survey and Report. 2006 Revenues from www. metrics2.com, "US consumer electronics Revenue will surpass $155 billion in 2007." 2006 Market Shares from ilounge. com, "ipod maintains 75.69. Share of US mp3 player market.

[a] HP briefly produced iPod-type MP3 players licensed from Apple.

portable MP3 player. It was introduced by the tiny computer equipment company Rio. Sony and Thomson followed with their own products. Sony, however, was hampered by the demands of its own music division for strong security against piracy. In 2001, Apple entered the market with the iPod and the music store iTunes and quickly became the dominant force in the market with a share of 35% in 2004, 65.8% in 2005 and 72.7% in 2007, according to Bloomberg Online. Through innovations such as the iPod Mini and Nano, and later the iPhone, Apple was able to keep charging a premium price (table 9.12, figure 9.8).

Audio Systems

Japanese firms have long dominated the U.S. radio industry. In 1951, Sony was the first Japanese firm to build transistor radios, based on semiconductor technology licensed from AT&T (which did not manufacture radios itself). The Japanese share of the U.S. radio market grew from 2% in 1955 to 93% in 1973.[17] Table 9.13 provides market shares for radio equipment. Table 9.14 expands this to include a broad set audio equipment.

As table 9.14 shows, in 2004 the market in the audio sector was concentrated; Sony accounted for 20% of the market, with 12% more than in

1984. Matsushita was second with 9.5%, followed by Sanyo (9.2%), Philips (7.9%), and Aiwa (7.9%). Overall concentration declined after 1988 to 768 in 2004 (see also figure 9.9).

Foreign firms dominate the overall market for stereo systems. Several small U.S. firms (for example, Bose) are prominent manufacturers of high-end audio components. However, such components account for an insignificant percentage of total stereo equipment sales.

Table 9.13 AM/FM Radio (Market Shares by Shipments)

Manufacturer	1984	1995	2000[a]
Sony	20	22	28
Matsushita	10	11	18
Pioneer	10	11	10
Kenwood	10	13.4	15
Philips	15	14.3	13
Others	35	56	16
U.S. Total Rev($ bil)	6	8.5	9.2
C4	55	60.7	74
HHI	925	1,110	1,602

Sources: Dealerscope, July 1995, p. 38. Kenwood and Philips 1995 market shares extrapolated.

[a]Euromonitor, "Audio Products in USA," July 2001 http://www.euromonitor.com.

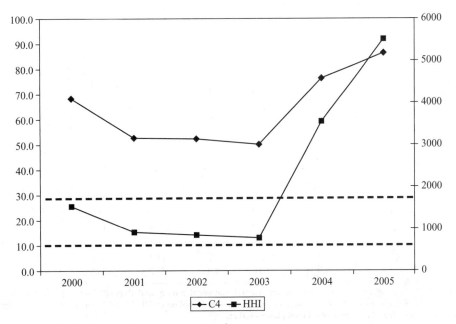

Figure 9.8 MP3 Players: Concentration Trend

Table 9.14 Consumer Audio Equipment, (Market Shares by Shipments)

	1984	1986	1988	1990	1992	1995	1996	2000	2001	2004
Sony	8.0	9.0	16.0	23.0	22.0	20.6	20.6	20.7	19.6	20.3
Aiwa[a]					4.0	5.0	5.2	6.2	7.5	Sony
Matsushita/Panasonic	14.0	13.8	13.6	13.5	9.7	9.0	8.5	6.3	8.5	7.8
JVC			12.0	9.0	9.1	4.8	4.0	0.7	Matsushita	
Sanyo[b]		10.0	9.7	9.3	8.9	8.3	8.4	8.8	8.8	8.7
Philips/Magnavox	10.3	7.0	3.6	2.7	2.7	2.5	3.2	6.2	7.5	5.6
Lennox Sound							1.3	6.3	5.8	4.5
Audiovox[c]						0.1	0.6	2.4	3.5	2.2
Thomson/RCA				Thomson						
RCA	10.6	11.0	8.0	9.0	10.0	11.8	10.9	7.5	5.6	8.0
GPX							0.6	3.1	4.2	2.6
Pioneer/Sharp	20.0	19.0	18.0	17.0	11.1	2.2	2.4	3.3	3.5	3.1
Mitsubishi					4.0	4.9	4.6	3.6	3.5	3.9
Kenwood	9.0	9.0	9.0	9.0	6.0	3.3	3.3	3.3	3.5	3.4
Toshiba					4.0	4.0	3.8	3.0	2.9	3.2
Bose	1.3	3.4	3.9	4.2	4.3	6.4	5.4	1.4	1.1	2.6
Yamaha						0.3	0.3	0.1	0.2	0.2
Zenith/LG Electronics						3.6	7.7			
Sylvania (Siemens)						4.4	3.5			
Emerson		4.3	3.8	3.0	2.3	2.2	1.8			
Others	26.8	13.6	2.5	0.3	1.9	6.6	3.9	17.1	14.3	17.6
Total U.S. Rev. ($ mil)	6,497	7,980	8,637	9,294	9,952	10,609	10,664	10,882	10,828	10,774
C3/4	44.6	53.8	59.6	62.8	52.8	49.7	48.4	43.3	44.4	44.7
C8					81.1	70.8	71.4	65.6	67.5	65.1
HHI	961	1,013	1,190	1,364	1,080	902	900	780	788	768

Sources: Dealerscope, "2002 CE Stats," 2000. Revenue is based on 24% growth estimate from previous two five-year periods; 1986 Sony market share is based on Sony Corporation, 10-K SEC Filing, 1985; 1985 revenues plus growth are estimated at 13% based on previous three years for year 1986. Also using 1985 audio segment percent of revenue at 23.8%, and U.S. sales share of 33.6% of revenues in 1985. Data for 2004 are extrapolated from 2001 growth rates.

[a] In 2002, Sony acquired the near-bankrupt Aiwa.
[b] In 2008, Panasonic acquired Sanyo.
[c] Audiovox acquired Thomson's audio operations in 2007.

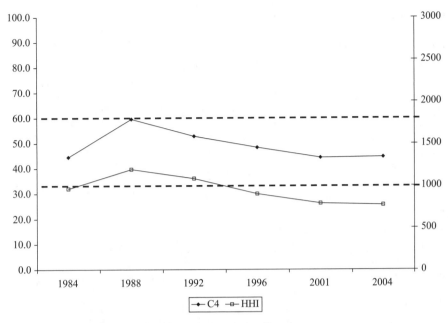

Figure 9.9 Audio Systems and Radios: Concentration Trend

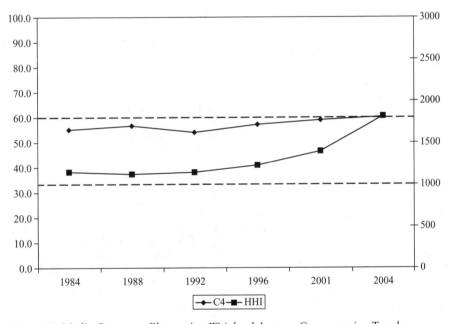

Figure 9.10 Media Consumer Electronics: Weighted Average Concentration Trend

CONCLUSION

The media consumer electronics industry is large and diverse in products. In 2004, its U.S. volume alone was $63 billion. Some firms are niche players, usually at the high-end of the price scale. But for the low and medium price ranges, the market is dominated by about 7–8 large, efficient firms with enormous economies of scale and scope. Several large firms were acquired or operated primarily as a brand. There is little middle ground in the industry. Average concentration is at the high end of moderate and was rising over the 20-year period, to a 2004 average weighted in C4 of 60.3% and an HHI of 1,815 (figure 9.10).

Sony is the largest consumer electronics firm in the U.S. market. Other Japanese firms are also strong, especially Matsushita/Panasonic. South Korean and Taiwanese firms have grown in importance. American firms survive in high-end segments such as speakers (Bose) or specialized products, or in nonconsumer products such as set-top boxes (Motorola/General Instrument). Although the rate of major business upheaval in the consumer electronics industry is slow, there is always a flurry of innovation, and countless new products are released annually.

The emergence of contract outsourcing manufacturers such as Flextronics and Solectron may lower entry barriers by giving smaller firms access to large, flexible manufacturing facilities with economies of scale. Even established giants such as Sony, Philips, and Motorola outsource the manufacturing of products to these firms. Computer makers Dell and Gateway embarked on this road after 2000, but their lack of success also pointed to the limits in this strategy. The best business model has been to build a strong brand name with a new product and then expand into multiple products while commanding a premium price.

Notes

1. We discuss related products—consumer computers, game consoles, and consumer telecom equipment—in separate chapters on computers and telecom.

2. As of 1921, General Electric owned 30.1% of RCA, Westinghouse 20.6%, AT&T 10.3%, United Fruit 4.1%, and others owned 34.9%. Gleason Archer, *Big Business and Radio*. New York: The American Historical Company, 1939, p. 8.

3. Curtis, Philip J., *The Fall of the U.S. Consumer Electronics Industry: An American Trade Tragedy*. Westport: Quorum, 1994, p. 194.

4. The definition of consumer electronics in table 9.4 is narrower than that in table 9.3, which also includes home security and accessories as well as batteries (not included in this book).

5. Kaufman Brothers, *Surfing with the Cable Guy*, November 21, 2000, p. 11.

6. *Matsushita Electric Industrial Co. v. Zenith Radio Corp.*, 475 U.S. 574 (1986).

7. "United States Color Television Shipments by Quarter in Units for 2003 and 2004, and forecast for 2005." *Appliance Design*, 52(12), December 8, 2004.

8. Mungwun, A. F., *Video Recording Technology: Its Impact on Media and Home Entertainment*. Hillsdale, NJ: Erlbaum, 1989, pp. 144–145.

9. Mungwun, A. F., "*Video Recording Technology: Its Impact on Media and Home Entertainment*." Hillsdale, NJ: Erlbaum, 1989, pp. 152–155.

10. Arensman, Russ, "Watch out Sony; Apex Already No. 1 in U.S. DVD Players, Is Taking Aim at TVs." *Business Trends*, May 1, 2002, p. 38.

11. Shankland, Stephen, "FAQ: HD-DVD vs. Blu-ray." 1 Oct. 2005. *CNET News*. July 17, 2006 http://news.com.com/FAQ+HD+DVD+vs.+Blu-ray/2100-1041_3-5886956.html.

12. "VCR's and Camcorders: Market Size." *Euromonitor*, July 2001.

13. Consumer Electronics Association, "Camcorder Popularity on the Rise," March 7, 2001, from http://www.ce.org.

14. Learmonth, Michael, "EchoStar Posts Loss, Marketing Costs Rise," Reuters, May 6, 2004 http://www.reuters.com/newsArticle.jhtml?type= topNews&storyID=5066135; SIA and Sky Research data as cited at "Facts & Figures," Satellite Broadcasting and Communications Association, SBCA.org.; Georg Mannes "DirecTV Posts Strong User Gain," *TheStreet.com*, August 5, 2004. Available at http://www.thestreet.com/_ yahoo/tech/georgemannes/10176654.html.

15. *Source:* Hoover's Company Profile.

16. Consumer Electronics Association of America, Digital American 2001 Report, "Hi Fi" as cited at http://www.ce.org.

17. Sobel, Robert, *RCA*. New York: Stein & Day, 1986, p. 211.

10

The Computer and Software Sector

INTRODUCTION

The computer has become the central device of the information age and of its media environment. For users it is the appliance that receives, accesses, and shares media information. For media providers, it is the facility that helps manage, collect, produce, and send out information streams. Computers have been at the core of the information sector, and they have penetrated devices and lifestyles.

The American information technology (IT) sector—hardware, software, and services—was $0.25 trillion in size in 2005. In 1984, it was $143 billion (in 2005 dollars). During these two decades, the hardware sector became less concentrated; the average HHI declined from 3,153 to 2,384. For computer software, average concentration decreased from 3,439 in 1984 to 1,963 in 2005 (figure 10.1).

Taken together, concentration for the entire IT sector—hardware and software—followed a U-shaped pattern, declining until about 1992, rising thereafter considerably, but lower in 2004 than two decades earlier. Average industry concentration dropped from 3,153 to 2,384. By the standards of the U.S. Justice Department, the aggregate IT sector is still highly concentrated.

This chapter is divided into sections on hardware and software. The hardware section discusses semiconductor components, computers, and peripherals. To readers more focused on media content, some of the discussion and differentiation might seem excessively detailed. But computers have increasingly become the gateway into the online information world. Film and music are uploaded from mainframes. Computer-like media devices are in every pocket. None of this would be possible without the basic building blocks—semiconductors, optical components, software, and mainframes. If the media sector is moving in the direction of the Internet, and if the Internet is spawned, sustained, and guided by IT developments, then the more classic media world cannot be set apart from IT.

The second reason for the inclusion of the computer sector is that it is a thesis of this book that with digital convergence, the dynamics of mass media increasingly converge to those of the information sector as a whole. Hence, to understand where media are going it is helpful to contrast and compare them with the other segments of the information sector. And in that sector, IT plays the central role. Once one engages in such comparison one cannot take shortcuts. The granularity of disaggregation has to correspond across sectors, or else a comparison becomes meaningless, since a wide aggregation (that is, a broad market definition) will lower each firm's market share and thus produce lower concentration numbers. This is a basic methodological point that must be kept in mind.

And the final reason, unapologetically, is that I find this sector endlessly fascinating and enormously

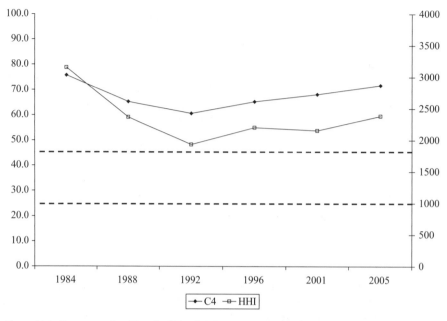

Figure 10.1 Concentration Trend of Total Information Technology Sector (HHI)

important. It has developed techniques to harness subatomic particles into purveyors and processors of information, and it is changing our lives, economies, media, and societies before our eyes.

COMPUTER HARDWARE:
COMPUTERS

Computer Industry Evolution: The Fall of IBM

In the 1980s, the computer hardware industry was completely transformed from being vertically integrated to specialized, from producing mainframes for businesses to making microcomputers for individuals, and from being dominated by one company, IBM, to a series of product-specific oligopolies served by a huge number of specialized firms.

IBM entered the 1980s dominating the computer industry. It had produced almost 72% of the installed base of U.S. computer equipment, more than twice the percentage of its competitors combined (table 10.1).

Until the 1980s, computer makers tended to be vertically integrated, that is, involved in most aspects of making and operating computers from

Table 10.1 U.S. Installed Computer Base in 1979 ($ Billion)

Company	$	%
IBM	37,651	71.6
Sperry Rand	3,510	6.7
Honeywell	3,281	6.2
Burroughs	3,242	6.2
Control Data	1,524	2.9
NCR	1,161	2.7
Amdahl	673	1.3
Digital Equipment	519	1.0
Xerox	397	0.8
Intel	358	0.7
Singer	150	0.3
Cray	74	0.2
Magnuson	15.2	0.03
Cambridge	1.3	0.002

Source: DeLamarter, Richard Thomas, *Big Blue: IBM's Use and Abuse of Power.* New York: Dodd, Mead, 1986, p. 232.

basic circuitry to components, peripheral equipment, operating software applications, software distribution, service, systems integration, and maintenance. Because the manufacturers used proprietary standards, they locked in customers to their software, peripherals, and service.

Table 10.2 U.S. Computer Equipment Market 1984–2004 (in $ million and %)

Item	Unit	1984	1988	1992	1996	2001	2004
Microcomputers	$	11,940	17,147	30,842	39,875	63,237	73,834
	%	30.7%	36.4%	59.4%	62.8%	78.1%	81.4%
Workstations	$	1,005	2,250	4,525	4,694	3,128	2,724
	%	2.6%	4.8%	8.7%	7.4%	3.9%	3.0%
Midrange Computers	$	10,400	14,183	8,575	7,800	7,949	8,101
	%	26.8%	30.1%	16.5%	12.3%	9.8%	8.9%
Mainframes	$	15,105	12,875	7,200	8,250	3,375	2,348
	%	38.9%	27.3%	13.9%	13.0%	4.2%	2.6%
Supercomputers	$	425	700	800	2,897	3,294	3,700
	%	1.1%	1.5%	1.5%	4.6%	4.1%	4.1%
Total U.S. Rev. ($ mil)	$	38,875	47,155	51,942	63,515	80,983	90,706

Sources: All data are compiled from the individual tables of this chapter. Microcomputer revenue for 2004 is extrapolated from 2005.

In 1981, IBM contributed to the end of its own dominance when it introduced its personal computer (PC) microcomputer. Forced to be on good behavior by a major federal antitrust challenge, IBM made two crucial strategic concessions in its PC. It designed it with a nonproprietary, open architecture, which made the PC easy to copy and ensured the compatibility of other manufacturers' products. And it farmed out the two key PC components—the microprocessor to Intel, and the operating system to Microsoft—without retaining exclusivity to the rights. IBM's failure to retain control over the essential elements of the PC expanded the hardware market to considerable competition. And the adoption of a ubiquitous operating system enabled software companies, at the time, to more easily develop and market new applications.

As computers evolved during the multichannel stage of media, product submarkets evolved, differentiated by operating power. The major categories within the general purpose computer industry, in the order of increasing computing power, are microcomputers, workstations, midranges, mainframes, and supercomputers.

Because of price declines, the overall computer equipment industry grew more slowly than is generally assumed. Its most dynamic segment, the microcomputer market, indeed exploded from under $1 billion in 1980 to $8 billion in 1984 to $18.4 billion in 1991. In the early 1990s, improvements in portability and the introduction of multimedia technology, such as CD-ROMs, expanded the market once again and spurred many households to buy or upgrade, causing microcomputer

revenues to more than double to $40 billion in 1995. The subsequent Internet revolution accelerated penetration of the consumer market, but by the late 1990s the PC industry had plateaued. The other main product line, mainframe computers, was in relatively constant decline from $15.5 billion in 1984 to $7 billion in 1995 to $4 billion by 2000 to less than $3 billion in 2003–2004. The shrinking market left IBM virtually in control of new mainframes by 2001. Table 10.2 charts the growth and decline of the various computer hardware submarkets since 1984.

The remainder of this section is divided into subsections on each of the computer segments, in order of calculating power.

Supercomputers

The first supercomputers were built in 1966 by Seymor Cray at Control Data Corporation (which later became the Ceridian Corporations). Cray started his own company, which dominated the field for a long time. Supercomputers are typically customized, state-of-the-art mainframes. They are generally used for large-scale scientific calculations and applications such as weather forecasting, code-breaking, nuclear engineering, and complex computer animation. Prices of supercomputers ranged from $350,000 to over $100 million.

Supercomputers tended to have special-purpose vector processors. These were often composed of multiple specialized processors that could perform certain calculations in parallel. A newer type of supercomputer, the massively parallel computer, uses a far larger number of standard (and thus far cheaper) microprocessors that function in parallel. Massively parallel computers are most effective for solving problems that can be broken down into discrete sections, and this technology simplifies editing.

For a long time, U.S. firms dominated the supercomputer market. Japanese firms rapidly gained market share for the fastest supercomputers in the 1990s. In 1996, 21 of the world's 50 fastest supercomputers were made in Japan. Even the U.S. government purchased its first Japanese-built system. This led to some alarm, and in 1997, the International Trade Commission in the United States levied punitive tariffs on a Japanese supplier for "dumping."

Owing to the limited customer base and the huge costs involved in development and production, manufacturing supercomputers is a risky and expensive proposition. In the early 1990s, the combination of these factors forced a number of U.S. firms out of the market. In 1996, Silicon Graphics purchased Cray, the leading supercomputer firm, but later sold it to Tera Computing. Concentration has historically been very high but has fallen as mainstream computing firms, including IBM, Sun, Hewlett-Packard (HP), and Compaq, introduced their own high-end machines. The HP-Compaq merger raised concentration again.

The title of most powerful supercomputer was captured by IBM, which reentered the market in 1997. Hitachi, NEC, SGI, and Fujitsu were competitors.[1] Since newer supercomputers derive their power not from a single, super-powerful processor but from thousands of off-the-shelf parallel RISC processors, with variants of UNIX and Linux as operating systems, the specialized hardware design expertise of a firm such as Cray grew to be less valuable. "Virtual supercomputers" were created by a "commodity clustering" of many PCs, workstations, and servers. Extreme clustering took place with the BOINC platform of over a million networked PCs, which jointly reached in 2007 a processing speed of 265 terra (that is, trillion) floating point operations (TFLOPS or "teraflops") for uses such as SETI@home, the search for extraterrestrial intelligence. It is a good example of the ability of small providers to cluster around integration in a nonprofit, volunteer fashion.

In 2002, the Japanese government financed the $350 million Earth Development (E-Simulator) supercomputer, a specialized clustered vector machine with a peak speed of 35.6 teraflops, built by NEC. Not to be outdone, IBM invested $100 million to build the fastest computer, code-named Blue Gene/L, with a speed of 12.3 teraflops achieved in 2004 and 280 teraflops in 2005, and with a sustaining speed of 70 teraflops. The U.S. government provided IBM with a $225 million contract for a massively parallel supercomputer for weather forecasting. IBM Roadrunner at Los Alamos National Labs reached a speed of 1.1 petaflops in 2008.

Although IBM dominates the special purpose high-performance computing market, HP, which acquired Convex in 1995 and then Compaq with its modest supercomputer line, is strong in the mini-supercomputer segment, which is much more affordable. Together, IBM and HP had a combined 79% of the top 500 supercomputers in the world. The market landscape has dramatically shifted from the days when Cray, Sun Microsystems, NEC, and others controlled the industry.[2]

Table 10.3 contains market share data for the leading supercomputer manufacturers. The market is highly concentrated, but less so than in the 1980s and 1990s. Market concentration is high, but declined in the early 1990s, together with Cray's dominance.

Mainframe Computers

From its beginning, the mainframe industry has been characterized by large, vertically integrated companies, high market-entry barriers, and proprietary systems. In the early stages of limited media, computers were synonymous with mainframes, there being no other type of general-purpose computer. Mainframes still can handle more and larger jobs than other computers. However, they are expensive and require substantial infrastructure. Networked workstations and PCs presented mainframes with substantial competition. In consequence, mainframes' share of aggregate computer hardware sales declined from 44% in 1984 to 19% in 1992 and 3.7% in 2004.

Although the mainframe market has been shrinking over time, it remains viable. Many large organizations have sunk large investments into proprietary systems and software that cannot easily be replaced. In addition, although mainframe hardware costs are high, the typical total cost of PC and workstation network computer power is higher still, per user or operation, especially if

Table 10.3 Supercomputers (Market Shares by Shipments)

Companies	1984	1987	1988	1992	1994	1996	2001	2004
Hewlett-Packard (Convex)			6.0	8.3	10.8	14.7	35.0	34.0
Compaq						10.0	HP	
IBM						14.0	16.0	28.0
Sun[a]						9.0	17.0	12.0
Cray/SGI/Tera	69.0	63.0	66.0	69.9	70.0	41.3	23.5	12.1
Fujitsu	1.0	15.0	12.0	15.3	14.0	8.0	4.0	
NEC		3.0	3.0	4.2	4.0	1.7	3.0	
Hitachi		5.0	5.0	2.3	1.0	1.0	1.0	
Control Data (ETA subsidiary/spin-off)		11.0						
Multiflow			7.6					
Others	30	3.0	0.4	0.0	0.2	0.4	0.5	13.9
Total U.S. Revenue ($ mil)	425	800	700	800	2,500	2,897	3,294	3,700
C4	70.0	94.0	91.6	97.7	98.8	80.0	91.5	86.1
HHI	4,762	4,349	4,628	5,212	5,230	2,368	2,348	2,088

Sources: Data are for technical high-performance systems that sell for $500,000 or more and represent global market shares. 1994 and 1996 HP figures are extrapolated from 1992 and 2000 figures. 2001 figures are from the companies' respective annual 10-k reports. Sun Microsystem's 2001 figure is from Runkel, Rebecca, "Sun Microsystems," Morgan Stanley, p. 28, March 27, 2001. In 1996 Silicon Graphics acquired Cray Research. In 2000 Tera Computer bought Cray Research from Silicon Graphics and changed its name to Cray. ETA, a unit of Control Data Corp., began shipping computers in 1986. See Sanger, David E., "A High-Tech Lead in Danger," *New York Times*, Dec. 19, 1988, p. A2. "Computers and Office Equipment," *Standard and Poor's Industry Survey*, Nov. 6, 1986, p. C80; Computers, *Standard and Poor's Industry Surveys*, Dec. 28, 1995, p. C92.; John Jones, "Server & Enterprise Hardware," Salomon Smith Barney, p. 88, May 24, 2001. Data for 2004 are from Cavalli, Mario. "HyperTransport Technology Consortium Report," July 8, 2005, HyperTransport Technology Consortium, May 31, 2006 http://www.hypertransport.org/docs/pres/ISC2005_WebReport.pdf. Cray's market share is calculated from the 2004 revenue figure (Cray.com); U.S. accounts for 68% and supercomputers account for 76% of total revenue (Hoover's Company Profile). Global revenue figures are from Morgan, Timothy Prickett, "HPC Server Market Explodes to $9.1 Billion in 2005," April 2006, ITJungle. May 31, 2006 http://www.itjungle.com/tlb/tlb040406-story08.html.: Strohmaier, Erich, "20 Years Supercomputer Market Analysis," May 2005. Lawrence Berkeley National Laboratory, 31 May 2006. http://amrit.ittc.ku.edu/tclark/class2005fall/eecs700/papers/strohmaierSC2005.pdf.

[a] Sun was acquired by Oracle in 2009.

application development and technical support is factored in. There will always be a need for the shared use of sophisticated applications on powerful equipment, as the Internet demonstrates with its portals, applications service providers, and e-commerce sites. These Internet mainframes are often called servers, though that term also encompasses computers of lesser power.

After eclipsing Univac's early lead, IBM has been the dominant mainframe marker, with its system/360 becoming the ubiquitous business machine. IBM's market share survived a dip in the late 1980s and grew from 76.8% in 1984 to 78% in 1996 to over 96% in 2004. Challenges to IBM in the late 1980s failed. Rivals experienced declining sales and profit margins, and were less able to absorb these losses than was IBM. The market structures became known as "IBM and the Seven Dwarfs" (Burroughs, Control Data, General

Electric, Honeywell, NCR, RCA/AT&T, and Univac.) Foreign entrants, equally unsuccessfull, were Siemens, ICL, and Groupe Bull. The Japanese firms Hitachi and Fujitsu developed small market niches, as did Bull, Unisys, and Hewlett-Packard. In addition, the shrinking mainframe market does not offer the opportunities for growth and profits that are present in more open, less expensive computer technology.

In consequence, the mainframe market has remained highly concentrated, with an HHI consistently above 5,000, rising to over 8,000—the most concentrated industry found in this entire analysis of the information sector (table 10.4, figure 10.3).

As shown in table 10.4, the mainframe market contracted sharply from 1987 to 2004, in both revenues and number of participants. As the market contracted, NEC abandoned the mainframe

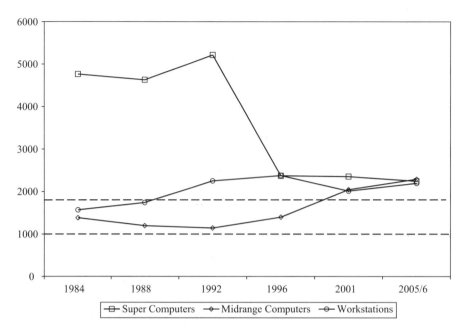

Figure 10.2 Computers (Supercomputers, Midrange, and Workstations): Concentration

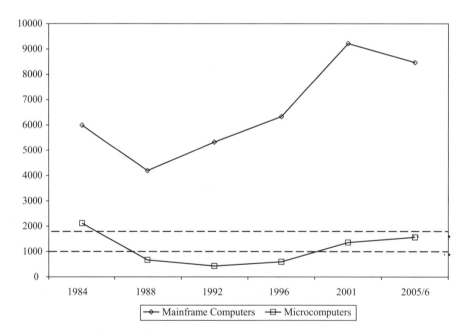

Figure 10.3 Mainframes and Microcomputers: Concentration

market. IBM's market share rose after 1994, when it introduced the faster, more efficient complementary metal oxide semiconductor (CMOS) S/390 mainframe with a 64-bit architecture, followed by its ZSeries and System Z9 servers. In the past, over 85% of all mainframe programs were written in COBOL, but Java, C, and C++ have gained share. Many mainframes are now running Linux. CMOS systems are built around arrays of mass-produced microprocessors. By 1996, there were only three

Table 10.4 Mainframe Manufacturers (Market Shares by Revenues)

Companies	1984	1987	1988	1992	1995	1996	1998	1999	2001	2005
IBM	76.8	71.0	62.7	71.4	80.0	78.0	73.0	79.0	96.0	92.0
Hitachi			9.0	8.0	7.0	13.5	20.0	13.0		
Fujitsu (Amdahl, ICL, Siemens)	5.0	6.1	10.5	11.3	12.0	8.0	7.0	8.0		1.0
NEC			3.0		6.0		Packard Bell			
Honeywell	3.3	2.2	2.2	Bull/NEC		0.2			1.0	1.0
Unisys/Burroughs	5.6	11.9	7.0	3.0						1.0
Sperry Rand	2.8	Unisys								
Control Data/Ceridian	3.0	2.3	2.0							
NCR	0.2									
Cray	1.1	2.8	1.5							
NAS/Itel	2.2	3.2	1.6							
Hewlett-Packard/ Tandem				2.0		2.0			1.0	1.0
Others	0.0	0.5	0.5	0.4	1.0	0.5	2.0	2.0	4.0	5.0
Total U.S. Rev. ($ mil)	15,105	18,550	12,875	7,200	8,000	8,250	8,500	4,163	3,375	2,348
C4	90.7	92.2	89.2	96.6	99.0	99.5	100.0	100.0	96.0	95.0
HHI	5,988	5,248	4,194	5,326	6,593	6,330	5,778	6,474	9,216	8,467

Source: 1984 data from DeLamarter, Richard Thomas, *Big Blue*, 1986. New York: Dodd, Mead, p. 288. 1988 data are from Mattera, Philip, *Inside U.S. Business, 1994 Edition*, Burr Ridge, Ill.: Irwin, 1994, *Source:* Dataquest. 1995 and 1996 data are from Zuckerman, Laurence, "Adding Power: Hitachi Becomes No. 2 to IBM in Mainframes," *New York Times*, July 7, 1997, p. D1, *Source:* Meta Group. Barr, James, "New Mainframe Developments," *Faulkner Information Services*, February, 2001, and Sacconaghi, Toni, "IBM," *Sanford Bernstein Equity Research*, 5, March 7, 2000. Dataquest data are as cited in "IBM Highlights Database Strength with 10,000th Mainframe Licensee," IBM Press Releases, http://www.ibm.com/Press/prnews.nsf/jan/ 5CF0E884D6C6829F85256A0700758ECC, March 6, 2001. MIPS and revenue market share statistics are cited or calculated from statistics in Sacconaghi, Toni, "IBM," *Sanford Bernstein Equity Research*, p. 4, May 4, 2001 and p. 6, March 7, 2000. Fujitsu, which had owned a stake in Amdahl since 1972, acquired the final 58% of Amdahl in 1997 for $850 million. 2001 U.S. revenue is based on IBM's revenue for 2001.—indicates shares of less than 2%. Both Hitachi and Amdahl left the mainframe production market in 2000. Mainframe revenues and market shares are extracted from a table in "IBM prepares for 40th anniversary of 360 mainframe with good news," Apr. 2004, http://www.findarticles.com/p/articles/mi_m0PAT/is_2004_April/ai_n6011108. Global revenue based on a 9.5% yearly decline in revenue, from Burt, Jeffrey,"Gartner: IBM, HP Tops in Server Revenue, Shipments," February 22, 2006 http://www. eweek.com/article2/0,1895,1930156,00.asp.

significant mainframe manufacturers left: IBM, Hitachi, and Amdahl (Fujitsu).[3] Thus, by 2000, after decades of fighting the competition and antitrust authority, IBM finally came to completely dominate the mainframe market, albeit a shrinking segment that is under threat from other types of computing hardware.

New software enabled mainframes to function as large servers for the Internet and corporate intranets. This breathed new life into the mainframe industry. Mainframe revenues actually increased again in 1998. One factor resulting in the sales increase was price. The prices for System/390 machines dropped by 35% per year. But after this spurt, sales declined again.[4] Even so, the segment is profitable to IBM. Total revenues that are related to mainframe sales (which include software, maintenance, service, and peripheral sales) are four to

five times mainframe hardware sales alone. These sales represented 48% of IBM's operating profit in 2000, but only 26% of its revenues.

Midrange Computers and Work Stations

Midrange computers are used for tasks ranging from control of manufacturing processes to capturing retail chain store data to operating as servers for networking arrangements. However, the definition of the midrange market is blurred, overlapping with both larger (mainframe) and smaller computers (networked high-end workstation). The midrange market was also being reshaped by the trend toward multiplatform environments (systems capable of running multiple operating systems).

In 1965, Digital Equipment Corporation (DEC) introduced the first minicomputer, the PDP-8. Other early market leaders included IBM, Wang, and Data General. After a period of rapid growth, the midrange market declined. Wang went bankrupt. DEC and IBM lost $9 billion in a single year and laid off tens of thousands of employees. In 1998, Compaq acquired DEC for about $9 billion, before being acquired itself by Hewlett-Packard (HP)/AT&T spun off NCR.

Table 10.5 and figure 10.2 chart the U.S. market share of U.S. midrange manufacturers by units shipped.

Figure 10.2 shows the concentration trend line for this industry. After a period of moderate and declining concentration, it rose again after 1992 as a result of Compaq's and HP's acquisitions in the industry. In addition, Sun Microsystems' (owned by Oracle after 2009) increase in market share further raised the HHI into the highly concentrated range after 1996.

Table 10.5 Midrange/Computers (Market Shares by Shipments)

Companies	1984	1987	1988	1990	1992	1996	2001	2004
IBM	28.8	27.6	25.6	21.6	23.1	23.7	26.1	28.2
Hewlett-Packard	9.1	6.5	7.1	8.4	12.1	19.5	29.0	31.7
Compaq			3.0	6.0	8.0	11.3	Hewlett-Packard	
Tandem		4.9	4.9	4.9	4.9	Compaq		
Digital Equipment	14.7	21.6	18.2	15.4	14.0	12.6	Compaq	
Dell						3.0	2.9	3.4
AT&T					9.7			
NCR	5.0	4.0	5.6	7.2	AT&T	2.8	3.1	3.3
Sun Microsystems[a]				1.8	4.4	10.3	21.3	20.8
Acer / Altos			2.0	3.9	4.1	3.2		
Unisys/Burroughs	6.7	8.4	7.3	5.7	5.2	4.6	4.2	4.1
Wang	9.3	3.4	2.3			Unisys		
Data General	8.0	2.5	2.2	1.6	1.8	1.2	0.3	
NEC			2.4	2.1	1.8	2.8	2.0	2.4
Packard Bell	5.0	5.0	3.0	2.5	1.0	NEC		
Honeywell	2.5	2.5	Bull/NEC					
Prime		3.2	3.2	DR				
Fujitsu							1.9	1.0
Siemens Nixdorf						4.5		
Silicon Graphics	1.0	1.0	1.0	4.0	4.0	2.0	2.0	1.8
Other	9.9	9.4	12.2	14.9	6.0	3.0	2.7	1.2
Total U.S. Rev ($ mil)	10,400	15,950	14,183	10,650	8,575	7,800	7,949	8,101
C4	61.9	64.1	58.2	52.6	58.8	67.1	80.9	84.9
HHI	1,381	1,441	1,195	966	1,143	1,396	2,044	2,289

Note: Based on percentage of units shipped, except 1984 and 1987, whose figures are based on percentage of revenues. *Sources:* 1990 and 1994 data are from Juliussen, Egil, and Karen Petska-Juliussen, *The Computer Industry 1994–95 Almanac*, Austin, Tex.: 1994. 1984 data are from Archbold, Pamela, and Verity, John, "Global Industry...The Datamation 100," *Datamation*, June 1, 1985, p. 37. 1987 data represent world market shares of medium-scale systems, *Standard and Poor's Industry Survey*, Jan. 1990, p. C84. *Source:* International Data Corp. 1996 data are from "Computers: Hardware," *Standard and Poor's Industry Survey*, July 1998, pp. 2, 7. 2000 statistics are based on IDC data cited in "Server and Enterprise Hardware and PC Hardware Quarterly," Salomon Smith Barney, April 24, 2001, p. 80. 2000 U.S. segment revenues are based on assumption that midrange sales follow the global distribution of sales of the top four vendors, using data from Runkel, Rebecca, "Sun Microsystems," Morgan Stanley, p. 28, March 27, 2001; Compaq Corporation, "2000 Annual Report," p. 60, 2001; IBM Corporation, "2000 10-K," p. 92, March 1, 2001; Hewlett-Packard Corporation, "2000 10-K," p. 85, April 2001. 2004 data with Hewlett-Packard/Compaq combined. Compaq purchased DEC in 1998. In 1996 Japan-based NEC merged its international operations with Packard Bell. Prime Computer was acquired by DR Holdings in 1989. Davis, Dwight B., "Gone Missing," *Electronic Business*, July 23, 1990, p. 102. Tandem merged with Compaq in June 1997. 1988, 1992, and 2001 figures are extrapolated from 1987, 1990, 1994, and 2000. Industry revenue data for 2004 are calculated from the growth percentages of the companies.

[a] Sun was acquired in 2009 by Oracle.

In 1985, Sun Microsystems introduced a new type of computer—the workstation, a type of single-user computer that was based around a powerful microprocessor, making it suitable for business and technical users whose requirements exceeded microcomputer capabilities. Workstations are typically used for computation-intensive tasks such as design automation, software development, and geographic information systems. After 1988, 64-bit RISC processors became standard, and after 2001, 128-bit processors were introduced.

Workstation servers were much cheaper than mainframes or midrange computers (between $20,000 and $100,000), and their sales grew rapidly in the late 1980s[5] but then fell to 1.7 million units in 2000 as PCs kept advancing in performance and as the growth of the Internet slowed.

The U.S. workstation market is more highly concentrated than the microcomputer market. The combined market share of the top four companies (Sun, Hewlett-Packard, DEC, and IBM) was 80% in 1990. In the next decade, after mergers and Dell's entry, the combined market share of the top four companies (Dell, Sun, Hewlett-Packard, and IBM/(Lenovo)), after an initial decline, rose to 90% in 2004 (table 10.6, figure 10.2).

Concentration has been high (HHI greater than 1,800) because entry by simple cloning is more difficult for workstations than for PCs.

Table 10.6 Workstations (Market Shares by Shipments)

Company	1984	1986	1988	1990	1992	1994	1996	1999	2000	2002	2004
Dell								14.0	23.0	26.0	28.6
Hewlett- Packard	24.0	17.0	16.9	19.5	21.5	23.4	27.0	19.0	18.0	22.0	24.1
Apollo	21.0	26.0	13.5	HP							
Compaq							1.0	10.0	10.0	HP	
Digital Equipment	12.0	10.0	18.6	17.8	15.7	13.5	6.0	Compaq			
Sun Microsystems[a]		23.0	28.3	36.3	37.9	39.5	36	27.0	19.0	24.0	23.7
IBM	7.0	5.0	5.0	6.3	8.0	9.6	9.0	15.0	17.0	15.0	14.0
Silicon Graphics		4.0	3.5	2.9	4.8	6.6	15.0	8.0	6.0	7.0	6.1
NCR	18.9	10.4	9.3	4.0	AT&T						
Intergraph				6.2	4.4	2.5	2.0	1.0			
TriStar					0.7	1.4	1.0				
NEC				1.7	1.5	1.2					
Tatung				0.3	0.4	0.4					
Data General				0.5	0.5	0.4					
Others	17.1	4.6	5.0	4.5	5.0	1.5	3.0	6.0	7.0	6.0	3.5
U.S. Rev. ($ mil)	1,005	1,500	2,250	3,250	4,525	5,800	4,694	5,733	3,592	3,128	2,724
C4	75.9	76.4	77.3	79.9	82.9	86.0	87.0	75.0	77.0	87.0	90.4
C8				94.7	94.2	97.7	97.0				
HHI	1,567	1,743	1,738	2,121	2,249	2,436	2,373	1,676	1,639	2,010	2,193

Note: Market share is based on shipments of both branded personal and traditional workstations. Sources: 1988 data are from Datamation, June 15, 1989, p. 150. 1984 and 1986 market shares were calculated based on the companies' revenues taken from "Electronics Current Analysis," Standard & Poor's Industry Surveys, June 7, 1984, September 3, 1987. 2002 data combines 2000 Compaq and HP due to 2002 acquisition. 1999 and 2000 U.S. market size was calculated based on 42% U.S. market share of global market. "Industry Survey. Computers: Hardware," Standard & Poor's Industry Surveys, May 23, 2002. 1996 data for U.S. market size are from "Server/Enterprise Group FX Sensitivity Outlook-Industry Report," Salomon Smith Barney, December 1997. 1999 and 2000 statistics are based on global unit sales data from Gartner/Dataquest 2001 as cited in "2000 Workstation Sales," Computer Monthly Magazine Online, March 2001. 1999 and 2000 segment revenues are from IDC, as cited in, "Server & Enterprise Hardware and PC Hardware Quarterly," Salomon Smith Barney Securities, May 24, 2001, p. 93. The 1990 U.S. revenue figure is extrapolated from 1988 and 1992 figures, the 1994 U.S. revenue figure is extrapolated from 1992 and 1996 U.S. figures. 1999–2001 market share data are provided by International Data Corp, 2002. The 1988 Silicon Graphics market share figure is extrapolated from 1986 and 1990 market share figures. Industry size for 2004 is extrapolated from companies' growth percentages.

[a] Sun was acquired by Oracle in 2009.

Workstation servers typically ran on Unix operating systems, though with different versions to prevent easy cross-use of software between different manufacturers' systems. In 1996, workstation platforms based on the Intel Pentium processor (a CISC architecture) and the Windows NT operating system were introduced by Compaq, Hewlett- Packard, and Intergraph, and by 1997, such workstations accounted for the bulk of units sold. Linux emerged in the 1990s as an increasingly utilized operating system.

Microcomputers

A microcomputer (often called a personal computer or PC) is a general applications computer designed for use by an individual, and operating on a single, integrated microprocessor chip. Each unit has a resident software operating system (for example, MS-DOS, Windows, Macintosh OS, or Linux) that governs the machine's internal functions and enables it to run a wide range of applications software. Microcomputers come in both stationary (desktop and tower) and portable (notebook, laptop, and subnotebook) models. Standardization of microprocessors and operating systems has enabled the markets for applications, peripherals, and networking capabilities to flourish.

Table 10.7 shows the increase of U.S. microcomputer shipments and installations from 1984 to 2005.

Increasing standardization reshuffled industry leader line-ups and blurred the boundaries of this submarket. Although the actual number of U.S. microcomputers shipped increased, as did the market share of the microcomputer segment in relation to the computer industry as a whole, the success of individual manufacturers was fragile. In the late 1980s, hardware sales sagged, prices dropped, and companies failed (software development and chip technology proved more resistant, as discussed in the software section).[6] In the early years of the microcomputer industry (late 1970s, early 1980s) three firms (IBM, Apple, and Commodore) dominated. The market became fragmented in the early 1990s but then gradually reconcentrated.

The largest closed-system manufacturer to survive is Apple, but its market share, in 2008, was 6%, a fraction of its 1984 share, though better than in the 1990s, and higher for the US consumer segment.

Table 10.7 PC Shipments (Millions of Units)

Year	U.S. Units in Use	U.S. Shipments	Global Shipments
1984	16	5	9
1988	23	7	14
1992	36	12	31
1995	74	25	50
1998	129	39	96
2000	164	48	125
2001	177	43	131
2002	206	42	138
2003	255	53	155
2004	280	58	178
2005	320	60	195
2006		62	239
2007		63	271
2008		68	293

Sources: "Computers: Hardware," *Standard & Poor's Industry Surveys*, December 11, 2003. Morgan Stanley Research, Infotrac Database, Information Access Co., 1996; Morgan Stanley Estimates, IDC, TrendFocus, "PC and Data Focus," Morgan Stanley, June 18, 2001, p. 4. UBS Warburg, "PC Outlook," June 18, 2001, p. 26. Global Industry Analysts, "Intel," August 1, 2000, p. 33; 2000 data on U.S. PCs in use are from *Computer Industry Almanac* as cited by Parks Associates, "Digital Lifestyles at Home: United States." 2001, 2002 figures are from Computer Industry Almanac, Inc., "Worldwide Cumulative PC Sales Exceed 1 billion." http://www.c-i-a.com/pr0203.htm. Information on shipments for 2003–2005 are from IDC, March 23, 2005: "Short-term PC Outlook Weakens Slightly While Long Term Growth Looks Solid."

The top four companies' combined market share fell from 82.7% in 1984 to 38% in 1990 and rose again to 64.3% in 2005. The PC market became more consolidated after 1992 as Dell and HP increased their market-share, but as reflected by the HHIs the concentration has been still moderate, although growing (table 10.8, figure 10.3).

A key dynamic at work has been the entry of PC "clonemakers" and the consequent commoditization of the PC. The most successful early manufacturer cloning IBM's PC was Compaq, followed by the direct-to-customer manufacturers/retailers Gateway and Dell. They sold computers through mail-order catalogs, phone orders, or over the Internet. Dell became the largest PC maker in 2001 and more profitable than Gateway through a low-cost structure. Packard Bell succumbed in the late 1990s after briefly being the leading vendor of consumer PCs. In 1995, NCR (formerly AT&T GIS) pulled out of the PC market entirely, having lost huge amounts of money.[7] IBM withdrew from the consumer market in 2000

Table 10.8 Microcomputer (Market Share by Revenues)

	1984	1986	1988	1990	1992	1994	1996	2002	2005	2007
Dell				1.4	3.1	5.8	6.8	25.5	33.1	31.4
Hewlett-Packard	5.0	4.0	3.0	2.0	2.2	2.4	5.3	24.0	19.0	26.1
Compaq	4.0	4.0	4.0	4.0	3.9	12.3	14.0	HP		
Digital Equipment								Compaq		
Lenovo (China)									5.4	5.4
IBM	32.0	28.0	23.0	18.0	13.4	8.8	8.0	6.0	Lenovo	
Apple	18.0	9.0	10.0	11.0	11.4	11.7	6.4	4.0	3.7	6.1
Tandy	7.0	6.0	3.0							
Toshiba (Japan)				2.0	2.3	2.5	5.0	2.5	3.8	5.4
Epson (Japan)	4.0	3.0	2.0							
AST Research (US)				2.0	3.0	3.9	4.8			
Sony (Japan)								2.5		
eMachines								2.5		
Acer (Taiwan)							4.7	2.0	5.7	9.0
Gateway				1.0	3.1	5.1	6.3	7.5	6.9	Acer
Packard Bell				5.0	8.3	11.5	11.4	0.5		
NEC (Japan)										
Commodore	25.7									
Others	4.3	46.0	55.0	53.6	49.6	36.0	32.0	23.0	28.2	16.8
Units Shipped (in thousands)	5,190	5,850	7,390	9,248	11,844	18,289	26,583	42,158	60,228	68,152
U.S. Rev. ($ mil)	11,940	13,941	17,147	23,584	30,842	35,358	39,875	63,237	73,834	83,548
C4	82.7	47.0	40.0	38.0	36.9	44.3	40.2	63.0	64.3	72.6
HHI	2,114	942	667	501	429	585	593	1,358	1,561	1,845

Sources: 1984–1986 data for market shares and total U.S. PC market size are from "IBM and Apple Continue to Dominate U.S. Market," *Personal Computer Markets*, May 13, 1986. The global PC market values for 1984 and 1986 are from "Computers & Office Equipment. Industry Surveys," *Standard & Poor's*, October 1, 1987, p. C92. 1990 and 1994 data are from *Information Technology Industry Statistics, 1960–2004*. Washington, D.C.: Computer and Business Equipment Manufacturers Association, Industry Statistics Program, 1994, p. 60; *Edge Work Group Computing Report*, Edge Publishing, April 3, 1995. Market shares for 1996–1998 are from Dataquest, International Data Corporation and Deutsche Bank Securities estimates. 2001 U.S. market share is from "Special Report: 2002 Market Profile," *Appliance Manufacture*, 50(4), April 2002. 2002 data assume those of 2001. Compaq was acquired by Hewlett-Packard in 2002. Data for 1990 U.S. global market size are from "Taste of Apple at IBM," *Financial Times*, October 2, 1991. 1994 and 1996 global market data are from *Server/Enterprise Group FX Sensitivity Outlook, Industry Report*, December 11, 1997, p. 30. 1998 and 2001 global market values were estimated based on the global shipment and dollar price per PC unit. The total shipments in 1998 and 2001 were 89.722 million and 133.5 million, respectively. The source for 1998 unit shipment is "Server and Enterprise and PC Hardware Quarterly," September 2002, p. 99, and the 2001 total global sales in units are from "Despite Slump Niche PC Makers Are Flourishing," *New York Times*, June 24, 2002. The average price per unit is $1,500.00. "Computer Hardware. Industry Surveys," *Standard & Poor's*, May 23, 2002. p. 1. U.S. units are from The Information Technology Industry Counsel, *Databook: U.S. Computer Consumption. Databook: 65+*, January 1, 1998. Market shares for 2005 are based on 1Q05 and 1Q06 percentages from *IDC Worldwide Quarterly PC Tracker*, April 19, 2006. 2005 industry revenue is calculated by using 5.3% sales growth. 2007 from Gartner, www.gartner.com/it.

and sold its PC operations in 2004 to the Chinese Lenovo Group for $1.25 billion. And Gateway was bought in 2008 by the Taiwanese firm Acer for $710 million.

Manufacturers with proprietary platforms (Apple, NEC, and Commodore) saw their market shares drop sharply over time. The Macintosh's user-friendliness and the innovativeness of its machines helped Apple hold on to some of its customer base. It remained the platform of choice for certain niche applications (e.g., education, desktop publishing, graphic design), and is popular in the research community and with computer professionals. However, it is much weaker in the corporate market.

By the turn of the century, the U.S. market for microcomputers had become, to a large extent, an upgrade market. Penetration was high at the business and middle-income household levels. For a long time, computer makers upgraded performance rather than reduced price, and this slowed penetration to lower-income households. However, new patterns of microcomputer usage emerged as networked PCs replaced many mainframes and midrange computers, and as it became the primary access node to the burgeoning Internet. Internet and multimedia use increased requirements for processor and memory power. The Internetworking encouraged some manufacturers to design simplified computers ("dumb" or "thin" clients) to access the Internet. The theory was that all applications would be run off the network from central servers. But the dropping PC prices kept even internetworked computers pretty smart.

The emerging PC market structure followed the classic U-pattern of a competitive phase followed by a consolidation. The top four firms account for almost two-thirds of the market, even more for business customers. These firms also become less vertically integrated, with much of the production outsourced to specialized providers. Dell, in particular, pioneered this as a business method. Since the main components are widely available to all, much of competition lies in early deployment and in price. This favors firms with large scale. At the same time, several of the major providers used their strong brands to expand horizontally to related product lines.

Video Game Hardware[8]

Video games have become a new mass media—increasingly sophisticated, interactive, feature rich, and popular. They have received increased attention by media scholars as more than a kids' toy.

Video game hardware for home use was pioneered in the United States in the mid-1970s by Nolan Bushnell, who invented Pong (an early arcade video game machine) and founded Atari. Atari was jointly acquired by Warner Communications and American Express, and became the dominant home video game vendor by developing the first successful programmable video game machine (using a 4-bit Central Processor Unit, or CPU). Development of the programmable machine created a new market for video game software. By 1983, Atari had close to 86% of the $2.2 billion global video game hardware and software markets. However, by 1984, consumers became bored with Atari and other consoles, and Atari was sold. In 1985, U.S. video game industry sales plunged to $100 million and Atari was soon wiped out.

A new entrant, the Japanese Nintendo Entertainment System (NES) took Atari's position in 1985. The higher quality of Nintendo games and 8-bit CPU and later 16-bit machines reinvigorated the industry. In 1990, Nintendo machines accounted for 90% of the $4 billion global hardware and software markets.[9]

In 1993 Nintendo lost its leadership to Sega's new machine that was based on a 32-bit microprocessor. Sega, in turn, lost out to Sony, which enjoyed quick success with its own 32-bit machine released in 1995, Playstation. The following year, Nintendo regained leadership with a 64-bit machine, until it was Sega's turn in 1999 with its 128-bit Dreamcast. This, too, was a short-lived success, and Sega left the video console business altogether, leaving Nintendo and Sony to duke it out with newcomer Microsoft, which entered the market in 2001 with its Xbox console. In 2005, Microsoft ushered in the seventh generation of consoles with the Xbox360. However, Sony and Nintendo were not far behind, continuing the fight for market share with their respective Playstation 3 and Wii consoles released in 2006.

As can be seen from its history, this market is unforgiving. New technology, expressed in processor complexity, drives console adoption. The first to market with the latest processor technology will sell many consoles in its first year, but sales will quickly fall in succeeding years as the novelty declines and rivals catch up.

Another factor for success is game titles. Nintendo's success was largely attributed to its innovative game titles such as *Mario Bros.*, *Zelda*, *Metroid*, and *Pokemon*. The Sega Dreamcast console scored disappointing sales because of a shortage of major game titles. This forced Sega out of the hardware market in 2000. Microsoft experienced similar problems. Although its Xbox was technically superior to Sony's, it lacked Sony's extensive library and backward compatibility to older but more popular games (table 10.9, figure 10.4).

The intense competition in gaming consoles and the high demand for the latest game releases has led industry participants to adopt a razor-and-blades business model. Manufacturers are willing to make little or no money on video game hardware sales to quickly build a large installed hardware base, thereby boosting profitable game or cartridge (software) sales. Microsoft's Xbox, released in 2001, retailed for $300 (including retailer markup), even though the gross cost to

Table 10.9 Video Game Hardware (Market Shares by Revenues)

Company	1981	1984	1987	1988	1992	1994	1995	1996	1997	1998	2000	2001	2004	2005	2007
Sony (Japan)						0.5	16.7	33.9	51.0	68.7	64.0	61.0	41.7	44.1	43.3
Nintendo (Japan)		41.0	82.0	85.5	63.7	35.0	28.3	37.2	46.0	31.0	21.0	22.0	41.0	42.2	37.0
Microsoft (US)												17.0	16.5	13.6	19.8
Sega (Japan)				6.0	30.0	56.0	47.3	24.8	2.3	0.3	15.0				
3DO (Japan/ US)						5.0	5.6	2.8							
Atari (US)	75.0	40.0	5.0	4.6	3.1	2.0	0.9	0.5							
Other	25.0	19.0	13.0	3.9	3.2	1.5	1.2	1.0	0.7	0.0	0.0	0.0	0.8	0.1	0.0
U.S. Rev. ($ mil)	290	445	600	740	1,300	1,575	1,127	1,464	1,800	2,114	1,473	3,125	2,600	3,200	7,040
C4	75.0	81.0	87.0	96.1	96.8	98.0	97.9	98.6	99.3	100.0	100.0	100.0	99.2	99.9	99.6
HHI	5,625	3,281	6,749	7,367	4,967	4,390	3,349	3,149	4,722	5,681	4,762	4,494	3,692	3,911	3,630

Source: 1987–1994 data are compiled from company reports. Data for 1981 are taken from "History of Atari and the Gaming Console Industry," at http://www.atarihistory.de, 2001. Data for 1998 are extrapolated from global data and geographical sales data from "Video Games," Schroder Salomon Smith Barney, February 2001, p. 18. 2000 data are extrapolated from global data and geographical sales data from "Video Games," Schroder Salomon Smith Barney, February 2001, p. 18. 2001 data reflect only consoles, not portable units. *Sources:* "Quick News," *Video Game News Online,* http://www.videogamenews.com, April 10, 2002; "First Quarter Video Game Industry 2002 Fact Sheet," *NPD Intellect,* May 20, 2002. 1984, 1988, and 1996 figures are extrapolated from 1981, 1987, 1992 and 1997 figures. Gikas, Anthony N., and Stephanie S. Wissink, "The Video Game Industry," PiperJaffray Equity Research, April 2005. 2004 market shares are based on hardware sales for February 2005 in UBS Equities "Video Game Update," March 11, 2005. Global revenue for 2004 are from Gikas, Anthony N., and Stephanie S. Wissink, "The Video Game Industry," PiperJaffray Equity Research, April 2005, pp. 4, 12, and 16. Figures for 2005 are from Osur, Elizabeth, "Sony Reiterates Video Game HW Forecasts; CIR Industry Model Unchg'd," January 26, 2006, Citigroup, May 30, 2006. Data for 2007 is from NPD Group, January 2008.

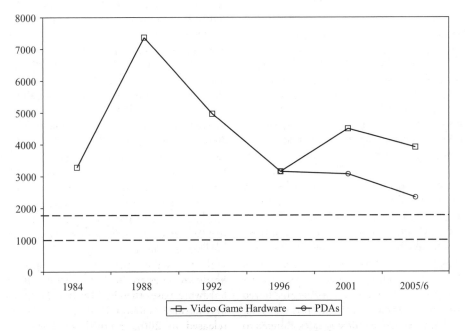

Figure 10.4 Video Games and PDA Hardware: Concentration (HHI)

produce each console was estimated to be $350. Microsoft, trying to enter a brand new business, accepted a per-sale loss on its Xbox.

Gaming consoles are becoming more than just gaming machines. Newer machines from Microsoft and Sony function as new generation DVD players and enable users to access the Internet, especially for online games. The transformation of gaming consoles from single-purpose hardware to PC-like functionality drew the attention of Microsoft, the dominant PC software provider. If gaming consoles became multitask computing machines, they would threaten Microsoft's core business of providing PC operating system software. Conversely, it was a logical expansion route for Microsoft, just as were its operating software for cell phones, PDAs, and TV set-top boxes.

Microsoft was one of the few firms globally able to enter the market for gaming consoles and compete with Sony, given the tremendous resources required to be successful and attract developers, coupled with the considerable risk of failure. Merrill Lynch estimated that Microsoft would lose a cumulative $2 billion in the games sector before its Xbox business turned profitable. When introduced, Microsoft's Xbox was the most powerful gaming console on the market. Approximately 200 developers created software for the Xbox.

Nintendo was for a time the leader in handheld consoles with nearly a 100% market share. Different from earlier handhelds, the Game Boy featured cartridges. Being thus similar to regular consoles, the handheld's success was driven by hit titles such as *Tetris* and *Pokemon*. The Game Boy's popularity forced every other major market competitor, including Atari and Sega, to exit the handheld console segment. Nintendo's market share in the handheld gaming market was threatened by the convergence of technologies, until it released in 2006 its highly successful Wii console.

The combination of PDA functionality, telecommunications, and gaming created several hybrid devices to compete with Nintendo. Nokia, the Finnish cell phone maker, in 2003 launched the N-Gage, a wireless game console, but failed to obtain a significant market share. Sony released a portable Playstation in 2005, which became successful, owing to its library of gaming titles and features such as MP3 and movie clip playback capability. The video game hardware industry is deeply competitive but sustains only three firms.

These big tentpole companies are surrounded by small game developers, which jointly create the network effects and scale necessary for success with a very finicky and volatile user base. Entry barriers are high for the hardware consoles but much less so for the game applications. The industry is totally global on the hardware side.

Personal Digital Assistants (PDAs) and Handheld Computers

Personal digital assistants (PDAs) are small, handheld computing devices that store and display alphanumeric information for scheduling and some computing applications. Following a British firm, Psion, in 1984 and Apple's $500 million failure with the Newton, the first Palm Pilot was released in 1996. Palm's founders had difficulty raising funding and sold the firm in 1996 for $44 million to U.S. Robotics, which in turn was bought by 3Com. A critical design feature of the Palm Pilot was its open operating system. Palm Pilot users could install software on their unit and were free to develop their own programs. The open system led to a grassroots software development movement, as well as developments by numerous software professionals. Palm licensed out its operating system to other hardware developers. Its mass market success attracted other entrants, most notably Microsoft, which began to license its own PDA operating system software. By 2001, despite numerous innovative products, no firm had taken significant market share from Palm except Handspring, started by the former co-founders of Palm, which allowed hardware features to be added to a PDA through a special slot.[10] Handspring was acquired by Palm in 2003, which split itself into an operating software company (Palm) and a hardware company (PalmOne). After 2005, PDAs were increasingly being merged into smartphone devices, thus greatly declining as stand-alone devices. (table 10.10, figure 10.4).

COMPUTER HARDWARE: COMPUTER PERIPHERAL AND STORAGE DEVICES

Having gone over the various computing devices, we now move on to devices that are connected to them. Computer peripheral devices include printers, disc drives, monitors, modems, scanners, and other equipment connected or integrated to

Table 10.10 PDA Equipment (Market shares by Revenues)

	1995	1996	2000	2001	2004	2005
PalmOne		51.0	61.2	50.0	43.4	37.3
Handspring			28.7	15.0	Palm	
Hewlett-Packard	28.0	14.0	3.5	6.3	15.2	11.6
Compaq			3.6	11.3	HP	
Research In Motion				1.8	7.5	27.7
Sony			2.3	13.2	8.4	discontinued
Dell					7.4	6.6
Toshiba					3.1	
Psion	33.0	16.0		discontinued		
Sharp	14.0	7.0		discontinued		
Apple	14.0	7.0		discontinued		
Others	11.0	5.0	0.7	2.4	15.0	16.9
Total U.S. Rev. ($ mil)	300	390	1,640	1,480	1,450	1,846
C4	89.0	88.0	97.0	89.5	82.0	93.4
HHI	2,265	3,151	4,600	3,070	2,306	2,332

Notes: Rifkin, Glenn, "A Very Small Computer's Big Numbers," *New York Times*, April 29, 1996, p. D23. *NPD Intellect* as cited by Prudential Securities, "Palm Inc.," May 17, 2001, p. 3. *Top Sellers,* February 2002, *New York Times,* Monday, April 15, 2002. Palm income information is from "Palm Inc. Strong Q 02 Results," Morgan Stanley, March 22, 2002. Palm Sales US is from Palm Inc., 10k July 30, 2002, Edgar file SEC. 1996 figures are extrapolated from 1995 and 2000 figures. Data for 2004 are based on unit shipments. *Sources: TWICE* 19 (4), February 9, 2004. 2005 market shares are based on *Gartner Dataquest* (February 2006). Data do not include smartphones, such as Palm Treo 650 or BlackBerry 7100, but include wireless PDAs, such as Hewlett-Packard's iPAQ 65xx and BlackBerry 8700. Sony pulled out of the PDA market in 2005: "Sony Officially Departs U.S. PDA Market," Dec. 17, 2005, About.com, May 30, 2006 [http://palmtops.about.com/od/palmarticles/a/Sony_Departs.htm]. 2005 global revenue is based on the 40% U.S. global market share and 7.3% worldwide revenue increase for 2005 from Gartner Dataquest (February 2006). The 2004 revenue of $4.3 billion is from Kerner, Sean Michael, "PDA Market Up or Down?," February 18, 2005. *InternetNews,* May 24, 2006 http://www.internetnews.com/stats/article.php/3484291.

Table 10.11 Computer Peripheral (Market Shares by Revenues)

	1984	1988	1992	1996	2001	2004
Xerox	4.0	6.7	9.2	8.8	10.1	15.0
Seagate	1.6	4.1	6.1	12.2	8.5	11.5
Maxtor	0.0	0.0	2.9	3.1	5.5	9.0
Hitachi	2.6	2.7	3.6	1.5	1.3	5.0
IBM	3.7	5.5	5.4	3.5	4.9	Hitachi
Hewlett-Packard	3.3	7.2	16.2	22.1	12.2	10.4
Fujitsu	4.7	2.7	2.8	2.0	5.2	3.5
Others	80.1	71.1	53.8	46.9	52.3	45.5
Total U.S. Rev. ($ mil)	6,568	11,498	15,526	22,222	22,844	19,830
C4	15.7	23.5	36.9	46.5	36.3	46.0
HHI	72	158	442	741	406	586

Note: Computer peripherals industries, for purposes of this section, are hard disk, optical storage drives, printers, copiers, and modems.

computing devices. The total value of the U.S. peripheral market grew from $6.6 billion in 1984 to $19.8 billion by 2004.

Table 10.11, which seems to indicate low (but rising) concentration, understates the concentration of individual peripheral markets. Most firms specialize and have a higher market power in their respective markets.

The following sections break down market shares for three of the most important segments of the peripheral market: disc drives, printers and copiers, and modems.

Disc Drives

There are several basic types of disk drives. Floppy drives provide portable magnetic storage for small quantities of data. Hard disk drives can store more data. CD-ROMs store and record data optically. DVD drives are capable of storing still more information and can hold a full-length movie on a single disc. The next DVD generation is based on light-blue lasers.

The hard disk market has been dominated by a shifting handful of firms providing devices to computer manufacturers with fickle requirements. The major suppliers are Seagate, Maxtor, Western Digital, Hitachi, and Fujitsu. Conner and Quantum grew in the 1980s by becoming suppliers of Compaq and Apple, respectively.[11] The pace of technical advancement is rapid and has destabilized market shares. Price competition is fierce, especially since most sales are to a handful of computer makers who themselves are engaged in energetic competition. In the early 1990s, market leader Seagate lost substantial market share to Quantum. Seagate regained the lead by acquiring in 1996 third-place Conner Peripherals. Maxtor

responded by purchasing Quantum in 2001 for $2.3 billion. This consolidating trend continued with Hitachi acquiring 70% of IBM's disk drive business in 2003.

There were eight major hard drive manufacturers globally in 2005, down from 20 in 1989. There were three or four primary vendors in each of the three hard drive segments of mobile (Hitachi, Maxtor, and Toshiba), desktop (Hitachi, Seagate, and Samsung) and enterprise (IBM, Seagate, and Maxtor) (table 10.12, figure 10.5).[11]

As seen in figure 10.5, market concentration exhibits a U-shaped trend after 1988. The combined share of the top four firms increased from 63% in 1984 to 78% in 2006.

During the 1990s, the CD-ROM market more than doubled annually. Matsushita assumed early leadership by supplying the computer makers Apple and Compaq microcomputers.[12] Some manufacturers specialized in component parts sold to computer makers.

In 1997, the next optical storage generation was introduced through DVD-ROM, which supplied up to 4.7 gigabytes of storage capacity (compared to the typical half a gigabyte for a CD-ROM). Blue-laser DVDs contested each other in two major technology alliances, one centered around Toshiba (HD-DVD), the other around Sony and

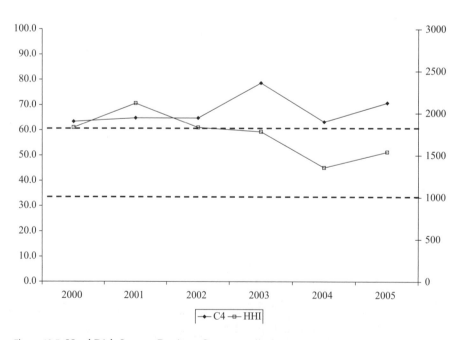

Figure 10.5 Hard Disk Storage Devices: Concentration

Table 10.12 Hard Disk Drive (Worldwide Market Shares by Shipments)

	1984	1988	1990	1992	1993	1996	1997	1998	1999	2001	2003	2005	2007
Seagate Tech.	2.5	6.6	10.3	11.0	13.5	26.8	23.4	20.8	21.4	21.0	20.6	27.7	34.6
Conner Periph.			5.2	9.1	8.3	Seagate							
Maxtor			3.0	5.3	5.5	3.7	6.6	11.8	13.3	13.7	23.5	14.3	Seagate
Quantum			2.7	6.2	9.2	15.2	20.3	17.5	17.0	15.7	Maxtor		
Western Digital				3.0	5.1	12.3	18.8	13.6	11.2	10.3	9.5	13.3	21.5
Hitachi	4.2	4.3	4.6	5.1	4.4	3.3	1.1	1.9	1.9	3.3	13.0	15.5	17.2
IBM	39.5	43.9	46.8	38.2	34.5	24.4	11.2	12.6	13.8	12.4	Hitachi		
Fujitsu	7.4	8.3	7.4	6.5	4.1	4.5	8.7	11.9	12.3	12.9	9.0	6.7	7.1
Toshiba					2.1	5.7	4.2	3.7	3.5	4.2	4.7	7.7	7.3
Samsung Electronics							3.6	5.9	5.3	5.0	3.0	6.9	11.0
Burroughs	2.1												
Control Data/MPI	11.1												
Digital Equipment	5.3	4.4	4.7	3.6	2.8								
Hewlett-Packard	2.7	2.1	2.1	2.1	4.3								
NEC	5.4	6.0	5.3	2.5	2.5	2.5							
Other	19.8	24.4	7.9	7.4	3.7	1.6	2.1	0.3	0.3	1.5	16.7	7.9	1.3
Global Rev ($ mil)	11,866	20,424	25,578	24,550	21,730	28,820	29,448	30,076	28,188	26,300	21,800	27,257	32,800
Est. U.S. Rev. ($ mil)	4,153	7,148	8,952	8,593	7,606	10,087	10,307	10,527	9,866	9,205	7,630	9,540	11,361
C4	63.4	64.8	69.8	64.8	65.5	78.7	73.7	64.5	65.5	63.3	66.6	70.8	84.3
HHI	1,831	2,118	2,470	1,830	1,655	1,780	1,590	1,416	1,435	1,355	1,348	1,541	2,076

Notes: Data were compiled with the help of Bruce Porter, Disk/Trend, Inc. Total share for the U.S. market were averaged as 35% of global revenues. Shares shown are *global* market shares.

Sources: Data for 1984 are from "Computers & Office Equipment," *Standard & Poor's Industry Surveys,* June 15, 1989. Data for 1990 are from *Electronic Business,* January 7, 1991, p. 30. Data for 1993 are from International Data Corp., 1993. Data for 1996 are from "Hard Disk Drive Market Poised for Robust 1997," *Business Wire,* January 30, 1997; *TrendFOCUS;* Costlow, Terry, "Hot Market Seen for Drives," *Electronic Engineering Times,* July 29, 1996, p. 26. Data for 1997–1999 are from SG Cowen Securities, "Global Top Nine Computer Disk Drive Companies Ranked by 1999 Shipments in Units and Market Share in Percent, with Each Firm's Shipments and Market Share in 1997 and 1998," August 16, 2000, SG Cowen Securities Corporation. Data for 2001 and 2003 are from "When Slower Is Better: Slowing Capacity, Consolidation and Better Corporate Behavior Rejuvenate the Once Cutthroat Disk Drive Industry. (Storage)," *Electronic Business,* March 2003, 29(3), 52. 2005 market shares for Seagate, Maxtor, and Western Digital are taken from 2005 revenues figures (Hoover's Company Profiles); market shares for Hitachi, Fujitsu, Toshiba, and Samsung taken from midyear estimates from Cassell, Jonathan, "Seagate Expands Lead in Hard Disk Drive Market," August 17, 2005, iSuppli Market Watch. May 25, 2005 http://www.isuppli.com/marketwatch/default.asp?id=312. 2005 global revenue is taken from Gartner Dataquest (August 2005) estimate. In May 2006, Seagate acquired Maxtor http://www.seagate.com/newsinfo/about/milestones/index.html. 2007 global revenue taken from Gartner.com – "Market share: Hard Disk Drives worldwide, 1Q.4Q 2007." 2007 Market shares taken from ITFacts.biz, "Top Hard Drive Manufacturers in Q1 2007."

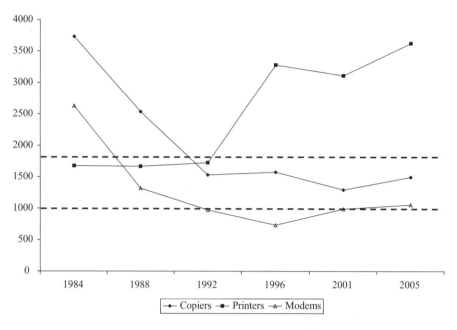

Figure 10.6 Printers, Copiers, and Modems: Concentrations (HHI)

Matsushita (Blu-Ray DVD), the eventual winner. As this battle progressed, hard disk drives were making big strides in increasing their storage capacity to levels much higher than optical discs, although at a higher price.

Printers and Copiers

The printer market includes printers of several technologies, including dot matrix, line, laser, highlight color, and inkjet printers. Overall revenues for the printer industry dropped from $8–9 billion in the 1990s to less than half of that by 2004, $3.8 billion, due to falling component costs, market saturation, and competitive pricing pressure.[13] The razor/blades nature of selling printers/cartridges makes the printer market a lucrative segment in the usually low-margin peripherals industry.

The inkjet market has been heavily dominated by the three manufacturers who own patents to inkjet print head designs, Hewlett-Packard (HP), Canon, and Epson. Adding Lexmark, those four firms regularly accounted for more than 80% of the market.[14]

The laser printer market has been even more concentrated than the inkjet market (figure 10.6). HP dominates that market, too.[15] Xerox and HP developed the first laser printers in the 1970s, and

Canon introduced the first desktop laser printers in 1982. HP entered into a partnership with Canon. By 1985 the HP Laserjet dominated the market.[16]

Table 10.13 shows the overall printer market. HP has been dominant since the early 1990s. Lexmark, Epson, and Canon make up the mid-rank.

The copier market is dominated by five large firms: Canon, Xerox, Ricoh, Sharp, and Toshiba. The result is a moderate level of concentration. In 1984, the market had been dominated by Xerox, the company that invented xerography and that held a 60% share. Poor strategy by Xerox and increasing competition saw it decline to below 20% by 2000. Canon took the lead in 1996 and held about a third of the market in 2004. Concentration dropped, with the HHI declining from 1984's high of 3,732 to a moderate 1,494 in 2004, but started to rise again after 2000 (table 10.14, figure 10.6).

Modems

Modems are devices that enable computers to transmit digital data as analog signals that can be sent over telephone networks designed to carry audio signals. To do this, they *modulate* an analog carrier wave at the transmitting end (breaking it into pulses that correspond to digital data), then

Table 10.13 Printers (Inkjet, Laser and Serial Dot Matrix) (Market Shares by Shipments)

	1984	1986	1988	1992	1995	1996	1997	2001	2004	2005	2006
Hewlett-Packard	5.0	6.0	18.0	37.75	57.5	55.3	53.0	52.0	55.8	56.5	52.9
Lexmark				1.6	3.2	4.1	5.0	7.7	18.0	16.7	11.2
Epson	33.0	27.0	23.0	13.8	4.6	9.8	15.0	13.1	10.4	10.3	5.3
Canon (with Apple)				2.8	5.6	8.8	12.0	11.1	6.4	6.8	5.6
Dell											7.0
Brother											1.6
Okidata				3.9	7.8	4.9	2.0	2.2			
Xerox						1.5	3.0	7.0			
Panasonic				2.3	4.6	3.3	2.0				
Apple	21.0	19.0	12.0	6.0							
IBM	11.0	13.0	13.0	6.5							
Other	30.0	35.0	34.0	25.4	16.7	12.4	8.0	6.9	9.4	9.7	16.1
U.S. Rev. ($ mil)	2,144	2,836	3,750	6,168	8,586	8,879	9,173	5,364	3,820	3,850	3,850
C4	70.0	65.0	66.0	64.1	75.5	78.8	85.0	83.9	90.6	90.3	76.7
HHI	1,676	1,295	1,166	1,725	3,451	3,280	3,220	3,112	3,587	3,623	3,035

Sources: Data for 1984–1986 are from "Those Makers Who Lead the Printer Marketplace," *Computer & Software News,* February 13, 1989; *StoreBoard Views,* 7 (7), 12. The U.S. market value for 1984 was calculated based on 33% of the U.S. market share within the global market (6,497 million in 1984), from "Getting Serious about Printers," *Computerworld,* August 5, 1985. Data for 1986 and 1988 U.S. market size were calculated based on the 15% annual compound rate of U.S. printer industry. "Aspen-Ribbons," *Business Wire,* October 23, 1986. Data for 1995 are from *Consumer Reseller News,* December 25, 1995, p. 115, and from *Market Share Reporter,* 1999, Table 844, p. 198; *Investor's Business Daily,* February 25, 1998, p. A8, from Computer Intelligence InfoCorp. Data for 2000 assumes the U.S. market as it is based on Global IDC data cited in Salomon Smith Barney, "Server and Enterprise Hardware and PC Quarterly," p. 104, May 24, 2001. Data for 2000 and 2001 for U.S. market size are from Morgan Stanley Research and IDC from "Systems & Enterprise Hardware," Morgan Stanley, June 26, 2002, p. 3. Data for 1995 and 1996 U.S. market size were calculated based on the 2.5% growth rate in 1996. Data for 1995 U.S. market size are from "Server/Enterprise Group FX Sensitivity Outlook—Industry Report," Salomon Smith Barney, December 1997, p. 82. Data for 1997 for U.S. total market revenue are from "Server and Enterprise Hardware Quarterly Review," Salomon Smith Barney, 1998, p. 90. 2004 and 2005 market shares are based on Runkle, Rebecca, and Kathryn Huberty, "June Printer Data Reflects Tough Market, but Overall Supports LXK Trademark," July 21, 2005. Morgan Stanley, July 12, 2006. Reuters Research-On-Demand. Dell resells Lexmark printers and its market share is factored into Lexmark's: Krazit, Tom. "Dell Will Resell Lexmark Printers," September 24, 2002, *PCWorld.* Revenues for 2004 and 2005 are from Gartner Dataquest (April 2006), report on U.S. inkjet and multifunction printer market, July 12, 2006. 2008 data from Gartner Dataquest (June 2008).

demodulate the carrier wave at the receiving end, converting it back to a digital data stream. Hence the term *modem.*

Early modems operated at 300 bits per second (bps). In 1978, D. C. Hayes introduced a $300 modem whose protocol quickly came to dominate the industry. The growth of commercial computer services sparked demand and upgrades to 1,200, and 2,400 bps. Data-compressing chip sets from Rockwell enabled bit rates to increase to 28 kbps. 56 kbps modems appeared in 1998 as the V.90 standard became widely accepted after considerable dispute among vendors. An estimated 70 million sold in 1999 alone.

The growth of the Internet and of bandwidth-intensive applications drove the need for still faster connections. DSL, ISDN, and cable modems raised the data speed of connections. DSL (digital subscriber line) takes unused higher-frequency portions of a phone line for data transmission. There are several competing DSL standards. HDSL provides speeds of around 2 Mbps over 3 miles of copper wire. VDSL enables speeds of up to 52 Mbps but with a still shorter range.

Dial-up lines that are all-digital ISDN (integrated services digital network) lines transmit data at a standardized speed of 64 Kbps per line. Several such channels can be put together for much faster rates. Cable modems, introduced in 1996, transmit data over cable's coaxial lines at rates up to 32 Mbps. This data stream is typically shared among several users at a lower actual rate.[17] Market demand and competition have been driving connection speeds up briskly.

The market for modems was relatively small until the mid-1990s, when the explosion of the

Table 10.14 Copiers (Market Shares by Revenues)

	1984	1988	1991	1992	1995	1996	1998	2000	2001	2004	2008
Canon	9.5	12.6	15.0	20.4	25.8	26.8	28.8	22.3	23.2	33.0	21.6
Xerox	60.0	48.0	39.0	31.0	23	24.7	28.2	18.5	16.5	9.7	8.7
Sharp	2.6	3.4	4.0	7.6	11.1	10.6	9.7	10.2	10.3	10.5	3.9
Hewlett-Packard										6.4	15.6
Ricoh				3.4	6.8	6.0	4.4	13.2	15.0	7.0	12.0
Toshiba	3.3	4.3	5.0	3.9	2.7	2.9	3.2	4.6	4.6	3.5	3.2
Mita (Kyocera)	2.6	3.4	4.0	5.2	6.4	6.1	5.4	7.0	7.0	3.8	2.7
Konica				2.1	4.1	4.1	4.0	5.8	5.8	7.2	5.7
Minolta	2.6	3.4	4.0	4.4	4.7	4.6	4.4	6.0	6.0	Konica	
Lanier						0.9	2.7	3.6	3.6	3.6	
Savin	3.3	4.3	5.0	4.4	3.7	3.3	2.4			4.4	
Brother											11.4
Pitney Bowes						0.7	2.1				
Others	16.1	20.6	24.0	17.9	11.7	9.4	4.7	8.8	8.0	10.9	15.2
U.S. Rev. ($ mil)	437	1,611	2,491	4,611	6,731	7,344	8,569	10,408	10,728	11,924	
C4	76.1	69.2	64.0	64.2	66.7	68.2	72.1	64.2	65.0	60.4	60.6
HHI	3,732	2,535	1,844	1,530	1,465	1,574	1,830	1,271	1,294	1,494	1,125

Source: The U.S. revenue and shares for 2001 is extrapolated from companies' annual revenues from SEC filings. Lynn Ritter, "Market Statistics: U.S. Copier 1996 Market Share and Forecast," April 21, 1997, Dataquest. Data for 2003 are from Dataquest, February 2004. Data from 2008 from Gartner Dataquest (June, 2008).

Internet and World Wide Web made them an essential item for computer owners. As a result, the U.S. modem market grew from $930 million in 1993 to $2.5 billion in 1995 to $8.3 billion in 2001. The analog modem industry witnessed a major decreasing concentration, with the HHI dropping from 2,629 in 1985 to 1056 in 2004, a level somewhat higher than in the early 1990s (figure 10.6).

Whereas it had been mostly a consumer market, it became increasingly characterized by bulk purchases by cable TV telecom companies for DSL equipment and by computer makers. Motorola, in particular, gained market share when it acquired General Instrument, traditionally a major supplier to the cable industry (table 10.15).

As shown in figure 10.6, the U.S. modem market declined in concentration in a U-shaped pattern. Hayes was the market leader from the 1980s until 1994, when it was surpassed by Maxtech and U.S. Robotics, the only firms with substantial shares of the 1995 market. Hayes was not able to keep up in the highly competitive modem market and declared bankruptcy in 1999. U.S. Robotics (later 3Com) became the new market leader in 2000, but sold its dial-up modem business to the Taiwanese firm Accton, The competition in the modem markets, as well as their fast commoditization, tended to make this a difficult business. 3Com left both the

cable and DSL modem businesses in 2001. Alcatel sold its market-leading DSL modem business to Thomson Multimedia. The primary chip suppliers to modem manufacturers have also grown into large firms, such as Broadcom, the dominant cable modem chip supplier, and Globespan, a DSL modem chip supplier.

COMPUTER HARDWARE: SEMICONDUCTORS

The majority of semiconductors are for computer- and communications-related uses (65%), as well as consumer products (17.6% in 2005). Table 10.16 provides an overview of the end markets.

The semiconductor industry tends to follow a boom-bust cycle driven by innovation, high demand, and investment, followed by overcapacity and dropping sales. From 1992 to 1995 there was a boom period for the industry, followed by three years of stagnating revenues. Similarly, 1999 and 2000 were boom years, followed by a bust cycle starting in 2001.

As the semiconductor industry grew, it disintegrated vertically. In the 1960s, a computer company (often part of a larger electronics firm) would build its own manufacturing equipment, design its own chips, manufacture them, and so

Table 10.15 Modems (Market Shares by Revenues)

Manufacturers	1985	1988	1992	1993	1995	1996	1997	2001	2004
Cable Modem CPE									
Motorola							4.3	4.0	23.7
(General Instrument)									
Ambit									5.9
Terayon							0.7	1.7	5.7
Thomson								4.3	5.5
Scientific Atlanta									5.1
DSL CPE									
Thomson (prev. Alcatel)									8.5
Siemens								4.0	7.5
DLink									4.7
ZyXEL									4.5
Westell								2.7	4.3
Dial-Up Modem									
Accton (Taiwan)									12.4
3Com							29.8	29.5	Accton
U.S. Robotics	8.3	10.6	12.5	14.3	21.9	21.9	3Com		3.1
Maxtech/GVC					18.4	12.6	6.8	5.0	2.6
Technologies									
Hayes	48	33.6	26.4	19.2	8.6	6.0	3.4	Bankrupt	
Microcom	10								
Ven-Tel	8								
Novation	6.7								
Boca Research					5.8	4.3	2.7	3.0	1.6
Global Village					5.1	3.3	1.4	Boca	
Compaq					5.1	2.5			
Zoom Telephonics			3.0	5.9	5.1	3.3	1.5	3.0	1.6
IBM	3.1								
Cardinal					1.9	0.9			
Multi-Tech Systems			2.6	5.1	1.0	1.3	1.5	3.5	1.8
Orckit								1.0	0.5
Com21							1.0	1.3	0.7
Other	9.8	47.0	45.3	44.0	25.1	40.7	46.9	37.0	0.2
U.S. Rev. ($ mil)	271	600	765	930	2,500	3,256	4,011	6,143	8,275
C3/4	74.3	53.0	52.1	50.9	54.7	44.8	44.3	42.8	52.2
HHI	2,629	1,319	973	766	1,012	734	980	989	1,056

Sources: Data for 1998 market shares are from Information Access Company; IAC Newsletter Database, EDGE Publishing. The source for 1997 data is *In-Stat* extrapolated from "V.90-Based Modems on the Way," *Electronic News,* New York, July 13, 1998. Data for 1993 are from *New York Times,* November 18, 1994, p. C1 (*source:* Dataquest). Data for 1995 are from *Computer Reseller News,* April 1, 1996, p. 87 (*source:* Dataquest). 2001 data are from "2001 Analog and Digital Modem Quarterly," *In-Stat.* 2001 data are from Dataquest based on mid-year 2000 unit sales data as cited in "Surfing with the Cable Guy," Kaufman Brothers, November 21, 2000, p. 76, and Dataquest data cited at CATV Cyberlab Modem Market, "CATV Cyberlab Modem," GecKo Research & Publishing, as cited online at [http://www.catv.org], February 2001; Motorola Corporation, "Schedule 14A," Motorola SEC Filings, p. F-8, April 2, 2001; Terayon Corporation, "10-K405," Terayon SEC Filings, p. 63, April 2, 2001; Com21, "10-KA," Com21 SEC Filings, p. 50, July 31, 2001. 1998 data is from Dell'Oro Group, using Morgan Stanley Dean Witter. Data for U.S. Cable market size are from Multimedia Telecommunications Association, *Multimedia Telecommunications Market Review & Forecast,* 142, January 1, 2000. Source for global market size is Pioneer Consulting from "Global Cable Modem Services Market," *PC Newswire,* February 17, 1999. 2001 Data from Joseph Bellace, "DSL Industry Update," *Jefferies & Co Equity Research,* pp 8–9, February 20, 2001. The U.S. market share was estimated from shares of Efficient, Westell, and Thomson Multimedia. Statistics from Westell Corporation, "10-K," Westell Corporation SEC Filings, p. 68, June 15, 2001; Efficient Corporation, "10-K," Efficient SEC Filings, p. F-22, September 9, 2000; Luc Mouzon, "Thomson Multimedia," *BNP Equity Research,* p. 48, December 20, 2001. 1988 and 1996 figures are extrapolated from 1985, 1993, 1995 and 1997 figures. Data for 2004 was compiled with the help of Dave Burstein (DSL Prime), Steve Noznik and Tam Dell'Oro (Dell'Oro Group), and Gauri Pavata (Gartner). Numbers for 2004 assume no changes in dial-up modem market shares and adds shares for DSL and cable modems.

Table 10.16 Global Semiconductor Consumption by Use (%)

	1991	1995	1996	1997	2000	2003	2005
Computers	40.8	51.1	50	50.3	42.0	42.0	40.7
Consumer Products	26.8	17.5	17.3	16.7	13.0	16.6	17.6
Communications	13.4	14.7	15.9	16.5	24.0	23.0	24.6
Automotive	5.5	5.2	5.5	5.6	6.0	8.0	7.1
Industrial/ Military/Other	13.5	11.4	11.3	10.8	15.0	10.0	10.0
Total ($ billion)	56.8	147.7	135.5	146.1	204.8	163	235.3

Source: "ICE Status 1997," *Integrated Circuit Engineering Corporation,* 1997, www.ice-corp.com/home/; Dataquest estimates as cited in Peck, Drew, "Semiconductor Primer," *SG Cowen Securities,* January 2001, p. 11.; Gartner Dataquest, February 2006.

forth. By 2000, however, the industry had splintered into subindustries of increasingly specialized firms. Manufacturing chips requires various equipment, from photolithography to design automation to wafer fabrication machines. Many firms selling equipment for the manufacturing of semiconductors appeared in the early 1980s. The firm Applied Materials emerged as the leader in this manufacturing equipment market with the largest range of products.[18] But there were dozens of companies with substantial market shares in their respective niches.

The deverticalization of the semiconductor industry includes foundries, "fabless" firms, and semiconductor intellectual property (SIP) firms. A foundry is a firm that specializes in producing chips for other firms on a contractual, outsourced basis. Equipment sophistication and manufacturing scale grew, and by 2001, the average cost of a new semiconductor fabrication facility ("fab") was over $2 billion. Some of the big foundries are located in South Asia, for example, TMCS and Winbond (Taiwan). Because of the enormous capital requirements for building a chip fabrication facility, it is uneconomical even for many large firms to build their own facilities. Contract foundries accounted for 5% of semiconductor output in 1995 and 12% in 2000; they are expected to account for 50% by 2010.[19]

Fabless semiconductor companies are the flip side of the giant foundries. They design, organize, and market. Most new semiconductor companies are fabless, subcontracting manufacturing to the foundries. Some such new-style companies became quite large, for example, the Internet chip firm Broadcom.

The trend toward semiconductor design firms took a further step with the SIP business model, in which a developer company licenses its designs to other designers or manufacturers. The firm MIPS, for instance, helped Nintendo design the processor for its N64 gaming console. The SIP business model is still less risky and capital intensive than the fabless model, since a firm does not manufacture—not even through subcontractors—nor does it have to market any goods or maintain inventories.

Table 10.17 shows world market shares of the leading semiconductor manufacturers from 1983 to 2005 in the overall semiconductor world market. Concentration in the overall semiconductor market remained at a fairly low level (well under 1,000). The combined share of the top four companies rose slightly (from 17.4% in 1983 to 28.7 in 2003/2004). But the aggregated market data do not reveal market power in specialized products. Firms tend to focus.

Texas Instruments and Fairchild Semiconductors invented the integrated circuit in the early 1960s. American firms dominated the industry through the mid-1970s. In the 1980s, Japanese companies developed superior manufacturing and distribution capabilities and benefited from their government's umbrella. These developments enabled Japanese firms to surpass American semiconductor production in 1986. A 1986 trade agreement with Japan created market share goals (that is, quotas) and mechanisms to establish "fair market values" for prices. The major U.S. semiconductor firms, with government assistance, also formed a collaborative R&D consortium to improve manufacturing.[20] American companies rebounded in the 1990s, helped by aggressive trade negotiations, a weaker dollar, and specialized high-value products.

Memory Chips

The capability of memory chips has increased exponentially, along the exponential path of "Moore's Law," doubling every one to two years.

Table 10.17 Semiconductors (World Market Shares by Revenues)

Company	1983	1987	1992	1996	2000	2003	2005	2007
Intel (U.S.)	3.9	3.2	6.5	13.5	16.6	14.9	15.0	12.6
Toshiba (Japan)	4.6	7.8	5.6	6.2	5.6	4.2	3.9	9.6
Texas Instruments (U.S.)	8	5.4	5.3	5.2	5.8	4.3	4.8	4.6
Samsung (S. Korea)			2.4	6.1	5.3	5.3	7.6	7.3
NEC (Japan)	6.9	8.5	6.4	8.3	5.2	3.1	2.4	2.1
STMicroelectronics (France)	2	1.8	2.6	3	3.9	4.0	3.8	3.7
Motorola (U.S.)	8	6.6	6	6	3.9	2.5	0.4	
Micron (U.S.)				1.2	3.7	1.9	2.1	1.8
Renesas Technology (Japan)						4.4	3.5	3.0
Hitachi (Japan)	5.4	6.7	5	5.7	3.6	Renesas		
Mitsubishi (Japan)		3.6	3.7	2.9	2.3	Renesas		
Infineon, spun off from Siemens (Germany)	1.7	1.4	2.2	2.2	3.4	3.9	3.5	2.3
Philips (the Netherlands)	4.9	3.3	3.6	3.1	3.2	2.5	2.4	
Hynix, formerly Hyundai and LG (S. Korea)				1.2	3.2	1.7	2.4	3.4
LG Semicon/Lucky Goldstar (S. Korea)				1.4	Hynix			
Taiwan Semiconductor or TSMC (Taiwan)					2.5		3.5	
AT&T/Lucent/Agere (U.S.)		1.4	1.6	1.7	2.4	2.0	0.7	
AMD (U.S.)				1.4	2.3	2.2	1.7	2.2
Fujitsu (Japan)	2.7	3.8	3.7	2.8	2.2	1.5	1.4	
Matsushita (Japan)		3.4	3.8	1.6	2.1	2.2	1.7	1.4
IBM (U.S.)		5.8	5.2	1.1	1.7	1.4	1.5	1.1
Sharp (Japan)		1.5	2.2		1.3	1.7	1.2	1.3
Others	51.9	35.8	34.2	25.4	19.8	36.3	37.6	48.6
Global Rev. ($ bil)	17	48	73	136	205	182	235	269
C4	28.3	29.6	24.5	34.1	33.3	28.9	31.3	29.1
HHI	279	354	310	475	521	386	407	311

Notes: Calculated based on separate data for actual sales (primarily from Integrated Circuit Engineering Corp.) and for in-house distribution (primarily from *Standard & Poor's Industry Surveys,* Annual. *Sources:* Integrated Circuit Engineering Corp., *Electronic News*). Data for additional companies are from *Financial Times,* April 5, 1988; *Electronic Business Buyer,* August, 1995; Lehman Brothers, "Chips with Everything," *Lehman Brothers Equity Research,* April 2001; Salomon Smith Barney, "ST Microelectronics," *Salomon Smith Barney Equity Research,* July 1998; "Semiconductor Industry: 3rd Quarter 2000," *Morningstar Review,* Fall 2000; Salomon Smith Barney, "IBM," *Salomon Smith Barney Equity Research,* May 8, 2001, p. 68; and Salomon Smith Barney, "IBM" *Salomon Smith Barney Equity Research,* February 17, 1999, p. 16; Cahners In-Stat as cited by the Semiconductor Online Resource Center, 2001, http://www.seminconductorsonline.com. U.S. revenues are estimated using the North American share of the aggregate, global semiconductor market. 1983 statistics were estimated based on North America's 1982 market-share. Sources include "ICE Status 1997," *Integrated Circuit Engineering Corporation,* www.ice-corp.com/home/. 2000 data from SIA are as cited in "Semiconductor Analyst," *Dresdner Kleinwort Research,* April 9, 2001, p. 9. 2003 are data from "Top 20 Chip Companies to Boost Capital Spending: Purchasing," 133(11): 38, June 17, 2004. 2005 data are based on total semiconductor industry revenue from Gartner Dataquest (February 2006), and individual company revenues from: Edwards, John. "The Secret of SEMI Success," *Electronic Business* 32(2006): 51–55; *Business Source Premier,* May 23, 2006, http://search.epnet.com/login.aspx?direct=true&db=buh&an=20727738&site=ehost. 2007 revenue and marketshare from isuppli, "Top 25 suppliers of Semiconductor Worldwide in 2007."

For dynamic random-access memory (*DRAM*), it grew from 256 bits in 1968 to 1,024 bits (1K) in 1970, 4K chips in the early 1970s, 16K chips in 1979, 64K in 1980, 256K in 1982, 1MB (1,000K) in 1986, 4MB in 1993, 16MB in 1995, 64MB in 1996, 128MB in 1998, 256MB in 2000, 1,024 MB in 2004, 2,048 in 2006 and 4,096 in 2008.

Table 10.18 contains capacity and price data for DRAM chips and normalizes them for price/MB.

Competition hastened technical advances and decreased the cost per megabyte of memory from $100 in 1982 to $.02 and less by 2008, a reduction of over 5,000-fold in 25 years, a doubling every two years. What cost $100 25 years ago can now be bought retail at almost a penny. This rate would be higher still if inflation were factored in, and if it had not been slowed by price-fixing among the ten firms in 1999–2002 that resulted in criminal conviction and near-record antitrust fines. Intense competition led to rapid technological change, often making a firm's DRAM obsolete before its R&D investments and capital expenditures were recouped.

When demand decreased in the mid-1980s, the resulting glut of chips caused memory component manufacturers to lose billions. Firms manufacturing commodity products such as DRAM experienced the boom/bust cycle especially severely. By the mid-1980s seven of the nine American firms making DRAM had left the business to focus on other segments of the semiconductor market (for example, microprocessors for Intel and digital signal processors [DSPs] by Texas Instruments). As a result, Asian companies held 56% of the total memory-chip market by the late 1980s[21] and retained over 50% in the 2000s. Intense competition also drove firms into multinational joint ventures to develop new generations of DRAMs (for example, Hitachi and Texas Instruments; or Toshiba, IBM, and Siemens).

Table 10.19 contains market shares for the largest memory chip firms. In 2004, U.S. firms (mostly Micron) accounted for 17% of the worldwide market production of MOS (DRAM and ROM) memory, Japanese firms accounted for 7%, Taiwanese firms for 10%, Korean firms for over 47%, and Europeans (Infineon/Qimonda) 13%.

Figure 10.7 shows the zigzagging concentration trend line for computer memory. As a result of Toshiba's growth, the industry became moderately concentrated by 1988. But with more competitors entering the market, concentration declined again to low levels, then once again moderately concentrated. Samsung, the market leader, held 31%, followed by Micron, Hynix and Infineon/Qimonda with about 15% each.

The concentration of the top four firms dropped from 69.0% in 1975 to 44.1% in 1984 to 46.5% in 1992, then grew to 76.2% in 2004. Basically, then, the industry is dominated by four firms, surrounded by specialist providers. The four firms have tried to stabilize the market to the point of price-fixing. After an investigation and prosecution by the U.S. Department of Justice, Samsung agreed in 2005 to pay a $300 million criminal penalty—the second highest in U.S. antitrust history. Four Infineon executives were convicted

to jail sentences. Hynix paid $185 million, and Infineon $160 million, while Micron cooperated and was not fined.

Central Processors

Central processors are the "smart" elements of electronic equipment. They calculate, direct, and transform. They include general-purpose microprocessors (MPUs), as well as the related microcontrollers (MCUs), microperipherals (MPRs), and digital signal processors (DSPs). MPUs, in particular, are the essential element of microcomputers. They retrieve, decode, and execute the instructions stored in programs. MCUs are microcomponents that are designed for specific purposes in noncomputer hardware and embedded in it (for example, digital watches, automobiles, appliances).

Microprocessors MPUs function as a microcomputer's central processing units. More than any technical building block, microprocessors are the heart of the information revolution. A key indicator of their power is the length of the bit strings they process. Microprocessors expanded from 8-bit capability in the 1970s to 16-bits in the 1980s to 32-bits in 1993 to gaming consoles in 2001 sporting 128-bit processors; Intel's 128 bit PC processors and server processors (Itanium) arrived in 2001. By 2004, 256 and 512-bit processing power appeared.

Table 10.20 summarizes the power and prices of succeeding generations of Intel MPUs. The power of MPUs is measured by the number of millions of instructions per second (MIPS) they can process. Original list prices are provided for comparative purposes. However, the price of each generation of chips dropped rapidly after release. Based on original list prices, the cost of 1 MIPS of computing power dropped 4,000-fold from 1982 to 2000 and 6,500-fold by 2006 (if inflation is factored in).

Intel was founded in 1969 by Robert Noyce, Andrew Grove, and Gordon Moore to manufacture cheaper memory, but the company's work in designing generic logic chips that could be used for multiple applications in the early 1970s led the company into what became its core business, microprocessors. The company's 4-bit processor, the 4004, was released in 1971 through an ad in a Popular Electronics magazine; an 8-bit version, the 8008, was released the next year. Ten years later, the

Table 10.18 DRAM ASP (Average Sale Price) Trends in Dollars

Capacity		1984	1986	1988	1990	1992	1994	1996	1997	2001	2004	2006	2008
256K	$	21.76	2.25	3.84	2.69	1.70	2.15	1.95	2.00				
	$/MB	85.00	8.79	15.00	10.51	6.64	8.40	7.62	7.81				
1MB	$		35.00	17.00	5.54	3.01	3.60	2.85	2.56				
	$/MB		35.00	17.00	5.54	3.01	3.60	2.85	2.56				
4MB	$				36.43	11.72	12.00	5.31	2.42				
	$/MB				9.11	2.93	3.00	1.33	0.61				
16MB	$					205.00	61.85	16.11	7.60				
	$/MB					12.81	3.87	1.01	0.48				
64MB	$						575.00	100.35	51.54	38.77	25.99		
	$/MB						8.98	1.57	0.81	0.61	0.41		
128MB	$										27.99		
	$/MB										0.22		
256MB	$										46.99	23.61	6.48
	$/MB										0.18	0.09	0.025
512MB	$										86.99	39.83	8.49
	$/MB										0.17	0.08	0.016
1,024MB	$										215.00	85.90	27.9
	$/MB										0.21	0.08	0.026
2,048MB	$											288.50	64.0
	$/MB											0.14	0.03
4,096 MB	$												73.2
	$/MB												0.02

Sources: Integrated Circuit Engineering Corporation, ICE Status 1998, www.ice-corp.com/home/, and median of ten lowest prices for PC133 DRAM as researched at prices-can.com, and reported by [etelint.com], an Asian technology research firm ($2.50 per 64Mbit chip as of January 20, 2001, with eight chips going into a single 64MB unit). 2001 and 2004 data for smaller units are sporadic due to the relative shrinking of markets for smaller memory modules. The price for 64MB in 2001 is extrapolated from 1997 and 2004. Data for 2004 are based on sale prices as found on www.epinions.com and www.cnetshopper.com. 2006 and 2008 data are based on sale prices from www.pricewatch.com (the average of five brands' DDR SDRAM PC3200 modules).

Table 10.19 Memory chips (MOS/ROM/DRAM) (Global Market Shares Based on Revenue)

	1975	1984	1988	1991	1992	1996	2001	2004
Samsung (S. Korea)		2.2	4.3	12.3	14.0	15.6	22.0	30.8
Micron (U.S.)		1.6	3.0	4.8	8.5	12.2	16.0	15.8
Texas Instruments (U.S.)	11.0	6.4	7.7	7.6	7.6	Micron		
Toshiba (Japan)		13.7	25.6	14.0	11.6	9.1	5.8	Micron
Infineon/Qimonda, spun out from Siemens (Germany)					2.0	4.0	8.0	13.3
Hynix (formerly Hyundai, S. Korea)				2.9	4.3	8.5	10.9	16.3
LG (S. Korea)					5.2	7.5	Hynix	
Nanya (Taiwan)							1.8	4.5
Elpida (Japan)							6.1	5.9
Mitsubishi (Japan)		6.4	12.6	7.0	5.0	3.0	3.4	Elpida
NEC (Japan)		6.6	12.8	10.0	10.7	11.4	4.0	Elpida
Hitachi (Japan)		5.8	10.9	10.2	10.3	10.4	4.3	Elpida
Mosel Vitelic (U.S.)							2.4	1.0
Powerchip (Taiwan)							0.8	4.3
Oki (Japan)		2.7	5.3	5.2	4.8	4.3	2.5	0.6
Intel (U.S.)	33.0	16.0						
Mostek (U.S.)	13.0	7.2						
AMI (U.S.)	12.0	7.2						
Intersil (U.S.)	7.0	3.2						
National Semiconductor (U.S.)	3.0	2.0						
Other	21.0	14.0	17.8	26.0	16.2	14.0	12.0	7.5
Global Rev. ($ mil)		7,600	8,800	12,300	21,150	30,000	26,800	26,718
Est. U.S. Rev. ($ mil)		3,300	4,400	4,800	7,200	9,600	8,330	8,305
C4	69.0	44.1	61.9	46.5	46.5	49.6	56.9	76.2
HHI	1,581	735	1,212	717	775	885	1,055	1,716

Sources: Company Reports, and "Semiconductor Industry," *Standard and Poor's Industry Surveys*, McGraw Hill, 1996. 1984 figures are extrapolated from 1975 and 1988 figures. Market share percentages and global revenue for 2004 are taken from Gartner Dataquest's February 2005 report on the DRAM market, assuming that the ROM market, with total revenue of less than $1 billion, has an insignificant effect on these numbers.

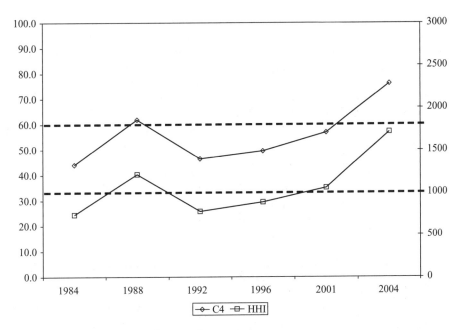

Figure 10.7 Memory Semiconductors: Concentration

Table 10.20 Power and Prices of Intel Microprocessor Generations

Chip	Launch Date	Original Price	Adjusted for Inflation (2006 $)[a]	Transistors/ chip	MIPS	$/MIPS	$/MIPS (adj. for inflation)
8086/8088	1978	$360	$1,113	60,000	0.3	$1,200.00	$3,710.00
80286	1982	$360	$752	134,000	0.9	$400.00	$835.56
80386	1985	$299	$560	275,000	6	$49.83	$93.33
80486	1989	$950	$1,544	1,000,000	20	$47.50	$77.20
Pentium	1993	$878	$1,224	3,200,000	100	$8.78	$12.24
Pentium Pro	1995	$974	$1,288	5,500,000	440	$2.21	$2.93
Pentium II	1997	$725	$910	7,500,000	600	$1.21	$1.52
Pentium III	1999	$790	$955	9,500,000	760	$1.04	$1.26
Pentium IV	2000	$819	$958	42,000,000	2,661	$0.31	$0.36
Pentium M[b]	2003	$672	$736	77,000,000	5,500	$0.12	$0.13
Core Duo	2006	$637	$637	151,600,000	20,000	$0.03	$0.03

Source: Early data based on Hill, G. Christian, "Bringing It Home," *The Wall Street Journal,* June 16, 1997, p. R1. *Sources:* Kleiner Perkins Caufield & Byers; Intel Corp.; Dataquest Inc. and *Plunkett's Information Technology Almanac,* Houston: Plunkett Research, p. 26, 2001; "Evolution of Intel Microprocessors: 1971 to 2003," *Archive Builders,* last updated March 1, 2000, p. 1; "Pentium, Pentium II Hit New Highs," April 18, 1997, *CNET* http://www.news.com; "Pentium III Is Now on Sale," January 29, 1999, *CNET,* http://www.news.com; "Intel Pentium 4," 2001, http://www.DansData.com; Lima, Cassio, "All Core Duo Models," April 6, 2006 http://www.hardwaresecrets.com/article/311/1.

[a] Calculated using the "CPI Inflation Calculator" for buying power, provided by the U.S. Department of Labor Bureau of Statistics. Available at http://data.bls.gov/cgi-bin/cpicalc.pl.
[b] After 2001 Intel started to use different measurements for its processors, such as WebMark instead of MIPS standard.

company introduced its breakthrough 80286 processor, which first appeared in the IBM PC microcomputer in 1984. To ensure a supply of MPUs, IBM bought one-third of Intel for $250 million in 1983, but sold it again in 1987.

In 1985, Intel introduced the 386 family of processors (the first 32-bit MPUs, much faster than the 286). Soon thereafter, Compaq released its Deskpro 386, the first to use the new generation chip, ahead of IBM.

Intel dominated the industry as the result of a combination of factors: an early lead, scale, brand identity, and market power. The firm was threatened with several antitrust investigations. In 1998 the Federal Trade Commission filed an antitrust action against Intel alleging that when the computer makers Compaq, DEC, and Intergraph refused to license patents on Intel's terms, Intel retaliated by withholding technical information—and threatening to cut off chip supplies. After 2000, AMD gained on Intel. Computer vendors were attracted by its second-sourcing role and lower prices. In 2006, it even surged ahead in product performance with its Opteron line, which beat Intel to the 64-bit chip design. As a result, AMD increased its share in the important server market.[22]

VIA Technologies, a Taiwanese chipset manufacturer, bought Cyrix from National Semiconductor in 1999 after the company proved unable to survive against Intel's low-end Celeron chip. Transmeta, a Silicon Valley startup, developed an Intel-compatible processor that consumes less power than Intel processors, thus enabling battery-powered notebooks to run longer than with Intel processors.

Table 10.21 shows the shares in the microprocessor market from 1984 to 2005. Concentration was high in this industry. Throughout the period Intel remained market leader, with a peak of 82.1% in 2000. AMD and Motorola held small-sized positions.

Figure 10.8 depicts the high-concentration trend of this industry. The increase in concentration after 1988 was the result of Intel's share increase. After 1996, the market stabilized at a very high concentration level.

In the mid-1980s, Intel developed the i860 RISC chip (reduced instruction-set computing). RISC chips use far fewer transistors than CISC (complex instruction-set computing) chips and therefore work much faster. Sun Microsystems, Hewlett-Packard, and IBM also introduced RISC microprocessors. Their competition led Intel to

scale back RISC production and focus on its traditional CISC architecture.[23] CISC chips remain the standard for microcomputers, whereas RISC chips became the standard for workstations which demand greater processing speed. Concentration levels dropped from high to low, but the market size is modest (table 10.22, figure 10.8).

Microcontrollers (MCUs) are microcomponents that are preprogrammed to perform specific functions in noncomputer devices ranging from digital watches to automobiles. The U.S. market for MCUs grew significantly in the 1990s. The proliferation of intelligent equipment has led to a plethora of non-PC computing devices, including PDAs, cell phones, gaming machines, and others, produced previously by Japanese consumer electronics firms (Table 10.23, figure 10.8).

COMPUTER SOFTWARE

Since the ascendancy of microcomputers in the 1980s and the creation of a mass market for computing, the software industry has become a vibrant sector in the economy. Many creative new companies and products have emerged. For a long time the global industry was dominated by U.S. firms. In 2004, U.S. software industry revenues totaled $96.5 billion in the U.S. alone. The worldwide computer software industry had 2004 revenue of about $190 billion.

Computer software falls into two broad categories: systems software and applications software. Systems software includes database-management software, operating systems and their enhancements, and networking software. Applications software perform specific functions (for example, word processing) and can be either customized for individual users or sold in standardized packages. The sharp growth in personal computers has changed the nature of the software industry from a low-volume, high-price business to one of high volume and low price.

Systems Software

Computer Operating Systems An operating system manages a computer's activities and its user interface. Microsoft had over 90% of the market of all operating systems on PCs worldwide in 2004. When IBM introduced its first PC in 1981, it used Microsoft's MS-DOS operating system. Apple's

Table 10.21 Microprocessors (Global Market Shares by Shipments)

Company	1984	1986	1988	1992	1994	1995	1996	1997	2000	2001	2003/4	2005	2008
Intel (U.S.)	66.0	61.0	64.0	68.0	73.1	75.6	78.7	81.7	82.1	77.1	78.7	80.3	79.7
AMD (U.S.)	7.0	9.0	10.0	11.0	9.0	6.1	4.7	3.3	8.1	9.6	13.9	18.1	13.0
Motorola (U.S.)	15.0	13.1	12.0	11.0	7.5	5.5	4.9	4.3	6.1	4.0	1.8		
IBM (U.S.)			1.5	3.0	2.7	3.3	2.9	2.4	1.0				
Texas Instr. (U.S.)	0.4	2.0	2.0	2.0	1.8	1.5	1.3	1.0	1.4				
VIA												1.4	
National Semiconductor/ Cyrix (U.S.)					2.2	1.5	1.5	1.5	Via				
Hitachi (Japan)	0.1	1.2	1.2	1.1	0.6	1.3	1.3	1.3					
NEC (Japan)	1.5	2.0	1.5	1.0	0.7	0.7	1.0	1.2	1.0				
Others	10.0	11.7	7.8	2.9	2.4	4.5	3.9	3.3	0.3	9.3	5.7	0.2	7.3
Global Rev. ($ mil)	746	907	2,881	4,855	10,950	14,300	18,900	23,500	26,955	21,354	22,000	30,000	34,660
Est. U.S. Rev. ($ mil)	321	390	1,627	2,864	4,928	6,149	8,127	10,105	11,591	9,609	9,900	13,500	15,597
C4	89.5	85.1	88.0	93.0	92.3	90.5	91.1	91.7	97.7	86.7	92.5	98.4	92.7
HHI	4,632	3,983	4,350	4,881	5,497	5,800	6,246	6,716	6,847	6,053	6,389	6,778	6,521

Sources: 2002 data are from Walter Smith, Thomas, "Semiconductors Industry Surveys," *Standard & Poor's*. 1999 data are from Market Share Reporter, "PC Processor Market 0 1999," Gale Group, 2001. 1998 data are from Market Share Reporter, "Top Microprocessor Makers—1998," Gale Group, 2001; Integrated Circuit Engineering Corporation, ICE Status 1997, [www.ice-corp.com/home/]. 2001 data are from SEMICONDUCTORS—Microprocessor Market Share Summary, CIBC World Markets Corp, Jan 17, 2002. Market shares for 1984–1992 were calculated based on the companies' microprocessor revenues extracted from "Electronics Current Analysis," *Standard & Poor's Industry Surveys*, June 7, 1984, September 3, 1987, January 12, 1989, June 10 1993, August 3, 1995. National Semiconductor purchased Cyrix in 1997. Via Technologies purchased Cyrix division from National Semiconductor in 1999. 1988 and 1996 figures were extrapolated from 1986, 1992, 1995, and 1997 figures.—indicates a market share smaller than 1%. Data for 2004 are estimated based on Hoover's Company Profile. Data for 2005 are from "Intel and AMD: Part I—Microprocessor Volumes, Pricing, and Share Trends—AMD Looks Better," Feb. 6, 2006; Sanford Bernstein and Co., Adam S. Parker, May 31, 2006; Reuters Research-on-Demand. 2005 global revenues are from Gartner Dataquest, August 2005. 2008 Data from iSuppli corporation, Q12008. Global revenues extrapolated from company reports.

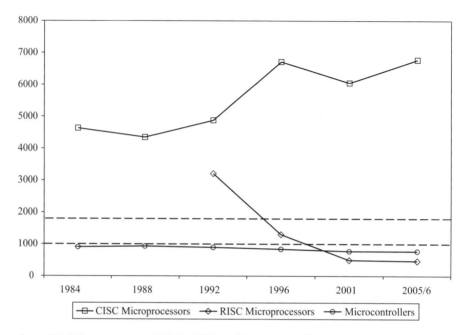

Figure 10.8 Microprocessors (CISC, RISC, and Microcontrollers): Concentration (HHI)

Table 10.22 RISC Microprocessors (Global Market Shares by Shipments)

	1993	1994	1995	1996	1997	1998	1999	2000	2001	2003/4
ARM	1.0	2.5	1.6	2.7	3.3	6.6	9.6	13.1	17.0	17.0
Motorola									10.0	10.0
Hitachi		9.0	41.0	31.0	24.0	17.0	13.0	7.0	7.0	7.0
MIPS	5.1	4.7	3.2	3.5	2.8	5.3	6.9	7.8	6.8	3.8
IBM	3.0	7.0	10.0	7.0	4.0	5.0	3.0	3.0	3.0	3.5
Intel	55.0	40.0	17.0	16.0	10.0	6.0	2.0	1.0	1.0	1.0
Sun	5.0	6.0	2.0	2.0	1.0	1.0	2.0	1.0	1.0	1.0
AMD	11.0	12.0	5.0	3.0	2.0	1.0	0.0	0.0	0.0	0.0
Other	19.9	18.8	20.2	34.8	52.9	58.1	63.5	67.1	54.2	56.6
Global Rev. ($ mil)	650	721	1,631	1,862	2,334	1,910	1,979	2,048	2,232	2,433
Est. U.S. Rev. ($ mil)	182	202	457	521	654	535	520	573	625	681
C4	76.1	68.0	73.0	57.5	41.3	34.9	32.5	30.9	40.8	37.8
HHI	3,207	1,938	2,112	1,299	716	424	326	292	495	468

Source: "Server & Enterprise Hardware and PC Hardware Quarterly," Salomon Smith Barney, September 2000, p. 105. U.S. market size is based on 28% share of the global market. "Industry Survey. Semiconductor Equipment," *Standard & Poor's*, February 14, 2002. 1993 data for market share is from "Server and Enterprise Hardware", Salomon Brother, March 1996. Data for 1993, 1994, and 1998 market size of global RISC chips are from Vanhaverbeke, Wim, Niels G. Noorderhaven, "Competition Between Alliance Blocks: The Case of the RISC Microprocessor Technology." *Organization Studies*, vol. 22, No. 1, 2001, pp. 1–30. Data for 1995 and 1997 global RISC chips market was estimated based on the 4% RISC market value within the worldwide RISC systems market. Data for 2004 use company growth percentages from Hoover's Company Profiles.

Table 10.23 Microcontrollers (Market Shares by Shipments)

	1984	1986	1988	1990	1992	1994	1996	1997	2001	2005
Motorola	11.6	12.4	12.0	11.6	13.7	15.7	16.9	16.5	24.0	15.1
Renesas										16.8
Mitsubishi	8.0	8.4	9.5	10.5	10.2	9.9	8.6	8.2	9.4	Renesas
Hitachi	9.7	10.0	12.8	15.6	14.0	12.3	11.0	11.3	10.0	Renesas
Intel	2.3	1.3	1.6	1.9	2.7	3.4	5.0	5.4	10.6	9.3
NEC	23.2	22.0	20.6	19.2	17.0	14.8	14.9	13.9	12.0	8.0
ST Micro					1.0	2.0	2.7	3.8	8.8	7.0
Microchip Tech.					0.8	1.5	2.0	2.7	4.5	5.8
Philips	0.8	2.0	3.1	4.2	5.0	5.8	5.6	4.7	5.6	5.2
Toshiba	5.0	6.0	6.3	6.6	6.5	6.3	6.0	5.5	2.8	1.1
Fujitsu	2.2	2.0	2.5	3.0	3.4	3.8	3.8	5.0	2.5	1.0
Matsushita	6.0	7.7	6.8	5.9	5.3	4.7	4.0	3.3	1.7	0.7
Texas Instruments	1.0	1.2	1.5	1.7	2.0	2.2	2.0	2.3	1.2	0.6
Other	30.2	27.0	23.4	19.8	18.7	17.6	17.5	17.4	17.4	26.1
Global Rev. ($ mil)	717	1,550	2,725	3,900	6,200	8,500	9,904	10,791	11,808	13,230
Est. U.S. Rev. ($ mil)	394	853	1,499	2,145	2,433	2,720	3,169	3,453	3,779	4,234
C4	52.5	52.8	54.9	56.9	54.8	52.7	51.4	49.9	56.6	49.2
C8	68.0	70.5	73.6	76.6	75.0	73.3	72.0	70.5	84.9	68.3
HHI	904	915	928	968	893	847	841	805	1,168	773

Note: Integrated Circuit Engineering Corp., Dataquest ST microelectronics was formed through the 1987 merger of SGS Microelettronica and Thomson-CSF (later Thales). *Sources:* 1996 and 1997 market shares are from Paine Webber, "Semiconductor Industry: Microcontroller Market Analysis," March 23, 1999, p. 11. Market shares for 1984–1992 were calculated based on the Microcontroller revenues extracted from "Electronics Current Analysis," *Standard & Poor's Industry Surveys,* June 7, 1984, September 3, 1987, January 12, 1989, June 10 1993, August 3, 1995. U.S. market size for 1984–1990 was estimated based on 55% U.S. share of the global market. "Electronics. Current Analysis," *Standard & Poor's Industry Surveys,* May 30, 1991, p. E31, declining 32%. Data for 2004 were extrapolated from growth rates for the periods 2001–2003 and 1997–2001. 2004 figures for Motorola and Renesas were taken from "MCU/MPU Market Keeps Growing," *Electronic News* (North America) 51, 2005; *Business Source Premier,* EBSCO, New York, May 24, 2006, http://search.epnet.com/login.aspx?direct=true&db=buh&an=17126409&site=ehost; "Hitachi and Mitusbishi Electric Sign Joint Venture Agreement for Establishing Renesas Technology," Dec. 26, 2002. Hitachi, Ltd., May 24, 2006 http://www.hitachi.com/New/cnews/E/2002/1226/1226.pdf. Global revenue figures are from Gartner Dataquest, August 2005.

Macintosh had its own preloaded operating system. DOS emerged as the industry standard, riding on IBM's reputation. Later, IBM developed its own operating system, OS/2. In 1991, Microsoft introduced Windows, an operating system that followed the user-friendly Macintosh graphic interface. Windows became the industry standard (table 10.24).

Unix, another operating system, was developed by AT&T in 1969 and was designed for multiusers (many people at one time); it became popular for Internet servers. The popularity of Unix led several firms to develop proprietary versions of Unix, which created compatibility problems.

In 2007, Microsoft dominated the computer operating system market with 91.8%, and Apple's share was 7.3%, but growing again. Linux had a small but loyal following. On the whole, the market was dominated by Microsoft, making its principal owners, Bill Gates and Paul Allen, into the richest men in the world and the target of governmental antitrust actions in the United States and Europe.

After the U.S. Department of Justice and 20 states brought a second antitrust suit against Microsoft in 1998, Judge Thomas Penfield Jackson found in 1999 that Microsoft had monopolized the market, had abused its power, and was engaged in unlawful business practices. He recommended restrictions on the conduct of Microsoft's business and splitting the firm into an operating system software company and an

Table 10.24 Computer Operating Systems (PC)—(Market Shares by Shipments)

Company	1984	1988	1992	1996	1998	1999	2000	2001	2004	2005	2007
Microsoft (DOS & Windows)	40.5	82.4	81.8	85.5	86.3	87.0	90.0	91.0	96.4	94.9	91.8
Apple (Macintosh)	13.0	13.0	11.8	6.2	4.6	5.0	3.0	3.0	3.3	4.3	7.3
Unix	2.3	3.6	3.3	3.0	2.5	2.5	2.0	2.0			
IBM OS/2		1.0	3.1	4.5	2.0						
Linux Providers[a]								0.1	0.29	0.5	0.6
Digital Research (CP/M & CP/M 86)	33.6										
Other	10.6	0.0	0.0	0.8	4.6	5.5	5.0	3.9	0.1	0.3	0.3
Global Rev. ($ mil)	1,526	2,232	2,585	3,815	5,778	7,395	9,011	9,286	9,569	10,047	
Est. U.S. Rev. ($ mil)	1,068	1,562	1,810	2,670	4,045	5,177	6,308	6,500	6,698	7,033	
C4	97.7	100.0	100.0	99.2	95.4	94.5	95.0	96.1	99.9	99.7	99.7
HHI	3,056	6,973	6,851	7,379	7,500	7,631	8,138	8,309	9,304	9,025	8,481

Sources: New York Times, December 31, 1989, citing International Data Corporation; *New York Times,* March 15, 1991, p. C1, citing Shearson Lehman; "Dataquest Downgrades Forecast for Windows 95," Dataquest Inc., August 12, 1996. 2000 data show global market shares and IDC and Merrill Lynch estimates as cited in Merrill Lynch, "Microsoft," *Merrill Lynch Securities,* February 8, 1002, p. 41. The 1995–1997 total global revenue figure is calculated from Microsoft's market share and desktop operating system revenues in "U.S. Investment Research," Morgan Stanley Dean Witter, November 6, 1997. Estimated 1997 U.S. revenue is based on SIIA's (Software & Information Industry Association) assumption that the United States held approximately a 70% share of the world market that year. The 1997 Unix market share figure is the average of 1995 and 2000 Unix market share figures. The 1995 Apple, Unix, and IBM OS/2 market share figure is from Newsport, [www.newsport.org/archive/s97/ms/mshare/opsys.html]. 1988, 1990, and 1996 global revenues are extrapolated from 1983, 1995, and 1997 global revenue figures. 1998 figures are from *Wall Street Journal,* November 28, 2000, from International Data Corp. 2001 figures are extrapolated from 2000 figures and companies' revenues from 2001. Data for 2004 and 2005 are based on market share percentage reported by Net Applications http://market-share.hitslink.com/report.aspx?qprid=2&qptimeframe=M&qpsp=83. 2005 Global and U.S. revenue is based on 5% growth fore-cast by Software and Information Industry Association. Elmer-DeWitt, Philip. "Survey: Mac OS hit record 7.3% share in December, iPhone up 33%." *CNN Money.* CNNMoney.com. January 1, 2008. Last accessed on January 24, 2008, from http://apple20.blogs.fortune.cnncom/2008/01/01/survey-mac-os-hit-record-73-share-in-december-iphone-up-33/

[a] Includes Red Hat, Debian, Fedora, Gentoo, Stackware, and Ubuntu.

applications software company. In early 2001, a Federal Court of Appeals upheld Judge Jackson's findings but not necessarily his prescribed remedy. Judge Jackson was replaced. The case was on its way to the Supreme Court when the Justice Department, now under the Bush administration, settled with Microsoft. The remedy left Microsoft intact but required it to provide information to software developers. The various states that were also litigants grumbled but eventually settled. This left the EU Commission to keep the case alive. In 2004, the EU ruled that Microsoft put its competitors at an unfair disadvantage by embedding free media-playing software in its Windows operating system and by withholding technical information needed by rival software developers. The decision obliged Microsoft to create an instruction manual on its Windows OS and discontinue packaging the free media-player into Windows OS, which prevented rivals such as RealNetworks from selling their own media-playing programs. Microsoft paid over $3 billion to settle with Sun, RealNetworks, and Novell. It unsuccessfully appealed the EU's ruling. In 2006, the EU found that Microsoft had not complied with the mandate, and fined the increasingly unpopular American company $357 million, a record fine by far, from that body.[24] In 2007, the EU fined Microsoft $613 million, and in 2008, it intiated two investigations against the company on the same issues: bundling of browser and operating system and refusal to disclose information enabling competitors' applications to easily interoperate with the Windows Office Suite. In 2008, the EU fined Microsoft yet again for continuing to ignore the remedies prescribed in the 2004 ruling, in the record amount of $1.35 billion.[25]

Linux, a new operating system, was born of the open source movement, which makes the source code available to software developers. Linux, an offspring of Unix, was originally written by the Finnish software developer Linus Torvalds and released to the open source community, where it was reworked through voluntary efforts of a wide community of programmers. Linux has a freely available source code with a General Public License, that requires subsequent developers to provide the original source code to their customers. Linux is offered as prepackaged software with some PCs, workstations, and other computing devices. Linux has been embraced by large companies such as IBM, Hewlett-Packard, Dell, and by several governments for their procurement, often to reduce their dependence on Microsoft products and to lower cost. Linux achieved a strongly committed following. But its market share among desktop microcomputer users has been low. Worldwide shipments and deployments of Linux-based PCs totaled only 6 million, in 2007 perhaps because most PC users do not have the expertise and time to install and modify the Linux kernel or download it from Linux providers and also lack system support. Linux's share was much more substantial for more powerful servers and networks. Linux firms such as Red Hat concentrated on the server, not the desktop.[26]

In the late 1990s, there were new developments in operating system software. The first and most potentially challenging development for operating system providers was the growth of the Internet. As transmission bandwidth grew cheap and plentiful, many observers expected that users would only need a so-called "thin client" with which to access the Internet, with the intensive computing done at a distance by more powerful servers. One of the key enablers of the thin-client or network computer vision was Java software by Sun,

introduced in 1995. Programs written in Java can run on a computer regardless of its operating system—they are platform independent. Java's platform independence enables a developer to write code in only one language (without having to prepare different versions for Linux, Windows, Mac OS, and so forth), and also frees software developers and users from being shackled to a particular operating system. By reducing the need for a standardized operating system, platform independent languages enable operating systems to compete with one another based only upon their price and performance criteria such as speed, reliability, and ease of use. Operating systems then cease to set the standards to which application developers must adhere.

The thin-client network computer concept failed to live up to expectations, and sales floundered in the United States because of the decreasing price of personal computers. Network computers' global sales represent 1% of the desktop PC market. Nevertheless, NC proponents predict a comeback in the form of affordable laptops for developing nations.

Network Operating Systems Network operating systems (NOS) set communication protocols and govern the use of shared resources by network users. NOS provide the backbone of local area networks (LANs). As the number of LANs increased, the NOS market increased rapidly. The percentage of PCs that are networked in some way increased from 33% in 1992 to 80% by 1999 to over 90% in 2008.

The NOS market is highly concentrated. The combined share of the top four firms providing networking software remained steady from 77% in 1988 to 75% in 2004 (table 10.25).

Figure 10.9 shows this initial increase and subsequent decrease in concentration. Novell dominated this industry until 1996, with a peak share of 59%. Microsoft, Sun, Hewlett-Packard, and Compaq entered and temporarily lowered the level of concentration. Microsoft subsequently achieved major market power as its share rose to almost half of the market. Linux reached a combined 28.4% in 2004 through a variety of providers. The two major commercial Linux distributors are Red Hat and Novell (which acquired SUSE Linux in 2004).[27] Noncommercial Linux providers include Debian, Fedora, Gentoo, Slackware, and Ubuntu.[28]

Applications Software

In the days of mainframes, much of the software used to be written as custom jobs by manufacturers or by the users themselves. In contrast, packaged applications software is prewritten for numerous users. The industry consists of two segments, client and enterprise software. Client software runs on PCs and usually serves an individual user. Examples are word processors, spreadsheets, and personal productivity tools. Enterprise software includes categories for departmental, enterprise, Internet, intranet, and extranets.

Microsoft achieved dominance of PC software applications because it bundled a complete applications "suite" of multiple programs, which displaced the specialized titles such as those of WordPerfect and Lotus.

By 2008, about 80% of U.S. homes had a PC, and the demand for user-friendly platforms grew enormously.

As software became more complex, the software industry separated itself from the hardware industry. Independent software companies increasingly wrote the application programs for the equipment.

Table 10.25 Network Operating Systems (Market Shares by Shipments)

Company	1988	1992	1995	1996	2000	2001	2004
Microsoft (Windows NT and Windows 2000)			13.0	17.0	38.0	41.9	46.2
Free Linux providers[a]					14.9	15.9	13.4
Novell (NetWare, SUSE Linux)[b]	46.0	57.0	59.0	55.0	15.0	13.4	8.7
Red Hat (Linux)					5.1	5.5	6.3
Sun				0.5	5.0	5.6	5.0
IBM	10.0	7.0	10.0	9.0	4.0	4.0	4.0
Hewlett-Packard				0.5	3.0	3.0	3.7
Compaq				0.5	1.0	0.7	HP
Banyan (Vines)	6.0	11.0	6.0	5.0			
Artisoft (LANtastic)			5.0	4.0			
Apple (AppleShare)	15.0	7.0	4.0	3.0			
Digital (Pathworks)		4.0	3.0	2.0			
Others	23.0	18.0	3.0	3.5	14.0	10.0	12.6
Global Rev. ($ mil)	685	788	1,652	2,372	3,092	3,100	3,132
Est. U.S. Rev. ($mil)	480	552	1,156	1,660	2,164	2,170	2,192
C4	77.0	82.0	88.0	86.0	73.0	76.8	74.7
HHI	2,477	3,484	3,836	3,454	1,968	2,275	2,485

Sources: Market Share Reporter, 1991, Table 1854, Source: PC Week, March 12, 1990, p. 133. Revenue information from Carr, Jim, "Forecast: Growth: The LAN Market Just Keeps Getting Bigger and Bigger," The Local Area Network Magazine, May 1990, p. 48, Source: Solomon Brothers. Financial World, April 12, 1992, p. 22, Source: Computer Intelligence. Revenue estimate from McMullen, Melanie, "Serving Two Masters," Local Network Magazine, June 1992, p. 55, Source: Dataquest. Computer Reseller News, June 3, 1996. Revenue estimate from "The LAN Market," Computer Industry Report, Aug. 31, 1995, p. 1, Source: International Data Corp. 2000 market share data assume that U.S. market shares mimic global market shares and are based on 2000 unit sales. McPeake, John, "Microsoft," Prudential Securities, p. 40, July 13, 2001. Novell Corporation, "2001 10-K," Novell, p. 17, December 31, 2001. "Sun Undisputed Unix Server Market Leader," System News, December 13, 2000 http://sun. systemnews.com/system-news/jobdir/submitted/2001.02/2956/2956.html. 2000 global revenue is extrapolated from Microsoft's Windows NT Server and Windows 2000 revenues, which account for 38% market share. Estimated U.S. revenues is based on SIIA's assumption that the United States market accounts for 70% of global software revenues. 1995 global revenue figure is extrapolated from 1992 and 2000 figures. 2001 figures are extrapolated from 2000 figures and 2001 revenues as stated in companies' 10-k reports. Global revenue and U.S. revenue are estimates based on the stagnant growth rate of the total software industry during 2000–2001. 1996 data are extrapolated based on 1995 and 2000 data. Red Hat's market share is calculated from 2004 revenue of $196.5 million. Market share of SUSE Linux, acquired by Novell in 2004, is calculated by subtraction from free Linux providers. Overall Linux providers experienced a 14% increase in market share from 2001 to 2004, Larry Greenemeier, "Linux Going Mainstream," Information Week, May 24, 2004.

[a] Includes, in the U.S., Debian, Fedora, Gentoo, Slackware, and Ubuntu.

[b] Novell lost significant market share to Microsoft and free Linux providers. In 2004, it acquired SUSE Linux and regained marked some share. "Novell Acquires SUSE and IBM Tosses In," Nov. 4, 2003. internetnews.com, July 18, 2006 http://www.internetnews.com/dev-news/article.php/3103951.

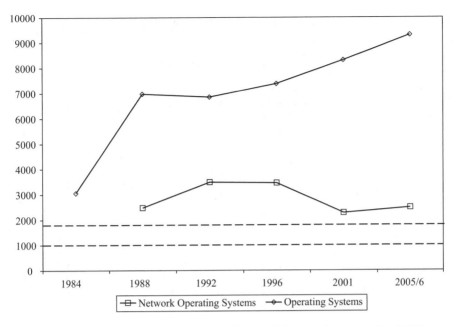

Figure 10.9 Computer and Network Operating System Software: Concentration (HHI)

Table 10.26 provides a market share breakdown of the enterprise application software market.

The industry grew from $233 million to $3.2 billion in the United States in the period 1984–1996, and $13 billion by 2004. Most entrants were small. Significant market shares were held by Microsoft, IBM, and Oracle (which acquired PeopleSoft). Concentration hovered around 900 and rose to 1,117. It is moderately concentrated as a whole, although it's often a different story in subsegments (figure 10.10). Here, many applications segments became concentrated; for example, the word processing software is dominated by Microsoft's Word. There are advantages for a single platform so that documents are easily exchanged and users can move from machine to machine.

Another submarket is applications for computer mainframes (table 10.27). Here, IBM's huge installed hardware base gives it major advantages in software. Computer Associates is a distant second, and has been racked by corporate problems after 2004.

Software Services

Software service providers do not sell products but deliver a service, such as processing or special programming.

This is a large and growing industry. Revenues have increased substantially. IBM has historically dominated this market, but other major providers emerged, in particular, Oracle, EDS and SAP. This led to a lowering of HHI from 2,254 to 1,487 in 2004 (table 10.28, figure 10.10).

Video Game Software

In the U.S., video game software was an $11 billion business in 2004. This number can be divided into two segments: game console software and PC game software. The former accounts for about three-quarters of the market and is discussed first.

Because each video game machine is a proprietary platform, these machines will only run software that is either produced in-house by the hardware manufacturer or produced by small third-party publishers (who pay license fees to the game companies and earn royalties on cartridge sales).

The game software industry is fragmented. The industry's fairly low barriers to entry, the programmers' creative potential, and gamers' obsessive nature attract numerous participants. Gaming software is much more of a media industry than a technology industry.

Table 10.26 Enterprise Application Software (Market Share by Shipments)

Company	1984	1988	1992	1996	1998	2000	2001	2004
Microsoft	0.2	1.4	3.3	7.4	13.9	15.2	19.7	21.9
IBM	28.9	27.6	28.2	28.7	21.7	19.0	18.1	18.3
Lotus	6.4	9.1	6.5	IBM				
Oracle	0.9	11.0	9.5	9.9	9.9	12.2	10.5	13.0
PeopleSoft		0.1	0.3	1.3	2.1	1.4	1.5	Oracle
SAP	2.8	3.5	4.0	6.0	4.7	5.6	5.6	6.0
EMC				2.1	2.7	3.6	3.8	3.8
Verisign				0	0.1	1.3	2.4	3.8
Symantec			2.7	1.9	1.7	2.3	2.4	3.0
Veritas			0.1	0.2	0.5	2.5	2.7	3.3
Adobe	0.5	1.5	4.0	3.4	2.8	3.0	3.0	3.0
Intuit	3.7	3.0	2.3	2.3	1.8	2.3	2.7	3.0
Siebel				0.2	0.9	2.8	2.5	2.6
Computer Associates	0.9	2.7	2.1	4.2	4.0	4.4	2.8	2.5
Autodesk			2.0	2.6	2.4	2.1	2.3	2.4
Cadence			1.6	1.8	2.4	1.6	2.1	2.1
BEA Systems				0.1	0.3	0.7	1.2	1.4
Network Associate			1.0	1.2	2.1	1.4	1.2	1.2
Rational	0.2	0.2	0.3	0.5	0.6	0.9	1.2	1.2
I2 Tech				0.2	0.7	2.0	1.1	1.1
JD Edwards		0.2	0.4	0.8	1.2	1.1	0.7	0.7
Others	55.5	39.7	31.7	25.2	23.5	14.6	12.5	5.7
Global Rev. ($mil)	349	783	1,757	4,775	8,564	12,545	16,716	18,571
Est. U.S. Rev. ($mil)	233	522	1,171	3,183	5,709	8,363	11,144	13,000
C4	41.8	51.2	48.2	52.0	50.2	52.0	53.9	59.2
C8	44.3	59.8	60.5	64.5	62.1	65.8	66.2	73.1
HHI	900	998	996	1,069	845	857	939	1,117

Note: This table reflects enterprise software from 18 separate vertical markets. These application software markets include analytical, application server, application development tool, computer aided design (CAD), content management, customer relationship management (CRM), education and learning, enterprise resource planning (ERP), entertainment, financial, health care, integration, personal productivity, relational database management (RDBMS), security, storage, supply chain management, and telecommunications. *Sources:* Figures from 1996, 1998, 2002, and 2004 companies' license revenues and software industry trends from *Standard and Poor's Industry Surveys*, McGraw Hill, Annual.; *Softletter*, Annual; p. 47; *1986 U.S. Industrial Outlook;* Thomas, Donald A. Jr., "History of the When of the Integrated Circuit," http://www.icwhen.com/book/the%201980s/1984.html, March 2002; "Worldwide Software Market," Salomon Brothers Equity Research, p. 51, March 1996; and *Datamation,* June 15, 1990, p. 195. The source for U.S. market size 1995–2001 is from Icon Group Ltd., [www.incongroupedition.com]. 1984–2004 figures are based on revenues from companies' respective annual reports and "A Complete Competitive Analysis of the U.S. Software Market," ABN-AMRO, March 18, 2002. 1984 Microsoft data cited by Thomas, Donald A. Jr., "History of the When of the Integrated Circuit" http://www.icwhen.com/book/the%201980s/1984.html, March 2002. Estimated U.S. revenue is based on SIIA's (Software & Information Industry Association) estimate that the United States account for 70% of the world market. Data for 2004 are calculated from preceding five-year growth rates. 1984 and 1988 are extrapolated from trend of later years.

There is considerable activity in mergers and acquisitions in the gaming software industry, although most deals are small. Microsoft and Sony made acquisitions of gaming software firms, since fans are loyal to software titles rather than to hardware consoles. Acquisitions of software firms by console or hardware firms enable them to offer that title exclusively on their system.

Both Sony and Microsoft had to catch up with Nintendo's proprietary library of hit games. Microsoft bought several game developers, such as FASA Interactive, Access Software, Digital Anvil, Bungie Software Products, and Ensemble Studios.

Maxis, manufacturer of the hit game SimCity, was bought by Electronic Arts in 1997 for $125

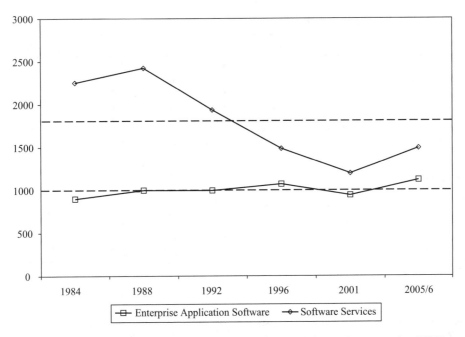

Figure 10.10 Enterprise Application Software and Software Services: Concentration (HHI)

Table 10.27 Mainframe Software (Market Share by Revenues)

Company	1984	1988	1992	1996	1999	2000	2001	2004
IBM	79.2	76.3	70.8	52.8	47.9	52.4	60.1	64.0
Computer Associates (CA)	3.4	6.4	10.2	25.5	21.2	24.9	20.4	18.2
Compuware	1	0.8	1.6	2.8	11.8	10.9	12.5	11.0
BMC	0.6	0.6	1.4	2.9	8.1	8.9	7.0	6.8
Others	15.8	15.9	16	16	11	2.9	0.0	0.0
Total U.S. Rev. ($ mil)	3,150	7,678	7,117	7,983	8,676	8,700	8,033	8,554
C4	84.2	84.1	84.0	84.0	89.0	97.1	100.0	100.0
HHI	6,286	5,864	5,121	3,454	2,949	3,564	4,233	4,595

Source: 1984–2001 figures are based on revenues from companies' annual reports and "A Complete Competitive Analysis of the U.S. Software Market," ABN-AMRO, March 18, 2002. 1999 and 2000 U.S. revenue figures are from "Packaged Software Industry Revenue and Growth," The Software & Information Industry Association, 2000. Data for 2004 are calculated from adjusted growth rates (MSN Money).

million. In 2000, the company bought DreamWorks Interactive, a joint venture between Microsoft and DreamWorks SKG. In 1998, Vivendi acquired Cendant Software (which included industry pioneer Sierra) for $985 million and Mattel bought the Learning Company or TLC for $3.8 billion. That deal proved disastrous and Mattel subsequently resold it. Activision made seven acquisitions between 1997 and 1999.[29] In 2005, it bought the game studios Vicarious Visions, Toys for Bob, and Beenox. The publisher Take-Two, successful with the *Grand Theft Auto* series, sought to expand by purchasing the studios Visual Concepts Entertainment and Kush Games from Sega in 2005, as well as Firaxis Games (table 10.29).

Gaming consoles had 41.1% penetration of American homes (45 million households) in 2006,

Table 10.28 Software Services (Market Share by Revenues)

Company	1984	1988	1992	1996	1998	1999	2001	2004
Oracle	2.0	1.9	1.9	11.4	14.7	16.2	16.3	20.4
IBM	43.1	44.7	36.4	24.5	26.8	25.4	21.8	20.0
EDS	15.3	17.0	18.5	20.0	16.0	14.6	14.2	17.8
SAP	6.8	4.7	12.4	15.7	10.4	10.6	12.5	15.6
Accenture	8.0	7.9	7.8	7.7	7.6	7.4	7.5	8.0
Computer Sciences	6.9	6.9	6.9	6.9	6.5	6.3	6.2	7.0
Others	17.9	16.9	16.1	13.8	18.0	19.5	21.5	11.3
Global Rev. ($ mil)	1,862	4,016	7,654	18,028	26,938	32,152	37,920	44,723
Est. U.S. Rev. ($ mil)	931	2,008	3,827	9,014	13,469	16,076	18,960	22,361
C4	73.3	76.5	75.1	71.6	67.9	66.8	64.8	73.8
HHI	2,254	2,423	1,933	1,484	1,399	1,328	1,194	1,487

Note: Software services figures are based on both professional services and maintenance revenues. *Sources:* Data for 1992–2004 are extracted from companies' 10-k reports. 1984 and 1988 figures are extrapolated as a percentage of companies' total revenues and from total global software industry growth figures. 1999–2000 U.S. revenue figures are based on "Packaged Software Industry Revenue and Growth," The Software & Information Industry Association, 2000. 2001 estimated U.S. revenue is based on 2000 data and growth rate.

and the revenue of the video gaming industry—both hardware and software—was often said to exceed that of movie theater ticket sales.[30] This was incorrect since U.S. theatrical box office revenues accounted for about $9 billion, almost twice as high as the U.S. video game software market. The gaming and movie industries are, in fact, often related through licensing. Game titles have made it to the big screen and vice versa. *Star Wars, Star Trek, James Bond, Indiana Jones,* and the Matrix trilogy were developed into video games, and game titles such as *Tomb Raider* and *Doom* have been made into films.

The dependency on successful game titles caused the market shares of many companies to fluctuate severely (figure 10.11). The HHI value for 1981, 5,932, shows a highly concentrated industry dominated by Atari. By 1988, with Atari's collapse, the industry became unconcentrated by Department of Justice (DOJ) standards. Nintendo became the market leader in 1992 and Electronic Arts after 1997, with 24% in 2004, followed by Take-Two and Activision, with 9% each. Concentration increased mildly after 2002 but was still in the unconcentrated range with an HHI of 930 in 2004.

In addition to console games there is also the PC entertainment market, the second segment of the game software industry. Since the early 1980s this industry has had a steady but small growth, to about $1.3 billion, with a moderate but rising concentration. Following the string of acquisitions

in the late 1990s, this industry started to become more concentrated. Unlike the overall video game market, whose concentration zigzags, this industry shows a steady increase in concentration since 1984. The market leaders in 2004 were Electronic Arts (25%), Vivendi (Havas) with 21%, Infogrames (Hasbro) with 19%, and Microsoft (11%). HHI concentration rose steadily from a low 346 in 1984 to 1,592 in 2004 (table 10.30, figure 10.11).

Acquisitions enabled some companies to significantly increase their stake in the market. Havas Interactive was essentially nonexistent in the U.S. PC software market prior to its 1998 acquisition of Cendant Software. Electronic Arts grew through its acquisition of Maxis and Westwood Studios.[31] In 1999, GT Interactive sold a majority stake to France's Infogrames Entertainment for $135 million. In 2001, Infogrames purchased Hasbro Interactive, and its market shares rose from 5% in 2000 to 17.2%.[32] In 2002 Infogrames purchased Interplay Entertainment's Shiny Entertainment subsidiary for $47 million, raising its market share to 19% in 2004.

CONCLUSION: THE COMPUTER HARDWARE AND SOFTWARE MARKETS

Subsequent to our base year of 1984, the use of computers decentralized and the IT industry vertically

Table 10.29 Video Game Software (Market Share by Revenues)

Manufacturer	1981	1984	1988	1992	1994	1995	1996	2001	2002	2003	2004	2007
Electronic Arts			3.5	7.0	14.0	16.0	17.1	18.0	20.0	24.0	24.0	16.5
Take-Two								5.0	10.0	6.0	9.0	3.5
Activision	1.0	1.0	1.0	1.0	1.0	1.0	1.0	7.0	7.0	6.0	9.0	8.8
Microsoft								3.0	3.0	3.0	7.0	8.2
Nintendo			14.0	28	23	30.4	21.5	11.0	5.0	6.0	6.0	9.3
Sony			2.1	4.2	3.8	4.3	4.5	9.0	8.0	7.0	6.0	7.5
THQ			1.0	2.0		0.7	1.0	4.0	4.0	4.0	5.0	4.0
Ubisoft								1.7	3.0	4.0	4.0	3.9
Konami								3.0	3.0	3.5	4.0	1.6
GT						4.0	7.7	4.0	3.0	4.0	3.0	
Interactive/												
Infogrames												
Atari	75	42.9										
Sega of America			6.0	12.0	19.0	28.0	20.1	4.0	4.0	3.0	2.0	
Acclaim			5.0	10.0	15.0	8.0	6.2	3.0	2.0	1.5	1.0	
Mattel	15	11.8	7.5									
Odyssey	9.0	7.1	4.5									
Other	0.0	37.2	55.4	35.8	24.2	7.6	21.1	27.3	28.0	28.0	20.0	36.0
Total U.S. Rev. ($ mil)	1,160	1,362	1,631	2,101	2,832	2,127	2,734	3,672	4,652	4,898	5,242	8,640
C4	100.0	62.8	32.5	57.0	71.0	82.4	66.3	45.0	45.0	43.0	49.0	43.0
HHI	5,932	2,031	352	1,100	1,326	2,064	1,275	678	710	814	930	609

Sources: 1997 figures are from *Packaged Facts,* "Video Games and PC Entertainment Software," June 1998. Figures for 2000 and 2001 are from "Video Games: Where Do We Go from Here?" UBS Warburg LLC, March 21, 2002. 1995 figures are from *Packaged Facts,* "Video Games and PC Entertainment Software," July 1996; *Packaged Facts* (1995, 1997), NDP Group (2000, 2001). Data for 2001–2004 are from Prudential Equity Group, LLC, *Entertainment Software Industry Overview,* June 15, 2005, p. 68. 2007 data from Company Reports; NPD Group (2007); Wikinvest.com/industry/video-Games; isuppli Corporation, 2007 report; and Edge&Online.com, "Top 20 publishers, 2007."

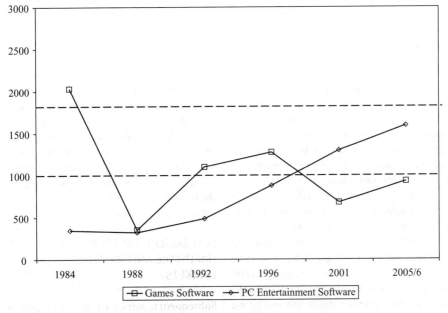

Figure 10.11 Video Game and PC Entertainment Software: Concentration (HHI)

Table 10.30 PC Entertainment Software (Market Shares Based on Revenues)

	1982	1984	1988	1991	1992	1996	1998	1999	2000	2001	2004
Electronic Arts	n/a	10.0	13.0	15.0	13.7	12.3	13.2	14.4	20.7	22.7	25.0
Vivendi									13.2	19.0	21.0
Universal											
Havas Interactive							18.5	15.6	12.0	Vivendi	
Cendent					7.8	15.6	Havas				
Sierra	11.0	11.0	11.5	12.0	12.0	10.0	Havas				
Infogrames[b] Interactive							8.3	5.7	5.0	17.2	19.0
Hasbro (Microprose, Atari)					1.1	2.2	9.3	12.4	12.2	Infogrames	
GT					4.5	9.0		Infogrames			
Microsoft					3.0	6.0	7.7	8.4	8.6	9.0	11.0
Activision[a]					2.0	4.0	5.6	5.1	5.6	5.0	6.0
Mattel							11.5	9.9	6.9	3.9	1.2
Disney					0.6	1.2	1.3	1.7	3.2	2.1	2.5
Broderbund	6.0	5.0									
Sirius	11.0	10.0									
Others	72.0	64.0	75.5	73.0	47.6	24.1	24.6	26.8	12.6	21.1	14.3
Total U.S. Rev. ($mil)	94	137	179	265	507	748	1,273	1,390	1,461	1,282	1,082
C4	28.0	31.0	24.5	27.0	41.3	53.5	52.5	52.3	58.1	67.9	76.0
HHI	278	346	323	369	487	877	896	834	1,084	1,298	1,592

Sources: 1982 data is from "Fun and games and profits," Fortune, May 2, 1983. 1991 data is taken from "New On-Line Network For Computer Games / System subscribers can dial for a duel," San Francisco Chronicle (Pre-1997 Fulltext); San Francisco, Calif.; Mar 23, 1992. PC Data, as cited by UBS Warburg, "PC/Video Game Industry," 3/5/01. 1996 data from PC Data as cited in Screen Digest Magazine, "Retail Sales of PC Games Software," Screen Digest, p. 72, March 1998. 1988 figures extrapolated from 1982 and 1991 figures. 2001 Mattel Interactive figure is extrapolated from 2000 and 1999 figures.; PC Data (1996, 1997, 2001); NPD (1998–2000). For 2004, company reports.

[a] Vivendi acquired Activision in 2007 and merged it with its Blizzard.

[b] In 2008, Infogrames changed name to Atari.

deintegrated. Whereas it was previously dominated by IBM (which made components, peripherals, computers, and software), it now spawned several new specialist giants dominating their U.S. niche: Intel in microprocessors, Microsoft in operating system software, and Cisco in data network equipment. In most other markets the trend has been to a small group of large providers with some strong participants such as Hewlett-Packard in peripherals and many other IT products and Dell in microcomputers. Those firms create strong brands and significantly rely on specialist suppliers to provide technology building blocks.

One major trend in hardware has been commoditization. This led first to a drop in concentration as competitors entered, and then to a reconsolidation around major firms that stabilized the rapidly dropping prices and provided platforms that facilitated interoperability. Entry barriers are lower in the sense that it is fairly easy to design and to assemble a PC from off-the-shelf components or to design new semiconductors. But these entry barriers are dwarfed by the scale economies that large providers enjoy. This is reflected in the overall concentration trends (weighted average) of the IT industries, with a U-shaped trend and high level (figure 10.12, table 10.31).

The revenue of the IT sector derives predominantly from hardware sales. But since 1984 the gap between hardware and software has closed significantly, from a 6:1 ratio to 6:4 in 2004. As a result, the aggregate trend line in figure 10.12 initially follows the hardware sector in its decline toward 1992, but as the software segment grew in size, it affected the aggregate trend. The overall IT sector shows a U-shape trend line for concentration, rising to 2,158 in 2004. Overall, the total information technology sector is highly concentrated, increasingly so after 1992. However, it is much less concentrated than it used to be in 1984.

In 1965, the computer electronics pioneer Gordon Moore observed that the power of semiconductors doubled every one to two years, and he predicted that this trend would continue. This rate of progress—about 50% a year—became famous as "Moore's Law." And indeed, it described the progress over the next decades pretty well. Computer components became smaller or more powerful or cheaper at roughly the predicted rate.

Whereas in 1970 a memory chip could store 1,000 bits, in 2006 it held 32 billion. Such progress enables marvels of technology, from CAT scans to video over cell phones.

Almost immediately, however, people questioned the validity of the law. Some objections were based on specifics of physics, electronics, systems design, and software. But the basic objection required no knowledge of advanced technology. It was simply that an exponential trend of this magnitude could not continue into the far future. Eventually, improvements would become harder, costlier, less important, less profitable, and hence slower.

And yet confounding the predictions of its imminent demise, Moore's Law has shown remarkable resiliency. Further progress will come from a variety of exotic sources, such as three-dimensionality of components, carbon nano tubes, quantum

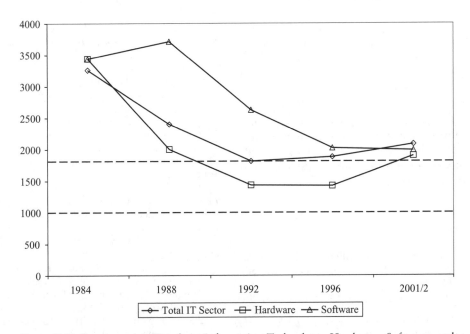

Figure 10.12 Concentration Trends in Information Technology: Hardware, Software, and Total (HHI)

Table 10.31 U.S. IT Revenues ($ Million)

	1984	1988	1992	1996	2001	2004
Hardware	50,340	68,530	86,057	117,933	139,826	156,060
Software	7,280	14,904	18,330	30,915	60,161	66,759
Total	57,620	83,434	104,387	148,848	199,987	222,819

computing, x-ray lithography, system-on-a-chip, and new fabrication systems.

Part of the secret of the success of Moore's Law has been that it has moved from prediction to self-fulfilling prophecy. It establishes a time line for progress that everyone in this highly decentralized industry understands. When a company is engaged in developing the next generation of its components, software, or hardware, it knows that the overall pace of technology progresses at the rate of Moore's Law, and it must plan to match it. If it falls behind that pace it must add engineers, money, and partners to its development effort. If it is too far ahead, it might end up designing products that are too far ahead of the market to find buyers. If its production costs do not drop fast enough it must compensate by gaining scale or moving to cheaper shores. Like a giant bell tower, Moore's Law has helped synchronize global electronics.

Thus, in the technology realm Moore's Law is alive and well. But technology does not operate in a vacuum. It has become increasingly expensive to squeeze higher performance and lower cost out of components and systems. No industry can progress in its performance at the rate of 50% a year without underlying change.

This is reflected in the industry's structural dynamics—first away from the slow system of vertically integrated industry, then to a system of a few large firms with resources and scale and a large number of specialist suppliers exercising scale in their respective niches.

Notes

1. Universities of Mannheim and Tennessee, Top 500, June 21, 2000, from http://www.top500.org/list/2001/06/.

2. Vance, Ashley. "IBM and HP Monopolize Top 397 Supercomputers List." June 28, 2006. *Register.* 13 Jul. 2006. http://www.theregister.co.uk/2006/06/28/top500_june_06/. "TOP500 List—November 2007 (1–100)." *Top500 Supercomputer Sites.* Top500.org. November, 2007. Last accessed on January 10, 2008, from http://www.top500.org/list/2007/11/100.

3. Zuckerman, Laurence. "Adding Power, Hitachi Becomes No. 2 to IBM in Mainframes." *New York Times,* July 7, 1997, p. D1.

4. "IBM Corporation." *SG Cowen Securities Corporation:* New York. February 7, 2002. p. 6.

5. U.S. Department of Commerce. *1994 U.S. Industrial Outlook.* Washington, DC: January 1994.

6. "Computer Equipment and Software." *1988 U.S. Industrial Outlook,* U.S. Department of Commerce, pp. 30–31.

7. Zuckerman, Laurence, "Stepping Out of the AT&T Nest." *New York Times,* October 21, 1996, p. D1.

8. Joost van Dreunen contributed to the narrative of the game section.

9. *Standard and Poor's Industry Survey.* New York: McGraw-Hill, annual.

10. Shim, Richard. "Palm has the PDA world in its hands." *ZDNet News.* ZDNet.com. September 28, 2000. Last accessed on January 10, 2008, from http://news.zdnet.com/2100-9595_22-524245.html.

11. Siegmann, Ken. "Conner, Quantum Tie for First." *San Francisco Chronicle,* April 15, 1991, p. C1.

12. Bobba, Naveen. "Maxtor Corporation." *Bear Stearns Equity Research,* p. 3, December 18, 2001; Blincoe, Alana. *"A Fight for Survival."* *ComputerWeekly.com,* October 16, 2001, from http://www.computerweekly.com/Article106918.htm.

13. Mayer, John H. "CD-ROM Drive Standards." *Electronic Buyers News,* August 28, 1995, p. 46. Source: Information Data Corporation.

14. IDC and Salomon Smith Barney , (SSB). *Server and Enterprise Hardware and PC Quarterly,* May 24, 2001.

15. Salomon Smith Barney, "Imaging & Visual Media," February 15, 2002. IDC.

16. Elling, George. "Enterprise Hardware." *Deutsche Bank Alex Brown Equity Research,* June 20, 2001, p. 30.

17. "HP: History of Laser Printer Development." *PrinterWorks Online,* 1996. http://www.printerworks.com/Catalogs/CX-Catalog/CX-HP_LaserJet-History.html.

18. http://www.cabledigitalnews.com/cmic/cmic1.html.

19. Company profile by Hoover, 2005. Available at www.hoovers.com. Applied Materials' revenues grew from $567 million in 1990 to $5.1 billion in 2002 to $8 billion in 2004.

20. "Chips Quo Vaditis." *Sarasin Research Group,* November 2000, p. 27.

21. Helms, Leslie. "America's Semiconductor Industry Again Leads the World. But New Asian Competitors Are Gaining Strength." *Los Angeles Times,* March 5, 1995, p. D1.

22. Warshofsky, F. *The Chip War: The Battle for the World of Tomorrow.* New York: Charles Scribner's Sons, 1989, p. 12.

23. "Intel's 64-bit Technology: Come Late, Stay Quiet." *PCStats,* March 1, 2005. http://www.pcstats.com/articleview.cfm?articleID=1736, Accessed July 13, 2006.

24. Burgelman, Robert, and Andrew Grove, "Strategic Dissonance." *California Management Review,* Winter 1996, pp. 8–9.

25. "Second Front: Why Microsoft Battles Europe Years After Settling With U.S.; Suspicions and Missteps Keep Its Antitrust Case Alive; Guarding Rival Engineers; Spat Over Encrypting a Disk." *Wall Street Journal,* May 5, 2006.

26. Castle, Stephen. "Europe Fines Microsoft $1.35 billion," *New York Times,* February 27, 2008.

27. Source: http://www.osdl.org/docs/linux_market_overview.pdf.

28. Smaller commercial Linux distributors tend to compete on a regional level: Mandriva Linux (Brazil and Latin America), Turbolinux, Red Flag, and Sun Wah (China).

29. Hubley, Mary I., and Cynthia Lubrano, "Linux Operating Systems Distributions: Perspectives." Gartner https://www1.columbia.edu/sec/cu/lweb/eresources/databases/gartner/index.html; Hubley, Mary I. "Red Hat Enterprise Linux Operating System." Gartner https://www1.columbia.edu/sec/cu/lweb/eresources/databases/gartner/index.html.

30. "Activision." *Bear Stearns,* February 31, 1999, p. 16.

31. "Gaming Goes to Hollywood." *Economist,* March 27, 2004.

32. The PC/Video Game Industry. "Starting a New Console Cycle." *UBS Warburg Equities,* March 2001, p. 72.

33. Infogrames Inc. *Hoover's Company Profile Database: American Public Companies,* June 2002.

PART IV

TELECOMMUNICATIONS

11

Telecommunications Services and Equipment

TELECOMMUNICATIONS SERVICES

There was a time when telecom was a world apart from mass media. Today, the distinction blurs. Cable TV and Internet, straddling both sides, illustrate the proximity.[1]

Everybody uses telecommunications—two-way individualized electronic communication—more than ever: at home, in the office, on the road, at the beach, when Web surfing, chatting with friends, e-mailing, downloading music and video clips, holding a meeting, or conducting business. The U.S. telecommunications industries generated in 2007 revenues of $300 billion for services[2] and $62 for equipment. This chapter deals with this large, growing, and changing industry.

To anticipate the "bottom line": the overall concentration trend of the telecom industry has been strongly U-shaped: a huge decline in 1983 with the AT&T divestiture; a gradual decline from 1984 to 1996, the multichannel phase of communications media; and a pronounced reconcentration thereafter (figure 11.1).

History

If a single date for the beginning of the multichannel stage of U.S. telecommunications needs to be selected, 1984 is the most appropriate. In 1984, AT&T's monopoly was broken up. For years, AT&T's ability to undercut its nascent rivals

concerned the federal government. AT&T could subsidize its competing long-distance operations with profits from its monopolistic local services and discriminate against its long-distance competitors' access to its local customers. To prevent such cross-subsidization and discrimination, the government and private companies such as MCI brought antitrust lawsuits in the mid-1970s. After adverse rulings in the lower court in 1981, AT&T settled the case by entering into a consent decree, which with early modification came to be known as the Modified Final Judgment (MFJ).[3] The divestiture decree divided the U.S. telecommunications industry into its then existing competitive and monopolistic segments. AT&T retained the competitive segments: equipment manufacturing and long-distance service. Local telephone service, including short-haul regional long-distance, was severed from AT&T because of its monopolistic attributes.

Local Services

Since the late nineteenth century, AT&T possessed franchise monopolies on the local services territories, comprising about 80% of the population, 90% of the business activity, and 50% of the land area. Several thousand independent local exchange companies served the rest of the country, with their number steadily declining with consolidations into firms such as GTE and United Telecommunications.

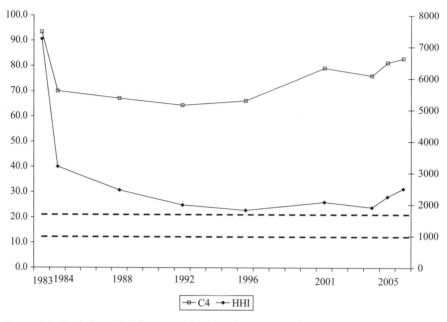

Figure 11.1 Total Overall Telecommunications Sector (21 Telecom Industries): Weighted Average Concentration Trends

The national market became significantly less concentrated in 1984 with the creation of the seven divested regional Bell operating companies (RBOCs), each holding approximately 11% of the market share nationally but nearly 100% in their respective service areas. GTE, the largest of the independent local exchange carriers, possessed a similar size. Several of the RBOCs merged after 1997, and concentration increased again. Yet the local telecommunications market did not return to the *national* concentration level of pre-divestiture days. More significant, however, was the state of *local* markets. Here, local competition increased from zero to a more competitive structure number as new firms entered the local market, in particular cable television operators. (That aspect is discussed in chapter 15.)

Even so, traditional "incumbent" local exchange companies (ILECs) continue to claim the bulk of the nationwide local market, in particular the largest two such firms, the new AT&T (SBC) and Verizon. Competitive LECs (CLECs) occupy only a small, though growing, share of the business market, but some of their activity is based on the use of the facilities of the ILEC rather than on separate infrastructure.

Local Exchange Carriers (LECs)   Traditionally, local telephone service was provided by companies that held legally exclusive franchises. Single-company supply seemed most efficient due to the high costs of duplicating local wireline infrastructure. In contrast to most countries, there was never a national monopoly over local service in America, apart from the first years of the Bell patents. The various local exchange companies (LECs) received monopoly franchises for various territories within states, but they were tightly regulated. These incumbent LECs became later known as ILECs.

Before its 1984 divestiture, AT&T accounted for nearly 77% of local telephone revenues nationally. As mentioned, the divestiture decree separated AT&T's 22 local operating companies and reorganized them into seven independent RBOCs: Ameritech (14%), Bell Atlantic (15%), BellSouth (16%), NYNEX (11%), Pacific Telesis (PacTel; 8%), Southwestern Bell (SBC; 10%), and U.S. West (10%). In addition, well over 1,500 independent LECs existed at the time, of which GTE and United Telecommunications were the largest. These independent LECs were not subject to the restrictions of the divestiture decree. None of the LECs faced competition from each other. The seven successor

RBOCs—the so-called "Baby Bells"—and GTE had relatively equal shares among local companies at the time: approximately 10–13% each of the national market but about 100% in their service territory.

Led by New York, several states began to allow competitive entry into regional long-distance and local service in the 1980s. The ILECs quickly faced competition for business services from competitive local exchange carriers (CLECs). CLECs gained market share, particularly in dense metropolitan areas. They were less actively seeking residential customers. In addition, CLECs successfully signed up Internet service providers as customers.

The 1996 Telecommunications Act aimed to encourage local competitors to enter the market in several ways. They could build complete telecommunications networks with their own facilities and interconnect them to the ILEC networks at regulated rates; or, alternatively, they could resell ILEC services, which they bought at discounted wholesale rates; or they could lease unbundled network elements ("UNEs") of facilities from ILECs and provide a portion of their facilities themselves. The 1996 Act prohibited ILECs from entering the long-distance market until they complied with a set of requirements to open their local networks to effective competition. The law thus provided incentives for the Baby Bells to cooperate with the introduction of local competition by making it a precondition for their entry into the long-distance service, which they desired in order to offer full service.

In 2004, ILECs accounted for 81.5% of switched access lines. This was down from the 85.3% they reported a year earlier. Independent ILECs accounted for $9 billion (8.9%), $2 billion (1.8%) for competitive local exchange carriers (CLECs), and had 6.5% or $6 billion for cable companies. Broadband Internet-based Voice over IP service (VoIP), was gaining share; it required, however, an underlying telecom DSL or cable broadband connection over their infrastructure, for which these two types of carriers charged users a flat monthly fee. Cable companies rapidly gained VoIP customers.

Competitive LECs used for their service ILEC-owned lines 73% of the time in 2004. Thus, from an infrastructure perspective, in 2004 ILECs accounted for 95.2% of the nation's local voice phone system, slightly down from 2003 (96%), but still dominant. But another type of infrastructure, other than cable-based VoIP, grew rapidly. Mobile wireless communications became a major alternative to wireline, convenient in its ubiquity

and capabilities of its handset, but at a higher price with lower voice and data quality.

Before the AT&T divestiture, the national HHI was at almost 8,000. The divestiture radically dropped that number to less than 1,080. The subsequent trend was a reconsolidation. Around 1996, the major RBOCs began to merge into two major groupings, SBC (AT&T) and Verizon.

In the Southwest, one Bell company (SBC) acquired another one (PacTel) in 1996, and in 1999 added the midwest Bell company (Ameritech) and the Connecticut regional firm *SNET*. In 2005, it acquired the remainder of the old AT&T and renamed itself AT&T. (It is therefore easy to confuse the old "Ma-Bell" AT&T for the new one, which is really SBC, the daughter.) In 2007, AT&T/SBC also acquired Bell South, the third-largest LEC.

In the Northeast, Bell Atlantic merged with another Bell company, NYNEX, in 1996 and with GTE in 2000. GTE, in turn, had bought Contel. Qwest, a new-style long distance company, bought U.S. West in 2000, using its high-priced stock. The same type of deal led to Global Crossing's acquisition of Frontier (formerly Rochester Telephone). When Global Crossing filed for bankruptcy, Frontier was bought by Citizen Communications, another independent ILEC. United Telecommunications, an independent local company, bought the long distance company Sprint, whose name it then took. Sprint also bought Centel in 1993. In 2006, Sprint spun off its wireline business as a new company named Embarq. Alltel, too, spun off its wireline business in 2005 as Windstream, and its mobile business was bought out in 2007 by a private equity group, and aquired in 2008 by Verizon Wireless. Verizon, in turn, sold about seven million of its lines to FairPoint (2008) and Frontier (2009). Thus, of the top dozen local firms in 1984, not a single one remained without major transformations.

Nationally, the major ILECs were rivals of each other in new types of business, such as mobile telephony and directory services, and in international acquisitions, but rarely in traditional local telephony. Merging with other ILECs, by itself, did not decrease actual competition in the local markets, though it eliminated potential competitors. Competition among Baby Bells became more of a possibility with VoIP (AT&T's CallVantage, and Verizon's VoiceWing), which potentially enabled national footprints and, with them, head-to-head competition of the major LECs.

Competitive Providers In the mid-1980s, a combination of regulatory, technical, and market-based factors led to the emergence of local telephone competitors commonly known as competitive access providers (CAPs) or competitive local exchange carriers (CLECs). CAPs provide alternate physical access links. CLECs, the broader category, also include resellers or repackagers of ILEC service, with limited or no infrastructure of their own. Still other CLECs are hybrids.

To support competitive entry, regulators set liberal collocation and interconnection rights, following New York and Illinois' lead in 1989. By 1992, five states had opened their markets to permit local competition. By 1995, 40 states permitted local competition. The Federal Telecommunications Act of 1996 expanded local competition to the rest of the country, under more uniform conditions.

In 1987, only five cities were served by CLECs.[4] In 1996, before the new Telecommunications Act was passed, 30 CLECs operated in 91 cities. New York City had the most CLECs (seven), and 33 cities had three or more.[5] CLEC revenues increased forty-fold from 1990 to 1995. The average annual growth of the CLEC industry between 1993 and 1996 was 76%.[6] In 1999, CLEC total market revenues were $5 billion out of $112 billion local services. In 2001, CLECs reported 17.3 million (9%) of the 192 million nationwide local telephone lines in service to end-users, and about $7.5 billion revenues from switched local access. By 2003, CLECs reported 26.9 million (or 14.7%) of the approximately 183 million nationwide local wireline telephone lines, but this number then declined. It should be noted that in the numbers game, there are incentives to inflate the competitors' line count by almost every party: entrants, incumbents, financiers, and regulators.

The new local entrants greatly varied in size and type. On the one end of the spectrum were telecom long-distance giants such as AT&T or MCI. But both of these firms ended up failing in their efforts and were absorbed by Bell companies by 2006. On the other end of the spectrum were tiny start-ups serving a handful of business customers in a single local market. In 1998, the largest CLEC was MFS, acquired in 1996 by the long-distance carrier, WorldCom, which joined with MCI's Metro MCI and later Brooks Fiber. The second largest was Teleport Communications Group (TCG), acquired originally in 1991 by four cable MSOs—TCI, Continental Cablevision, Comcast, and Cox—and then sold in 1998 to AT&T. AT&T also aimed, without much impact, to provide local telephony through its huge cable TV acquisitions TCI and MediaOne. The Telecommunications Act of 1996 made it easier for cable firms to use their networks to provide broadband and voice service. Cable companies can provide service in three major ways: (a) through separate telecom wires that share the conduit space with their cable TV infrastructure (this was the early type of approach of the cable phones in the UK), (b) through the dedication, on the TV cable platform itself, of circuits for circuit-switched telephony, as for example by the cable MSO Cablevision, and (c) through the use, as part of cable's cable modem broadband service, of Voice over Internet Protocol (VoIP). Such service did not require the more elaborate circuit-switching facilities of the second alternative. With cable-modem service booming after 2000, it was only a matter of time for the cable to become a significant local telecom contender by using the latter approach.

The 1996 Telecommunications Act and its implementation by the FCC and the states facilitated entry in several ways and produced incentives for ILECs to cooperate with competition by tying compliance with permission to enter national long-distance service from their service territory. There were three ways for competitors to enter: (a) through their own network "facilities," such as in the case of cable TV companies or fiber-based companies serving central business districts, (b) through the resale of ILEC services, based on an established "wholesale discount," and (c) through the ability to lease from the ILECs "unbundled network elements" (UNEs), of which seven (later eight) were defined, such as local loops, operator service, and later high-frequency "line sharing" use of local loops. The CLECs could bundle such elements into "UNE platforms" and link them to their own network elements such as switches or trunks. CLECs could place their equipment into the ILEC central offices. These arrangements, in which the established firms had to service their own competitors, led to unceasing acrimony. Hardest fought over were the prices for accessing the UNEs. The FCC established a regime of "TELRIC" (Total Elemental Long Run Incremental Cost) prices based on the incremental costs of a hypothetical advanced network, whereas the ILECs argued for the use of actual ("historic") cost as the basis for charges. TELRIC prices tended to be much lower and enabled entrants to gain a foothold.[7] Conversely, the subsidy system to independent rural telecom companies provided an incentive for the large carriers to sell off some of their rural operations.

National Concentration   Mergers caused the national market share of the top four firms to grow from 55% in 1984 to almost 86% in 2006. By the HHI measure, concentration in the national LEC market doubled from moderate (after 1984) to high again after 1996. Thus, the extreme national concentration of this sector was diminished by regulatory action, rose again briefly, while they experienced competition from CLECs and cable companies. But with CLECs beaten back in the market place and the regulatory arena, and with mergers between major companies, the HHI rose again to a high 2,850 in 2006 (table 11.1, figure 11.2).

Local Concentration   The national concentration measures overstate the options available to users since the major local carriers do not usually compete. This leads us to analyze and present local market shares in a different way, on the basis of selected local markets. (For more details, see the chapter on local concentration.)

Table 11.2 shows the extent of local concentration, based on the allocation of telephone numbers (see also chapter 15). In defining local market share, one question is whether to count physical facilities (actual access lines) or subscribership, including those of resellers. We use the second and wider definition. The table is based on 30 local markets.

Table 11.2 and figure 11.3 show that local telecom concentration, once a monopoly (HHI = 10,000), declined in the 1990s. While still very high, it was 6,067 in 2002. The top firm's share is 75%, down from 100% in 1984 and 1988. Concentration has been declining in large markets, but also, a bit later, in small and medium-sized cities.

Perhaps the major alternative to the ILECs emerged in the form of cellular mobile wireless. As penetration zoomed and prices dropped, many users opted for wireless service as a substitute for wireline and dropped the latter altogether.

Voice over Internet Protocol (VoIP), especially offered by cable television firms as part of cable modem broadband service, became an increasingly important alternative to traditional telephony. And cable broadband connectivity, even without VoIP, is often substituted for second telephone lines used for the slower dial-up Internet connectivity.

Long-Distance Services

The concentration story of long-distance telecommunications services follows a trajectory from

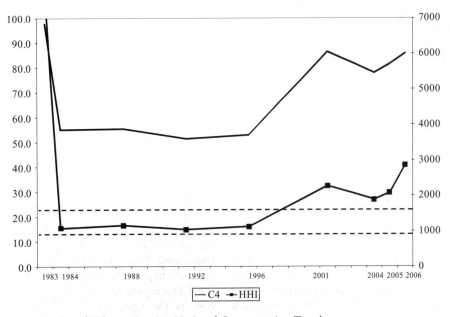

Figure 11.2 Local Telecom Service: National Concentration Trend

Table 11.1 Local Telecom Service (Market Shares by Subscribers)

Service Provider	1983	1984	1988	1990	1992	1996	1997	1999	2000	2001	2004	2006
SBC ("AT&T")	0	10	10.3	9.6	9.4	9.9	18.2	25.5	30.1	31.5	28.0	42.8
Ameritech	0	14	12.4	11.8	11.2	11.2	11.1	SBC				
Pacific Telesis		8	9.4	8.6	8.2	8.3	SBC					
SNET	1.3	1.3	1.3	1.3	1.3	1.3	SBC					
AT&T	88.3							2.8	2.9	2.8	2.8	SBC
BellSouth	0	15	15.3	15.2	14.8	15.4	15.5	15.7	15.6	14.9	13.4	SBC
Verizon[a]									31.3	30.6	27.9	30.1
Bell Atlantic	0	15	12.5	12.1	12.2	11.5	24.2	23.8	Verizon			
NYNEX	0	11	15.3	14.5	13.2	13	BellAtl					
GTE (incl Contel)	6.5	6.5	8.6	10.6	10.8	13	12.3	13	Verizon			
MCI Worldcom (MFS)								1.4	1.9	2.0	2.2	Verizon
Intermedia								0.1	Worldcom			
Qwest									10.2	9.3	8.5	8.5
U.S. West	0	10	10.3	9.8	9.5	10	10	10.2	Qwest			
Citizens Telecom/Frontier[a]								0.6	1.0	1.3	4.3	4.3
Global Crossing								0.3	0.3	Citizens		
Frontier (Rochester)						0.5	0.5	Global Crossing				
Alltel (Windstream)			0.2	0.3	0.3	0.3	0.3	0.8	0.6		0.2	0.2
Broadwing								0.4	1.1			
Cincinnati Bell	0.7	1	0.7	0.6	0.6	0.7	0.7	0.7	Broadwing		0.8	0.1
Embarq												4.3
Sprint (incl Contel)					1.5	4.1	4.2	4.3	4.4	3.1	4.3	Embarq
United Telephone		2	2.4	2.4	2.4	Sprint						
McLeodUSA								0.3	0.3	1.4	1.7	1.7
Electric Lightware										0.1	0.1	0.1
Commonwealth Tel						0.1	0.1					
Cablevision								0.000	0.000	0.1	0.2	0.1

Cox Communication							0.003	0.005	0.003	0.03	0.03	0.03
Time Warner Telecom										0.09	0.18	0.18
BrightHouse											0.0001	0.0002
Insight											0.0001	0.0002
Charter											0.0001	0.0002
Comcast												0.0001
Vonage										0.1	0.2	0.2
Skype (eBay)											0.0002	0.0004
Packet8										0.000	0.000	0.000
Net2Phone							0.000	0.000	0.000	0.0003	0.0001	
Primus (Lingo)							0.000					
VocalTech (DT)							0.000					
NetSpeak							0.000					
Voxware							0.000					
Total U.S. Rev. ($ mil)	49,243	50,871	58,066	62,004	72,120	80,453	84,105	93,725	96,539	99,300	98,504	98,504
C4	97.5	55.0	55.4	53.6	51.3	52.9	70.2	78.0	87.2	86.3	77.8	85.7
C8	99.0	89.5	93.9	92.2	89.2	92.3	96.2	96.7	97.5	95.6	91.4	92.1
HHI	7,841	1,080	1,155	1,109	1,038	1,119	1,550	1,766	2,267	2,262	1,867	2,850

Sources: FCC, Statistics of Common Carriers, 1986, 1990, 1995, 1996, 1997, 1998, 1999, 2000/2001. FCC. Bell Operating Companies aggregated to post-divestiture model for comparability. Figures include Network Access Revenues. The FCC's listed ILEC revenues are higher because they also include regional long distance service (intra-LATA interexchange service). These revenues are excluded here and are part of the long distance telecom market table below; market shares for 1988 and 1992 extrapolated based on adjacent years; Revenue from "Acquisition of Teleport Communications" in: CLEC Report 2000, New Paradigm Resources Group, INC. Figures for 2000 for McLeadUSA, Time Warner Telecom, and NextLink are based on "CLEC Revenue" as listed in CLEC Report 2000, New Paradigm Resources Group; SNET figures estimated based on population served. 2001 figures for small companies are extrapolated; Global Crossing bought Frontier in 1999. VoIP revenues are allocated 60% to local, 40% long distance and international. 2006 includes the mergers between AT&T/SBC and Verizon/MCI, assigning 50% of AT&T local share in 2004 to SBC in 2006. Assigned 33% of overall VoIP revenue to local service. 2006 data includes only mergers.

[a] Verizon sold 4.8 million of its lines to Frontier in 2009. In 2008, it sold 1.8 of its landline customers to the holding companies FairPoint. This reduced its national market share by about 5%

Table 11.2 Telecom Local Concentration

	1984	1988	1992	1996	2002	2006
C1 Concentration						
C1 Large Cities	100	100	97.5	90.0	74.9	69.5
C1 Medium Cities	100	100	100	93.5	78.3	72.7
C1 Small Cities	100	100	100	97.2	71.7	64.7
Weighted Average	100	100	99.0	93.1	75.1	69.2
C4 Concentration						
C4 Large Cities	100	100	98.5	93.9	84.8	81.7
C4 Medium Cities	100	100	100	97.4	91.4	87.8
C4 Small Cities	100	100	100	99.3	92.5	88.4
Weighted Average	100	100	99.4	96.5	89.1	85.5
HHI Concentration						
HHI Large Cities	10,000	10,000	9,571	8,285	5,713	4,971
HHI Medium Cities	10,000	10,000	10,000	8,876	6,255	5,387
HHI Small Cities	10,000	10,000	10,000	9,636	6,364	4,584
Weighted Average	10,000	10,000	9,827	8,852	6,067	4,993
Avg. Annual Rev. per Household						
Large Cities	197	239	290	351	426	437
Medium Cities	191	231	280	340	412	410
Small Cities	192	233	282	342	414	424

Source: Reports, North American Numbering Plan Administration, http://www.nanpa. com/.

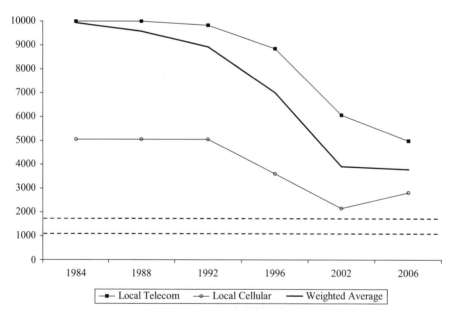

Figure 11.3 Local Telecom and Internet Concentration: Local HHI Trends

monopoly to oligopoly, strong competition, and reconcentration. In 2006, the market for U.S. long-distance (inter- and intra-LATA toll service) was a declining $84 billion,[8] down from $108 billion in 1999. This was caused by dropping prices; actual usage by minute was growing rapidly.

AT&T's market share dropped from 99.2% in 1978 and from 90% in 1984 to 36% in 2004.[9] MCI (with WorldCom) and Sprint grew from 5 to 21% (2001) and from 3 to 9%, respectively, during the same period. After 1998, a second wave of long-distance carriers also entered, with a wholesale strategy based on private circuits and bulk capacity that aimed mostly at large corporate users and service providers such as Internet backbones and mobile carriers. Such new carriers included Level 3, Qwest, Williams, and Global Crossing. By 2001, the ILEC had begun to enter, too, having gained admission in the states and then on the Federal level. In the process, all of these firms added capacity and unleashed further price competition. Prices dropped rapidly, and by 2002, most long-distance firms were either in bankruptcy proceedings (WorldCom, ICG, WilTel, Allegiance), tottering, or under investigation for accounting irregularities (WorldCom, Qwest). It was therefore not surprising that AT&T succumbed in 2005 and was acquired by SBC. MCI WorldCom's CEO Bernard Ebbers was sentenced to 25 years of prison time for fraud. The company was acquired by Verizon. XO bought Allegiance, and Level 3 acquired WilTel.

Domestic Long Distance   The 1984 AT&T divestiture divided the United States into 161 geographic regions known as local access and transport areas (LATA). There was at least one LATA in each state. Domestic long-distance calls were known as inter-exchange service, and they could be either intra-LATA (short-haul) or inter-LATA (usually long-haul). The latter services were initially provided by inter-exchange carriers (IXCs) such as AT&T or MCI, whereas the former were provided by the LECs. Over time, the distinction blurred but did not disappear. The 1984 AT&T divestiture accelerated inter-LATA competition by requiring the RBOCs to offer access to all IXCs on an equal basis in terms of price, type, and quality. Previously, customers of rival long-distance carriers had to enter an extra 10-digit access code before each call. The divestiture decree also barred the RBOCs (known as the "Baby Bells") from providing inter-

LATA services. They could, however, offer intra-LATA service (short-haul long-distance).

Restrictions on the Baby Bells' activity proved contentious from the beginning. For these companies, restrictions meant exclusion from what they perceived to be potentially lucrative long-distance services. They also could not be one-stop, full-service providers of telecom. LATAs often had artificial geographic boundaries. For example, a call from New York City to Montauk, Long Island, a distance of some 100 miles, is an intra-LATA call on a national level, and was hence provided by the Baby Bell NYNEX. However, a call from New York City across the Hudson River to New Jersey, a distance of one mile, was usually an inter-LATA call and had to be handled by two or three separate phone companies, thereby raising its cost. In time, these market separations blurred as states allowed the IXCs to enter intra-LATA and local service, which are under primary state jurisdiction. The Telecommunications Act of 1996 extended this to the entire United States and, subject to a number of conditions, opened inter-LATA long-distance service to the Baby Bells (table 11.3).

After 1984, the AT&T divestiture accelerated long-distance competition, and prices fell. The top three long-distance carriers lowered their rates by over 80% from 1984 to 2000 alone. For example, AT&T's rates for a five-minute regular residential toll call from Philadelphia to San Francisco decreased from $2.53 in 1984 to $0.35 in 2001 and $0.25 in 2004, not even accounting for an inflation of 77% over that period.[10] Actual rates dropped even more steeply, as the numbers do not reflect widespread discounting and bonuses that all the IXCs offered to gain or retain customers. One of the purposes of the formal rates was to make the discounts look large.

Price competition allowed the average subscriber's volume of long-distance calls to increase greatly. For example, from 1985 to 1995, AT&T's minute volume increased by 83% while its number of presubscribed lines remained relatively stable (about 101 million).[11] Increased calling volume caused total IXC long-distance revenues to grow from $51.2 billion in 1984 to $108.2 billion in 1999, when they peaked. After 1999, however, the total revenue declined again.

After the AT&T divestiture, the number of long-distance carriers registered with the FCC increased from 54 in 1984 to several hundred in 1990 and more than 700 in 2000.[12] Of these, only a handful

Table 11.3 Telecom Long Distance (Market Shares by Users)

Service Provider	1983	1984	1988	1991	1992	1995	1996	1997	1998	1999	2001	2004	2006
SBC AT&T		1.8	1.6	1.5	1.4	1.0	2.7	2.3	2.2	3.2	3.8	3.9	39.1
AT&T	85.4	68.3	56.3	50.2	48.9	44.9	42.1	39.2	38.6	36.9	36.7	36.5	SBC
Alascom		0.7	0.5	0.5	0.6				AT&T				
Ameritech		2.0	2.1	1.9	1.9	1.8	1.6	SBC					
PacTel	0.0	3.5	3.5	3.2	3.0	1.4	1.3	1.2	1.1	SBC			
Bell South	0.0	2.7	2.4	2.0	1.8	1.2	0.9	0.7	0.6	0.6	0.6	0.6	SBC
Verizon											9.3	9.2	24.6
WorldCom/LDDS		0.0	0.1	0.4	1.0	4.3	4.8	5.9	21.1	21.6	20.8	20.0	Verizon
MCI	3.4	3.4	8.0	12.1	13.3	17.1	17.6	17.0					
Intermedia									0.2	0.2		Worldcom	
Metromedia		0.4	Metr									Worldcom	
ITT			0.1	0.2	LDDS								
WilTel			0.5	0.7	LDDS								
Comsystems		0.2	0.3	0.7	LDDS								
Bell Atlantic	0.0	2.6	2.5	2.2	2.2	1.7	2.5	2.1	3.1	2.9	Verizon		
NYNEX	0.0	2.5	2.2	1.8	1.7	1.2	1.1	Bell Atl					
GTE[a] (Sprint)	3.6	3.6	6.4	3.2	3.0	3.0	2.7	2.4	0.8	0.6	Verizon		
Qwest								Qwest			2.8	2.5	2.5
LCI			0.2	0.7	0.5	0.9	1.4	1.2	Qwest				
US West	0.0	2.0	2.2	2.2	2.1	2.1	3.3	2.8	3.0	2.9			
Other LECs		5.7	4.1	2.6	2.6	1.9	1.2	2.0	2.3	1.4	0.9	0.7	0.7
Sprint[b] (United)		0.2	0.4	7.8	8.0	8.5	8.5	8.5	7.6	9.0	8.4	8.5	8.5
Frontier/Citizens												Citizens	
Global Crossing						1.6	1.7	1.3	1.3	1.4	2.5		
Frontier/Rochester			0.1	0.3	0.3	1.9	1.9	1.5	Global Crossing	Global Crossing		2.1	2.1
Allnet			0.8	0.6	0.7	Frontier							

Level 3													1.6
WilTel							0.1	0.2	0.2	0.3	0.2	0.1	0.1
XO									0.3	0.3	0.4	0.4	
Allegiance									0.3	0.4	0.1		
ICG							0.2	0.3	0.4	0.1	0.1	0.1	
Vonage								0.2	0.3	0.1	0.3	0.3	0.2
Skype (eBay)[a]												0.0002	0.0006
Other IXC's	7.6	0.6	4.4	4.9	5.8	4.1	3.7	11.9	17.8	18.8	13.0	15.4	21.9
Total U.S. Rev. ($ mil)	48,767	51,200	62,250	68,500	71,900	85,500	93,300	100,800	105,100	108,200	99,301	83,697	83,697
C4	92.4	80.9	73.8	73.3	73.1	74.8	73.0	70.6	70.4	70.7	75.2	74.2	74.6
HHI	7,311	4,760	3,322	2,780	2,675	2,437	2,226	1,967	2,026	1,941	1,967	1,917	2,218

Sources: Figures include, for early years, both inter- and intra-LATA calls. Federal Communications Commission, Common Carrier Bureau, *Long-Distance Market Shares*, Washington DC, July 12, 1996. FCC, *Statistics of the Long Distance Telecommunications Industry*, January 2000. *CLEC REPORT 2000*, 11th edition, New Paradigm Resources Group. FCC "Study of Telephone Trends," May, 2004. Revenues for period 1992–2002 from FCC, "*Trends in Telephone Service*" May 6th, 2004. 2004, 2005 and 2006 figures only incorporate the mergers SBC/AT&T, Verizon/Worldcom, and AT&T/Bell South. Mergers subtract resale share to avoid double-counting. Assigned 40% of VoIP revenues of cable and VoIP firms to domestic long distance service. 2006 data includes only mergers.

[a] Sprint was owned from 1982 to 1989 by GTE, when control shifted to United Telecom, which renamed itself Sprint. GTE kept, however, some of its short-haul long distance. eBay bought skype in 2007 for $4.1 billion.

of carriers had national physical infrastructures. Another two dozen companies are a mix of facilities-based carriers and resellers (which lease lines by minute volumes from carriers and retail them). The rest of the 600-plus carriers either had minimal facilities or were resellers (table 11.4, figure 11.4).

In the long-distance private line market, AT&T similarly lost market share to its competitors. Its share dropped from 90% to 37% between 1983 and 2006. Figure 11.4 shows an enormous decline in market concentration of domestic public and private-line long-distance service. Its HHI remained highly concentrated, but barely so. In 2005, the concentration rose again as a result of the SBC/AT&T and Verizon/MCI mergers.

International Long Distance   With communications prices declining and the globalization of economic transactions, international calling volume skyrocketed. New calling alternatives for users abroad,

Table 11.4 Telecom Private Line (Market Shares by Lines)

	1983	1984	1988	1990	1992	1996	1999	2000	2002	2004	2006
SBC								0.2	1.1	1.2	36.8
AT&T	90.1	90.1	74.6	65.0	57.7	44.4	39.9	37.0	36.3	35.6	SBC
BellSouth									0.6	0.6	SBC
Verizon								1.1	1.8	2.0	26.2
WorldCom			0.1	0.2	1.7	4.8	23.4	21.9	23.5	25.2	Verizon
MCI	4.5	4.5	10.2	11.1	13.5	17.6	World Com				
Sprint	2.7	2.7	7.2	9.7	9.1	9.0	9.7	8.8	9.0	9.0	9.0
Qwest								3.0	4.1	4.1	4.1
Other	2.7	2.7	7.9	14.0	18.0	24.2	27.0	28.2	24.7	22.3	23.9
No. of Carriers			257	325	411	582	651	808	932	900	
Total U.S. Rev ($ mil)	5,743	5,743	6,889	7,543	7,783	10,665	13,169	16,189	16,402	16,618	16,618
C4	97.3	97.3	92.1	86.0	82.0	75.8	73.0	67.7	72.9	73.9	76.1
HHI	8,146	8,146	5,722	4,442	3,597	2,385	2,234	1,927	1,971	2,008	2,140

Source: See Table 11.3

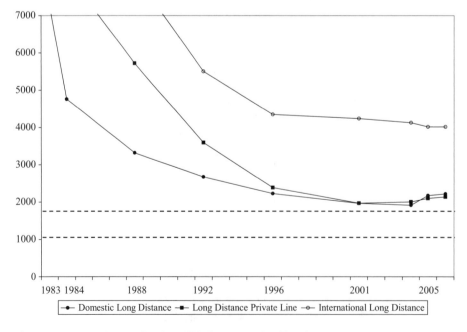

Figure 11.4 Long-Distance Service: HHI Concentration Trend

such as callback services and later VoIP also fueled growth. The number of calls made from the United States to other countries increased from 200 million in 1980 to 1.4 billion in 1991, 5.3 billion in 1999, 7.4 billion by 2003, and 10.9 billion by 2004.[13] This does not even include the huge volume of calls made over private networks and through Internet-telephony. Due to falling prices, however, international revenues billed by IXCs increased by a much slower rate.[14] During the period of analysis, the historical mainstays of text messaging—international telex and telegraphy—entirely disappeared, dropping from $421 and $37 million in 1984 to $24 and $2 million in 2001, respectively.

Prior to its 1984 divestiture, AT&T accounted for over 95% of the international voice telephone service. By 2004, AT&T's share in this voice segment had fallen to 49%; MCI had 21%, and Sprint 18% (table 11.5).

Figure 11.4 also shows the weighted aggregated trend line for market concentration for the four major (in 1984) international telecommunications services: International Voice, International Private Line, International Telex, and International Telegraph.

In the 1990s, long-distance telecommunication, despite enormous growth in transmission volume, became a largely unprofitable commodity business. WorldCom, Qwest, and Global Crossing hid this

Table 11.5 Telecom International Services (Market Shares by Revenue)

International Service	1984	1988	1992	1994	1996	2001	2005
Verizon							20.8
Worldcom/LDDS			0.46	1.7	3.7	24.7	Verizon
MCI	6.0	10.3	20.7	23.4	27.9	Worldcom	
RCA Globecom	6.8	4.5	MCI				
Western Union	2.1	5.2	MCI				
GTE	1.8	4.0	0.5	0.4	0.1	Verizon	
SBC (AT&T)	73.4	69.8	66.3	61.4	54.0	45.2	49.0
AT&T							SBC
Alascom	0.2	0.1	0.1	0.1			
FTC Communications	0.8	0.8					
Sprint			7.0	9.3	9.6	12.7	18.2
TRT Telecom	2.5	2.1	0.9				
ITT/Worldcom	6.5	0.8					
US Liberia	0.01						
IXC						1.3	
Global Crossing						0.2	
Level 3						0.1	0.1
Vonage							0.016
Skype (eBay)							0.004
Other	0.2	2.4	3.5	3.7	4.7	15.7	11.9
Total U.S. Rev. ($ mil)	2,610	3,431	7,477	8,713	6,262	12,810	9,178
C4	92.6	89.8	94.9	95.8	95.2	83.9	88.1
HHI	5,518	5,047	4,877	4,404	3,802	2,815	3,166

Notes: Includes voice, telex, private line, and telegraph services for those years when offered. Data for 1984 are estimated, since the FCC data only reports weighed totals. AT&T market share for 1988 is estimated from http://www.bellsystemmemorial.com/pdf/tattc.pdf. Data for 1996 and 2001 are extrapolated and adjusted to include the 1.4% "other carrier" category as found in FCC reporting. Assigned 30% of VoIP revenues for cable and VoIP firms to international long distance service.

Source: Federal Communications Commission, Trends in International Telephony Report, July 2nd, 2004, Table 3.

from investors in ways that, for WorldCom, led to criminal charges and prison convictions. Global Crossing went into bankruptcy, and Qwest was penalized by the SEC. By 2005 the independent long-distance firms threw in the towel. AT&T, the grandest brand in the world of telecommunications for over a century, was acquired by SBC for a mere $16 billion. MCI was courted by two other Bell companies, with Verizon prevailing. Sprint spun off its local exchange operations, perhaps in anticipation of future mergers. Thus, the vertical consolidation of the long-distance industry with the main local telecom firms was nearly complete. The AT&T divestiture had been reversed, with a structure of two major (and a handful of minor) regional firms) which also provided national long-distance and mobile services.[15]

Mobile Services

AT&T's Bell Labs were instrumental in the early development of invented cellular radio telephony in the 1960s and readied it for application in the 1970s. Because the FCC was slow to settle policy over licensing, commercial cellular service did not begin in the United States until 1983 amid the confusion of the AT&T divestiture. With some delay, mobile services grew tremendously and diversely. By 2009, over 85% of Americans owned a cellular telephone. The result was intra-platform competition among mobile service providers, and inter-platform competition with traditional wireline telephony.

The concentration of local cellular service will be discussed at greater length in chapter 15. This section discusses mobile telephony, paging, and other wireless platforms, with a final segment on wireless data and computing.

Cellular Telephony   The development of cellular radio increased the utilization of frequencies by dividing a service area into small sections or "cells." Each cell uses a low-power transmitter, rather than the high-power transmitter of previous mobile communications. The same frequency can be reused in multiple cells in nearby (through noncontiguous) areas, and this greatly increases system capacity. Although AT&T and Motorola first successfully tested cellular radio in 1962, regulatory hurdles prevented any commercial offering of cellular service for two decades. In 1970, the FCC tentatively allocated 75 MHz (later reduced to 50

MHz) in the 800 MHz band for cellular-mobile telephone systems. Political maneuvering among industry players impeded the regulatory process. As a result, more than 10 years elapsed between the initial allocation and the processing of applications for cellular systems.

Initially, in 1974, the FCC had wanted to license only one cellular operator per market, that is, the local phone companies. But small wireless firms, so-called "radio common carriers" (RCCs) that provided radio services to taxi cabs and trucking companies, or paging services, wanted licenses, too. The FCC eventually decided to allocate, after 1982, two licenses for each of 734 territories. One of the two licenses went to the local LEC, while the other had to be assigned to an independent operator not affiliated with the local LEC. Appeals by losing applicants significantly delayed the process. Eventually, beginning in 1986, the FCC awarded licenses for the remaining contested 276 markets through a lottery system.

With several waves of competition, prices dropped. In addition, handset prices also fell. The average price for a cellular handset moved from $1,800 in 1984 to $200 in 2000, and soon $100. And the service providers offered heavily discounted handsets if the subscriber signed up for a long-term contract. Demand for cellular services grew rapidly in the number of subscribers and minutes of use. Most of the original independent cellular operators were bought out by local and long-distance telephone companies. AT&T purchased the independent cellular company McCaw, which had earlier consolidated many of the small independents. The LECs, similarly, purchased independent cellular companies and merged or joint-ventured with each other, thus establishing national footprints.

Personal Communications Services (PCS)   The large companies also grew their coverage by acquiring more spectrum when the FCC allocated licenses for PCS. PCS differed from the previously existing analog cellular service (the "first generation" of mobile service using the AMPS standard). Its frequency range is higher, necessitating more cells. Although licensees were free in the technology they deployed for PCS service, they invariably used a digital system, with a greater number of channels, higher signal quality, better security, and a more rapid data transfer. Perhaps even more important, this established competition beyond the previous duopoly.

In Europe, a simple digital standard (global system for mobile communication, or GSM) was mandated for second-generation (digital) mobile service. But in America, four distinct and rival digital standards emerged: time division multiple access (TDMA), code division multiple access (CDMA), GSM, and I-DEN (integrated dispatch enhanced network). TDMA, a variant of the European GSM, was chosen by AT&T and Cingular (the joint mobile operation of SBC and Bell South), and eventually transitioned to GSM. T-Mobile (acquired by Deutsche Telekom as Voicestream) used the GSM standard from the beginning. Both TDMA and GSM operate on dividing transmission time among multiple users. CDMA, the major alternative, is a technology developed by Qualcomm that splits each signal into packets with unique identification codes, allocates the packets among multiple channels according to availability, and then reassembles the signal at the receiving end based on their codes. The major U.S. firms using the technology are Verizon and Sprint. The so-called "third generation" (3G) of mobile wireless is based worldwide on CDMA, though two competing variants have emerged, one for Europe and Japan (W-CDMA) and another for North America (CDMA 2000). All handset manufacturers—grudgingly—pay license fees to Qualcomm for the technology that many of them had denigrated for years as unworkable and inferior.

This means that competition in U.S. mobile communications occurs on two levels: among cellular firms and among several transmission standards.

The FCC allocated PCS licenses by assigning them to the winner of auctions. The first broadband PCS auction (for the wide-area A and B blocks) began in 1994. The top three bidders were Sprint Spectrum (a joint venture of Sprint and the three cable TV companies TCI, Cox, and Comcast); AT&T Wireless and PCS PrimeCo (a consortium of Bell companies that converged into Verizon). They accounted for 62% of the 99 licenses auctioned and 70% of the revenue raised.[16]

The second set of 30 MHz broadband auctions (the C block) was reserved for smaller business enterprises and smaller areas. Eighty-nine companies paid an aggregate of $10.2 billion for the 493 (BTA) licenses. Unlike the first auction, where telcos focused on filling gaps in their

national wireless coverage, the leading participants in the second auction focused on large city markets, such as New York City, Los Angeles, and Chicago.

Although the firms that participated in the second auction had to be "small entities," many were in fact backed by large firms or foreign groups. Often they were later bought out, or their capacity leased, by the large service providers.

Before the advent of PCS, the cellular market was a duopoly with fairly high prices and contractual agreements. Competition by additional service providers changed the face of the wireless market. In most major markets, five competitors emerged, plus the SMR operator Nextel (discussed below). New entrants typically underpriced the established duopoly providers by 15–20%. Prices dropped steadily, especially through the use of various marketing discounts and billing plans. Since the introduction of one-rate, distance-insensitive minute "bucket" packages by AT&T in 1998, prices for wireless calls fell by as much as 80%.

Specialized Mobile Radio Another provider of mobile service emerged from a different direction. In 1974 the FCC conceived of "specialized mobile radio" (SMR) as a commercial private land mobile radio service. Customers were utility and delivery companies, taxi services, and other firms whose personnel spent considerable time in the field. In the early 1990s, private SMR carriers began to offer wide-area (regional) services previously offered only by common carriers. The FCC opened private radio frequencies to common carrier competition in 1995.

This led to Motorola's development of digital "enhanced" SMR (ESMR) technology. After the FCC authorized ESMR in 1991, Fleet Call (renamed Nextel) launched the service in 1992. By the late 1990s Nextel owned almost three quarters of this industry, and established it, in effect, as an alternative mobile phone system.

SMR, beyond its dispatch service role, is also a substitute for cellular telephony. In 2001 Nextel held 7.7% of the national cellular market with the most loyal customer base. Even so, Nextel's size was apparently too small for holding off the ever-growing Verizon and SBC (Cingular and AT&T wireless), and it was merged in 2005 into Sprint PCS, as the main non-Bell mobile operation, in close alliance with the cable TV industry.

Overall Mobile Concentration   A large wave of mergers and acquisitions among cellular carriers after 1998 redefined the mobile market in the United States. Deals between SBC (with Ameritech) and Bell South created Cingular, to which AT&T was added in 2004–2005. Verizon Wireless was created out of the cellular operations of Bell Atlantic,

NYNEX, GTE, U.S. West, and PacTel (Airtouch), the latter owned by the UK's mobile phone giant Vodafone. Sprint acquired Nextel. By 2005, four companies, all with nationwide footprints, held much of the market (89% in 2005). The two Bell company operations accounted for 63%. (Table 11.6, Table 11.7).

Table 11.6 Selected Mergers and Acquisitions in Mobile Cellular Industry

Buyer	Acquisition	Transaction ($ million)	Year
PacTel Comm	Communications Industries	$429	1987
SBC	Metromedia	$1,400	1987
BellSouth	Mobile Communications	$710	1988
Centel	United TeleSprectrum	$796	1988
McCaw	51% of LIN Broadcasting	$3,400	1990
GTE	Contel (Incl. wireline)	$6,250	1991
AT&T	McCaw	$11,500	1994
AT&T	48% of LIN Broadcasting	$3,300	1995
Bell Atlantic	NYNEX (Incl. wireline)	Merger	1995
AirTouch	U.S. West (mob ile operations)	$5,700	1995
SBC	Pacific Telesis (Incl. wireline)	$16,500	1997
AirTouch Comm	U.S. Cellular	$243	1997
McCaw Family	Nextel Communications	$232	1997
SBC	Southern New England Telecom. (Incl. wireline)	$5,800	1998
ALLTEL	360 Degrees Communication	$6,000	1999
Vodafone	AirTouch.	Merger	1999
SBC	Ameritech (Incl. wireline)	$62,000	1999
Verizon	Vodafone/Airtouch	Merger 55:45	1999
Qwest	U.S. West(Incl. wireline)	$36,500, Merger	2000
Bell Atlantic (Verizon)	GTE (Incl. wireline)	$74,000	2000
Verizon	Price Communications' Cellular One brand	$1,500	2000
Voicestream	Omnipoint	$7.2 billion	2000
Voicestream	Aerial	Stock swap	2000
SBC, BellSouth	Cingular	Joint Venture 60:40	2000
Deutsche Telekom	Voicestream	$51,000	2001
Nextel	Arch	$250	2001
Cingular	AT&T Wireless	$41,000	2004
Alltel	Western Wireless	$6,000 Merger	2005
Sprint	Nextel	$35,000 Merger	2005
Verizon	Cal North Wireless		2006
SBC (AT&T)	Bell South (Incl. wireline)	$86,000	2007
TPG Capital and Goldman Sachs	Alltel	$27,500	2007
United Wireless	Velocita		2007
Deutsche Telekom	SunCom	$2,400	2007
Verizon WL	Rural Cellular	$757	2007
AT&T	Dobson	$2,800	2007
Verizon	Alltel	$28,100	2008

Sources: Notes: Information from *Cellular Telecom Mergers and Acquisitions,* by Date, 1988–1998, Copyright 1998 Paul Kagan Associates, Inc., *Standard & Poor's Stock Reports,* May, 8 1999, Moody's, AirTouch Webpage, Telegeography, and Bell Atlantic webpage [http://www.nanpa.com/]. *RCR Wireless News,* November 18, 2002. "The Wireless EDGE," Salomon Smith & Barney, April 3, 2003.

Table 11.7 Mobile Cellular Telephone Service (Market Shares by Subscribers)

	1983	1984	1988	1992	1996	1998	2000	2001	2004	2005/2006
SBCᵃ (AT&T)										35.0
Cingular							18.5	19.9	21.2	
SBC		5.4	6.0	7.4	7.5	11.0	Cingular			
Ameritech		6.5	7.5	6.5	5.5	SBC				
BellSouth		5.2	5.3	6.0	6.0	7.0	Cingular			
AT&T (McCaw)ᵇ	44.5	0.9	2.0	10.8	11.0	12.0	16.0	14.0	14.0	Cingular
SNET		0.8	0.9	1.0	1.0	0.5	Cingular			
Vanguard/Cellular										
One										
Verizon Wireless							24.4	27.9	27.9	28.0
Bell Atlantic		7.6	6.3	8.9	10.0	12.0	Verizon			
Metro Mobile	2.0	3.4	3.2	2.6	2.5	Bell Atlantic				
NYNEXᶜ		6.5	6.5	6.5	Bell Atlantic					
GTE Mobilenet/	6.8	6.8	7.3	8.8	9.0	8.0	Verizon			
Contelᵈ										
Vodafone						12.0	Verizon			
Air Touch (Pac Tel)ᵉ	0.0	7	7.1	10.3	11.0	Vodafone				
U.S. West	0.0	5.5	4.1	3.9	Airtouch					
New Vector										
MCI				1.6	2.0	*	0.2	0.1	0.1	Verizon
Alltelʲ	1.4	1.4	1.2	1.8	2.0	6.0	5.7	6.5	6.5	6.5
Sprint PCSᶠ	1	1	1.0	4.6	5.0	6.0	7.5	11.2	11.2	18.9
Centel			4.5	3.5	Sprint					
Nextel				3.1	3.9	4.7	5.5	7.7	7.7	Sprint
T-Mobile							4.3	5.9	5.9	5.9
Voicestreamᵍ					0.2	2.0	T-Mobile			
Century	1.2	1.2	1.0	0.4	0.3	1.0	0.8	0.7	0.7	0.7
U.S. Cellular (TDS)ʰ				0.9	1.0	3.0	2.8	3.3	3.3	3.3
Other	43.1	40.8	36.1	11.4	22.1	14.8	14.3	2.8	1.5	1.5
Total subs		0.1	2.1	16.0	44.0	69.2	109.4	128.4	182.1	194.6
Total U.S. Rev. ($ mil)ⁱ	200	340	1,959	12,253	26,415	36,633	51,908	61,051	102,121	108,535
C4	54.7	27.9	28.4	38.8	41.0	47.0	53.6	72.9	74.3	88.6
HHI	2,035	341	362	627	602	774	997	1,642	1,697	2,469

Sources: Table compiled from revenue data in industry tables throughout this chapter.

ᵃ In 2006, SBC acquired Bell South and its part of Cingular. It merged these wireless operations with the acquired from AT&T and renamed all of it AT&T Mobil.
ᵇ AT&T, prior to the 1984 divestiture, owned the RBOC licenses for mobile telephony and transferred them to these firms in 1984. It acquired McCaw in 1994.
ᶜ ell Atlantic and NYNEX merged their cellular operations in 1995.
ᵈ In 1991, GTE Mobilnet merged with Contel Cellular.
ᵉ irTouch and U.S. West NewVector merged in 1995.
ᶠ Sprint acquired Centel in 1993, then spun it off to create 360 Degrees Communications in 1995.
ᵍ Voicestream (1999) was spun off from Western Wireless and acquired Omnipoint Communications and Aerial Communications in 2000. T-Mobile bought Suncom for $2.4 billion in 2008.
ʰ U.S. Cellular Corp is owned by TDS (80.9%), an LEC that serves about 28 states.
ⁱ CTIA *Wireless Quickfacts*, April 2006. Available at http://files.ctia.org/pdf/Wireless_Quick_Facts_April_06.pdf.
ʲ Verizon wireless acquired Alltel in 2008/9 for $28.1 billion, giving it, for 2009, about 34% of the US market. Alltel had bought in 2007 Western Wireless for $6 billion.

The concentration trend line is depicted in figure 11.5. The industry had consolidated after 1984 and 1995, when it was licensed in a purposefully decentralized fashion on a national level. The subsequent first wave of consolidation was then offset by a new set of PCS licenses. This led to a second wave of consolidations, in which the telecom firms sought to create national "footprints." Concentration rose after 1996 to six and then four national footprints. A few regional

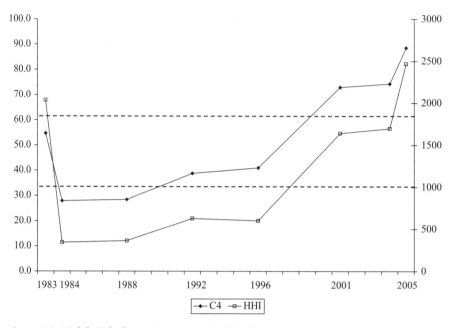

Figure 11.5 Mobile Telephony: Concentration Trends

companies still exist, often as partners of the national firms.

The market in 2006 was led by SBC (which acquired AT&T) and renamed itself with a 35% market share, and Verizon Wireless with a share of 28%, to rise to about 35%, too, with the Alltel acquisition in 2008/9. Several companies attempted to provide mobile service on a resale basis. MCI's strategy was to be a reseller under its brand name, but the strategy proved unsuccessful. After 2004, this approach was resumed by so-called MVNOs (mobile virtual network operators) such as Virgin, 7-Eleven, or Buzz mobile.

On the local level, concentration declined initially, with the replacement of the duopoly system by typically five to six providers, but it rose again with mergers to about four per market. This can be seen in table 11.8, based on 30 local markets.

Local market concentration dropped from a highly concentrated HHI of 5,050 in 1984 to 2,814 in 2006 (see chapter 15 and Table 11.9). The market leader's share (C1) fell from about 55% to 31%. Local concentration started out much higher than national concentration, as can be expected in an initially fragmented national market. However, as companies consolidated into national footprints, the gap between local and national concentration narrowed and disappeared.

Radio Paging   Paging used to be a major communications industry in America, much bigger than in Europe. It emerged after 1949 when the FCC allocated radio frequencies for one-way and two-way mobile communications. Nationwide paging was introduced in 1986 but was not met with great success. Market concentration in local areas varied widely but was low. In 1993, the average local market had eleven paging companies. In some local markets there were as many as 75 providers and resellers. In 1993, the FCC reclassified different types of carriers (RCCs and PCPs) as commercial mobile radio services (CMRS), a new class of common carrier.

In the late 1980s, the Bell companies tried unsuccessfully to enter the paging market. SBC purchased Metro Media's paging operations for $1.38 billion in 1987, but sold it later to Mobile Media Communications. BellSouth bought MobileComm and DialPage, but sold them to Mobile Media in 1995. In 1994, AT&T purchased McCaw and its paging operations, with little success. In 1998, Arch bought Mobile Media and its 3.1 million subscribers. Metrocall acquired AT&T's wireless messaging unit, giving Metrocall 5.3 million subscribers to make it the third largest U.S. paging carrier.[17] In 1999, SkyTel Communications was acquired by MCI WorldCom for $1.3 billion. Arch Communications

Table 11.8 Mobile Cellular Communication: Local Concentration

	1984	1988	1992	1996	2002	2006
			C1 Concentration			
C1 Large Cities	55	55	55	40.6	26.2	35.1
C1 Medium Cities	55	55	55	46.2	37.4	42.7
C1 Small Cities	55	55	55	43.7	32.3	42.1
Weighted Average	55	55	55	43.2	31.4	39.5
			C4 Concentration			
C4 Large Cities	100	100	100	91	81.9	92.3
C4 Medium Cities	100	100	100	94.1	88.2	96.1
C4 Small Cities	100	100	100	90.7	81.4	92.4
Weighted Average	100	100	100	91.9	83.8	93.5
			HHI Concentration			
HHI Large Cities	5,050	5,050	5,050	3,499	1,949	2,564
HHI Medium Cities	5,050	5,050	5,050	3,776	2,502	3,142
HHI Small Cities	5,050	5,050	5,050	3,561	2,073	2,805
Weighted Average	5,050	5,050	5,050	3,604	2,158	2,814
			Avg. Annual Rev. per Household			
Large Cities	4	36	110	312	859	880
Medium Cities	4	36	109	309	849	844
Small Cities	4	35	107	304	835	854

Sources: The local shares were obtained, for each of 30 markets, by looking at the distribution of telephone numbers by the North American Numbering Association (NANPA). *Source:* the North American Numbering Plan Administration, http:// www.nanpa.com/. *RCR Wireless News*, November 18, 2002. "The Wireless EDGE," Salomon Smith & Barney, April 3, 2003. For details, see chapter 15 of this book.

purchased USA Mobile, and through several acquisitions and mergers it eventually became the market leader, renamed USA Mobility.

Fierce competition drove paging prices down and reduced profits. With prices dropping, the number of subscribers tripled from 1991 to 1995. By 1998, the U.S. paging industry had an extraordinary 50 million subscribers with their ubiquitous "beepers", far and away more than anywhere else in the world.

In 1994, the FCC auctioned off 10 national and 30 regional "narrowband" PCS licenses, which provide additional frequencies for advanced paging, messaging, and other nonvoice wireless services. However, such frequency acquisitions did not protect paging firms from intermodal competition from cellular carriers. As miniaturization continued to decrease the size of cellular phones and as competition led to lower cellular prices and more text features, the market for paging-only services melted away. Thus, the number of one-way pager users in 2002 dropped to 30 million, from a high of 50 million in 1998.

The concentration of the paging industry had been low but increased steadily in the 1990s. Much of the paging business has traditionally been held by small local and regional firms. The combined share of the top four companies rose from 16.1% in 1984 to 29.8% in 1990 to 36.6% in 2004. Figure 11.6 shows the concentration trends in the paging industry. The low entry barriers for small local competitors largely prevented a consolidation along the lines of local wireline service and mobile cellular. Arch is the market leader under the name USA Mobility. Arch's acquisition of Mobile Media, PageNet, and Metrocall resulted in a 59% market share. Concentration rose significantly, but in a greatly diminished market that consisted mostly of medical, emergency, and IT personnel (Table 11.9).

Total Telecom Services So far, we have looked at all telecom subindustries separately. We can now present these industries together and observe their average concentration trend. This is shown in figure 11.7. The trend of each of the six subindustries is U-shaped, as is their weighted average. The

Table 11.9 Radio Paging (Market Shares by Subscribers)

Company	1983	1984	1988	1992	1996	2001	2005
USA Mobility (previously Arch Wireless)				1.2	7.3	16.5	59.4
USA Mobile				1.8	Arch		
PageNet				13.6	19.7	12.7	
Mobile Media				7.0	10.5	Arch	
MobileComm (Bell South)		3.7	6.0	6.4	MobileMedia		
Metrocall Inc.				1.3	4.9	9.4	
AT&T (McCaw)	16.1	2.0	2.5	2.7	2.6	Metrocall	
ProNet Inc.				0.7	2.7	Metrocall	
Verizon Wireless Messaging Services					BellAtl.	6.3	13.4
Airtouch Paging		5.0	5.3	5.4	6.3		
GTE	3.7	3.7	3.7				
SkyTel Comm Inc. (MTEL) (Worldcom)				1.3	2.2	·2.8	8.7
PageMart Wireless/ Weblink BellSouth Wireless Data					3.7	3.8	2.0
Teletouch Communications					0.7	0.6	1.8
Aquis Communications						0.7	
Bell Atlantic Paging / NYNEX		3.7	3.7		0.4		
SourceOne Wireless Inc.					0.8		
Network Services						0.5	0.5
American Paging				2.1	1.8		
Preferred Networks Inc.					0.7	0.8	
SBC (AT&T)		3.7	3.7			2.0	
Ameritech Paging					2.6		
TSR Wireless					2.3	4.1	
Others	80.2	78.2	75.2	56.5	30.8	39.9	14.2
Total U.S. Rev. ($ mil)	1,065	1,200	1,332	2,261	4,410	2,197	1,050
C4	19.8	16.1	18.7	32.4	43.8	44.9	83.5
HHI	273	84	111	324	665	606	3,791

average declined and in 1996 briefly reached a moderate level. Since then it has climbed strongly to an HHI level of almost 3,000. This will be further discussed in chapter 13, as well as at the conclusion of this chapter (figure 11.7).

TELECOMMUNICATIONS EQUIPMENT

After analyzing the various telecom services, we now examine the equipment side of the sector. Traditionally, telecommunications equipment industries were divided into two categories based on the destination of their products: fairly simple consumer and office-oriented "customer premises equipment" (CPE), and carrier-oriented network or infrastructure equipment. Because increasingly sophisticated equipment has migrated to the user edge of the network, with intermediate service providers and large customers establishing network operations, the distinction between CPE and network equipment has blurred.

AT&T dominated all sectors of the U.S. telecommunications equipment market from the 1880s until it spun off its equipment operations in 1996. By that time its control had declined. Several court and FCC decisions that go back to 1950 had increasingly opened the CPE segment to AT&T's competitors. But most dramatically, the 1984 AT&T divestiture created independent Bell companies with the freedom to purchase network equipment from manufacturers other than AT&T. In addition, advances in digital technology helped companies outside the traditional telecommunications vendors to contest AT&T. AT&T's vertical integration, once a major source of strength,

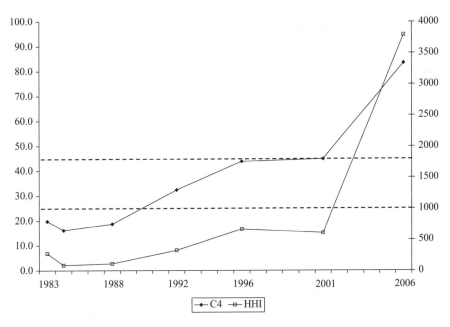

Figure 11.6 Paging: Concentration Trends

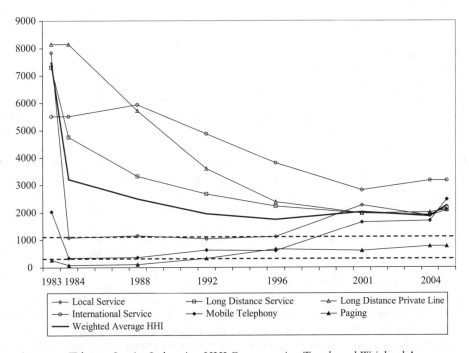

Figure 11.7 Telecom Service Industries: HHI Concentration Trends and Weighted Average

became a liability under competition. AT&T was engaged in an increasingly bitter service rivalry with its own largest customers, the Bell companies and various foreign telecom operators. In consequence, an equipment firm—Lucent—was spun off from AT&T to better retain the business of the Bell companies. AT&T also spun off its computer equipment division, which it had acquired only a few years earlier when it bought NCR for over $9 billion and merged it with its own existing

Table 11.10 Telecom Customer Equipment—Market Segments ($ Million)

	1984	1988	1992	1996	2001	2004
Corded Handsets	700	660	580	515	320	264
Cordless Handsets	511	730	949	1,424	1,585	1,149
Fax Machines	500	685	826	1,143	518	242
Mobile Handsets	200	614	1,146	3,291	11,135	14,513
PBXs	1,600	2,600	2,550	3,210	4,524	6,077
Total U.S. Rev.	3,511	5,289	6,051	9,583	18,083	22,245

Sources: The table was compiled from revenue data in industry tables throughout this chapter.

computer activities. Now, NCR became independent again. This move was significant insofar as AT&T, in 1982, had agreed to its own radical divesture in order to be allowed into the computer business, with all its future potential. Spinning off NCR signified that this strategy had failed miserably, and that the entire divesture may have been, from AT&T's perspective, a needless sacrifice. Neither Lucent nor NCR attained anything close to the dominance in the market that AT&T had possessed in the past. Soon things got worse. After 2001, with the general downturn of the telecom business, Lucent was near insolvency and frantically selling off parts. It hung on until 2006, when it agreed to consolidate with the French firm Alcatel in a $13.4 billion acquisition/merger in which it was the junior partner. The new firm was in trouble, too. And the traditional German market leader Siemens, number 3 in the U.S. market and ailing too, merged its network equipment business in 2006 into a company dominated by Nokia.

The following sections discuss the two major equipment subsectors—customer premises equipment (CPE) and network equipment—and their respective subindustries.

Customer Premises Equipment (CPE)

Customer premises equipment (CPE) is a broad category that includes numerous products in particular handsets, cell phones, facsimile (fax) machines, answering machines, modems (discussed elsewhere in this book), and the more complex private branch exchanges (PBXs). All are connected to the telecommunications network at the user's end (table 11.10).

AT&T used to have a near-monopoly in CPE. It actually owned the telephones in most homes and businesses, renting rather than selling such equipment. The rental of such CPE was a price-regulated

part of its service. No equipment could be connected to AT&T's network unless approved by AT&T. In such a way AT&T leveraged its control over networks into control over equipment nationally. Four fundamental FCC and court decisions changed AT&T's restrictive policy and required AT&T to permit interconnection of non-AT&T equipment to its networks: the 1956 *Hush-a-Phone* decision, the 1968 *Carterfone* decision, the 1977 *North Carolina Utilities Commission* decision, and the 1980 *Computer Inquiry II*.[18] These decisions, together with the FCC's implementations of required technical specifications, permitted widespread interconnection of equipment.

With the equipment market forced open, a flood of new competitors entered. Asian consumer electronics manufacturers, in particular, benefited from the opportunity. By 1987, 49% of new CPE certifications went to Far East firms.[19] Such increased foreign entry caused the U.S. balance of trade for telecommunications equipment to decline steadily throughout the 1980s, reaching a deficit of $2.6 billion in 1989,[20] and $21.8 billion in 2005.[21]

Telephone Handsets Because entry barriers are lower for simple CPEs such as telephone handsets, these markets tend to be less concentrated than the markets for more sophisticated equipment such as PBXs. Thus, the telephone handset market is one of the most competitive, with hundreds of firms (most of whom are non-U.S.) contesting each other. AT&T's share of the corded telephone handset market dropped from 60% in 1984 to 18% in 2001. The lowering of the technological threshold attracted a plethora of competitors in this market. Although the overall revenues declined from $700 million to $320 in the period 1984–2002, the market shares among the largest competitors stabilized. GE, AT&T (Lucent/Avaya), Sony, and Panasonic (Matsushita) all held market shares of equal size in 2004, hovering around 17% each (table 11.11).[22]

In the *cordless* handset market, AT&T/Lucent's market share fell from 38% in 1984 to 6% in 2005. GE held more than a quarter of the market, and HHI concentration rose again to 1,636 in 2005. Vtech held 17% of the market and Uniden about 10%. (table 11.12).

Fax Machines   Japanese consumer and office electronics firms dominate the fax machine market,

with eight of the top ten manufacturers, all but Xerox and Hewlett-Packard. Heightened competition caused prices and revenues to drop with increased market saturation. The combined C4 market share of the top four firms increased from 56.2% in 1984 to 81% in 1999 and declined to 71% in 2004. Sharp and Brother were the market leaders with 27% and 22%, respectively. Hewlett-Packard and Panasonic formed the second tier. The growth of Brother and Panasonic is the main reason for the increase in the overall concentration.

Table 11.11 Corded Telecom Handsets (Market Shares by Shipments)

	1984	1988	1989	1992	1993	1996	2001	2004
GE	2.0	4.8	5.5	8.2	9.1	16.2	17.2	17.3
Lucent[a]							18.0	18.1
AT&T	60.0	50.6	48.3	39.5	36.6	18.8	Lucent	
Sony	5.0	9.5	10.6	13.9	15.0	15.8	16.2	16.3
Panasonic (Matsushita)	10.0	11.9	12.4	13.8	14.3	14.5	14.7	14.8
Bell South		2.2	2.8	4.8	5.5	5.5	5.5	5.5
Radio Shack/Tandy	10.0	7.6	7.0	4.8	4.0	4.0	4.0	4.0
Other	13.0	13.3	13.4	15.0	15.5	25.2	24.4	23.8
Total U.S. Rev. ($ mil)	700	660	650	580	557	515	320	264
C4	85.0	79.6	78.3	75.4	75.0	65.3	66.1	66.6
HHI	3,829	2,882	2,686	2,060	1,898	1,122	1,145	1,162

Sources: Electronic Market Data Book, Consumer Electronic Association, p. 26; *Market Share Reporter* 1991, Gale Research; *New York Times,* December 27, 1989, p. 28; Appliance, *Telephone Market Shares; Telecommunication Products,* 51(8), p. 13, August 1994; Numbers for GE and AT&T/Lucent: Appliance, *Telephone Market Shares; Telecommunication Products,* 53(11), p. 106, November 1996.

[a] In 2006, Alcatel merged with Lucent.

Table 11.12 Cordless Telecom Handsets (Market Shares by Shipments)

	1984	1988	1992	1995	1996	1997	1999	2001	2003	2005
GE	3.0	7.7	12.5	16.0	15.5	15.0	21.3	27.6	28.6	28.6
Vtech								9.0	15.1	15.4	15.4
Panasonic	19.0	14.6	10.3	7.0	6.5	6.0	8.0	13.8	14.0	14.0
Sony			11.0	11.0	10.5	10.0	11.0	12.0	12.2	12.2
Uniden	7.0	8.5	9.9	11.0	11.0	11.0	10.0	9.8	10.5	10.5
Lucent								8.8	9.0	9.0
AT&T	38.0	34.0	30.0	27.0	22.0	17.0	13.0	Lucent		
SBC	4.0	4.0	4.0	4.0	4.0	4.0	4.0	4.0	3.0	6.0
Bell South				8.0	10.0	12.0	12.0	4.7	3.0	SBC
Radio Shack				4.0	4.0	4.0	4.0	4.0	3.0	3.0
Others	29.0	31.2	22.4	12.0	16.5	21.0	7.7	0.2	1.3	1.3
Total U.S. Rev. ($ mil)	511	730	949	1,168	1,424	1,679	1,700	1,585	1,149	1,149
C4	68.0	64.8	63.7	65.0	59.0	55.0	57.3	68.5	70.2	70.2
HHI	1,879	1,517	1,396	1,372	1,130	947	1,164	1,552	1,618	1,636

Sources: Keller, John J., "Lucent, Philips to Produce Phones Jointly," *Wall Street Journal,* June 18, 1997, p. A3; Personal Technology Research, Framingham, Mass.; *Market Share Reporter* 1991, Gale Research, Source: *New York Times,* December 27, 1989, p. 28; Data for 2003 uses growth percentages for individual companies.

Table 11.13 Fax Machines (Market Shares by Shipments)

	1984	1988	1990	1992	1995	1996	1997	1998	1999	2001	2004	2008
Sharp	20.8	20.8	22.9	23.3	24.0	24.5	25.0	19.8	23.2	24.8	26.5	2.4
Brother				5.6	14.0	19.0	24.0	25.8	23.0	24.6	21.5	26.2
Muratec	15	15.0	18.9	13.7	6.0	3.0						
Hewlett-Packard				4.4	11.0	12.0	13.0	17.3	15.0	11.9	11.3	19.2
Canon	10.5	10.5	9.8	9.9	10.0	10.5	11.0	10.5	10.0	7.5	5.0	28.0
Ricoh	9.9	9.9	8.4	6.2	3.0	2.0	1.0					5.4
Panasonic	5.3	5.3	6.8	10.5	16.0	16.5	17.0	16.6	20.0	13.8	12.0	4.9
Toshiba	5	5.0	6.0	3.6								
Xerox	3	3.0	3.5	2.9	2.0	2.5	3.0	3.0	3.0	3.0	3.0	1.3
Fujitsu	3.2	3.2	2.5	1.5								
Others	27.3	27.3	21.2	18.3	14.0	10.0	6.0	7.0	5.8	14.4	20.7	12.6
Total U.S. Rev.												
($ mil)	500	685	869	826	919	1,143	1,367	776	546	518	242	
C4	56.2	56.2	60.0	57.4	65.0	72.0	79.0	79.5	81.2	75.1	71.3	78.8
HHI	938	938	1,149	1,054	1,298	1,507	1,790	1,752	1,801	1,618	1,471	1,900

Sources: Dealerscope Merchandising, April 1990, May 1991, Dataquest. Figures for 1995, 1998: *2001 Market Share Reporter*. Detroit: Gale Research. Figures for 1999: *2002 Market Share Reporter*. Detroit: Gale Research. Figures for 2001: *US Business Reporter*, MetricMedia Group, Inc.; *New York Times*, Sept. 16, 2002, p. C8 (Market Share Reporter); *Wall Street Journal*, June 24, 2004, p. B6 (Market Share Reporter); Reed Business Information, *Twice* 19, Sept. 20, 2004. 2008 Data from Gartner Dataquest (June 2008).

Hewlett-Packard, Xerox, and Canon, in particular, serve the higher-end business market (table 11.13).

Wireless CPE Phones The first commercial cellular system was a payphone set up by AT&T on a New York to Washington, D.C. Metroliner train. Four years later, in 1973, Motorola created the first consumer cellular phone. Motorola committed large resources to wireless R&D. In 1975, the FCC allowed AT&T to begin a trial cellular system after a lengthy regulatory review process lasting nearly a decade. But the world's first commercial network, NMT, began operating in Scandinavia in 1981. A 150-year-old Finnish company with origins in paper manufacturing, Nokia, made the first mobile car phones for the network.

The U.S. market for cellular telephones grew from $200 million in 1984 to over $4.6 billion in 2005. The U.S. cellular service market alone exploded from 92,000 subscribers paying $340 million in 1984 to 195 million subscribers paying $108 billion in 2005. Motorola and Nokia, along with Ericsson, dominate the market for cell phones. Ericsson, the Swedish company founded in 1876, is the only one of the big three with origins in the traditional telecommunications industry.

Manufacturing cell phones was initially a booming business, but the average prices for cellular handset declined steadily, making it a $2 billion industry in 2004.[23] Only manufacturers with very deep pockets were able to devote sufficient resources to research and product development efforts, as well as ramping up manufacturing capacity quickly to meet demand.

Nokia was the first manufacturer to market cell phones as a fashionable consumer device. Nokia's vision paid off in its stock price, which experienced some of the largest gains of stock in the 1990s. Ericsson, lagging, entered into collaboration with the unsuccessful Sony to improve its own market share. The Korean firm Samsung also became a significant player.

The average weight of cellular phones has fallen from 40 pounds (built into a car) in 1986, to less than one pound by 1996 and to around 2 ounces in 2006. Prices for cellular phones also fell sharply, with new phones dropping from an average of $3,000 in 1986 to less than $100 in 2006, often subsidized by service providers to show lower prices.[24] Falling prices, coupled with smaller phone sizes and new features, also prompted many users to upgrade their cell phones every few years.

Although the cellular CPE market has been competitive, it has also consolidated. The combined market share of the top four manufacturers increased from 65% in 1984 to 79% in 1996, and to 77% in 2005. Nokia, Motorola, Samsung, and Sony Ericsson have been the top four cellular phone suppliers to the U.S. market. The overall revenues

Table 11.14 Mobile Cellular Handsets (Market Shares by Shipments)

	1984	1985	1988	1991	1992	1996	2001	2005	2008
Motorola/Pulsar	21.0	21.0	25.1	29.2	29.5	31.0	30.5	29.9	23.4
Nokia/Mobira	13.0	13.0	13.5	14.0	15.3	22.0	19.0	15.9	9.3
Samsung					0.3	2.0	8.8	15.5	19.3
Sony Ericsson (GE)	6.0	6.0	17.3	28.6	27.2	20.0	11.7	16.1	9.0
Sanyo								4.8	
Qualcomm						6.0	5.2		10.5
LG									8.8
RIM									3.3
HTC									6.5
Apple									
UTStarcom (Audiovox)						4.0	4.0	3.0	
BenQ/Siemens	3.0	3.0					1.6	1.6	
Mitsubishi	5.0	5.0	5.2	5.4	5.1	4.0	2.0		
OKI	15.0	15.0	9.5	4.0	3.8	3.0	1.5		
NEC America	16.0	16.0	10.8	5.6	2.5	2.0	2.5		
Philips	5.0	5.0							
Other	16.0	16.0	18.6	13.2	15.3	6.0	13.4	5.4	6.5
Total U.S. Rev. ($ mil)	200	266	614	962	1,146	3,291	11,136	17,933	20,500
C3	52.0	52.0	55.9	71.8	72.0	73.0	61.1	61.9	63.2
C4	65.0	65.0	66.7	77.4	77.5	79.0	69.9	77.4	75.45
HHI	1,186	1,186	1,345	1,943	1,914	1,960	1,558	1,712	1,595

Sources: 1985 Figure estimated from Global Sales Mobira/Nokia, as cited in Steinbock, Dan, "The Nokia Revolution," 2001, p. 102; *Investor's Business Daily,* February 20, 1997, p. A6. (Market Share Reporter); Paine, Webber, "Mobile Phone Market Transitioning Again," December 8, 2001; Credit Suisse First Boston, *High Grade Trading Daily,* August 30, 2001. Data for 2005 are based on third-quarter unit sales from "The NPD Group: U.S. Mobile Phone Sales Reached 31.6 Million Units in Third Quarter 2005," Oct. 26, 2005, NPD Group. Accessed May 2006 from http://www.npd.com/dynamic/releases/press_051026.html. Revenue taken from TIA's 2006 *Telecommunications Market Review and Forecast.* In 2004, UTStarcom purchased Audiovox http://investorrelations.utstar.com/ReleaseDetail.cfm?ReleaseID=147043, and in 2005, BenQ, a Taiwanese company, purchased Siemens mobile division. Qualcomm, pioneer of CDMA technology, stopped its own handset manufacturing and focused on design, chipset manufacture, and technology licensure to other manufacturers. http://www.benqmobile.com/cds/frontdoor/0,2241,hq_en_0_119246_rArNrNrN,00.html. Data for 2005 are based on global shares as reported in "Global top Six Handset Manufacturers by Market Share Percentages Estimated for 2004 and 2005," *Wireless Week,* 11(7), 27, March 15, 2005. 2008 figures from NPD Group study, www.NPD.com, and Strategy Analytics, www.cn-c114.net/s83/a336685.html. Bloomberg.com, Ville Heiskanen, LG surpasses Samsung in US. HTC data from Krazit, Tom, "Apples iPhone loses US market share in Q1", C-NET News, news, cnet.com/8301-13579-3-995-7776-37.html, and applying share of smart phones in total. Sony Ericsson 2008 market share used global share. Fiercewireless.com/shary/sony-ericsson-g-profit-market-share-g-down-17/2008-09.

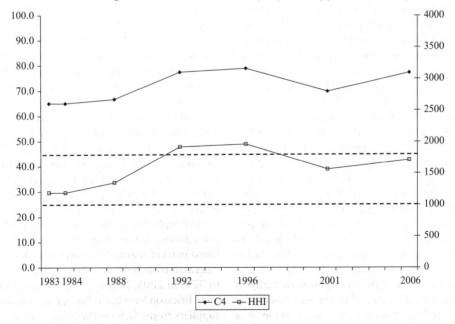

Figure 11.8 Mobile Handsets: Concentration Trends

of mobile handsets stabilized after 1996 at around $3.5 billion, as did market concentration. Ericsson saw its share halved in this period while it joined forces with Sony (table 11.14, figure 11.8).

To make things more complicated, in the United States, different service providers implemented (as discussed) four different digital transmission standards: GSM, TDMA, CDMA, and iDEN. All are multiplexing schemes that increase the number of conversations that a given spectrum allotment can carry. Hence, different firms had different strengths in each of these standard's submarkets. iDEN equipment was dominated by Motorola, whereas CDMA equipment, whatever its manufacturer, requires licensing by its prime developer Qualcomm. The GSM standard equipment market was more competitive, though it lacked in most countries the interstandard rivalry. TDMA eventually merged into GSM, and iDEN was being phased out. Thus GSM and CDMA were the main survivors. GSM was globally dominant, but the next generation ("3G") of mobile phones all adopted flavors of CDMA.

Private Branch Exchanges   One of the most concentrated CPE submarkets is that of private branch exchanges (PBXs). A PBX is a switch located on a user's premises that routes calls within an office or to a different branch office within a private network. The FCC's 1959–1981 decisions to permit equipment interconnection allowed competitors into the U.S. PBX market. AT&T's share fell from nearly 90% in 1968 to 20% in 1984. Several American entrants, including ITT, Rockwell, United Technologies, Memorex, TRW, Wang, and even Exxon, attempted to capture PBX market share. Most were unsuccessful in keeping up with the rapid advances in the field.

In the early 1980s, the Canadian-firm Northern Telecom (renamed Nortel) was the first to offer a complete line of digital switches and transmission products. Nortel's market shares grew from 8% in 1980 to 20% in 1994. Between 1986 and 1989, ITT sold its large equipment operations, mostly located across Europe and including PBXs, to the French firm Alcatel. GTE sold its PBX business to Fujitsu, and IBM sold its Rolm PBX division to Siemens of Germany. Thus, by the 1990s, AT&T (Lucent) was the only significant U.S. PBX firm left. Lucent led the PBX market with a 33% share in 1999, and then spun off this line of business as Avaya. The combined share of the top four firms

rose from 64% in 1984 to 80% in 2001. The low point in concentration occurred soon after AT&T was split up, but consolidation has increased ever since. A significant contributor to this was the purchase of NEC's American PBX business by Siemens in 1990. The U.S. market was dominated by two companies—Lucent/Avaya and Nortel—with a combined share of more than 62% in 2001, and the remainder was divided up by several other companies. With new technologies such as packet switching and mobile communications emerging, Lucent's and Siemens' market shares declined and the industry's concentration dropped back to its early 1990s levels (table 11.15).

A PBX, which is a user-based switch, also competes with network-based switching. After 1984, PBX sales stagnated for a decade as a result of the Bell companies' promotion of Centrex, a competing switching system based in the telephone company central offices. This trend continued with "hosted PBXs" offered by traditional and new providers from a distance which substantially diluted the "private" element of PBXs. More recently, many PBXs are IP or LAN based. 3Com dominated this niche with a 53% market share. Vertical Networks and Cisco followed with 20% and 19% of the market, respectively, in 2000, with total revenues of $125 million.[25] By 2004 this market had significantly expanded to $1.5 billion, and the main competitors were Cisco (29.9%), Avaya (22.4%), Nortel (17.7%), 3Com (7%), and Mitel (6.2%).[26]

Network Equipment

Unlike CPE, most categories of network and transmission equipment are sold primarily to carriers and service providers, not to the end users themselves (unless they are quite large). Telephone companies have the largest installed base of infrastructure and are by far the largest buyers of network equipment. Transmission equipment, a subset of network equipment, includes the multiplexers that combine and separate signals, different types of wires, and wireless equipment used to carry signals. The other major segments of network equipment are the switches and Internet working routers that direct calls through the network, as well as the transmission media themselves—wires, cables, fibers, and wireless transceivers (figure 11.9).

In the limited stage of the communications sector, the network equipment market was vertically integrated and closed to competitors. AT&T's

Table 11.15 Telecom Private Branch Exchange Equipment (Market Shares by Revenues)

	1983	1984	1988	1990	1992	1994	1996	1998	1999	2001	2002	2003	2004
Lucent/Avaya								32.0	33.0	34.0	36.1	32.7	27.0
AT&T	30.0	20.0	22.0	26.9	29.5	32.0	32.0					Lucent	
Nortel	10.0	20.0	19.1	23.9	25.0	26.0	26.8	27.5	28.0	28.2	30.3	27.2	24.0
Cisco												7.4	12.0
Siemens	4.0	4.0	4.0	16.0	15.5	15.0	12.4	9.8	9.8	9.9	13.9	10.5	8.0
Rolm	14.0	14.0	23.2	Siemens									
NEC	8.0	8.0	7.3	5.8	6.4	7.0	8.6	10.2	8.8	7.7	6.7	5.0	8.0
Mitel (Canada)	10.0	10.0	8.3	9.3	7.7	6.0	7.2	8.4	8.8	7.4	1.9	3.0	7.0
GTE/Fujitsu	5.0	5.0	3.6	3.6	3.7	3.7	2.9	2.0	2.1	2.3	2.6	2.9	2.9
Intecom			2.1	1.2	1.2	1.2	1.1	1.0	1.5	2.0	2.9	2.2	2.2
3Com												1.5	1.0
Others	49.0	39.0	32.4	40.2	40.7	41.1	41.1	41.1	41.0	42.5	41.7	7.7	7.9
Total U.S. Rev. ($ mil)	1,350	1,600	2,600	2,300	2,550	2,800	3,210	3,620	4,900	3,900	3,750	4,200	4,600
C4	64.0	64.0	72.6	76.1	77.6	80.0	79.8	79.5	79.6	79.8	87.0	77.8	71.0
HHI	1,401	1,201	1,543	1,685	1,844	2,025	2,028	2,056	2,131	2,173	2,478	2,023	1,640

Sources: Data for 1984: McInerney, Francis, "PBX Market Analyses," *Teleconnect,* September 1, 1985, p. 90. Data for 1988: *North American Telecommunications Association, Telecommunications Market Review and Forecast: Annual Report of the Telecommunications Industry,* 1990 edition, Washington, 1989, p. 120; *Business Week,* August 14, 1989, pp. 84–85; Coy, Peter, "For PBX Makers, the Future Is Later," *Business Week,* February 25, 1991, p. 88; *PC Computing,* May 1995, p. 154, Source: Dataquest; *InfoTrack for Enterprise Communications, Phillips Consulting,* 2001; Estimated share of PBX was 20% in 2001 and 10% in 1998. Data for 2002 are from *The Telecom Manager's Voice Report,* January 13, 2003, p. 3. Data for 2003 from *Annual PBX Report;* Jennifer Hagendorf Follet, "Avaya, Nortel Vie for Cisco Share," *CRN,* August 25, 2003, Iss. 1059; p. 5. Data for 2004 are from Sulkin, Allan, "2004 USA PBX Market Review: IP Telephony Drive PBX Market Resurgence," 2004. TEQConsult Group. May 18, 2006, pp. 11–12, http://www.avaya.com/master-usa/en-us/resource/ assets/whitepapers/teqconsult_2004pbxwp-pdf.. In 2007, Siemens merged its telecom equipment operations with Nokia's.

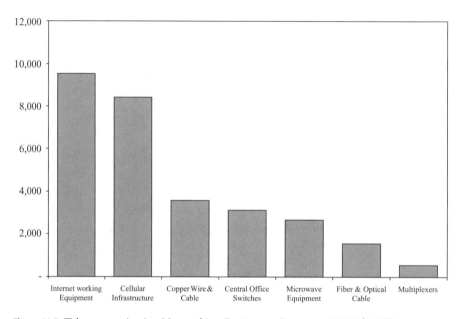

Figure 11.9 Telecommunication Networking Equipment Revenues 2004 ($ Million)

Western Electric division was nearly the exclusive supplier of network equipment to AT&T's local and long-distance service subsidiaries, accounting for 80% of the network equipment. It had several key advantages: economies of scale; access to its operating LECs; a stellar industrial lab; construction forecasts; and power over network designs, standards, and protocols. GTE, the second largest phone company, similarly owned its own manufacturing company. Thus, competition in the U.S. network and transmission equipment markets existed only for sales to smaller independent telephone companies, comprising less than 10% of the market. In that market, Stromberg-Carlsson was a large supplier.

The 1984 divestiture decree mandated that the Bell companies provide all IXCs with equal access in their central offices, which necessitated equipment and upgrade purchases. New competing telephone service providers required equipment to build their facilities. Carriers upgraded their networks by deploying fiber-optic cable. The overall network equipment market grew enormously from $5.4 billion in 1984 to over $41 billion in the boom years up to 2001 (even with the substantial price declines), but then strongly retreated to $30 billion in 2004.

Despite many predictions to the contrary, the Bell companies were quick to embrace new

equipment suppliers beyond AT&T, particularly Nortel's digital switches. Starting in 1989, many Bell companies gained a further incentive to buy equipment at the best available prices due to the partial substitution of price cap regulation for rate-of-return regulation, which had often provided incentives to "gold-plate" the network.

The newly opened U.S. market attracted international network equipment vendors. Some foreign companies entered the U.S. market by charging low prices, having covered the development cost by sales to their domestic phone monopolist. Equipment firms that were under political pressure to buy from domestic manufacturers in less competitive markets could therefore charge their domestic telecom monopoly high premiums. For example, Siemens' price per line in Germany, in 1990, when it was still shielded from competition, was 350% higher than its international bids, and Alcatel's were 204% higher (table 11.16).[27] These enormous premium prices declined rapidly after the privatizations of operating companies gave them an incentive to pursue the best prices.

For about a decade the problem for U.S. manufacturers was that foreign telecommunications equipment markets were not reciprocally open to U.S. producers, because the still existing state monopolies preferred to buy domestic products. Thus from 1981 though 1987, U.S. telecommunications

Table 11.16 Domestic vs. International Prices for Telecom Switches (1990)

Company	Market Share in Home Market	Home Price ($/Line)	Intl. Lowest Bid ($/Line)	Home Market Premium (%)
Alcatel (France)	84	335	110	204
AT&T (U.S.)	42	110	100	10
Ericsson (Sweden)	100	325	130	150
Fujitsu (Japan)	24	290	110	164
NEC (Japan)	25	290	140	107
Nortel (Canada)	80	250	100	150
Siemens (Germany)	83	450	100	350

Source: Noam, Eli. *Telecommunications in Europe.* New York: Oxford University Press, 1992.

imports increased by 320%, whereas exports increased by only 41%. The main U.S. exporters of the early 1980s, ITT and GTE, were squeezed out in Europe, and they eventually sold out to the French firm Alcatel and to the German firm Siemens, respectively. The U.S. government pushed increased liberalization of procurement and a competitive carrier system, with the expectation that this would lead to a greater market for U.S. providers. Many but not all of the domestic preference issues declined with privatization, liberalization, and World Trade Organization (WTO) trade agreements.

Demand for networking equipment grew at a rapid rate in the 1990s, especially for optical equipment and routers. A period of intense merger activity ensued. This boom ended abruptly after 2000, when the market demand for network equipment collapsed with overcapacity and dropping transmission prices of telecom service providers. In 2006, AT&T successor company, Lucent, threw in the towel and merged into Lucent-Alcatel, dominated by the French company. In 2009, the number 2 vendor, the Canadian firm Nortel, went into a Chapter 11 bankruptcy reorganization.

Central Office Switches The most significant category of traditional fixed-line network equipment is the central office switch that connects subscribers' lines to each other and to trunk lines (which transport traffic to other network nodes of the same network, as well as to other networks) (table 11.17).[28]

The combination of AT&T's divestiture and its temporary failure to keep up with the digital advances of Northern Telecom (owned by the Canadian telecom incumbent Bell Canada Enterprises [BCE]), drove AT&T's national market share down from 88% in 1983 to 40% in the late 1980s. Nortel almost became AT&T's equal in size in this market. Siemens (which had acquired

the GTE and Stromberg Carlsson operations) was a distant third. Ericsson, Alcatel, and NEC each held small but growing shares. In 2006, Alcatel merged with Lucent as the dominant partner, and the Siemens network equipment business became part of a partnership dominated by Nokia. The Chinese firm ZTE was becoming active in the world market, but had no impact in the U.S. yet. With the bulk of the market divided among three companies, the concentration was high, with an HHI of about 2,750. The overall market declined dramatically in size after 2000 (figure 11.10).

Multiplexers Multiplexers enable simultaneous transmission of multiple voice and data signals over a single transmission line. To do this, multiplexers converge the signals at the sender's end and separate them at the receiver's end. This has been a fairly crowded industry, with Alcatel (after buying Newbridge and DSC) and AT&T as the market leaders at about 22% and 16%, respectively. AT&T used to dominate, but its spin-off Lucent faded to 10–15%. The remainder of the industry is divided among many smaller providers. In the early 1990s several of the smaller companies, such as Fujitsu, Harris, Plessy-Stromberg, and Siemens, left this market. But several medium-sized companies remain, such as Cisco, Tellabs, and Nortel. After AT&T's share dwindled, the HHI reached the low concentration threshold in 1992 and stayed relatively flat thereafter. However, with the acquisition of Lucent by Alcatel in 2006, the industry consolidated again (table 11.18).

Internetworking Equipment Internetworking equipment is widely sold to customers other than telephone and cable companies. An internetwork is a private data network, usually within a company. The major piece of internetworking equipment is the

Table 11.17 Telecom Central Office Switches (Market Shares by Lines)

Company	1983	1984	1987	1988	1989	1991	1992	1994	1996	1998	2001	2004	2006
Alcatel (France)		1.0	2.5	2.1	1.7	1.3	1.2	0.9	0.95	1.0	1.0	6.4	41.4
Lucent (USA)										Lucent			Alcatel
AT&T (USA)	88.3	64.0	39.6	40.0	40.4	40.7	41.3	43.2	42.6	42.0	41.0	35.0	
Nortel (Canada)	3.0	11.2	36.2	37.2	38.2	38.6	38.3	37.4	37.8	38.2	39.0	29.8	29.8
Siemens[a] (Germany)		1.0	2.0	6.5	11.0	10.0	9.8	9.0	9.0	9.0	10.0	8.7	8.7
Stromberg Carlsson (USA)	3.2	4.0	4	4	Siemens								
GTE (USA)	5.5	6.8	6	6	Siemens								
Ericsson (Sweden)				0.1	0.2	1.1	1.2	1.4	1.6	1.8	2.0	8.2	8.2
NEC (Japan)		1.0	1.2	1.1	1	0.9	0.8	0.6	0.7	0.8	1.0	1.0	1.0
Others	0.0	11.0	8.5	3.0	7.5	7.4	7.4	7.5	7.4	7.2	6.0	10.9	10.9
Total U.S Rev. ($ mil)	2,900	3,143	4,033	4,317	4,600	5,300	6,100	8,500	8,950	9,300	8,191	3,168	
Total Lines (1,000)			45,982	58,136	70,289	90,595	100,484	130,152	136,660	143,167	141,736	163,157	
C4	100	86.0	85.8	89.7	90.6	90.4	90.6	91.0	91.0	91.0	92.0	81.7	88.1
HHI	7,846	4,286	2,936	3,079	3,213	3,250	3,273	3,349	3,329	3,309	3,308	2,298	2,746

Sources: Northern Business Information estimates, Industry Analysis, 1988, 1990, 1992, 1994, 1995; Henry, John, *"Telephone and Telegraph Equipment,"* United States Industrial Outlook, January 1992, p. 29; Egan, Bruce L., and Leonard Waverman, "The State of Competition in Telecommunications," Barry G. Colein, ed., *After the Breakup: Assessing the New Post-AT&T Divestiture Era.* New York: Columbia University Press, 1991, pp. 285–304; 1998 data assume a 10% increase in total lines as well as in total revenue, based on the stability between the price and number of lines; 2001 data assume a 10% increase in total lines as well as in total revenue, based on the stability between the price and number of lines from 1998 to 1999, a 0% change between 1999 and 2000, and finally a 10% decrease in both total number of lines and total revenue; Gartner Dataquest, 2004, by special communication. 2006 Figure uses 2004 data only to estimate impact of Alcatel-Lucent merger, controlled by Alcatel.

[a] Merged in 2007 into the joint firm Nokia Siemens, controlled by Nokia (Finland).

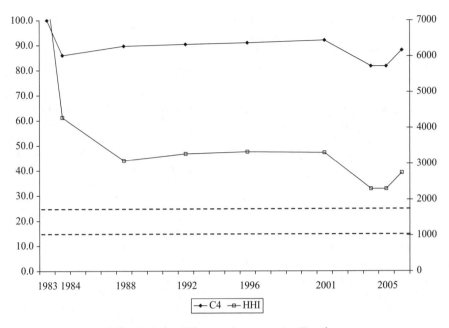

Figure 11.10 Central Office Switches Telecom: Concentration Trends

Table 11.18 Telecom Multiplexers (Market Shares by Shipments)

	1984	1988	1990	1992	1994	1996	2001	2004	2006
Alcatel-Celwave (FR)	0.5	0.8	1.0	4.0	2.8	8.0	28.3	22.0	38.0
Newbridge (Canada)		3.6	5.4	11.8	22.5	22.5	Alcatel		
AT&T/Lucent (USA)	53.6	38.0	30.3	13.3	7.3	8.3	9.8	16.0	Alcatel
DSC (USA)					2.6	2.0	1.4	Alcatel	
Ascom Timeplex (Canada)	11.7	13.9	15.0	14.0	14.0	13.6	13.0	12.0	12.0
NET (USA)	4.4	8.1	10.0	11.0	11.2	9.0	8.3	8.3	8.3
Motorola (USA)		1.5	2.2	1.6	8.2	7.4	7.2	7.2	7.2
Nortel (Canada)	4.9	3.8	3.3	1.5	1.1	1.3	2.5	5.0	5.0
Cisco (Stratacom) (USA)	0.1	2.2	3.2	6.0	6.2	6.1	6.0	6.0	6.0
Telco Systems (BATM) (USA)	1.0	1.0	1.0	2.1	2.5	2.8	3.1	3.1	3.1
NEC (Japan)	8.8	6.0	4.6	0.5	0.8	0.6	0.6	2.0	2.0
Tellabs (USA)				5.8	4.2	4.5	4.8	2.0	2.0
Siemens (Germany)[a]	1.0	0.5	0.2						
Others	14.2	20.6	23.9	28.3	16.6	14.0	15.0	16.4	16.4
Total U.S. Rev($ mil)	426	631	734	1,307	961	590	570	585	
C4	78.9	66.1	60.7	50.1	55.8	53.4	59.4	58.3	65.5
HHI	3,128	1,778	1,320	730	1,025	1,031	1,264	1,083	1,787

Note: Numbers combine both T1 and T3 multiplexers.

Sources: Northern Business Information estimates, Industry Analysis, 1987, 1991, 1993, 1995. Northern Business Information, Industry survey estimates, 1987, 1989, 1991, 1993, 1995; "Timeplex Rules T-1 Schoolyard," *Data Communications,* November 1988, p. 113; Revenue 1998–2004 from Multimedia Telecommunications Association, *Multimedia Telecommunications Market Review and Forecast,* 133, February 13, 2001; 2004 market shares from Gartner Dataquest figures by special communication. 2006 Figure uses 2004 data for illustrative purposes only to estimate impact of Alcatel-Lucent merger.
[a] Nokia Siemens Networks after 2006.

router, which enables fast, accurate packet exchange between computers. They are the key devices in ethernet networks, the most popular form of inter-network. Routers (and their cousins, hubs and gateways) are an essential component of computer-based networks such as local area networks (LANs), wide area networks (WANs, which are privately owned by many large firms), organizational intranets and extranets, and especially the Internet.

Other types of internetworking equipment include internetworking software (generally bundled with routers), LAN and WAN switching equipment, and remote-access server computers. Table 11.19 and figure 11.11 display the concentration trend for the overall Internetworking equipment market.

Cisco Systems is by far the leading vendor in internetworking devices, with a 56% market share in 2004. As a result, concentration is high. In certain submarkets, Cisco was even more dominant. It accounted for almost 80% of all routers in 2004. Starting in 2002, however, Chinese vendors, in particular HuaWei, began to challenge Cisco around the world, although less in the United States. As shown in the figure 11.11, the concentration trend in this market is U-shaped. AT&T's share dropped from a high 45% in 1984 to around 19% in the early 1990s, when the market grew enormously and Cisco became the dominant player. Concentration was high, with an HHI of 3,544. The merger of Alcatel and Lucent in 2006

caused the concentration to increase even further to 3,707.

Wireline Equipment Wireline equipment includes copper wire, coaxial cable, and optical fiber. Coaxial cable is a copper conductor surrounded by shielding, thus protecting it more from outside interference and enabling a greater transmission capacity. Optical fiber transmits information via modulated light pulses and can use different color light frequencies (windows). A half-inch-thick optical fiber cable may have several dozen pairs of fiber, each with dozens of windows, and can simultaneously transmit vast amounts of information. Optical/electrical conversion and installation costs make fiber comparatively expensive to put directly into each customer's home.

Due to high start-up, R&D, and manufacturing plant cost, fiber manufacturing is concentrated. The top four firms' fiber market share was near 90%. Corning Glass, the technology leader, held 48% in 2004. After 2001, industry revenues collapsed by over 75% (table 11.20).

Corning's dominant share dropped after 1984 from 84% as competitors entered the market. This deconcentration trend continued throughout the 1980s. AT&T (Lucent) grew in share and peaked with a market share of 51% in 1990. In 2006 it merged with Alcatel, which became the market leader. Other companies in this market—Pirelli,

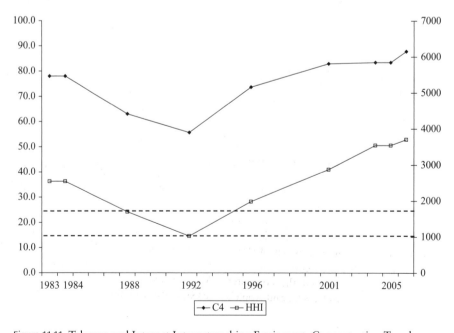

Figure 11.11 Telecom and Internet Internetworking Equipment: Concentration Trends

Table 11.19 Telecom and Internet Internetworking Equipment (Market Shares by Revenues)

Company	1984	1988	1990	1992	1993	1995	1996	1999	2000	2001	2004	2006
Cisco (USA)		0.5	6.0	20.0	30.0	33.3	36.6	40.0	41.0	48.0	56.0	56.0
Alcatel (France)[a]	3.0	1.7	1.0	1.0	1.0	1.0	3.7	4.0	5.0	5.0	4.5	22.5
Newbridge (Canada)		1.3	2.0	3.3	4.0	2.9	Alcatel					
Ungerman Bass (USA)			13.0	4.3		Alcatel						
Lucent (USA)								26.0	27.0	20.0	18.0	Alcatel
AT&T (USA)	45.0	37.7	34.0	21.7	19.0	21.0	22.0	Lucent				
Ascend (USA)						1.9	Lucent					
Nortel (Canada)	10.0	8.0	7.0	4.3	3.0	2.9	11.0	12.0	10.5	7.0	5.0	5.0
Wellfleet/Bay Networks (USA)				7.0	7.0	9.5	Nortel					
Siemens (Germany)[b]	2.0	3.3	4.0	2.7	2.0	1.9	1.9	2.0	2.0	2.0	1.0	1.0
Marconi[c] (UK)							0.5	2.0	5.0	8.0	4.4	4.4
IBM (USA)	20.0	14.0	11.0	7.0	5.0	3.8	4.1	5.0	5.0	5.0	4.3	4.3
HuaWei (China)											1.0	1.0
Other	20.0	33.5	22.0	28.7	29.0	21.9	20.2	9.0	4.5	5.0	6.8	6.8
Total U.S. Rev. ($ mil)	550	963	1,170	1,376	1,479	1,687	3,853	10,350	12,600	11,085	9,571	
C4	78.0	63.0	65.0	55.7	61.0	67.6	73.7	83.0	83.5	83.0	83.5	87.9
HHI	2,538	1,695	1,552	1,025	1,365	1,680	1,979	2,469	2,599	2,871	3,545	3,707

Sources: Market Share Reporter, Annual from The Wall Street Journal, July 14, 1992, p. 31; "Internetworking, Data Communications," August 21, 1996, p. 103; Dataquest. 1990 revenue from Mulqueen, John T., "Data Communications 1991 Market Forecast," Data Communications, Dec. 1990, p. 95; 1999 and 2000 figures are from Merrill Lynch, "Data Networking Market Share/Trends: Review and Outlook," June 2000. Prorated to U.S. of 45% global estimated and extrapolated. Market shares for 2004 use data on worldwide router, ethernet, and port switches from Nortel by personal communication. HuaWei was assigned a share of 1% in the United States, because of its production joint venture with 3Com and distribution agreement with IBM. Its total 2004 revenue outside of China was $552 million (according to Hoover's), with its sales in the U.S. around $100 million. 2006 Figure uses 2004 data for illustrative purposes only to estimate impact of Alcatel-Lucent merger. Siemens is part of Nokia Siemens Networks after 2006.

[a] Alcatel controls the merged firm Lucent Alcatel.
[b] Nokia controls the merged equipment firm Nokia Siemens Networks
[c] Marconi's business were acquired by Siemens and by Ericsson.

Table 11.20 Fiber and Optical Cable (Market Shares by Revenues)

	1984	1986	1988	1990	1992	1994	1996	2001	2003/4	2006
Corning/Siemens (U.S./Germany)	83.6	36.0	36.3	26.1	28.1	23.2	23.6	32.2	33.0	33.0
Alcatel (France)		5.0	10.3	8.7	21.9	19.9	18.8	19.6	20.1	40.1
AT&T/Lucent (U.S.)		40.0	34.5	50.9	12.5	11.0	11.9	19.6	20.1	Alcatel
Nortel (Canada)		4.0	4.8	2.0	12.5	15.4	14.8	12.6	13.0	13.0
Sumitomo (Japan)		1.0	0.4	0.7	10.9	12.7	12.0	10.3	8.7	8.7
Pirelli (Italy)		2.0	6.0	6.7	12.5	16.6	17.8	4.7	4.3	4.3
Ericsson (Sweden)	16.4	6.0								
General Cable (U.K.)		5.0								
Others	0.0	1.0	7.7	4.9	1.6	1.2	1.2	1.1	0.9	0.9
Total U.S. Rev. ($ mil)	120	650	496	690	3,202	4,531	5,057	6,362	2,304	2,304
C4	100.0	87.0	87.1	92.3	74.9	75.0	75.0	83.9	86.1	94.8
HHI	7,260	3,003	2,671	3,393	1,855	1,727	1,729	2,089	2,156	2,960

Sources: Northern Business Information, estimates, "Industry Analysis," 1987, 1989, 1991, 1995; "Ericsson Inc. Will Sell Fiber-Optic Equipment in $19.5 Million Accord," *Wall Street Journal,* New York, Feb. 2, 1984; Berg, Eric N., *"Gains Foreseen in Fiber Optics."* New York:, Market Place, May 21, 1985. Market shares based on 1998 revenue, share of market, and product line contribution in Hoover's Company Profile Database (World Companies). 2006 Figure uses 2004 data for illustrative purposes only to estimate impact of Alcatel-Lucent merger.

Table 11.21 Copper Wire and Cable (Market Shares by Revenues)

	1984	1986	1988	1989	1991	1992	1993	1996	1998	2001	2003	2006
General Cable (U.K.)	1.1	1.1	5.3	8.7	16.9	19.3	21.6	22.0	21.9	24.2	28.4	28.4
Alcatel (France)	3.4	4.5	6.4	6.8	10.0	11.7	13.3	18.8	20.2	15.6	12.9	38.7
AT&T/Lucent (U.S.)	63.9	62.9	56.6	52.1	44.9	41.3	37.7	39.1	35.7	33.5	25.8	Alcatel
Superior/Essex (U.S.)	3.4	4.5	8.2	9.2	8.3	8.8	9.3	12.5	14.6	19.2	25.5	25.5
Essex	6.8	9.0	11.1	11.4	9.3	8.1	6.9	Superior				
Nortel (Canada)	8.0	6.7	5.1	4.2	3.1	3.3	3.5					
Others	13.3	11.2	7.2	7.5	7.5	7.5	7.5	7.5	7.5	7.5	7.5	7.5
Total U.S. Rev. ($ mil)	526	712	973	1,092	1,319	1,256	1,193	1,845	2,533	3,053	3,588	
C4	82.1	83.1	82.3	81.4	81.1	81.1	82.0	92.5	92.5	92.5	92.5	92.?
HHI	4,216	4,127	3,491	3,070	2,565	2,369	2,218	2,526	2,381	2,320	2,284	2,948

Sources: Northern Business Information, 1987, 1990, 1992, 1994; market share percentages based on company SEC filings for 1998 and 2001; data for 2003 are based on total sales in North America, company annual reports. In 1993, the Alpine Group, a holding company bought Superior Tele-Tec. In 1995 Alpine purchased the Alcatel's North American operations, as well as Philips Cable's Vancouver operations, making Alpine the largest U.S. maker of copper cable and wire for outside plant. Kraph, Eric, "Why They're Buying Cable," *America's Network,* Nov. 1, 1995, p. 12. 2006 Figure uses 2004 data for illustrative purposes only to estimate the impact of Alcatel-Lucent merger. Category of "Other" estimated for several years, based on data for 1988.

Sumitomo, and Nortel—made their presence felt after 1992.

The copper wire and coaxial cable market is similarly more concentrated than the fiber market. The top four copper and cable companies accounted for about 90% of the revenues (table 11.21).

Wireless Transmission Equipment Microwave equipment consists of the towers located along the transmission routes (usually spaced about 20 miles apart) and the associated radio equipment. Traditional microwave customers, such as phone or cable companies, use microwaves for long-haul

Table 11.22 Microwave Communications Equipment (Market Shares Revenues)

	1986	1988	1990	1992	1994	1996	2001	2004	2006
Alcatel (Fr)	1.0	0.5	0.4	15.0	15.9	16.1	20.0	20.3	45.3
Rockwell (U.S.)	17.1	13.0	12.5	Alcatel					
AT&T/Lucent (U.S.)	40.1	40.1	25.8	20.7	18.5	19.8	24.8	25.0	Alcatel
Harris (U.S.)	1.9	8.8	21.6	28.5	33.2	30.9	30.2	29.6	29.6
Tadiran (Isr.)			1.7	3.6	3.6	4.8	8.3	8.3	8.3
Calif. Microwave (U.S.)	7.8	7.0	6.7	15.2	12.6	12.2	Tadiran		
TeleSciences	0.0	5.9	6.6	Calif. Microwave					
Nortel (Canada)	10.8	3.4	5.4	4.9	4.7	4.3	4.0	3.7	3.7
DMC Stratex Networks (U.S.)	1.0	2.9	4.6	4.7	4.0	4.2	5.2	5.6	5.6
Motorola (U.S.)	0.0	0.9	6.6						
NEC (Japan)	8.2	9.6	0.5						
Siemens (Germany)	0.0	0.4							
Fujitsu (Japan)	2.9								
GTE-Milano (US/Italy)	1.6								
Ericsson (Sweden)	1.0								
Others	6.8	7.5	7.5	7.5	7.5	7.5	7.5	7.5	7.5
Total U.S. Rev. ($ mil)	528	609	483	470	510	1,079	2,500	1,675	1,675
C4	76.1	71.5	66.7	79.3	80.2	79.1	83.3	83.2	88.8
HHI	2,158	2,055	1,479	1,751	1,908	1,820	2,038	2,026	3,042

Sources: Market shares are based on 2001 revenue and relative share of market and product, as provided in Hoover's Company Profile Database (World Companies). 2006 Figure uses 2004 data only to estimate the impact of Alcatel-Lucent merger.

focused directional transmissions, but microwave equipment is also used for local communications and for satellite transmission (table 11.22).

Mobile Wireless Network Equipment The wireless network equipment industry includes three major segments: cellular sites, cellular switches, and cellular transmission systems. As the cellular mobile industry grew enormously, so did wireless network equipment sales: from $2.5 billion in 1990 to $9.6 billion in 2001. The cellular network equipment sector has been highly concentrated. Significant entry barriers exist in the form of high start-up costs and alliances between service providers and equipment suppliers.

By 2004, four firms—Motorola, Nortel, Nokia, and Lucent—all held similar market shares, around 15%. Ericsson led the market with more than a quarter market share, and the overall HHI declined to moderate concentration levels at 1,521 (table 11.23).

Concentration of Telecom Equipment—Overall Figure 11.12 shows the concentration trends for telecom customer equipment, network equipment, and their aggregate. Customer equipment, on the one hand, hovers between moderate and high concentration. The trend, mostly flat, shows a slight U-shaped trend line. Network equipment, on the other hand, shows a tremendous decline, followed by a flattening in concentration, and a rise after 2004. It remained highly concentrated throughout the period. Aggregating both segments shows the aggregate trend line for the entire telecom equipment sector: a steep decline initially, a stable period between 1988 and 1996, and a moderate rise in concentration after 2004.

CONCLUSION: CONCENTRATION IN THE TELECOM SECTOR

What then is the overall trend of concentration for the telecom sector? Figure 11.13 sums it up.

After a steep decline after the divestiture of AT&T in 1984, weighted average concentration for both the equipment and services industries kept decreasing. Services even became moderately concentrated—just barely so—in 1996, and then rose again. After 2004 the entire sector increased more steeply in concentration. Equipment industry concentration was fairly flat after 1988, at a high level.

A similar picture emerges if we pool all the segments of the telecom services sector into a single industry, rather than averaging the several industries. The calculation is done as part of Chapter 13, "National Concentration Trends." We anticipate the results in figure 11.14. Here, too, we observe

Table 11.23 Mobile Cellular Network Infrastructure (Market Shares by Revenues)

	1984	1987	1988	1990	1992	1995	1996	1997	1998	2001	2004
Ericsson (Sweden)	6.0	10.0	11.9	15.8	30.0	27.3	23.2	23.0	31.0	37.0	26.0
Motorola (US)	22.0	36.0	34.3	31.0	16.0	19.2	14.5	13.0	17.0	22.0	16.0
Nortel (Canada)	7.0	11.0	11.0	11.0	13.0	15.6	19.2	21.0	12.0	11.0	14.7
Nokia (Finland)							3.7		11.0	15.0	20.5
Siemens										6.5	
AT&T/Lucent/ Alcatel (US/France)	62.0	29.0	32.5	39.5	41.0	36.7	37.2	38.0	26.0	14.0	13.3
Qualcomm							1.5				
Others	3.0	14.0	10.2	2.7	0.0	1.2	0.7	5.0	3.0	1.0	9.5
Total U.S.											
Rev. ($ mil)	120	267	1,011	2,500	2,800	6,400	6,723	7,046	7,379	9,600	8,448
C4	97.0	86.0	89.8	97.3	100.0	98.8	94.1	95.0	86.0	88.0	70.7
HHI	4,413	2,358	2,498	2,892	3,006	2,704	2,515	2,583	2,191	2,389	1,621

Sources: Bradshaw, Della, "Mobile Communications," *Financial Times*, September 12, 1988, p. 6.; "Ericsson Remains Top Network Manufacturer," *FinTech Mobile Communications*, July 4, 1991; *Communications Daily*, February 11, 1993; "On and About AT&T," *Edge*, April 1, 1996; Source: Dataquest; *1999 Market Reporter*, citing RCR, March 23, 1998, p. 1, Yankee Group; Merrill Lynch's Global Securities Research and Economics Group, *Telecommunications Equipment. Industry Handbook*, 1999; Merrill Lynch's Global Securities Research and Economics Group, *Wireless Equipment Industry: What's in the Air For 2001"* 2001. Shares for 2004 are based on global shares. Walko, John. "Cellular Infrastructure Market Fell 12 Percent in '03, Says Gartner," *Networking Pipeline*, May 20, 2004. Available at http://nwm.networkingpipeline.com/news/20900084. Data for 2004 assume that North American companies' domestic share is one third larger than their worldwide share.

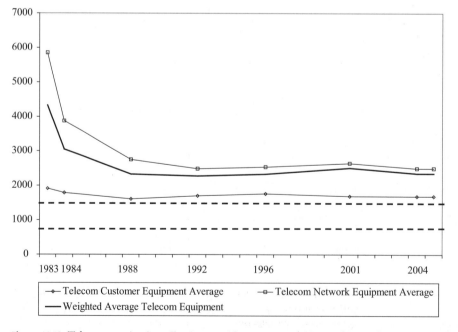

Figure 11.12 Telecommunications Equipment (Customer and Networking): Concentration Trends

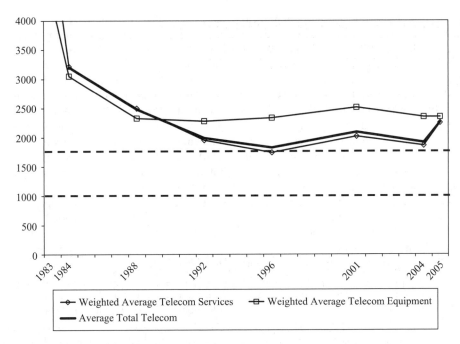

Figure 11.13 Total Telecommunications Sector

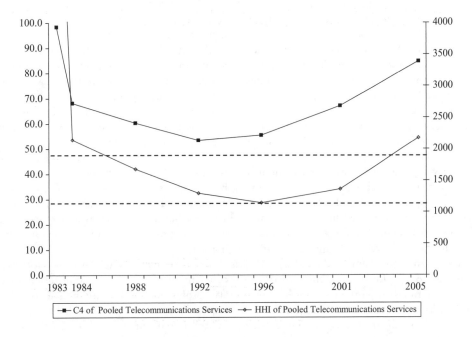

Figure 11.14 Pooled Telecom

a U-shaped concentration trend, though, as one could expect, at a somewhat lower level.

The overall concentration trend of the telecom services industry has been strongly U-shaped: a huge decline in 1983 with the AT&T divestiture; a gradual decline from 1984 to 1996 in the multichannel phase of communications media; and a pronounced reconcentration thereafter as the industry entered its digital phase.

Concentration levels in the telecommunications services market rose after 1996 with the major Baby Bell mergers. Nonetheless, the C4 remains well below the 1983 level. These mergers caused the national market share of the top four firms to grow from 69.4% in 1984 to almost 83.3% in 2006, from moderate to high. But this should also be contrasted with pre-1984, when AT&T's near-monopoly had been overwhelming at 89.3% for that firm alone, plus part ownership in another 2%.

The telecom sector's rising concentration seems in part a return to the earlier highly concentrated AT&T system that prevailed for over a century. Two major vertically integrated network firms offering a full menu of services have emerged. What do we make of this trend, which seems to contradict a pronounced and long-standing public policy of creating greater competition in telecommunications?

For several decades, U.S. policy in telecommunications and electronic mass media focused on the encouragement of competition. This policy, usually known as deregulation but more accurately described as liberalization, of entry aimed at an opening of the market to competitors and a reduction of market power. There were numerous elements and proceedings to this policy by the Federal Communications Commission, the states' Public Service Commissions and legislatures, the courts, and Congress.

The issue of concentration has acquired importance in light of the meltdown in the telecom sector after 2000. The telecommunications industry— old and new type network operators, equipment suppliers, and Internet service providers—became mired in an unprecedented and worldwide crisis. Worldwide, the industry shed hundreds of thousands of jobs, lost trillions of dollars in stock market capitalization, endured a continuous stream of bankruptcies, and was besmirched by scandals.

According to *The Economist*, the global telecom crash—10 times bigger than the better-known dotcom crash—may qualify as the largest bubble in history. Many of the new telecom entrant firms went through various stages of bankruptcy. Established incumbents lost revenues, lines, and customers. All long-distance companies were on the ropes, and AT&T and MCI were soon sold to the Bell companies. As network firms sought survival rather than expansion, the telecom equipment-manufacturing sector collapsed.

It is possible that the telecom downturn was only temporary. The problem for the industry, however, was not a one-time recovery from a one-time boom and bust. The more fundamental problem is that the telecom industry entered a pattern of volatility, with boom-bust patterns becoming potentially a common occurrence rather than an aberration. The telecommunications industry environment had moved from a utility to volatility.

Although business cycles are not new to many industries, in telecom they were an entirely new phenomenon. In the past, the network industry progressed in only one direction: up. Telecom used to be less volatile than the economy as a whole. It grew steadily, with long planning horizons hardly ruffled by the business cycle. But more recently, in sharp contrast, it is becoming more like the construction business, and less like water utilities.

One major reason for instability has been overcapacity. Overexpansion is a fundamental economic characteristic of competitive network industries with high fixed costs and low marginal costs. The telecommunications industry is characterized by huge investments followed by tiny costs of serving additional customers. This gives incentives to be large and to expand early and thus creates overcapacity, as it becomes firms' strategy across an entire industry. Price competition then drives down prices to unprofitable levels. This creates boom-bust cycles. The factors of instability will remain: low marginal costs, high fixed costs, inelastic demand, and lags in supply, in disinvestment, and in regulation.

As instability became part of the environment, what was telecom companies' response? One textbook response was to cut costs and prices. A second approach was to differentiate the product and services. But these strategies were quickly matched by competitors, thus creating commodity-style markets.

The other main strategy was therefore to reduce competition and the commoditization that lowered profitability and future investments. To do so required market power, which led to consolidation of firms into oligopoly. This is a main driver of concentration trends in the telecommunications sector.

But why did the U.S. government acquiesce? First, because of a laissez-faire attitude toward letting the dynamics of the market place deal with market power, and second, because a volatile telecom market cannot be easily accepted by the political process. Given the realities of the policy process, and the undesirability of having essential industries with a high failure rate, stability won over competitive efficiency.

Notes

1. Noam, Eli M., "Reconnecting Communications Studies with Communications Policy." *Journal of Communications*, 43, no. 3 (Summer 1993), 199–206.
2. Federal Communications Commission. "December 2007 Monitoring Report." Washington: Federal Communications Commission. FCC.gov. December 28, 2007. pp. 1–13. Last accessed on January 8, 2008, from http://hraunfoss.fcc.gov/edocs_public/attachmatch/DOC-279226A3.pdf.
3. Cole, Barry G., ed., "After the Break-Up: Assessing the New Post-AT&T Divestiture Era." New York: Columbia University Press, 1991.
4. Huber, P., M. Kellog, and J. Thorne. "The Geodesic Network II: 1993 Report on Competition in the Telephone Industry," pp. 2–35, Washington, DC, 1992.
5. Federal Communications Commission. *U.S. Competitive Local Loop Market: 1996*, MTA-EMCI, Washington, DC: FCC, 1996.
6. Federal Communications Commission. *Trends in Telephone Service 1998*, Table 9.1.
7. Noam, Eli M. *Interconnecting the Network of Networks*. Cambridge: MIT Press, 2001.
8. Federal Communications Commission. *Trends in Telephone Service,* May 2004, Table 9.1.
9. Federal Communications Commission. *Trends in Telephone Service,* May 2004, Wireline Competition Bureau, Table 9.7.
10. http://www1.jsc.nasa.gov/bu2/inflateCPI.html.
11. Federal Communications Commission, Common Carrier Bureau. *First Quarter 1996 Long-Distance Market Shares*, Washington DC: FCC, July 12, 1996, Tables 2 and 4.
12. Federal Communications Commission, Common Carrier Bureau, *Long Distance Telecommunications Industry*, January 2001.
13. Federal Communications Commission, *Trends in Telephone Service*, May 2004, p. 38. Federal Communications Commission. "Trends in Telephone Service." Washington: Federal Communications Commission. FCC.gov. February, 2007. pp. 6–3. Last accessed on January 8, 2008, from http://hraunfoss.fcc.gov/edocs_public/attachmatch/DOC-270407A1.pdf.
14. Before 1991, "U.S. traffic" refers to calls originating in the United States. Since 1991, "U.S. traffic" refers to calls billed to a customer by the IXC serving the U.S. location. For example, before 1991 an international collect call originating in the U.S. could be included in U.S. traffic.
15. Qwest, weaker than AT&T, Verizon, and Sprint, offers resold wireless service.
16. Wang, Michael, and William J. Kettinger. "Projecting the Growth of Cellular Communications." *Communications of the ACM,* October 1995, p. 119.
17. "Paging and Land Mobile Radio in 1998: What It Was, What It Wasn't." *Land Mobile Radio News*, December 18, 1998.
18. The 1956 *Hush-A-Phone* case forced AT&T to allow the attachment of nonelectrical devices (*Hush-A-Phone Corporation* v. *United States of America and Federal Communications Commission,* 238 F.2d 266 [1956]). The 1968 *Carterfone* decision allowed electrical devices to interconnect to the telephone network, but allowed AT&T to require use of an AT&T-supplied connector. *In the Matter of Thomas F. Carter and Carter Electronics Corp., Dallas, Tex.* (Complainants), v. *American Telephone and Telegraph Co., Associated Bell System Companies, Southwestern Bell Telephone Co., and General Telephone Co. of the Southwest* (Defendants), Docket No. 16942; Docket No. 17073, 13 FCC 2d 420 (1968)]. In 1977 the *North Carolina Utilities Commission* decision that AT&T lost the ability to use state regulation to restrict interconnection of non-AT&T equipment (*North Carolina Utilities Commission* v. *Federal Communications Commission,* 552 F.2d 1036 [4th Cir. 1977]). The *Computer II* decision deregulated all CPE and unbundled and detariffed it (Computer II, Final Decision, 77 FCC 2d 584 [1980]). AT&T was also forced, in several proceedings, to reduce the strictness of its technical interface requirements in favor of FCC-set standards, together with self-certification.
19. Von Alven, William H., ed. *The Billboard: A Newsletter for Part 68 Applicants,* February 1992.
20. Noam, Eli M. "Assessing the Impacts of Divestiture and Deregulation in Telecommunications." *Southern Economic Journal,* January 1993, 59(3), p. 445.
21. Telecommunications Industry Association "Annual Report 2004," p. 6; http://www.tia-online.org/business/media/reports/documents/AnRpt04.pdf.
22. Similarly, AT&T's share of the answering machine market fell from near 100% in the early 1970s to 13% in 1999 (GE was first with 16%). Source: *Market Share Reporter,* 2002. Gale Research, source: "Appliance," Sept 2000, p. 84.
23. Number of additional cellular subscribers from 2003 to 2004 (179.5−158.5 = 21) plus 56% replacement of existing phones ("United States Annual Wireless Telephone

Market Size by Subscribers, Sales, Prices, and Market Penetration in Units, Dollars, and Percent Change for 2003 to 2004, and Forecast for 2005 to 2010." *TWICE*, March 7, 2005, 20(6), p. 1.)

24. "United States annual wireless telephone market size," *TWICE*, 20 (6), p. 1.

25. *Market Share Reporter,* 2002. Gale Research, Source: Network World, August 7, 2000.

26. Follet, Jennifer Hagendorf. "Avaya, Nortel Vie for Cisco Share." *CRN*, August 25, 2003, Iss. 1059; p. 5.

27. Noam, Eli. *Telecommunications in Europe.* New York: Oxford University Press, 1992.

28. Central office switches include Class 5 (or end-office) switches, community dial offices, tandem switches, remote switching modules, and cellular mobile telephone switching systems.

PART V

INTERNET MEDIA

12

The Internet: Still Wide Open and Competitive?

DIGITAL PRESENT

Although the three major subsectors of the information sector—mass media, telecommunications, and information technology (IT)—developed at different times and paces, technological and regulatory tendencies affected them in roughly the same periods. In the 1990s, a fourth subsector emerged—Internet media. Has it been subject to similar dynamics of market structure?

For a period, the Internet was celebrated as open, free, and competitive. Entrepreneurialism was high, financing easy, and entry barriers were low. But in the wake of the Internet's bursting bubble, after 2000, the reality of that competition deserves a second look: is the Internet still as open and competitive as it used to be, or is it becoming concentrated and dominated by a few firms with market power?

To even ask this question often raises emotional responses, so deep is the self-image of openness and competitiveness (in contrast to the perceived stodginess of the telecom, print, and TV industries).

Many people even had difficulty with the very concept of looking at the Internet as an industry. And it is true that the early phases of the medium were dominated by government, universities, and nonprofit entities, all operating outside of the market. Even when the Internet became commercialized it was frequently asserted that the bit economy operated on fundamentally different principles than the atom economy. Today, a more balanced perspective has emerged. This includes the recognition, first, that the Internet is a set of interacting activities provided by a variety of commercial firms operating in a set of interacting submarkets. The structure of those markets affects, in the classic paradigm of industrial economics, the behavior and hence the performance of these firms. A prime measure for market structure is the extent of market concentration; it is an indicator and predictor of competitive behavior. Since the Internet has been arguably the major force for economic, societal, and cultural innovation in society in recent years, the extent of competitive forces driving it is significant far beyond the sector itself.

Traditional media were separated by delivery technology—printed paper, film on celluloid, broadcast amplitudes, telephone wires, vinyl discs, computer discs, and so forth. Similar specializations separated the provision of content from conduit. Within these separate markets, a firm could achieve market power. In the 1980s and accelerating in the 1990s, however, a technical convergence of media began to gradually blur the clear lines between segments, thereby creating potentially more rivalry. The major technological trend behind this convergence is well known: the increased use of digital electronics to create, store, transmit, and display information. The elements of digital electronics use many common hardware elements and similar formats for the coding of information.

The various forms of content—text, still pictures, moving images, sound—can be variations of the same basic information technology. This fundamentally affects media, the borders between them, and the market structures in which they operate.

THE INTERNET

The Internet was initiated by the United States Department of Defense (DoD).[1] In the 1960s, the RAND Corporation presented the concept of its researcher Paul Baran for a command and control center following a hypothetical nuclear attack on the United States. Text messages would be divided into small "packets," with each packet separately winding its way through the network. The Pentagon's Defense Advanced Research Projects Agency (DARPA) funded a substantial project based on this concept. DARPA hired the firm Bolt, Beranek, and Newman (BBN) to develop the first packet-switched network, initially to link major defense-oriented research facilities. By 1969 there were four such nodes linked in an embryonic network designated ARPANET. ARPANET grew rapidly. It could interconnect local computer networks provided the individual machine could speak a common digital language known as TCP/IP (Transmission Control Protocol/Internet Protocol).

In 1975, BBN started a similar commercial packet-switched network for the civilian sector. But Telenet was a financial flop and was soon bought out by GTE. Tymnet, started by the computer time-sharing firm Tymshare, entered as a competitor. The aircraft manufacturer McDonnell Douglas bought Tymnet, then sold it in 1989 to British Telecom. GTE Telenet, together with GTE's Sprint long-distance company, was spun off to a medium-sized telephone company, United Telecommunications, which renamed itself Sprint, and Telenet became Sprintnet.

With the proliferation of microcomputers in the 1980s, an increasing number of research users linked themselves to ARPANET.

The system outgrew its defense link and financing. In 1986, the National Science Foundation (NSF) therefore created and funded the NFSNET for the civilian part of ARPANET. The network was managed by nonprofit Advanced Network and Services (ANS), which in turn contracted with commercial carriers, especially MCI.

The number of host networks and domains increased exponentially. Whereas there were about 313,000 hosts and 9,000 domains in 1990, by 2007 there were 489 million hosts and 138 million domains worldwide.[2] In 1995, almost 50 million people were online, primarily in the United States, Canada, and Europe. By 2006, that number had increased to 694 million.[3]

The original NSFNET was replaced in 1995 by a collection of commercial Internet backbones, while the NSF established a second-generation NSFNET for ultraspeed applications.

In the 1990s, everything related to "the Net" seemed certain of success. The financial markets were welcoming almost every Internet-related firm with open arms. Applications such as Internet telephony and webcasting began to attract the attention and funds of telecommunications companies and venture capitalists alike.

Plummeting computer and Internet access prices coupled with growing access, increased transmission, and faster processing speeds drove Internet usage. New applications such as portals, streaming media, interactive gaming, online banking, e-auctions, commerce, and social networks made the Internet increasingly popular. Online advertising revenue grew from $267 million in 1996 to $16.9 billion in 2006.[4]

But exponential growth cannot go on forever, and the Internet bubble promptly burst in 2000. A recorded 494 online companies laid off 41,515 people in 2000 alone.[5] And in 2001, over one hundred thousand Internet jobs were eliminated in the United States.[6]

Most of the Internet's history, including the boom and bust cycle, is well known. But what has been the trend of the market concentration during that entire period? To answer this question, we look at the empirical data, and discuss in greater detail the Internet's key components—backbones, ISPs, and portals.

Internet Backbone Infrastructure

Internet backbones transport the Internet data streams close to the user, to local area networks or Internet service providers (ISPs). Backbones are often (but inaccurately) also referred to as ISPs, because some firms provide both ISP services and backbones. But the functions are different.

The government-supported Internet had a three-level hierarchical structure. Advanced Network and Services (ANS)[7] operated the core NSFNET national backbone network for NSF.[8] In turn, ANS was provided for by MCI and IBM. NSFNET connected a set of regional access providers (for example, the New England area's NEARNet network, the San Francisco Bay Area's BARNet, or New York's NYSERNet). Numerous local area networks, such as those of universities and later of commercial Internet service providers (ISPs), linked to the regional providers,[9] constituting the third tier of networks.

In 1995, the Internet structure changed. With the take-off of commercial service provision, major commercial Internet service providers would now be interconnected directly with one another at about a dozen designated sites. Soon, this system evolved further, with backbones interconnecting with one another at private "peering" exchange points throughout the country.

Within this network architecture, the national Internet backbone providers were firms that located high-speed routers in cities across the country and linked them by leasing (sometimes owning) high-speed trunk data lines from telecom carriers.

Backbones, in transporting and routing traffic between and among ISPs and other backbones, are at the core of the Internet.[10] However, due to the absence of reporting, the integration of revenues in larger entities, and the presence of governmental providers (that often subcontract with private carriers), the backbone market is difficult to assess. Table 12.1 and figure 12.1 show the market shares of backbone providers.

From the mid-1980s until 1996, the concentration in the backbone industry was decreasing from its original government-sponsored centralism. After 1996, concentration began to rise again. In 2004 the HHI value stood at a medium concentration of 1,610. The advent of commercial networks (replacing the early role of governmentally sponsored backbones, and the relatively undeveloped commercial user market) and the explosion in personal computing expanded the backbone industry from $300 million in 1984 to $13.8 billion in 2004. The price of bandwidth dropped substantially, spurring demand further. In the second half of the 1990s, the industry consolidated as UUNET and MCI were bought by WorldCom, while Genuity consolidated others. The industry experienced a wave of bankruptcies and reorganizations, including WorldCom's spectacular one. WorldCom was acquired by Verizon in 2005, and AT&T, having acquired IBM's global backbone operations, was bought by the other major Bell company, SBC. The fundamental problems for the industry were a glut in supply, a decrease in pricing power, and a slowing of Internet subscriber growth. However, growing broadband penetration led to another growth phase in backbone capacity needs, requiring large capital investment. Both trends are likely to lead to further consolidation and higher concentration in the backbone market, with the major telecom companies as the primary providers.

Internet Service Providers

Internet service providers link computer users to the Internet, and may provide additional services such as email. Small users typically connect to an ISP by dialing up its node over their regular local telephone lines, or by using "always-on" high-speed broadband connectivity such as a digital subscriber line (DSL), a fiber line, or a cable modem connection. Broadband wireless such as WiMax, or power-grid lines are other options. The ISP connects to the Internet by high-capacity links that reach the backbones, which in turn connect directly or over still other backbones to various Web sites and other Internet nodes.

With the development of the Web, the number of ISPs initially exploded from 230 in 1994[11] to 9,335 in 2000 then dropped rapidly to 4,327 in 2004, 2,437 in 2005.[12]

Originally, most consumers accessed the Internet via computer online service providers (COLS).[13] This was due largely to their user friendliness and large subscriber base. The major COLS were AOL, The Source, CompuServe, Prodigy, Delphi, and Genie. The total number of COLS subscribers rose from 51,000 in 1982 to over 12 million in 1996.

AOL was founded in 1985 by Steve Case and partners as Quantum Computer Services. Its competitor, Prodigy, was formed in 1984 as the joint venture Trintex of IBM, Sears Roebuck & Co., and CBS (which soon dropped out). IBM and Sears invested an estimated $1.2 billion in Prodigy, but it never showed a profit. Prodigy was the first to introduce a flat monthly fee. It was also the first online service to use a graphic user interface rather than text commands, and the first to include advertising. But, Prodigy kept losing money. Control for the U.S. operations eventually shifted to the telecom giant SBC, which

Table 12.1 Internet Backbone Providers (Market Shares by Revenues)

Company	1984	1987	1988	1992	1995	1996	1997	1999	2001	2005
Verizon							29.0	36.0	32.5	28.0
WorldCom							8.0			Verizon
MCI		5.0	5.5	6.0	7.0	10.5		WorldCom		
UUNet			3.0	8.0	11.0	16.5	WorldCom			
CompuServe	8.3	5.0	4.0				WorldCom			
Level 3										
Genuity								4.0	4.0	12.0
GTEi							6.0	Genuity	13.0	11.0
BBN			3.0	8.0	15.0	7.5	GTEi			
Sprint Nextel							7.0	8.0	9.0	9.4
Telenet (GTE)	11.7	16.0	15.5	13.0	11.0	9	Sprint			
Qwest				3.0	8.0	6.0		4.8	4.0	8.0
PSINet/Cogent							5.0	4.5	5.0	7.0
SBC/AT&T										21.0
AT&T							7.5	8.0	14.0	13.0
IBM				4.0	4.0	4	3.0	AT&T		
Cerfnet					1.6	1.6	ICG/AT&T			
Netcom (ICG)				10.0	10.0	7.7	AT&T			
Cable & Wireless (CWIX)										
Prodigy		3.0	2.0	SBC	10.0		5.0	5.0	6.0	SBC

France Telecom										4.0
XO Nextlink								9.0		4.0
Gov't networks (ARPAnet, NSFNet, etc.)	30.0	28.0	26.0	19.9	15.0	13	12			
Regional science networks	16.7	16.0	15.0	10.0	7.0	6	5.0		6.0	2.0
Tymnet (BT)	8.3	8.0	7.0	4.0						
Frontier (Citizens / Global Crossing)						1	2.0	3.0	3.0	2.0
Other/SAVVIS	25.0	19.0	19.0	14.1	10.4	9.7	6.0	2.7	6.5	2.6
Total U.S. Rev. ($ mil)	300	1,200	1,300	1,700	2,000	2,400	2,664	8,011	10,500	13,762
C4	66.7	68.0	63.5	52.9	52.0	49.0	57.0	72.0	65.5	70.4
HHI	1,454	1,419	1,259	970	973	896	1,302	1,883	1,565	1,610

Sources: Curley, John. "McDonnell Is Taking a Risk on Tymshare." *Wall Street Journal*, March 20, 1984, 35; *Market Share Reporter*, Gale Research Inc., 1998, p. 273; *Market Share Reporter*, Gale Research Inc., 1999, p. 415; Abramson, Bram Dov. "Interpreting Current Statistics: Internet Backbone Market Shares." *TelecomReform*, 1(2), July 2001, p. 7; *Market Share Reporter*, Gale Research Inc., 2002, p. 318; "Backbone Democracy," *America's Network*, 106(3), 21, February 15, 2002; *Top ISP Providers, 2001* (Boardwatch, ISP Directory 13th ed., 2001), available at http://www.boardwatch.com; Kraft, Jeffery. "Measuring Internet Backbone Market Shares." Paper presented at the Internet Convergence and Self-Governance OECD/OSIPP Workshop, Osaka University, June 9, 1998, available at www.oecd.org//dsti/sti/it/cm/act/kraft.pdf; Kraft, Jeffery. *Business Communications Review*, March 1, 2002, 32(3), 6; Stapleton, Paul. *The 1997 Year End Recap and 1998 Prognosis* (ISP Report.com); "ICG Sells off More Netcome." *Wired News*, Wired.com, January 1998; *Top Internet Backbone Companies 1999*. (Boardwatch and International Data Corp, February 1, 1999). 2002 data are from www.cybertelecom.org/data/backbones.htm; "US Top Three Internet Backbone Operators by Percent Market Share of Internet Service Provider Revenues, Reported as of February 15, 2002." *America's Network*, 106(3), 21, February 15, 2002. ISSN: 1075–5292. Share for 2004 AT&T is estimated."Evolution of the Internet." *ICT Regulation Toolkit.* ICTRegulationToolkit.com. October 29, 2007. Last accessed on January 11, 2008, from http://www.ictregulationtoolkit.org/en/Section.2189.html. Horrigan, John B., and Smith, Aaron. "Home Broadband Adoption 2007. June 2007." *Pew Internet and American Life Project.* PewInternet.org June 2007. Last accessed on January 11, 2008, from http://www.pewinternet.org/pdfs/PIP_Broadband%202007.pdf. 2005 figures already includes 2006 mergers.

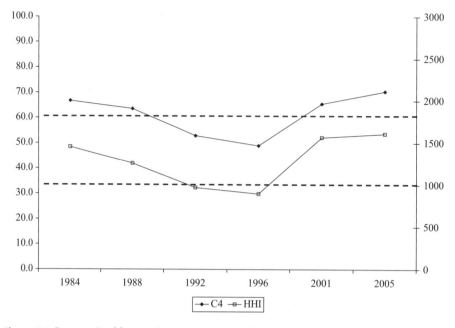

Figure 12.1 Internet Backbones: Concentration Trend

absorbed its subscribers and then stopped using the Prodigy brand name altogether.

The narrowband ISP market evolved into three tiers. The top tier consisted of AOL, with its 22.8 million subscribers in 2004, down to 13 million by 2007.[14] Some of these accounts are part of corporate bulk arrangements and are inactive. This led to an overreporting of actual subscriptions by AOL, which resulted in government investigations of its accounting practices. AOL lost millions of customers with the rapid rise of broadband connections, an area in which it was lagging, and was in serious trouble. The second ISP tier consists of United Online (9.7%), a merger of NetZero and Juno Online, and Earthlink (7.3%), which merged with Mindspring. Also in the second tier are Microsoft's MSN (9.7%)[15] and AT&T/SBC (formerly Prodigy) with 1.9% (table 12.2, figure 12.2).

Figure 12.2 shows that the ISP industry underwent a drastic change in structure from 1984 to 1996, from high concentration to fairly high competition, mostly by the entry of numerous small new firms. Many of the small firms established local dial-up arrangements across the country. By 2000, most metropolitan areas had hundreds of ISPs that were reachable through a local connection. Many of these firms were part of larger national operations, leaving their local designation more as a local brand identity than a corporate one. For a while, some ISPs such as NetZero, Juno, and Blue Light tried to

be free of charge, with no subscriber fees, generating revenues from the advertising content delivered to these users. That free ISP model quickly fell apart when advertising revenues declined. Through it all, AOL dominated the dial-up ISP market. It maintained 30+% market share in a period of exponential Internet subscriber growth. New users, in particular, favored the large firms with brand recognition. In 2004, the dial-up ISP market was moderately concentrated with an HHI value of 1,356. But it was also shrinking rapidly as users upgraded to broadband, where an entirely different market structure exists.

Broadband Service

In the late 1990s, the speed of dial-up connectivity was inadequate for many users who had become used to the higher speed, service quality, and advanced Web site features available at their office. This opened the way for residential higher-speed broadband Internet connectivity. Such connectivity was offered by several sets of providers, including:

- Local telephone companies, offering digital service, subscriber line (DSL) service, and later fiber-to-the-home (FTTH) or to a nearby node (FTTN).
- Independent DSL providers, such as Covad, which use the facilities of the phone companies

Table 12.2 Narrowband Internet Service Providers (Market Share by Subscribers)

Company	1984	1988	1992	1995	1996	1998	1999	2000	2001	2002	2003	2004
America Online/Time Warner			7	27.5	33.9	46.6	39.6	35.6	33.6	31.5	34.2	33.2
Road Runner								1.3	America Online			
CompuServe	76.0	61.0	39.0	30.3	18.3	America Online						
The Source	17.0	12	CompuServe									
United Online									5.8	5.9	7.5	9.7
Juno							3.3	5.3	United			
Netzero								4.6	United			
Bluelight.com								3.7	0.2	United		
Earthlink						3.0	6.7	6.1	5.0	5.9	7.3	7.4
MindSpring						2.2	Earthlink					
AT&T/SBC (incl. Prodigy)		3	36	19.3	13.9	3.2	2.5	2.9	2.3	2.1	1.9	2.1
AT&T WorldNet						5.0	3.5	2.5	1.5			
Gateway.net								2.3	1.1			
MSN (Microsoft)				0.9	2.7	6.4	4.6	5.3	7.6	9.3	9.7	10.0
At Home							1.7	3.8	Bankrupt			
Delphi (News Corp)	6.0	5.0	4.0	1.2								
Genie (GE)	1.0	16.0	14.0	0.9		IDT						
Other	0.0	3.0	0.0	19.9	31.2	33.6	38.1	26.6	43.0	45.3	39.4	37.6
Total U.S. Rev. ($ mil)	47	359	672	1,416	3,072	6,384	8,376	10,920	23,064	20,184	17,064	16,896
C4	100.0	94.0	96.0	78.3	68.8	61.2	54.4	52.3	51.9	52.6	58.7	60.3
HHI	6,102	4,155	3,078	2,050	1,683	2,262	1,666	1,432	1,251	1,153	1,377	1,356
Total Subscribers	0.34	1.6	2.8	9.6	15.8	28.2	45.2	68.4	96.1	84.1	71.1	70.4

Notes: For 1984, and 1992, one-third of COLS revenues allocated toward their ISP services. *Sources: Internet Service Updated: Part 6,* S.G. Cowen Securities Corporation, December 16, 1999. *Business Wire,* January 16, 1986; 1998 market shares for CompuServe and Genie based on percentage of total subscriber base. Prodigy market share is estimated from Crain Communications, "GE Plugs into Home Shopping," August 29, 1988. Genie from Burnett, Richard. "Computer Sales Boots On-Line Market." *Orlando Sentinel Tribune,* February 17, 1993, p. C1. Prodigy numbers from Hoover's Company Profile Database, 1996, The Reference Press, Inc., Austin, Tx.; CompuServe numbers are from company; 1995 subscriber data: Based on numbers in "MSN Promises an Ease of Multitasking." *Orange County Register,* August 21, 1995. MSN subscribers revenue number is based on Vohra, Neeraj K. "The Internet, the Dawn of a New Medium," *Industry Report,* March 4, 1996, p. 38; 1996 CompuServe subscribers are estimated at 3 million. Some 1996 market share and revenue are extrapolated between 1995 and 1998. "AOL to Swallow CompuServe Deal Steps up On-line Battle. *USA Today,* September 9, 1997. 1998, 1999, 2000 and 2001 Subscriber data: Total subscriber numbers are from TR's Online Census, found in "Internet Audience Growth Sharply in 2001," report by Peter Loftus, Dow Jones News Service, February 22, 2002. "A Sobering Look at Internet Advertising." *Cable World,* Dec. 2, 2001. Revenues estimated at $240 per subscriber ($20 month). Market shares for 2001–2004 based on subscriber numbers reported by ISPplanet http://www.isp-planet.com.

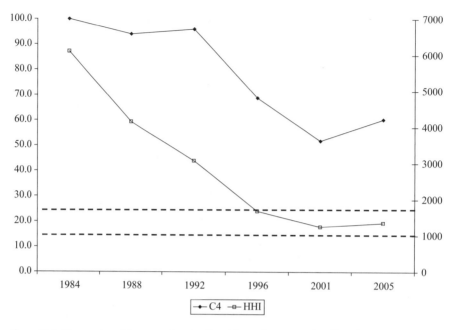

Figure 12.2 Narrowband Internet Service Providers: Concentration Trend

(networks elements), together with their own infrastructure and equipment,
- Cable TV companies, offering cable modem services,
- Other delivery technologies such as satellite operators, electric utility powerline service, fixed wireless, such as WiMax, and third-generation mobile data service from cell phone companies.

Broadband Internet access grew rapidly and served about 64.5 million households in the United States by 2007.[16] Cable TV companies provided almost 60% of this service, and the rest was offered mostly by the incumbent local telephone companies (ILECs). The share of independent DSL providers dropped rapidly as both the dot-com crash and the ILECs' resistance squeezed their business. Some ISPs such as AOL or Earthlink resell re-branded DSL service of provider companies such as Covad or of the ILECs.

Table 12.3 shows this industry as moderately concentrated. But this measure is understated because it reports national rather than local shares. In most areas, only one cable company and one telecom firm exist, and they provide the vast bulk of broadband service. Users face mostly a duopoly. Another alternative is independent DSL provided mostly over telecom infrastructure. WiMax and

Powerline service are in early stages only, and satellite service and mobile data are slower, more expensive and suffer greater latency. In rural areas, there might be no service option at all, or only that of a costly and slow satellite service.

If we assume that in a given area there is no competition among cable providers and among telecom firms, and report concentration in that fashion, we find a much higher concentration, with an HHI of about 4,245 (figure 12.3).

Navigational Software

Although the original Internet grew by leaps and bounds, it was still confined to the research community and relatively sophisticated users. It was complex to use and its content was essentially text. Far from a mass medium, its economic foundation was largely governmental and nonprofit, with little consumer or commercial involvement. This changed dramatically with the introduction of the World Wide Web.

The World Wide Web uses additional protocols to transmit color graphics beyond plain text. The Web's key ease-of-use feature is *hypertext*, developed at Geneva's CERN laboratory in 1989 to allow researchers to reference other documents available on the Internet. This means that any data

Table 12.3 Broadband Internet Providers (National Market Shares by Subscribers)

	1999	2000	2001	2002	2003	2004	2005	2006
					DSL			
SBC/AT&T	5.1	11.7	10.9	10.2	12.5	14.9	15.5	19.9
Bell South	1.3	3.2	5.0	5.7	5.2	6.1	6.5	AT&T
Verizon	3.9	8.2	9.8	9.9	8.3	10.3	11.4	12.6
Qwest	4.9	3.4	3.5	3.4	2.3	3.0	3.4	3.8
Covad	2.5	4.2	2.8	1.9	1.8	1.8	1.3	0.9
					CableModem			
Comcast	6.4	6.1	7.8	7.7	18.8	21.0	19.0	20.7
AT&T Broadband	8.7	10.6	12.4	10.1	Comcast			
Adelphia	1.7	2.3	3.1	3.7	3.2	4.1	TW/Comcast	
Time Warner	14.8	14.5	15.7	15.4	11.5	12.4	11.2	10.1
Cox	8.4	7.4	7.3	7.4	7.1	7.8	6.9	5.5
Charter	3.8	3.9	5.2	5.1	5.4	6.0	4.9	4.3
Cablevisions	2.3	3.7	4.0	3.8	3.8	4.1	3.8	3.6
					Satellite			
HughesNet (prev. DirecWay)			1.4	1.4	1.4	1.4	0.6	0.5
WildBlue					0.01	0.01	0.1	0.2
Starband					0.02	0.03	0.1	0.1
Total U.S. Rev. ($ mil)	1,162	2,322	4,762	7,444	10,125	15,930	19,291	35,493
C4	38.3	45.0	48.8	45.6	51.0	58.6	57.1	67.3
HHI	502	693	828	759	851	1,105	999	1,163

Sources: CSFB, "RBOC/ILEC Update-Fourth Quarter DSL and Cable Modem Update," April 5, 2002. And also Morgan Stanley, "Broadband Cable Television-Broadband: Grabbing a Bigger Piece of the Pie," June 21, 2002 (Market Share by total DSL Subscribers). 2003 data are based on Wachovia Securities, "North American Broadband Update," June 1, 2004. Total revenues for 2003 are extrapolated, from growth percentage in subscriber numbers. 2002 revenue is extrapolated from 2001 and 2003. "Teletruth News Analysis". *Teletruth.* NewNetworks.com. 29 November 2007. Last accessed on 8 January 2008 at http://www.newnetworks.com/parttwosummary.htm.
Friedland, Jim and Kopelman, Kevin. "Q1:07 Residential Internet Access & VoIP Survey." *Cowen and Company.* 29 May, 2007. Hoorigan, John B., and Smith, Aaron. "Home Broadband Adoption 2007, June 2007." *Pew Internet & American Life Project.* PewInternet.org. June 2007. Last accessed on January 11, 2008, from http://www.pewinternet.org/pdfs/PIP_Broadband%202007.pdf. Goldman, Alex. "Top 21 U.S. ISPs by Subscriber: Q4 2005." ISP-Planet. ISP-Planet.com. May 4, 2006. Last accessed on January 11, 2008, from http://www.isp-planet.com/research/rankings/2005/usa_history_q42005.html. "Status Update From WildBlue." *WildBlue.* Wildblue.com. December 15, 2005. Last accessed on January 11, 2008, from http://www.wildblue.com/company/doPressReleaseDetailsAction.do?pressReleaseID=11. Grant, August E., and Meadows, Jennifer H. "Communication Technology Update, 10/e, Tenth Edition." *Elsevier/Focal Press*: Burlington, MA. 2006. Pp. 290. Horan, Timothy, Anantha, Srinivas, Baramov, Ned, and Maheshwary, Suneer. "Telecommunications Services: 3Q07 Preview." *CIBC World Markets*: New York, October 4, 2007. Pp 12. Accessed through Reuters Research on Demand database on November 5, 2007. "Top Telecommunications, Media and Technology Companies." *The Center for Public Integrity.* PublicIntegrity.org. 2007. Last accessed on January 11, 2008, from http://www.publicintegrity.org/telecom/rank.aspx?act=industry. Smith, Steve. "Ready, aim, segment: adventures in search targeting." *OMMA: The Magazine of Online Media, Marketing, and Advertising.* Mediapost.com. November 2006. Last accessed on November 5, 2007, from http://publications.mediapost.com/index.cfm?fuseaction=Articles.showArticle&art_aid=50238. Belson, Ken. "With a Dish, Broadband Goes Rural." *New York Times.* November 14, 2007. Last accessed on November 5, 2007, from http://www.nytimes.com/2006/11/14/technology/14satellite.html.

need only be stored on one server to be accessible by any computer connected to the Web.

Because of the intuitive nature of hypertext, even those with little computer experience were able to quickly make use of the Web. In addition, due to the low computing power required to run a Web server and the simplicity of creating Web pages, even individuals and small organizations could become Web information providers, and could do so on an international scale. Thus, the Web gave large segments of society the ability to access and distribute information.

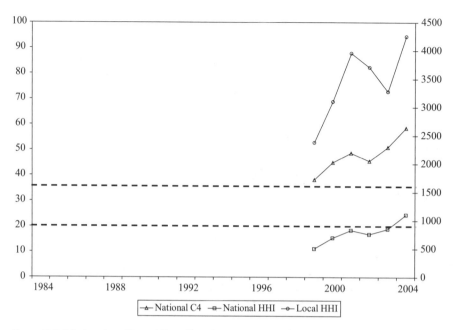

Figure 12.3 National and Local Broadband Internet Providers: Concentration Trends

The 1991 introduction of the Web was followed by the development of important software such as browsers and search engines. The original Web browser was Mosaic, created in 1993 at the University of Illinois for nonprofit use. One of its programmers, Marc Andereesen, then commercialized the development in a version called Netscape Navigator, made available for free over the Internet. Its record-breaking IPO in 1995 is often considered the starting point of the Internet frenzy by the financial markets. Control shifted to AOL and subsequently to Time Warner. In response to the overnight success of Netscape Navigator, Microsoft introduced its own browser, Internet Explorer, in 1995. Generally, browser firms distribute their user-level software for free. This strategy is intended to build market share and create a dominant platform. Money is then made by selling Web server or enterprise software (which enables servers to house Web sites and conduct and manage business on the Web) and from advertising revenues on the associated default portals of the browsers (for example, Netcenter.com and MSN.com). Because of incompatibility, dominance over the browser market gives a company a leg-up in the server software market.

The two major Web browser developers engaged in intense competition. Netscape Navigator's dominance was replaced by Microsoft's, which increased its market share from 36% in 1997 to 56% in 1999 and from 86% in 2001 to over 90% in 2002 (figure 12.4).[17] This led to a major antitrust lawsuit.

Not until the end of 2004 was Microsoft again challenged in its position in this market. The emergence of Firefox, a browser equipped with a pop-up advertising blocker, in combination with the prolonged delay in the release of Microsoft's next-generation operating system, led to a decrease in its market share (table 12.4).

The Firefox developer is the Mozilla Foundation, a nonprofit organization created to finance and support open-source work. AOL's Netscape division launched the Mozilla project in 1998 to create and distribute open source software, then spun it off in 2003 as the Mozilla Foundation. Despite Firefox's rise to over 14% in 2007, this market remains highly concentrated with an HHI value of 7,892 in 2005 (figure 12.5). Smaller browsers include Safari (Apple) and Opera, as well as the independent SeaMonkey and Camino, allied with Mozilla.

Microsoft's competitive advantage was its ability to bundle its browser with its Windows operating system and have it preloaded by PC makers. The result was a browser software market dominated by Microsoft. This did not go unnoticed. In 1998, the U.S. Department of Justice, along with 20 states and the District of Columbia, filed suit

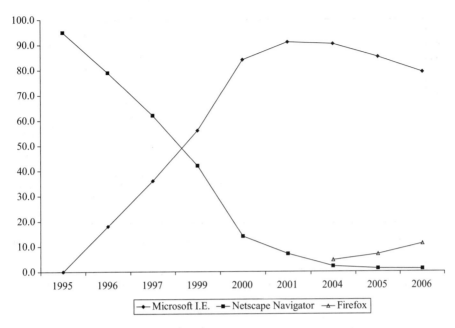

Figure 12.4 Internet Browsers: Market Share

Table 12.4 Web Browsers (Market Share by Users)

	1995	1996	1997	1999	2000	2001	2004	2005	2006	2008
Microsoft	0.0	18.0	36.0	56.0	84.0	91.0	90.3	85.1	79.1	68.2
Netscape (Time Warner)	95.0	79.0	62.0	42.0	14.0	7.0	2.1	1.2	1.1	0.6
Mozilla/Firefox				0.1	0.1	0.3	4.6	6.9	11.1	21.3
SeaMonkey									0.1	
Opera			0.1	0.1	0.2	0.3	0.6	0.6	0.6	0.7
Apple (Safari)							1.0		4.8	7.9
Camino							0.1		0.1	
Other	5.0	3.0	2.0	2.0	2.0	2.0	2.4	2.6	2.7	0.2
Total U.S. Rev. ($ mil)	77.5	92.0	105.5	225.0	275.0	300.0	275	275	250	
C2	95	97	98	98	98	98	94.9	92	90.2	97.4
HHI	9,025	6,565	5,140	4,900	7,252	8,330	8,181	7,291	6,405	5,164

Sources: 1995 market share is estimated based on entry of Microsoft in 1995; 1997 market share: Cavallone, Mark. "Computer: Consumer Services and the Internet." *Standard and Poor's Industry Survey,* March 25, 1999; 1998 market share: Cavallone, Mark. "Computer: Consumer Services and the Internet." *Standard and Poor's Industry Survey,* March 28, 2000; 2000 market share: "Computer: Consumer Services and the Internet." *Standard and Poor's Industry Survey,* September 28, 2000; 2001 market share: "Computer: Consumer Services and the Internet." *Standard and Poor's Industry Survey,* October 4, 2001; March 28, 2002 revenues: "10-K Annual SEC Filing." Netscape Corporation. 1996 revenue and market share numbers are an extrapolation from the 1996–1998 numbers. Data for 2005 are from "Mozilla's Browsers Global Usage Share Is 7.35 Percent According to OneStat.com." *OneStat.com Press Box,* November 22, 2004, Amsterdam. Available at http://www.onestat.com/html/aboutus_pressbox34.html. Revenue for 2005 is estimated. Safari and SeaMonkey market shares from NetApplications. Market shares from Net Applications – "http://market share.hitslink.com/report.aspx?qprid=0".

against the firm alleging anticompetitive behavior.[18] Specifically, the government argued that Microsoft's bundling of its Web browser (Internet Explorer) with Windows 95 and Windows 98, its dominant PC operating systems, represented a deliberate effort to crush Netscape, its chief rival in the Web browser market. The government charged that Microsoft provided discounts to ISPs for favoring Explorer, even offering to illegally split the Web browser market with Netscape (during a secret meeting of Microsoft and Netscape managers on June 21, 1995).

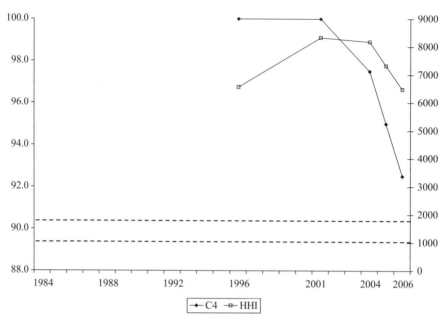

Figure 12.5 Browser Software: Concentration Trend

Microsoft rejected the assertion that its bundling of browser with operating system was a ploy to destroy Netscape. It argued that it had planned to integrate Internet features into its operating systems long before Netscape's existence. Microsoft further argued that the tight integration of browser with operating system offered technological and economic efficiency.[19] It also argued that the market for operating systems was not monopolized by Windows but instead faced stiff competition from Apple, IBM, and increasingly Linux.[20] Several of the conditions supporting the government's case against Microsoft changed during the case. The purchase of Netscape by AOL, and AOL's subsequent merger with Time Warner in 2000, had created a more formidable browser competitor to Microsoft. Sun Microsystems developed Java, a "platform-independent" programming language, thereby reducing Windows' role as an operating system. And the "open software movement," which promoted free software, especially the Linux operating system had achieved some success. But much more importantly, the more Microsoft-friendly Bush Administration replaced the Clinton White House, and pursued a settlement rather than a structural breakup as originally decided upon by Judge Thomas Pennfield Jackson. Jackson was removed from the case by the appellate court after giving incautious newspaper interviews. His findings of fact, however, were left standing. In the end, Microsoft agreed to an independent panel to oversee its practices rather than having to split up, as sought earlier by the U.S. Department of Justice,[21] and settled also with the states. Microsoft fared less well in Europe, where challenging it was politically popular. The company was fined in 2006 a record $357 million and had to reveal the code and unbundle. In 2007, the EU fined Microsoft an additional $613 million. It lost its appeal in September 2007, and was fined $1.35 billion.

Web Directories and Search Engines

Web directories and search engines let users find information. Without such software, users can only find a Web site if they already know its address or happen upon a hyperlink.

Web directories (for example, Yahoo, Google, Infoseek) let users search for information by category. By arranging Web sites into multiple, hierarchically arranged categories, directories enable users to make ever more specific category selections on a series of menus. Web directories typically allow users to directly search the sites listed in their directories for specified words. The search sites earn revenue by selling advertising space, and increasingly by selling preferred placement to Web sites eager for users' clicks.

The search engine industry has always been concentrated, with only a few firms getting involved with the massive task of designing, setting up, and maintaining the search process. The engines of the past often provided results that were not efficiently filtered. The usage for search engine services is mainly driven by portals. These sites pay search engines for every visitor that performs a search. The search engine industry was initially dominated by Yahoo, Excite, AltaVista, and Infoseek. Google became popular by using a rank-based search algorithm. By 2001 Infoseek and Excite dropped entirely out of the search market and the newer companies Overture and Google captured significant market share. The market, however, is concentrated. In 2003, Yahoo acquired Overture, and with it AltaVista and Inktomi. Microsoft's MSN Search, renamed Live Search in 2007, was number three, followed by IAC's Ask.com, formerly Ask Jeeves. There are also specialized search engines for jobs, blogs, news, pictures, health, shopping, business, etc. And there are "metasearch engines" that direct a request to multiple search engines. But despite all of these options Google was increasingly dominant, raising its share from 31.5% in 2004 to 53.6% in 2007 and 61.2% in 2008 (table 12.5, figure 12.6).

Table 12.5 Internet Search Engines (Market Shares by Unique Users)

Company	1997	2001	2004	2006	2008
Google		4.5	31.5	43.7	61.2
AOL (Time Warner)[a]		7.4	3.5	5.9	4.3
Yahoo	27.4	14.9	20.1	28.8	16.9
Overture		7.4	Yahoo		
FAST		0.0	Yahoo		
AltaVista	12.1	7.4	Yahoo		
Inktomi	2.3	5.3	Yahoo		
Go.com/Infoseek (Disney)	13.2	7.4[b]			
MSN (Microsoft) (Live Search)		3.7	17.7	12.8	11.4
IAC Search & Media			4.9	5.4	2.3
Ask.com (previously Ask Jeeves)		3.6	IAC		
Excite	20.3	7.4	IAC		
LookSmart		5.2			
FindWhat (MIVA)		1.5			
Lycos (Terra/Telefonica/Daum)	4.5	4.1			
HotBot		0			
Other	20.0	20.0	20.0	3.4	2.0
Total U.S. Rev. ($ mil)	193	1,000	2,047	6,800	
C4	73.1	37.2	74.2	91.2	93.8
HHI	1,515	619	1,746	2,967	4,185

Sources: Revenues include the following categories: banner ads, buttons, and sponsorships on search pages; license fees; maintenance fees; and paid placement. 1997 "total revenue" is the sum of the 10K revenues (minus non-U.S. revenues) of the following companies: Excite, Infoseek, Lycos, Yahoo, Search.com, and Inkitomi. Calculation based on Alta Vista's revenues of 30 million. 2001 total revenue and market shares from "The Internet Search Market," Salomon Smith Barney, October 1, 2002. In 2002 Infoseek was part of Disney's Go.com, Excite used other search services for its portal, and Lycos was part of terra.com. 2004 data are compiled from Nielsen Netratings and SearchEngineWatch.com, 2005. Market shares from Nielsen methodology, which measures "time spent." 2008 figures from Nielsen, as reported in www.itfacts.biz/category/search-engines.

[a] AOL "enhanced" by Google. Allocated two-thirds of market share to Google. Sullivan, Danny. "ComScore Media Metrix Search Engine Ratings." *SearchEngineWatch*. SearchEngineWatch.com. August 26, 2006. Last accessed on January 11, 2008, from http://searchenginewatch.com/showPage.html?page=2156431. "2006 Full Year Results IAB Internet Advertising Revenue Report." *PricewaterhouseCoopers, Sponsored by the Interactive Advertising Bureau (IAB)*. IAB.net. May 23, 2007. Last accessed on November 5, 2007, from http://www.iab.net/resources/adrevenue/pdf/IAB_PwC_2006_Final.pdf. Google's market share further increased after 2006.
[b] Provided by Yahoo.

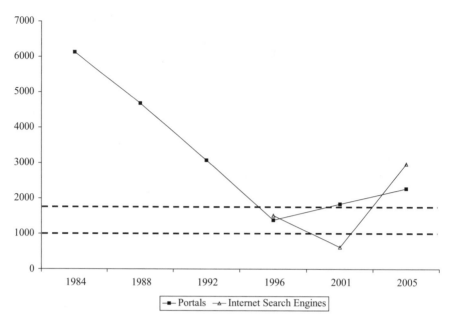

Figure 12.6 Internet Search Engines and Internet Portals: HHI Concentration Trends

Concentration is based on large economies of scale. The cost of creating the database and search algorithms is high, but the usage cost is minimal. Rival search sites compete in the efficiency of the search, or in their specialization. Users quickly drop an engine if another gets the search done better. This requires the constant development of more advanced filtering intelligence. A second level of competition is in features. Search engines offer additional, search-related services. Google, for example, allows users to search for news on a specific topic, along with such features as shopping, images, and academic studies. Soon, Google added advertising services and became a powerhouse in online advertising. Its share prices soared. It began acquisitions that included, in 2007/8, web security firm Postini; Adscape and DoubleClick (advertising, for $3.2 billion); YouTube (video, for $1.6 billion); and 5% of AOL ($1 billion). AOL bought ad search firm Quigo ($340 million). Yahoo countered by buying Right Media (advertising, $680 million). Microsoft acquired aQuantive (advertising, for $5.7 billion) and unsuccessfully tried to buy Yahoo for 44.6 billion. Google then entered into a deal with Yahoo for an advertising partnership but ran into trouble with Washington antitrust agencies.

Web Portals

The World Wide Web led to major growth in central Web sites known as "portals." Firms compete to be users' home page, or at least their preferred destination, and thus the entry point for further Web activities. This competition led firms to provide numerous services such as e-mail, news, stock quotes, movie listings, search engines, shopping, and so forth linked to their main home page. This concept became known as a portal. The portal market was highly concentrated in the pre-Internet era. Computer online service providers (COLS) such as CompuServe, Prodigy, and AOL were portals, though the term was not yet used. The market changed with the introduction of the World Wide Web, which allowed users to pick portals and content providers separately from their ISP. Although concentration in the industry dropped, it was not low by U.S. Department of Justice standards. New portal sites were started during the dot-com boom of the late 1990s, but declining advertising revenues allowed only those companies with strong advertising streams and high page hit volumes to survive. This led again to a reconcentration, with the C4 share at 86% by 2002. AOL was the market leader for a long time, but in 2004 it lost its position to Yahoo. Disney and AT&T failed in their web-portal efforts Go.com and Excite.

The market for portals closely follows the overall trend of the online media industry: strong initial concentration as an industry was dominated by early entrants and market size was small. Then, with the spread of Internet connectivity and personal

Table 12.6 Internet Portals (Market Shares by Unique Users)

Company	1984	1988	1992	1996	1997	1998	2000	2001	2004[b]
AOL/Time Warner			7.0	19.2	20.4	28.7	28.4	29.1	28.0
Netscape				17.7	20.4	13	AOL		
CompuServe	76.0	64.9	39.0	AOL					
The Source	18.0	12.8	CompuServe						
Yahoo				18.6	21.4	19.4	20.2	21.6	28.1
MSN (Microsoft)							17.4	19.7	25.5
Lycos (Terra/Telefonica/ Daum)				8.0	9.2	14.9	10.2	9.8	4.8
Iwon							3.7	2.7	1.5
Prodigy (SBC)[a]		3.2	36.0	13.1	6.1	1.9	1.8	2.7	2.0
Infospace (Excite)				10.6	12.2	12.0	5.5	3.6	2.3
Go2net.com									Infospace
IGN								2.7	3.0
BONZI.com								1.8	1.8
Juno (United Online)								1.9	1.5
Delphi (News Corp)	1.0	2.1	4.0	0.9					
Genie (GE)	5.0	17.0	14.0	3.0					
NBCi (GE)							5.5		
Snap						2.7	NBCi		
Go.com (Disney)							7.3	4.4	
Infoseek				8.9	10.3	7.4	Go.com		
Total U.S. Rev. ($ mil)	96	148	200	336	370	1,161	1,976	2,791	6,200
C4	100.0	97.9	96.0	68.6	74.4	76.0	76.2	80.2	86.4
C6				88.1	93.9	95.4	89.0	88.2	91.7
HHI	6,126	4,680	3,078	1,386	1,561	1,739	1,669	1,839	2,272

Notes: 1984, 1992 allocated two-thirds of COLS revenues toward portal services. *Sources:* Unique visitor data are from Media Metrix http://cyberatlas.internet.com/big_picture/stats_toolbox/article. Revenue estimates are calculated based on Yahoo's and Excite's revenues per unique visitors. 2002 revenues are based on Q1 revenues. Data for 2004 are based on unique visitor number, "Consumer Services and the Internet." *Standard and Poor's Industry Surveys,* March 3, 2005.

[a] Discontinued.

[b] After 2004, the concept of "portals" as a market seperate from websites declined, and our data collection has not continued.

computers, industry revenues grew exponentially, resulting in an influx of new firms with often fierce competition in the marketplace. But only a few companies were able to survive this competition, since economies of scale and network effects were high. This resulted in consolidation and greater concentration (table 12.6, figure 12.6).

Internet Telephony Applications

Two promising convergence-driven Internet mass media applications have been Internet telephony (VoIP) and webcasting, discussed next.

Voice telephone service over the Internet was introduced in 1995. Unlike standard telephony, which transfers voice communications over circuit-switched networks, packetized voice communication translates voice into packets traveling over packet-switched networks.

For a time, Internet telephony required a computer, microphone, speakers, special software at both ends of the call, and an Internet subscription via an ISP. Such requirements limited the potential market. But soon, calls could terminate within the public (circuit) switched telephone network. After 1996, Internet phone gateways (IPGs) overcame these access obstacles by enabling users to use regular telephone sets to place calls through the Internet.

IP telephony's advantage was in pricing, especially for the traditionally high-priced international long-distance voice calls.

The use of voice over the Internet grew dramatically in the late 1990s. Between 1998 and 1999 alone, usage of Internet telephony soared from 310 million minutes to over 2.7 billion worldwide.[22] In 2004, most of the business of IP telephony was realized in countries where international telephone rates were high, such as India.

At first, the Internet telephony service market was led by small firms such as Net2Phone (a division of IDT), NetSpeak (WebPhone), Voxware and VocalTec. Soon, AOL, Yahoo, Microsoft, Netscape, Intel, and IBM offered IP-telephony service, though usually as resellers. In an effort to hedge risk, some larger telecommunications firms invested in Voice over IP (VoIP) providers. Deutsche Telekom purchased 20% of VocalTec. They also began to test and route traditional voice calls using the IP protocol and packet switching instead of circuit switching to cut costs and add features. The rapid rise of broadband Internet gave additional stimulus to voice services. Vonage became the trend-setter for a subscription-based service. But more successful was Skype, a free Web-based service whose basic tier was free when calling other Skype-accounts. The calling of non-Skype numbers, however, was being charged. In 2008 Skype had 309 million accounts world wide, of various activity levels. In 2007, the online auction giant eBay bought Skype for $2.4 billion.

Telecommunication services became more competitive as the Internet telephone service providers took market shares from the major telecommunication companies. The major cable TV companies' broadband Internet service provides a platform for this service. At the same time, Internet telephony also enables traditional telecom companies

Table 12.7 Web-Based IP Telephony (Market Share by Revenue)

	1997	2001	2003	2004	2005
Cable					
Time Warner (Digital Phone)			8.6	18.4	23.3
Cablevision (Optimum Voice)			20.7	17.2	17.7
Cox			3.4	3.4	4.1
BrightHouse			2.6	2.6	3.0
Insight			3.4	4.4	2.8
Charter			3.4	3.1	2.3
Comcast			0.9	0.9	2.3
Telecom					
AT&T CallVantage			2.0	3.6	2.7
Voice Wing (Verizon)					2.4
Independent VoIP					
Skype (eBay)[a]				7.1	5.7
Vonage				22.2	22.8
Packet8			0.3	2.7	0.8
Primus (Lingo)			4.3	3.4	
VocalTech (DT)	20.0	10.0	10.0		
NetSpeak	10.0				
VoxWare	10.0				
Net2Phone (IDT)	20.0	20.0	1.2	1.0	
Other	40.0	50.0	50.0	10.1	10.2
Total U.S. Rev. ($ mil)	17	263	291	413	1,240
C4	60.0	50.0	43.5	64.9	69.5
HHI	1,000	500	668	1,258	1,466

Sources: Table based on subscriber numbers. Data for the period 1997–2003 are estimated using company information. Data for 2004 from Deutsche Bank. "The Hotline. VoIP: State of Play," June 22, 2005, pp. 3–4. 2004 Skype market share is averaged from 2003 and 2005 figures. Cablevision's early large market share is based on its offering of cable phone service to its subscribers earlier than other cable companies. Telecom and independent data for 2005 are based on "Vonage Stays No. 1 in VoIP Competition," May 22, 2006. Business Source Premier. CO. July 19, 2006. http://search.epnet.com/login.aspx?direct=true&db=buh&an=21034243. 2005 cable market shares and total revenue from "24 mln VOIP subscribers in 2008, Vonage, Time Warner, Cablevision Market Lead," Jan. 15, 2006. *ZDNet Research,* Jul. 19, 2006. http://blogs.zdnet.com/ITFacts/?p=9925.

[a] Skype is a largely free service and its revenue share is therefore lower than its user share.

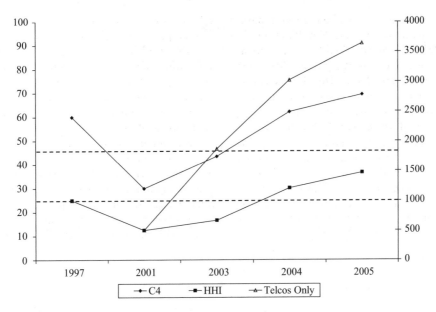

Figure 12.7 Internet Telephony: Concentration Trend

to extend their service footprint from regional to national and international (table 12.7).

As this market grew, the small companies were joined by large cable firms such as Cox, Time Warner, and Comcast. As a result, the overall concentration in the VoIP industry increased again after 2003. However, this understates concentration insofar as cable companies do not offer telephone service outside their service territory and thus do not compete with each other. The major telecom firms did not compete much with each other for residential non-mobile service, even after they acquired national VoIP operations by buying MCI and AT&T. When we factor this in, concentration is higher (figure 12.7).

But one can also make the case that VoIP is not an industry apart from voice telephony more generally, and as such part of a vastly larger market. This was incorporated in the analysis of local and long-distance service in chapter 11 of this book.

Media Player Software

New software had, by the mid-1990s, enabled the provision of audio and limited video over the Internet. Broadcasts for audio and video are often facilitated by a "streaming" of packets. As with the case of Internet telephony, packets are sent in fragments rather than in a continuous stream. "Streaming" works by storing enough data in advance, so as to provide a continuous stream if some packets are delayed. The leading Web audio software became Progressive Networks' Real Audio, which after 1997 was distributed freely over the web. Server software is then sold to Web broadcasters.

In addition to RealPlayer, Microsoft's Media Player and Apple's Quick Time also hold strong market shares, because these software programs are tied in with their respective operating system (OS) software. There are also a good number of small media players (table 12.8, figure 12.8).

CONCENTRATION OF THE INTERNET SECTOR

We are now ready to put the various elements together and address the broader question of whether the Internet has become less or more concentrated. We define the Internet sector as the core instrumentalities and infrastructure components underlying the Internet's basic functioning. This definition excludes applications, content, computer hardware, and telecom/cable conduits. It

Table 12.8 Internet Media Players (Market Share by Usage)

	1996	1999	2000	2001	2004	2006
Microsoft (Windows Media)[a]	5.0	17.1	27.1	27.6	38.2	48.6
RealNetworks (RealPlayer/Real Jukebox)	90.0	54.3	50.0	49.8	29.5	19.6
Apple (Quick Time and iTunes)	2.5	13.0	13.0	13.5	15.3	21.5
AOL (Winamp)			6.5	6.2	6.2	
Other	2.5	15.6	3.4	2.9	10.3	10.3[b]
Total U.S. Rev. ($ mil)	11	50	216	153	108	
C4	97.5	87.0	96.6	97.1	89.2	89.7
HHI	8,131	3,410	3,446	3,462	3,538	2,987

Sources: 1996 revenues are estimated by extrapolating from RealNetworks 1996 U.S. revenues. *HBW*, "RealNetworks Inc." June 11, 1998. Market share for Microsoft and Apple are estimated from revenues in "Media Players U.S. Usage." *Deal Memo*, October 23, 2000. U.S. Revenues are based on share of 44% of global volume: RealNetworks. "10-K Annual Report," 2001. 2001 market share from Nielsen/NetRatings, December 2001. 2006 data from Nielson//Netratings, "Streaming Media Pwlayers," 2006.

[a] Microsoft acquired 10% of RealNetworks in 1997.
[b] 'Other' market share for 2006 extrapolated from 2004 data.

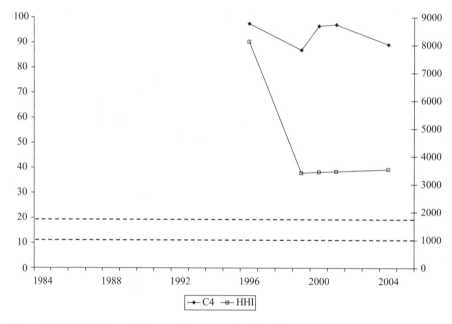

Figure 12.8 Media Player Software: Concentration Trend

does include the basic infrastructure components of the Internet through the following eight industries discussed above: Internet backbones, Internet dial-up service providers (ISPs), broadband providers, search engines, browser software, portals, IP telephony, and media player software.

In the previous sections, we looked at the market concentration trends for these eight Internet-sector industries in America. For each of these industries, we tracked their revenue and calculated individual firms' market shares for a period of up to 20 years. These market shares were then used to calculate concentration indices and track them over time (table 12.9, table 12.10, figure 12.9).

We also calculate concentration assuming that cable and local telecom companies in different franchise territories do not compete within each subindustry for broadband and VoIP services. With this assumption, we obtain an "Adjusted Weighted HHI" for the Internet sector.

Table 12.9 Summary: Concentration of 8 Major Internet Industries

	1984	1988	1992	1996	2001	2004
Backbone	1,454	1,259	970	896	1,565	1,610
ISPs	6,102	4,155	3,078	1,683	1,251	1,377
Broadband Providers				502	828	1,163
Browser Software				6,565	8,330	8,177
Search Engines				1,515	619	2,967
Portals	6,126	4,680	3,078	1,386	1,839	2,272
IP Telephony				1,000	500	1,466
Media Player Software				8,131	3,462	3,538
Weighted Average, With No *Intra*-Platform Competition of Telco and Cable, Respectively, In Same Territory	3,230	2,276	1,751	1,580	1,675	2,180

Table 12.10 Revenues Of Major Internet Industries ($ mil)

	1984	1988	1992	1996	2001	2004
Backbone	300	1,300	1,700	2,400	10,500	13,762
ISPs	47	359	672	3,072	23,064	16,896
Broadband Providers				1,162	4,762	15,930
Browser Software				92	300	275
Search Engines				193	1,000	2,047
Portals	96	148	200	336	2,791	6,200
IP Telephony				17	263	1,240
Media Player Software				11	153	108
Total U.S. Rev.	443	1,807	2,572	7,283	42,833	56,459

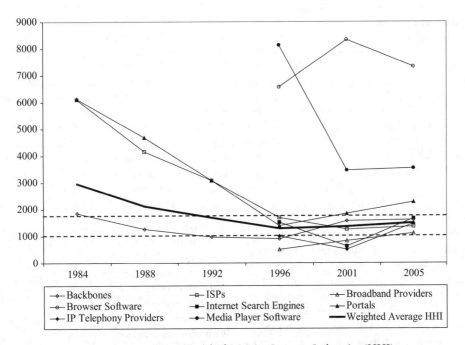

Figure 12.9 Average Concentration Trend of 8 Major Internet Industries (HHI)

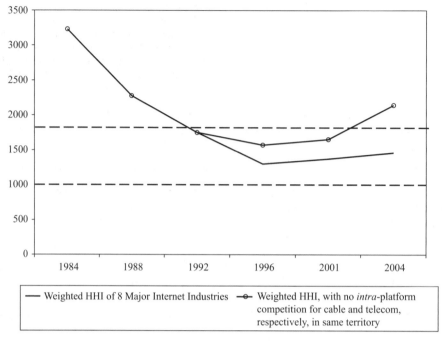

Figure 12.10 Average Concentration Trend of 8 Major Internet Industries (Weighted HHI)

The aggregates are provided in figure 12.10. They show that

1. The Internet sector's overall concentration has never been low.
2. Concentration declined in the 1980 and into the mid-1990s, but in the mid-1990s it increased again.
3. If we assume reasonably that cable and local telecom firms do not compete among each other within a platform type due to non-overlapping franchise territories, the concentration in the Internet sector is actually quite high again, and now for a sector vastly larger than before.

What are some of the factors leading to higher concentration in the Internet's industries? Each of its component industries has a different story. But the common elements are high economies of scale (scalability), based on high fixed costs and low marginal costs, and often complemented by network effects (positive externalities) on the demand side. These characteristics encouraged rapid expansions and created a period of intense competition in which prices were driven

to levels that could not sustain total costs. The eventual result was the failure of some market participants, and efforts at consolidation by the survivors with the aim of reducing competition and creating a market structure that could sustain higher prices. Such firms can also maintain access to financial markets, access that has shut down for most entrants in the competitive segments. The Internet's business downturn of the early 2000s therefore accelerated the concentration trends.

When the Internet business revived with "Web 2.0" activities that stressed community, dominant firms quickly emerged by the same logic: in social networking, Facebook (140 million user worldwide) and MySpace (acquired in 2006 by News Corp for $580 million, 120 million users worldwide); and in video sharing, where YouTube dominates. It was bought in 2006 by Google for $1.65 billion.

Similar concentration trends can be observed for industries closely related to the Internet core: e-commerce applications (for example, online book retailing, auctions, and travel services), operating system software, microprocessors, microcomputers and workstations, and telecommunications.

Therefore, a broader definition of the Internet sector does not change the results.

IMPLICATIONS

Thus, there have been pronounced horizontal and vertical trends of concentration in the Internet sector that challenge the view of the Internet as a highly competitive medium.

What are the implications? On the business end:

1. Intra-firm cross-subsidies are likely within major Internet firms from segments with market power to segments that are more competitive. Microsoft's alleged role in browsers and media server software is an example.
2. Relatively higher user prices.
3. Increased power of major Internet firms over:
   - Governance, standards, and protocols of the Internet
   - Access by content and applications providers
   - Hardware providers

If the Internet becomes concentrated and dominated by a few firms, given its centrality to commerce, culture, and politics, it is not likely to be left alone by government. The debates over the "net neutrality," that is, over the Internet access to broadband connectivity, or over vertical integration of operating systems software and Internet application, are early examples. Others are likely to follow.

These findings and conclusions may not fit the Internet's self-image of being wide-open and competitive, but business strategies and public policies will benefit from a realistic rather than wishful assessment.

Notes

1. For a history of the Internet and its technological elements, see Leiner, Barry M., Vinton G. Cerf, David D. Clark, Robert E. Kahn, Leonard Kleinrock, Daniel C. Lynch, Jon Postel, Larry G. Roberts, and Stephen Wolff. "A Brief History of the Internet." *Internet Society,* December 10, 2003. http://www.isoc.org/internet/history/brief.shtml. See also Cerf, Vinton, as told to Bernard Aboba, "How the Internet Came to Be." *The*

Online User's Encyclopedia, Bernard Aboba. Addison-Wesley, November 1993.

2. Nua Industry Surveys, *How Many On-Line?,* 2001. Available at http://www.nua.ie/surveys/analysis.../total_revenue_generated_2002.html. "ISC Internet Domain Survey, Jul 2007" *Internet Systems Consortium.* ISC.org. July, 2007. Last accessed on January 11, 2008, from http://www.isc.org/index.pl?/ops/ds/reports/2007-07, "Latest VeriSign Domain Name Industry Brief Underscores Growth of Internet Internationally." *VeriSign.* VeriSign.com. August 29, 2007. Last accessed on November 5, 2007, from http://www.verisign.com/press_release/pr/page_042743.html

3. Lipsman, Andrew. "694 Million People Currently Use the Internet Worldwide According to ComScore Networks." *ComScore.* ComScore.com. May 4, 2006. Last accessed on November 5, 2007, from http://www.comscore.com/press/release.asp?press=849

4. Trono, Lynn (IAB), and Suzanne Dawson (PwC). "IAB/PwC Release First Half 2005 Internet Ad Revenue Figures," http://www.iab.net/news/pr_2005_9_26.asp. "2006 Full Year Results IAB Advertising Revenue Report." *PricewaterhouseCoopers, Sponsored by the Interactive Advertising Bureau (IAB).* IAB.net. May 23, 2007. Last accessed on November 5, 2007, from http://www.iab.net/resources/adrevenue/pdf/IAB_PwC_2006_Final.pdf

5. From December 1999 to December 2000, 41,515 people were laid off from dot-com jobs. Source: "Layoffs at Internet Firms Jump 19 Percent, Startups Continue Shut-Down Trend as Quepasa.com Sells Assets," *St Louis Post,* December 28, 2000, p. C1.

6. "Dot-com Job Cuts Headed by Consumer, Services Firms." *Silicon Valley/San Jose Business Journal* (August 27, 2002. Accessed June 3, 2004. Available at http://sanjose.bizjournals.com/sanjose/stories/2002/08/26/daily13.html.

7. ANS was a nonprofit organization spun off by IBM, MCI, and MERIT Network, until America Online acquired it in 1995.

8. Richard, Jack. *Directory of Internet Service Providers: May/June 1997.* (Internet Architecture)

9. Meeker, Mary, and Chris Deputy of Morgan Stanley. *The Internet Report.* New York, Harper Business, 1996, pp. 5–13.

10. Kraft, Jeffery. "Measuring Internet Backbone Market Shares." Paper presented at the Internet Convergence and Self-Governance OECD/OSIPP Workshop, Osaka University, June 9, 1998. Available at www.oecd.org//dsti/sti/it/cm/act/kraft.pdf.

11. Booker, Ellis. *Web Week,* January 29, 1996, p. 48.

12. "Local ISPs Continue to Thrive in U.S." *Nua Internet Surveys,* August 1, 2002. "Teletruth

News Analysis". *Teletruth.* NewNetworks.com. 29 November 2007. Last accessed on 8 January 2008 at http://www.newnetworks.com/parttwo summary.htm

13. *American Internet User Survey: Management Report,* February 1996.

14. Borland, John. "Broadband Leaps Ahead of AOL." *CNET News.com.* May 13, 2004. Available at http://news.com.com/2100-1038_3-5212122.html?tag=nefd.top.

15. Hoover's Online, Fact Sheet, United Online, Inc. Available at http://www.hoovers.com/united-online/--ID__103858--/free-co-factsheet.xhtml.

16. Friedland, Jim and Kopelman, Kevin. "Q1:07 Residential Internet Access & VoIP Survey." *Cowen and Company.* May 29, 2007.

17. Metz, Cade. "Whither Netscape?" *PC Magazine,* January 11, 2003.

18. Shiver, Jube. "Changes in Industry Dim Relevance of Microsoft Trial." "Technology: Allegation of Unfair Use of Dominance Is Undermined as AOL-Netscape Merger Strengthens Rivals." *Los Angeles Times.* December 14, 1999. South Carolina dropped its antitrust suit against Microsoft in 1999, reducing the number of states to 19 and the District of Columbia.

19. Oldham, Jennifer. "Summary of Both Sides' Arguments." http://www.latimes.com/business/microsoft/arguments.htm.

20. Paltridge, Sam. "Internet Infrastructure Indicators." *Directorate for Science Technology and Industry, Organization for Economic Co-Operation and Development,* October 1998.

21. "Information on the *United States v. Microsoft* Settlement." Antitrust Case Filings. United States Department of Justice, Antitrust Division. 3 June 2004. http://www.usdoj.gov/atr/cases/ms-settle.htm.

22. Dennis, Sylvia. "Intranets & IP Telephony Are King Says IDC." *Newsbytes.* September 1, 1999. http://www.newsbytes.com.

PART VI

NATIONAL CONCENTRATION TRENDS: SUMMARIES

13

National Horizontal Concentration

HORIZONTAL CONCENTRATION TRENDS

Concentration within the same industry, for example for film production, is generally referred to as "horizontal," in contrast with a "vertical" concentration across the chain of production and distribution, or in contrast with "local" concentration in geographic submarkets such as a city's radio stations. The large number of mergers in information industries raises the question of whether the information sector as a whole, and which of its constituent industries, has become more concentrated and by how much. This chapter examines these questions—summarizing the results of the preceding industry chapters and aggregating them—and investigates horizontal concentration on a national level. Vertical concentration is discussed in chapter 14 and local concentration in chapter 15.

Has horizontal concentration increased? This is an empirical question that we will address by using HHI figures for specific industries and sectors. The characterizations of the index numbers as being highly concentrated, moderately concentrated, or unconcentrated follow the definitions of the *Horizontal Merger Guidelines* of the U.S. Department of Justice (DOJ). These characterizations should not be read as conclusive. (See the earlier discussion on the limitation of antitrust measures for media industries in chapter 1.) The measures provide a useful tool, however, for observing

trends and making comparisons, if employed consistently over time and across industries, as we have tried to do.

We now proceed more methodically through the subsectors, assembling many of the earlier findings that we developed in the industry chapters, repeating some of them, and aggregating them. We begin with the mass media industries.

The Mass Media Sector

The industries of electronic mass media distribution include radio station groups, TV station groups, direct broadcasting satellite (DBS) providers, and cable TV operators. (We also include, for illustrative purposes, the category of multichannel TV, which combines cable TV and DBS.) As can be seen, all industries involved have increased in concentration after 1996, and basically have increased in concentration since 1984 (figure 13.1, table 13.1).

Most noticeable is the steep increase in concentration in radio station ownership. Clear Channel and Viacom increased their market shares significantly since 1996 as a result of a loosening of regulations by the FCC and Congress in the middle of the 1990s. Clear Channel owns over 1,200 radio stations. However, since the total number of stations is also large (12,932 in 2004), national concentration for radio still remains moderate in DOJ terms in comparison to most other media industries. Clear Channel's market share in 2004, by

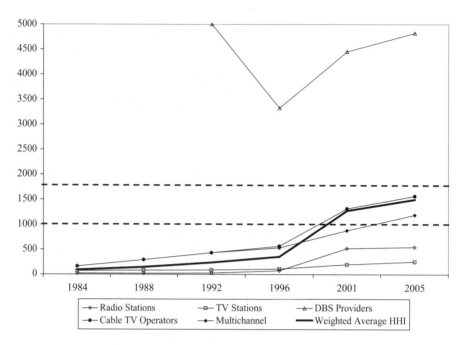

Figure 13.1 Mass Media Distribution: Concentration Trends

Table 13.1 Electronic Mass Media Distribution (HHI Concentration)

MM Distribution	1984	1988	1992	1996	2001	2005
Radio Stations	20	20	25	75	519	545
TV Stations	73	80	88	110	199	253
DBS Providers			5,000	2,342	4,454	4,498
Cable TV Operators	162	292	430	565	1,316	1,568
(Multichannel)	162	292	430	532	876	1,189
Weighted Average HHI	91	147	237	354	1,274	1,499
Weighted Average C4	15.2	18.6	23.0	30.3	52.5	58.3

Note: Not part of weighted aggregates in this table.

revenues, was 19% (and dropped after 2007 when the company was acquired by private equity financers who sold off several hundred of its stations to pay for the purchase).

The TV station industry saw its national concentration grow significantly in the period between 1984 and 2004—from 73 in 1984 to 110 in 1996 to 253 in 2005—enabled by the loosening of ownership caps set by the FCC. News Corp's acquisition of New World and Chris-Craft in particular raised concentration, with its market share increasing from 1.9% to 9.1%. Nonetheless, the industry's

level of concentration remains low by DOJ terms, with an HHI of 253. The C4 was 27.7%, also a low figure.

DBS provision, in contrast, is a highly concentrated industry in which EchoStar and DirectTV (News Corp) account for over 90% of revenues. This industry exhibits huge economies of scale and high entry barriers.

Lastly, the cable TV operators experienced a dramatic increase in national concentration, far greater than that of radio or TV stations. With an HHI of 1,568 and a C4 value of 68.1, it is a highly concentrated industry nationally (and still more so locally, as will be discussed in chapter 15). But even here, concentration levels were in the intermediate range of national concentration by DOJ definitions.

If we pool DBS providers and cable multiple system operators (MSOs) into one industry—multichannel TV—their combined national HHI is of course lower. But even so, the HHI rises steadily. We can also observe the relative size of the four industries—with cable TV accounting for one-half after 1992 (table 13.2).

In figure 13.1, the weighted average concentration for electronic mass media distribution is indicated by the bold line. It shows a steady increase from 1984, accelerating after 1996. This is mainly driven by DBS and cable TV. Radio and TV stations, which have received most of the attention in the media concentration policy debate, have contributed much less to the increase.

The preceding analysis averaged and weighted the concentration in the several industries. One can also aggregate in a different way, not by averaging several industries, but by combining the various forms of retail TV/video distribution into one pool. This includes TV stations, cable MSOs, DBS providers, and also video stores, which are an alternative form of video distribution. We do not average separate industries but consider them to be a single video retail distribution industry with the major firms active in several of its segments. Figure 13.2 and tables 13.3 and 13.4 show the trends for the pooled sector. (See also figure 4–7 for retail video distribution without video stores.)

We observe in table 13.4 that among these combined video distribution firms, cable MSOs have by far the major and fastest-growing shares: Comcast 18% and Time Warner 11.1%. No other firm has more than 10%, not even News Corp (8.5%), CBS (1.7%), or GE (also 1.7%). Mid-sized cable firms also have a presence near the top: Cox and Charter near 5% and Cablevision 2.3%.

The concentration of the pooled TV/video distribution sector shows a steady increase after 1992. But they do not show high numbers. The HHI is in low-concentration range (627, although up from 48); and the C4 is up, from 10% to 43.0%, a very high rise but still at a moderate level for most non-media industries. The overall HHI concentration is fairly low, but that could be expected in a market purposely defined quite broadly. What is striking is the decline of the share of the smaller firms, subsumed under "others." These small broadcasters and cable firms used to account for over 70% of video distribution revenues. By 2005, this share had dropped to less than 30%.

The electronic mass media programming sector consists of the aggregators of programs: radio and TV networks, syndicators, cable (and DBS) channels, and pay-TV. The graph below shows relatively high—but declining—levels of concentration in this sector. TV networks experienced a decline in concentration since the late 1980s. For radio and pay-TV networks, and for syndication, concentration increased. Cable channels zigzagged, declining in overall concentration since 1984 but increasing after 1992 (figure 13.3, table 13.5).

Radio networks show a high level of concentration, declining after 1996. This is the result of Unistar's purchase of United and TransStar in the late 1980s and its own acquisition by Westwood in 1996, enlarging the latter's market share to 31% by 2004. However, the relative importance

Table 13.2 Electronic Mass Media Distribution Revenues ($ Million)

	1984	1988	1992	1996	2001	2005
Radio Stations	5,596	7,511	8,378	11,947	17,450	18,932
TV Stations	10,572	14,417	15,630	20,747	21,479	25,613
DBS Providers			5	1,293	10,748	15,350
Cable TV Operators	8,331	13,409	21,079	27,706	49,427	57,600
(Multichannel)	8,331	13,409	21,081	28,649	53,788	72,566
Total U.S. Rev.	24,999	35,337	45,092	61,693	99,104	117,495

Note: "Multichannel data" not used as part of total revenues and are provided for illustrative purposes only.

Table 13.3 TV/Video Retail Distribution: Pooled Revenue ($ Million)

	1984	1988	1992	1996	2001	2005
Comcast	83	402	717	1,635	5,570	18,317
Jones Intercable	8	54	127	305	Comcast	
Lenfest Communications		107	190	388	Comcast	
Storer (50% interest)	75	KRR	316	443	Comcast	
AT&T Broadband						Comcast
MediaOne				2,854	10,009	
Continental Cablevision	258	778	1,117	MediaOne	AT&T	
TCI	450	1,703	3,309	3,740	AT&T	
Viacom Cable	192	335	401	471	TCI	
TCI Entertainment/ Tempo/ Primestar			5	417		
US Satellite Broadcasting Corp				192		
Storer (50% interest)	125		316	443	TCI	
Heritage		241 TCI		TCI		
Storer Communications	350	KKR	TCI/Comcast			
Time Warner			2,087 TW	3,823	5,222	11,290
American TV & Com	367	818		416		
Adelphia	75	161	295		2,959	TW/Comcast
Century		161	316	360	Adelphia	
Newhouse (ex-TWE)/Bright House	142	241	506	TWE		1,843
Cox Communications	408	496	653	1,468	3,786	4,954
TCA Group	25	67	148	249	Cox	
Times Mirror	250	335	443	Cox		
Charter				360	3,699	4,723
Marcus Cable			443	443	Charter	
Bresnan		40	84	249	Charter	
Falcon	83	27	42	222	Charter	
Cablevision Systems	117	496	569	277	740	2,304
News Corp (Fox)			358	601	1,550	8,634
DirecTV (Hughes)/Liberty					618	News Corp
Pegasus				6	838	News Corp
Chris-Craft	66	250	377	446	News Corp	
EchoStar/Dish Network				60	3,606	5,603
CBS (ex-Viacom)						1,760
Viacom				2,790 Viacom	5,655	CBS, Blockbuster
Westinghouse	845	420	519	Viacom		
CBS	353	382	503	Westinghouse		

Blockbuster (ex-Viacom)	6	284	1,024	Viacom	1,233	3,411
GE		590	585	1,000		1,743
RCA/NBC	335	GE			315	
Movie Gallery			22	216	1,137	1,402
Video Update				8	1,184	MG
Hollywood Entertainment			7	254	1,130	MG
Tribune	259	400	500	861	920	1,250
Disney				950		1,171
CapCities		770	767	Disney		
ABC	482	CapCities				
Mediacom				55	566	1,152
Insight					653	979
Gannett	353	367	371	641	662	821
Hearst-Argyle	NA	10	27	73	642	753
Belo	163	178	201	333	598	679
Saban Ent.						644
Univision	NA	28	100	193	335	Saban
CableOne	117	148	169	222	348	518
Paxson	NM	NM	NM	15	200	111
Netflix					86	508
Family Video				15	134	131
Others	15,942	22,997	46,359	29,190	27,811	27,281
Total U.S. Revenue ($ million)	21,928	33,286	63,971	56,837	81,270	101,990

Note: This composite table includes TV stations, DBS, cable TV operators, and video rental.

Table 13.4 Pooled TV/Video Retail Distribution: Market Shares by Revenues)

	1984	1988	1992	1996	2001	2005
Comcast	0.4	1.2	1.1	2.9	6.9	18.0
Jones Intercable		0.2	0.2	0.5	Comcast	
Lenfest Communications	0.3	0.3	0.3	0.7	Comcast	
Storer (50% interest)		KRR	0.5	0.8	Comcast	
AT&T Broadband					12.3	Comcast
MediaOne				5.0	AT&T	
Continental Cablevision	1.2	2.3	1.7	MediaOne		
TCI	2.1	5.1	5.2	6.6	AT&T	
Viacom Cable	0.9	1.0	0.6	0.8	TCI	
TCI Entertainment/ Tempo/ Primestar				0.7		
US Satellite Broadcasting Corp				0.3		
Storer (50% interest)		0.7	0.5	0.8	TCI	
Heritage	0.6	TCI				
Storer Communications	1.6	KKR	TCI/ Comcast			
Time Warner	0.0	0.0	3.3	6.7	6.4	11.1
American TV & Com	1.7	2.5	TW			
Adelphia		0.5	0.5	0.7	3.6	TW/ Comcast
Century	0.3	0.5	0.5	0.6	Adelphia	
Newhouse	0.6	0.7	0.8	TWE		1.8
Cox Communications	1.9	1.5	1.0	2.6	4.7	4.9
TCA Group	0.1	0.2	0.2	0.4	Cox	
Times Mirror	1.1	1.0	0.7	Cox		
Charter				0.6	4.6	4.6
Marcus Cable			0.7	0.8	Charter	
Bresnan		0.1	0.1	0.4	Charter	
Falcon	0.4	0.1	0.1	0.4	Charter	
Cablevision Systems	0.5	1.5	0.9	0.5	0.9	2.3
News Corp (Fox)			0.6	1.1	1.9	8.5
DirecTV (Hughes)/Liberty					1.0	News Corp
Pegasus					0.9	News Corp
Chris-Craft	0.3	0.8	0.6	0.8	News Corp	
EchoStar/Dish Network				0.1	4.0	
CBS (ex-Viacom)						1.7
Viacom				4.9	7.0	
Westinghouse	3.9	1.3	0.8	Viacom		
CBS	1.6	1.1	0.8	Westinghouse		
BlockBuster		0.9	1.6	Viacom		3.3
GE		1.8	0.9	1.8	1.5	1.7
RCA/NBC	1.5	GE				
Tribune	1.2	1.2	0.8	1.5	1.4	1.2
Disney				1.9	1.1	1.1
CapCities		2.3	1.2	Disney		
ABC	2.2	CapCities				
Mediacom					0.7	1.1
Insight				0.1	0.8	1.0
Gannett	1.6	1.1	0.6	1.1	0.8	0.8
Hearst-Argyle		0.0	0.0	0.1	0.8	0.7
Belo	0.7	0.5	0.3	0.6	0.7	0.7
Saban Ent.						0.6
Univision		0.1	0.2	0.3	0.4	Saban
CableOne	0.5	0.4	0.3	0.4	0.4	0.5

Table 13.4 *(Continued)*

	1984	1988	1992	1996	2001	2005
Paxson		NA	NA	0.0	0.2	0.1
Movie Gallery				0.4	0.4	1.4
Video Update				0.0	0.2	MG
Hollywood Entertainment				0.4	1.3	MG
Netflix					0.1	0.5
Family Video					0.2	0.1
Others	72.8	69.1	72.5	51.4	34.2	26.7
Total U.S. Rev. ($ mil)	21,928	33,286	63,971	56,837	81,270	101,990
C4	10.0	12.2	11.8	23.2	32.6	43.0
HHI	48	63	55	172	381	627

Note: This composite table includes TV stations, DBS, and cable TV operators.

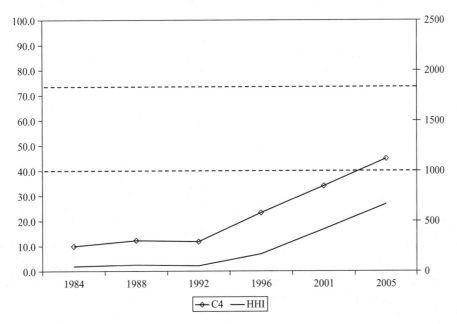

Figure 13.2 Concentration of Pooled Retail Distribution of TV/Video (Including Retail Home Video)

and size of networks in radio is modest. The traditional three major TV networks, in contrast, have declined in share and even in size after Fox, WB, UPN, and Paxson, entered the market after 1988, and the demand for Spanish language networks grew. Together, these developments created a 10-network system in TV broadcasting, dominated by four firms. The industry remained highly concentrated in 2005 with an HHI of 2,159, but this is down from an HHI of 3,228 in 1984.

The cable TV channels industry grew enormously in size and scope. It saw its concentration levels reaching a low of 906 in 1992. Subsequently,

concentration increased through acquisitions, especially of Turner by Time Warner. As a result of additional entries, the HHI declined again somewhat and the industry remained moderately concentrated by DOJ standards.

Pay TV (table 13.6) was increasingly dominated by Time Warner, whose market share in 2005 was 38%. After 2001, digital cable, with its added options such as video-on-demand, began to eat into this market share.

Figure 13.3 shows the average weighted concentration of the overall electronic mass media programming sector as the bolded line. The overall

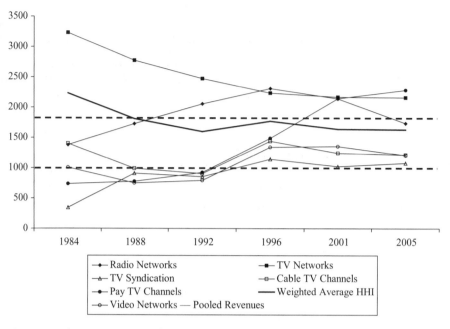

Figure 13.3 Electronic Mass Media Programming Concentration

Table 13.5 Electronic Mass Media Networks (HHI Concentration)

HHI	1984	1988	1992	1996	2001	2005
Radio Networks	1,380	1,728	2,055	2,309	2,141	1,736
TV Networks	3,228	2,775	2,474	2,234	2,168	2,159
TV Syndication	345	911	854	1,145	1,024	1,079
Cable TV Channels	1,403	992	906	1,443	1,244	1,214
Pay TV Channels	738	776	924	1,489	2,143	2,282
Weighted Average HHI	2,233	1,811	1,601	1,771	1,639	1,633
Weighted Average C4	77.4	71.8	70.2	73.4	71.9	71.6

trend has been downward after 1984, from a high HHI of 2,233 in 1984 to a moderate-level 1,771 in 1996 and 1,633 in 2005. As broadcast TV networks and cable channels make up the bulk of the subsector, the overall trend is downward, in spite of the increase in concentration in radio, syndication, and pay-TV.

Whereas so far we averaged the several industries' concentration, we now proceed again also somewhat differently, by aggregating all TV/video program provisions into a single "pooled TV/video programming networks" market, which combines TV broadcast networks, cable

channels, TV syndicators, and pay-TV channels. In other words, we look at all types of TV channels as one market and measure the share of major media companies in it (tables 13.7–13.10, figures 13.4, 13.5).

We observe that the concentration has been zigzagging within a fairly steady band, holding steady by the HHI measure, an increasing in C4 and C6 over the 20-year period. Both HHI and C4 measures show declines after 1996. The top firms in 2005 were Time Warner and GE (both at 17%); and CBS, Viacom, News Corp, and Disney with 10–14% each. Together, these top six firms

Table 13.6 Electronic Mass Media Network Revenues ($ Million)

	1984	1988	1992	1996	2001	2005
Radio Networks	388	382	377	465	919	1,081
TV Networks	8,318	9,320	10,149	13,081	14,300	16,713
Syndication	420	901	1,370	2,218	3,102	3,674
Cable TV Channels	2,466	4,261	6,504	10,906	22,917	26,879
Pay TV Channels	3,410	4,491	5,140	4,757	5,873	6,778
Total U.S. Rev.	15,002	19,355	23,540	31,427	47,111	55,125

Table 13.7 Pooled TV/Video Programming Networks ($ Million)

	1984	1988	1992	1996	2001	2005
CBS (ex-Viacom)						6,337[a]
Viacom	843	1,356	1,725	6,161	10,609	6,200
Westinghouse				2,736	Viacom	
CBS	2,390	2,602	2,955	Westinghouse		
King World	80	280	503	663	CBS	
UPN				883	Viacom	
Paramount			600	Viacom		
Spelling Ent.	100	120	258	Viacom		
Republic	3	13	45	Viacom		
Time Warner	810	1,122	1,776	5,326	8,715	9,296
Turner	672	1,264	1,745	TW	TW	
Newline Cinema	4	12	45	TW		
WB[b]				(680)	(910)	(1,290)
Lorimar Telepic		494	TW			
Telepictures	73	TW				
Lorimar	206	TW				
GE/Universal		3,107	2,970	4,430	5,161	9,201
RCA/NBC	2,425	GE				
Vivendi					931	GE
USA	99	170	260	502	Vivendi	
Seagram					Vivendi	
Universal/MCA	163	200	Matsushita	Seagram		
News Corp		757	1,713	2,472	4,076	5,329
Disney	760	747	1,061	4,871	6,972	7,745
Cap Cities		2,660	2,612	Disney		
ABC	2,800	CapCities				
Discovery Networks		9	194	473	1,223	1,717
Liberty Media			157	199	863	1,022
Cablevision				360	501	750
PBS	163	194	236	285	348	445
Sony			97	119	154	199
Columbia Pictures		79	Sony			
TriStar	64	Sony				
Gannett				150	155	181
Multimedia	40	66	129	Gannett		
Paxson				10	103	56
Saban						257
Univision				57	116	Saban
Comcast					100	200
Others	6,317	8,954	8,925	5,137	5,751	4,389
Total U.S. Rev. ($ mil)	14,767	19,927	21,700	30,552	44,773	53,324

Note: This table is a composite of TV networks, cable networks, pay-TV networks, and syndication.

[a] Viacom and CBS, although separated, were still controlled by the National Amusements Co., Sumner Redstone's investment entity.
[b] WB is part of TW and included in the parent company. Its revenues were $684 mil in 1992, $966 mil in 2001, and $1,187 mil in 2005. It subsequently merged with UPN into a joint channel, The CW.

Table 13.8 Pooled TV/Video Programming Networks (Market Shares by Revenues)

	1984	1988	1992	1996	2001	2005
CBS (ex-Viacom)						11.8[a]
Viacom	5.7	6.8	7.9	20.3	23.2	11.6
Westinghouse				9.0		
CBS	16.2	13.1	13.6	Westinghouse		
King World	0.5	1.4	2.3	2.2	CBS	
UPN				2.9	Viacom	
Paramount			2.8	Viacom		
Spelling Ent.	0.7	0.6	1.2	Viacom		
Republic		0.1	0.2	Viacom		
Time Warner (TW)	5.5	5.6	8.2	17.4	19.0	17.4
Turner	4.6	6.3	8.0	TW		
NewLine Cinema		0.1	0.2	TW		
WB[b]				(2.2)	(2.2)	(2.3)
Lorimar Telepic		2.5	Time Warner			
Telepictures	0.5	TW				
Lorimar	1.4	TW				
GE/Universal		15.6	12.8	14.5	11.3	17.2
RCA/NBC	16.4	GE				
Vivendi					2.0	GE
USA	0.7	0.9	1.2	1.6	Vivendi	
Seagram					Vivendi	
Universal/MCA	1.1	1.0	Matsushita	Seagram		
News Corp		3.8	7.9	8.1	9.1	10.3
Disney	5.1	3.7	4.9	15.9	15.2	14.5
Cap Cities		13.3	12.0	Disney		
ABC	19.0	CapCities				
Discovery Networks			0.9	1.5	2.7	3.2
Liberty Media			0.7	0.7	1.9	2.8
Cablevision				1.2	1.1	1.4
PBS	1.1	1.0	1.1	0.9	0.8	0.8
Sony			0.4	0.4	0.3	0.4
Columbia Pictures		0.4	Sony			
TriStar	0.4	Sony				
Gannett				0.5	0.3	0.4
Multimedia	0.3	0.3	0.6	Gannett		
Paxson				0.03	0.2	0.1
Saban						0.5
Univision				0.2	0.3	Saban
Comcast					0.2	0.4
Others	20.9	23.5	13.0	2.8	12.6	8.2
Total U.S. Rev. ($ mil)	14,767	19,927	21,700	30,552	44,773	53,558
C4	57.3	48.8	46.6	68.0	68.7	60.9
C6	67.9	60.8	62.6	85.1	80.3	82.4
HHI	1,007	750	793	1,342	1,355	1,206

Note: Table is composite of TV Networks, Cable Networks, Pay-TV Networks, and Syndicators.

[a] Viacom and CBS, although separated, were still controlled by the National Amusements Co., Sumner Redstone's investment entity. If one considers them to be a single company, the C4 and the HHI rise to 72.5 and 1,480.

[b] WB is part of TW and included in the parent company. Its revenues were $684 mil in 1992, $966 mil in 2001, and $1,187 mil in 2005. It subsequently merged with UPN into a joint channel, The CW.

Table 13.9 Pooled TV/Video Mass Media Programming and Distribution ($ Million)

	1984	1988	1992	1996	2001	2005
Time Warner	810	1,122	3,863	9,149	13,937	20,586
American TV & Comms	367	818 818	TW			
Newhouse Broadcasting	142	241	506	TWE		1,843
Adelphia		161	295	416	2,959	TW/Comcast
Century	75	161	316	360	Adelphia	
Turner	663	1,084	1,505	TW		
Newline Cinema	4	12	45	TW		
Lorimar Telepic		494	TW			
Telepictures	73	TW				
Lorimar	206	TW				
Comcast	83	402	717	1,635	5,670	18,517
Jones Intercable	8	54	127	305	Comcast	
Lenfest Communications	75	107	190	388	Comcast	
Storer (50%)		KKR	316	443	Comcast	
AT&T Broadband					10,009	Comcast
MediaOne				2,854	AT&T	
Continental Cablevision	258	778	1,117	MediaOne		
TCI	450	1,703	3,309	3,740	AT&T	
Viacom Cable	192	335	401	471	TCI	
TCI Entertainment/Tempo/Primestar			5	417		
US Satellite Broadcasting Corp				192		
Storer (50% interest)		241	316	443	TCI	
Heritage	125	TCI				
Storer Communications	350	KKR	TCI/Comcast			
News Corp	757	757	2,071	3,073	6,244	13,963
DirecTV (Hughes)[a]/Liberty					618	News Corp
Pegasus				6	838	DirecTV
Chris-Craft	66	250	377	446	News Corp	

continued

Table 13.9 (*Continued*)

	1984	1988	1992	1996	2001	2005
GE/Universal	2,760	3,697	3,355	5,430	6,394	10,944
RCA/NBC		GE				GE
Vivendi	99	170	260	502	931	
USA					Vivendi	
Seagram					Vivendi	
Universal/MCA	163	200	Matsushita	Seagram		
CBS (ex-Viacom)						6,960
Viacom	843	1,356	1,725	6,161	10,981	6,200
Westinghouse	845			2,736	Viacom	
CBS	2,743	2,984	3,458	Westinghouse	CBS	
King World	80	280	503	663		
UPN				883	966	1,137
Paramount	100	120	600	Viacom		
Spelling Ent.		13	258	Viacom		
Republic	3		45	Viacom		
Group W	345	420	519	809	Viacom	
Disney	760	747	1,061	5,971	7,892	8,916
CapCities	3,282	3,430	3,379			
ABC		CapCities		Disney		
Cox Communications	408	496	653	1,468	3,786	2,660
TCA Group	25	67	148	249	Cox	4,954
Times Mirror	250	335	443	Cox		
Charter				360	3,699	4,723
Marcus Cable			443	443	Charter	
Bresnan		40	84	249	Charter	
Falcon	83	27	42	222	Charter	
Cablevision Systems	117	496	569	277	740	2,304

Discovery Networks	259	9	194	473	1,223	1,717
Tribune		400	500	861	1,130	1,250
Mediacom					566	1,152
Insight				55	653	979
Liberty Media	353	367	157	199	863	964
Gannett		66	371	641	662	821
Multimedia	40	10	129	Gannett		
Hearst-Argyle	163	178	27	73	642	753
Belo			201	333	598	679
Saban Ent.					Saban	644
Univision	117	28	100	193	335	518
CableOne	163	148	169	222	348	445
PBS		194	236	285	348	199
Sony			97	119	154	
Columbia Pictures		79	Sony			
TriStar	64	Sony				
Paxson				25	303	167
EchoStar				60	3,606	5,603
All Others	19,365	26,775	29,080	29,093	30,196	30,260
Total U.S. Revenue ($ mil)	37,374	51,839	64,237	83,812	121,193	158,568

Note: Table includes the following industries: TV networks, syndication, cable TV channels, pay TV, TV stations, cable TV operators, and DBS providers.

[a] In 2007, News Corp sold DirecTV to Liberty Media in exchange for News Corp stock held by Liberty.

Table 13.10 Pooled TV/Video Programming and Distribution (Market Shares by Revenues)

	1984	1988	1992	1996	2001	2005
Time Warner	2.2	2.2	6.0	10.9	11.5	13.0
American TV & Comms	1.0	1.6	TW	TW		
Newhouse Broadcasting	0.4	0.5	0.8	0.5		
Adelphia		0.3	0.5	0.4	2.4	1.2 TW/Comcast
Century	0.2	0.3	0.5	0.4	Adelphia	
Turner	1.8	2.0	2.3	Time Warner		
Newline Cinema	0.01	0.02	0.1	Time Warner		
Lorimar Telepic		1.0	Time Warner			
Telepictures	0.2	Time Warner				
Lorimar	0.6	Time Warner				
Comcast	0.2	0.8	1.1	2.0	4.7	11.7
Jones Intercable		0.1	0.2	0.4	Comcast	
Lenfest Communications	0.2	0.2	0.3	0.5	Comcast	
Storer (50% interest)		KKR	0.5	0.5	Comcast	
AT&T Broadband					8.3	Comcast
MediaOne				3.4	AT&T	
Continental Cablevision	0.7	1.5	1.7	MediaOne		
TCI	1.2	3.3	5.1	4.5	AT&T	
Viacom Cable	0.5	0.7	0.6	0.6	TCI	
TCI Entertainment/Tempo/Primestar			0.01	0.5		
U.S. Satellite Broadcasting Corp				0.2		
Storer (50% interest)	0.3	0.5	0.5	0.5	TCI	
Heritage		TCI				
Storer Communications	0.9	KKR	TCI/Comcast			
News Corp	0.9	1.5	3.2	3.7	5.2	8.8 News Corp
DirecTV (Hughes)					0.7	News Corp
Pegasus					0.6	DirecTV
Chris-Craft	0.2	0.5	0.6	0.5	News Corp	
GE/Universal	6.5	6.1	4.3	5.3	4.3	5.1
RCA/NBC	0.9	GE				
USA	0.3	0.3	0.4	0.6		
Universal/MCA	0.4	0.4	Matsushita	Seagram	Vivendi	
CBS (ex-Viacom)						4.6
Viacom	2.3	2.7	2.7	7.4	9.1	8.2
Westinghouse	2.3	Viacom				
CBS	7.4	5.9	5.4	Westinghouse		
King World	0.2	0.5	0.6	0.8	CBS	

	C1	C2	C3	C4	C5	C6
UPN			0.9	1.1	0.8	0.7
Paramount	0.3		0.4	Viacom		
Spelling Ent.			0.1	Viacom		
Republic		1.5	1.6	Viacom		
Disney	2.1	6.7	5.2	7.1	6.5	5.6
CapCities	8.9	Cap Cities		Disney		
ABC	1.1	0.9	0.7			
Cox Communications			0.2	1.6	2.8	3.3
TCA Group	0.1	0.1	0.7	0.2	Cox	
Times Mirror	0.7	0.7	1.0	Cox		
Charter	1.1	1.0	0.7	1.8	3.1	3.1
Marcus Cable				0.5	Charter	
Bresnan	0.2			0.3	Charter	
Falcon	0.3	0.1	0.1	0.3	Charter	
Cablevision Systems	1.0	1.0	0.9	0.3	0.6	1.5
Discovery Networks	0.3	0.02	0.3	0.6	1.0	1.1
Tribune	0.7	0.8	0.8	1.0	0.9	0.8
Mediacom	1.0		0.2	0.1	0.5	0.7
Insight				0.1	0.5	0.6
Liberty Media		0.7	0.6	0.2	0.7	0.6
Gannett	0.1	0.1	0.2	0.8	0.5	0.5
Multimedia		0.02	0.0	Gannett 0.1	0.5	
Hearst-Argyle	0.4		0.3	0.1	0.4	0.4
Belo		8.3	0.1	0.4	0.3	0.4
Saban Ent.				0.2		Saban
Univision	0.3	0.1	0.3	0.3	0.3	0.3
CableOne	0.4	0.3	0.4	0.3	0.3	0.3
PBS	0.2	0.4	0.1	0.1	0.1	0.1
Sony			Sony			
Columbia Pictures		0.2				
TriStar		Sony				
Paxson				0.03	0.3	0.1
EchoStar				0.1	3.0	3.5
All Others	59.9	55.6	60.2	38.4	24.5	21.0
Total U.S. Revenue ($ mil)	370,374	51,839	64,237	83,812	121,193	158,568
C4	25.1	22.0	21.7	30.7	35.3	41.7
C5	27.3	24.7	26.0	35.1	40.5	47.3
HHI	205	155	173	325	440	572

Note: Table includes the following industries: TV networks, syndication, cable TV channels, pay TV, TV stations, cable TV operators, and DBS providers.

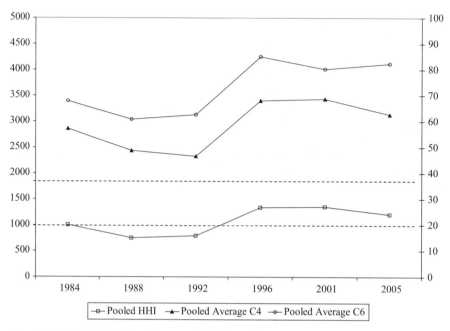

Figure 13.4 Pooled TV/Video Programming Networks

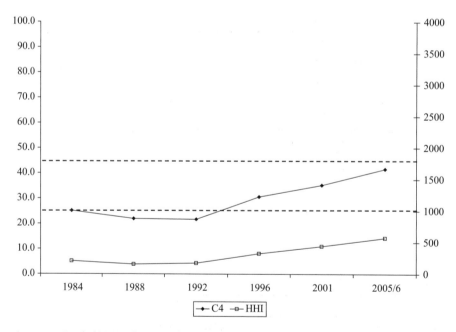

Figure 13.5 Pooled TV/Video Distribution

account for 82% of the overall TV/video network market. This is not a low concentration. But it has not been increasing over the 20 year period. Of the six major TV channel companies, five are vertically integrated into production. Sony is the one major Hollywood production/distribution company with no role in the TV channel markets. Conversely, CBS owns none of the major Hollywood film production studios.

Figure 13.4 shows that the pooled TV/video *programming* networks industry (including cable TV networks) has been zigzagging and declining after 1996 to an HHI of about 1,200. In contrast, the pooled TV/video retail *distribution* sector (TV stations, cable MSOs, DBS providers) has steadily increased in concentration after 1996. But it is much less concentrated, reaching an HHI of about 777 in 2005. Thus, after 1996 the two trends have run in opposite directions. How do they add up when pooled, as the major media firms tend to be on both sides? Taken together, TV/video programming and retail distribution is not concentrated, reaching 572 in 2005. However, the trend has been upwards since 1988, when the HHI was 155.

Moving to the film industry: The subindustries are film production/distribution (the two are functionally too intertwined in Hollywood to separate); TV prime-time production; movie theaters; home video distribution; and video rental. Figure 13.6 shows the concentration trends (see also table 13.11).

The key industry—movie production/distribution—has been moderately concentrated since the 1970s by DOJ standards, divided among six main "studio" companies, controlled today by Disney, Time Warner, Viacom, News Corp, GE, and Sony. Some independent studios were acquired by the

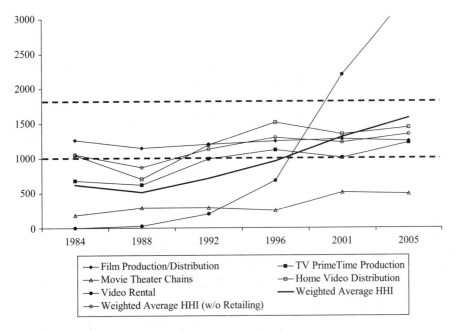

Figure 13.6 Film Sector Industries: Concentration Trends

Table 13.11 Film Sector HHI Concentration

HHI	1984	1988	1992	1996	2001	2005
Film Production/Distribution	1,262	1,146	1,198	1,245	1,278	1,248
TV PrimeTime Production	681	618	991	1,119	1,005	1,223
Movie Theater Chains	182	286	288	249	509	490
Home Video Distribution	1,048	702	1,191	1,516	1,347	1,443
Video Rental		27	199	679	2,201	3,346
Weighted Average HHI	620	513	712	958	1,306	1,581
Weighted Average C4	34.4	33.5	40.4	48.4	57.3	60.9
Weighted Average Production and Distribution HHI, without Retailing (film theaters and video rental)	1,054	868	1,131	1,299	1,226	1,347

main firms, but new ones also entered. The HHI for this oligopolistic distribution industry has remained moderately concentrated and remarkably stable over most of the two-decade period at an HHI of about 1,250 and a C6 of 80%.

After the FCC's 1995 repeal of rules preventing vertical integration, the major Hollywood firms acquired the major TV networks or created new ones and also became dominant in TV prime time production. News Corp and Disney became the largest in that industry, with about 19% each, followed by Viacom (14%), Time Warner (10%), and GE (10%) in 2005. The shift of production toward these five companies led to a doubling of the HHI for TV prime time production from 681 in 1984 to an intermediate level of 1,223 in 2005 and to significant vertical integration with TV networks.

Movie theater chains experienced a significant increase in concentration, primarily as a result of the trend to large multiplex chains. Regal and AMC acquired several smaller theater owners and reached market shares of 19.4% and 13%. Concentration grew from a low HHI of 182 in 1984 to a still low 490 in 2005. Concentration slightly declined after 2001. The industry remains nationally unconcentrated despite this increase.

Video rental shows the steepest increase in concentration. The industry formerly comprised thousands of mom-and-pop stores. Blockbuster had an insignificant market share of 0.2% in 1985, but grew to 53% in 2004. With the purchase of Hollywood Entertainment by Movie Gallery, raising its share to 22%, the HHI increased further to 3,346 in 2005. But the industry as a whole was in decline, and Viacom spun off Blockbuster in 2005 (table 13.12).

In the aggregate (the bold line of figure 13.6), the film industry has grown steadily in average concentration, shifting from unconcentrated to moderately concentrated, in DOJ terms (HHI = 1,581

in 2005). Much of that increase came from the retailing segment, that is, from home video rentals and movie theaters. Without these retail industries the film sector would have increased modestly in concentration from 1,054 to 1,347, mostly from TV production.

Most print publishing industries are only moderately concentrated by DOJ standards. Educational books and online book retailing are the exception. Book retailing has grown significantly in concentration but is still in the DOJ's moderately concentrated range. Although trade and paperback, other books, academic journals, printing services, daily newspapers, and magazines all show fluctuations in concentration, none of them became significantly more concentrated over the 20-year period on the national level (figure 13.7, tables 13.13 and 13.14).

Trade and paperback books reached in 2005 an HHI of 693, about the same as in 2001 and in 1988. The largest firm, Bertelsmann, has a market share of 16.1%. The academic journals industry has two strong players, Reed Elsevier and Wolters Kluwer, but here, too, there are many other small participants. The HHI tripled from 110 to 347. However, this understates reality since there are many specialized segments in which concentration is much higher. In contrast, educational books show a high degree of concentration, after a series of acquisitions by Pearson, Reed Elsevier, Scholastic, and McGraw-Hill.

Newspaper concentration is low on the national level. A similar trend is observable for magazines. But newspapers are highly concentrated locally, as discussed in Chapter 15.

The weighted average concentration trend line for the print publishing industry is shown in figure 13.7. With daily newspapers and magazines representing the bulk of this sector, their HHI values weight is heaviest. Average concentration remains well below the DOJ threshold of moderate

Table 13.12 Film Industries: Revenues ($ Million)

	1984	1988	1992	1996	2001	2005
Film Production/Distribution	4,031	4,458	4,871	5,912	8,413	9,406
TV PrimeTime Production	2,236	3,122	4,358	6,083	6,430	6,776
Movie Theater Chains	3,116	4,460	4,870	5,910	8,410	9,530
Home Video	1,014	2,773	4,616	6,530	8,146	18,515
Video Rental	2,900	5,460	7,260	7,710	9,551	8,200
Total U.S. Revenue	13,297	20,273	25,975	3,2145	40,950	52,427

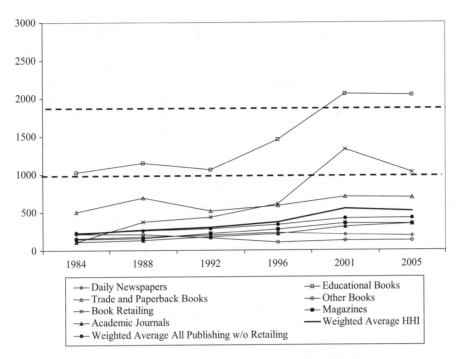

Figure 13.7 Print and Publishing Sector Industries: Concentration Trends

Table 13.13 Print and Publishing HHI Concentration

HHI	1984	1988	1992	1996	2001	2005
Daily Newspapers	155	176	200	230	208	191
Educational Books	1,024	1,148	1,061	1,458	2,061	2,046
Trade and Paperback	505	692	518	588	704	693
Other Books	214	208	164	104	127	127
Retailing Books	109	376	438	612	1,330	1,025
Magazines	146	157	220	276	355	347
Academic Journals	110	132	179	215	312	347
Weighted Average HHI	217	270	303	371	547	512
Weighted Average C4	24.4	26.6	28.6	30.9	36.7	35.2
Print Publishing Weighted Average HHI (All Print w/o Retailing)	229	259	286	337	420	424

Table 13.14 Print Publishing Revenues ($ Million)

	1984	1988	1992	1996	2001	2005
Daily Newspapers	25,170	32,280	30,639	38,075	44,300	46,700
Educational Books	2,469	3,034	4,165	5,373	7,652	8,820
Trade and Paperback	3,217	4,043	5,914	7,159	8,657	9,044
Other Books	3,903	4,490	5,664	7,697	9,787	9,787
Retailing Books	5,163	5,900	8,433	11,767	17,239	19,412
Magazines	8,191	11,681	14,284	21,498	29,479	31,611
Academic Journals	2,247	2,782	3,317	5,237	6,506	7,368
Total U.S. Revenue	50,360	64,210	72,416	96,806	123,620	132,743

concentration, doubling from 217 in 1984 to 512 in 2005, although still a low number.

This increase in concentration is partly the result of the increase in consolidation and revenue growth in educational books and academic journals. But even more, it is driven by the increase in retailing concentration in traditional and online book retailing. The book distribution channels are consolidating more than the any other part of the print publishing industry. If one excludes these retail channels, the concentration in the print and publishing sector is lower, although still doubling, rising from 229 in 1984 to 424 in 2005.

In the music sector, concentration has increased slightly, except for performance rights. Music cable channels show a steep increase. The remainder of the industries show a more stable and intermediate trend line. Record labels/distributors, music publishing, and music retailers all steadily increased in concentration during the period but are not at high levels in DOJ terms (figure 13.8, table 13.15).

Music publishing is a fairly unconcentrated industry whose concentration peaked in 1996. The performance rights industry has historically known only three serious participants, and the decrease of the HHI for this industry is the result

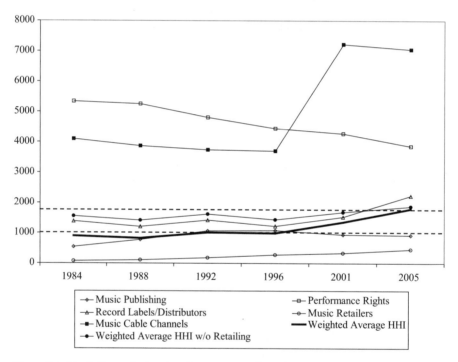

Figure 13.8 Music Sector Industries: Concentration Trends

Table 13.15 Music Industry HHI Concentration

HHI	1984	1988	1992	1996	2001	2005
Music Publishing	541	778	1,066	1,081	941	920
Performance Rights	5,340	5,256	4,810	4,445	4,273	3,855
Record Labels/Distributors	1,389	1,203	1,420	1,221	1,525	2,224
Music Retailers	74	106	183	278	339	456
Music Cable Channels	4,096	3,864	3,737	3,700	7,225	7,054
Weighted Average HHI	899	823	1,012	988	1,352	1,790
Weighted Average C4	42.9	42.1	47.7	48.0	56.6	61.5
Music Industry Weighted Average HHI without retailing	1,554	1,411	1,619	1,437	1,662	1,871

of a reshuffling of the market shares among those firms. The key music industry is record labels/distribution, which has been controlled by four to five firms with fairly similar market shares. This resulted in moderate but not high HHI numbers in DOJ terms. In 2004, after several attempts by EMI to merge, the consolidation of Sony's and Bertelsmann's music production and distribution raised concentration substantially. In addition, both EMI and Warner Music (which had been sold off by Time Warner) were seeking to buy each other. The trend line for this industry shows a steady increase after 1996, approaching the DOJ's high concentration range.

Music retailing increased steadily in concentration. However, it is still low, with an HHI of 447. The smallest industry in the music sector (table 13.16),

music cable channels, shows by far the highest concentration levels, because of Viacom's dominance.

From 1984 to 1996 the weighted average concentration of the music industry stayed fairly stable, hovering below the threshold for moderate concentration. After 1996, this was followed by a significant rise. If we omit the music retailing industries—retail stores/online and cable channels—from the averaging, the HHI increases from 1,554 in 1984 to 1,871 in 2004, reaching a high level of concentration by DOJ standards.

We can now aggregate the results of all 27 mass media industries into an overall trend for the entire mass media sector (figure 13.9, table 13.17) and compare the trends of different mass media categories such as print and music.

Table 13.16 Music Industries Revenues ($ Million)

	1984	1988	1992	1996	2001	2005
Music Publishing	523	641	1,007	1,462	1,939	1,314
Performance Rights	319	414	640	921	1,301	1,537
Record Labels/Distributors	4,109	5,697	7,468	10,425	12,389	11,449
Music Retailers	4,370	6,435	7,941	10,758	12,389	11,053
Music Cable Channels	113	211	388	698	1,260	1,470
Total U.S. Rev.	9,435	13,397	17,443	24,264	29,278	26,823

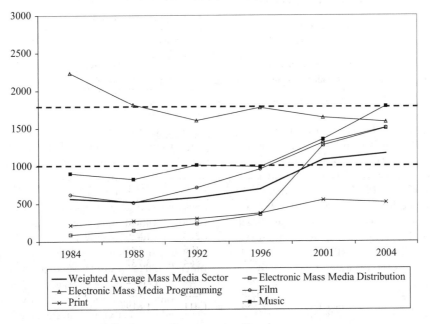

Figure 13.9 Mass Media Sectors: Concentration Trends

Table 13.17 Mass Media Sectoral and Overall Concentration (HHI)

Mass Media Sector (HHI)	1984	1988	1992	1996	2001	2005
Mass Media Electronic Distribution	91	147	237	354	1,274	1,499
MM Electr Prog	2,233	1,811	1,601	1,771	1,639	1,633
Film	620	513	712	958	1,306	1,581
Print	217	270	303	370	547	512
Music	899	823	1,012	988	1,352	1,790
Weighted Average HHI	564	520	580	693	1,084	1,209
Weighted Average C4	32.2	32.8	36.1	40.2	50.4	52.9

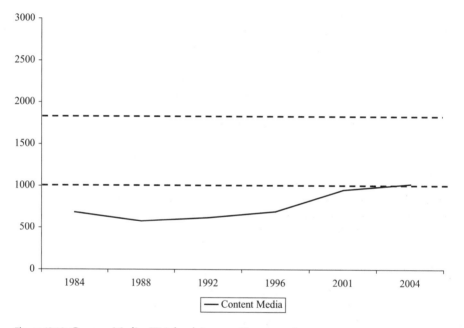

Figure 13.10 Content Media: Weighted Average Concentration

The average trend line in figure 13.16 indicates that until 1996, the weighted average concentration in the mass media sector industries had been low by DOJ antitrust standards. It was basically stable from 1984 to 1992. It even declined slightly during that period. However, after 1992, concentration of the mass media sector accelerated and rose to 1,202 by 2004. The primary spurt was between 1996 and 2001. Overall concentration is still in the moderate range by DOJ standards.

Although many industries contribute to the overall trend, this aggregate growth trend in concentration of the mass media sector is driven primarily by concentration increases for TV stations and cable TV operators, which exhibit both rising concentration and large size.

We can also report concentration trends in somewhat different ways. First, we can aggregate just the "content media industries," leaving out retailing but also including video games and software (which are discussed further below, under IT). The result of this aggregation, figure 13.10, shows that the average concentration for these content industries has slightly but steadily increased but is at an unconcentrated level.

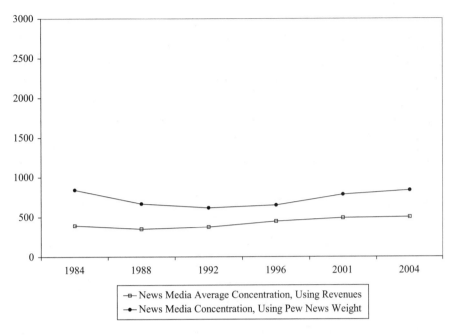

Figure 13.11 News Media: Average Concentration

A second way to aggregate media industries is to group together the set of "news media" and exclude pure entertainment media. Here, we skate on methodologically thin ice and provide at this time no more than a brief suggestion to respond to a frequently raised question. News media here include newspapers, magazines, TV networks and stations, cable networks, and radio networks and stations. We first use their relative revenues as the weight. If we proceed in that fashion, averaging and weighting these media, we find a low concentration and a flat trend, not indicating a rise in concentration (figure 13.11, the lower line).

On the other hand, the news component of these news media differs considerably. TV, radio, and cable channels are to a substantial extent entertainment media, with news a modest component. Therefore, we also use a somewhat different weighing scheme, according to a medium's importance as a news vehicle. How can one determine this importance? One way is to look at the users' news-gathering activities. To do so, we use the news weight of media, according to periodic surveys conducted by the Pew Research Center and the Project of Excellence in Journalism on news

habits of Americans.[1] The results, using these weights in the averaging of the news media, are also shown in figure 13.11. They, too, do not indicate high or rapidly rising concentration in news media. This analysis requires additional work to be more definitive.

Finally, we also pool all mass media industries—electronic, print, film, music—and determine the various companies' overall shares in the total mass media industry. (This is developed and discussed in chapter 14.)

Telecommunications

Figure 13.12 shows the concentration trends in telecommunication services. We include calculations up to the year 2006, when SBC absorbed AT&T and Bell South, and Verizon acquired MCI. The 1984 breakup of AT&T transformed the telecommunications services industry from a virtual nation-wide monopoly to a set of medium-large companies which were at times rivals to each other, such as in mobile telephony. This trend reversed itself in the mid-1990s (see also table 13.18).

This development applied to the subindustries of telecommunications. Cellular (mobile) carriers

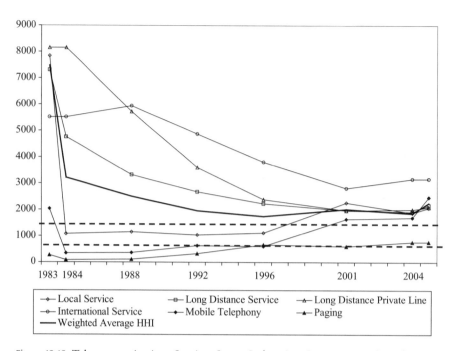

Figure 13.12 Telecommunications Services Sector Industries: Concentration Trends

Table 13.18 Telecommunications Service Concentration (HHI)

HHI	1983	1984	1988	1992	1996	2001	2004	2005	2006
Local Service	7,841	1,080	1,155	1,038	1,119	2,262	1,867	2,062	2,850
Long Distance Service	7,311	4,760	3,322	2,675	2,226	1,967	1,917	2,172	2,218
Long Distance Private Line	8,146	8,146	5,722	3,597	2,385	1,971	2,008	2,097	2,140
International Service	5,518	5,518	5,047	4,877	3,802	2,815	3,166	3,166	3,166
Mobile Telephony	2,035	341	362	627	602	1,642	1,697	2,469	2,469
Paging	273	84	108	324	665	606	3,791	3,791	3,791
Weighted Average HHI	7,475	3,216	2,475	1,955	1,745	2,027	1,877	2,269	2,528
Weighted Average C4	94.2	69.4	65.9	62.4	63.5	78.5	75.8	81.8	83.3

Notes: The source is chapter 11 of this book. 2005 and 2006 data incorporate only mergers (SBC/AT&T; Verizon/MCI, AT&T/BellSouth), and spin-offs (Sprint/Embarq).

experienced the biggest growth in size and concentration after 1996, shifting from a regionalized and nationally unconcentrated industry that was a result of the licensing system to consolidated national footprints. The paging industry also saw its overall concentration quadruple, although its overall size collapsed as cell phones became ubiquitous.

Likewise, an increase in national concentration took place in the local services as several of the Baby Bells merged with each other and their competitors. SBC tripled its market after 1996, and Verizon served almost a third of the U.S. by 2006. (table 13.19).

These telecom service industries are averaged into one trend line, shown in figure 13.12 in bold. The aggregate concentration drops steeply in 1984 due to the AT&T divestiture, followed by a period of declining concentration until

Table 13.19 Telecom Services Revenue ($ Million)

	1983	1984	1988	1992	1996	2001	2004	2005	2006
Local	49,243	50,871	58,066	72,120	80,453	99,300	98,504	98,504	98,504
Long Distance	48,767	51,200	62,250	71,900	93,300	99,301	83,697	83,697	83,697
Long Distance Private Line	5,743	5,743	6,889	7,543	10,665	16,402	16,618	16,618	16,618
International	2,610	2,610	3,431	7,477	16,262	12,810	9,178	9,178	9,178
Mobile	200	340	1,959	12,253	26,415	61,051	102,121	108,535	108,535
Paging	1,065	1,200	1,332	2,261	4,410	2,197	1,050	1,050	1,050
Total U.S.	107,628	111,964	133,927	173,553	231,505	291,061	311,168	317,582	317,582

Note: 2005 and 2006 data incorporate only mergers (SBC/AT&T; Verizon/MCI, AT&T/BellSouth), and spin-offs (2006 Sprint/Embarq).

1996 to an average HHI of 1,745. It then rose again in steps to 2,528 by 2006. The drivers of the aggregate concentration trend were primarily the mergers in the local services (nationally) and mobile services industries, which make up the bulk of the revenue (table 13.19). Mobile service, having become the largest segment of the telecom sector, is pulling down average industry concentration, since even after its consolidation it is still less concentrated nationally than local service is nationally.

Concentration of local services is actually higher on the local level, which is the more meaningful market measure for users. This is discussed and analyzed in Chapter 15. That concentration, while high, has been declining due to the emergence, in particular, of mobile and cable telephony as viable options.

Telecom companies tend to be active in several subindustries, and increasingly so. Table 13.20 incorporates all telecom services in one big "pooled" market and shows overall market shares. The development is depicted in figure 13.13. Here, too, can we observe a strong U-trend. After 1984 and the AT&T Divestiture, the pooled industry concentration dropped steadily until 1996, almost reaching an unconcentrated level. Thereafter, concentration rose again pronouncedly until 2005 with an HHI level of almost 2,100, into the DOJ's range of high concentration.

For customer telecom equipment, all five major segments have had a stable but high level of concentration since 1996 (figure 13.14, table 13.22).

Telecommunications customer equipment (consumer and business) is moderately concentrated, with a flat trend around HHI = 1700. In contrast, telecommunication network equipment industries are highly concentrated, as can be seen in figure 13.15 and table 13.23. AT&T saw its market share halved between 1983 and 1988, and Nortel gained tremendously. In 2006, Siemens partnered with Nokia and Lucent with Alcatel, and control shifted to the new partners. The average concentration of all industries in the telecom networking equipment sector stabilized after 1992 at a high level of about 2,500. Most of these industries remained heavily concentrated.

We can now aggregate concentration for the entire telecom sector (figure 13.16, table 13.24). Telecom services show a trend line similar to that of telecom equipment. The overall trend shows a U-shape, dropping radically from 1983 to 1984 as a result of the AT&T divestiture. After the divestiture, concentration kept dropping with liberalization and deregulation, but rose again after 1996 with the mergers among the Baby Bells and the consolidations in the cellular industry. In 2006 the HHI stood at a high 2,475. This sector has become highly concentrated again, after briefly flirting with entering (almost) moderate concentration, around 1996.

Table 13.20 Pooled Telecommunications Services ($ Million)

	1983	1984	1988	1992	1996	2001	2005	2006
SBC Communication (AT&T)		6,027	7,143	8,664	12,524	43,068	96,999	96,999
Ameritech		8,168	8,623	10,211	11,956	SBC		
PacTel		1,792	2,148	2,157	1,213	SBC		
SNET	640	664	772	1,060	1,310	SBC		
AT&T	85,300	42,059	42,773	44,572	52,800	50,968	SBC	
AT&T Wireless (McCaw)		27	72	1,384	3,020	8,547	Cingular	
AT&T CallVantage						53	SBC	
AT&T Broadband						590	SBC	
Vanguard/Cellular One					101			
BellSouth		9,031	10,453	12,674	28,589	20,576	37,691	37,691
Cingular (Bell S. 40%, SBC 60%)[a]						*(12,119)*	*(38,204)*	*(38,204)*
Verizon[b]						57,416	86,832	86,832
VoiceWing(Verizon)						Verizon	*(10)*	*(10)*
Air Touch (Pac Tel)		24	139	1,262	2,906	Verizon		
Bell Atlantic		8,988	8,878	11,449	14,226	Bell Atlantic		
NYNEX		6,898	10,321	11,488	11,485	Bell Atlantic		
Metro Mobile	4	12	63	319	660	Verizon		
GTE (incl Contel)	4,005	4,152	6,631	9,983	12,999			
GTE Mobilenet/Contel	14	23	143	1,078	2,377			
MCI Worldcom (MFS)	2,074	2,157	5,971	12,355	23,363	29,720	Verizon	
RCA Globecom	177	177	130	MCI				
Western Union International	54	54	153	MCI				
Metromedia		215	MCI					
ITT	168	168	78	3				
Comsystems		97	174	LDDS	LDDS			
Alltel[b]	3	5	500	753	931			
Qwest			93	324	1,363	3,968	7,252	7,252
LCI			219	760	3,070	12,854	11,610	11,616
U.S. West		6,111	7,350	8,340	9,072	Qwest		
U.S. West New Vector		19	80	478	Airtouch	Qwest		
Citizens Telecom/Frontier[b]				58	161	1,291	4,236	4,236
Global Crossing				324	1,586	2,515	1,745	1,745
Frontier (Rochester)			149	421	2,014	Global Crossing		

Broadwing						Broadwing		
Cincinnati Bell	345	509	377	433	563	730	896	896
Embarq								4,236
Sprint (incl Contel and United)	1,191	1,242	3,962	8,053	13,750	21,367	34,955	30,754
Contel	(2)	(3)	(20)	(564)	(1,321)			
Sprint PCS			88	429	Sprint	(6,838)	(20,513)	(20,513)
Nextel				380	1,030	4,701	Sprint	
United Telephone		1,017	1,394	1,731	Sprint			
McLeodUSA						1,390	1,675	1,675
Electric Lightware						99	136	136
Commonwealth Tel					80			
Alascom	4	352	344	418				
Level 3						11	1,347	1,347
WillTel			324			199	Level 3	
XO						298	335	
Allegiance						298	XO	
ICG						397	84	84
FTC Communications	21	21	27					
TRT Telecom	64	64	72	66				
US Liberia	0	0	0					
IXC						172	6,404	6,404
T-Mobile						3,602		
Voicestream					53	T-Mobile		
Century	2	4	20	49	79	427	760	760
US Cellular(TDS)				110	264	2,015	3,582	3,582
USA Mobility (prev. Arch Wireless)				27	322	363	624	624
Cablevisions Systems					71	246	1,608	1,608
Skype (eBay)							169	169
Vonage						79	120	120
Primus (Lingo)							20	20
Packet8							16	16
VocalTec (DT)					3	26		

continued

Table 13.20 (Continued)

	1983	1984	1988	1992	1996	2001	2005	2006
NetSpeak					2			
VoxWare					2			
Net2Phone (Liberty Media)					3	53	7	7
Covad					29	133	286	286
Comcast					74	370	3,345	3,345
AOL Time Warner					172	748	1,974	1,974
Cox Communications					97	347	1,250	1,250
Adelphia Communications					19	149	650	650
HughesNET (prev. DIRECWAY)						67	223	223
WildBlue							1	1
Total U.S. Revenue ($ million)	94,066	100,077	119,665	151,811	214,386	269,849	306,925	306,631

Note: Data reflect mergers and spin-offs up to 2006.

[a] Ownership of Cingular is split between Bell South (40%) and SBC (60%). Cingular revenues have been proportionately allocated.

[b] Alltel was acquired by Verizon in 2009. Verizon sold off parts of its local wireline operations to Frontier and FairPoint in 2009 and 2008.

Table 13.21 Pooled Telecommunications Services (Market Shares by Revenues)

	1983	1984	1988	1992	1996	2001	2006
SBC Communication (AT&T)		6.0	6.0	5.7	5.8	16.0	31.6
Ameritech		8.2	7.2	6.7	5.6	SBC	
PacTel		1.8	1.8	1.4	0.6	SBC	
SNET	0.7	0.7	0.6	0.7	0.6	SBC	
AT&T	90.7	42.0	35.7	29.4	24.6	18.9	SBC
AT&T Wireless (McCaw)		0.0	0.1	0.9	1.4	3.2	Cingular
AT&T CallVantage						0.0	SBC
AT&T Broadband					0.0	0.2	SBC
Vanguard/Cellular One					0.0		
BellSouth		9.0	8.7	8.3	13.3	7.6	12.3
Cingular (Bell S. 40%, SBC 60%)[a]						(4.5)	(12.5)
Verizon[b]						21.3	28.3
VoiceWing(Verizon)						Verizon	0.003
Air Touch (Pac Tel)		0.0	0.1	0.8	1.4	Verizon	
Bell Atlantic		9.0	7.4	7.5	6.6	Bell Atlantic	
NYNEX		6.9	8.6	7.6	5.4	Bell Atlantic	
Metro Mobile		0.0	0.1	0.2	0.3	Verizon	
GTE (incl Contel)	4.3	4.1	5.5	6.6	6.1		
GTE Mobilenet/Contel	0.0	0.0	0.1	0.7	1.1		
MCI/Worldcom (MFS)	2.2	2.2	5.0	8.1	10.9	11.0	Verizon
RCA Globecom	0.2	0.2	0.1	MCI			
Western Union International	0.1	0.1	0.1	MCI			
Metromedia		0.2	0.1	MCI			
ITT	0.2	0.2	0.1	0.0	LDDS		
Comsystems		0.1	0.4	LDDS			
Alltel[b]			0.1	0.5	0.4	1.5	2.4
Qwest		0.0		0.2	0.6	4.8	3.8
LCI		0.0	0.2	0.5	1.4		
U.S. West		6.1	6.1	5.5	4.2		
U.S. West New Vector		0.0	0.1	0.3	Airtouch		
Citizens Telecom/Frontier[b]				0.0	0.1	0.5	1.4
Global Crossing				0.2	0.7	0.9	0.6
Frontier (Rochester)			0.1	0.3	0.9	0.0	0.0

continued

Table 13.21 (*Continued*)

	1983	1984	1988	1992	1996	2001	2006
Broadwing	0.4	0.5	0.3	0.3	0.3	0.3	0.3
Cincinnati Bell						Broadwing	
Embarq (out of Sprint)							1.4
Sprint (incl Contel and United)	1.3	1.2	3.3	5.3	6.4	7.9	10.0
Centel			0.1	0.3	Sprint		
Sprint PCS			0.0	0.4	0.6	2.5	6.7
Nextel				0.3	0.5	1.7	Sprint
United Telephone		1.0	1.2	1.1	Sprint		
McLeodUSA						0.5	0.5
Electric Lightware					0.0	0.0	0.0
Commonwealth Tel					0.0		
Alascom		0.4	0.3	0.3			
Level 3							0.4
WillTel			0.3			0.1	Level 3
XO						0.1	X0
Allegiance						0.1	
ICG						0.1	0.03
FTC Communications	0.02	0.02	0.02				
TRT Telecom	0.1	0.1	0.1	0.04			
IXC							
T-Mobile						0.1	2.1
Voicestream						1.3	T-Mobile
Century			0.02	0.03	0.02	0.2	0.2
U.S. Cellular(TDS)				0.1	0.04	0.7	1.2
USA Mobility (prev. Arch Wireless)				0.02	0.1	0.1	0.2
Skype (eBay)							0.05
Vonage						0.03	0.04
Primus (Lingo)							0.01

Packet8							0.01
VocalTec (DT)						0.01	
NetSpeak					0.0008		
VoxWare					0.0008		
Net2Phone (Liberty Media)					0.01	0.02	
Covad					0.03	0.05	0.1
Comcast					0.1	0.1	1.1
Time Warner					0.05	0.3	0.6
Cox Communications					0.01	0.1	0.4
Adelphia Communications					0.03	0.1	
Cablevision Systems						0.1	0.5
HughesNET (prev. DIRECWAY)						0.02	0.1
WildBlue		0.00					0.0004
Total U.S. Revenue ($ million)	94,066	100,077	119,665	151,811	214,386	269,849	306,631
C4	98.4	68.2	60.3	53.4	55.5	67.1	84.7
HHI	8,248	2,145	1,681	1,299	1,148	1,364	2,176

Note: Data reflect mergers and spin-offs up to 2006.

[a] Ownership of Cingular is split between Bell South (40%) and SBC (60%). Cingular revenues have been proportionately allocated.

[b] Alltel was acquired by Verizon in 2009. Verizon sold off parts of its local wireline operations to Frontier and FairPoint in 2009 and 2008.

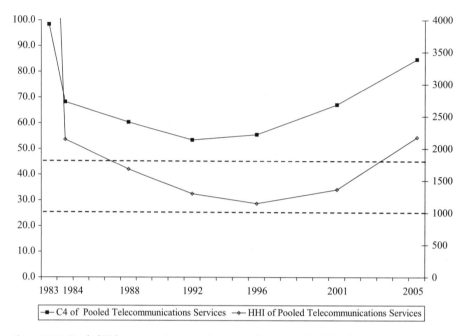

Figure 13.13 Pooled Telecommunications Services: Concentration Trend

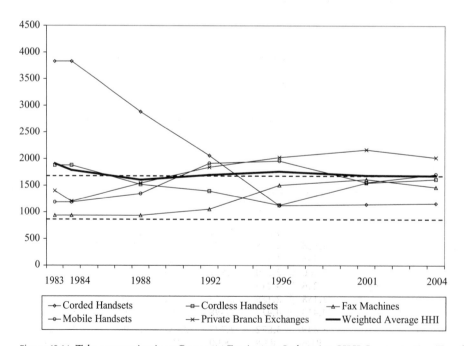

Figure 13.14 Telecommunications Customer Equipment Industries: HHI Concentration Trend

Table 13.22 Telecommunications Customer Equipment HHI Concentration

HHI	1983	1984	1988	1992	1996	2001	2004	2006
Corded Handsets	3,829	3,829	2,882	2,060	1,122	1,145	1,162	1,162
Cordless Handsets	1,879	1,879	1,517	1,396	1,130	1,552	1,618	1,618
Fax Machines	938	938	938	1,054	1,507	1,618	1,471	1,471
Mobile Handsets	1,186	1,186	1,345	1,914	1,960	1,558	1,712	1,712
Private Branch Exchanges	1,401	1,201	1,543	1,844	2,028	2,173	1,640	1,640
Weighted Average HHI	1,913	1,785	1,605	1,700	1,761	1,689	1,685	1,696
Weighted Average C4	68.0	67.7	69.6	72.4	74.7	72.0	75.1	76.8

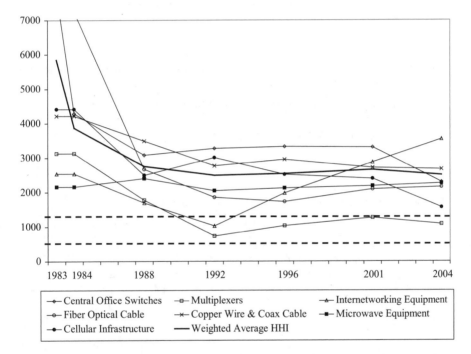

Figure 13.15 Telecommunications Networking Equipment Industries: HHI Concentration

Table 13.23 Telecommunications Networking Equipment (HHI Concentration)

HHI	1983	1984	1988	1992	1996	2001	2004	2006
Central Office Switches	7,846	4,287	3,079	3,273	3,329	3,308	3,168	2,298
Multiplexers	3,128	3,128	1,778	730	1,031	1,264	1,083	1,083
Internetworking Equipment	2,538	2,538	1,695	1,025	1,979	2,871	3,545	3,545
Fiber Optical Cable	7,260	7,260	2,671	1,855	1,729	2,089	2,156	2,156
Copper Wire and Coax Cable	4,216	4,216	3,491	2,369	2,526	2,320	2,284	2,284
Microwave Equipment	2,158	2,158	2,055	1,751	1,820	2,038	2,026	2,026
Cellular Infrastructure	4,413	4,413	2,498	3,006	2,515	2,395	1,563	1,563
Weighted Average HHI	5,849	3,872	2,727	2,452	2,502	2,614	2,441	2,441
Weighted Average C4	91.6	83.8	83.0	81.9	85.3	86.5	80.4	80.4

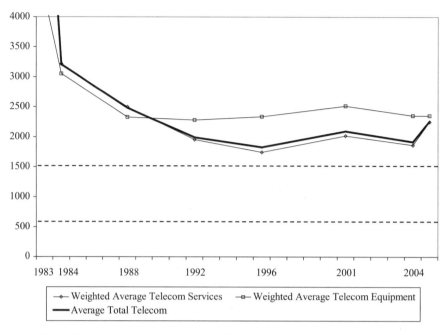

Figure 13.16 Telecom Industry Concentration (Average Services and Equipment)

Table 13.24 Telecom Sector Overall Concentration (Services and Equipment)

HHI	1983	1984	1988	1992	1996	2001	2004	2005
Weighted Average Telecom Services	7,475	3,216	2,475	1,955	1,745	2,027	1,877	2,269
Weighted Average Telecom Equipment	4,327	3,050	2,312	2,250	2,313	2,373	2,130	2,130
Weighted Average Total Telecom	7,247	3,204	2,459	1,989	1,824	2,083	1,912	2,251
Weighted Average C4	93.4	70.0	67.1	64.4	66.2	79.2	76.1	81.3

Information Technology

With digital convergence, traditional media are becoming IT-rich and IT-dependent. At the same time, the IT sector converges in its computer and consumer electronics devices and software and is becoming part of media. Nokia and Microsoft make game consoles. Consumer electronics giant Sony produces film and music. Google and Yahoo, basically software companies, are increasingly the gateway into the online content world. Film and music are uploaded from mainframes. Computer-like devices are in every pocket and become media terminals. As the media sector is moving into the direction of the Internet, and as the Internet is spawned, sustained, and guided by IT developments, then the traditional media world cannot be apart from the IT world.

Let us begin with consumer electronics (figure 13.17, table 13.25).

The Television Sets industry zigzags at fairly unconcentrated levels. Home Video Equipment shows a similar trend line at a higher level. TV Reception Equipment (DBS equipment and cable TV set top boxes) are highly concentrated, partly given the absence of a consumer market (the boxes are usually bought by the cable MSOs and DBS providers and rented out as part of regular or digital service).

The concentration trend line for Audio Equipment (CD Players, MP3 Players, and Audio Systems and

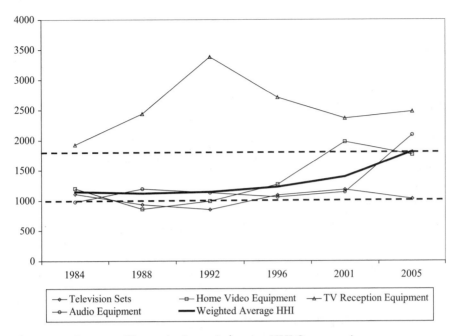

Figure 13.17 Consumer Electronics Sector Industries: HHI Concentration

Table 13.25 Major Segments of Consumer Electronics (HHI Concentration)

HHI	1984	1988	1992	1996	2001	2005
Television Sets	1,108	936	851	1,090	1,180	1,028
Home Video Devices	1,199	860	992	1,267	1,975	1,759
TV Reception Equipment	1,927	2,439	3,382	2,710	2,362	2,475
Audio Equipment	979	1,194	1,130	1,059	1,141	2,088
Weighted Average HHI	1,146	1,120	1,144	1,226	1,396	1,815
Weighted Average C4	55.1	56.7	54.0	57.1	58.9	60.3

Radios) is N-shaped and shows an increase. Sony holds leading positions in these industries.

Overall, the consumer media electronics sector has been only moderately concentrated, with a slight growth after 1996. The sector is competitive. However, several well-known consumer brands exist, such as Sony, Panasonic, and Samsung, and the combined average market shares of the top four firms is above 55%.

Semiconductors are the heart of IT developments. There are significant differences among the several semiconductor industries, as shown in figure 13.18. Microprocessors (CISC) have a very high concentration, dominated by Intel. The HHI for this industry increased steadily to well above

6,000 after 1996, one of the highest of all industries. Computer memory and microcontrollers have been fairly steady in their market concentration, with Samsung (24%), Micron (16%), and Hynix (12%) dominating the memory market. The weighted average concentration in the semiconductor sector rose significantly to a highly concentrated 3,407 in 1996 and 3,532 in 2005. The aggregate concentration trend for semiconductors is led by computer memory and CISC microprocessors. As the microprocessors grew in revenue, their influence on the overall trend increased even as their market concentration stabilized after 1996.

Most computer industries were highly concentrated in 2005. However, the trend lines follow

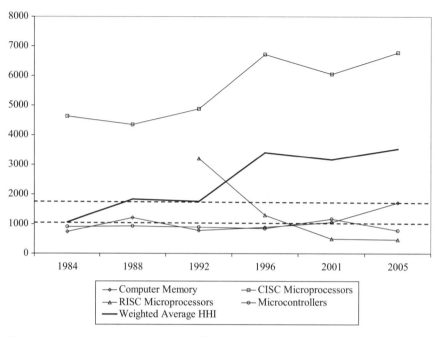

Figure 13.18 Computer Semiconductors: HHI Concentration

Table 13.26 Computer Semiconductors Concentration (HHI)

HHI	1984	1988	1992	1996	2001	2005
Computer Memory	735	1,212	775	885	1,055	1,716
CISC Microprocessors	4,632	4,350	4,881	6,716	6,053	6,778
RISC Microprocessors			3,207	1,299	495	468
Microcontrollers	904	928	893	841	1,168	773
Weighted Average HHI	1,063	1,834	1,760	3,407	3,167	3,532
Weighted Average C4	48.6	66.1	59.0	67.9	69.0	82.2

different patterns, as can be seen in figure 13.19 and table 13.27.

Microcomputers, far and away the largest IT hardware segment, were initially highly concentrated, but this changed as the industry grew and clones entered. Concentration bottomed out in 1992 with an HHI of 429. Subsequently, Dell, Compaq, and Hewlett-Packard increased significantly in market presence, with the latter two merging in 2002. Dell and Hewlett-Packard accounted for 50% of the market. Market concentration, having followed a U-shaped trend pattern, is in the moderate DOJ range.

A similar U-shaped trend characterizes the mainframe industry, too, though at a much higher level. IBM lost some market share in the late 1980s to "plug-compatibles" and other firms. By 2005, this industry, much diminished in size (table 13.28), became almost totally concentrated, with IBM holding 96% of the market, resulting in an HHI of 9,216.

The weighted average concentration trend line (bold in figure 13.19) is U-shaped. To a good extent this can be attributed to the weight of microcomputers, which represents two-thirds of the total revenue in this subsector. But several other computer industries show a similar pattern, and all but work stations rose in concentration after 1996.

Computer peripherals include, in particular, storage devices, printers, copiers, and modems

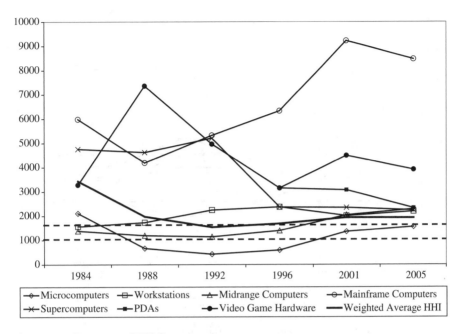

Figure 13.19 Computers: HHI Concentration

Table 13.27 Computers Industries' Concentration (HHI)

	1984	1988	1992	1996	2001	2005
Microcomputers	2,114	667	429	593	1,358	1,561
Workstations	1,567	1,738	2,249	2,373	2,010	2,193
Midrange Computers	1,381	1,195	1,143	1,396	2,044	2,289
Mainframe Computers	5,988	4,194	5,326	6,330	9,216	8,467
Supercomputers	4,762	4,628	5,212	2,368	2,348	2,241
PDAs				3,151	3,070	2,332
Video Game Hardware	3,281	7,367	4,967	3,149	4,494	3,911
Weighted Average HHI	3,436	1,983	1,544	1,688	1,937	1,929
Weighted Average C4	79.9	62.0	54.8	57.5	69.7	70.2

Table 13.28 Computer Industries' Revenues ($ Million)

	1984	1988	1992	1996	2001	2005
Microcomputers	11,940	17,147	30,842	38,875	63,237	73,834
Workstations	1,005	2,250	4,525	4,694	3,128	2,724
Midrange Computers	10,400	14,183	8,575	7,800	7,949	8,101
Mainframe Computers	15,105	12,875	7,200	8,250	3,375	2,348
Supercomputers	425	700	800	2,500	3,294	3,700
PDAs				390	1,480	1,846
Video Game Hardware	445	740	1,300	1,464	3,125	3,200
Total	39,320	47,895	53,242	64,972	85,588	95,752

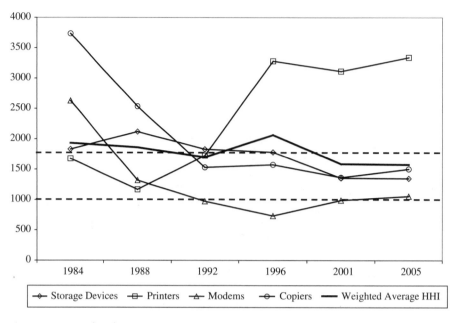

Figure 13.20 Peripheral Computer Equipment: HHI Concentration

Table 13.29 Computer Peripheral Equipment (HHI Concentration)

HHI	1984	1988	1992	1996	2001	2005
Storage Devices	1,831	2,118	1,830	1,780	1,355	2,333
Printers	1,676	1,166	1,725	3,280	3,112	3,623
Modems	2,629	1,319	973	734	989	1,056
Copiers	3,732	2,535	1,530	1,574	1,294	1,494
Weighted Average HHI	1,933	1,860	1,697	2,064	1,563	1,869
Weighted Average C4	66.6	65.1	63.9	72.4	63.4	66.9

(figure 13.20, table 13.29). The markets for storage devices and modems show a U-shaped concentration. For printers, concentration rose strongly after 1988, as Hewlett-Packard's market share grew from 5% in 1984 to 55% in 1996. Copiers, which became the largest segment, strongly declined in concentration in the 1980s, as Xerox's dominance ebbed, and stabilized at an intermediate level. The aggregated concentration for the peripheral industries shows an S-shaped trend at the low end of high concentration.

We can now take stock of the hardware subsector. The overall IT Hardware industry—comprising consumer media electronics, computers, peripherals, and semiconductors—shows a distinct U-shaped graph. After a sharp decline

from 1984 to 1992, average concentration increased again to a high HHI of 2,200 in 2005 (figure 13.21, table 13.30).

We now move to computer software. Of the various segments of the software subsector, the software for computer operating systems, network operation, and mainframes are highly concentrated (figure 13.22, table 13.31). Other software segments are much less concentrated, though specialized niches exist that are dominated by specialist firms.

The concentration of the microcomputer operating system software industry is well known. Microsoft dominated this industry with 92% market share. In the 1990s, Linux emerged, an operating system developed by a community of users and programmers. Its 2005 share was still small,

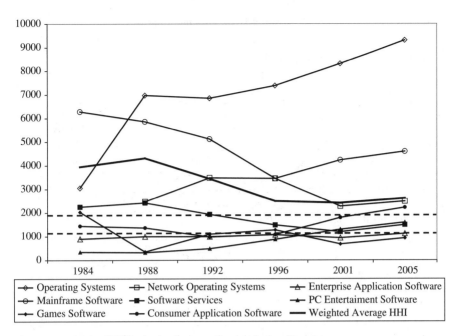

Figure 13.21 Major IT Hardware Sectors: Concentration Trends

Table 13.30 IT Hardware Industries (HHI Concentration)

	1984	1988	1992	1996	2001	2005
Semiconductors	1,063	1,834	1,760	3,407	3,094	4,092
Computers	3,436	1,983	1,544	1,688	1,937	1,929
Peripherals	1,933	1,860	1,697	2,064	1,563	1,869
Consumer Electronics	1,146	1,120	1,144	1,226	1,396	1,815
Weighted Average HHI	2,536	1,746	1,503	1,937	1,920	2,200

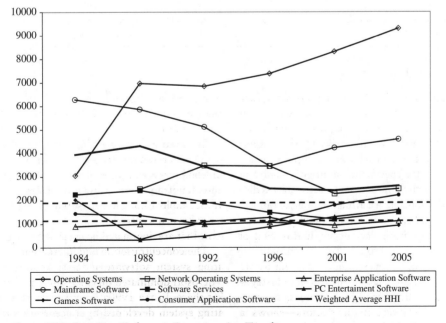

Figure 13.22 Computer Software: Concentration Trend

Table 13.31 IT Hardware Sectors' Revenues

IT Hardware	1984	1988	1992	1996	2001	2005
Semiconductors	4,015	7,526	12,679	23,395	22,798	26,719
Computers	39,320	47,895	53,242	64,972	85,588	95,752
Peripherals	7,005	13,109	20,136	29,566	31,440	33,589
Consumer Electronics	18,167	21,571	26,053	30,756	32,284	35,089
Total	77,255	108,298	139,634	216,147	258,096	272,695

Table 13.32 Computer Software Concentration (HHI)

	1984	1988	1992	1996	2001	2005
Operating Systems	3,056	6,973	6,851	7,379	8,309	9,304
Network Operating Systems		2,477	3,484	3,454	2,275	2,485
Enterprise Application Software	900	998	996	1,069	939	1,117
Mainframe Software	6,286	5,864	5,121	3,454	4,233	4,594
Software Services	2,254	2,423	1,933	1,484	1,194	1,487
PC Entertainment Software	346	323	487	877	1,298	1,592
Games Software	2,031	352	1,100	1,275	678	930
Consumer Application Software	1,443	1,367	981	1,082	1,796	2,220
Weighted Average HHI	3,951	4,313	3,443	2,494	2,415	2,612
Weighted Average C4	77.4	75.8	74.7	73.0	68.3	72.1

Table 13.33 Computer Software Revenues ($ Million)

	1984	1988	1992	1996	2001	2005
Operating Systems	1,068	1,562	1,810	2,670	6,500	6,698
Network Operating Systems	—	480	552	1,660	2,170	2,192
Enterprise Application Software	233	522	1,171	3,183	11,144	13,000
Mainframe Software	3,150	7,678	7,117	7,983	8,033	6,852
Software Services	931	2,008	3,827	9,014	18,960	22,361
PC Entertainment Software	137	179	507	748	1,282	1,082
Games Software	1,362	1,631	2,101	2,734	3,672	5,242
Consumer Application Software	400	844	1,245	2,923	8,400	9,332
Total	7,280	14,904	18,330	30,915	60,161	66,759

however, in contrast with its growing share in network operating system software.

Because of the specialized nature of mainframe software and the concentrated hardware market, this industry has historically known few competitors. Computer Associates and Compuware held a smaller position in the face of dominance by IBM (63% in 2005). This brought concentration down significantly, but it remains high.

In the very large industry of software services, concentration shifted from high to moderate levels as Oracle and SAP successfully entered the market. IBM lost about half of its share to 20%. The market concentration in this industry is moderate.

In video game software, Atari initially held a 75% market share but lost it when the industry crashed in 1984. Nintendo became market leader in the video game hardware industry and lost it to Sega and Electronic Arts. The market reached unconcentrated levels.

The consumer application software industry experienced several mergers that caused it to become concentrated. IBM acquired Lotus, but Microsoft was the only company that succeeded significantly—its market share expanded from 24% to 47%, raising concentration to 2,220 and resulting in a U-shaped trend (tables 13.32, 13.33).

The overall aggregation for the software industry is shown in the bolded trend line in figure 13.21. Concentration declined significantly after 1988 and stabilized after 1996 at a fairly high level around an HHI of 2,100.

We can now aggregate both the hardware and the software parts of the IT sector (figure 13.23).

The overall information technology sector shows a U-shaped trend line, too. After an initial decline, concentration increased again after 1992 to a level that is in the low end of the high range but still below that of 1984 (tables 13.34, 13.35).

The decline of IBM in many of the IT segments outside of mainframe computers reduced overall concentration initially. After 1992, the growth of Dell, the failure of many small entrants, the mergers of HP, Compaq, and DEC, and other stock

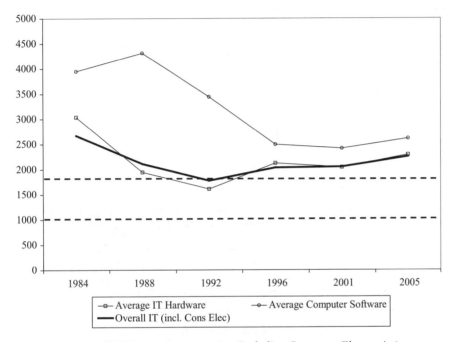

Figure 13.23 Overall IT Sector Concentration (Including Consumer Electronics)

Table 13.34 Concentration of the Major IT Sector

	1984	1988	1992	1996	2001	2005
IT Hardware	3,038	1,943	1,611	2,123	2,042	2,287
Consumer Electronics	1,146	1,120	1,144	1,226	1,396	1,815
Software	3,951	4,313	3,443	2,494	2,415	2,612
Weighted Average HHI	2,672	2,110	1,775	1,881	2,053	2,047

Table 13.35 Revenues of Major IT Sectors (Including Consumer Electronics)

	1984	1988	1992	1996	2001	2005
Aggregate IT Hardware	50,340	68,530	86,057	117,933	139,826	156,060
Consumer Electronics	18,167	21,571	26,053	30,756	32,284	33,063
Computer Software Aggregate	7,280	14,904	18,330	30,915	60,161	66,759
Total IT Sector	75,787	105,005	130,440	179,604	232,271	255,882

market–fueled deals drove concentration up again. Overall, the IT sector is highly concentrated by DOJ standards.

The Internet Sector

Industries associated with the Internet have grown considerably in size. These industries can either be considered part of the traditional sectors—mass media, telecom, and IT—or treated separately. We have chosen to do the latter.

The core Internet sector comprises eight industries that provide the basic instrumentalities for online users. Their concentration trends are shown in figure 13.24 (see also tables 13.36, 13.37).

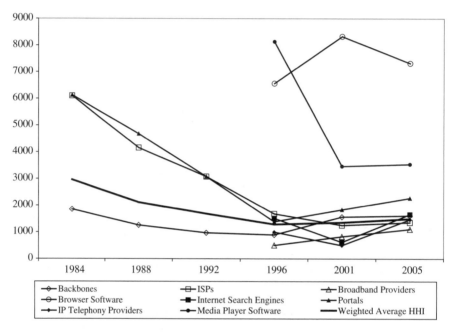

Figure 13.24 Cybermedia Industries Concentration (HHI)

Table 13.36 Internet Industries Concentration (HHI)

	1984	1988	1992	1996	2001	2005
Backbones	1,454	1,259	970	896	1,565	1,610
ISPs	6,102	4,155	3,078	1,683	1,251	1,356
Broadband Providers				502	828	1,163
Browser Software				9,025	8,330	7,325
Internet Search Engines				1,515	619	2,967
Portals	6,126	4,680	3,078	1,386	1,839	2,272
IP Telephony Providers				1,000	500	1,466
Media Player Software				8,131	3,462	3,538
Weighted Average HHI	2,959	2,114	1,685	1,287	1,357	1,494
Weighted Average C4	77.4	72.4	67.5	57.9	56.8	66.2

Table 13.37 Internet Industries Revenues ($ Million)

	1984	1988	1992	1996	2001	2005
Backbones	300	1,300	1,700	2,400	10,500	13,762
ISPs	47	359	672	3,072	23,064	16,896
Broadband Providers				1,162	4,762	15,930
Browser Software				92	300	275
Internet Search Engines				193	1,000	2,047
Portals	96	148	200	336	2,791	6,200
IP Telephony Providers				17	263	1,240
Media Player Software				11	153	108
Total	443	1,807	2,572	7,283	42,833	56,459

ISPs, Portals, search engines, and backbones show U-shaped concentration trends. ISPs, although initially highly concentrated, drop to moderate levels in 1996 and then rise again, with AOL becoming the market leader. In 2005, AOL held a declining share of 33% of the ISP market. For portals, three companies, Time Warner (AOL), Yahoo, and MSN (Microsoft), had a combined share of almost 82% in 2005.

For broadband providers, the market is split between cable and DSL, and concentration is moderate nationally (though essentially duopolistic locally). Internet backbones show a different trend. After a decrease of the HHI to an unconcentrated level in 1996, the subsector rose to 1,610 in 2004, the result of a string of acquisitions by WorldCom in the late 1990s.

The aggregate trend line for the Internet industries is U-shaped, too. After declining to a low of 1,287 in 1996, the trend line rises, reaching a moderately concentrated HHI of 1,494 in 2004.

HIGH- AND LOW-CONCENTRATION INDUSTRIES

We can identify which industries have been particularly pronounced in their growth and decline of concentration in the two-decade period of 1984 to 2005. This is provided in the next two tables. Table 13.38 shows the concentrating industries in descending order of their 20-year C4 concentration gain. We use the gain in C4 concentration to calculate the extent of change, since using the HHI with its exponent nature would distort comparisons of growth percentages. At the top of concentration are video rental (a 64.8% gain in share for the top four companies, as the industry changed from mom-and-pop to a national chain structure) and cable TV operators (whose national C4 gain was large, 47.4%, and which is also locally highly concentrated). Other high-gain industries are mobile telephony (46.4%), PC entertainment software (45%), pay-TV (35.1%), radio stations (29.6%), and local phone service (22.8%). Additional important mass media industries with high concentration gain are prime-time TV production (25.4%), educational books (23.1%), movie theater chains (14.3%), TV stations (13.2% but low in absolute terms), magazines (9.7%), academic journals (8.4%), and trade and paperback books (8.4%).

And what are the industries with low or negative growth of concentration? Table 13.39 shows that of 85 industries analyzed that existed both in 1984 and 2005, 23 industries have deconcentrated over the 20-year-period, and 22 in the period 1996–2005. The largest meaningful decreases were for Fiber Optical Cables, (–47%) in the technology field (though rising after 1996) and ISPs (mostly in the 1990s due to the emergence of commercial entrants). Of mass media industries, reductions in concentration over the 20-year period were in TV networks (–11%) and cable TV channels (–4.3%, and before 1996). This is not a long list.

Table 13.38 Industries with Growing Concentration (C4)

Industry	1984	1996	2005	Gain of Top 4 Firms (1984–2005)	Gain of Top 4 Firms (1996–2005)
Video Rental	0.2	32.0	64.8	64.6	32.8
Cable TV Operators	20.7	43.5	68.1	47.4	24.6
Mobile Telephony	27.9	41.0	74.3	46.4	33.3
PC Entertainment Software	31.0	53.5	76.0	45.0	22.5
Pay TV Channels	36.9	53.0	72.0	35.1	19.0
Camcorders	60.4	83.4	93.9	33.5	10.5
Computer Memory	44.1	49.6	76.2	32.1	26.6
Radio Stations	8.3	13.6	38.0	29.6	24.4
Syndication	33.3	61.1	61.2	27.9	0.1
TV PrimeTime Production	37.0	55.0	62.4	25.4	7.4
Music Retailing	15.4	26.7	38.8	23.4	12.1
Educational Books	57.8	69.6	80.9	23.1	11.3
Midrange Computers	61.9	67.1	84.9	23.0	17.8
Local Service	55.0	52.9	77.8	22.8	24.9
Paging	16.1	43.8	36.6	20.5	−7.2
Printers	70.0	78.8	90.3	20.3	11.5
Video Game Hardware	81.0	98.6	99.9	18.9	1.3
DBS Equipment	65.0	80.8	83.6	18.6	2.8
Copper Wire & Coax Cable	82.1	100.0	100.0	17.9	0.0
Enterprise Application Software	41.8	52.0	59.2	17.4	7.2
Retailing Books	18.5	44.1	35.2	16.7	−8.9
Home Video	52.8	69.0	69.0	16.2	0.0
Supercomputers	70.0	80.0	86.0	16.0	6.0
Mainframe Software	84.2	84.0	100.0	15.8	16.0
Radio Networks	39.5	60.8	55.1	15.6	−5.7
Fax Machines	56.2	72.0	71.3	15.1	−0.7
Hard Discs	63.4	78.7	78.5	15.1	−0.2
Workstations	75.9	87.0	90.4	14.5	3.4
Movie Theater Chains	24.5	26.8	38.7	14.3	11.9
Private Branch Exchanges	64.0	79.8	77.8	13.8	−2.0
TV Stations	14.5	18.2	27.7	13.2	9.5
Microwave Equipment	76.1	85.5	88.0	11.9	2.5
Magazine	21.0	26.3	30.7	9.7	4.4
Record Labels/Distributors	67.0	61.1	76.0	9.0	14.9
CISC Microprocessors	89.5	91.1	98.4	8.9	7.3
Mobile Handsets	65.0	77.9	73.8	8.8	−4.1
Music Publishing	64.9	85.4	73.6	8.7	−11.7
Academic Journals	18.0	26.3	26.4	8.4	0.1
Trade and Paperback	37.7	40.2	46.1	8.4	5.9
Cable TV Set Top Converters	79.0	93.0	85.0	6.0	−8.0
Internetworking Equipment	78.0	73.7	83.5	5.5	9.8
Mainframe Computers	90.7	99.5	95.0	4.3	−4.5
Daily Newspapers	21.7	25.6	24.2	2.5	−1.4
Operating Systems	97.7	99.2	100.0	2.3	0.8
Cordless Handsets	68.0	59.0	70.2	2.2	11.2
Movie Production/Distribution	60.7	62.0	62.8	2.1	0.8
Software Services	73.3	71.6	73.8	0.5	2.2
Audio Systems & Radios	44.6	48.4	44.7	0.1	−3.7
Media Player Software		97.5	100.0		2.5
Broadband Providers		38.3	58.6		20.4
IP Telephony Providers		60.0	69.5		9.5
PDAs		88.0	93.4		5.4
Internet Search Engines		73.1	76.8		3.7
DBS Providers		95.3	98.0		2.7
PVR Players			92.0		92.0
MP3 Players			71.0		71.0

340

Table 13.39 Industries with Declining Concentration (C4)

Industry	1984	1996	2005	Loss of Top 4 Firms (1984–2005)	Loss of Top 4 Firms (1996–2005)
Performance Rights	100.0	100.0	100.0	0.0	0.0
Music Cable Channels	100.0	100.0	100.0	0.0	0.0
CD Players	70.0	61.2	67.8	−2.2	6.6
Television Sets	56.0	56.0	53.2	−2.8	−2.8
Microcontrollers	52.5	51.4	49.2	−3.3	−2.2
Central Office Switches	86.0	91.0	81.7	−4.3	−9.3
Cable TV Channels	66.4	61.7	62.1	−4.3	0.4
International Service	92.6	95.2	88.1	−4.5	−7.1
Long Distance Service	80.9	73.0	74.2	−6.7	1.2
Other Books	28.0	16.9	20.4	−7.6	3.5
Backbones	78.4	49.0	70.4	−8.0	21.4
Consumer Application Software	66.3	49.7	57.2	−9.1	7.5
TV Networks	100.0	92.2	88.8	−11.2	−3.4
VCR Players	62.1	40.0	48.9	−13.2	8.9
Portals	100.0	68.6	86.4	−13.6	17.8
Games Software	62.8	66.3	49.0	−13.8	−17.3
Copiers	76.1	68.2	60.4	−15.7	−7.8
Microcomputers	82.7	40.2	64.3	−18.3	24.1
Corded Handsets	85.0	65.3	66.6	−18.4	1.3
Multiplexers	78.9	53.4	58.3	−20.6	4.9
Modems	74.3	44.8	52.2	−22.1	7.4
Long Distance Private Line	97.3	75.8	73.9	−23.4	−1.9
Cellular Infrastructure	97.0	94.1	70.7	−26.3	−23.4
ISPs	100.0	68.8	60.3	−39.7	−8.5
Fiber Optical Cables	100.0	42.4	53.0	−47.0	10.7
Browser Software		100.0	94.6		−5.4
Network Operating Systems		86.0	74.7		−11.3
DVD Players		71.0	41.5		−29.5
RISC Microprocessor		57.5	37.8		−19.7

Notes

1. Averages use weight for each news industry as reported in *Online Newspaper Readership Countering Print Losses: A Survey Conducted in Association with the Project for Excellence in Journalism.* June 26, 2005. The Pew Research Center, Washington, D.C. The survey goes back to 1991. For 1988 and 1984, we extrapolated from 1991 and 1993 figures. The weight is based on surveyed responses to the question: "How have you been getting most of your news about national and international issues? From television, from newspapers, from radio, from magazines, or from the Internet?"

14

Vertical and Cross-Industry Concentration

THE ECONOMICS OF VERTICAL INTEGRATION

The Nature of Synergies

Mergers among content providers, distributors, retail outlets, and technology firms raise questions about vertical integration. The fear is the extension of market power from one industry to a related one. But even if a firm does not dominate any specific market, its presence in several markets interlinked along the chain of production and distribution might create an overpowering combination. Whatever one might think of remedies to a threat, the first question is whether empirical data show its existence, or of trends in that direction. This empirical question must be answered prior to any policy debate.

Firms integrate vertically for several reasons. Owning key inputs can help control costs and reduce the risk of disruption in production. Integration might also provide a way to hide the profits of regulated activities by shifting them into unregulated ones. Media and entertainment companies seek vertical integration as a way of ensuring market outlets and input supply. And this desire to expand vertically has been facilitated by relaxation of regulatory restrictions. Yet the economic logic behind vertical integration is not obvious. Why should Warner Bros. Television productions earmark its best TV shows for its

sister TV network CW if other networks offer more money, for example because their audience is larger? Conversely, should Warner Bros. force its weak shows on the CW television network? In a competitive environment, firms' divisions must cut the best deals. Warner Bros. sold its hit series "Friends" to NBC rather than to the CW. Thus, the different parts of a vertically integrated company subject to competition would act to a significant extent independently of each other.[1]

There may be efficiency gains, however, commonly referred to as synergies. These consist most directly of reductions in duplicative administrative functions. Synergies may promote economies of joint operation (scope). Transaction costs are reduced and coordination enhanced. For example, by coordinating effort, each division of a company could benefit from the promotional efforts of another division.

Synergies may also exist in the ability to create cross-business opportunities, that is, using one part of a business to promote or benefit from another. Synergies may also arise from cost savings on transactions such as the substitution of untaxed internal transactions for taxable transactions between separate firms, the reduction of transaction costs, and from the ability to assure constant supply of necessary inputs and constant consumption of outputs.

How real are synergies? They have often been asserted rather than proven. In announcing its 1996 megamerger with ABC, Disney CEO Michael

Eisner invoked the word, like a mantra, no less than five times in four consecutive sentences. Yet most of the purported cross-promotional benefits of such synergy for films, books, or toys, could be established by simple contracts rather than full-scale mergers. Nor are the efforts to create synergies new. In the 1970s, CBS bought the New York Yankees baseball team and the book publisher Simon & Schuster in pursuit of the supposed benefits from vertical integration with content providers. The results were disappointing. In the 1980s, Sony bought Columbia Pictures and Records in order to merge film and music with consumer electronics. A main reason was the desire to affect future technical standards in consumer media electronics and to avoid a repeat of the business defeat of its technically superior Betamax VCR standard. But the acquisition of content companies turned out to be a double-edged sword. In time, Sony's consumer electronics divisions were held back by its music division's fears of digital piracy. This slowed down introduction of MP3 players and opened an opportunity for Apple's iPod. Apple could also gain the cooperation of Sony's music rivals where Sony might not have. There are also other negative synergies to consider. For example Time Warner's music division released an inflammatory "cop-killer" rap music record which dragged down the respectability of its newsmagazines and also brought down the wrath of Washington politicians whose support was needed for various regulatory battles.

Vertical integration might increase operating costs by eliminating competition from external suppliers. Inefficiencies might also arise if economies of scale make the optimal size of one stage of the production chain exceed the optimal size of another stage. In that case, the optimally larger stage might be better spun off.[2]

In sprawling media conglomerates, different divisions of the same company will follow different objectives. To act with optimal efficiency in an open competitive environment, each segment of a company must be willing to buy, sell, or partner with businesses that offer the most profitable terms, even if those companies are in direct competition with the parent corporation. A vertical strategy would only work if a firm had market power in the production market that it could leverage into the distribution side by denying attractive programming to competing distributors. Some companies are likely to follow a "systems integration"

or "packager" approach, in which they do not own or operate the various activities of production and distribution. Rather, a packager selects optimal elements in terms of price and performance, bundles them together, manages these bundles, and offers them to the customer, often on a one-stop basis. In this model, actual ownership of the various elements is not required.

The economic literature of vertical integration is voluminous, and will be only touched lightly here. In standard equilibrium economic analysis, assuming that a firm has market power—that is, it can influence product price—the dominant firm may use its power to exact some degree of economic rents.[3] That is, it will sell at a price above the minimum it would take, which would be marginal cost. Furthermore, it could price discriminate both as a seller (toward consumers) and as a buyer (toward program providers). Thus, equilibrium would be the price at which most program producers could sell their product for more than the acceptable minimum. A vertically integrated distribution firm could therefore appropriate part or all of this rent to itself by purchasing from its own program subsidiaries. But this is not an instance of synergy efficiencies but rather of its market power in one of the stages of production.[4]

Where markets are truly competitive there are few benefits to vertical integration that could not be gained by contracts. Some synergies may exist but they may be offset by a loss of focus and specialization. Vertical integration makes sense for a firm if it has substantial market power in at least one critical market, and could then leverage such market power into other markets. First, by gaining a monopoly position in an input market, a firm could secure a dominant position in a downstream market by limiting the supply of the input to its competitors. Second, a firm could restrict access to an input unless favorable contract terms were offered for one of its "downstream" products. Third, vertical integration can result in cross-subsidization. This occurs either when a firm in a profit-regulated market absorbs some of the costs of its competitive downstream operations, giving it a competitive advantage downstream, or when it pays inflated prices to its own supplier upstream.

There is a vast literature on vertical integration.[5] Economists have mostly turned away from the notion of leverage and foreclosure. The exceptions are where inputs are provided in variable proportions, and where two or more monopolies follow each other in the vertical chain.[6] In other situations, the economic analysis sees no advantage and predicts an eventual devolution. One economic perspective on vertical integration is that where it exists, it reflects efficiencies such as synergies. Another view is that such integration is used for strategic foreclosure of rivals and is anticompetitive in nature.[7] In the media sector, for example, the integration of book publishing with film distributors and TV networks makes no long-term sense. The same goes for TV networks and media electronics devices.

EMPIRICAL MEASURES OF VERTICAL INTEGRATION

Given the controversies over vertical integration, it is important to look at vertical merger activity in the information industry in an empirical way. To what extent is the American information sector vertically integrated? And how much more now than 20 years ago?

It turns out that "vertical integration" is not easy to define in an operational sense and is even harder to measure. Suppose a telephone company also makes light bulbs, as GTE did when it owned the lightbulb manufacturer Sylvania. Since GTE's offices used plenty of light bulbs, and indeed could not conveniently function without them, the company could then be viewed as vertically integrated. But is this incidental vertical relationship meaningful? By comparison, consider GTE's concurrent ownership of telecom equipment manufacturing. Here, one could speak of a genuine vertical integration. A useful empirical measure of vertical integration would therefore have to consider the relative magnitude of the interaction.

The U.S. government's antitrust enforcement guidelines evaluate vertical mergers by a variety of factors.[8] Mergers between vertically related firms "raise concern" only if (1) the two markets are so interdependent that a new firm seeking to enter one market would have to enter the other simultaneously (either because one industry supplies an essential input for the other industry, or because one industry consumes almost the entire output of the other industry, thereby significantly raising entry barriers), and (2) one of the markets is highly concentrated (with an HHI greater than 1,800). That is, there would have to be a significant likelihood that a firm could leverage market power from one market to another. Both factors require judgment calls. This is especially true for condition (1), the relative proximity of the given markets.

How would one measure "proximity?" Ideally, one would begin by measuring the flow of inputs and outputs between each pair of subindustries, and also within each integrated firm's divisions. However, such data is rarely available.

In contrast to horizontal integration, where indices such as the HHI or the C4 readily exist, there are no similar government-sanctioned indices established for vertical integration. Part of the reason must be that no index for vertical integration has been found that is satisfactory.

One type of "vertical HHI" that has been proposed is VHHI $= \Sigma\ s_i \max (s_i, \sigma)$, where s_i is the market share of firm i in one market A and σ_i the market share of the firm in upstream market B. But this methodology focuses on downstream firms and their market concentration. It is not symmetrical for upstream or downstream markets. A simpler and more robust measure for a vertical HHI would be the following:

$$VHHI = W_A \sum s_{Ai}^2 + W_B \sum \sigma_{Bi}^2 + W_{AB} \sum (s_{ABi})^2:$$

s_{ABi} are the combined shares of each of the firms present in both markets.

The weights W are

$$W_A = \frac{a}{a+b}; W_B = \frac{b}{a+b}; W_{AB} = \frac{\alpha+\beta}{a+b}$$

α, β are the sizes of firms' activity in both industries where such cross-industry activity exists; a and b are the sizes of markets A and B.

This measure is the sum of each market's HHI concentration, each weighed by its relative size, plus the shares of firms active in both markets. For example, suppose there are two markets. Market A, of size \$10 billion, has five firms, each with an equal market share of 20%, for an HHI $= 2,000$. Market B is \$20 billion in size, has four firms with 25% each and an HHI of 2,500. Suppose one firm of industry A merges with a firm of industry B. Its size would then be \$7 billion.

The Vertical HHI would then be

$$VHHI = \frac{10}{30}\sum_1^5 20^2 + \frac{20}{30}\sum_1^4 25^2 + \frac{7}{30}(20+25)^2$$
$$= 2805$$

This index's magnitude should not be strictly compared to the regular HHI in its scale. A two-industry vertical relation with a VHHI of 2,305 is not necessarily less concentrated than a single-industry HHI of 3,000. Also, the weights add up to more than 1, for simplicity's sake. The limitation of this measure of vertical integration is that it is defined for two-industry pairs. Where there are dozens of industries, there are hundreds and even thousands of such pairs.

It is possible to calculate a global measure that incorporates all pairs. Computationally this is possible. Our data would go some way to support it. It would require, however, a computational effort for 10,000 industry pairs, as well as additional data, and would result in nontransparent findings. For now, we assume for greater simplicity that within the information sector all of the subindustries are, in principle, vertically related to each other, either as suppliers or as buyers or both, and build several vertical indicators. None of them is fully explanatory, but together they help identify trends.

Our analysis focuses on the largest 50 information industry firms, as well as the top 25 mass media companies, for the year 1984 and subsequent years. These firms are ranked according to their information sector revenue and are listed in table 14.1. All revenues are those in the United States, whether by American or non-American firms. Revenues by U.S. firms realized abroad are not included, nor are noninformation revenues, such as GE's jet engines or refrigerators.

In 1984, of the top 50 information sector companies, 12 were telecom firms, 14 IT firms, and 24 mass media companies. By 2005, the balance among the sectors had changed noticeably. Using a firms' primary activity as its identifier, among the top 50 firms were six telecommunications companies, including telecom equipment makers. There were 20 IT (and Internet) related firms, five consumer media electronics firms, and 23 mass media companies. Among these firms, telecommunications' share of the overall information industry declined from 39.6 to 19.4% and IT and Internet companies increased from 13.1 to 19.1%; mass media firms, however, increased from 9.1 to 20.3%. Telecom companies still occupy the top two ranks of information sector firms.

Of the top 50 information sector firms in 1984, an extraordinary 23 firms had ceased to exist by 2005: most by mergers and acquisitions and one by bankruptcy. Applying a more generous definition

to survival in a merger of equals, 19 firms of 1984's top 50 ceased to exist, still a remarkable fraction. Conversely, of the top 50 firms in 2005, 28 were not in the top 50 in 1984 or did not even exist. If we extend the analysis by one year to 1983, prior to the divesture of AT&T, that number rises to 33.

Table 14.2 shows the top 25 firms in a narrower sub-sectors, that of mass media. Only U.S. revenues are included, and only revenues derived from mass media activities. Thus, for that list Sony's non-U.S. income is not counted, nor is its U.S. consumer electronics business.

THE PARTICIPATION INDEX (PI)

The first measure for vertical integration is the participation of the major firms in many of the industries of the sectors.

We define a Participation Index (PI) of the top 50 information sector firms in the 100 industries of the information sector

$$PI_{100} = \left(\frac{1}{m}\right)\sum_i^m PI_i = \left(\frac{1}{50}\right)\sum_i^{50} \sum_i^{100} 0,1$$

where

i = firm (top 50 firms in terms of information revenues)
j = industries
n = number of industries
m = number of top firms

The PI tallies the number of subsectors in which each firm participates, without regard for market share or market size. For example, Viacom had a presence in seven of the 100 industries in 1984. The overall PI is the average PI score of each of the top 50 firms in the index. Table 14.3 shows the PI for the top 50 firms for the years 1984–2005.

Figure 14.1 shows the trend. The average participation increased from an average 5.3 to 7.4 industries over the period 1984–2005, falling slightly after 2001 (figure 14.1.) The median participation among the top 50 firms increased from 4 to 6.5. Thus, many of the 50 largest firms expanded into other industries during the period examined, but not dramatically so, into two to three new industries. A few firms, most prominently Microsoft (from 1 to 12), Sony (from 6 to 16) and Disney (from 4 to 10) expanded their

Table 14.1 Top 50 Companies of the U.S. Information Sector (U.S. Information Sector Revenues only, in $ Million)

	1984		1988		1992		1996		2001		2005	
	Company	Rev	Company	Rev	Company	Rev	Company	Rev	Company	Rev	Company	Rev
1	AT&T	60,318	AT&T	61,756	AT&T	64,904	AT&T	52,184	AT&T	62,776	SBC (AT&T)[b]	71,324
2	IBM	25,882	IBM	27,399	IBM	23,328	IBM	29,395	Verizon	52,050	Verizon	74,764
3	NYNEX	9,573	BellSouth	13,600	Bell South	12,498	MCI	20,976	SBC	45,908	Time Warner	39,269
4	BellSouth	9,519	NYNEX	10,496	Bell Atlantic	12,145	Time Warner	20,390	IBM	35,215	IBM	35,637
5	Ameritech	8,347	Bell Atlantic	9,051	GTE	11,821	GTE	15,187	AOLTime War	34,690	Sprint	31,632
6	Bell Atlantic	8,090	Ameritech	8,713	NYNEX	11,309	Ameritech	14,924	Worldcom	24,474	HP	29,362
7	Pacific Telesis	7,800	SBC	8,569	Time Warner	10,680	BellSouth	14,818	HP/Compaq	24,264	Microsoft	25,340
8	USWest	7,280	Pacific Telesis	7,800	Ameritech	10,667	Sprint	14,544	Sprint	23,612	Bell South	24,848
9	SBC	7,191	USWest	7,463	MCI	10,562	SBC	13,141	Viacom	21,718	Dell	22,386
10	GTE	7,000	GTE	7,260	Motorola	10,232	Bell Atlantic	13,081	BellSouth	21,119	Comcast	19,190
11	RCA	6,352	Motorola	7,017	SBC	9,845	NYNEX	11,501	Microsoft	20,958	Sony	18,342
12	Motorola	5,040	Xerox	6,866	USWest	9,134	Motorola	11,190	Sony	16,679	Disney	16,195
13	Xerox	3,692	Sprint	6,493	Pacific Telesis	9,108	USWest	11,168	Dell	13,288	Motorola	14,722
14	ABC	3,291	MCI	5,137	Sprint	9,026	HP	10,841	Disney	13,063	News Corp	13,992
15	Sprint	2,856	General Electric	4,261	Xerox	8,705	Xerox	10,426	Qwest	12,931	Viacom	11,623
16	CBS	2,715	Warner Comm	4,134	Sony	7,478	Compaq	10,122	Lucent	12,059	Qwest	11,541
17	Warner Comm	2,629	Unisys	4,053	HP	5,435	Disney	9,943	Motorola	12,002	General El.	9,340
18	NCR	2,546	CBS	3,894	CBS	5,173	Lucent	9,789	Xerox	10,487	CBS	8,905
19	Gannett	2,274	ABC	3,889	Matsushita	5,042	Pacific Telesis	9,455	News Corp	10,268	Intel	8,423
20	Burroughs	2,195	DEC	3,645	News Corp	4,694	Sony	9,323	Comcast	9,674	Lucent (Alcat.)	7,954
21	MCI	2,157	Sony	3,492	General Electric	4,219	Intel	8,688	Intel	9,382	Xerox	7,838
22	DEC	2,032	HP	3,078	ABC	4,157	Viacom	7,690	Vivendi	8,107	Oracle[b]	7,717
23	Time	1,962	Matsushita	3,062	Apple	3,878	CBS	7,026	Oracle	6,972	Gannett	7,381
24	HP	1,926	Gannett	2,999	Gannett	3,763	News Corp	6,838	General El.	6,423	Cox	6,598
25	Apple	1,908	NCR	2,953	Thomson	3,456	TCI	5,954	Hughes	6,180	Toshiba	6,295
26	Matsushita	1,881	Thomson	2,944	TCI	3,312	General Electric	5,946	Gannett	6,016	Cisco	5,843
27	Knight Ridder	1,664	Apple	2,670	Samsung	3,186	Worldcom	5,292	Cox	5,956	Tribune	5,783
28	Times-Mirror	1,551	Time	2,523	Viacom	3,154	Gannett	5,063	Cisco	5,443	Apple	4,858
29	Viacom	1,470	Viacom	2,505	Disney	3,074	Samsung	5,053	Toshiba	4,935	Bertelsmann	4,831
30	Tribune	1,422	MCA	2,401	Intel	3,018	Toshiba	4,903	Bertelsmann	4,728	Samsung	4,743
31	Sony	1,410	Knight Ridder	2,083	Unisys	2,862	Microsoft	4,877	Barnes&Noble	4,206	Vivendi	4,688
32	MCA	1,403	Times-Mirror	1,866	Toshiba	2,812	Thomson	4,300	Sun	3,864	Gateway	4,212

Rank	Company	Value	Company	Value	Company	Value	Company	Value	Company	Value	Company	Value
33	McGraw-Hill	1,097	News Corp	1,837	Dun&Bradstreet	2,600	Apple	4,247	Tribune	3,807	Hearst	4,100
34	General Electric	1,049	Bertelsmann	1,819	Knight Ridder	2,324	Matsushita	3,708	Samsung	3,692	Barnes&Noble	3,999
35	Disney	1,032	Dun&Bradstreet	1,741	Times-Mirror	2,271	Dell	3,540	Matsushita	3,667	McGraw-Hill	3,857
36	Cox	1,032	TCI	1,703	Microsoft	2,190	Sun	3,226	Border/Walden	3,640	Advance	3,844
37	Westinghouse	989	Intel	1,639	Sun	2,186	Seagram	3,113	McGraw-Hill	3,609	KnightRidder/McClatchey	3,820
38	Washington Post	984	Toshiba	1,629	DEC	2,082	Unisys	3,070	Advance	3,457	Matsushita	3,685
39	WangLabs	967	Tribune	1,588	Compaq	2,061	Bertelsmann	3,044	Avaya	3,397	Blockbuster	3,518
40	Dun&Bradstreet	957	Disney	1,581	Bertelsmann	1,974	NCR	2,994	Hearst	3,300	Reed Elsevier	3,331
41	Thomson Corp.	947	McGraw-Hill	1,463	Hearst	1,973	Knight Ridder	2,904	Reed Elsevier	3,232	Sun[b]	3,259
42	Sperry	903	Hearst	1,398	TBS	1,768	Oracle	2,868	Thomson Corp.	3,160	Borders Group	3,203
43	Gulf+Western	903	Washington Post	1,367	McGraw-Hill	1,723	Computer Ass.	2,817	EDS	3,042	Avaya	3,083
44	Hearst	884	Gulf+Western	1,280	Gulf+Western	1,649	Cox	2,615	NewYork Times	2,865	Wash Post	3,014
45	NewYork Times	849	Cox	1,272	Thomson Corp.	1,644	Hearst	2,568	Knight Ridder	2,821	NY Times	2,966
46	Intel	815	NewYork Times	1,201	Tribune	1,641	Reed Elsevier	2,479	Apple	2,761	EDS	2,923
47	Reader's Digest	679	Reader's Digest	1,172	Cox	1,545	McGraw-Hill	2,474	Agere	2,700	Unisys	2,636
48	TBS	663	Thomson Corp.	1,134	Reader's Digest	1,465	EDS	2,103	Computer Ass.	2,674	Thomson	2,621
49	Toshiba	620	Compaq	1,079	Washington Post	1,450	Gateway	3,844	Unisys	2,595	NCR	2,551
50	Bertelsmann	563	TBS	805	NewYork Times	1,433	Barnes&Noble	1,930	Gateway	4,743	Thomson Co.	2,413
Total		221,309		269,780		326,656		437,572		608,609		628,663
Average		4,426		5,396		6,533		8,751		12,172		12,573
Median		1,895		2,949		3,384		5,950		6,098		6,069

Note: Figures for 2005 are 2004 data updated for mergers and spin-offs in 2005.

[a] SBC/AT&T merger with Bell South announced in 2006.
[b] Oracle acquired Sun in 2009.

Table 14.2 Top 25 Mass Media Companies U.S. Mass Media Revenues

1984		1988		1992		1996		2001		2004		2005	
RCA	$4,214	Warner Comm	$4,134	Time Warner	$10,680	Time Warner	$20,390	AOL Time Warner	$34,690	Time Warner	$39,269	Time Warner	$39,269
ABC	3,291	General Electric	4,091	CBS	5,173	Disney	9,943	Viacom	21,718	Viacom	20,528	Comcast	19,190
CBS	2,715	CBS	3,894	News Corp	4,694	Viacom	7,690	Disney	13,063	Comcast	19,190	Disney	16,195
Warner Comm	2,629	ABC	3,889	General Electric	4,219	CBS	7,026	AT&T	10,732	Disney	16,195	News Corp	13,992
Gannett	2,274	Gannett	2,999	ABC	4,157	News Corp	6,838	News Corp	10,268	News Corp	13,992	Viacom	11,623
Time, Inc.	1,962	Time, Inc.	2,523	Gannett	3,763	TCI	5,954	Comcast	9,674	General Electric	7,681	CBS	8,905
Knight Ridder	1,664	Viacom	2,505	TCI	3,312	General Electric	5,946	Vivendi	8,107	Gannett	7,381	General Electric	7,681
Times-Mirror	1,551	MCA	2,401	Sony	3,168	Gannett	5,063	General Electric	6,423	Cox	6,598	Gannett	7,381
Viacom	1,470	Knight Ridder	2,083	Viacom	3,154	Sony	3,790	GM/Hughes	6,180	Sony	5,924	Cox	6,598
Tribune	1,422	Times-Mirror	1,866	Disney	3,074	Thomson Corp.	3,160	Gannett	6,016	Tribune	5,783	Sony	5,942
MCA	1,403	News Corp	1,837	Dun & Bradstreet	2,600	Seagram	3,113	Cox	5,956	Charter	4,918	Tribune	5,783
McGraw-Hill	1,097	Bertelsmann	1,819	Knight Ridder	2,324	Bertelsmann	3,044	Bertelsmann	4,728	Bertelsmann	4,831	Charter	4,918
Disney	1,032	Dun & Bradstreet	1,741	Times-Mirror	2,271	Knight Ridder	2,904	Charter	4,223	Vivendi	4,688	Bertelsmann	4,831
Cox	1,032	TCI	1,703	Bertelsmann	1,974	Cox	2,615	Sony	2,615	Hearst	4,207	Vivendi	4,688
Westinghouse	989	Tribune	1,588	Hearst	1,973	Hearst	2,568	Tribune	2,568	Barnes & Noble	3,807	Hearst	4,100
Washington Post	984	Disney	1,581	TBS	1,768	Reed Elsevier	2,479	McGraw-Hill	2,479	McGraw-Hill	3,609	Barnes & Noble	3,999
Dun & Bradstreet	957	McGraw-Hill	1,463	McGraw-Hill	1,723	McGraw-Hill	2,474	Advance	2,474	Advance	3,457	McGraw-Hill	3,857

Thomson Corp.	947	Hearst	1,398	Gulf + Western	1,649	Barnes & Noble	1,930	Hearst	3,300	Knight Ridder	3,820	Knight Ridder	3,844	Advance
Gulf + Western	903	Washington Post	1,367	Thomson Corp.	1,644	New York Times	1,922	Clear Channel	3,250	Clear Channel	3,752	Clear Channel	3,820	Knight Ridder
Hearst	884	Gulf + Western	1,280	Tribune	1,641	US West (MediaOne)	1,912	Reed Elsevier	3,232	Blockbuster	3,518	Blockbuster	3,752	Clear Channel
New York Times	849	Cox	1,272	Cox	1,545	Washington Post	1,853	New York Times	2,865	Reed Elsevier	3,331	Reed Elsevier	3,518	Blockbuster
Reader's Digest	679	New York Times	1,201	Reader's Digest	1,465	Tribune	1,851	Knight Ridder	2,821	Border/Walden	3,203	Border/Walden	3,331	Reed Elsevier
TBS	663	Reader's Digest	1,172	Washington Post	1,450	Times-Mirror	1,826	Thomson Corp.	2,301	Washington Post	3,014	Washington post	3,203	Border/Walden
Bertelsmann	563	Thomson Corp.	1,134	New York Times	1,433	Comcast	1,635	Washington Post	1,924	New York Times	2,966	New York Times	3,014	Washington post
News Corp	463	TBS	805	Reed Elsevier	1,226	Dun & Bradstreet	1,564	Reader's Digest	1,524	Thomson Co.	2,413	Thomson Co.	2,966	New York Times

Note: U.S. mass media activities only.

Table 14.3 Participation of Top 50 Information Sector Firms in 100 Information Industries, 1984–2005

	1984		1988		1992		1996		2001		2005	
1	IBM	12	IBM	15	IBM	16	IBM	16	AOL Time Warner	18	Sony	16
2	RCA	11	AT&T	13	AT&T	14	Sony	14	Sony	15	Time Warner	16
3	AT&T	11	Sony	8	Matsushita	13	Time Warner	13	IBM	14	IBM	14
4	GTE	8	Viacom	8	Sony	13	Viacom	12	Viacom	14	Microsoft	12
5	Warner Comm.	8	Matsushita	7	Time Warner	11	Disney	10	Microsoft	12	News Corp	11
6	Viacom	7	Motorola	7	Toshiba	8	Lucent	9	Disney	10	General Electric	11
7	CBS	6	Warner Comm	7	Viacom	8	Motorola	9	Vivendi	10	Disney	10
8	Matsushita	6	CBS	6	Motorola	7	News Corp	9	Bertelsmann	8	Bertelsmann	8
9	Sony	6	GTE	6	News Corp	7	HP	8	HP/Compaq	8	HP/Compaq	8
10	Toshiba	6	HP	6	CBS	6	Matsushita	8	Lucent	8	Lucent	8
11	SBC	5	Toshiba	5	Disney	6	CBS	7	Matsushita	8	Matsushita	8
12	Motorola	5	ABC	5	General Electric	6	Compaq	7	Motorola	8	Motorola	8
13	General Electric	5	Bertelsmann	5	HP	5	Toshiba	7	News Corp	8	Toshiba	8
14	HP	5	Disney	5	ABC	5	Bertelsmann	6	Toshiba	8	Viacom I	8
15	Burroughs	4	General Electric	4	Bertelsmann	5	Sun	6	AT&T	7	SBC	7
16	Bell Atlantic	4	News Corp	4	GTE	5	AT&T	6	SBC	7	Verizon	6
17	Disney	4	SBC	4	Apple	5	General Electric	5	Bell South	6	Samsung	6
18	NCR	4	Apple	4	Bell Atlantic	4	GTE	5	General Electric	6	Sprint	6
19	Westinghouse	4	Bell Atlantic	4	Bell South	4	Microsoft	5	Samsung	6	Thomson	6
20	McGraw-Hill	4	Bell South	4	DEC	4	Seagram	5	Sprint	6	Tribune	5
21	ABC	4	Gannett	4	Gannett	4	Ameritech	4	Verizon	6	Comcast	5
22	Washington Post	4	Gulf + Western	4	Hearst	4	Apple	4	Worldcom	6	Viacom II	6
23	NYNEX	4	Hearst	4	Microsoft	4	Bell Atlantic	4	McGraw-Hill	5	McGraw-Hill	5
24	Ameritech	3	NCR	4	Samsung	4	Bell South	4	Dell	4	Vivendi	5
25	Hearst	3	NYNEX	4	SBC	4	Gannett	4	Gannett	4	Bell South	4
26	Gulf + Western	4	Thomson	4	Sprint	4	Hearst	4	Qwest	4	Dell	4
27	Tribune	3	Washington Post	4	Thomson	4	McGraw-Hill	4	Reed Elsevier	4	Gannett	4
28	Reader's Digest	3	Ameritech	3	Washington Post	4	Reed Elsevier	4	Cox	4	Qwest	4

29	Cox	3	Cox	3	Ameritech	3	Samsung	4	Hearst	3	Reed Elsevier	4
30	MCA	3	DEC	3	Compaq	3	SBC	4	Thomson Corp.	3	Washington Post	4
31	Thomson Corp.	3	MCA	3	Cox	3	Sprint	4	Xerox	3	Cox	3
32	Time, Inc.	3	McGraw-Hill	3	Gulf + Western	3	Thomson	4	Advance	3	Hearst	3
33	Pacific Telesis	3	MCI	3	McGraw-Hill	3	Cox	3	Apple	2	Thomson Corp.	3
34	DEC	3	Pacific Telesis	3	MCI	3	Dell	3	Barnes & Noble	2	Xerox	3
35	Apple	3	Reader's Digest	3	NYNEX	3	MCI	3	Cisco	2	Advance	3
36	Times-Mirror	3	Sprint	3	Reader's Digest	3	NYNEX	3	Computer Ass.	2	Apple	2
37	Bertelsmann	3	Thomson Corp.	3	Sprint	3	Worldcom	3	Hughes	2	Barnes & Noble	2
38	Sprint	3	Time, Inc.	3	Thomson Corp.	3	Xerox	3	Intel	2	Cisco	2
39	Gannett	3	Times-Mirror	3	Times-Mirror	3	Barnes & Noble	3	NCR	2	Gateway	2
40	Intel	3	Tribune	3	Tribune	3	Computer Ass.	3	Oracle	2	Intel	2
41	MCI	3	Unisys	3	Unisys	3	Gateway	3	Sun	2	NCR	2
42	Bell South	3	US West	3	US West	3	Intel	3	Tribune	3	Oracle	2
43	Sperry	2	Compaq	2	Intel	2	NCR	3	Agere	1	Sun	2
44	US West	3	Intel	3	Pacific Telesis	2	Oracle	2	Avaya	1	Avaya	1
45	New York Times	2	Xerox	2	TCI	2	Pacific Telesis	2	Border/Walden	1	Blockbuster	1
46	Dun & Bradstreet	1	Dun & Bradstreet	1	Xerox	1	TCI	2	Comcast	3	Border/Walden	1
47	TBS	1	Knight Ridder	1	Dun & Bradstreet	1	Unisys	2	EDS	1	EDS	1
48	Xerox	2	New York Times	2	Knight Ridder	2	US West	2	Knight Ridder	1	Knight Ridder	1
49	Wang Labs	1	TBS	1	New York Times	1	EDS	1	New York Times	2	New York Times	2
50	Knight Ridder	1	TCI	1	TBS	1	Knight Ridder	1	Unisys	1	Unisys	1
Average		4.1		4.3		4.8		5.1		5.2		5.2
Median		3.0		4.0		4.0		4.0		4.0		4.0

Continued

Table 14.4 Participation of 1984's Top 50 Information Sector Firms in 100 Information Industries, 1984–2005

1984 Rank	Company	1984	1988	1992	1996	2001	2005
1	AT&T	11	13	14	7	4	SBC
2	IBM	12	15	16	16	14	14
3	NYNEX	4	4	3	3	Verizon	
4	Bell South	3	4	4	4	4	SBC 2006
5	Ameritech	3	3	3	4	SBC	
6	Bell Atlantic	4	4	3	4	Verizon	6
7	GTE	9	8	6	6	Verizon	
8	Pacific Telesis	3	3	2	2	SBC	
9	US West	3	3	3	2	Qwest	
10	SBC	5	5	4	4	7	AT&T 2006 7
11	RCA	10	3	Thomson/GE/MCI			
12	Motorola	5	7	7	9	8	8
13	Xerox	2	2	2	3	3	3
14	ABC	4	5	5		Disney	
15	Sprint	3	3	4	4	6	6
16	CBS	6	6	6	7	Viacom	
17	Warner Comm.	8	7	Time Warner	13	18	16
18	NCR	4	4	AT&T	2	2	2
19	Gannett	3	4	4	4	4	4
20	Burroughs	4	Unisys				
21	MCI	6	6	7	7	Worldcom	Verizon
22	DEC	3	3	4	5	Compaq	
23	R.R. Donnelley & Sons	1	1	1	1	1	1
24	Time, Inc.	3	3	Time Warner			
25	HP	5	6	6	8	8	8
26	Apple	3	4	4	4	2	2
27	Matsushita	9	10	15	10	8	8
28	Knight Ridder	1	1	1	1	1	McClatchey 2006
29	Times-Mirror	3	3	3	2		
30	Viacom	7	8	8	12	14	14
31	Tribune	3	3	3	3	2	2
32	Sony	8	10	16	18	16	16
33	MCA	3	3	2	UMG Vivendi		
34	McGraw-Hill	3	3	3	4	5	5
35	General Electric	6	6	7	6	7	7
36	Disney	4	5	6	10	10	10
37	Cox	3	3	3	3	3	3
38	Westinghouse	3	2	2	2	Viacom	
39	Washington Post	2	2	2	2	2	4
40	Wang Labs	1	1	Bankrupt			
41	Dun & Bradstreet	1	1	1	1	1	1
42	Thomson Corp.	3	3	3	3	3	3

Continued

Table 14.4 *(Continued)*

1984 Rank	Company	1984	1988	1992	1996	2001	2005
44	Hearst	3	4	4	4	3	3
45	New York Times	2	2	2	2	2	2
46	Intel	3	2	2	2	2	2
47	Reader's Digest	3	3	3	3	3	3
48	TBS	1	1	1		Time Warner	
49	Toshiba	6	6	8	7	9	8
50	Bertelsmann	3	5	5	6	8	8
	Average	4.2	4.4	4.8	5	5.7	5.8
	Median	3	3.5	3	4	3.5	4

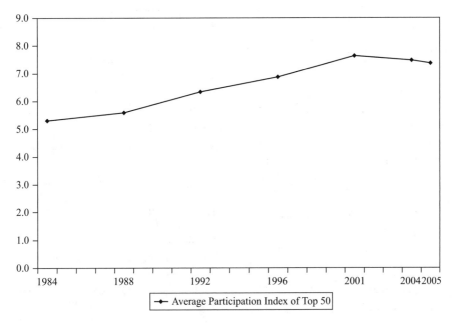

Figure 14.1 Average Participation Index of Top 50 Information Sector Firms: 1984–2005 (Presence in 100 Industries)

presence considerably. Other notable expanders included Hewlett-Packard (from 5 to 8) and Sprint (from 3 to 6). (Sprint, however, spun off its local telecom operations in 2006, reducing its PI to 5.). AT&T, however, declined from 11 in 1984 (and 14 in 1983) to 4 in 2004, before disappearing entirely. Taken as a whole, 22 of the top firms in 2005 were present in five or more industries of the information sector. In contrast, in 1984, 14 firms participated in five or more industries.

We next look at the evolution of the formerly largest information sector firms during a twenty-year period. Table 14.4 traces the diversification of 1984's top 50 firms (as opposed to the top 50 firms in each point of time, which is a changing set). If we trace the 1980 top 50 to the survivors of 2005, their PI increased from 4.2 to 5.7. Thus, for 1984's top 50 companies, participation across industries increased by about 36%, or about one and a half new industries.

The companies tend to participate within similar sectors, for example, in telecommunications services, computer equipment, or mass media. Few of the top 50 firms participate in more than one of the major subsectors. AT&T, for example, tried unsuccessfully to enter IT (through NCR) and mass media (through the cable firms TCI and Media One), before retreating back into telecom services. Disney spectacularly increased its presence in the overall information industry, from 4 in 1984 to 10 in 2005, but the company remained firmly rooted in the mass media subsector. Viacom similarly expanded only into industries closely related to its core business, such as music and print publishing, and even left the cable MSO part of the business. With the merger with AOL, Time Warner crossed into the Internet zone, which for a while represented almost a quarter of the company's total revenues. IBM briefly tried to enter telecommunications but left the field.

Of the top 50 companies, Sony forms the main exception for its intersectoral activities, with its expansion from 6 to 16 markets, moving beyond its consumer electronics base into mass media and telecommunications (cell phones). However, the company was, by 2005, not doing well; its far-flung product lines were not well coordinated and at times were even in each other's way. Thus, most diversification has been *intrasectoral* rather than *intersectoral*.

We now look, similarly, at the top 25 mass media firms and their diversifications in mass media and the Internet. Table 14.5 and figure 14.2 show the findings.

There was an increase in the average mass media participation from 3.1 to 4.8 industries in the 20-year period. These were lower numbers than those of the information sector as a whole, which were 4.2 in 1984 and 5.8 in 2005. The change was entry into about one to two new industries over 20 years. Most of the change took place between 1996 and 2001. Thereafter, diversification was flat. However, (see figure 14.2) for the top five media firms, participation changed more pronouncedly. Whereas it was 4.6 mass media industries in 1984, it was 9.6 in 2005.

THE SECTOR SHARE INDEX (SSI)

The Participation Index has its limitations. It only indicates a firm's presence in various industries within the overall information sector. It does not tell us about the magnitude of a firm's involvement in a particular industry. Therefore, we define a second measure for a vertical integration, the Sector Share Index (SSI).

In constructing the SSI, we take, for each of the top firms, the sum of its market share in each subindustry, weighed by the share of the respective subindustry in the overall information sector. This is equal to the share of that firm of the entire information sector. Then, these firm-specific measures are averaged over the top $n = 50$ firms and their trend observed over time.

$$SSI = \frac{1}{n}\sum_i SSI_i = \frac{i}{n}\sum_i \frac{R_i}{M}$$

where

R_i = Firm i's total information sector revenues
M = Revenues of total information sector

The results for the top 50 information sector firms are provided in table 14.6, which shows their share in the overall information sector in each of the years 1984–2005. Table 14.7 provides a similar calculation for the top 25 mass media firms only, as a share of overall mass media subsectors. We can then calculate the HH1 for the entire information and media sector.

Table 14.6 shows that the HHI concentration within the total information sector declined from 519 in 1984 to 169 in 2001 and 176 in 2005, after bottoming out in 1996.

Figure 14.3 shows the aggregate SSI for the top 50 and the top 10 companies in the information sector as a whole. For the top 50 firms, that share has declined from 71.1% in 1984 to 59.6% in 1996 to 59.1% by 2005. The share of the top three firms, at the same time, declined from 30.8% to 17.4%—by almost half.

The trend line of the SSI of the 50 largest information sector companies (figure 14.4) shows a steady but slight decline, but it is fairly stable. Much more telling is the trend line of the top 10 companies. It shows a decrease in SSI of the biggest 10 companies. Their share was 48.5% in 1984 and declined fairly strongly by 1996, when it was 28%. Thereafter, it rose again to 35%. Thus, the overall hold of the top 10 firms declined rather than increased. Although the share of the top 10 firms increased again, one must also observe its significant decline since 1984, by almost 40% to 1996, and by 25% to 2005. If we go back a year further to 1983, the top 10 firms (including the undivested AT&T) accounted for 54% of the information sector, with AT&T at 34.8%.

However, the share of companies ranked 11–50 show the opposite trend. The year 1996 was the low point for the total share of the top 10 companies.

Table 14.5 Participation Index for Top 25 Mass Media Firms in Mass Media Industries, 1984–2005

1984		1988		1992		1996		2001		2005	
Company	PI	Company	PI	Company	PI	Company	PI	Company	PI	Company	PI
RCA	3	Warner Comm.	7	Times-Mirror	3	Time Warner	13	AOL Time Warner	12	Time Warner	11
ABC	4	General Electric	4	CBS	6	CBS	7	Viacom	15	Comcast	3
CBS	6	CBS	6	News Corp	6	New York Times	1	Disney	9	Disney	9
Warner Comm	8	ABC	5	General Electric	5	Gannett	2	AT&T	1	News Corp	11
Gannett	2	Gannett	2	ABC	5	Barnes & Noble	2	News Corp	10	Viacom	9
Time, Inc.	3	Time, Inc.	3	Gannett	2	Dun & Bradstreet	1	Comcast	3	CBS	6
Knight Ridder	1	Viacom	8	Thomson Corp.	3	TCI	2	Vivendi	7	General Electric	5
Times-Mirror	3	MCA	3	Sony	7	Seagram	5	General Electric	4	Gannett	2
Viacom	7	Knight Ridder	7	Viacom	8	Viacom	12	GM/Hughes	2	Cox	3
Tribune	3	Times-Mirror	3	Disney	5	Cox	3	Gannett	2	Sony	6
MCA	3	News Corp	3	Dun & Bradstreet	4	Disney	9	Cox	3	Tribune	5
McGraw-Hill	5	Bertelsmann	5	Knight Ridder	1	Knight Ridder	2	Bertelsmann	8	Charter	3
Cox	3	Dun & Bradstreet	3	Tribune	3	Times-Mirror	3	Charter	2	Bertelsmann	8
Disney	4	TBS	1	Bertelsmann	5	Bertelsmann	5	Sony	7	Vivendi	6
Westinghouse	3	Tribune	3	Hearst	4	Hearst	4	Tribune	3	Hearst	3
Washington Post	3	Disney	5	TCI	5	Sony	2	McGraw-Hill	4	Barnes & Noble	3

Continued

Table 14.5 (*Continued*)

1984		1988		1992		1996		2001		2005	
Company	PI	Company	PI	Company	PI	Company	PI	Company	PI	Company	PI
Dun & Bradstreet	1	McGraw-Hill	3	McGraw-Hill	3	McGraw-Hill	4	Advance	3	McGraw-Hill	4
Thomson Corp	3	Hearst	4	Gulf + Western	4	General Electric	4	Hearst	3	Advance	3
Gulf + Western	4	Washington Post	3	Time Warner	11	Thomson Corp.	3	Clear Channel	3	Knight Ridder	2
Hearst	3	Gulf + Western	4	US West (MediaOne)	1	Tribune	3	Reed Elsevier	4	Clear Channel	3
New York Times	2	Cox	3	Cox	3	Comcast	2	New York Times	2	Blockbuster	1
Reader's Digest	3	New York Times	2	Reader's Digest	2	News Corp	8	Knight Ridder	2	Reed Elsevier	4
TBS	1	Reader's Digest	1	Washington Post	3	Washington Post	3	Thomson Corp.	3	Borders Group	2
Bertelsmann	3	Thomson Corp.	3	New York Times	2	New York Times	2	Washington Post	3	Washington Post	3
News Corp	1	TBS	1	Reed Elsevier	3	Reed Elsevier	4	Reader's Digest	3		
Average	3.1	Average	3.5	Average	4.0	Average	4.6	Average	4.6	Average	4.8
Median	3	Median	3	Median	3	Median	3	Median	3	Median	3

356

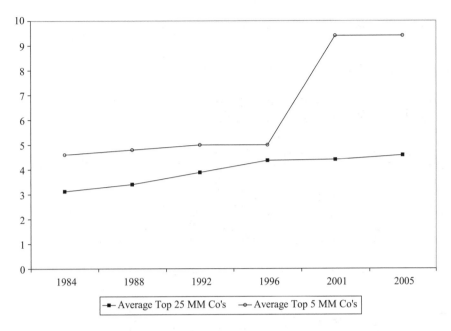

Figure 14.2 Average Participation Index for Top 5 and Top 25 Mass Media Companies 1984–2005 (Presence in 30 Mass Media Industries)

But it forms a high point for the remainder of the top 50. For both groups the year 1996 forms a turning point in the total information sector revenue (figure 14.4). After 1996, the top 10 firms increase their combined share, which is approximately of the same size as that of the next 40 firms (about 25–30% since 1992). The share of firms 11–50 throughout the 20-year period has been relatively stable at about 25%.

For the top 50 firms, the average share steadily declined from 1.4 in 1984 to 1.2 in 2005. After 20 years and many mergers, the average top 50 firm in 2005 had a *lower* share than in 1984, essentially unchanged since 1996. Median shares for the top 50 firms (that is, the share of firm number 26) stayed stable, from 0.6 in 1984 to 0.5 in 2004.

Table 14.1 shows that the average size of a top 50 firm almost tripled from $4.4 billion in 1984 to $12.6 billion in 2005, and that the median grew from $1.9 billion to $6.1 billion. Even so, the information sector as a whole grew faster still, from $311 billion to $1.1 trillion, more than triple. Thus it cannot be said that the top 50 firms, or the top 10, have increased their hold over the sector.

Vertical Concentration in the Mass Media Sector

We also look at the share of the top mass media firms (a) in the overall information sector and (b) in the mass media subsector. Figure 14.5 and Table 14.6 show that the share for the top 10 mass media companies in the overall information sector has clearly increased in the two-decade period. After a slight decline from 7.5 to 7.4 in the late 1980s, the share increased, reaching 12.9 in 2005.

The aggregate share of the overall information sector of the top 25 mass media firms increased from 11.8 to 18.5 between 1984 and 2005. Time Warner, Viacom, Bertelsmann, Disney, and GE all show an increase in SSI, particularly after 1996. Medium-sized companies, such as The New York Times Company, the Washington Post Company, and several of the other publishers, show only small SSIs. The average SSI for top-25 mass media companies increased from 0.5 to 0.7.

More important is the share of the top 5, 10, and 25 mass media firms in the *mass media sector*. This is shown in figure 14.6, which is based on table 14.7.

Figure 14.6 shows a steady and clear upward trend in the shares of the top five media firms from

Table 14.6 Shares of the Top 50 Information Sector Firms in the Information Sector

	1984		1988		1992		1996		2001		2005	
1	AT&T	19.4	AT&T	15.0	AT&T	12.4	AT&T	7.1	AT&T	6.4	Verizon	7.0
2	IBM	8.3	IBM	6.7	IBM	4.5	IBM	4.0	Verizon	5.3	SBC/AT&T	6.7
3	NYNEX	3.1	Bell South	3.3	Bell South	2.4	MCI	2.9	SBC	4.7	Time Warner	3.7
4	Bell South	3.1	NYNEX	2.6	Bell Atlantic	2.3	Time Warner	2.8	IBM	3.6	Sprint	3.4
5	Ameritech	2.7	Bell Atlantic	2.2	GTE	2.3	GTE	2.1	AOL Time Warner	3.5	IBM	3.3
6	Bell Atlantic	2.6	Ameritech	2.1	NYNEX	2.2	Ameritech	2.0	Worldcom	2.5	HP	2.8
7	Pacific Telesis	2.5	SBC	2.1	Time Warner	2.0	Bell South	2.0	HP/Compaq	2.5	Microsoft	2.4
8	US West	2.3	Pacific Telesis	1.9	Ameritech	2.0	Sprint	2.0	Sprint	2.4	Bell South	2.3
9	SBC	2.3	US West	1.8	MCI	2.0	SBC	1.8	Viacom	2.2	Dell	2.1
10	GTE	2.2	GTE	1.8	Motorola	2.0	Bell Atlantic	1.8	Bell South	2.1	Comcast	1.8
11	RCA	2.0	Motorola	1.7	SBC	1.9	NYNEX	1.6	Microsoft	2.1	Sony	1.7
12	Motorola	1.6	Xerox	1.7	US West	1.7	Motorola	1.5	Sony	1.7	Disney	1.5
13	Xerox	1.2	Sprint	1.6	Pacific Telesis	1.7	US West	1.5	Dell	1.3	Motorola	1.4
14	ABC	1.1	MCI	1.3	Sprint	1.7	HP	1.5	Disney	1.3	News Corp	1.3
15	Sprint	0.9	General Electric	1.0	Xerox	1.7	Xerox	1.4	Qwest	1.3	Viacom I	1.1
16	CBS	0.9	Warner Comm	1.0	Sony	1.4	Compaq	1.4	Lucent	1.2	Qwest	1.1
17	Warner Comm	0.8	Unisys	1.0	HP	1.0	Disney	1.4	Motorola	1.2	General Electric	0.9
18	NCR	0.8	CBS	0.9	CBS	1.0	Lucent	1.3	Xerox	1.1	CBS	0.8
19	Gannett	0.7	ABC	0.9	Matsushita	1.0	Pacific Telesis	1.3	News Corp	1.0	Intel	0.8
20	Burroughs	0.7	DEC	0.9	News Corp	1.0	Sony	1.3	Comcast	1.0	Lucent	0.7
21	MCI	0.7	Sony	0.8	General Electric	0.8	Intel	1.2	Intel	1.0	Xerox	0.7
22	DEC	0.7	HP	0.7	ABC	0.8	Viacom	1.0	Vivendi	1.0	Oracle[a]	0.7
23	Time, Inc.	0.6	Matsushita	0.7	Apple	0.7	CBS	0.7	Oracle[a]	0.8	Gannett	0.7
24	HP	0.6	Gannett	0.7	Gannett	0.7	News Corp	0.7	General Electric	0.7	Cox	0.6

#												
25	Apple	0.6	NCR	0.7	Thomson	0.7	TCI	0.8	Hughes	0.6	Toshiba	0.6
26	Matsushita	0.6	Thomson	0.7	TCI	0.6	General Electric	0.8	Gannett	0.6	Cisco	0.5
27	Knight Ridder	0.5	Apple	0.6	Samsung	0.6	Worldcom	0.7	Cox	0.6	Tribune	0.5
28	Times-Mirror	0.5	Time, Inc.	0.6	Viacom	0.6	Gannett	0.7	Cisco	0.6	Apple	0.5
29	Viacom	0.5	Viacom	0.6	Disney	0.6	Samsung	0.7	Toshiba	0.5	Bertelsmann	0.5
30	Tribune	0.5	MCA	0.6	Intel	0.6	Toshiba	0.7	Gateway	0.5	Samsung	0.4
31	Sony	0.5	Knight Ridder	0.5	Unisys	0.5	Microsoft	0.7	Bertelsmann	0.5	Vivendi	0.4
32	MCA	0.5	Times-Mirror	0.5	Toshiba	0.5	Thomson	0.6	Barnes & Noble	0.4	Gateway	0.4
33	McGraw-Hill	0.4	News Corp	0.4	Dun & Bradstreet	0.5	Apple	0.6	Sun[a]	0.4	Hearst	0.4
34	General Electric	0.3	Bertelsmann	0.4	Knight Ridder	0.4	Gateway	0.5	Tribune	0.4	Barnes & Noble	0.4
35	Cox	0.3	Dun & Bradstreet	0.4	Times-Mirror	0.4	Matsushita	0.5	Samsung	0.4	McGraw-Hill	0.4
36	Westinghouse	0.3	TCI	0.4	Microsoft	0.4	Dell	0.5	Matsushita	0.4	Advance	0.4
37	Disney	0.3	Intel	0.4	Sun	0.4	Sun	0.4	Border/Walden	0.4	Knight Ridder	0.4
38	Washington Post	0.3	Toshiba	0.3	DEC	0.4	Seagram	0.4	McGraw-Hill	0.4	Matsushita	0.3
39	Wang Labs	0.3	Tribune	0.3	Compaq	0.4	Unisys	0.4	Advance	0.4	Blockbuster	0.3
40	Dun & Bradstreet	0.3	Disney	0.3	Bertelsmann	0.4	Bertelsmann	0.4	Avaya	0.3	Reed Elsevier	0.3
41	Thomson Corp.	0.3	McGraw-Hill	0.4	Hearst	0.4	NCR	0.4	Hearst	0.3	Sun[a]	0.3
42	Gulf + Western	0.3	Hearst	0.3	TBS	0.3	Knight Ridder	0.4	Reed Elsevier	0.3	Border/Walden	0.3
43	Sperry	0.3	Washington Post	0.3	McGraw-Hill	0.3	Oracle	0.4	Thomson Corp.	0.3	Avaya	0.3
44	Hearst	0.3	Gulf + Western	0.3	Gulf + Western	0.3	Computer Ass.	0.4	EDS	0.3	Washington Post	0.3

Continued

Table 14.6 (*Continued*)

	1984		1988		1992		1996		2001		2005	
45	New York Times	0.3	Cox	0.3	Thomson Corp.	0.3	Cox	0.4	New York Times	0.3	New York Times	0.3
46	Intel	0.3	New York Times	0.3	Tribune	0.3	Hearst	0.3	Knight Ridder	0.3	EDS	0.3
47	Reader's Digest	0.2	Reader's Digest	0.3	Cox	0.3	Reed Elsevier	0.3	Apple	0.3	Unisys	0.2
48	TBS	0.2	Thomson Corp.	0.3	Reader's Digest	0.3	McGraw-Hill	0.3	Agere	0.3	Thomson	0.2
49	Toshiba	0.2	Compaq	0.2	Washington Post	0.3	EDS	0.3	Computer Ass.	0.3	NCR	0.2
50	Bertelsmann	0.2	TBS	0.2	New York Times	0.3	Barnes & Noble	0.3	Unisys	0.3	Thomson Corp.	0.2
	Aggregate SSI %	71.1		65.7		62.5		59.6		61.8		59.1
	Average SSI %	1.4		1.3		1.2		1.2		1.2		1.2
	Median SSI %	0.6		0.7		0.6		0.8		0.6		0.6
	HHI	518.5		334.6		240.0		136.7		168.5		176.5

[a] Oracle acquired Sun in 2009.

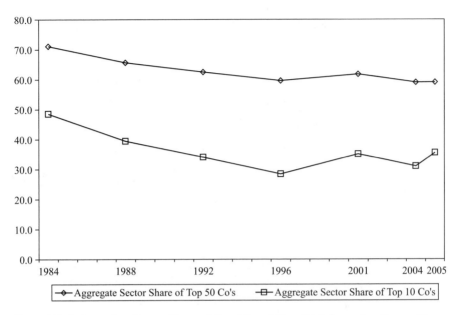

Figure 14.3 Information Sector Share of Top 10 and Top 50 Information Sector Firms: 1984–2005

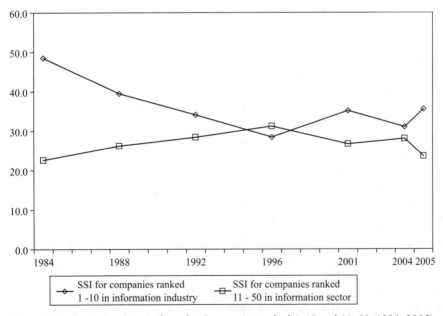

Figure 14.4 Information Sector Share for Companies ranked 1–10 and 11–50 (1984–2005)

1988 to 2001. This trend deserves attention. The top five firms accounted for about 13.4% in 1984, and by 2001, their share had almost doubled to 22.8%. By 2005, their share had grown to 26.2%. (There was a decline over 2004 resulting from the Viacom spin-off of CBS.) The share of the top 10 mass media firms rose from 20.6 to 37.3% in 2001 and then plateaued. And for the top 25 firms, it

rose from 32.5 to 52.4% in 2001 and similarly stabilized. Thus, the increase was largest for the top five firms, between 1988 and 2004.

The share of the top 25 media companies in 2005 in the total mass media sector was 51.3%, which is 18.8 percentage points higher than in 1984 when it was 32.5%. This is a major increase. However, this share is not high in comparison to most sectors of

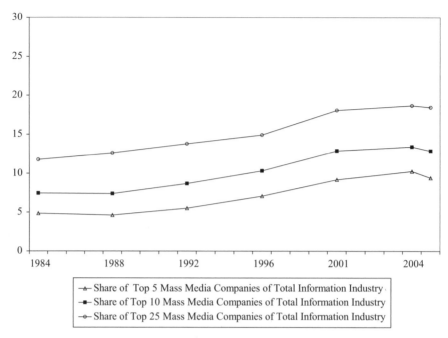

Figure 14.5 Share of Top Mass Media Companies in Overall Information Industry

the economy, where such a market share would be accounted for by 3–5 firms, not 25. Why is it lower than many people's intuition would suggest? The overall mass media sector is quite large, about $385 billion in 2005 U.S. revenues. Thus, even the largest media companies, in the order of $10–40 billion U.S. revenues, account for only a fraction. Since some of the sectoral size may double count retailers' revenues, we also calculated the percentages after eliminating retailing companies and other companies' retail operations. (Retailers were film theaters, as well as video, book, and music stores.) With this narrower definition of mass media, the share of the then 25 top firms rises somewhat to 57.6%.

For 25 companies to account for about half of the sector implies the participation of numerous other firms for the other half. Each of them has only a small share but they add up. Many of these firms are well known and may have a good-sized market share in a particular media industry. But in the overall mass media market they do not make it to the top 25. These companies include: in radio: Citadel and XM Sirius. In TV and cable TV: Sinclair, Paxson/ION, Belo, Saban, Cablevision, Dish Network, Liberty, PBS, and Discovery. In film and music retailing: Regal, AMC, Cinemark, Carmike, Netfix, Movie Gallery, Apple i-Tunes, and Amazon.com. In music: EMI,

and Warner Music, In newspapers: McClatchey. In book publishing: Holtzbrinck, Pearson, Scholastic, Thomson, and Torstar/Harlequin. In magazines: Legardere/Hachette, Reader's Digest, Primedia, IDG, and Ziff-Davis.

In order to generalize we look at the aggregate share of *non*-top 25 companies in various mass media industries. We find that their revenue share for 2005 is high in the following:

Move Theaters	96.9%
Daily Newspapers	70.1%
Magazines	66.2%
All Books	70.1%
Radio Stations	66.6%
TV Stations	71.6%

On the other hand, the market share of non-top 25 mass media companies is lower for these industries:

TV Broadcast networks	4.1%
Cable Channels	31.7%
Cable TV Operators	31.6%
Film Production/Distribution	15.6%
TV Primetime Production	23.0%
Record Labels/Distribution	37.9%

Table 14.7 Share of the Top 25 Mass Media Companies in the Mass Media Sector, 1984–2005

1984		1988		1992		1996		2001		2005	
Company	SSI	Company	SSI	Company	SSI	Company	SSI	Company	SSI	Company	SSI
RCA	3.7	Warner Comm	2.7	Time Warner	5.8	Time Warner	8.5	AOL Time Warner	10.2	Time Warner	10.3
ABC	2.9	General Electric	2.7	CBS	2.8	Disney	4.1	Viacom	6.4	Comcast	5.0
CBS	2.4	CBS	2.6	News Corp	2.5	Viacom	3.2	Disney	3.8	Disney	4.2
Warner Comm	2.3	ABC	2.5	General Electric	2.3	CBS	2.9	AT&T	3.2	News Corp	3.7
Gannett	2.0	Gannett	2.0	ABC	2.0	News Corp	2.8	News Corp	3.0	Viacom	3.0
Time, Inc.	1.7	Time, Inc.	1.7	Gannett	1.8	TCI	2.5	Comcast	2.8	CBS	2.3
Knight Ridder	1.5	Viacom	1.6	TCI	1.7	General Electric	2.5	Vivendi.	2.4	General Electric	2.0
Times-Mirror	1.4	MCA	1.6	Sony	1.7	Gannett	2.1	General Electric	1.9	Gannett	1.9
Viacom	1.3	Knight Ridder	1.4	Viacom	1.7	Sony	1.6	GM/Hughes	1.8	Cox	1.7
Tribune	1.3	Times-Mirror	1.2	Disney	1.7	Thomson Corp.	1.3	Gannett	1.8	Sony	1.6
MCA	1.2	News Corp	1.2	Dun & Bradstreet	1.4	Seagram	1.3	Cox	1.8	Tribune	1.5
McGraw-Hill	1.0	Bertelsmann	1.2	Knight Ridder	1.2	Bertelsmann	1.3	Bertelsmann	1.4	Charter	1.3
Disney	0.9	Dun & Bradstreet	1.1	Times-Mirror	1.1	Knight Ridder	1.2	Charter	1.2	Bertelsmann	1.3
Cox	0.9	TCI	1.1	Bertelsmann	1.1	Cox	1.1	Sony	1.2	Vivendi	1.2
Westinghouse	0.9	Tribune	1.0	Hearst	1.0	Hearst	1.1	Tribune	1.1	Hearst	1.1
Washington Post	0.9	Disney	1.0	TBS	1.0	Reed Elsevier	1.0	McGraw-Hill	1.1	Barnes & Noble	1.0

Continued

Table 14.7 (Continued)

1984		1988		1992		1996		2001		2005	
Company	SSI	Company	SSI	Company	SSI	Company	SSI	Company	SSI	Company	SSI
Dun & Bradstreet	0.8	McGraw-Hill	1.0	McGraw-Hill	0.9	McGraw-Hill	1.0	Advance	1.0	McGraw-Hill	1.0
Thomson Corp	0.8	Hearst	0.9	Gulf + Western	0.9	Barnes & Noble	0.8	Hearst	1.0	Advance	1.0
Gulf + Western	0.8	Washington Post	0.9	Thomson Corp.	0.9	New York Times	0.8	Clear Channel	1.0	Knight Ridder	1.0
Hearst	0.8	Gulf + Western	0.8	Tribune	0.8	US West (MediaOne)	0.8	Reed Elsevier	1.0	Clear Channel	1.0
New York Times	0.8	Cox	0.8	Cox	0.8	Washington Post	0.8	New York Times	0.8	Blockbuster	0.9
Reader's Digest	0.6	New York Times	0.8	Reader's Digest	0.8	Tribune	0.8	Knight Ridder	0.8	Reed Elsevier	0.9
TBS	0.6	Reader's Digest	0.8	Washington Post	0.8	Times-Mirror	0.8	Thomson Corp.	0.7	Border/Walden	0.8
Bertelsmann	0.5	Thomson Corp.	0.7	New York Times	0.7	Comcast	0.8	Washington Post	0.6	Washington Post	0.8
News Corp	0.4	TBS	0.5	Reed Elsevier	0.5	Dun & Bradstreet	0.7	Reader's Digest	0.4	New York Times	0.8
Top 25 Aggregate SSI %	32.5		33.9		39.1		45.4		52.4		51.3
Average SSI %	1.30		1.36		1.56		1.82		2.10		2.05
Median SSI %	0.95		1.15		1.25		1.25		1.35		1.25
Top 25 Aggreg. SSI%, excluding retail industries companies, and activities	37.8		40.9		46.3		51.9		61.1		57.6
CPI	11.3		10.5		13.4		18.7		33.6		33.2
HHI	57		55		88		149		218		205

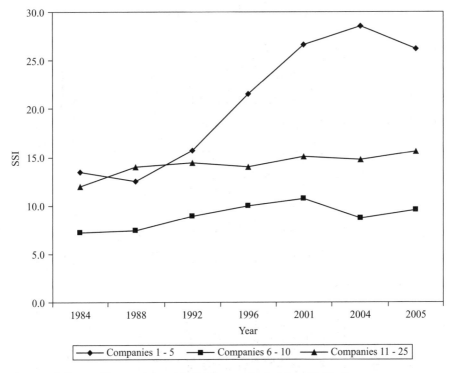

Figure 14.6 Share of Largest Mass Media Companies in Mass Media Sector

To conclude: taken together, the top 50 firms accounted for a smaller percentage of the total information sector, declining from 67.5% in 1984 to 59.1% in 2005. The surviving top-50 firms of 1984 had, by 2005, 37.3%, down from 67.5% in 1984. The top five firms had 36.5% in 1984 and 24.1% in 2005. The share of the top 10 firms similarly declined.

But for the mass media subsector we find a very different picture. The top five firms doubled from 13.4% in 1984 to 26.2% in 2005, whereas the share of the next 20 firms rose only slightly after 1988.

The top fifty information sector firms control a smaller share of the overall information sector than before, and the disparity in market share has narrowed. In 1984, the largest firm's share was 30 times as great as the median score for the top 50, and the median score was 3 times greater than the score of the smallest firm. By 2005, these figures had dropped to 12.3 and 2.5 times, respectively. The disparity between the largest and the smallest firms in the top 50 decreased from 18 in 1984 to 6.8 by 2005. The average sector share for the smaller firms (ranked 11–50) in the top 50 increased slightly, from 0.54 to 0.59%. For the information sector as a whole, then, the relative share of the 10 largest firms diminished; the average share

of the next 40 firms increased slightly, and the share of the rest of the information sector firms increased substantially (from 32.4 to 40.9%). Thus, the information sector has become less dominated by its top firms.

It is quite different for the mass media sector. Here, the share of the top 10 firms doubled from 17.7 to 35.5%, and most of the growth was accounted for by the top five firms.

THE COMPANY POWER INDEX (CPI)

Although presence in multiple industries may widen the reach of a firm, commanding market share in one or two industries allows a company to leverage and strengthen its role. The Sector Share Index discussed in the previous section shows the share of a firm in the overall information sector. However, it ignores a company's dominance in particular industries. Suppose there are two firms with the same revenue earnings and the same market share in the overall information industry. Firm A participates in one industry, in which it has a dominant share of 50%, while it holds a modest 10% in the second industry. Firm B, in contrast,

Table 14.8 Top 50 Information Sector Firms' Power Index, 1984–2005

1984		1988		1992		1996		2001		2005	
AT&T	963	AT&T	597	AT&T	453	AT&T	283	AT&T	152	SBC	254
IBM	395	IBM	272	IBM	157	IBM	128	Verizon	121	Verizon	196
RCA	50	NYNEX	31	MCI	31	Intel	60	Microsoft	82	Microsoft	100
Bell Atlantic	35	Bell South	30	Time Warner	30	Time Warner	54	IBM	81	Time Warner	80
Bell South	35	General Electric	30	Bell South	28	MCI	46	SBC	81	IBM	78
Ameritech	30	Bell Atlantic	22	General Electric	23	Lucent	42	AOL Time Warner	79	Dell	61
ABC	24	Ameritech	20	Intel	23	HP	35	Worldcom	77	Comcast	60
CBS	21	ABC	20	Microsoft	23	Microsoft	29	HP	76	Intel	58
NYNEX	19	CBS	16	Sony	23	General Electric	27	Intel	49	Sony	36
US West	15	Warner Comm	15	NYNEX	22	Bell South	25	Viacom	49	HP	34
SBC	15	Intel	15	Bell Atlantic	22	Disney	24	Comcast	46	Bell South	30
Warner Comm	14	US West	14	CBS	19	Sony	21	Sony	36	Viacom I	27
Pacific Telesis	11	SBC	14	GTE	18	GTE	20	Hughes	30	Disney	24
Apple	10	Pacific Telesis	13	Ameritech	17	NYNEX	17	Lucent	25	Sprint	22
Matsushita	10	DEC	12	ABC	16	Bell Atlantic	16	Bell South	25	General Electric	18
Dun & Bradstreet	9	Sony	11	HP	15	Compaq	16	Dell	24	Vivendi	17
GTE	7	GTE	11	SBC	15	Motorola	15	Disney	20	Lucent	14
DEC	7	Thomson	11	US West	12	SBC	14	Sprint	19	Viacom II	13
Intel	6	MCI	11	Sun	11	Ameritech	13	General Electric	15	News Corp	10
Time, Inc.	6	Dun & Bradstreet	10	Sprint	11	Viacom	13	Samsung	12	Oracle	8
HP	5	Xerox	8	Matsushita	10	Sprint	13	Motorola	12	Qwest	7
Viacom	4	Viacom	7	Thomson	9	CBS	13	Vivendi	10	Barnes & Noble	7
Xerox	4	Unisys	7	Pacific Telesis	9	US West	10	Barnes & Noble	9	Xerox	6
Gannett	4	Matsushita	7	Dun & Bradstreet	9	Thomson	9	Qwest	8	Blockbuster	6
McGraw-Hill	3	Toshiba	6	TCI	9	Sun	9	Oracle	8	Samsung	6
General Electric	3	Apple	6	Disney	8	Samsung	9	Bertelsmann	7	Bertelsmann	5
Sony	3	Time, Inc.	6	Xerox	7	Pacific Telesis	7	Border/Walden	7	Sun	5
Burroughs	3	Bertelsmann	5	Viacom	7	Computer Ass.	6	News Corp	6	Matsushita	4
MCI	2	Sprint	5	Apple	7	TCI	6	Sun	6	Border/Walden	4

Rank	Company	Value	Company	Value	Company	Value	Company	Value	Company	Value	Company	Value
1	Wang Labs	2	TCI	4	Samsung	7	Gannett	5	Gannett	5	Tribune	4
2	Knight Ridder	2	Motorola	4	Gannett	5	Matsushita	5	Matsushita	5	Cox	4
3	Times-Mirror	2	Disney	4	Motorola	4	Xerox	5	Cox	3	Gannett	4
4	NCR	2	Gannett	3	DEC	4	News Corp	5	EDS	3	Toshiba	4
5	Toshiba	1	McGraw-Hill	3	TBS	3	EDS	4	Computer Ass.	3	McGraw-Hill	4
6	TBS	1	HP	3	Bertelsmann	3	Seagram	4	Gateway	3	Thomson Corp.	3
7	Tribune	1	Knight Ridder	2	Toshiba	2	Oracle	3	Thomson Corp.	3	Reed Elsevier	3
8	Bertelsmann	1	Times-Mirror	1	McGraw-Hill	2	Dell	3	Xerox	3	Knight Ridder	3
9	Thomson Corp.	1	MCA	1	Knight Ridder	2	Bertelsmann	3	McGraw-Hill	3	EDS	2
10	Disney	1	Gulf + Western	1	Compaq	1	Toshiba	3	Toshiba	1	Motorola	2
11	Westinghouse	1	TBS	1	Times-Mirror	1	Barnes & Noble	2	Reed Elsevier	1	Thomson	2
12	Reader's Digest	1	Reader's Digest	1	Gulf + Western	1	McGraw-Hill	2	Tribune	1	Gateway	2
13	MCA	0.9	Thomson Corp.	1	News Corp	1	Worldcom	2	Advance	1	Advance	2
14	Gulf + Western	0.9	Tribune	0.9	Hearst	1	Knight Ridder	2	Knight Ridder	1	New York Times	1
15	Cox	0.9	NCR	0.9	Thomson Corp.	1	Reed Elsevier	2	Hearst	1	Apple	1
16	Motorola	0.8	News Corp	0.8	Reader's Digest	1	Gateway	2	New York Times	1	Hearst	1
17	Sprint	0.8	New York Times	0.8	New York Times	0.9	Apple	1	Avaya	1	Avaya	1
18	New York Times	0.7	Compaq	0.8	Tribune	0.8	Cox	1	Apple	0.9	Unisys	1
19	Hearst	0.5	Hearst	0.7	Unisys	0.6	Hearst	1	Agere	0.2	Cisco	0.3
20	Washington Post	0.3	Cox	0.7	Cox	0.6	Unisys	0.2	Unisys	0.1	Washington Post	0.2
21	Sperry	0.3	Washington Post	0.3	Washington Post	0.2	NCR	0.0	Cisco	0.0	NCR	0.0
Average		35.10		25.78		22.15		9		8		24.72
Median		3		6		9		9	Average Median	9		6

Continued

368 National Concentration Trends

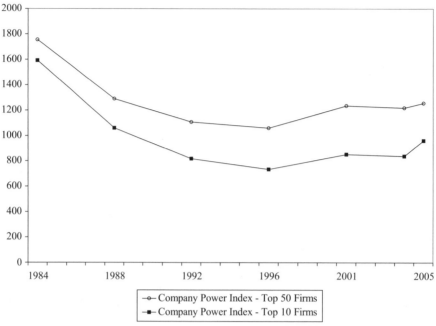

Figure 14.7 Aggregate Company Power Index of Top 10 and Top 50 Total Information Sector Firms (1984–2005)

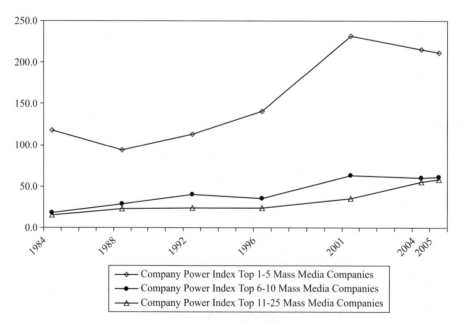

Figure 14.8 Aggregate Company Power Index of Top 5, 10, and 25 Mass Media Companies in the Total Information Sector (1984–2005)

is present in two industries with a 30% share in each. Whereas Company B is more vertically integrated, one might argue that Company A has more power, assuming that the industries are equally important. We define as a measure a Company Power Index (CPI) to capture such differences. It gives a greater weight to the larger market shares that a firm commands. The CPI is defined as:

$$CPI_{industry} = \sum_i CPI_{firm} = \sum_i \sum_j \frac{s_{ij}^2 m_j}{M}$$

where

s_{ij} = firm i's share in market j
m_j = total revenue of submarket j
j = subindustries, ranging from 1 to 100 (comprising the 100 industries)
i = firm
M = Revenues of total information sector

In effect, the CPI is the sum of a company's HHI scores in its various industries, each weighted by that industry's share in the overall information sector.

The Company Power Indices for the top 50 companies from 1984 to 2005 are shown in table 14.8 and figure 14.7

To illustrate the findings: Comcast and Sony had in 2005 fairly similar SSI scores (that is, share in the overall information sector) of 1.8 and 1.7, respectively. But Comcast participates in 5 industries, one of which it dominates. In contrast, Sony participates in 16 industries, all of which are fairly competitive (the music industry oligopoly being an exception). Consequently, Comcast's CPI score is 60 whereas Sony's is much lower at 36, even though it is present across more industries.

Figure 14.7 shows that the average Company Power Index levels are lower in 2005 than they had been two decades earlier. Numerically, this was primarily due to the significant drop in AT&T's and IBM's power index. In contrast, mass media companies such as Viacom and Time Warner show large increases in their CPIs over the period. Disney shows an increase of its CPI from 1.5 in 1984 to 24.2 in 2005.

Figure 14.7 shows a pronounced initial decline in aggregate CPI of the top 10 and top 50 firms, followed by a gradual increase after 1996, although to a lower level than it had been in 1984. Since the two lines are fairly parallel to each other, the share of firms 11–50 is fairly steady, increasing gradually until 2004. For mass media firms, the CPI of the top five firms rose steeply, as seen in Figure 14.8, after a slight decline after 1984. The rise was much lower for companies ranked 6–10 and 11–25 in size.

CONCLUSIONS

The several indices used in this chapter show the following trends:

- The aggregate share of the top 50 and 10 firms in the overall information sector did not increase, but declined, then stabilized at around 60% and 30%.
- But the share of the top five mass media companies increased considerably as a share of the mass media sector, doubling to 26.2%.
- The average top 50 companies in the information sector were active in 2.5 more industries on average in 2005 than in 1984.
- Most companies expanded only within their own subsector.

Notes

1. For an analysis of the issues, the economics, and legal schools of thought, both on vertical integration generally and media industries specifically, see Yoo, Christopher S. "Vertical Integration and Media Regulation in the New Economy," *Yale Journal on Regulation*, Winter 2002: 171–300. Joskow, Paul L. "Asset Specificity and the Structure of Vertical Relationships: Empirical Evidence." *Journal of Law, Economics and Organization* 4 (1988): 95, 107–11; Waterman, David, & Weiss, Andrew A. *Vertical Integration in Cable Television*. La Vergne, Tennessee: AEI Press, 1997; Bhagwat, Ashutosh. "Unnatural Competition?: Applying the New Antitrust Learning to Foster Competition in the Local Exchange." *Hastings Law Journal* 50 (1999): 1479; Olson, James W., & Spiwak, Lawrence J. "Can Short-Term Limits on Strategic Vertical Restraints Improve Long-Term Cable Industry Market Performance?" *Cardozo Arts and Entertainment Law Journal* 13, no.2 (1995): 283–315; Blair, Roger D., & Kaserman, David L. *Law and Economics of Vertical Integration and Control*. New York: Academic Press, 1983, pp. 20, 82; Williamson, Oliver E. *Markets and Hierarchies, Analysis and Antitrust Implications*. New York: Free Press, 1975, pp. 29–30, 35–37; Milgrom, Paul, & Roberts, John. *Economics, Organization and Management*. Englewood Cliffs, NJ: Prentice Hall, 1992, pp. 552–69; Larner, Robert J., & Meehan Jr., James

W. "The Structural School, Its Critics, and Its Progeny: An Assessment," in Larner, Robert J., & Meehan Jr., James W., eds. *Economics and Antitrust Policy.* New York: Quorum Books, 1989, pp. 179, 180–91; *Antitrust Law: An Economic Perspective.* Chicago: University of Chicago Press, 1976; McGee, John S., & Bassett, Lowell R. "Vertical Integration Revisited." *Journal of Law and Economics* 19, no. 1 (1976): 17–38; Graham, Daniel A., & Vernon, John M. "Profitability of Monopolization by Vertical Integration." *Journal of Political Economy* 79, no. 4 (July/August 1971): 924–925; Abiru, Masahiro. "Vertical Integration, Variable Proportions, and Successive Oligopolies." *Journal of Industrial Economics* 36, no. 3 (1988): 315–325; Perry, Martin K. "Vertical Integration: Determinants and Effects," in Schmalensee, Richard & Willig, Robert D., eds. *Handbook of Industrial Organization.* 1st ed. Amsterdam: North Holland, 1989; Hay, George A."An Economic Analysis of Vertical Integration." *The Industrial Organization Review* 1 (1973): 188–198; Schmalensee, Richard. "A Note on the Theory of Vertical Integration." *Journal of Political Economy* 81, no. 2 (1973): 442, 448; Warren-Boulton, Frederick R. "Vertical Control with Variable Proportions." *Journal of Political Economy* 82 (July 1974): 783, 794–96, 798, 799; Joskow, Paul L. "Asset Specificity and the Structure of Vertical Relationships: Empirical Evidence." *Journal of Law, Economics and Organization* 4 (1988): 95, 107–11; Hovenkamp, Herbert. "Post-Chicago Antitrust: A Review and Critique." *Columbia Business Law Review,* 2001, pp. 257–337; Hart, Oliver, & Jean Tirole, "Vertical Integration and Market Foreclosure," in Brookings Papers on Economic Activity. Washington DC: Brookings Institution Press, 1990, p. 205; Ordover, Janusz A., Saloner, Garth, & Salop, Steven C. "Equilibrium Vertical Foreclosure." *American Economic Review* 80, no. 1 (March 1990): 127–142; Riordan, Michael H. "Anticompetitive Vertical Integration by a Dominant Firm." *American Economic Review* 88, no. 5 (1998): 1232–1248; Riordan, Michael H., & Salop, Steven C. "Evaluating Vertical Mergers: A Post-Chicago Approach." *Antitrust Law Journal* 63 (1995): 513; Salinger, Michael A. "Vertical Mergers and Market Foreclosure." *Quarterly Journal of Economics* 103, no. 2 (May 1988): 345–356; Williamson, Oliver E. "Assessing Vertical Market Restrictions: Antitrust Ramifications of the Transaction Cost Approach." *University of Pennsylvania Law Review* 127 (April 1979): 953, 965; Carlton, Dennis W., & Perloff, Jeffrey M. *Modern Industrial Organization.* 3rd ed. Reading, MA: Addison Wesley Longman Inc., 2000, pp. 157, 165, 167, 175; Chipty, Tasneem. "Vertical Integration, Market Foreclosure, and Consumer Welfare in the Cable Television Industry."

American Economics Review 91, no. 3 (June 2001): 428–453.

2. Scherer, F. M., and David Ross. *Industrial Market Structure and Economic Performance.* Boston: Houghton Mifflin, 1990.

3. Given the scarcity of superior talent and outstanding programs, an increase in programs ought to lead to an increase in their average and marginal cost. A monopolist thus faces an upwardly sloping supply curve.

4. While most economists have approached this matter theoretically, there has also been empirical research. A study commissioned by the FCC finds that TV networks do not discriminate against independent producers of TV shows but that they discriminate against shows created by the owners of rival broadcast networks. And where cable TV operators favor their own cable program channels, it tends to be in places where competition from satellite broadcasters is low. Goolsbee, Austan. "Vertical Integration and the Market for Broadcast and Cable Television Programming," Federal Communications Com-mission. FCC. gov, September 5, 2007. Accessed on January 6, 2008, from http://www.fcc.gov/ownership/studies.html.

5. See Yoo, Christopher S. "Vertical Integration and Media Regulation in the New Economy." *Journal on Regulation,* 2002. pp. 171–300.

6. Tirole, Jean. *The Theory of Industrial Organization,* Cambridge: MIT Press, 1988.

7. For the literature, see Motta, M. "Competition Policy: Theory and Practice, "Cambridge: Cambridge University Press, 2004; Rey, and Tirole, J. "A Primer on Foreclosure," *Handbook of Industrial Organization, volume 3.* Amsterdam: Elsevier Science, B. V. 2005; and Goolsbee, Austan, and Amil Petrin. "The Consumer Gains from Direct Broadcast Satellites and the Competition with Cable TV," *Econometrica,* 2004. For vertical integration in cable TV, see also Chen, D., and D. Waterman. "Vertical Integration, Market Foreclosure, and Consumer Welfare in the Cable Television Industry," *American Review,* 2001; Ford, G. S., and J. D. Jackson. "Horizontal Concentration and Vertical Integration in the Cable Television Industry, "Discussion Paper, Osaka University, 2006: Waterman, D., and Weiss. "The Effects of Vertical Integration Between Cable Television Systems and Pay Cable Networks," *Journal of Econometrics,* 1996; Waterman, D. and Weiss. *Vertical Integration in Cable Television,* Cambridge: MIT Press, 1997.

8. For an elaboration, see Department of Justice and Federal Trade Commission, *Horizontal Merger Guidelines* (April 2, 1992; revised April 8, 1997); also, for the case of telecommunications, Department of Justice, *Opening Markets and Protecting Competition for America's Businesses and Consumers* (April 7, 1995), especially Parts II and IV.

15

Local Media Concentration

Where companies compete against each other across the country—such as Dell vs. Apple; HBO vs. Showtime; Paramount vs. Universal—one must analyze an industry's market structure on a national scale. But in other situations, the relevant geographic markets are not national or international but local. A cable company may be small nationally, yet in the city that it serves, it is likely to be the only cable provider and hold dominant market share. A newspaper chain may only account for 2% of newspapers sold across the country but for 90% of the papers in the cities in which it publishes. Conversely, a company may have only modest shares in each local market, but those small slices may add up to a large national role. The TV station group Paxson Communications (now ION Media), for example, owns tiny UHF stations all across the country, and their aggregate gives it a national presence. It is therefore important to distinguish local and national concentration, investigate the extent and direction of local concentration trends in the information sector, and go beyond national figures.

Despite the importance of this question, little systematic research has been done on it. There was a FCC study on local cable TV competition, part of a Congressional mandate following the 1992 Cable Act, in order to roll back prices of monopolistic cable markets to the levels prevailing in

competitive markets.[1] The FCC found that for over 12,000 cable TV franchise areas, only a few dozens were served by more than one firm, mostly as a result of some historical accident. But it identified neither market shares nor trends.

In 2003, the FCC, as part of its media ownership proceeding, ventured into local markets. As part of this effort the FCC established the Diversity Index (DI).[2] The DI was calculated from five local media: TV, radio, cable, newspaper, and the Internet. Local markets were defined as the Nielsen Designated Market Area (DMA).[3] Each DMA was divided up equally among the number of local television stations. For example, the FCC counted 23 television stations in the New York market. It then divided 100% by 23, and gave every station the same market share, 4.3%. Then, a weight was assigned to each medium, as determined by a study presented to the FCC by Nielsen Media Research that shows what media people use as a source for their news.[4] The market share for each company was then multiplied by this weight.

There are several problems with this methodology. One is that it assigns the same market share to companies of unequal size. In the New York City DMA, for instance, according to the FCC's methodology, Columbia University's tiny campus radio station is treated equally with CBS' flagship radio station WCBS. CBS, by that methodology, holds a radio market share that is six times larger than the market share of The New York Times Company, since the former owns six radio stations and the latter only one. In reality, however, CBS holds a 34.3% audience share and The New York Times Company only 2%.[5] The Columbia station WKCR's audience is below 0.1%. (In 2008 New York City had a total of 45 radio stations.)

The FCC simply counts each radio and TV station and each newspaper as "voices" available to the community, then weighs its news significance for an overall aggregation. The FCC approach—which happens to magnify media diversity—is not the methodology of antitrust analysis. The U.S. government does not count the mere numbers of, say, computer companies or film producers to determine market power. There are hundreds of them, but only a handful have significant audiences and revenues. The concept of "availability" that the FCC favored is not containable to a local market. There are hundreds of short-wave radio stations "available" over the air, many of them in foreign languages. If a station transmits in the forest and nobody hears it, is it a voice?

Another problem is that the FCC counts newspapers as competitors even if they serve distinct submarkets within a region. The *Poughkeepsie Journal* and the *Newark Star-Ledger,* both in the New York metropoliton region, are hardly rivals to each other or to the *New York Post.* Nor do they have identical market shares. Furthermore, the FCC does not provide a trend, because it does not look into the past. Its study focused on the year 2001/2002 and had no historical dimension.

The main reason that the FCC and other researchers have shied from a more thorough approach has been the difficulty of the task—conceptually as well as in terms of data availability. The task of the present study is therefore to overcome this gap and to provide an analysis of local media concentration trends for several local media over 20 years, with aggregations that permit some general observation. Some of the results have already been reported in earlier chapters.

First we need to define local media. The relevant industries of local mass media that are being analyzed are:

Radio stations
TV stations
Newspapers
City magazines and periodicals
Cable TV operators

But the following are also local distribution media, although of a different kind and dynamics.

Local wireline telephone networks
Cellular mobile networks

Most of these local media have experienced public policy conflicts concerning their local market power, with the exceptions of city periodicals.

The definition of a local medium is not always straightforward. Cable TV is a local distribution medium but it faces competition from direct broadcasting satellites (DBS), which are largely a national distribution medium, with a few local channels. To ignore the competition by DBS as a rival medium would overstate cable's share. (Therefore, we reduce cable's local share by the DBS penetration.) For the category "local periodicals" we included general audience glossy city magazines as well as alternative and free local periodicals, but not specialized local periodicals (*LA Dentist*).

The second step in the analysis is a determination of the relevant local market. In a metropolitan region, there may be a dozen cable companies, each with exclusivity in its franchise territory, and a dozen suburban papers, each with its own locality. If we defined a local market broadly, such as being a metropolitan statistical area or Nielsen DMA, this would overstate competition. We therefore define the local market as the city itself.

A third question is the selection of localities. There are many hundreds of cities large and small in the United States, and it would be impractical to seek the media concentration trends for each. We have therefore selected 30 markets to be representative of their categories. Ten large cities stand for major media markets (market rankings of 1–20), 10 medium-sized cities stand for the next tier (20–60), and 10 small local markets (above 60) represent small cities.[6]

Large Markets

New York, New York
Los Angeles, California
Chicago, Illinois
Houston, Texas
Philadelphia, Pennsylvania
Phoenix, Arizona
San Francisco, California
Boston, Massachusetts
Atlanta, Georgia
Miami, Florida

Medium Markets

Indianapolis, Indiana
Jacksonville, Florida
Portland, Oregon
Tucson, Arizona
New Orleans, Louisiana
Tulsa, Oklahoma
Richmond, Virginia
Grand Rapids, Michigan
Salt Lake City, Utah
Dayton, Ohio

Small Markets

Lincoln, Nebraska
Spokane, Washington
Boise, Idaho
Amarillo, Texas
Topeka, Kansas
Ft. Collins, Colorado
South Bend, Indiana
Green Bay, Wisconsin
Lancaster, Pennsylvania
Morgantown, West Virginia

LOCAL RADIO

The concentration of local radio stations has received much attention, since the abolition of national ceilings enabled one company, Clear Channel, to acquire over 1,500 stations for a time. On the local level, ownership restrictions were loosened in 1996 to a maximum number of local stations that could be owned by a single firm of eight in the largest of media markets and fewer in smaller markets.

The mere number of stations, however, does not fully convey market power, since some stations have much larger audiences and revenues than others. We use audience shares.

Table 15.1 shows local radio concentration trends. Local concentration in 2006 was significantly higher than it was in 1984. The weighed average share of the top firm in a market (C1) grew from about 19.9 to 33.8% and for the top four firms from 52.6 to 83.8%; the HHI index rose from a fairly unconcentrated 939 to a highly concentrated 2,326. These are large increases. However, if we compare this with the findings presented in figure 15.1, radio is still among the least concentrated of

Table 15.1 Radio Local Concentration

Local Radio Markets	1984	1988	1992	1996	2002	2006
	C1 Concentration					
C1 Large Cities	14.1	14.6	14.4	32.3	34.3	29.9
C1 Medium Cities	22.3	22.2	25.0	34.8	37.8	37.5
C1 Small Cities	25.6	24	23.5	35.6	31.8	35.5
Weighted Average	19.9	19.7	20.3	34	34.7	33.8
	C4 Concentration					
C4 Large Cities	43	42.2	45.8	67.7	80.3	78.8
C4 Medium Cities	57.2	62.6	68.0	88.8	91.8	87.1
C4 Small Cities	61.4	60.5	64.6	77.4	82.1	87.3
Weighted Average	52.6	53.8	58.1	77.1	84.4	83.8
	HHI Concentration					
HHI Large Cities	592	756	816	1,733	2,139	1,989
HHI Medium Cities	1,094	1,298	1,572	2,457	2,798	2,569
HHI Small Cities	1,263	1,238	1,333	2,173	2,330	2,537
Weighted Average	939	1,062	1,200	2,085	2,400	2,326
	Avg. Annual Rev. per Household					
Rev. Large Cities	41	55	62	92	144	200
Rev. Medium Cities	32	41	46	63	90	120
Rev. Small Cities	26	33	41	57	72	82
Weighted Average Revenue	34	44	51	73	106	142

Sources: Duncan's Radio Market Guide; 1985, 1989, 1994, 1997, and 2002 editions, respectively. Copyright James H. Duncan, Jr. Local market concentration was established using the *Broadcasting & Cable Yearbook* (1984, 1988, 1992, 1996, and 2001, respectively), R. R. Bowker, New Providence, N.J. For 2006, Arbitron local market ratings used. 2006 revenues based on population growth in each market.

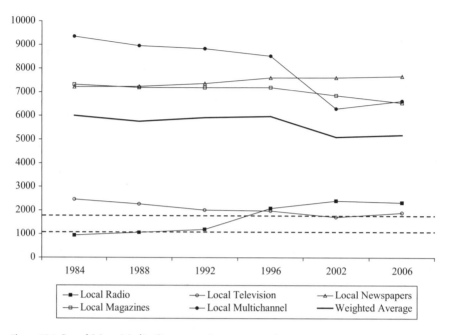

Figure 15.1 Local Mass Media Concentration

local media. Local media concentration in 2006 was much higher for multichannel TV (6,629) and newspapers (7,676).

When we look at the three market-size categories (large, medium, and small), we observe what we will find for other media, too: although the large markets are the least concentrated, as one would expect, the small markets have actually a slightly lower concentration than the medium-sized ones. The likely explanation is that in small markets, audiences also listen more to stations from adjacent cities, whereas audiences in medium-sized cities, given that there are more directly local choices, listen more to their own local stations.

LOCAL TELEVISION STATIONS

There are few issues in media policy that are more contentious than control over local television. Politicians consider local TV their primary access to voters and resent its gatekeeping power. Citizens concerned with diversity of content and political viewpoints have similarly been vigilant against local power. Businesses fear high prices for commercial advertisements. This has led to

strong coalitions opposed to the raising of the number of stations that any single company can own in the same market. This opposition exists even though many channels are available over cable and satellite, which is the way most people (85%) watch TV in America. But there is a logic to it: cable and DBS channels are mostly national, not local. (Cable has some local public access, education, and governmental channels, and in large metropolitan areas all-news cable channels.) Even though local TV stations air predominantly national programs delivered by networks and syndicators, localism nevertheless exists in local TV news—mornings, evenings, late night, and special programming—and is significant to the local political process, given that TV is most peoples' major source of news. This issue is different from the one about overall national ownership of local stations, another major bone of contention, which has been discussed in the chapter on TV station ownership.

The results for television local concentration are provided in table 15.2 as well as in figure 15.1. The findings show that concentration of local TV has actually declined over the past two decades, from a C4 of 89.8% in 1984 to 73.1% in 2006 (62.0% in large markets). For the market leader, the share

Table 15.2 TV Station Local Concentration

Television	1984	1988	1992	1996	2002	2006
			C1 Concentration			
C1 Large Cities	29.1	27.9	23.6	24.5	18.4	24.1
C1 Medium Cities	37.1	32.6	30	28.7	27.7	31.4
C1 Small Cities	35.9	36.3	32.9	31.3	31.2	37.6
Weighted Average	**33.5**	**31.8**	**28.2**	**28**	**24.9**	**30.2**
			C4 Concentration			
C4 Large Cities	84.5	80.1	72.5	73.3	61.8	62.0
C4 Medium Cities	95.1	90.9	87.6	88.0	78	77.1
C4 Small Cities	91.4	91.4	90.1	89.0	85.2	84.5
Weighted Average	**89.8**	**86.7**	**82.2**	**82.4**	**73.5**	**73.1**
			HHI Concentration			
HHI Large Cities	2,108	1,910	1,581	1,594	1,256	1,361
HHI Medium Cities	2,756	2,437	2,212	2,179	1,859	1,930
HHI Small Cities	2,634	2,595	2,384	2,306	2,207	2,619
Weighted Average	**2,460**	**2,269**	**2,006**	**1,979**	**1,714**	**1,895**
			Avg. Annual Rev. per Household			
Rev. Large Cities	111	146	158	200	258	264
Rev. Medium Cities	80	104	110	134	167	166
Rev. Small Cities	47	59	67	82	102	104
Weighted Average Revenue	**83**	**108**	**118**	**146**	**185**	**188**

Sources: Local television revenues are based on *Duncan's Radio Market Guide;* 1985, 1989, 1994, 1997, and 2002 editions, respectively. Copyright James H. Duncan, Jr. Concentration values C4 and HHI use Nielsen TV shares, from Nielsen Media Research . The chosen time period on deciding the television shares was 8:00–11:00 p.m. (and 8:00–10:00 p.m. if not available) from Monday–Friday; data used was for July except for 1996 due to the Olympic games held in Atlanta that year. (NBC had exclusive rights, and which increased its market share for that period.) In consequence, for 1996 the November period was chosen. 2000 data from Nielsen ratings.

dropped on average from 33.5 to 30.2% (24.1% in large markets). The HHI declined from 2,460 to 1,895.

The numerical reasons for this decline are a somewhat large number of local TV stations and a lessened audience share of the top three (and later four) stations affiliated with the major national TV networks, relative to other stations. It must be understood, furthermore, that these erosions would show as much larger if the major stations' audience shares were taken among *all* channels, including cable channels. In that case, they decline collectively by still another 50%. However, given our focus on local media and local news, we did not measure local TV market power in such a way, and looked only at the shares among local broadcast stations, whatever the platform they use to reach their audience. The decline of the broadcasting TV station audience is reflected in the revenue figures relative to local multichannel TV.

The level of local TV station concentration is the lowest among all of the five local mass media (figure 15.1). Although most cities must be content with one newspaper and one local magazine (if at all), there are likely to be half a dozen or more TV stations. Radio used to be less concentrated than TV but more recently has overtaken it, with a much greater disparity among companies' market shares.

MULTICHANNEL TV PROVIDERS

Multichannel TV used to be entirely provided by a cable TV operator, of which there was hardly ever more than one in each franchise territory. Large cities were often divided into several franchise territories, each with a single operator, and companies did not compete across franchise lines. In a few areas there were more than one cable operator, but those tended to be historic aberrations. Local franchises often consolidated into larger regional coverage by the same cable MSO. In time, direct broadcast satellites emerged as alternatives. Their share has gradually increased to about 15% nationally, and more in rural areas. Cable TV and DBS are not perfect substitutes. Cable carries local TV stations (DBS carries some, but fewer) and local PEG channels. Cable's interactivity enables it also to be a platform for broadband, Internet, and telephony. DBS, on the other hand, is geographically more widely available. These features, however, were not factors in the period before 2002. Market concentration trends can be seen in table 15.3.

The findings show that concentration is enormous but declining, with the market share of cable declining especially after 1996. The C1 dropped from 96.6 to 80.5%, HHI from 9,344 to a still quite high 6,629. Also, the size of the industry has

grown to make it by far the largest of local mass media ($1,765 million).

From the perspective of local media source diversity, cable has more competition than it used to have in local multichannel distribution. Telecom- delivered video services, such as Verizon's FiOS and Internet TV, will further add to the options. But this segment still is heavily concentrated, and its importance in terms of sheer size as a medium has grown.

LOCAL NEWSPAPERS

The local newspaper concentration trends can be seen in table 15.4 and figure 15.1. Local newspapers are the most concentrated of all local content media and distribution. Once one goes beyond the biggest cities, a single newspaper system prevails. A few papers (USA Today, the Wall Street Journal, and the New York Times) are widely available nationally, but their local readership is small. Their coverage of local news is minor, and their relevance to local advertisers nonexistent. It is best to

Table 15.3 Multichannel TV Local Concentration

Multichannel	1984	1988	1992	1996	2002	2006
	C1 Concentration					
C1 Large Cities	97.6	96.1	95.7	94.6	78.9	84.3
C1 Medium Cities	95.9	93.3	92.6	90.6	76.5	78.1
C1 Small Cities	95.9	93.3	92.6	90.6	77.8	77.8
Weighted Average	96.6	94.5	93.9	92.2	77.8	80.5
	C4 Concentration					
C4 Large Cities	100	100	100	98.9	99.3	99.4
C4 Medium Cities	100	100	100	97.9	99.3	99.6
C4 Small Cities	100	100	100	97.8	99.5	99.6
Weighted Average	100	100	100	98.3	99.4	99.5
	HHI Concentration					
HHI Large Cities	9,539	9,264	9,179	8,962	6,454	7,090
HHI Medium Cities	9,213	8,755	8,605	8,238	6,101	6,322
HHI Small Cities	9,211	8,752	8,602	8,234	6,302	6,313
Weighted Average	9,344	8,960	8,836	8,529	6,300	6,629
	Avg. Annual Rev. per Household					
Rev. Large Cities	100	132	205	298	456	469
Rev. Medium Cities	118	132	200	269	446	442
Rev. Small Cities	97	107	151	215	383	390
Weighted Average Revenue	105	125	188	266	432	437

Sources: Television and Cable Factbook: 1983, 1989, 1993, 1997, and 2002, respectively. Warner Communications and News Telecom and Media Intelligence. The Cable TV Financial Databook—2000. Paul Kagan Associates. www.NCTA.com accessed December 2007. www.SBCA.com accessed December 2007.

Table 15.4 Newspaper Local Concentration

Newspapers	1984	1988	1992	1996	2002	2006
	C1 Concentration					
C1 Large Cities	60.1	59.4	58.9	64	64.6	62.0
C1 Medium Cities	93.3	93.6	97.3	97.4	97.6	97.5
C1 Small Cities	94.8	94.9	95	95.2	94.4	97.3
Weighted Average	80.3	80.2	81.1	83.3	83.4	83.1
	C4 Concentration					
C4 Large Cities	98.3	97.4	95.9	96.3	96.4	96.1
C4 Medium Cities	100	100	100	100	100	100
C4 Small Cities	100	100	99.6	99.8	100	100
Weighted Average	99.3	99	98.2	98.4	98.6	98.4
	HHI Concentration					
HHI Large Cities	5,047	5,081	4,996	5,571	5,562	5,464
HHI Medium Cities	9,064	9,083	9,588	9,602	9,629	9,622
HHI Small Cities	8,267	8,271	8,280	8,311	8,325	8,670
Weighted Average	7,219	7,239	7,367	7,612	7,621	7,676
	Avg. Annual Rev. per Household					
Rev. Large Cities	125	163	160	184	220	213
Rev. Medium Cities	93	119	114	130	148	147
Rev. Small Cities	56	68	68	88	92	98
Weighted Average Revenue	95	122	120	140	161	160

Sources: Local newspaper revenues and concentration are based on *Duncan's Radio Market Guide*, 1985, 1989, 1994, 1997, and 2002 editions, respectively. Copyright James H. Duncan, Jr. Gale Broadcasting & Publishing Directory, annual editions. For the years in question, local newspaper companies and revenues were also published in DRMG. We differentiate between local and peripheral papers. The latter are newspapers from a larger city nearby. Conversely, city papers are also sold out of town. We therefore use 70% of a city paper and 20% of the adjoining peripheral paper.

think of them (except for the *New York Times* in New York itself) as a kind of daily national magazine, without a local dimension.[7] For local newspapers, too, we find that concentration is highest in medium-sized markets. The reason, again, is that readers in small cities such as Lancaster, Green Bay, or Fort Collins are more likely to buy a paper from a bigger, nearby city such as Philadelphia, Milwaukee, or Denver than readers in medium-sized markets tend to do.

The local concentration of newspapers has further increased in the past two decades, as many secondary papers have fallen by the wayside. The C1 concentration grew from 80.3 to 83.1% for the market leaders, and the HHI grew from 7,219 to 7,676.

Newspapers are arguably the most important of local media when it comes to local news and public affairs. TV and radio rarely allocate more than a few seconds to a story and tend to avoid

sticking out their necks in order not to alienate audience segments. Newspapers are also the main outlet for local advertising. The high concentration of the medium is hence a particular problem in terms of its political gatekeeper role and economic power.

LOCAL MAGAZINES AND PERIODICALS

This medium is somewhat hard to define. However, it is often described as another source of local diversity of news, and should therefore not be omitted from this study.

Local periodicals include only those of general readership. Special-audience local publications are not considered.[8]

The findings presented in table 15.5 and figure 15.1 show that local periodicals exist in the largest

Table 15.5 Magazines and Publications Local Concentration

Magazines	1984	1988	1992	1996	2002	2006
			C1 Concentration			
C1 Large Cities	55.2	54.1	51	48.0	46.8	42.3
C1 Medium Cities	88.9	88.9	94.5	100.0	92.5	91.6
C1 Small Cities	70.2	68.1	68.5	68.9	69.5	89.6
Weighted Average	**70.0**	**69.0**	**69.6**	**70.3**	**67.6**	**71.1**
			C4 Concentration			
C4 Large Cities	98.9	98.4	98	97.7	97.4	98.0
C4 Medium Cities	100	100	100	100	100	100
C4 Small Cities	100	100	100	100	100	100
Weighted Average	**99.6**	**99.3**	**99.2**	**99.1**	**98.9**	**98.9**
			HHI Concentration			
HHI Large Cities	4,344	4,036	3,851	3,665	3,546	3,291
HHI Medium Cities	9,505	9,505	9,753	10,000	9,063	8,944
HHI Small Cities	9,145	9,125	9,131	9,137	9,143	8,533
Weighted Average	**7,321**	**7,191**	**7,196**	**7,201**	**6,859**	**6,547**
			Avg. Annual Rev. per Household			
Rev. Large Cities	34	38	40	43	48	50
Rev. Medium Cities	2	3	3	3	10	9
Rev. Small Cities	3	3	4	5	8	6
Weighted Average Revenue	**15**	**17**	**18**	**20**	**25**	**25**

Sources: Gale Broadcasting & Publishing Directory; annual editions. Data for local magazines was collected with the help from the City and Regional Magazine Association. After identifying the appropriate magazines concerned with local news and events, we collected the circulation data on each magazine's Web site and marketing reports.

of cities, typically two in number. Thereafter, the numbers drop off rapidly, although in some cases regional magazines fill a similar function. Concentration of local periodicals declined slightly from an HHI of 7,321 to a 6,547 in 2006. In terms of revenues, this medium is by far the smallest of local media.

The findings for all five local mass media are as follows (see figure 15.1):

1. All local mass media are highly concentrated.
2. Radio and TV are the least concentrated, relatively speaking, with the former trending pronouncedly up and the latter trending down gradually.
3. Print media are among the most highly concentrated, with newspapers the most concentrated local medium by 2002.
4. Multichannel TV is highly concentrated but is trending downward as a result of the inroad of DBS (which is not really a local medium), but its revenues are trending upward.

5. A weighted average (figure 15.2) of all local mass media shows a decline in concentration for several years after 1996, after being essentially flat before. Yet the overall level is still high at an HHI 5,185 and C4 of 91.7. If we omit multichannel cable TV from content media, given that it is also a distribution medium, the trends show a lower level and a decline in concentration after 2001 (figure 15.2). The HHI decreases from 4,436 in 1984 to 4,042 in 2006; the C4 declines from 88.9 to 85.2.

WIRELINE TELECOMMUNICATIONS

This section discusses local telecom networks. Here, the local media provide transmission channels for all kinds of content, mostly provided by others. These media are two-way and individualized, in contrast to the mass media discussed above. Cable TV is a hybrid, serving as a local

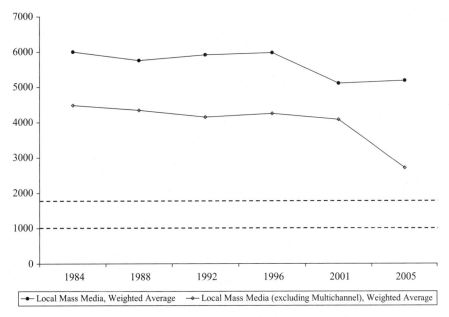

Figure 15.2 Local Mass Media Concentration Weighted Average Market Concentration

distribution network as well as content medium, and with some two-way capabilities (which are accounted for in the section on wireline telephony and Internet).

The wireline market has been the subject of much regulatory attention. Historically, except for a brief period over a century ago, this segment had been monopolistic. It has been opened in recent years through the requirement on the incumbent telecom companies to share their infrastructure with competitors, as well as through network unbundling and prices that made competition feasible. These and other rules have opened local markets to resale and facilities-based entrants. In defining local market share, one question is whether to count physical facilities (actual access lines) or subscribership, including those of resellers. We use the second and wider definition, not only because it is more relevant for business competition, but also because it is the measure used by the FCC (to show success for its policy), by the entrants (to dazzle investors) and even by incumbents (to argue for their deregulation).

The results in table 15.6 and figure 15.3 show

1. Local telecom concentration, once a monopoly in economic and legal terms, (HHI = 10,000), declined in the two decades under

observation. Although still quite high, it was 4,993 in 2006. The C1 is 69.2%, down from 100% in 1984 and 1988. A large share of the new entrants' revenues comes from large business accounts, and much of the rest from voice telephony over cable.

2. Concentration has been declining in large markets but also, a few years later, in small and medium-sized cities.

MOBILE COMMUNICATIONS

For several years, mobile phones were a formal local duopoly. Later, cellular telephony became diversified with often four or more additional "PCS" providers, for a total of often six or more providers before the market consolidated to four major national footprints.

The results, table 15.7 and figure 15.3 show that market concentration dropped from a highly concentrated HHI of 5,050 in 1984 to 2,158 in 2002 and then rose to 2,814 in 2006. The market leader's share (C1) fell from about 55 to 31.4% and rose again to 39.5%.

Consolidation has affected this industry both nationally (large footprints) and locally (through mergers and acquisitions among competitors). In

Table 15.6 Telecom Local Concentration

Telecom	1984	1988	1992	1996	2002	2006
			C1 Concentration			
C1 Large Cities	100	100	97.5	90	74.9	69.5
C1 Medium Cities	100	100	100	93.5	78.3	72.7
C1 Small Cities	100	100	100	97.2	71.7	64.7
Weighted Average	100	100	99.0	93.1	75.1	69.2
			C4 Concentration			
C4 Large Cities	100	100	98.5	93.9	84.8	81.7
C4 Medium Cities	100	100	100	97.4	91.4	87.8
C4 Small Cities	100	100	100	99.3	92.5	88.4
Weighted Average	100	100	99.4	96.5	89.1	85.5
			HHI Concentration			
HHI Large Cities	10,000	10,000	9,571	8,285	5,713	4,971
HHI Medium Cities	10,000	10,000	10,000	8,876	6,255	5,387
HHI Small Cities	10,000	10,000	10,000	9,636	6,364	4,584
Weighted Average	10,000	10,000	9,827	8,852	6,067	4,993
			Avg. Annual Rev. per Household			
Rev. Large Cities	197	239	290	351	426	437
Rev. Medium Cities	191	231	280	340	412	410
Rev. Small Cities	192	233	282	342	414	424
Weighted Average Revenue	**194**	**235**	**285**	**345**	**418**	**425**

Sources: Reports from the North American Numbering Plan Administration, allocation of numbers available at http://www.nanpa.com/. Data on local telecom markets collected using the local area codes for each local market, enabling finding the number of telephone lines within such markets. NANPA listed the companies to which the telephone lines are assigned, which permits the calculation of market shares, by lines. Revenues were calculated by using the FCC's *Reference Book of Rates, Price Indices, and Household Expenditure for Telephone Service* (July 2002).

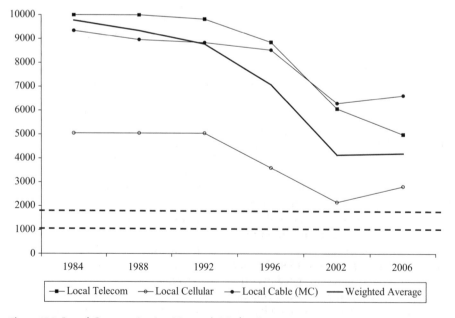

Figure 15.3 Local Communication Network Media Concentration

Table 15.7 Mobile Communication Local Concentration

Cellular	1984	1988	1992	1996	2002	2006
			C1 Concentration			
C1 Large Cities	55	55	55	40.6	26.2	35.1
C1 Medium Cities	55	55	55	46.2	37.4	42.7
C1 Small Cities	55	55	55	43.7	32.3	42.1
Weighted Average	55	55	55	43.2	31.4	39.5
			C4 Concentration			
C4 Large Cities	100	100	100	91	81.9	92.3
C4 Medium Cities	100	100	100	94.1	88.2	96.1
C4 Small Cities	100	100	100	90.7	81.4	92.4
Weighted Average	100	100	100	91.9	83.8	93.5
			HHI Concentration			
HHI Large Cities	5,050	5,050	5,050	3,499	1,949	2,564
HHI Medium Cities	5,050	5,050	5,050	3,776	2,502	3,142
HHI Small Cities	5,050	5,050	5,050	3,561	2,073	2,805
Weighted Average	5,050	5,050	5,050	3,604	2,158	2,814
			Avg. Annual Rev. per Household			
Rev. Large Cities	4	36	110	312	859	880
Rev. Medium Cities	4	36	109	309	849	844
Rev. Small Cities	4	35	107	304	835	854
Weighted Average Revenue	4	36	109	309	849	861

Sources: The North American Numbering Plan Administration, allocation of numbers available at http://www. nanpa.com/, for number block allocation. Also, *RCR Wireless News,* November 18, 2002. *"The Wireless EDGE"* Salomon Smith & Barney April 3, 2003.

terms of dollar volume, the industry has grown enormously, from $4 on average annually per household in 1984 to over $861 in 2006 for all three categories. It has surpassed every other local medium in size.

OVERALL LOCAL MEDIA CONCENTRATION

We are now able to average all of the seven local media by using weights based on their revenue volumes. (In a later section we will use a different weighting system for mass media, based on their importance as a news source.)

The findings are shown in figure 15.4. Average concentration (the bold line) has dropped over the past 20 years, mostly due to the decline in concentration on the network side (telecom, mobile, and cable TV's losses to DBS).

We can also differentiate between three types of cities/markets: large, medium, and small. The result can be seen in figure 15.5. As expected, large cities are less concentrated, because they can support more media and because of their larger diversity. But the concentration in small markets is not much higher than in medium-sized markets, and often indeed smaller. The reason is likely to be their audiences' reaching beyond the small markets to the media of nearby larger cities, whereas audiences in medium-sized cities might be more self contained.

To repeat some of the overall findings:

1. All local media are strongly concentrated, with most HHI values either within the Department of Justice classification of "moderately concentrated" or well above it.
2. Of the local electronic mass media, broadcast television stations and multichannel

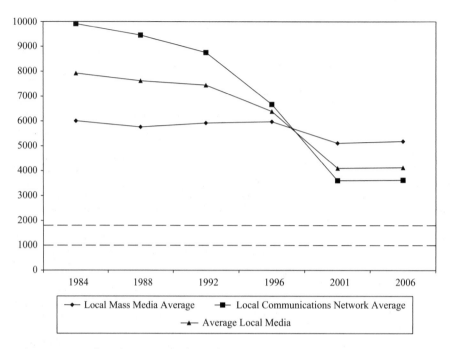

Figure 15.4 Local Media: Mass Media and Communications Networks

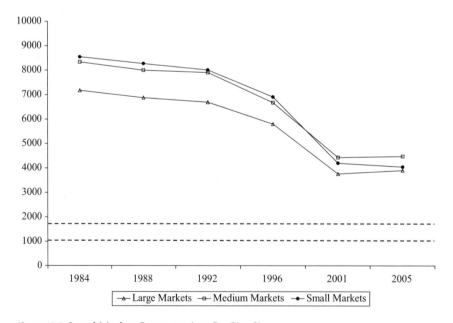

Figure 15.5 Local Market Concentration, By City Size

TV are experiencing the biggest declines in concentration.

3. Local print media are highly concentrated, and the local newspaper industry also shows an upward trend in concentration.

4. The local telecom market is less concentrated than it used to be, but still remains at a high level.

5. Radio is growing fastest in concentration, but remains well below the concentration levels prevailing in most other local media.

6. Averaging all (weighted) seven local media shows a decline of local concentration from an average HHI of an astonishing magnitude of almost 8,000 in 1984 to about half the magnitude at about 4,000. This is mostly the result of the declines in concentration of wireline and cellular telephony, and of multichannel stemming from the rise of DBS. If we instead only look at local mass media, without the two telecom media, the trend is high (6,000) and flat until 1996, and then drops to about 5,000. This is again mostly the result of the decline of concentration in multichannel due to DBS, which could be classified as a distribution rather than content medium. If that medium, too, is excluded, the remaining mass media decline gently from 4,500 in 1984 to a still high 4,000 in 2006.

Notes

1. "Second Order on Reconsideration, Fourth Report and Order, and Fifth Notice of Proposed Rulemaking," MM Docket No. 92–266, FCC 93–177, 8 FCC Rcd 5361.

2. "Report and Order and Notice of Proposed Rulemaking," June 2, 2003. FCC 03–127.

3. Available at http://www.nielsenmedia.com/DMAs.html.

4. The weights assigned to each medium in the local markets were television, 33.8; radio, 24.9; newspaper, 28.8; Internet, 12.5. For an explanation see http://www.fcc.gov/Daily_Releases/Daily_Business/2003/db0702/FCC-03–127A2.pdf.

5. *Duncan's Radio Market Guide,* 2002 Edition, Copyright 2002, James H. Duncan Jr.

6. Available at http://www.nielsenmedia.com/DMAs.html.

7. Methodologically, therefore, we count for the *New York Times* only its New York circulation as part of that city's calculative newspaper concentration.

8. In the case of the *New Yorker* magazine, which has a wide national readership, only its New York City circulation is counted for the concentration in New York.

9. Local online news sites accounted in 2004 for 2% of their print newspaper cousins.

16

The Ownership Structure of the American Information Sector

In this chapter we examine the composition and structure of ownership in the American information sector. For media, the ownership and control are arguably more important than in other industries, given the role of information in social, economic, and political life. In the past, when a political or military coup took place somewhere in the world, the rebels gave priority to taking control over broadcast stations and telephone exchanges.

There are several forms of *noncommercial* ownership in America. They include direct governmental ownership (for example, Voice of America for foreign broadcasts); indirect control by lower levels of government, such as a broadcast station licensed to a state university; nonprofit public TV stations; and some newspapers owned by foundations set up by the original owners. But more significant in terms of size, impact, and prevalence are the several types of *private* ownership—by individuals, families, partnerships, publicly held corporations, institutional investors, and venture capitalists.

American newspapers and magazines have often been owned and controlled by individuals and families through closely held (that is, largely nontraded) corporations or special voting stock. Other media firms relied on outside financing through a more "public" ownership of shares, or from "private equity" funds. This, in turn, has led to a significant ownership role by institutional investors that buy stakes in companies on behalf of smaller investors.

INDIVIDUAL AND INSIDER OWNERS

Media owners can influence people's minds: Benjamin Franklin shaped the emerging American republic via his newspapers and magazine. William Randolph Hearst used his newspapers to fight for policy and war and to promote his unsuccessful bids for high office; and Henry Luce, owner of *Time*, advanced his strong views on U.S.-China foreign policy through his magazines. The power of media owners has always been worrisome to the public, although in other cases that same power is called "independence" and viewed as a positive check on self-serving politicians and overreaching officials.

The information sector has been the foundation of some of America's largest fortunes. Table 16.1 lists a subset of the 400 wealthiest individuals in the United States in 2005, selecting those individuals who earned or inherited their fortunes from activities of media and communications companies.

This list does not include the non-American owners of large media operations in the United States, such as the Mohn family, which controls, through a foundation, the Bertelsmann company that owns in America the media firms BMG and Random House. The list demonstrates the extraordinary wealth that has been amassed in the information industries: 21 out of the 50 largest American fortunes originate in the information sector. Five years earlier, in 2000, at the height of the Internet boom, an amazing 22

Table 16.1 Media and Information Fortunes among Forbes' 400 Wealthiest Americans, 2008

Rank	Name	Net Worth ($ million)	Industry/Firm
1	William Gates III	57,000	Microsoft
3	Lawrence Ellison	27,000	Oracle
8	Michael Bloomberg	20,000	Bloomberg
11	Michael Dell	17,300	Dell Computer
12	Paul Allen	16,000	Microsoft, Charter Cable
13	Sergey Brin	15,900	Google
14	Larry Page	15,800	Google
15	Steven Ballmer	15,000	Microsoft
19	Anne Cox Chambers	13,000	Cox Enterprises
27	Kirk Kerkorian	11,200	Entertainment
32	John Kluge	9,000	Metromedia
33	James Goodnight	8,700	SAS Institute
33	Jeffrey Bezos	8,700	Amazon
35	Charles Ergen	8,100	EchoStar/Dish Network
36	Philip Anschutz	8,000	Entertainment, Telecommunications
36	Donald Newhouse	8,000	Publishing
36	Samuel Newhouse Jr	8,000	Publishing
47	Rupert Murdoch	6,800	News Corp
49	Blair Parry-Okedon	6,500	Cox Enterprises
49	David Geffen	6,500	Movies, Music
49	James Kennedy	6,500	Cox Enterprises
54	Pierre Omidyar	6,300	Ebay
59	Eric Schmidt	5,900	Google
61	Steven Jobs	5,700	Apple Computer, Pixar
66	Sumner Redstone	5,100	Viacom/CBS
68	Henry Ross Perot Sr	5,000	Computer Services, Real Estate
84	Gordon Moore	4,400	Intel
84	John Sall	4,400	SAS Institute
89	Patrick McGovern	4,100	IDG
91	David Sun	4,000	Computer memory
91	George Lucas	4,000	Film
91	John Tu	4,000	Computer memory
97	Daniel Ziff	3,700	Publishing
97	Dirk Ziff	3,700	Publishing
97	Robert Ziff	3,700	Publishing
131	A Jerrold Perenchio	3,100	Univision
131	Steven Spielberg	3,100	Movies
144	Ray Dolby	2,900	Dolby Laboratories
147	Amos Hostetter Jr	2,800	Cable Television
147	Mortimer Zuckerman	2,800	Real Estate, Media
155	Oprah Winfrey	2,700	Television
161	Mark Cuban	2,600	Broadcast.com
163	Leonore Annenberg	2,500	Publishing
187	William Randolph Hearst III	2,400	Hearst Corp
190	Frank Batten Sr	2,300	Landmark
190	John Malone	2,300	Cable Television
190	Craig McCaw	2,300	McCaw Cellular
190	Robert E "Ted" Turner	2,300	Cable Television
205	Henry Ross Perot Jr	2,200	Computer Services, Real Estate
215	Austin Hearst	2,100	Hearst Corp
215	David Hearst Jr	2,100	Hearst Corp
215	George Hearst Jr	2,100	Hearst Corp

continued

Table 16.1 *(Continued)*

Rank	Name	Net Worth ($ million)	Industry/Firm
215	Phoebe Hearst Cooke	2,100	Hearst Corp
246	Irwin Jacobs	1,900	Qualcomm
246	Omid Kordestani	1,900	Google
246	Thomas Siebel	1,900	Siebel Systems
262	Henry Nicholas III	1,800	Broadcom
262	Henry Samueli	1,800	Broadcom
262	Min Kao	1,800	navigation equipment
281	David Filo	1,700	Yahoo
281	Dean White	1,700	lboards, hotels
281	Jerry Yang	1,700	Yahoo
281	Kavitark Ram Shriram	1,700	Google
281	Stanley Hubbard	1,700	DirecTV
281	Walter Scott Jr	1,700	construction, telecom
301	Alan Gerry	1,600	cable television
301	James Kim & family	1,600	microchips
301	John Morgridge	1,600	Cisco
301	Michael Krasny	1,600	CDW Corp
321	Alexander Knaster	1,500	Oil, Telecom, Banking
321	Amar Bose	1,500	Bose
321	Bharat Desai & family	1,500	Syntel
321	Edmund Ansin	1,500	Sunbeam Broadcasting
321	Mark Zuckerberg	1,500	Facebook
321	Todd Wagner	1,500	Broadcast.com
355	Barry Diller	1,400	IAC/InterActiveCorp
355	Richard Egan	1,400	EMC Corp
355	Theodore Waitt	1,400	Gateway
355	Vinod Khosla	1,400	Sun Microsystems, venture capital
377	Kenny Troutt	1,300	Excel Communications
377	Peter Thiel	1,300	Paypal, Facebook
377	Thomas Secunda	1,300	Bloomberg

Source: Forbes, "400 Richest People in America," 2008. Available at http://www.forbes.com.

of the 30 wealthiest Americans had made their fortune in the information sector. Most interesting is the presence of individuals on this list whose companies were nascent a dozen or so years earlier, such as the major owners of Microsoft, Dell, Oracle, Google, eBay, and EchoStar, Dish Network. Table 16.1 shows that in 2008, 80 individuals (20%) of the Forbes 400 richest Americans earned their wealth in the media, information, and communications fields. (In 2000, at the height of the boom, that number had been almost 25%, at least on paper.)

(The table lists only those who earned their fortunes in the media and communications industries. Individuals who attained their wealth through other sources, even those that include substantial media and communications investments, such as in the case of the investment guru Warren Buffett, were not included.)

It is also perhaps no accident that individual wealth in the information sector is tied to relatively new industries, for example, computers, cable television, Internet, and cellular communications. Individual entrepreneurial activity is often strongest at the early phases of a new industry, and the capitalized value of expected future above-normal returns can create enormous instant wealth.

Table 16.2 shows the level of "insider" ownership of the largest information sector firms. Such ownership generally refers to the officers, directors, and those that hold more than 5% of shares in a company ("significant shareholders").[1] The table shows a considerable decrease in insider ownership for mass media firms from 1988 to 2005, dropping from a weighted average of 30.4 to 15.0%. In contrast, the insider ownership for IT and telecom firms, while much lower, increased somewhat, rising from 2.2 to 4.5% over the

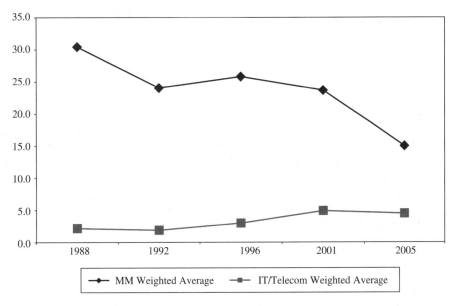

35.0

30.0

25.0

20.0

15.0

10.0

5.0

0.0

1988   1992   1996   2001   2005

◆ MM Weighted Average   ■ IT/Telecom Weighted Average

Figure 16.1 Weighted Average of Insider Ownership, Mass Media and IT/Telecom, 1988–2005, by Percentage

same period (see also figure 16.1). However, the trends are converging. In 1988, this ratio had been 15 times as high. Since then, IT/telecom insider ownership has doubled, whereas that of mass media was cut by half.

Insider ownership declined in several major IT firms; over 50.8% of Microsoft was owned by insiders in 1992, dropping to 23.6% by 2005. For Hewlett-Packard, insider ownership declined from 25.9% in 1998 to 10.1% in 2005. This decrease in insider ownership largely stems from the growth cycle of such companies. Generally, new-venture companies start out as privately owned and then go public in order to raise additional capital to develop their products (and enrich their founders, backers, and investment bankers), while still retaining as much control as possible by the founders. Over time, some of the technology or new media companies became stock market favorites, causing their insider ownership to decrease further as insiders sold out. However, the share of newer IT firms within the overall sector increased, and thus the weighted average rose slightly.

In the mass media, firms with an intermediate insider share are those led by their founders or builders—News Corp 27.4% (Rupert Murdoch); Viacom/CBS 36% (Sumner Redstone); Comcast (Roberts family owns 1–2% of outstanding shares but 33% of voting stock); Barnes & Noble 19.8% (Leonard Riggio). In other cases, companies are held by dynasties: Cox (66%); The New York Times Company 35% (Ochs/Sulzberger); Washington Post Company 35.4% (Meyer/Graham); Bertelsmann (100% through a Mohn family-dominated foundation); Hearst 47.8%; Advance 75%, (Newhouse family); and Tribune 27%, (Medill and Chandler families, with ownership transferred to Sam Zell and the employees' stock ownership plan). In some cases, control is actually higher because of different classes of stock with different voting rights and other control arrangements at tension with shareholder democracy.[2] Such arrangements are largely absent in telecom/IT.

INSTITUTIONAL OWNERS

Institutional ownership is not a recent phenomenon, but it has increased with the growth of mutual funds and pension funds. Mutual funds are companies that pool the money of investors and invest it in a portfolio of stocks, bonds, and other assets. They attempt to optimize returns for a given risk level. Complex rules limit investment in any single company and generally make it inadvisable to hold more than 5% of assets in any one company and no more than 10% of any company's outstanding shares.[3] This limits the capacity of any individual fund to exercise much control over a firm, with the specific limitations determined by the kind of fund

Table 16.2 Insider Ownership in Major Media and Communications Companies

1988 Mass Media		1988 IT/Telecom		1992 Mass Media		1992 IT/Telecom	
Company	Insiders (%)	Company	Insiders (%)	Company	Insiders (%)	Company	Insiders (%)
Bertelsmann**	100.0	HP	25.9	Bertelsmann**	100.0	Microsoft	50.8
TBS	100.0	Intel	22.5	Thomson Corp.***	70.0	HP	19.6
TCI	71.0	Compaq	21.5	Cox*	66.0	Unisys	13.4
Thomson Corp.***	70.0	Apple	14.3	Viacom*	60.0	DEC	10.0
Cox*	66.0	Motorola	13.2	TCI	49.0	Intel	7.9
Times-Mirror	51.0	DEC*	10.0	Hearst***	44.9	Apple	7.1
Hearst***	44.9	Sprint	5.0	Times-Mirror	37.9	Sun	6.9
New York Times^	44.2	MCI	2.4	Tribune	36.3	Motorola	4.7
Viacom^	41.3	Sony***	1.0	Knight Ridder	30.4	Sprint	3.8
CBS	37.8	Matsushita***	1.0	New York Times^	30.2	MCI	1.8
Tribune	34.4	Toshiba***	1.0	Washington Post*^	30.0	Matsushita***	1.0
Washington Post^	31.1	NCR	0.9	TBS	29.8	Sony***	1.0
Knight Ridder***	30.4	Xerox	0.7	News Corp***	27.4	Samsung***	1.0
News Corp***	27.4	Unisys	0.5	Reader's Digest	24.4	Toshiba***	1.0
Reader's Digest***	24.4	IBM	0.4	Disney***	20.0	IBM	0.1
ABC/Cap Cities	23.4	General Electric	0.3	ABC/Cap Cities	18.5	Bell Atlantic	0.1
Disney	19.2	Ameritech	0.1	Gannett	12.5	GTE	0.1
MCA	18.4	SBC	0.1	CBS	12.1	NYNEX	0.1
Gannett	12.5	US West	0.1	Time Warner	9.9	Ameritech	0.1
McGraw-Hill	5.2	AT&T***	0.0	McGraw-Hill	5.2	SBC	0.1
Warner Comm	5.0	Bell South	0.0	Gulf + Western	2.7	US West	0.1
Time, Inc.	2.9	NYNEX	0.0	Sony***	1.0	Xerox	0.1
Gulf + Western	2.7	Bell Atlantic	0.0	Dun & Bradstreet	0.5	AT&T***	0.0
Dun & Bradstreet	0.6	Pacific Telesis	0.0	Reed Elsevier***	0.5	Bell South	0.0
General Electric	0.3	GTE	0.0	General Electric	0.1	Compaq	2.0
Weighted Average	30.4	Weighted Average	2.2	Weighted Average	24.0	Weighted Average	1.9
Average	34.6	Average	4.8	Average	28.8	Average	5.1
Weighted Average of U.S.-Owned Firms	27.9	Weighted Average of U.S.-Owned Firms	2.2	Weighted Average of U.S.-Owned Firms	24.4	Weighted Average of U.S.-Owned Firms	1.9

Company	Insiders (%)	Company	Insiders (%)	Company	Insiders (%)	Company	Insiders (%)	Company	Insiders (%)
Bertelsmann**	75.0	HP	41.3	Bertelsmann**	75.0	Bertelsmann**	34.1	Oracle	43.3
Thomson Corp.***	70.0	Microsoft	38.6	Advance^^	75.0	Advance^^	23.7	Gateway	38.7
Cox*	66.0	Samsung***	10.7	Thomson Corp.***	70.0	Cox*	21.4	Microsoft	23.6
Seagram	61.3	Intel	5.5	Cox	59.7	Hearst	19.4	Qwest	17.4
TCI	49.0	Worldcom	5.4	Hearst	44.9	Washington Post^	11.6	Samsung	10.7
Hearst***	44.9	Motorola	3.1	Comcast	38.0	New York Times*^	10.7	HP	10.1
Comcast*^	38.0	Apple	3.0	Washington Post*^	35.0	News Corp	5.4	Dell	9.5
Barnes & Noble	33.9	MCI	1.6	Viacom	34.1	Tribune	2.2	Intel	5.9
Washington Post*^	32.7	Compaq	1.2	Knight Ridder***	30.0	Barnes & Noble	1.8	Sun	2.0
New York Times^	32.1	Sony***	1.0	News Corp***	27.4	Comcast	1.2	Sony*	1.0
Viacom^	30.5	Toshiba***	1.0	New York Times^	26.4	CBS	1.0	Toshiba*	1.0
Knight Ridder	29.1	Matsushita***	1.0	Tribune	24.6	Viacom I	1.0	Matsushita*	1.0
News Corp***	27.4	Xerox	0.6	Clear Channel	22.3	Charter	1.0	Avaya	0.7
Tribune	19.8	Sprint	0.3	Reader's Digest	18.9	Clear Channel	1.0	Apple	0.6
Times-Mirror	18.6	IBM	0.2	Disney***	7.0	Disney	0.7	Motorola	0.4
Disney	17.2	GTE	0.1	Charter	6.5	Time Warner	0.5	EDS	0.4
Gannett	14.4	Ameritech	0.1	AOL Time Warner	3.7	Blockbuster	0.5	Xerox	0.3
CBS***	12.1	SBC	0.1	Vivendi	3.0	Vivendi*	0.3	Lucent	0.2
Time Warner***	9.9	Bell Atlantic	0.1	AT&T	1.2	Gannett	0.1	NCR	0.2

continued

389

Table 16.2 (Continued)

	1996				2001				2005			
	Mass Media		IT/Telecom		Mass Media		IT/Telecom		Mass Media		IT/Telecom	
Company	Insiders (%)	Company	Insiders (%)	Company	Insiders (%)	Company	Insiders (%)	Company	Insiders (%)	Company	Insiders (%)
McGraw-Hill	2.2	NYNEX	0.1	Sony***	1.0	SBC	0.1	Border/Walden	1.2	SBC/AT&T	0.1
Sony***	1.0	US West	0.1	McGraw-Hill	0.6	Bell South	0.1	Sony*	1.0	Sprint	0.1
Reed Elsevier**	0.5	AT&T	0.0	Reed Elsevier***	0.5	Lucent	0.1	McGraw-Hill	1.0	IBM	0.1
Dun & Bradstreet	0.4	Bell South	0.0	Gannett	0.4	Cisco	0.1	Knight Ridder	0.6	Bell South	0.1
General Electric	0.1	Lucent*	0.0	GM/Hughes	0.2	Avaya	0.0	Reed Elsevier*	0.5	Cisco	0.1
US West (MediaOne)*	0.1	Pacific Telesis	0.0	General Electric	0.1	Apple	0.0	General Electric	0.1	Unisys	0.1
Weighted Average	25.8	Weighted Average	3.0	Weighted Average	23.7	Weighted Average	4.9	Weighted Average	15.0	Weighted Average	4.5
Average	27.4	Average	5.1	Average	24.2	Average	5.5	Average	19.6	Average	6.4
Weighted Average of US-Owned Firms	25.9	Weighted Average of US-Owned Firms	3.0	Weighted Average of US-Owned Firms	24.3	Weighted Average of US-Owned Firms	5.1	Weighted Average of U.S.-Owned Firms	14.0	Weighted Average of U.S.-Owned Firms	4.7

Notes: Insiders (%) include individuals with 5% ownership. Source for 1988–2005: "Compact D-SEC," Compact Disclosure Inc., 1988–2005.

Source for Mass Media 2005: MSN Money.

* Estimate.

** 76.9% of company is owned by the family-controlled Bertelsmann Foundation. The remainder is now owned by the Mohn family, descendants of the founder.

*** Extrapolated from other years.

^ Two Classes of stock consolidated, and assuming both classes are of equal weight.

^^ Advance is private, owned mostly by the Newhouse family [http://www.publicintegrity.org/telecom/analysis/CompanyProfile.aspx?HOID=8030].

and, in some cases, its location and purpose. With pension funds, for example, the state in which they are based is determinative.

The Growth of Institutional Investors

Institutional investment in the United States and in global markets has grown tremendously. Stocks are an attractive investment vehicle for institutions because of their liquidity, and media and computer technology stocks were frequent favorites based on perceptions of future growth potential. High-technology firms in the electronics sector were often set up through venture funding, which led to public stock offerings and often contributed to institutional ownership.

Institutional investors' assets in the United States grew from approximately $675 billion in 1970 to $24.1 trillion in 2005[4] and $35.5 trillion in 2007, 326% of the annual GDP. (This does not include hedge funds and private equity.) Mutual funds grew quickly throughout the 1980s and 1990s, and pension funds grew even faster. In 1980 there were approximately $70 billion in assets under management by mutual funds; by 2007, this figure had grown to $12.4 trillion. Meanwhile, pension fund assets increased from $213 billion in 1970 to $17.2 trillion in 2007. And insurance assets rose to $6.3 trillion.

The following tables take a more detailed look at the increase in institutional investment in communications and media industries. The term "institutional investors" formally applies only to entities that hold themselves out as primarily engaged in investing, reinvesting, or trading securities. Accordingly, actual institutional ownership of media companies may be understated by most data sources. For example, if Company A is partly owned by a Company B, which does not fall into the category of "institutional investor," then B's investment will not be counted in the overall institutional ownership figures for Company A, even though B may be largely owned by institutions. Moreover, the SEC does not require disclosure of institutional investors that own less than 5% of a company. However, many companies list such ownerships anyway.

Table 16.3 shows the share of institutional ownership in the largest information sector firms in the U.S.

Institutional investment in the largest domestic mass media companies grew steadily from 46.9%

in 1988 to 62.3% in 2005. The average level of institutional ownership in large U.S. IT firms also grew, from 42.5% in 1988 to 64.8% in 2005. Thus, institutional ownership increased over the 17 years by about 20% in absolute terms or 50% in terms of relative growth.

Table 16.4 shows similar data for a subset of institutional investors, mutual funds. The list is not a complete listing of institutional ownership, but it highlights the trend. (Firms are grouped by subsector.)

Tables 16.3 and 16.4 show a dramatic rise in institutional presence in information sector firms since 1990. As a whole, mutual funds' ownership in the information sector grew 445% between 1984 and 2005. The rise is most dramatic for ownership in telecommunications, which increased nearly 703% as compared to 430% for mass media and 336% for computers. Furthermore, mutual fund ownership increased particularly in the period after 1990.

The 20 largest mutual funds account for some 40% of overall mutual fund investment.[5] But there are numerous other funds. For example, nearly 250 mutual funds invested in AT&T in 1998, and more than 1,000 institutional investors overall held shares of AT&T in 2000. (None did well, one may presume.)

Thus, at the beginning of the twenty-first century, institutional interests owned almost two-thirds of the mass media and information sector firms. The major engine of such growth was the mutual and pension funds. Mutual funds owned, on average, almost 30% of the largest information companies.

Figure 16.2 summarizes the findings. Institutional ownership in the largest of media and IT/telecom firms increased considerably, whereas insider ownership dropped considerably for mass media firms.

The trend toward institutional ownership accelerated with the emergence of private equity (PE) funds as acquirers of stock market traded "public" media and communications firms. PE funds pool the financial resources of large investors, themselves often institutions such as pension funds. They then buy up companies, withdraw their shares from public trading, reorganize them, and eventually may sell them back to the wider investor public.

After 2005, large private equity firms such as Bain, Blackstone, Carlyle, KKR, Providence, or Texas Pacific—and their equivalents elsewhere—acquired major media and communications companies. These include Clear Channel, MGM,

Table 16.3 Institutional Ownership of the Largest Information Sector Firms

1988 Media Company	Institutions (%)	1988 IT/Telecom Company	Institutions (%)	1992 Media Company	Institutions (%)	1992 IT/Telecom Company	Institutions (%)
Knight Ridder***	69.0	Intel	72.2	Dun & Bradstreet	71.0	Xerox	77.5
CBS	67.6	Sprint	70.0	Knight Ridder	69.0	Sprint	74.7
Warner Comm	64.1	Unisys	69.2	Time Warner	67.3	Intel	73.6
Gannett	63.3	Xerox	66.5	Gannett	65.7	Motorola	73.0
ABC/Cap Cities	61.0	MCI	64.8	McGraw-Hill	63.5	Sun	67.1
Dun & Bradstreet	61.0	Apple	63.0	ABC/Cap Cities	56.9	MCI	65.3
Time, Inc.	59.8	Compaq	62.1	Gulf + Western	52.9	Apple	59.0
Gulf + Western	52.9	Motorola	60.7	General Electric	51.0	Hewlett-Packard	50.4
McGraw-Hill	51.9	NCR	60.4	Washington Post*^	50.6	DEC†	50.0
MCA	50.4	GTE	52.4	Tribune	48.4	GTE	48.3
News Corp***	48.1	DEC*	50.0	News Corp***	48.1	Sony***	47.9
General Electric	45.4	Sony***	47.9	Sony***	47.9	IBM	43.8
Times-Mirror	43.6	IBM	46.7	Times-Mirror	43.6	US West*	40.0
Disney	41.1	General Electric	45.4	CBS	42.9	Samsung***	40.0
Tribune	39.9	Hewlett-Packard	41.9	Disney***	39.5	AT&T***	38.6
Reader's Digest***	36.0	Pacific Telesis	41.1	Reader's Digest	36.0	Toshiba***	37.7
TCI	23.3	US West*	40.5	New York Times^	25.9	SBC	36.8
Hearst***	22.0	SBC	38.7	Hearst***	22.0	NYNEX	36.6
New York Times^	21.4	AT&T***	38.6	Viacom*	20.0	Matsushita***	36.3
Cox*	20.0	Toshiba***	37.7	Cox*	20.0	Pacific Telesis	35.6
Thomson Corp.***	19.2	Matsushita***	36.3	Thomson Corp.***	19.2	Microsoft	33.7
Washington Post^	18.0	NYNEX	32.3	Reed Elsevier***	17.4	Bell Atlantic	29.3
Viacom	11.3	Bell Atlantic	31.5	TCI	8.3	Ameritech	29.2
Bertelsmann**	0.0	Ameritech	31.3	TBS	3.8	Unisys	27.9
TBS	0.0	Bell South	24.3	Bertelsmann**	0.0	Bell South	24.9
Weighted Average	45.3	Weighted Average	42.5	Weighted Average	48.6	Weighted Average	44.3
Average	39.6	Average	49.0	Average	39.6	Average	46.8
Weighted Average of U.S.-Owned Firms	46.9	Weighted Average of U.S.-Owned Firms	42.5	Weighted Average of U.S.-Owned Firms	50.1	Weighted Average of U.S.-Owned Firms	44.5

Company	Institutions (%)	Company	Institutions (%)	Company	Institutions (%)	Company	Institutions (%)	Company	Institutions (%)	Company	Institutions (%)
CBS***	85.8	Xerox	76.0	Charter	79.0	EDS	81.1	Border/Walden	98.0	EDS	92.0
Dun & Bradstreet	73.6	Compaq	65.6	Gannett	76.6	Agere	80.4	Blockbuster	96.5	Xerox	86.0
Knight Ridder	70.9	Worldcom	61.0	Clear Channel	74.5	Xerox	63.1	Knight Ridder	92.1	Sprint	83.3
Gannett	68.8	Dell	56.4	McGraw-Hill	71.7	HP/Compaq	56.1	Clear Channel	87.5	SBC/AT&T	76.2
Time Warner***	67.3	MCI	55.7	Reader's Digest	62.3	Worldcom	54.7	Gannett	84.3	NCR	75.5
McGraw-Hill	63.1	Intel	54.6	AOL Time Warner	60.3	Motorola	54.6	McGraw-Hill	77.4	HP	72.7
Barnes & Noble	55.3	Sprint	49.2	Knight Ridder***	60.0	Cisco	53.1	Time Warner	74.7	Qwest	72.4
Tribune	55.2	HP	48.1	Washington Post*^	60.0	Apple	51.0	CBS	74.3	Apple	71.8
Comcast*^	51.7	Sony***	47.9	GM/Hughes	58.5	Dell	50.7	Barnes & Noble	73.6	Unisys	71.7
Washington Post*^	50.7	IBM	46.9	Disney***	55.2	Avaya	50.3	Viacom I	68.4	Avaya	71.3
General Electric	50.3	Motorola	46.3	Comcast	51.0	Sun	49.5	Disney	66.3	Motorola	71.1
News Corp***	48.1	GTE	41.5	General Electric	51.0	Intel	49.4	Washington Post^	64.2	Dell	64.6
Sony***	47.9	Pacific Telesis	41.2	News Corp***	48.1	Sprint	49.2	General Electric	55.2	Bell South	59.8
Disney	44.6	US West	40.0	AT&T	47.9	IBM	48.8	Tribune	54.6	Cisco	58.7
Times-Mirror	41.7	Samsung***	40.0	Sony***	45.9	Bell South	48.2	Charter	54.0	Gateway	56.1
USWest (MediaOne)*	40.0	NYNEX	39.3	Tribune	39.3	Microsoft	48.0	News Corp	48.1	Microsoft	55.9
New York Times^	26.4	AT&T	38.6	New York Times^	29.4	AT&T	47.9	Sony*	47.9	Intel	55.8

continued

Table 16.3 (Continued)

| | 1996 | | | | 2001 | | | | 2005 | | | |
| | Media | | IT/Telecom | | Media | | IT/Telecom | | Media | | IT/Telecom | |
Company	Institutions (%)	Company	Institutions (%)	Company	Institutions (%)	Company	Institutions (%)	Company	Institutions (%)	Company	Institutions (%)
Bertelsmann**	25.0	Lucent*	38.6	Cox	25.7	Sony***	47.9	Comcast	47.3	Verizon	55.4
Hearst***	22.0	Toshiba***	37.7	Bertelsmann**	25.0	Verizon	46	New York Times*^	40.0	Sun	54.2
Cox*	20.0	Apple	36.5	Advance^^	25.0	SBC	45.9	Bertelsmann**	25.0	Oracle	48.3
Thomson Corp.***	19.2	Matsushita***	36.3	Viacom	24.7	Qwest	45.7	Hearst	25.0	Sony*	47.9
Seagram	18.4	SBC	35.9	Hearst	22.0	Samsung***	40.0	Advance^^	25.0	IBM	46.9
Reed Elsevier***	17.4	Ameritech	35.1	Thomson Corp.***	19.2	Oracle	39.1	Cox*	20.0	Samsung	40.0
Viacom	14.3	Microsoft	34.5	Reed Elsevier***	17.4	Toshiba***	37.7	Reed Elsevier*	17.4	Toshiba*	37.7
TCI	8.3	Bell Atlantic	33.0	Vivendi	13.5	Matsushita***	36.3	Vivendi*	13.5	Lucent	36.7
Weighted Average	47.0	Weighted Average	44.1	Weighted Average	46.2	Weighted Average	48.8	Weighted Average	59.4	Weighted Average	63.2
Average	43.4	Average	44.8	Average	46.1	Average	50.3	Average	57.2	Average	61.5
Weighted Average of U.S.-Owned Firms	48.4	Weighted Average of U.S.-Owned Firms	44.2	Weighted Average of U.S.-Owned Firms	49.1	Weighted Average of U.S.-Owned Firms	49.1	Weighted Average of U.S.-Owned Firms	62.3	Weighted Average of U.S.-Owned Firms	64.8

Sources: Notes: Insiders (%) include individuals with 5% ownership. Source for 1988–2005: "Compact D-SEC," Compact Disclosure Inc., 1988–2005.

Source for 2005: MSN Money. European companies—assume one-third U.S. investors

*Estimate.

**Most of company is owned by family-controlled Bertelsmann Foundation.

***Extrapolated from other years.

^2 Classes of stock consolidated.

^^Advance is private, owned by the Newhouse family. See http://www.publicintegrity.org/telecom/analysis/CompanyProfile.aspx?HOID=8030. </TFN>

Table 16.4 Ownership of Top 30 Information Sector Firms by Major Mutual Funds (Firms Grouped by Sectors)

	Mutual Fund Ownership					
	1984	1990	1997	2000	2004	2005
Mass Media						
ABC	9.0					
CBS			28.8			25.9
Disney	3.0	3.5	10.1	10.5	24.5	24.8
Donnelley	4.4	2.5	22.7	23.2	12.8	35.9
Dun & Bradstreet	4.8	8.3	30.1	25.6	33.7	35.0
Gannett	3.2	6.5	17.9	23.1	26.1	26.9
RCA	6.7					
Time Inc.	4.9					
Time Warner		13.6	23.6	34.7	33.1	35.4
Times Mirror	6.8	4.8	25.2	28.6		
Tribune	1.8	2.6	15.5	18.5	17.1	20.6
Viacom	15.1		27.0	18.6		25.1
Warner	3.2					
Telecommunications						
Ameritech			14.4			
AT&T	0.9	1.5	12.7	28.6	34.7	34.7
Bell Atlantic	2.2	2.7	11.2	15.2		
Bell South	1.6	1.9	9.3	10.7		
Cisco			20.1	19.6	25.5	25.5
GTE		3.2	12.2	18.1		
Lucent			12.0	12.3	13.4	13.4
MCI		9.0	26.3			
Motorola	7.4	15.1	13.5		30.5	30.5
NYNEX	4.4	3.8				
Pacific Telesis	4.3	4.9				
SBC	4.1	6.9	13.9	15.7	23.6	23.6
Sprint	3.4		25.6	24.1		
US West	4.5	5.4	23.9			
Qwest Comm				8.5	24.2	24.2
Information Technology						
Apple	3.8	7.0	5.0	22.7	33.3	27.2
Burroughs	14.6					
Compaq	3.2	9.8	25.4	11.9		
Dell		1.6	17.8	13.6	26.6	28.0
Digital	12.3	7.2				
Gateway			6.7	21.1	16.3	11.4
Hewlett-Packard	2.1	2.7	11.0	16.3	27.8	29.7
IBM	3.0	5.1	17.5	16.8	18.2	18.8
Intel	4.3	13.2	13.6	14.8	21.4	22.5
Microsoft		5.0	9.2	14.5	22.8	25.0
NCR		7.2	16.6	20.6	26	58.3
Oracle		4.1	18.0	18.7	17.4	20.0
Seagate		16.0	24.5	21.7		19.2
Sperry	12.3					
Sun Microsystems		10.0	15.8	22.3	20.7	25.1
Texas Instruments	14.1	8.5	35.7	35.6	34.6	33.2
Unisys			15.4	33.2	24.7	23.3

continued

Table 16.4 (*Continued*)

	Mutual Fund Ownership					
	1984	1990	1997	2000	2004	2005
Averages	5.5	6	18.7	21.8	24.5	26.5
Mass Media	5.7	5.3	22.3	22.9	24.5	28.6
Telecom	3.6	5.4	16.3	22.3	25.3	25.3
IT	7.2	7.3	17.5	20.3	24.2	26.3

Sources: Vickers Facts on Funds. Vickers Stock Research Corporation, 1984, 1990, 1997 and 2000). Data for 2005 from MSN Money.

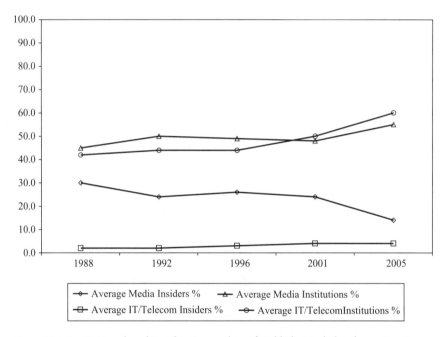

Figure 16.2 Institutional and Insider Ownership of Publicly Traded Information Sector Companies

Univision, Primedia, PanAmSat in America, and VNU in the Netherlands (which owns Nielsen Media Research in the US), and the main telecom companies in Ireland, Denmark, and Canada. Still other firms were taken fully private by their own majority shareholders, such as Bertelsmann and Cox.

In contrast to the public institutional funds with their numerous small investors, the private equity fund is limited by law and strategy to deep-pocket investors whose identities are not disclosed. The funds themselves keep a low profile. For example, Thomas H. Lee Partners is a $20 billion Boston

PE firm that has acquired singly or in partnership the media companies Clear Channel, Univision, VNU/Nielsen, Houghton Mifflin, Cumulus, and Warner Music. Yet the firm did not appear to even maintain a website until 2008 when a bare-bones website appeared. In general, little information is available to the press. Securities analysts do not follow the privately held stock. Activists have no shareholder meeting to speak at. And governments cannot evaluate the soundness of companies that may be essential national infrastructure providers.

Private equity has been in the ascendancy, buoyed by cheap debt, rising equity prices, and high liquidity. In 2006, almost a quarter of all M&As were financed in that way, with over 2,500 deals worth $655 billion worldwide. Talent flocked to PE firms, from ex-CEOs to ex-presidents, prime ministers, and regulators.

This trend has raised questions. Many PE deals are fueled by a desire to flee the closer regulation and disclosure requirements of public companies. In the aggregate this reduces the transparency of the economy, even as it may make some companies more efficient.

There are additional considerations for media firms. The PE deals often lead to a breakup of large media conglomerates to reduce debt that paid for the acquisition. Thus, radio company giant Clear Channel, the poster child for media concentration, was selling off almost half of its 1,100 radio stations. Similarly, private equity has been an instrument of deconcentration for the Tribune Co. and McClatchy newspaper divestitures, and for Time Warner music and The New York Times Company's TV station spin-offs. Where media conglomerates were part of empire building, they are likely to be dismantled by unsentimental cost-cutters installed by the PE owners.

But the same cost-cutting also impacts news rooms, film budgets, script selection, and R&D. PE is low on risk taking in content as it seeks the cash flows to meet debt payments and position the company for subsequent resale, just as venture capital is risk taking. PE, when aiming to resell, is short-term oriented and unlikely to undertake major upgrades of communications infrastructure that might have long-term benefits for the economy.

PE also changes the nature of media ownership. Public attention has centered on highly visible moguls such as Murdoch, Redstone, or Eisner. That personalized portrayal has a certain antiquated quality to it, given the prevalence of institutional investors, but these institutions rarely interfered with managers beyond a general pressure to keep the stock price up. Company management was accountable to all shareholders and scrutinized by the public, investment analysts, and the press.

But this changes under private equity. Now, a PE fund's management company controls the acquired media company fully and installs its management with tough performance mandates. Increasingly,

the PE fund partners play a hands-on operational role beyond the merely financial one.

Ownership Concentration within the Largest Information Sector Companies

In most cases, institutions are at the top of the ownership list, or near it. However, corporate founders or families still maintain a controlling presence in some companies. There may also be institutional owners with substantial ownership stakes.

We can construct for media companies an Ownership Concentration Index (OCI). This index is simply the combined share of ownership of the top five owners, that is, the C5 of ownership percentages.[6] Table 16.5 displays ownership concentration.

The data show an increase in the concentration of ownership of IT firms. For companies such as Microsoft and Dell, there was a sizable drop in ownership concentration. These increases can be accounted for by the rise in ownership by the largest of institutional investors. By contrast, the drop in the C5 scores of computer firms such as Dell and Microsoft can be accounted for by the sharp decreases in individual ownership as founders cashed in or sought new investments.

C5 scores for mass media remained relatively constant. Individuals did play a noticeable role in the declines in some of the C5 scores in mass media, accounting for much of the decreases for firms such as Viacom, Donnelley, Tribune, and Disney. In such companies the participation of individuals became less prominent. Institutions played a significant but ambivalent role in the C5 movements for Gannett and Dun & Bradstreet. In the former case, a bigger number of institutional investors, each with a smaller participation, led to a less concentrated equity structure. But in the latter case, an increase of the investments of major institutions, raised concentration.

Major Institutional Owners

Who owns the media? The next two tables shed light on thus question and are especially important. In table 16.6, we determine and compile the ownership interests of the ten major institutional investors in the top 50 American information companies. Since the exact number of shares held by institutions changes at any time, the date chosen was January 1, 2006.[7]

Table 16.5 Ownership Concentration (C5) of Top Media and IT/Telecom Companies

	1988				1992		
Media		IT/Telecom		Media		IT/Telecom	
Company	C5	Company	C5	Company	C5	Company	C5
Warner Comm	47.2%	AT&T^	6.7%	Time Warner	33.5%	AT&T**	11.3%
General Electric	12.4%	IBM	6.3%	CBS	42.3%	IBM	7.8%
CBS	41.9%	Bell South	5.3%	News Corp**	40.3%	Bell South	6.1%
ABC**	37.0%	NYNEX	6.2%	ABC	36.8%	Bell Atlantic	6.6%
Gannett	18.7%	Bell Atlantic	6.4%	Gannett	25.0%	GTE	16.6%
Time, Inc.	17.8%	Ameritech**	17.0%	General Electric	7.9%	NYNEX	7.9%
Viacom*	42.9%	SBC	8.1%	TCI	57.8%	Ameritech	16.6%
MCA	29.7%	Pacific Telesis	9.2%	Viacom	39.9%	MCI	15.4%
Knight Ridder	31.6%	US West***	6.0%	Disney	28.9%	Motorola	13.7%
Times-Mirror	43.9%	GTE	15.0%	Dun & Bradstreet	16.6%	SBC	8.9%
News Corp	43.8%	Motorola	78.7%	Knight Ridder	36.5%	US West	7.0%
Dun & Bradstreet	10.6%	Xerox	16.1%	Times-Mirror	47.5%	Pacific Telesis	9.8%
TCI	63.0%	Sprint**	17.0%	Bertelsmann***	100.0%	Sprint	17.0%
Tribune*	17.2%*	MCI	17.4%	Hearst**	27.0%	Xerox	32.1%
Disney	26.3%	General Electric	6.8%	TBS	31.2%	Hewlett-Packard	29.2%
McGraw-Hill	13.9%	Unisys	11.5%	McGraw-Hill	26.5%	Apple	21.6%
Hearst*	27.0%	DEC**	18.0%	Gulf + Western**	11.0%	Intel	17.1%
Washington Post*	34.3%	Hewlett-Packard	34.3%	Thomson Corp.**	71.0%	Unisys	33.0%
Gulf + Western	10.5%	NCR	15.6%	Tribune*	29.5%	Microsoft	52.4%
Cox**	69.0%	Apple	23.7%	Cox **	69.0%	Sun	24.9%
New York Times*	49.4%*	Intel	47.8%	Reader's Digest*	60.5%	DEC	18.2%
Reader's Digest**	60.5%	Compaq	28.3%	Washington Post*	19.2%	Compaq	13.2%
Thomson Corp.	70.8%			New York Times*	34.9%		
TBS	53.4%						
Average	36.6%	Average	18.2%	Average	38.8%	Average	17.6%

Company	C5	Company	C5	Company	C5	Company	C5	Company	C5	Company	C5
Time Warner	23.0%	AT&T	9.1%	AOL Time Warner	17.2%	AT&T	17.2%	Time Warner	23.4%	Verizon	9.0%
Disney**	29.0%	IBM***	10.6%	Viacom	43.0%	Verizon	11.4%	Comcast*	24.7%	SBC/AT&T**	8.0%
Viacom	34.0%	MCI**	15.0%	Disney**	29.0%	SBC	11.7%	Disney	15.5%	Sprint	24.4%
CBS	66.9%	GTE	22.8%	AT&T	17.2%	IBM	13.4%	News Corp	40.3%	IBM	17.3%
News Corp**	40.3%	Ameritech	17.4%	News Corp**	40.3%	Worldcom	15.1%	Viacom	41.3%	HP	24.9%
TCI	59.6%	Bell South	9.3%	Comcast*	16.9%	HP/Compaq	24.9%	CBS***	41.3%	Microsoft	22.2%
General Electric	9.2%	Sprint	31.7%	Vivendi	22.0%	Sprint**	17.0%	General Electric	14.3%	Bell South	29.9%
Gannett	24.3%	SBC	10.9%	GM/Hughes	18.2%	Bell South	23.3%	Gannett	23.4%	Dell	25.1%
Thomson Corp.**	71.0%	Bell Atlantic	10.8%	Gannett	24.1%	Microsoft	31.3%	Cox	69.1%	Motorola	19.0%
Seagram	41.6%	NYNEX	18.0%	Cox	76.3%	Dell	24.0%	Tribune*	27.9%	Qwest	53.7%
Knight Ridder	41.5%	Motorola	8.2%	General Electric	12.2%	Qwest	28.1%	Charter	38.8%	Intel	20.8%
Cox	89.3%	US West***	7.0%	Charter	41.6%	Lucent	9.1%	Hearst	39.5%	Lucent	14.1%
McGraw-Hill	28.0%	HP	27.0%	Tribune*	21.6%	Motorola	12.2%	Barnes & Noble	48.0%	Xerox	35.0%
Barnes & Noble	53.0%	Xerox	28.0%	McGraw-Hill	20.5%	Xerox	37.7%	McGraw-Hill	19.4%	Oracle	32.4%
New York Times*	25.3%	Compaq	3.0%	Advance***	80.0%	Intel	19.7%	Advance***	80.0%	Cisco	16.2%
US West (MediaOne)***	7.0%	Lucent	3.3%	Hearst	27.3%	Oracle	33.1%	Knight Ridder	45.7%	Apple	24.7%

continued

Table 16.5 (Continued)

1996 Media		1996 IT/Telecom		2001 Media		2001 IT/Telecom		2005 Media		2005 IT/Telecom	
Company	C5	Company	C5	Company	C5	Company	C5	Company	C5	Company	C5
Washington Post*	41.0%	Pacific Telesis	20.2%	Clear Channel	41.2%	Cisco	12.4%	Clear Channel	42.8%	Gateway	57.2%
Tribune	38.9%	Intel	17.4%	New York Times*	23.4%	Sun	22.1%	Blockbuster	26.0%	Sun	20.3%
Times-Mirror	43.9%	Worldcom	20.1%	Knight Ridder	44.0%	Avaya	36.4%	Border/Walden	41.4%	Avaya	29.6%
Dun & Bradstreet	25.1%	Microsoft	42.6%	Washington Post*	33.1%	Apple	22.9%	Washington Post*	17.1%	EDS	46.7%
Comcast*	18.5%	Apple	27.1%	Reader's Digest	26.4%	Agere	15.2%	New York Times*	20.3%	Unisys	40.3%
		Dell	48.3%							NCR	27.9%
Average	38.6%	Average	18.5%	Average	32.2%	Average	20.9%	Average	35.3%	Average	27.2%

Sources: Compact Disclosure Database, Compact D-SEC and MSN Money.

*Two Shares of Stock considered, families combined.

**Data from nearest year where otherwise unavailable.

***Estimate.

Table 16.6 Media Ownership by Ten Major Institutions (2005) ($ Million)

Mass Media Companies	Fidelity Management & Research		Mellon Bank		Vanguard Group		Capital Research & Management Group		Wellington Management	
	$	%	$	%	$	%	$	%	$	%
Time Warner	889	1.1	975	1.2	1,911	2.4	3,325	4.2	1,088	2.7
Comcast	419	1.2	425	1.2	1,148	3.3	880	2.5	1,088	3.1
Disney	1,236	2.7	610	1.3	1,107	2.4	965	2.1	396	0.9
News Corp	495	1.4	860	2.5	881	2.6	1,632	4.7	285	0.8
Viacom	677	1.5	542	1.2	1,136	2.5	347	0.8	982.7	1.9
General Electric	9,052	2.4	4,760	1.3	8,745	2.4	8,907	2.4	4,500	1.2
Gannett	259	1.8	141	1.0	341	2.3	358	2.5	338	2.3
Tribune	98	1.1	60	0.6	171	1.8	0	0.0	0	0.0
Charter	18	3.6	1	0.2	15	2.9	0	0.0	27	5.3
Hearst	0	0.0	6	0.5	13	1.0	0	0.0	0	0.0
Barnes & Noble	0	0.0	54	1.9	85	3.0	0	0.0	88	3.1
McGraw Hill	529	2.7	476	2.5	457	2.4	0	0.0	41	0.2
Knight Ridder	126	2.7	33	0.7	176	3.8	104	2.2	4	0.1
Clear Channel	2,410	14.2	260	1.5	378	2.2	1,895	11.1	13	0.1
Blockbuster	0	0.0	3	0.6	9	2.0	0	0.0	5	1.2
Borders Group	11	0.7	10	0.7	32	2.2	0	0.0	40	2.8
Washington Post	2	0.0	38	0.6	49	0.8	0	0.0	0	0.0
New York Times	327	8.6	57	1.5	134	3.5	0	0.0	55	1.4
Mass Media Total $	16,54		9,310		16,788		18,413		10,002	
Mass Media % Avg.		2.54		1.17		2.42		1.81		1.51

continued

Table 16.6 (Continued)

IT/Telecom Companies	Fidelity Management & Research $	%	Mellon Bank $	%	Vanguard Group $	%	Capital Research & Management Group $	%	Wellington Management $	%
Verizon	4,115	6.8	942	1.6	1,429	2.4	0	0.0	685	0.8
AT&T	173	3.5	32	0.6	134	2.7	0	0.0	1,796	1.9
IBM	101	0.9	82	0.7	284	2.4	0	0.0	2,115	1.4
Hewlett-Packard	5,302	3.5	2,400	1.6	3,571	2.4	1,264	0.8	443	0.5
Microsoft	2,065	3.7	993	1.8	1,323	2.4	717	1.3	4,848	1.7
Bellsouth	1,925	1.8	1,267	1.2	2,516	2.4	3,279	3.1	338	0.7
Dell	112	0.9	120	1.0	294	2.3	298	2.4	1,074	1.5
Motorola	676	10.8	250	4.0	212	3.4	0	0.0	713	1.3
Qwest	3,085	4.7	888	1.3	1,612	2.4	3,301	5.0	11	0.1
Intel	1,479	1.0	1,586	1.1	3,075	2.1	4,137	2.8	980	0.7
Lucent	57	0.1	0	0.0	0	0.0	0	0.0	0	0.0
Xerox	6	0.0	99	0.7	329	2.3	0	0.0	592	4.2
Oracle	1,254	11.9	61	0.6	278	2.6	1,410	13.4	22	0.0
Cisco	2,744	3.9	715	1.0	16	0.0	508	0.7	1,884	1.8
Apple	2,960	3.1	1,301	1.4	2,288	2.4	7,549	7.9	303	0.5
Gateway	1,897	2.3	822	1.0	1,936	2.4	3,469	4.3	0	0.0
Sun	2	0.1	20	1.0	57	2.9	0	0.0	0	0.0
Avaya	1,369	2.8	401	0.8	1,193	2.4	5,939	12.0	8	0.2
EDS	1	0.1	6	0.6	19	2.0	24	2.5	3	0.0
Unisys	1,478	1.8	911	1.1	1,988	2.4	2,276	2.7	60	3.0
NCR	1,704	2.7	526	0.8	1,098	1.7	3,174	5.0	50	0.8
IT/Telecom Total $	33,103		13,522		23,984		37,761		18,856	
IT/Telecom % Avg.		3.21		1.12		2.4		4.5		1.5
Total Media, IT Telecom	49,650		22,832		40,772		56,173		28,858	
(%)		2.9		1.2		2.1		3.3		1.2

Table 16.6 (Cont.)

Mass Media Companies	State Street Global Investors		Axa Financial		Barclays		Northern Trust		TIAA/CREF	
	$	%	$	%	$	%	$	%	$	%
Time Warner	2,466	3.1	3,329	4.2	2,728	3.4	875	1.1	1,786	2.2
Comcast	1,489	4.2	569	1.6	2,571	7.3	20	0.1	53	0.2
Disney	1,518	3.3	330	0.7	1,550	3.4	576	1.2	604	1.3
News Corp	1,018	3.0	610	1.8	1,188	3.5	392	1.1	289	0.8
Viacom	1,511.2	3.3	935	2.0	1,935	4.2	396.3	0.9	500	1.1
General Electric	10,826	2.9	8,300	2.2	14,205	3.8	5,543	1.5	2,994	0.8
Gannett	433	3.0	42	0.3	562	3.9	185	1.3	116	0.8
Tribune	219	2.4	16	0.2	394	4.2	144	1.5	72	0.8
Charter	5	1.0	0	0.0	21	4.1	6	0.8	2	0.4
Hearst	17	1.3	0	0.0	16	1.3	3	0.2	4	0.3
Barnes & Noble	199	7.1	16	0.6	145	5.2	0	0.0	59	2.1
McGraw Hill	595	3.1	38	0.2	634	3.3	349	1.8	208	1.1
Knight Ridder	118	2.5	8	0.2	152	3.2	54	1.2	25	0.5
Clear Channel	453	2.7	29	0.2	550	3.2	173	1.0	113	0.7
Blockbuster	10	2.3	2	0.5	22	4.8	0	0.1	5	1.1
Borders Group	24	1.7	49	3.3	53	3.6	9	0.6	9	0.6
Washington Post	80	1.3	13	0.2	136	2.2	27	0.4	29	0.5
New York Times	102	2.7	7	0.2	130	3.4	40	1.0	22	0.6
Mass Media Total $	21,084		14,293		26,991		8,796		6,889	
Mass Media % Avg		2.83		2.54		1.17		0.9		0.9
IT/Telecom Companies	$	%	$	%	$	%	$	%	$	%
Verizon	2,684	3.2	2,970	4.9	3,609	6.0	1,092	1.3	763	1.3
AT&T	3,252	3.4	8	0.2	165	3.3	1,149	1.2	815	16.2
Sprint	2,041	3.1	234	1.6	473	3.3	745	1.1	947	6.6
IBM	6,488	4.3	22	0.2	410	3.5	1,614	1.1	1,100	9.3
Hewlett-Packard	3,564	4.4	1,525	1.0	7,580	5.0	1,083	1.3	887	0.6
Microsoft	7,263	2.6	500	0.9	2,742	4.9	3,265	1.2	2,248	4.0
Bellsouth	3,104	6.3	387	0.4	5,564	5.3	672	1.4	490	0.5
Dell	2,160	3.1	844	6.7	441	3.5	1,016	1.4	610	4.9

continued

Table 16.6 (Continued)

	State Street Global Investors		AXA Financial		Barclays		Northern Trust		TIAA/CREF	
	$	%	$	%	$	%	$	%	$	%
Qwest	614	5.8	2,372	3.6	2,339	3.5	93	0.9	62	0.1
Intel	4,788	3.2	1,684	1.1	4,405	3.0	2,164	1.4	971	0.7
Lucent	309	2.6	1	0.0	3	0.0	123	1.0	94	0.2
Xerox	1,080	7.7	26	0.2	479	3.4	146	1.0	102	0.7
Oracle	1,369	2.2	16	0.2	309	2.9	591	0.9	405	3.9
Cisco	3,243	3.1	467	0.7	2,637	3.7	1,554	1.5	1,323	1.9
Apple	1,863	3.1	1,060	1.1	3,649	3.8	6	0.7	532	0.6
Gateway	22	2.3	3,236	4.0	2,832	3.5	10	1.0	88	0.1
Sun	380	2.7	6	0.3	69	3.5	151	1.1	122	6.1
Avaya	134	2.7	336	0.7	1,747	3.5	48	1.0	31	0.1
EDS	708	5.6	2	0.2	26	2.8	133	1.1	86	9.2
Unisys	54	2.7	963	1.2	4,739	5.7	20	1.0	20	0.0
NCR	159	2.5	548	0.9	1,609	2.6	65	1.0	54	0.1
IT/Telecom Total $	47,006		17,225		46,044		16,560		12,502	
IT/Telecom % Avg		3.6		3.21		1.12				
Total Media, IT, Telecom $	68,113		31,518		73,036		25,356		19,391	
(%)		2.9		2.9		1.2		0.9		1.4

Notes: Data in Thomson Financial Services.
% = % of company stock.
% Industry = % of top 50 media, IT, and communications companies.

The next table, table 16.7, shows the extensive aggregate ownership by the ten investment institutions in media companies. We can see from the numbers how large institutional ownership is. The total ownership stakes held by the top institutions in various media firms are significant. And even

Table 16.7 Aggregate Ownership of Major Telecom Sector and Media Sectors Firms by Ten Largest Institutional Investors Communications Companies

Mass Media Companies	Public Stock Owned by 10 Major Institutions (%)
Time Warner	25.6
Comcast	24.7
Disney	19.3
News Corp	22.2
Viacom	19.4
General Electric	20.9
Gannett	19.2
Tribune	12.6
Charter	18.3
Hearst	4.6
Barnes & Noble	23.0
McGraw Hill	17.3
Knight Ridder	17.1
Clear Channel	36.9
Blockbuster	12.6
Borders Group	16.2
Washington Post	6.0
New York Times	22.9

IT/Telecom Companies	Public Stock Owned by 14 Major Institutions (%)
Verizon	28.3
AT&T	33.0
Sprint	30.2
IBM	23.8
Hewlett-Packard	21.1
Microsoft	24.5
Bellsouth	23.1
Dell	27.7
Motorola	40.0
Qwest	27.4
Intel	17.1
Lucent	3.9
Xerox	20.0
Oracle	38.6
Cisco	18.3
Apple	24.6
Gateway	20.9
Sun	17.7
Avaya	26.2
EDS	24.1
Unisys	21.6
NCR	18.1

though the ownership percentages of individual institutions like State Street and Barclays in any single firm are usually intermediate or small in percentage terms, they are still often among the largest owners of the companies. As mentioned, institutional investors rarely have interests greater than 5% in companies since they seek diversification of their portfolios and are subject to a variety of legal limitations and reporting requirements.[8]

The large institutional investors in table 16.6 had a total investment of about $415 billion in each Media, Telecom and IT sector at the beginning of 2006. The average ownership interest of each of these ten institutions in the top Media companies (18 firms which are publicly traded) was 1.7%. Barclays has around $57 billion invested, $27 billion of it in mass media, with an average interest of 3.7% in the top media firms. Fidelity had around $41 billion invested, with about $17 billion in media, with an average interest of 2.54%. State Street had around $68 billion invested, with about $21 billion in media, with an average interest of 2.83%.

Each institution has a different investment strategy, leading to different ownership patterns. Capital Research & Management maintains ownership of 5% or more in five companies, with an interest of 10% or more in three of those (Clear Channel, Oracle, and Avaya). However, CRM holds no stake in many other media companies, making it one of the more focused institutions. Barclays, the biggest investor in the group, maintains a 5% or greater ownership interest in six companies, and significant shares in many other companies as well.

Generally, the stake of institutional investors is much larger than those of individuals. In 2005, State Street had over $68 billion invested in the major 50 information industry companies. Bill Gates, the country's richest man, had "only" $51 billion, some of it invested outside of the information sector, and at least 23 institutions had investments of over $10 billion in the information sector. In 2001, Janus Capital, with an over $10.1 billion ownership, had much more money tied up in Time Warner than Ted Turner, whose share of $6 billion was the largest individual stake. Yet hardly anyone outside the financial community has heard of Janus, whereas Turner is legendary. TIAA-CREF, an educators' pension fund, had over $19 billion invested in U.S. major information companies in 2005. In comparison, Sumner Redstone had "only" $8.4 billion and Rupert Murdoch $6.7 billion.

However, individual holdings tend to be more concentrated in one firm, whereas institutional investors' assets are scattered. The average number of information companies in the portfolio of the top 20 institutional investors in 2001 was 67. And the largest of institutional investors in media and communications held only between 4% and 30% of their total assets invested in the largest of information industry companies. In contrast, large individual owners are much more heavily focused in their ownership. For that reason they are usually much more involved in the day-to-day running of the firm and often control "their" companies.

The Implications of Institutional Ownership

Institutional investors are usually viewed as primarily concerned with short- or medium-term gain, gauging corporate performance solely according to stock price and earnings.

Individual ownership that reaches high levels in a company, such as Bill Gates's 10.12% interest in Microsoft in 2005, allows him to exercise considerable control over corporate decisions, but often it cannot be liquidated rapidly. Institutional investors with large ownership stakes also face this dilemma, but usually to a lesser degree.

Pension funds are often patient investors. The Council of Institutional Investors, the association of public pension funds, reported that its members maintain their investments for an average of over four years. The average holding period for the California Public Employee's Retirement System (Calpers), the largest public pension fund in the United States, is more than eight years. This contrasts with the typical view of institutional short-term orientation and explains why at least pension funds become increasingly interested in exercising "voice." Public employee pension funds have been more active in corporate management than other institutional investors.

Mutual funds tend to be less interested than public pension funds in politics. They usually avoid involvement in public policy issues for fear of alienating existing investors and discouraging the acquisition of new ones. (A few funds, however, may make policy presences a selling point.)

Institutional investor participation in corporate decision making takes various forms, ranging from direct personal contact by institutional investor management to formal proxy contests.

After 1992, changes in SEC regulations made it possible for institutional investors to discuss voting matters with each other without SEC filing requirements as long as no proxies are solicited. Capital Research & Management (CRM), past of the Capital Group is an example of activism by mutual fund managers through direct personal contacts. The chief media investor at CRM, Gordon Crawford, got directly involved in companies in which his fund had invested. CRM rejected in 1995 the slate for the CBS board of directors. CBS resisted and antagonized Wall Street, which contributed to its acquisition by Westinghouse a few months later. Crawford also successfully demanded the resignation of AOL Time Warner Chairman Stephen Case for various reasons, specifically after the company was charged for accounting irregularities in 2002.

Institutional investors at times have also focused on the structure of the corporate board of directors and on monitoring board performance and compensation. In 1997, institutional investors became dissatisfied with the composition of Walt Disney's board of directors, which *Business Week* had named the "worst board in America." It included individuals with close ties to CEO Michael Eisner, such as his personal attorney and his architect. Eisner was forced to make changes in response to the institutional investor criticism,[9] but his troubles with institutional and pension funds continued, and they led, eventually, to the end of his long reign. Yet the funds became active only after being mobilized by a relentless campaign of a classic insider, Roy Disney, a director, founding family member, large shareholder, and officers who had been pushed out by Eisner.

In 2003, U.S. mutual fund Tweedy Browne, which held 18% of the newspaper holding firm Hollinger International shares, initiated an investigation that uncovered misspending at the newspaper chain (*Chicago Sun-Times*, *Daily Telegraph*, and several other papers). The discovery led to the resignation of Lord Conrad Black from his position as CEO, the sale of the company, and to Black's criminal conviction.

In theory, fund managers might be tempted to oppose content that would negatively affect other holdings of their portfolio.[10] If Fidelity holds large ownership positions in tobacco companies and in Disney, it is possible that the ABC network management might pull its punches in producing programs about the addictiveness of nicotine.

Since direct intervention would often not stay confidential and backfire, either such instances are rare or they are implicit and require no direct communication. In contrast, there is evidence for direct intervention by the major individual owner on just that issue. CBS dropped in 1995 a negative story about a tobacco company executive. At the time, CBS principal owner was Laurence Tisch, who was also the principal shareholder of the large tobacco company Lorillard.

Generally, institutional investors will prefer safe mainstream content rather than controversy that may make some of their investors unhappy. Similar incentives for safe mainstream content exist also for corporate media management and for individual owners, unless they put their personal politics ahead of their commercial interests. Institutional ownership might affect content quality through greater pressures for short-term profitability. Yet it may also shield managers from control by erratic principal owners on the model of William Randolph Hearst or Colonel Robert McCormick.

Is greater institutional investor involvement in the decisions of media and communications companies a good or bad thing? Is the fund manager at Fidelity qualified to second-guess decisions in Disney's boardroom? In whose interests are institutional investors acting—that of their beneficiaries (fund participants), that of the institutional investor firm itself, or that of the media company's shareholders more generally? The public's interest in diverse media is not likely to be at the top. Nor is it the company itself, its employees, or the communities it serves. In most cases financial returns are paramount, often but not always with a short-term orientation. But this does not answer the question of whether such a profit orientation is different from that of an individually or family owned company.

Indeed, in media industries in which competition is weak, owners can afford to offer content that is based on their personal preferences, which may or may not include a sense of public service. The running of local newspapers by established families who exercise ownership and control is one example; the three TV networks' news programs in the 1960s and 1970s is another.

CONCLUSION

Decades ago, media ownership was primarily in the hands of a small group of individuals and families.

But by the late twentieth century, new technology and new media had created a massive need for capital, and this required many sources and hence a more widespread ownership. This trend has been most evident in the computer and high-technology industries, where relatively young companies need to rely upon equity capital—initially often by venture capital investment—to finance their future growth. A high degree of institutional ownership is an inevitable consequence of a burgeoning technology market.

In contrast, mass media companies relinquished ownership control to a lesser extent. This means that they are more able to self-finance, that they expand less aggressively, or that they use debt rather than equity. But they, too, have widened ownership.

Thus, the actual ownership of the U.S. media and information sector has shown two seemingly contradictory trends. On the other hand, it has become more fragmented—a large number of stakeholders with small stakes. On the other hand, some of these institutional owners have stakes in many media and information firms. If they acted in concert, they could exercise industry-wide power. But there is, so far, little evidence for such joint activity aimed at content.

Thus, as this chapter shows, the popular belief that convergence in the information industries has resulted in a small group of media moguls is not an accurate one. A better description is one of a large number of fund managers owning, on behalf of their fund investors, narrow slices of a big pie. They do not micromanage the companies' leadership terms, often in contrast to large individual owners, but put performance pressure on them through their buy and sell decisions. But such pressure arises from private firms in a profit-oriented market economy rather than from concentrated ownership. The same pressures would be brought to bear if there were 100 media companies or 10.

Notes

1. Also, beneficial shareholders who own the shares on behalf of another (such as when a trustee administers shares on behalf of a beneficiary or estate).

2. For purposes of Tables 16.2, 16.3, and 16.5, in those cases where different classes of stock exist, since there usually are no valuations for the nontraded special voting stock, we assume it to constitute half of the company's value.

3. Institutional investors are required to file disclosure information when they own 5% or more of a publicly traded company. They are limited in their ability to profit on shares held for less than six months once they reach the 10% ownership threshold. If a mutual fund wants to promote itself as "diversified" and gain pass-through tax benefits, then the regulated 75% of the fund cannot own more than 10% of a company in its portfolio. Also, a "diversified" fund cannot have more than 5% of its total assets invested in a single company by the Investment Company Act of 1940. Therefore, only 25% of a fund, the unregulated portion, can be concentrated in a single stock. Pension funds are generally less regulated than mutual funds and fall under the Employee Retirement Income Security Act of 1974 (ERISA), which require each fund to diversify. But under ERISA, pension fund managers are given some leeway to avoid diversification if it is "clearly prudent" not to do so.

4. Brancato, Carolyn, and Stephan Rabimov., "The 2005 Institutional Investment Report: U.S. and International Trends." *The Conference Board*, September 2005. 2007 figures from IFSL Research, *Fund Management 2008*, London 2008, www.ifsl.org.uk/research.

5. Blommenstein, Harold. "Impact of Institutional Investment on the Financial Markets." Blommenstein et al (eds.), OECD, 1998, p. 45.

6. Where several family members owned large parts of a company, we pooled their holdings. The C5 is used because it is more intuitive than the HHI and because in the averaging, one or two single-owner firms could distort the average.

7. To calculate the institutional investors' percentage ownership in some of the largest information industry companies, the number of shares held by the institutional investor in a particular company were taken as a percentage of the company's total outstanding shares for the fourth quarter of 2005. To determine the dollar amounts invested in these companies, the number of shares held by each institutional investor were multiplied by the price per share at close of the market on Dec. 31, 2005.

8. See note 3.

9. Byrne, John, Ronald Grover, and Richard Melcher. "The Best and Worst Boards." *Business Week*, December 8, 1997.

10. Soloski, John, and Robert Picard. "The New Media Lords: Why Institutional Investors Call the Shots." *Columbia Journalism Review*, September 19, 1996, p. 11.

PART VII

CONCLUSIONS

17

The Need for a New Concentration Index for Media

Media concentration has become a topic around the world. Both opponents and supporters of ownership restrictions for media have conducted the debate with considerable forcefulness, perhaps because both are partly correct. The data show that U.S. mass media have, in the aggregate, indeed steadily increased in concentration since 1988. But they also show that the concentration on a national basis is usually fairly low by the standards of U.S. antitrust. Here, the official U.S. Government guidelines define an unconcentrated industry as having a Hirschmann-Herfindahl Index of less than 1,000. The HHI is the sum of the squares of the market shares, or ΣS^2. For example, if a local radio station market comprised two companies with 40% each and two companies with 10% each, it would have an HHI of 3,400. Markets with an HHI above 1,800 are defined as highly concentrated, whereas markets with an HHI below 1,000 are deemed to be unconcentrated.

By that antitrust standard, many media industries are unconcentrated. The numbers show that even radio, the classic example for growing media concentration, had in 2005 a national HHI of only 545. For TV station ownership it was 253; for newspapers, 191; for film distribution, 1,248; and for cable TV, 1,568. (Concentration is much higher locally, given the smaller markets. For radio, it is 2,400, and for newspapers and cable distribution it has long been above 7,000. Rarely is there more than one local newspaper in a city. The relation

of concentration and market size is a separate but related question we will consider later.)

Compare these numbers with those of other industries. Just for example, video game consoles have an HHI of 3,911; microcomputers, 1,561; cellular handsets, 1,712—all much higher for products used daily, yet without unleashing the same passion about concentration.

The obvious reason for this discrepancy is that most people desire a greater diversity in their information sources than in their computer hardware. They wish more choices for themselves and for the political process. Therefore, the question arises of whether the traditional antitrust measure of the HHI that is used for other goods and services is also appropriate for media.

The issue is partly whether the concentration threshold for media should be lower, and partly whether the HHI methodology itself accounts sufficiently for media pluralism. For example, in the radio example above, if the two smaller stations were replaced by 20 stations, each with 1% of the market, the HHI would decline only slightly, from 3,400 to 3,220. Yet the diversity of the local radio market would clearly be significantly increased by the presence of 18 additional radio station providers.

Earlier, in the introduction, we discussed the question whether the traditional tools of antitrust—market analysis, a concentration index, and so forth—are appropriate for mass media.

Most people consider media to be a different category from other industries, given their role in politics and culture.[1] To most people, a TV set is more than a "toaster with pictures," the image famously given by a former FCC chairman, Mark Fowler. To avoid the difficult issues surrounding pluralism, the U.S. antitrust authorities have tried in recent years to stay on familiar ground and looked mostly at the impact of media mergers on advertising prices. This approach, focusing on economic effects, has been severely criticized for neglecting the dimension of diversity.

Yet the assurance of a diversity of perspectives and sources—"pluralism"—opens practical problems for an antitrust agency. How does one define a "viewpoint"? How does one measure it? Which viewpoints need to be assured a media outlet in order to find diversity? Just the major political parties or all the way to the White Supremacists and the Flat Earthers?

These differences then lead to an alternative approach, that of protecting opportunities rather than outcomes by assuring nondiscriminatory *access* to all voices and perspectives. Elements of such a policy are common carriage, access rights, interconnection rights, net neutrality, and so forth. All these are regulatory approaches, and they require a variety of interventions that may include controls over the price for such access,[2] its quality, and who must offer it.[3] These issues are not simple, and they get more complex over time as the participants learn to "game" the system.

Another option to promote access is more indirect, not by direct assurance but by reduction of gatekeeping powers. These are *structural* policies, aiming to create a competitive media system that is believed to result in a nondiscriminatory access. This includes limits on size, ceilings, or on the number of outlets, restrictions on cross-media ownership, etc. The underlying theory is that with a diverse media industry structure, if enough people like to speak out in favor of a point of view or to listen to that message, there would be media that would serve them. Ideas contest each other for audiences and acceptance, and media serve them, following commercial incentives. But the concept of the "marketplace of ideas" has problems, too. In a marketplace there are winners and losers, and some media critics therefore reject that approach toward diversity, since it can lead to an underrepresentation of unpopular or minority perspectives. The structural approach relies on the classic paradigm of industrial organization economics—structure, behavior, performance. That paradigm, not without its critics among economists, postulates that, generally speaking, different market structures create different behavioral and performance models. Thus, a media industry in which the top three firms have much market power leads to results different from those of one with wide-open competition.

One might agree to that proposition as a concept, but it still leaves the question of what to do about it. The primary tools of structural policies are ownership regulations and antitrust/antimonopoly law. Regulation puts numeric limits on ownership. Antitrust case law has tests of market power. Because such tests are vague and litigation-intensive, the U.S. Department of Justice issued in 1982 its "Merger Guidelines", with a yardstick, the Hirschmann-Herfindahl Index (HHI), in order to orient both government and industry.

The question is whether this traditional measure of concentration is appropriate for media. Adopting the HHI or any other measure does not by itself imply adopting a particular threshold definition as to what constitutes concentrated market for a medium. 1,000? 1,500? 2,000? That is a separate question. The DOJ measures are, in any event, not a binding rule but a guideline, to be supplemented by additional factors and be used with discretion. But should there be no numeric test at all? Or should it be a reasoned independent call by experienced public officials in government agencies and courts? But it is a real problem to let important decisions about media become the judgment calls of government officials, providing them with a tool to reward friends, punish enemies, and pacify critics. People tend to advocate subjective judgment calls—discretion—when the numbers come out against them. But they do so at their own peril when it comes, inevitably, to the next case. The relationship between media and government is inherently adversarial. It should not include discretionary powers by government over media, or, conversely, the ability of influential media firms to sway those officials. Therefore, if special considerations exist for media, the guidelines or methodology should be different but still clearly spelled out in advance. This argues for a relatively clear-cut test, with a relatively clear-cut methodology. (The qualifiers are used because competent legal counsel will undoubtedly manage to fuzzy up anything that is supposed to be "clear-cut.")

Over the time of this study, I have come to appreciate the robustness of the HHI measure. Some of its potential problems proved, when actual data work was done, to be more hypothetical than real. Running two other indices alongside proved largely unnecessary, except that the C4 is more intuitive and hence a better way to tell a story. But the problem with the HHI (and the C4) is that although it considers market power, which is essential, it does not make allowance for pluralism, which is also essential. That is, it looks only at actual choices rather than at options. As a radio listener, I am better off having 20 other stations on the air, even if I rarely tune in to them. As a citizen, I am better off if an alternative paper exists that keeps the city council, and the big paper, on their toes. As a moviegoer, I am better off having more options from which to choose even if I end up going to the latest blockbuster. As a cable TV viewer, I am better off by having obscure channels around: Who knows? Options matter, and they have concrete value. Billions of dollars traded daily in financial options attest to that, and an entire body of financial economics literature has grown around the concept.

But even with options, market power is still a factor. The FCC, in creating a Diversity Index (DI), ignored this. It aimed to measure local diversity by counting "voices" and then weighing it by the medium's generic importance as an information source. A voice was a radio station, a newspaper, a TV station, or a cable operator. Yet the FCC equated gnats with elephants, thus ignoring the resources of the large media outlets, the talents they can put into content production, their marketing strength in obtaining an audience and advertisers, and their brand value. Counting voices without accounting for their loudness is simplistic. It also created a higher diversity count that, given the FCC's desire to buttress a policy of liberalization, was useful as an argument. Partly for those reasons, the FCC's Diversity Index was resoundingly rejected by an appellate court in 2004.

[T]here is no dispute that the assignment of equal market shares generates absurd results. For example, in New York City, the Dutchess Community College television station and the stations owned by ABC each receive an equal 4.3% market share. Or compare the Dutchess Community College station's weighted share of 1.5% (4.3% times the 33.8% multiplier for television) to mere 1.4% weighted, combined share assigned to the New York Times Company's co-owned daily newspaper and radio station. A Diversity Index that requires us to accept that a community college television station makes a greater contribution to viewpoint diversity than a conglomerate that includes the third-largest newspaper in America (Source: Audit Bureau of Circulations) also requires us to abandon both logic and reality. (p. 68)[4]

The FCC lost in court mostly due to the inadequate evidence it provided as the basis for its decision to relax ownership rules. In anticipation of a second attempt, the agency sought to create such a fact base. In 2007, the FCC issued nine studies commissioned mostly from outside academics and consultants. Several of these studies dealt with ownership by racial minorities[5] and women.[6] Other studies dealt with impacts on news and public affairs,[7] on radio programming,[8] or on quantity and quality of TV programming.[9] These questions are outside the scope of the present book. Some of the results were supportive to the FCC's majority. One study found that TV stations that were cross-owned with newspapers had during the 2006 general election 4–7% more news coverage than non-cross-owned stations, and 30% more news coverage of state and local political candidates. The mechanism, presumably, is the greater news resources of locally cross-owned media.

Yet in fairness, the FCC's "voice count" measure is not without at least some merit. Diversity of media does not require that all available voices have equal weight. It is the nature of markets to coalesce around major choices and marginalize small ones. It is the very essence of popular media to be popular. Media audiences will always be unevenly distributed. As long as the small voices have an opportunity to speak up, they make a difference. Equality of opportunity does not mean an equality of outcomes. Yet merely counting the number of participants in a market is not the test applied in other industries. If antitrust authorities look at the Boeing's and Airbus's market power in the commercial jet airplane market, they will not be overly impressed by the presence of Fokker, Eclipse, or Cessna as alternative aviation options.

It is easy to dismiss the FCC's approach, and many have done so. It is harder to come up with an alternative. Few have tried. Mark Cooper proposes the following formula as a measure of voices.

Voice Count = [(Broadcast + Newspaper) / 0.8] − Jointly Owned Voices.

For example, if there are five TV stations and two newspapers in a city, and one paper is cross-owned with a TV station, the voice count would be = $[(5 + 2) / 0.8] − 2 = 8.75 − 2 = 6.75$. The 0.8 factor is based on a Nielsen showing that TV and newspapers represent 80% of the news market. Where Internet and radio have a bigger news role, that factor would be reduced. This formula means weights of 0.4 for TV and newspapers. Just as for the FCC's own weights for different media, this can be disputed with some of the same arguments that Cooper as a public interest litigator successfully made himself against the FCC's weights; and it would have to be regularly revised in light of changed usage patterns, thereby affording opportunities for litigators to continuously challenge the formula. Also, the subtraction of *both* parts of cross-owned media seems incorrectly specified. For example, if there were four TV stations and four newspapers, all cross-owned in pairs, the number of voices would be, by the formula, a mere 0.75 rather than something near the 4 that should be expected.

It can be seen by this example that it is not easy to construct a system that is robust, simple, and based on solid evidence that would stand up to challenge. Maybe none is possible. But that should not deter us from seeking approximations.

Most opponents of the FCC's voice-counting approach would dismiss its alternative, the market power test, when it is applied to the music or film industries and results in only moderate concentration numbers because the major market participants are fairly equally matched in size. For those industries, some of the same critics want to go beyond market concentration and consider voices. Yet no credible test can jump around ad hoc and be driven by the desire for outcomes. That game is usually won by those with the largest legal resources.

The question then is how to bridge the two concepts: market power and voices. The starting point should be to acknowledge that *both* market power and diversity are legitimate factors to consider, and that to omit one or the other leaves out a major factor and invites reasoned opposition.

The measurement of market power has been that of the HHI, which functions reasonably well, but how to go about diversity? As mentioned above, perhaps the best way to look at diversity is as having options. There is a benefit in options, even if unexercised. In the stock market, financial options to buy or sell in the future are created as instruments of value, and are widely traded. In film or publishing, "options contracts" are a main way to transact business.[10] Producers "option" the rights to scripts, distributors option the rights to a film, and so forth. Clearly, there is a value in having an option, and to ignore it is incorrect analysis. But how to value such options? Financial theory has come up with formulas for the valuation of financial options. The best known is the Black-Scholes-Merton model, which gained its authors a Nobel Prize in economics.[11] For nonfinancial assets, "real options" has been an approach that is increasingly popular.[12] Practically speaking, however, the real options approach would require us to determine a great many parameters. Such parameters will be difficult to determine unambiguously or will not be available, and in the legally and politically contentious situation of a merger, evaluation will lead to endless litigation. Therefore, a shorthand approach is needed for the diversity option. Such an approach would include the number of voices as well as the market concentration, and it must do so in a simple fashion.

The voice value index declines with the number of options, since, say, the third new radio station adds more value than the thirty-third station. To express this, let the "voice value" of a medium be v. v is defined as

$$v = Kn^{-1/2} = \frac{K}{\sqrt{n}}.$$

K is a constant, and n is the number of voices. For example, if the option value of the first station is 100, the incremental value of the second station is 70.7, of the tenth station is 31.6, of the twentieth station 22.3, and so forth.[13] Total option value of all stations is their aggregate. Using a continuous function this is the integral over n,

$$V = K\int_{1}^{n} n^{-0.5}dn = 2Kn^{1/2}.$$

The proposed Media Ownership Concentration and Diversity Index (MOCDI) is therefore defined as the following:

$$MOCDI = \frac{HHI}{V} = \frac{\sum_i^n S_i^2}{\sqrt{n}}$$

The numerator is the regular HHI for market power—the sum of squared market shares. The denominator is the square root of the number of voices in a media market.[14]

This means that total value v of media options is proportional to the square root of the number of these options. The larger the number n, the larger the aggregate value of the options, the "voice value." And the larger the market concentration, the larger the HHI. Hence, as one divides concentration by voice value, the ratio (the index) rises in size with more market concentration and with less diversity, and declines with less concentration and more diversity.[15]

For example, suppose there are eight separately owned radio stations, of which four have a share of 24% each and the remaining four stations have a share of 1% each. The regular HHI would then be 2,308. The existence of the four smaller stations would hardly affect it. If they did not exist at all, the HHI would be 2,500, not a very different result. But clearly, the small stations should be considered a factor. If we simply counted eight voices as if their respective size did not matter, however, we would overstate actual diversity. Instead, with the media concentration and diversity index above, we would find a MOCDI value of $\frac{2308}{\sqrt{8}} = 816$. But without the existence of the four small stations the MOCDI score would be 1,250, that is, a higher concentration measure that reflects the lower number of voices.

If all eight stations had the same market share, the MOCDI would be 442. On the other extreme, if one station had 90% and the other seven stations split the rest, the index would be 2,867. Thus, the index reflects an ordinal ranking that makes sense as we weigh both factors, market share and market participation.

For orders of magnitude, a national medium with ten equal-sized firms would have a media concentration index of 316. For a pure monopoly, $MOCDI = 10,000/\sqrt{1} = 10,000$. With five equal-sized firms, it would be about 900; with 20 firms, 112.

The MOCDI is numerically not comparable to the HHI. Thus, a media sector whose MOCDI is lower than its HHI is not "less concentrated." The two measures are on different scales with the $MOCDI = HHI * n^{-1/2}$, that is, smaller, and more so with the number of voices. For that reason, the HHI thresholds are not applicable to the MOCDI.

The next question is the practicality of the index. The numerator is the same as before for the HHI, providing no challenge that did not previously exist. The denominator requires us to identify participants. Should every high school paper be included, or every free supermarket paper? For practical reasons, there has to be a cutoff. We propose a minimum share of 1% as a reasonable floor: small but not trivial. But other minimum definitions can be readily used.

The MOCDI formula, slightly modified, could also be used for the concentration of all media in the aggregate, since a company might have no special market power in any particular medium but be involved in several media so that overall it would hold significant power, especially if it were to have multiple holdings in one city. For example, the merger of two local radio stations in a city where there are also two other radio stations, two newspapers, and seven TV stations is less of a reduction of diversity than when there is only one newspaper and only three TV stations. To deal with such cross-impacts, one could average the different local media into a single measure, consider them as a single market rather than segmented markets, and calculate the average HHI. A better approach would be to have a pooled local measure that takes into account all local media—TV, radio, newspaper, and magazines—and gives each a weight based on either revenues, news significance, or some other factor. In that definition, the number of newspapers in a city would make a difference to the question of how many radio stations another company should be able to own, because they are all part of the same media market.

A still better way would be to use the approach developed in this section, which is to consider both the overall number of voices and their market shares, weighted by revenues or other measures of relative importance. Using revenues as a weight across firms and media industries has its problems, of course. In particular, each medium is different in terms of its news richness vs. entertainment richness. An alternative way to weigh different media might be to look at the share of news and public affairs in a medium, for example, by counting its overall number of pages or broadcast minutes as a percentage of overall pages and minutes. A third way would be to weigh a medium by its subjective significance as a news and information contribution, based on public surveys.[16] We do not aim to resolve the question here of what these weights might be.

Whatever the weight—dollars, news content, or surveys—we could define an overall index of local media diversity that would provide a weight for each of radio, TV, newspapers, magazines, and local special cable channels.

$$\text{All-Media-}MOCDI = \frac{\sum w_j \sum S_{ij^2}}{\sqrt{n}}$$

where w_j is the informational weight of medium j, and S_{ij}^2 is the market share of firm i in medium j. Thus, in the example above (4 radio stations, 2 newspapers, and 7 TV stations, with 2 radio stations merging), suppose each radio station's revenues are 50, each TV station's 100, and each newspaper's 50. This would result in an overall media MOCDI[17] index of 236 for the situation preceding the proposed merger. The merger would raise the MOCDI by 24.[18] But in the case where only one newspaper and three TV stations exist, radio is as before with 4 stations, and the media industries are of the same size, the overall MOCDI starts out at 645,[19] and the merger would increase it by 26.

The special wrinkle of this measure is that it includes a firm's market share in other media, too, to account for cross-ownership. Thus, if a newspaper company with a 50% share in a local market also owns a TV station in the same market, with 14% of the market, these shares would be added; that is, $S_{ij} = S_{ij1} + S_{ij2}$, and S would become 64. The weight would be that of the higher-weight medium.

With this approach, it is reasonable to incorporate other changes in the media landscape. As new media emerge and smaller media grow or some of the larger firms stay stable in size, some others can own more than before, since overall market concentration would not increase from before.

This leaves the question of what the concentration thresholds ought to be. The actual threshold is a matter of policy, taste, and market size. To some

people, one voice is plenty so long as it agrees with them. Others would want to assure almost every perspective its voice, regardless of how minor. To get a sense for the order of magnitude, a MOCDI threshold of 500 would be the result of about 7.5 equal voices or of four voices with a market share of 20% each, with the remainder shared between seven other small players. Today, radio, TV stations, and newspapers, seen separately and nationally, are below that number, whereas cable TV is close to it, and TV networks are above. The music industry's merger between BMG and Sony exceeds that threshold. As a national figure, 500 seems in the ballpark for a single-medium threshold. At MOCDI of 300, there would be about ten equally sized companies, or a lot of small ones. The range between 300 and 500 is one of moderate concentration.

One could look at any past year and decide whether its media concentration had been comfortable in democratic and economic terms, and then aim for that level as the benchmark. An acquisition that would go beyond that mark would be closely scrutinized.

The desired media concentration threshold would have to depend on the size of the market. For a local market, or for a smaller country, it would be different than for the large American national market. As an illustration of the concept, such a function could be

$$\text{Diversity Threshold D} = 10{,}000 \times \text{Pop.}^{-.2}$$

Table 17.1 Media Concentration Index (MOCDI) for Equal-Sized Voices

Voices n	MOCDI
1	10,000
2	3,535
3	1,924
4	1,250
5	894
6	680
7	540
8	442
9	370
10	316
15	172
20	112
30	61

Such a formula would set the threshold, in a small local market of 100,000 population, at a MOCDI index of 1,000, which translates to about 4.6 independent voices. In a local market of a million people, the formula would result in 6.3 equal-sized local voices. And for the United States as a whole, the overall threshold would be an index of 200, the equivalent of 13.5 voices if they are of equal size, or, for example four companies of 15% each, four companies of 5% each, and 17 companies of 1.2% each. This is just an example. Whatever the numbers of voices are desired, one would simply modify the equation so the threshold number would be obtained by the formula.

Some people will oppose this approach. They might suspect darkly that it means a loosening—or tightening—of the existing rules. But that is a question of where the thresholds would be set, not of the methodology itself. Others might argue that no intervention at all is warranted, since markets will generate competitive entry and diversity. There would be no need to ever use any media diversity test. But suppose that market power does emerge? What then? After all, the economics of media and information, with their high fixed costs and low reproduction costs, create strong economies of scale that often favor concentration. In any event, such a laissez-faire approach is highly unlikely in the real world, considering the FCC's debacle in Congress and the courts in trying to loosen the rules.

To still others, any numerical test is suspect as mechanistic. They would prefer a case-by-case consideration of many factors relevant to a media market. But this would leave a judgment call over media ownership to government officials able to reward friends and punish enemies, or enable powerful media companies to thwart unfavorable decisions—both undesirable options given the inherently adversarial relationship of government and media. As mentioned before, this argues for a relatively clear-cut test, with a relatively clear-cut methodology. But to allow for special circumstances, it would not be an inflexible test but rather what lawyers call a rebuttable presumption, a benchmark. It would also create a tool to let local communities take a look at their own media situation and find out where they stand in terms of media diversity. Given the contentiousness of the issue, it would be best to create such a system in advance rather than to do so ad hoc, ad hominem, and ad infinitum.

Notes

1. Economists are used to the insiders of almost any industry considering their industry to be "different." The test might therefore be whether non-insiders also think so. By that test, the media is likely to be on the "special case" list, together with health care and a few others.

2. Noam, Eli. *Interconnecting the Network of Networks*. Cambridge: The MIT Press, 2001.

3. "Beyond Liberalization II: The Impending Doom of Common Carriage." *Telecommunications Policy*, 18(6) (1994), pp. 435–452.

4. *Prometheus Radio Project* vs. *Federal Communications Commission*; United States of America, United States Court of Appeals for the Third Circuit, June 24, 2004.

5. Hammond, Allen S., Barbara O'Connor, and Tracy Westin. "FCC Media Ownership Study #8: The Impact of the FCC's TV Duopoly Rule Relaxation on Minority and Women Owned Broadcast Stations 1999–2006," Federal Communications Commission. FCC.gov. July 31, 2007. Accessed on January 6, 2008, from http:// hraunfoss.fcc.gov/edocs_public/attachmatch/ DA-07-3470A9.pdf.

6. Beresteanu, Arie, and Paul B Ellickson. "FCC Media Ownership Study #7: Minority and Female Ownership in Media Enterprises," Federal Communications Commission. FCC.gov, June, 2007. Accessed on January 6, 2008, from http:// hraunfoss.fcc.gov/edocs_public/attachmatch/ DA-07–3470A8.pdf.

7. Shiman, Daniel, Kenneth Lynch, Craig Stroup, and Pedro Almoguera. "FCC Media Ownership Study #4: News Operations," Federal Communications Commission. FCC.gov, July 31, 2007. Accessed on January 6, 2008, from http://hraunfoss.fcc. gov/edocs_public/attachmatch/DA-07-3470A5. pdf. Milyo, Jeffrey. "FCC Media Ownership Study #6: The Effects of Cross-Ownership on the Local Content and Political Slant of Local Television News," Federal Communications Commission. FCC.gov, September 17, 2007. Accessed on January 6, 2008, from http://hraunfoss.fcc.gov/ edocs_public/attachmatch/DA-07-3470A7.pdf.

8. Chipty, Tasneem. "FCC Media Ownership Study #5: Station Ownership and Programming in Radio," Federal Communications Commission. FCC.gov, June 24, 2007. Accessed on January 6, 2008, from http://hraunfoss.fcc.gov/edocs_public/ attachmatch/DA-07-3470A6.pdf.

9. Crawford, Gregory S. "FCC Media Ownership Study #3: Television Station Ownership Structure and the Quantity and Quality of TV Programming," Federal Communications Commission. FCC.gov, July 23, 2007. Accessed on January 6, 2008, from http://hraunfoss.fcc.gov/ edocs_public/attachmatch/DA-07-3470A4.pdf.

10. Caves, Richard. *Creative Industries.* Cambridge: Harvard University Press, 2000.

11. Black, Fischer, and Myron Scholes. "The Pricing of Options and Corporate Liabilities." *Journal of Political Economy,* 1973, 81(3), 637–654; Merton, Robert C. "Theory of Rational Option Pricing." *Bell Journal of Economics and Management Science,* 1973, 4 (1), pp. 141–183.

12. See, e.g., Allemann, James, and Eli Noam. *The New Investment Theory of Real Options and Its Implications for Telecommunications.* Amsterdam and New York: Kluwer, 1999.

13. If one ignores diminishing incremental value added, the index loses persuasiveness. The exponential factor −0.5 is meant to be symmetrical to the HHI's squarings and it is computationally easy. If a more rapid or slower decline of options seems more reasonable, a different exponent can be used in the formula.

14. Since it is a dimensionless index we can ignore the constant 2K.

15. Noam, Eli. "How to measure media concentration." *Financial Times.* August 30, 2004. Last accessed on February 27, 2008 from http://www.ft.com/cms/s/2/da30bf5e-fa9d-11d8-9a71-00000e2511c8.html.

16. This approach was partly used by the FCC, by using Nielsen survey data on people's news use of various media. A separate question is whether the Nielsen survey that the FCC used was a good one, and whether it asked the right questions. A further question is whether such surveys should be part of an official index to determine policy, or whether its use should be left to research and studies.

17. The calculation:

$$MOCDI = \frac{4*(5\%)^2 + 2(5\%)^2 + 7(10\%)^2}{\sqrt{4+2+7}} = 236.11$$

18.

$$MOCDI = \frac{1*(10\%)^2 + 2(5\%)^2 + 2(5\%)^2 + 7(10\%)^2}{\sqrt{12}}$$
$$= \frac{900}{3464} = 360$$

19.

$$MOCDI = \frac{4*(5\%)^2 + 1*(10\%)^2 + 1*(23.3\%)^2}{\sqrt{8}}$$
$$= 645$$

18

Findings

THE OVERALL INFORMATION SECTOR

Undoubtedly, the coverage of 100 industries will be tedious at times to those interested in only a few of them. And at times the distinctions among industries might seem minor to those who are focused on other segments. Yet this book is about the information sector as a whole and it looks at media as part of that larger sector. Its thesis is that similar dynamics take place across industries, including mass media, and that they lead to further media concentration trends. Such an analysis cannot be done credibly with only a sketchy treatment of the other information industries. And once one deals with the telecom and IT sectors, one must disaggregate them to a comparable level to make comparisons meaningful.

Let us begin with a look at the size of the major segments of the information sector. Table 18.1 shows three segments—Mass Media, Telecom, and IT—to be of relatively similar size, about a quarter to a third of a trillion dollars. The Internet segment is still much smaller but growing rapidly. Combined, the U.S. Information sector accounts for over one trillion dollars, not including its considerable exports to other countries.

We can now do the final averaging across all 100 information sector industries, and also across the 27 mass media industries that we have investigated. We then proceed to an interpretation.

Figure 18.1 and table 18.2 show several findings for the overall information sector.

1. The average concentration of the information sector, in terms of the weighted average HHI trend of 100 industries, fell from 2,108 in 1984 to 1,631 in 2005 but varied considerably over that period. Before 1984, overall concentration was high (the weighted average for 1983 was HHI = 3,660, much of it as a result of AT&T.) Then, between 1984 and 1992, aggregate concentration declined fairly sharply, with new participants due to lower legal, technological, and economic entry barriers. Around 1996, concentration rose pronouncedly when several of the companies aggressively sought market share as competitive advantage, that is, to acquire scale economies and network effects. After 2001, concentration declined again somewhat as industries stabilized.

Thus, the average weighted HHI, our primary measure of sectoral concentration, was lower in 2005 than it was in 1984[1] by a good amount (from 2,108 down to 1,613). But it was higher in 2005 than it had been between 1992 and 1996, when it was about 1,400. Soon after 1984, the information sector as a whole moved into the range of concentration defined by the U.S. Justice Department as "moderately concentrated" and, with zigs and zags, remained there. Did concentration rise in the near past? *No*, if the baseline year is 1984 or earlier. *Yes*, if the baseline year is 1992.

Table 18.1 Revenues of U.S. Information Sector (in $ Billion)

	1984		1988		1992		1996		2001		2005
	Nominal	2005 $	Nominal	2005 $	Nominal	2005 $	Nominal	2005 $	Nominal	2005 $	Nominal
Media	113	213	153	253	184	254	246	304	340	372	385
Telecom	121	228	148	245	196	271	269	333	343	376	361
IT	76	143	105	174	130	180	180	223	232	254	258
Internet			2	3	3	4	7	9	43	47	56
Total	310	585	408	675	513	708	702	869	958	1,049	1,060

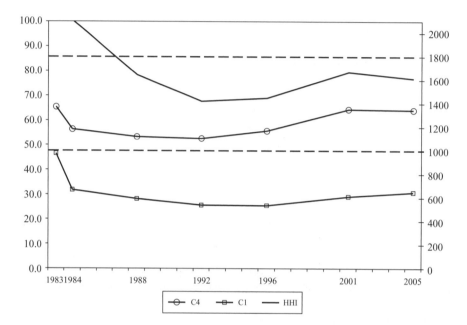

Figure 18.1 Average Concentration of the Entire Information Sector (100 Industries)

Table 18.2 Weighted Average Concentration in the Entire Information Sector (100 Industries)

	1983	1984	1988	1992	1996	2001	2005
HHI	3,660	2,108	1,645	1,421	1,448	1,670	1,631
C4	65.4	56.3	53.3	52.6	55.7	64.4	64.1
C1	46.5	31.8	28.2	25.7	25.5	29.1	30.8

2. The C4 index (the average share of the top four firms in each industry) followed a similar pattern. It first declined from 56.3 in 1984 to 52.4 in 1992, then rose again to 64.4% in 2001, and slightly declined thereafter. By that measure, overall concentration rose over the 20 years. This, together with the declining HHI, would indicate that single-firm control lagged and led to an overall lower HHI, whereas the ownership by the next tier of two to three firms increased on average and likely became more similar to each other

3. And indeed, as the C1 line shows in figure 16–1, the market share of the top company (the C1) also shows slight U-shape, although it is on the whole stable at about 30%.

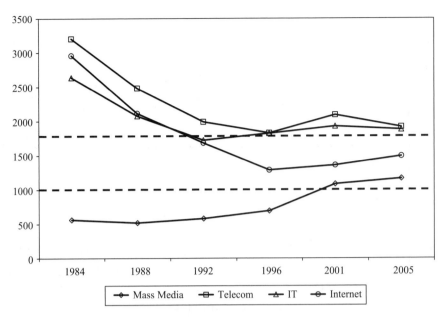

Figure 18.2 Sectoral Concentration Trends (HHI)

Table 18.3 Sectoral Concentration Trends (HHI)

	1984	1988	1992	1996	2001	2005
Mass Media	564	520	580	693	1,084	1,165
Telecom	3,204	2,482	1,992	1,828	2,093	1,917
IT	2,638	2,077	1,724	1,823	1,926	1,879
Internet	2,959	2,114	1,685	1,287	1,357	1,494

THE FOUR SUBSECTORS OF THE INFORMATION SECTOR

We can compare the four major subsectors of the information sector: mass media, telecommunications, IT, and Internet (figure 18.2, table 18.3).

1. The Internet, telecommunications, and IT sectors show a U-shaped trend line. For telecom and IT, it is at quite high a level, around 1,900. For the Internet sector, it is in the intermediate range, around 1,500. In distinct contrast, the mass media sector followed an S-shaped pattern, increasing in concentration steadily after 1988 and especially from 1996 to 2001. However, it remained lower in concentration than the other three sectors and moderately concentrated by the standards of the U.S. government's Antitrust Merger Guidelines, at an HHI of 1,165.

2. The concentration in telecommunications is higher once we consider the overall telecom services sector. In such a pooled sector, HHI concentration plummets with the AT&T divestiture in 1984 from 8,248 to 2,100. It keeps dropping steadily until 1996, when it almost reaches an unconcentrated level at 1,058. (This is nationally; locally it is a different story, see the local findings below.) Thereafter, concentration rises again to almost 2,100 in 2005.

3. Concentration in mass media has steadily increased over the 21-year period and come closer to the concentration levels prevailing in the rest of the information sector. Whereas in 1984 mass media HHI concentration was only one quarter (27%) of that of the overall information sector, it was 71% in 2005.

MASS MEDIA

Figure 18.3 and Table 18.4 show the overall concentration trends for the mass media sector, which

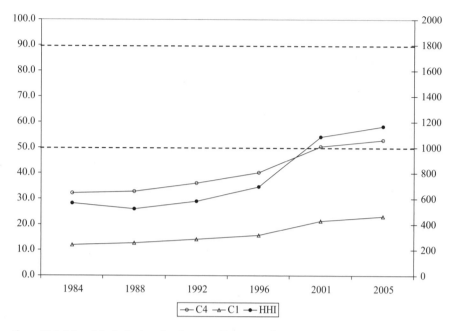

Figure 18.3 Mass Media Industries Average Concentration

Table 18.4 Mass Media Sector Concentration

	1984	1988	1992	1996	2001	2005
HHI	564	520	580	683	1,081	1,160
C4	32.2	32.8	36.1	40.2	50.4	52.9
C1	11.9	12.7	14.2	15.8	21.3	23.1

includes print, music, film, TV, radio, cable, DBS, and so forth.

1. For mass media, the concentration trend is not U-shaped but S-shaped. The average (weighted) HHI concentration of mass media as a whole was fairly flat in the 1980s, at first even declining a bit. It rose after 1993, and slowed after 2001. The C4 index shows a trend similar to that of the HHI measure. Whereas the top four firms accounted in 1984 for one-third of an average mass media industry, the C4 was about one-half in 2005. (The identity of these top four firms varies by industry.)

2. The average share of the leading company in a media industry almost doubled from about 12% to 23%.

3. At the same time, the average industry concentration, even after the steady rise subsequent to 1988, is well in the lower end of the range defined by the U.S. Department of Justice as "moderately concentrated." In 1988, the weighted average HHI had been at 520, well inside the "unconcentrated" range. Almost two decades later it stood at 1,165, at the low end of the U.S. Justice Department's range of moderate concentration.

4. Together with the requirement that all shares must add up to 100%, the average C1, C4, and HHI measure for mass media describe a typical market structure within a fairly well-defined band. It would be, approximately,

Top firm: 23%
Three firms, each 10%
Nine firms, each 6%
Small firms, totaling 2%

If firm 2 is larger than 10%, then mathematically firms 3 and 4 would have to be correspondingly smaller, and the third tier would consist of smaller but more numerous firms. (Example: $1 \times 23\%$, $1 \times 17\%$, $2 \times 6.5\%$, $10 \times 4.7\%$).

Looking at it positively, in most nonmedia industries, these would not be considered high levels of concentration. But one can also put it negatively—that in the average media industry, four firms control over one-half (53%) of what we read, watch, or buy. One must understand, though, that these are not always the same four firms. If we aggregate the largest the top 10 firms in the overall media sector, their combined share is 36%, much lower than for an average industry.

5. Thus, mass media have indeed been rising in concentration, but to repeat, their average level of concentration is not in the range that would normally raise antitrust action if encountered in other industries. Hence, if one seeks a systematic deconcentration of media to a level below the prevailing one, the general antitrust process will usually not work, except in extreme cases. This is why the preceding chapter proposes an alternative concentration index system.

Within the mass media sector we can look at the several media subsectors: figure 18.4 shows the national concentration trends for several categories of media: print,[2] film,[3] music,[4] broadcasting,[5] multichannel TV,[6] and the Internet.[7]

6. The findings show that, roughly, the more electronic and "digital" a media subsector is, the more highly it seems to be concentrated. Thus, print media are relatively unconcentrated, with its HHI rising only slowly. Film and broadcasting, historically the next entrants, are more concentrated in the order of their age. Multichannel TV national concentration is high. The Internet media is more concentrated, initially declining, then reconcentrating. Within the Internet, broadband, the newest of media, shows high concentration and increases after 1996, suggesting further rise in overall Internet concentration.

The inference (though not proof) is that as media become more electronic and technologically advanced, they become subject to the more general economic dynamics of the information sector. I have described these dynamics, in an introductory chapter 2, as those of increasing scale economies and lowering entry barriers, leading to more concentrated industries and to periodic instability that leads to still further concentration. Print media have lower fixed costs than film or Internet. They have higher marginal costs than these media. Hence, the scale economies are lower, and industry concentration lower. Film is somewhere in between, with high fixed costs and relatively high marginal

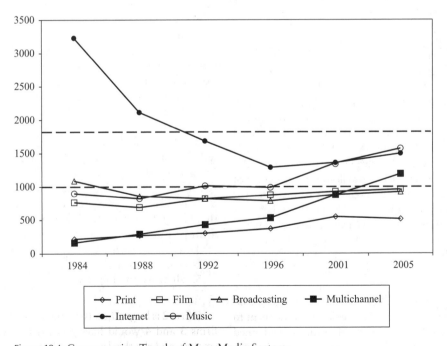

Figure 18.4 Concentration Trends of Mass Media Sectors

costs. Broadcasting has very low marginal costs. DBS has high fixed and low marginal costs. Cable also has high fixed/low marginal costs on a per channel/per user basis, and high scale economies. The ordering of industries by their fixed cost/ marginal cost ratio seems to correspond roughly to the industries' concentration levels, though this would have to be the subject of further research of the various cost elements.

THE INTERNET

In the debate over media concentration, the openness of the Internet has been a major argument for relaxing controls over traditional media. However, strong economies of scale, network effects, distance-insensitivity, and high complexity have led to a consolidation for the core of the Internet as well as for many major applications.

The aggregate concentration trend for the Internet industries, too, has been U-shaped, as the trends were for almost all of its major subindustries. Furthermore, most Internet industries were moderately concentrated in absolute terms, with the aggregate HHI at about 1,500 in 2005, well above the level of mass media. After 1996, concentration increased considerably.[8]

This pours some cold water over the hope that the Internet will solve the media concentration problem. This sector exhibits the same dynamics prevailing in the traditional media, leading to concentration. If anything, its greater dynamism gets it there faster. And the more advanced platforms for the Internet—broadband and fiber-based ultrabroadband—will strengthen that trend. Because this sector experiences bursts of innovation and entrepreneurship, the concentration trend will exhibit a zigzag pattern within the overall U-shaped trend.

It bears repeating that this concentration is not measured here for the many uses of the Internet, any more than those of telephone applications are measured when we discuss concentration for telecom services, or of advertising agencies when we analyze TV network concentration. A vast number of online applications have emerged, and they are lumped together in people's minds as "the Internet." These applications are outside the scope of this study.[9] But even here, concentration trends are evident. Network effects favor the Web sites that have somehow achieved scale

or critical mass in their particular niche, such as eBay's dominance in auctions, Napster (before it was shut down by the courts), Skype, YouTube, Monster, and Craigslist.com. Ninety-five percent of Web searches use Google or Yahoo. Economies of scale and network effects create a winner-take-all situation. Even for news, although in theory one can reach a vast panoply of news sites, the reality is that four sites get the overwhelming number of visits—in November 2007, Yahoo had 31 million visitors; MSNBC, 30 million; CNN, 33 million; and AOL News, 20 million. Everyone else's numbers drop off rapidly.[10] The top five news sites get more traffic than the next 15.[11]

One study shows how users flock to the most-frequented websites in a self-reinforcing pattern. There were, in 2003, 13,000 Web pages on the subject of gun control, but just 10 of them received two-thirds of all hyperlinks.[12] Studies show that concentration levels for users for particular applications such as news drop off following a power curve, that is, they decline exponentially.[13] Yes, there is a long tail.[14] But it is set on a squat body.

TOP COMPANIES

1. We rarely found market shares to be in the monopoly range. Table 18.5 shows the entire set of firms with 2005 market share of over 60%, in 100 industries.

For the other industries investigated, no such single-firm dominance exists. American information and media industries are not monopolies but more likely oligopolies. The average industry has an HHI of 1,631, a C4 of 64%, and a C1 of 31%, results that correspond numerically to top firms with 31%, one firm with 18% and another 4 firms with 7%, and a few small players. For mass media, as mentioned, the statistically typical industry structure is a top firm of 23%, 3 firms of 10%, 9 firms of 5%, (An alternative distribution that fits the data is four firms with about 13% each, six firms with 8%, and a few smaller participants.)

2. The role of the top single firm declined in Telecom, IT, and Internet. Figure 18.5 shows the trends in the average industry of the share of the market leader, the C1.

We can see a U-shaped decline in weighted average for three of the sectors. But it has increased for mass media, almost doubling to about 23%.

Table 18.5 Industries with Predominence by Top Company (Share of Over 60%)

Industry	Dominant Firm	Share	Rivals and Comments
Microcomputer Operating Software	Microsoft	95%	Linux (growing). MS under antitrust obligations from Brussels.
Mainframe Hardware and Software	IBM	92%	Networked smaller computers (growing). Declining industry.
Cable Music Channels	Viacom	84%	No direct rival, but MP3 downloads are growing. Declining industry.
CISC Microprocessors	Intel	80%	AMD (growing)
MP3 Players	Apple	74%	CE industry
Search Engines	Google	51% (61% in 2008)	Yahoo, MSN Live search and video
Video Rental Retail	Blockbuster	53.2	Netflix, VOD, streaming are destroying storefront industry

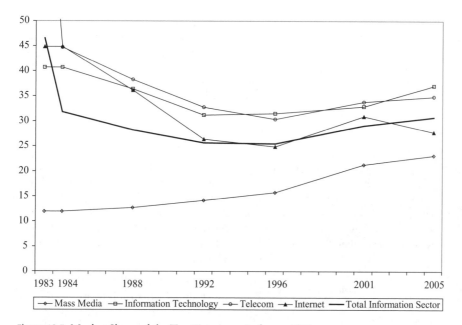

Figure 18.5 Market Share of the Top Firm in an Industry (C1)

This does not mean that one firm holds 23% of the total mass media sector; different media industries are led by different firms. The top firm in the mass media sector overall, Time Warner, accounts for 10.3% of the overall sector. After the Viacom split, no other firm has more than 5%.[15] Overall, for the entire information sector, the share of the top firm in an industry (the C1) has remained fairly constant from 1984 (31.8%) to 2005 (30.8%).

3. As the share of the top company rose (for mass media) or declined (for the other three

sectors), how has the share of the next few firms moved? Figure 18.6 shows a "Dominance Ratio" of the top firm's share relative to that of the next three firms combined: D = (C1/C(2–4)). When this ratio is high, and the C4 as a whole is high, the top single firm dominates the rest, and the market can be described as monopolistic. Where the ratio is low while the C4 is high, the four firms in the top group are more similar in size—and more likely to be an oligopoly.

We can see that the three sectors Internet,[16] telecom, and IT declined in their Dominance Ratio

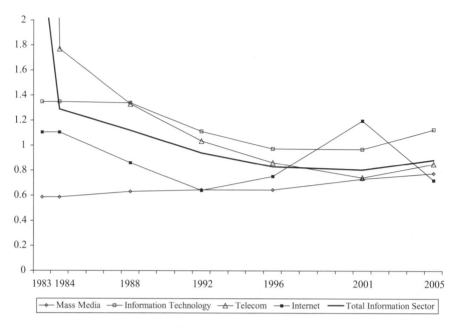

Figure 18.6 Dominance Ratio of the Top Company Relative to Firms 2–4, by Sector

considerably from single-firm dominance in the direction of oligopoly levels.

But for mass media, the Dominance Ratio stayed fairly level over 20 years, rising gently from 0.6 to 0.7, which means that the top firm did not lose out relative to firms number 2 through 4. They grew together, in contrast to the rest of the information sector.

Here, too, these are trends leading to a convergence of market structure across the four segments of the Information sector.

So far, much of this discussion centered on national concentration measures. But many of the problems in mass media concentration are (a) vertical and (b) local.

VERTICAL CONCENTRATION AND CONGLOMERATES

A purely horizontal concentration measure cannot take account of the growth of firms that are active across a host of industries, a characteristic that is the hallmark of media conglomerates.

1. Diversification. We find that the 50 largest firms of the overall information sector participated,

on average, in 5.2 information industries, 1.1 more than in 1984. The largest 25 mass media firms participated, on average, in 4.8 industries in 2005, 1.7 more than in 1984. And the top 5 mass media firms participated in 8.8 industries in 2005, whereas it was 4.6 in 1984. That number peaked at 9.4 in 2001.

2. Cross-sectoral convergence. We do not find much direct expansion by firms active in one traditional sector of the information sector (mass media, telecom, IT) into the other two main traditional sectors. Of the 50 largest firms in the information sector, none had a presence in all four sectors. Microsoft, Sony, AT&T, and Time Warner had a presence in three sectors. However, Sony largely left telecom, except for mobile handsets as the junior partner in a joint alliance with Ericsson. The old AT&T first entered, then left computers and cable TV; the new AT&T and Verizon are trying for a role in TV distribution. Time Warner's role in IT was minor, but its broadband and voice-over telephony are growing (and subject to shareholder pressure to spin off). The exception to the absence of cross-sectoral convergence has been the Internet, which drew many of the largest information firms from all sectors. It

seems the ground on which other firms from the more traditional sectors meet, test, and contest.

3. The combined share of the top 50 firms in the overall information sector did not increase, but declined from 68 to 58%. The average top-50 information sector firm in 1984 had 1.4% of the overall information market. Almost 20 years and countless mergers later, the average top 50 firms had a *lower* share at 1.1% in 2005.

4. More telling is the trend line of the top 10 information sector companies (see figure 18.7). It shows a substantial *decrease*, from 48 to 27%, in the aggregate share of the biggest ten companies until 1996, when it started to fluctuate around 30%. But companies ranked 11–50 show the opposite trend. Thus, the relative market share of the large firms became progressively more symmetric during this period. The smaller of the large firms increased in share, whereas the largest of firms saw it reduced.

5. For the top mass media firms, however, trends were, again, quite different. The numbers show a steady upward trend in overall sectoral share by the top firms. The top five mass media firms accounted together for about 13.4% of the mass media sector in 1984. By 2005, their share

had doubled to 26.2%.[17] The increase was largest for the top five firms, which each gained, on average, a 2.5% share for a total of 5.2% since 1984 (figure 18.8).

Figure 18.8 shows a continuous and pronounced upward trend of the top five firms after 1988 until 2004. Even so, their aggregate share, at 26.2% of the overall mass media sector, was much lower than that prevailing in the telecom and IT sectors, where the top five companies held in 2005 an aggregate share of 61.2% and 43.0%, respectively.

6. If we look solely at the electronic mass media, the top five firms' share was 42%, again double that of 1984 (21.6%).[18]

7. For the combined electronic video mass media market (TV and cable networks, TV stations, DBS, cable MSOs—the part of mass media most likely under the regulatory supervision of the FCC)—the market share of the top five firms slightly declined to 18.1% in 1992, then rose pronouncedly to 40.3 in 2001 and 42% in 2005.

8. For the combined telecom services market, also under FCC jurisdiction, the share of the top four firms dropped from 66% in 1984 to 52% in 1992 and 1996, then rose to 88% by 2005.

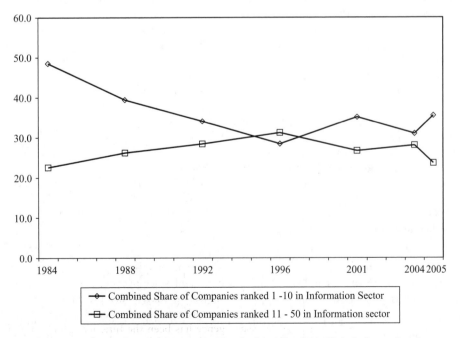

Figure 18.7 Aggregate Share of Companies Ranked 1–10 and 11–50 in Information Sector

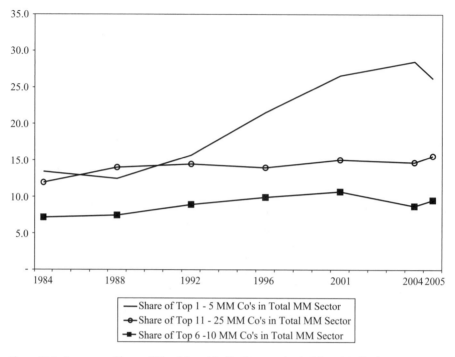

Figure 18.8 Aggregate Share of Top Mass Media Companies in Mass Media Sector

To conclude: in the overall information sector, vertical integration has increased in terms of participation but has declined in terms of overall share or leverage power. It has increased by all three measures for the mass media sector. Top firm market share also increased across the telecom sector.

LOCAL CONCENTRATION

1. We find that all local media are strongly concentrated, with newspapers at the top and rising (HHI = 7,676 in 2006). Broadcast television stations (1,895) and multichannel TV (6,629) experienced a decline in their (still high) concentration. Cable television, by itself and without the mitigating factor of including the two DBS rivals in the market definition, has a 100% product share.

2. Radio has grown fastest in local concentration, but remains, in absolute numbers (2,326), well below the levels of most other local media.

3. The local telecom market is less concentrated than it used to be, but remained in 2006 at a high

level (HHI = 4,993). Alternative telecom firms have faltered for economic and regulatory reasons, but cable as an alternative infrastructure and VoIP as an Internet application (on both cable and telecom broadband lines) have made major inroads. Mobile telephony, too, has been an increasingly popular alternative to local wireline connectivity, either for second or main lines. By itself, local mobile concentration is HHI = 2,814. Pooled with wireline service (and taking into account in shares that telecom companies provide both wireless and wireline), local concentration is about 3,788—high, but much lower than it used to be.

Small local markets are not more concentrated than medium-sized ones (and often even less so) because they partake in the media of other cities. (This, however, makes them not quite "local" anymore.)

Since the local concentration of each medium is high, and since everyone lives in some locality or another, does this mean that everyone's media are highly concentrated? One cannot jump to that conclusion. Many or most media are national in scope, whether TV and cable channels, magazines, or websites and are subject to much lower concentration. This still leaves local news/public affairs as a problem. To measure its concentration one would need to aggregate, not average, the different local news media in a local market. This was discussed in chapter 17, with a suggested methodology.

OWNERSHIP

1. Of the largest 30 American individual fortunes in 2005, half originated in the information sector. Of the largest 400 fortunes, 94 (almost a quarter) originated in the information sector. This sector shows some of the gold-rush aspects of railroads in the nineteenth century. A substantial part of the world's top wealth holders earned their wealth in the media, information, and communications fields.

2. But this wealth does not mean that ownership is in the hands of those billionaires. If anything, the opposite has been the case. The ownership by "insiders"—that is by shareholders with more than 5% or by managers or board members—declined significantly for most of the largest information sector firms. Even for mass media firms, where it is higher than in the rest of the information sector, it fell from 34.6% to 19.6% between 1988 and 2005. Technology and new media companies became stock market favorites, and inside ownership decreased as founders cashed out. For the IT/Telecom sector as a whole, it rose from 4.8 to 6.4%, much lower than for mass media.

3. Similarly, within the individual top-50 firms, the ownership concentration of the major five shareholders declined. The same holds mostly for top mass media firms. Ownership became more fragmented among more shareholders, often without a dominant shareholder.

4. One major change has been the greatly increased ownership by large institutional investors in the information sector. Decades ago, media ownership was primarily in the hands of a small group of individuals and families. But by the late twentieth century, new technology and new media had created a massive need for capital, and this required many sources and hence a widespread ownership. This trend has been most evident in the computer and high-technology industries, where relatively young companies need to rely upon

equity capital—initially by way of venture capital investment—to finance their future growth. A high degree of institutional ownership is an inevitable consequence of burgeoning technology and new media. Institutional investors are attracted to high-technology stocks because of their significant growth potential.

Information sector companies became an attractive investment vehicle for the ever-growing mutual and pension funds. Mutual funds' ownership of top information sector firms almost quintupled from 1984 to 2005, from 5.5% to 26.5%. Institutional ownership rose from 39.6% in 1988 to 57.2% in 2005 for the mass media sector and from 49.0% to 61.5% for the IT and telecom sector. Most of the increase was after 1990. The largest firms in mass media had the highest share of institutional investment during the same period: from 52.6% in 1988 to 65.3% in 2005.

5. However, some major mass media companies were reluctant to relinquish owner-family control. The print media industries, given the prevalence of family control, have generally received less institutional investment than technology companies.

6. Who then owns the media? The funds with the largest equity positions in the major media companies in 2005 were State Street Global Advisors ($68 billion), Barclays ($57 billion), Capital Research & Management ($47 billion), Fidelity Management & Research ($41 billion), Vanguard Group ($30 billion), and Wellington Management ($29 billion). Pension funds were also big investors, such as TIAA-CREF, the educators' retirement fund, which had $19 billion invested in the media and information sector. Several of these institutional investors invest very large amounts in some of the largest information sector firms. Moreover, they hold onto their shares for longer periods than in the past, and turn over their holdings more slowly, thus having more of a stake in company management.[19] They often also hold sizable chunks of media companies' debt in the form of long-term corporate bonds and short-term commercial paper.

7. However, even though the institutional owners hold only a few percentages (at most) of any single company, they often have stakes in many firms. Just 14 large institutional investors hold 21.2% of the average top 25 mass media

firms and hold 26.0% of IT and telecom companies. This is a remarkably high aggregate ownership. In addition, they set the tone for the many
smaller funds and can trigger market changes
for the major firms. If they acted in concert they
could exercise industry-wide power. But there is
little evidence for such coordinated and direct
activity, and especially not for activity aimed
directly at content.

Thus, the claim that convergence in the information industries has resulted in a small group
of media moguls is not an accurate one. A better
description is one of many institutions owning narrow slices of a big pie. Among them, a dozen or so
set the tone and have the highest stakes across virtually all media firms. Collectively, they let media
managers run their businesses in a micro-sense
but in a macro-sense put performance pressure
on them through their buy-and-sell decisions. But
such performance pressure, which can affect content decisions, arises from the existence of private
media firms in a profit-oriented market economy
rather than from concentrated ownership. Indeed,
strong owners with substantial control who run a
media company have been the most problematic to
many critics—owners such as Rupert Murdoch,[20]
Lowry Mays,[21] and the Smith brothers in the present, or of Laurence Tisch, William Paley, William
Randolph Hearst, and Colonel McCormick in the
past,[22] or of Silvio Berlusconi in Europe.[23]

Notes

1. To avoid a distortion in the comparisons, we
used 1984 as the baseline year. Had we started in
1983 or earlier, the huge AT&T would have been
reflected in a much greater overall concentration.
For 1983, the HHI would have been 3,660 and the
C4 65.4%, both well above the 2005 figures.
2. "Print" includes daily newspapers, educational books, trade and paperback books, other
books, book retailing, magazines, and academic
journals.
3. "Film" includes movie production/
distribution, TV prime time production, and movie
theaters.
4. "Music" includes music publishing, performance rights, distribution, retailing, and music
cable channels.
5. "Broadcasting" includes TV prime time production, radio stations, TV stations, radio networks, TV networks, and TV syndication.

6. "Multichannel TV" includes home video,
video rental, DBS providers, cable TV operators, cable TV channels, and cable TV set top
converters.
7. "Internet" includes backbones, ISPs, browser
software, Internet search engines, portals, IP telephony, media player software, and broadband
providers.
8. Clearly the embryonic years of the Internet
are of only limited informational value. But
they still show the pattern: from a limited
medium of high concentration and few providers, to a wide-open structure, and then to a
reconcentration.
9. The exceptions, due to their more fundamental applicability, are VoIP and search engines.
10. NYTimes.com, 12.1 million; Google News,
9.3 million; Washingtonpost.com, 8.8 million.
Source: Nielsen NetRatings as quoted by Jonathan
Dube in "CyberJournalist.net: Top news sites
for January 2006," http://www.cyberjournalist.
net/news/003335_print.php. Woodson, Alex.
"Yahoo, MSNBC and CNN Lead Online News."
Editor and Publisher. EditorandPublisher.com.
December 17, 2007. Last accessed on January 14,
2008, from http: //www.editorandpublisher.com/
eandp/departments/online/article_display.
jsp?vnu_content_id=1003686429.
11. Cukier, Kenneth Neil, and Mathew
Hindman. "Measuring Media Concentration
Online and Offline," Ford Foundation Conference
on Media Diversity, Dec. 2003. http://www.
cukier.com/writings/webmedia-jan04.htm.
12. Hindman, Matthew, Kostas
Tsioutsiouliklis, and Judy A. Johnson. "Measuring
Media Diversity Online and Offline: Evidence
from Political Websites." Proceedings of the 32nd
Annual Telecommunications Policy Research
Conference, September 17, 2004. http://web.
si.umich.edu/tprc/papers/2004/362/Hindman_
Media_Diversity_TPRC.pdf.
13. Hargittai, Eszter. "How Wide a Web?
Inequalities in Accessing Information Online."
Princeton University, 2003; Cukier, Kenneth
Neil, and Mathew Hindman. "Measuring Media
Concentration Online and Offline," Ford Foundation
Conference on Media Diversity, Dec. 2003 http://
www.cukier.com/writings/webmedia-jan04.htm.
14. Anderson, Chris. "The Long Tail." www.
wired.com/wired/archive/12.10/tail.html.
15. However, Sumner Redstone and his family's
privately held National Amusements firm was the
controlling shareholder of both Viacom and CBS,
and Redstone was chairman of the board of both
companies. Hence the two firms are independent
of each other only to a limited extent.
16. The 2001 spike in the Internet's Dominance
Ratio was caused by a special situation in the backbone industry.

17. The top five mass media companies for 2005/6 are the following (percentage of total mass media sector revenue): Time Warner (10.3), Viacom (3.0), plus CBS (2.3), Comcast (5.0), Disney (4.2), and News Corp (3.7).

18. This includes the following industries: radio stations, TV stations, DBS providers, cable TV operators, radio networks, TV networks, TV syndication, cable TV channels, and pay TV channels.

19. The average turnover time of the large capital funds, i.e., funds that specialize in Fortune 500 firms such as IBM, AT&T, and Time-Warner, as tracked by *Morningstar Mutual Funds*, has shown a decrease in its three-year moving average from 82.7% in 1988 to 66% in 1997. See chapter 16. *Morningstar Mutual Funds*, Dec 21, 1998, p. 179. *Morningstar Mutual Funds,* v 5, issue 2, Sep 21, 2007. Pp. 155.

20. See www.freepress.net/hallofshame.

21. See www.corporatewatch.org.

22. See *Sinclair and the Public Airwaves,* Report by Sinclairwatch.org, accessed at www.sinclairwatch.org/sinclair_report.pdf.

23. See www.democracynow.org/article.

19

The Findings and the Model

THE MODEL REVISITED

In the introductory chapter 2, we presented a simple model for the dynamics of the information sector. It is based on two variables: lower entry barriers, which induce a new entry, and growing scale economies, which lead to a more concentrated market structure.

Together, these two factors and their changes induce oscillations. The trend of scale economies defines the axis (angle) of the oscillations, whereas the entry barriers affect frequency and amplitude of oscillations. Figure 19.1 shows this conceptually.

A third factor is digital convergence. It means that as industries become more digital in their technical characteristics, they also become more "digital" in their fundamental economic characteristics and hence in their concentration characteristics. This is presented in figure 19.2, which shows schematically how the concentration of different sectors converges.

We find that this model describes well the two decades we investigated, shown in figure 19.1. At first, monopolies and tight oligopolies ruled the roost (Point A). Major players were AT&T, IBM, the three TV networks, and the six major film studios. Then concentration of the information sector dropped as both entry barriers and economies of scale dropped. New entrants emerged almost everywhere: in computers, Apple, Dell, Compaq, and a host of IBM clones; in telecommunications, MCI, Sprint, and many small networks and resellers; in cable TV distribution, numerous small firms; in TV and cable networks, Fox, Turner and small cable networks; in mobile communications, McCaw and numerous other new cell phone providers. On top of it there were the many new industries. This was the period of openness and competition. It was soon followed by the takeoff of the Internet and a boom period unparalleled in recent decades of American economic history. Concentration dropped (Point B). But this did not last.

The reason was that the growing competition destabilized the industry, and led to problems which in turn led to a reconcentration. After 2000, and again after 2008, there has been a panoply of calamities—a bursting dotcom bubble; a telecom industry crisis; a music industry meltdown; a newspaper advertising recession; a consumer electronics glut. Each industry has its own story. But there are also commonalities.

The problem for the industry has not been weak demand—more minutes and bits of almost everything are being consumed. The problem is the *price deflation* in the information sector. Information network services and devices have been becoming cheaper for a long time, and it became increasingly difficult to charge. The music industry was

Table 19.1 Concentration Trends: Impact of Economies of Scale and Entry Barriers

		Scale Economies	
		Rising	Declining
Entry Barriers	Rising	Higher Concentration	Inverted-U Concentration Trend
	Declining	U-shaped Concentration Trend	Lower Concentration

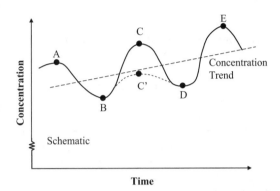

Figure 19.1 Concentration Trends, with Continuously Rising Scale Economies and Declining Entry Barriers

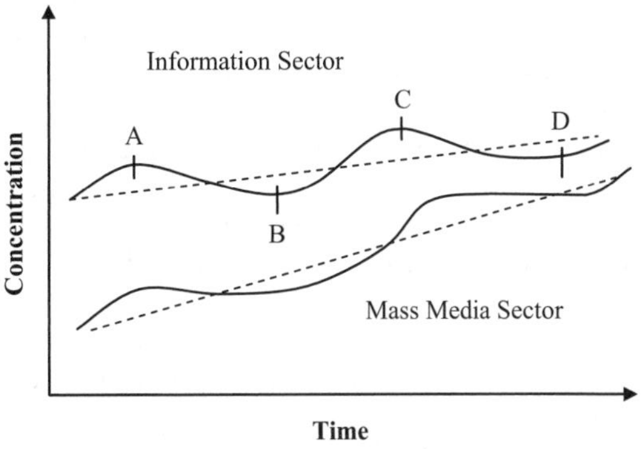

Figure 19.2 Convergence of Concentration of Overall Information Sector and Mass Media Sector

unable to maintain prices as users found alternative access to it. The online publishers could not charge information without losing their audience. (The major Texas newspaper, the *Dallas Morning News,* started to require payment for its online Texas Rangers football section, and its website dropped from 100,000 subscribers to 800.) The price of international phone calls declined enormously and, with VoIP, moves to near-zero. Cell phone prices dropped, from $.26 to $.06 per actual used minute on average, and prices for ISP and backbone services also declined steadily. Web advertising prices collapsed. Broadcast TV and radio have always been free in America, and with PVRs, viewers need not even pay with their attention. Much of the news is free, and much of software de facto so.

What has happened is that the entire information sector—from film to music to newspapers to telecom to Internet to microchips and anything in between—has been subject to a gigantic price deflation in slow motion. It is one of the fundamental trends of the digital environment.

The basic structural reasons are simple. Most information products and services are

characterized by high fixed costs and low marginal costs. They are expensive to produce but cheap to reproduce and distribute. The cost characteristics mean substantial economies of scale and incentives for each competitor to expand in order to gain them. Entrants are attracted by the growth characteristics and the lower entry barriers relative to the past. Collectively, this leads to expansion and eventually overexpansion.

The implication is a secular trend of price deflation in information products and services. This is a good deal for consumers. But it also creates problems for the suppliers. Under competitive pressures, the price for their information is marginal cost, which is close to zero.[1] It is most likely below average cost, which means that it does not cover total cost. One can do this only for so long before going out of business. And the more efficient the information market because of the technology, the faster this process.

The reaction of information and media companies is to try to escape commodification. The first basic strategy is one of product differentiation. Innovation in content and products is an important differentiator. But it is an expensive and risky way to go.

The second strategy is to be more efficient than rivals are. Firms therefore try to cut costs. But this is not easy beyond a point and soon may affect quality and credibility. The third main strategy is one of consolidation in order to actively maintain power and control over price. Cable TV and local newspapers, for example, are among the profitable segments of the information sector because they hold significant local market power. Microsoft is profitable because of its hold over PC operating software. Consolidation is much easier than product innovation. Firms therefore try to consolidate to create or restore pricing power.

In terms of Figure 19.1, industry concentration moves to Point C. If scale economies have risen, C will be higher than A has been, that is, the industry will trend to a higher concentration than before. But it is also possible that it will trend toward C', at a lower level than A, if the impact of rising scale economies is lower than that of lowering entry barriers, and as new entrants emerge with the rising profitability associated with concentration.

These are the factors underlying much of the consolidation in the information sector. Our empirical findings match the model well. If we look at figure 18-1 in the preceding chapter, which depicts the overall concentration trend, we find a strong correspondence after 1988 to the model of Figure 19.1. In terms of the HHI, it reaches Point C'. In terms of the C4, it reaches point C. And if we look at figure 18-2, of the four information subsectors, we see a converging trend similar to that postulated in Figure 19.2. The telecom and IT sectors are returning to a level of concentration out of which they were briefly pushed when a burst of regulatory liberalization and technological innovation lowered entry barriers and destabilized their previous industry structure. But the mass media sector has taken a different path, as figure 18-2 has shown. It has gone through only minor deconcentration in the multichannel stage of the 1980s and proceeded to rise over a longer period. It is not returning to a prior equilibrium but to a higher level. This matches our model's figure 19.2. The reasons are several. In the electronic media field the old unconcentration was partly based on regulatory ceilings that created barriers. Relaxation of these rules hence raised media structures to levels that are more market based.

But more important is the greater transition of mass media toward dynamics and structure of the other major segments of the information sector. And although mass media are not yet fully converged with each other or with the rest of the information sector, they are more so than in the past; they affect each other and are affected by similar dynamics. This process is most advanced for the highest-tech of mass media, online media. Other electronic and distribution media, as well as film and music, are following in that direction. Even newspapers and magazines are gradually following. Recall our earlier finding that the newer the medium (that is, the more electronic and digital it is), the more concentrated it becomes.

If this indeed is the underlying and driving force, it will lead to still further consolidation and concentration. In 2005, the combined and weighted concentration of the other three sectors was 1,807, whereas that of the mass media sector was 1,165. There are, of course, differences of content-producing media from network distribution or from the manufacturing or the software. But the commonalities and interactions are substantial, too, along with commonalities in industry dynamics, including concentration trends. These tendencies will be checked, from time to time, by bursts of new entry and innovation. But in most cases the newcomers eventually become part of the same consolidation process. Google and Yahoo are examples. The economic logic of the information environment seems to lead to oligopolistic consolidation. Where pricing power is lost, the industry's profitability declines quickly, as in the case of the music distribution. Their strategy then is either to consolidate horizontally still further, or to merge in a vertical integration with the hope of gaining gatekeeper power.

As companies consolidate, industry concentration rises to Point C in figure 19.1. But, counterforces gather that slow down the trend towards C and reverse it. On the policy level, there is government and political opposition which might resist consolidation. On the business side, the rising profitability creates opportunities for investment and entry. Depending on entry barriers, this entry can lead to a moderate or vigorous competition. The decline in concentration after 2001 (see in figure 18-1 above) is only shallow, at least until the end of our time series data, suggesting that entry barriers—financial and legal—have not been lowered by much or have stabilized.[2] In time, this decline in concentration will reverse direction again as the newcomers become themselves part of consolidation (Point D). A new cycle begins.

These are the dynamics of the media industry and, more generally, of the information sector. Media barons implement and take advantage of fundamental forces. The question then is whether regulatory barriers will block these forces if aggregate concentration exceeds a limit, and what those limits might be. To assist this determination and its implementation, a concentration index specific to media has been provided in chapter 17.

Notes

1. For hardware, too, the main cost is in the development, set-up, and marketing, not of the actual production.

2. Indeed, telecom regulations became less favorable to new entrants after 2001, and financing was hard to obtain.

20

The Future of Media Industries

One of the conclusions of this study is that the U.S. information sector as a whole—a $1 trillion part of the economy (about 10% of the GDP)—has become less concentrated in 2005 than it had been in 1984. However, it became more concentrated after 1996. Since 2001, this increase has flattened out and slightly declined.

We have identified concentration trends in the information sector and in its major constituent parts. For telecom, IT, and the Internet, in the two decades from 1984 to 2005, concentration first declined in a "multichannel" stage, then rose in the "digital" stage, then plateaued or declined. These three sectors thus followed the model of Chapter 2 pretty well, though it will take at least another cycle to verify its long-term validity. For mass media, concentration declined initially slightly and then rose rapidly, then more slowly.

We observe a U-shaped concentration trend pervading across the share of the information sector over the two decades. Of the 100 industries analyzed, we find it for 41%. It is a strong trend that cuts across numerous industries, and it characterizes three of the four subsectors of the information sector—IT, telecom, and the Internet.

But the important exception is the mass media sector. Because of the significance of media, much of the public debate has focused on it. (More recently, the debate has also reached the telecom industry as a carrier of Internet traffic). For the mass media sector as a whole, concentration increased steadily after 1988 and into the late 1990s. However, the sector also remained lower in concentration than the other three sectors and unconcentrated by the standards of the U.S. government's Antitrust Merger Guidelines.

This comparison does not imply that mass media concentration is low, since a strong case can be made for lower concentration thresholds for mass media than for other industries. (See chapter 17 for an alternative measure.)

Media free-marketeers who deny this concentration trend will need to deal with these facts. One can argue that counter-trends of competitive entry will emerge, but one cannot argue that no substantial rise has occurred.

Media reformers, on their part, need to deal with the fact that overall concentration, while clearly rising, is much lower than the alarmist rhetoric suggested. Criticism has been shrill even when media concentration was quite low. Ben Bagdikian wrote about "the Media Monopoly" and about the "private Ministry of Information and Culture" not as a prediction but as a description, and in a period when overall media concentration was actually declining.

Once we observe these numbers, the questions arise: What next? Will the concentration issue, by and large, take care of itself? Or, to the contrary, are fundamental forces at work that transform the structure of information and media industries?

Given the dynamics described in the preceding chapter, what will future media industries look like? In chapter 2 we concluded that the model and the underlying forces it described had several implications for information industries and firms. The main structural implication was a two-tier media system, based on

1. Large integrator firms, assembling and bundling elements mostly produced by others, operating in a oligopolistic industry structure.
2. Numerous specialist firms surrounding the integrators in geographic and functional clusters and providing much of actual production and service elements. Some of these specialists may be quite large themselves and/or dominate their niche.

We increasingly find these industry structures across many parts of the information sector, as described in various industry chapters. In some industries such as semiconductors, IT, consumer electronics, music, telecom services, software, games, and online portals, they already exist; in others they can be expected. I provide two examples in the chapter, about newspapers and film.

The emerging environment has a structure different from that of the past, with its emphasis on media and technology conglomerates operating along the value chain, that is, on vertical integration. The new environment will be based more on scale economies, that is, on horizontal integration. It is first necessary to shake the belief that existing large media firms have no way to go but to expand horizontally and vertically.[1] Industries and sectors could still increase in concentration even as old firms falter and new firms take over leadership. The failures of powerful firms are often overlooked in generic criticism of media firms' growth—such as the decline or fall of such formerly major diversified players as RCA, the old AT&T, the old CBS, Vivendi (as a global media firm), Maxwell, Gulf & Western, MCI WorldCom, Times Mirror, MGM, and others who seemed invincible for a time. This is to be distinguished from reasonably successful firms being acquired and disappearing inside the new entity, or from spin-offs. Companies and industries go through life cycles, and to focus on their vigorous growth phases alone gives a distorted view. What we observe instead is that the conglomerate and vertically integrated structure of major

media firms—in which the large firms produce most of their inputs and outputs—is tottering.

Of the 25 major media and information conglomerates of 2005, virtually all had been going through crisis or restructuring:

- *Time Warner* dropped AOL from its name to obliterate a reminder of a major merger gone spectacularly sour. After lowering the valuation of the assets on its balance sheet by a record-breaking write-off of $144 billion, and heavily in debt, it sold off its music division, book divisions, and many magazines. It had to beat back in 2005, at least temporarily, a serious challenge by dissident shareholders to spin off its cable group and other properties. It then spun off its huge cable operations in 2009. This was happening because the economic arguments for divestment were persuasive to many institutional investors.
- *AT&T* had spun off its telecom equipment and computer divisions. Then, having invested about $100 billion to become the largest U.S. cable TV company, it sold off these cable properties at half the acquisitions price, and disposed of its cellular operations (to whose invention it had contributed). In 2005, what was left of "Ma Bell" was acquired for a mere $16 billion by its former daughter SBC, which renamed itself AT&T.
- *Disney* was under sustained shareholder attack of its management's profit performance, and its long-time CEO Michael Eisner was forced out. It sold off its radio business.
- *Viacom* saw its heir-apparent ousted in 2004, spun off its dominating Blockbuster video store chain, and split itself up in 2005 by spinning off CBS. In 2008, under financial pressure, its controlling shareholder Sumner Redstone sold off parts of his holding, including most of his theaters, as well as the videogame firm Midway Game.
- *News Corp* was dominated by another aging empire-builder, Rupert Murdoch, with successor battles taking place, and its leadership prospects were as uncertain as those of CBS and RCA after their legendary leaders William Paley and David Sarnoff had left the scene. Murdoch had to give up the largest US satellite broadcasting provider, DirecTV.
- *GE*, the last of the 1970s-style conglomerates, has long been held together by super-CEO Jack Welch, but it is not a company whose structure makes long-term sense. What are

the synergies of film and TV production with jet engines, nuclear reactors, refrigerators, and financial services? In time, this structure will come apart.

- *The Tribune Company* went into Chapter 11 bankruptcy.
- *IAC/Interactive Corp.* media mogul Barry Diller's conglomerate was unraveling.
- *Clear Channel*, the radio giant, was being acquired by a private equity consortium, with over 400 stations scheduled for sale to help finance the deal.
- *Charter Communications*, the third largest cable TV company, filed for Chapter 11 bankruptcy protection in 2009 and sold off a number of cable properties.
- *Knight-Ridder*, the second largest daily newspaper chain which was in the financial doldrums, sold its papers in 2006 to McClatchy, which in turn spun off half of them to others.
- *The New York Times Company*, with more than $1 billion in debt and plunging revenues, sold off its TV stations, its new headquarters building, and other media properties. It also sold a 6.4% stake of the company to the Mexican telecom magnate Carlos Slim.
- *Sony* was undergoing considerable restructuring in order to stem its decline, and increasingly entered into major partnerships to lower its presence in the numerous fields it contested, such as in semiconductors, mobile phones, and TV screens.
- *Blockbuster*, the world's largest home video retailer, was teetering on the verge of bankruptcy, with no strong business model in sight.
- In Europe, *Bertelsmann* was subject to internal control battles among owner family members and management, and partly as a result was selling off its music business. *Kirch*, Germany's second largest media conglomerate, went bankrupt. *Vivendi* was tottering, its driving-force CEO Jean-Marie Messier ousted and under criminal indictment, its film unit Universal sold off to GE. *Siemens* sold off control over telecommunications equipment, and mobile handsets, and microcomputers.

The closer one observes many of the media emperors, the fewer new clothes one sees. Major media conglomerates have grown enormously in size but have also often reached the diseconomies of diversification. The Disney Corporation is an example. As mentioned, the main charge by

shareholders against CEO Michael Eisner was that he had been a poor leader, accumulating costly mistakes. Eisner is an experienced media manager. And yet, if one reads of James Stewart's painstakingly detailed chronicle *Disney Wars*,[2] one must wonder how anybody could run a company of Disney's complexity at all. Almost every day brought forth a plethora of decisions and crises—operational, financial, legal, artistic, contractual, international, technical—across multiple ventures, from animation to live action movies to hotels, theme parks in three continents, retail chains, TV networks, Internet portals, soap operas, cable channels, TV stations, radio network, and more. A similar narrative is told in the story of the AOL–Time Warner merger, *Stealing Time*, which shows Time Warner as a company that is barely manageable.[3]

Another indication of the problems of major media companies is their missing out on major new developments. None of the major media companies, on their own, made a dent in the Internet business.[4] Almost everything they do successfully in that space is by acquisition or by copying.

One need not feel sorry for Michael Eisner, Gerald Levin, or similarly overextended media empire builders such as Jean-Marie Messier, Robert Maxwell, or Leo Kirch. The broader question is whether the structure of the multimedia conglomerate is stable in the long term, or whether it is a temporary assembly willed by strong individuals but unable to survive them.

This suggests that the media conglomerate model does not work well long-term. But it does not mean that major media firms will become smaller. Instead, there is room for two kinds of potentially large firms: the *specialists*, and the *integrators*. The specialists focus on a narrow segment and may dominate it. Examples are Intel in microprocessors, Microsoft in operating software, Comcast in cable TV, or Nokia in mobile handsets.

Some firms, such as News Corp, have a mixed strategy, combining conglomerate aspects (film, books, newspapers) with specialization (global satellite TV). But in time, it is quite likely that the book part, for example, will not fit it anymore. Other specialist firms have diversified, like Microsoft did into game hardware, cable investments, and WebTV. But these moves rarely worked and are more often in the nature of a firm having to do something with the high profits from its dominated market. The proper business response would be to return these profits to shareholders and stick to one's knitting, but internal organizational dynamics often lead instead to an empire-building, based on often-flimsy arguments of synergy, and dilute the firm's performance.

Investors understand this. They know that in the absence of meaningful positive synergies (and even more so in the presence of negative ones) the diversified firm functions as an investment fund of sorts. Most serious investors believe that they can do a better job in selecting investments and assembling portfolios, and with much greater flexibility and liquidity. Hence, they increasingly prefer "pure plays" of specialist firms, which they can place within their portfolio strategy, and which they can also value more accurately than a hodgepodge of diverse divisions whose performance is hidden inside consolidated financial statements and internal transactions.

This has led to several breakups or attempts thereof. As mentioned, Viacom split itself up into a "high growth" and a "slow growth" company to raise its overall stock valuations. Time Warner was pressured by investors led by Carl Icahn to break up the company, since the parts were worth more than the whole. Sprint spun off its local telecom operations. AT&T split itself in 1996 into three parts in a voluntary "trivestiture." Other companies, feeling undervalued by the stock market, bought back their own shares and went "private," such as Cox, thereby reducing their potential for expansion.

In other cases, media firms—including Clear Channel, Univision, VNU/Nielsen, and parts of the Tribune Co.—were acquired by private equity funds such as Bain, Carlyle, or Blackstone. Such funds buy the companies with the intention of breaking them up, streamlining operations and costs, and reselling them. Clear Channel is an example. Similarly, private equity has been an instrument of deconcentration for the Tribune Co. and McClatchy newspaper divestitures, and for Time Warner music and The New York Times Company's TV station spin-offs. Where media conglomerates were part of empire building, they are likely to be dismantled by unsentimental cost-cutters installed by the PE owners. Thus, the performance pressures due to the increasing ownership by institutional investors—often seen as the cause for a decline in the quality of media—is also a force to undo the conglomerate structure of large media companies.

The second model for large media firms is to be an *integrator*. Integrator firms provide the focal point, the coordination for the production process that leads to consumer goods and services. They are the face that users see when they seek a media or information service. They design, assemble, bundle, promote, and brand. Sometimes they finance. Often they do not even design and assemble but outsource these activities to specialists. In the purest case, they are merely coordinators of others' activities. Normally, however, they contribute one or several key elements that are the basis of their brand value.

In the past, such coordination created high transaction costs. The results were organizations that produced and created internally many or all elements of a product or service. Economists have analyzed the business rationale of why firms exist as an institution. Firms are a command-and-control element inside an "invisible hand" market, and in tension to it. The reasons that firms exist were generally held to be to reduce transaction costs. This view was shared by Ronald Coase, Kenneth Arrow, Friedrich von Hayek, Herbert Simon, and Oliver Williamson.[5] Transaction costs are a function of technology. Change the underlying technology of transactions, and the structure of a firm will change, too. Advances in information technology reduce the transaction costs of dealing with outsiders to the firm. It becomes possible to move toward a larger reach geographically, greater decentralization, and a hub-and-spoke system based on outsourcing to suppliers.

In such an environment, what would traditional media industries look like? To get a sense of the emerging industry and company structure, we discuss two examples at some length: newspapers and film.

Newspapers

Newspapers, following a lively competitive pre-radio period, have been a stodgy industry for over 70 years. But now, as it is moving to electronic online delivery, the newspaper sector has become turbulent again. National electronic news "papers" became possible; customization and specialized news were added, requiring more resources or networked content production; advertising was offered in different and multimedia ways. As a result, the likelihood that the structure of this medium will remain as before is nil. It is likely to evolve over time into a few big national operations, often with locally branded editions, and with much content supplied by specialist news companies, such as trade publications on travel, automobiles, and so forth. On the other hand, new voices also emerged, such as bloggers and community publications (such as Newswiki or the Korean Ohmynews) . Not only will the newspaper industry be transformed (and more concentrated at its core, though also with lower entry barriers at the periphery), but it will have also become volatile and changeable, moving from periods of growth and profitability to periods of decline and crisis.

Why these changes? In the twentieth century, newspapers lost their primacy over the attention of mass audiences to broadcasting. But for politics, culture, or business, newspapers remained the central medium. Their circulation keeps sliding, however. In America, newspaper circulation was down 5% in 2004,[6] 2.6 % in the second half of 2005, 2.6% in the first 6 months of 2007, and another 4.6% in the first half of 2008. In Europe, circulation was down in 2004 by 3% and almost 2% in 2007. Japanese papers lost 2% in circulation in 2004, another 1% in 2006 and in subsequent years, and the actual loss could have been larger without below-cost subscription sales. Some print people believe that all that is happening is a migration from paper to online. But a print reader generates more than 20 times as much in revenues than an online reader, which means that a lost print reader requires at least 20 online readers to offset the revenue loss. If newspapers lose 5% of readers a year, they must double total readership—print plus online—every year just to stay even in revenues.[7] This growth rate is impossible to sustain. Where are all these new readers supposed to come from?

The problem of newspapers is not, as has often been claimed, generational and sociological[8] but technological and economical. Newspapers are under pressure, and will be still more, not because young (and older) people do not want to pay for news but because they do not have to.

The fundamental problems of newspapers are the basic economics of the information business, as described above—high fixed costs, low marginal costs, and commodification (for nonlocal content and for advertising). Online news sites accelerate these trends. In this, newspapers are not alone but in good company as part of a fundamental trend in the information sector.

The economic dynamics have led in the past to the collapse of most second-tier newspapers. In most American cities there used to be many dailies, often half a dozen in even fairly medium-sized places. But for decades now, usually only one newspaper has survived the price-cost squeeze.

The lone paper could therefore charge fairly high prices for advertising and subscriptions. TV and radio took away some news audience and advertisers, but they were not a substitute for longer news stories or many types of advertising, such as classifieds. The surviving papers were therefore profitable and could afford the production of the news content. But now, another generation of technology creates another wave of alternatives and undercuts the ability to charge the previous price for news and ads.

In any commodity situation, the business strategy advice is to seek a differentiation of the product. And if that is not possible, to be more efficient in cost. And if that is not possible, to try to reduce competition.

Some major newspaper chains are trying a cost efficiency strategy, but it is at best a short-term remedy.[9] The second strategy is to reduce competition by consolidation. And, indeed, there has been a good amount of regional clustering going on, which has more of an impact on news source diversity, and on advertisers, than a nationally scattered expansion.

And the third strategy is differentiation through customization. The traditional newspaper provides undifferentiated content to its readers because of the inherently limited technical nature of the paper medium. But with electronics, one can serve the reader's individualized particular mix of interests.

This editorial strategy has huge structural implications for the news organization itself. If one indeed lets users customize their content in a meaningful way, it requires huge informational resources—stories, details, updates, and expertise much beyond what is offered in the traditional environment. Realistically, no single news organization can do it, and do it well, through its own economic and editorial resources. To gain such diversity of information, the news organization must do far beyond internally produced content. Instead, it must rely substantially on others: on traditional syndicated and wire-service content, of course; on magazines, trade journals, newsletters; and on blogs and other nontraditional sources.[10]

And this leads to a new stage of the newspaper structure, that of the newspapers as *networks*. In this model, newspapers are not stand-alone operations; they resemble portals to which people go for news on many levels. In this network system, there are two basic tiers of participants who could be economically viable:

1. *The specialist content providers.* These are expert news operations in their field. They could be news providers about the airline industry, about film, or about Italy. Their information would be accessible from the larger news site. The models here are trade magazines, or the local newspapers of smaller cities. They would be selected by the integrator news portal, and their quality would be monitored by them. These specialist firms could also be bundled by larger firms into regular groups. The models here are magazine groups who often publish dozens of titles, or specialty TV documentary channels bundled by *Discovery*.
2. *News portal firms.* These are the integrators. They pick and choose the content elements of third parties such as specialist news firms, as well as of bloggers, syndicators, trade magazines, books, freelancers, and video and audio providers. Some of the content would be produced offshore. Some of the marketing, production, and advertising would be outsourced and offshored. Pure portals would be simply integrators and quality managers, plus rights managers, without any content production activity. More likely, however, is that they will provide some aspects of content production, because that is their differentiating factor, and because they can do so better than non-content producers.

In some cases, the specialist content providers are themselves little networks of subspecialists, so the network can have several levels—a network of networks.

In this system, the traditional separations of media will diminish. The distinction of news organizations by their temporal scope will make little sense. That distinction had newspapers providing mostly immediate information; magazines providing near-term information and analysis; book publishers providing long-term, long-format information; TV news stations and networks providing visual images; and radio stations providing audio. But there is no obvious reason for such distinction anymore on a news portal. Users want to be able to shift among them as needed. And news portals make an effective integration their differentiating factor.

Newspaper-based portals then need no longer concede breaking news to broadcasting. They can deal with perishable scoops. They can recombine audiences across several media. This makes sense from the perspective of newsgathering, editing, and distribution, as well as from an economic perspective. But it raises fundamental questions about local media diversity. True, there will be much easier access in such a structure for rival news portals. But the elements of localism will decline in favor of large national integrator news sites with perhaps a few local windows.

The problem for traditional news organizations is that such an integrator function can also be done by others. Today's bloggers, for example, already do so embryonically through the hyperlinking to chosen stories from other sources. In the future, some of them will expand into full-fledged, often commercial, news sites based on their integrator activity.

But more important, there will be the major portals based on search engines, such as Google and Yahoo. Search engine portals will not take over, though they will be big and have the cost advantage of not having to produce content on their own. The reason is the brand and the credibility of news organizations in screening and selecting. This is the editorial function on the micro level, and on the macro level, it is the selection of the partners and their content.

Such a future is not for everyone. Most news organizations will be unable to meet it. There are strong economies of scale and strong network effects, and this means that in time market leaders will emerge and drive traffic, advertising, and hence larger budgets. These economies of scale favor national and even global news firms and alliances. So the structure of the newspaper industry will change over time into a few big national and international brands, smaller local and subject-matter satellites, and much greater market concentration.

Film Industry

The Hollywood film industry has become so successful, for so long, in so many countries, and across so many distribution media that the economic reasons for its success are instructive to an understanding of the structure of future media firms. Explanations abound, of course, ranging from cultural imperialism, to language, to the vertical integration of production and distribution.

But the basic economic case for the importance of vertical or conglomerate integration is questionable to most economists, as was discussed earlier in chapter 14. Ultimately, the market power of Hollywood distributors depends on their access to attractive films, not vice versa.

The main success factor for content production is the organizational efficiency of Hollywood. This seems counterintuitive. Hollywood movies are vastly more expensive than European or Indian ones. A Hollywood film costs over $70 million to produce, 10 times as much as in Europe, 50 times as much as in India. The budget for 2 minutes of Hollywood film produces an entire feature film in India.

But cost is not the whole story. Hollywood's big budgets are spread over audience size and are actually smaller per ticket sold than for a European film. In Europe, it takes $12.50 of a film budget per ticket, whereas for Hollywood films, it is only $1.65, almost one eighth.

India's "Bollywood" is still much lower at $.43. But movie tickets in India are cheap. And its revenues outside of South Asian box offices are small. If one looks at revenues generated per average budget dollar. Hollywood and Bollywood are about equal ($1.20), and Europe is in the red.

The six major Hollywood firms, despite their high up-front cost, have strong scale economies because of their world-wide audiences and also because of portfolio diversification based on the slates of movies they distribute. Film projects are enormously risky: 80% of films lose money overall, even allowing for the elusiveness of the concept of profits in the film business. Hollywood firms create a portfolio of investments, each with a certain riskiness, which achieve a lower risk than any individual part of the portfolio. The studio distribution/financial (the studio) pools many risky projects, making their aggregate cash flow reasonably safe for the lenders. And this in turn generates investments into film projects of Hollywood.

But the main success factor of Hollywood's efficiency goes further; it has developed a new business model. This is important to all industries and all companies, not just in the media sector.

Hollywood has developed this model not because of superior strategy—never its strong suit—but because it has been engaged in a Darwinian process. Each year, over a hundred major films, and many small ones, are being produced. Each of the major films cost about $70–100 million to produce, and maybe $40 million or more to promote. The majority of these films sink within days after release with hardly a trace. Thus, under the pressures to perform or perish, companies and business practices evolve continuously.

Most people who still talk about the "studios" believe that a few highly concentrated conglomerates are producing all these movies. Not so. The big six are mostly distributing films made by small independent or semi-independent firms. The studios finance some of them. In some cases they rent them their production facilities. But their share in the actual production of the major films they distribute keeps declining and is probably less than 20% now. (There are many gray shades between outright studio production and truly independent production.)

Instead, Hollywood today is hundreds of small independent production companies, which in turn use thousands of specialized firms with particular skills. All use mostly free-lancers, that is, independent contract labor rather than regular staff. Even management staff is project based. The studio companies are the integrators of this system, but relative to their activity level and its riskiness, they are low-overhead,[11] low-risk, low-employee, and low-employee benefits. They shift risk, and transform discrete projects into a continuous flow of content.

This has restructured the industry from vertically integrated firms with in-house talent and skills—which is the traditional image of the Hollywood firms—to one of horizontal specialists, independent contractors assembled by integrators. It also favors geographical clustering, in which providers of physical inputs are near the integrators, and the integrators are near these specialists.

Between 1980 and 1995, entertainment-related companies in Southern California more than tripled. Over 100,000 of the film industry's workers are freelancers, or work for companies with fewer than 10 people.[12]

As this system evolves, it increasingly deploys in its network of specialists also the talent and creativity from everywhere—animators from Japan; special effects software in India; post-production in Shanghai; venture finance in London; government funding from Germany and Canada; advertising companies in New York.

The model of the project-oriented, almost "virtual" production firm is perhaps the forerunner for many business firms and industries in general. It combines the creativity of small organizations with the economies of scale of large ones.

We can see similar developments arising in consumer electronics, computers, games, semiconductors, book publishers, portals, and other industries. Specialist firms do the technical or content design. Others produce the elements. Still others assemble. Still others do the physical or electronic distribution and the storage function. The major firms then are mainly coordinators, integrators of the specialist firms, the branders of the final products, and often the marketers. Some of the specialists, too, can be quite large, since they may be providers to several integrators and to multiple industries. This will be, for many industries, the business model of the future.

It would not be the first time that media has led the way for a general business transformation. The printing press led the way for the industrial mass production system. And now, the film industry model, created in the Darwinian process described, may be a forerunner for the next stage, the post-industrial production system and economy.

Policies

In the preceding section, we provided two examples of how economic and technological forces transform two media industries, newspapers and films, in the direction of a two-tier structure with many specialists surrounding a few integrators in a network-like structure.

This structure gives a central role to the integrator firms, and hence much power. It also gives much influence to specialist firms that control their particular specialty. But it is not necessary for a society to accept this or any other structure and its market power. Yet it is difficult for government to alter after the fundamental structural trends of an industry, as opposed to mitigating their effects or dealing with abuse. When national grocery chains such as A&P emerged in force after World War I and evolved into supermarket chains after World War II, they harmed the numerous small Mom-and-Pop stores around the country. In consequence, a variety of laws and trade practice regulations were passed nationally and locally and by the states. Yet they had only little long-term impact on the structure of food retailing, which today is largely based on large national and regional chains,[13] supplemented by small and medium-sized local independents. Within that structure companies rise and fall. A&P, for example, dropped from 16,000 stores to about 500, and is now owned by a German chain.

Is a similar fate in store for media regulation of market structure? It is beyond this book's aim to propose specific policy solutions when media concentrations rise beyond the level that a society finds acceptable. But we can surely list the basic options.

They are variants of the following:

1. Laissez-faire
2. Access requirements
3. Public service institutions
4. Nonprofit providers
5. Behavioral regulations
6. Structural rules

The first is to do nothing and hope for competitive forces, technologies, entrants, and voices to emerge. But this might take a long time, and irreparable damage could be done by then. Also, incumbents will not sit idly by and could have the rules on entry rewritten while they are still influential. AT&T did so for decades to block entry into long distance and local service, as did the broadcast TV industry against the nascent cable industry. (Of course, in both cases the incumbents ultimately lost. But it took decades and much government-assisted opening.)

The second option is for government to assure the access of alternative voices, technologies, and providers. This has been the historical approach, through such policies as common carriage obligations, interconnection requirements, program access to channels, and now net-neutrality rules. There are a lot of positives in this approach, but there are also problems that must be understood.[14] The first is that it is difficult to do this only partially, for some types of companies, services, or industries. The reason is that in a head-to-head competition, companies without such obligations would outperform those with such obligations.[15] Thus, one should not institute sustainable access rules if one is not prepared to extend them widely.

The second problem is that the access policy entrenches market power in the segment where the access is mandated, though it might reduce it for the segments that are granted access. These providers, for example, will have their entry barriers lowered by reaching audiences more easily, but they also have now less incentive to create alternative means such as new networks. Thus, this policy will tend to reduce concentration in one part of a vertical chain at the same time that it also increases it in another.

The third option is to create new public-service voices, networks, or institutions that enable them. This would mean a form of subsidy, either financial or through other resource transfers such as frequencies, scarce licenses, opening of previously licensed spectrum bands, user subsidies, provider subsidies, or regulatory advantages. This approach, while perhaps the most direct, also has problems. It costs money or other scarce public resources.[16] It is easily politicized. And it must be reconciled with constitutional limitations on government media support policies that are not content neutral.

The fourth approach is to marshal the *civil society* sector. One way to deal with market structure problems might be to enable alternatives to the market mechanism altogether. Volunteerism might take up part of the slack. Examples for volunteerism and community building are the open source software movement, peer-to-peer and file sharing, P2P, and free websites. But volunteerism has structural problems too, the classic "tragedy of the commons" when some users diminish the credibility and reputation of the medium by their contributions. Also, it is hard to run large activities outside of economics over a long period. The volunteerist approach works best for text-based opinion pieces and for eyewitness information. For more complex and sustained efforts, a funding mechanism would be necessary. This would merge or overlap with the third approach of public service institutions. Beyond financial resources, there are other ways to facilitate nonprofit entry: spectrum (for example, unlicensed bands) and changes in the copyright law, such as on the fair use of copyrighted materials.

The fifth option is to establish *behavioral* requirements of content diversity on private media. These have been held unconstitutional in the U.S. for print media,[17] upheld weakly for licensed broadcasters,[18] and might well not survive a new constitutional challenge. Regulators whittled down requirements on licensed broadcasters to provide balance, fairness, and local coverage. An exception was a fairly weak requirement to add some quality children's programs. Even if passing constitutional muster, it is difficult to operationalize media's diversity of content, beyond the mandating of access (option 2).

The sixth major option is the *structural* approach. It means to intervene in media markets in order to make them less dominated by a few large participants. This could mean ownership ceilings, limitations on cross ownership among media, or other limits or restrictions on mergers and on market power. Free marketeers often believe that any government intervention in media activities is a potential violation of the First Amendment of the U.S. Constitution. But it is precisely the Amendment's severe restrictions of governmental intervention into media content and behavior that leaves intervention in the industry structure as a tool to deal with media problems.[19] This approach can be instituted either through regulation or general antitrust law. The regulatory approach has been used for many years, but the problem is that it covers only a part of the media, and a shrinking one at that, which the government licenses because it requires spectrum. These licensing powers cannot be applied to print media, film, or Internet media except where they intersect with a licensed media industry. This leaves the antitrust approach as the main structural tool. But here the problem, as our numbers show, is that many media industries are not concentrated according to the traditional thresholds that are applied to other industries. Also, courts have followed economists and have been reluctant to block or reverse vertical integrations.

The discussion of these options might give the impression that we have an effective set of policy tools and all we need to do is decide which to deploy. But the fact is that all of these policies will be quite hard to make stick.

In the past, for print media, a variety of prodiversity policies existed for a long time, such as below-cost postal rates and the Newspaper Preservation Act, which permits economic collaboration among competing local dailies. But this did not stop the erosion of second papers. For film, the dominance and practices of the major film companies were challenged by government in antitrust action, but the industry structure did not change much.[20]

Ownership ceilings on TV stations worked reasonably well originally when they were fairly simple. Then they were changed into national ceilings on "reach," which was more complicated already. They also required rules on "attribution" when ownership relations among companies (or family members) became murky.[21] But this is nothing in comparison to the complexities that would involve media that are outside the ordered broadcast licensing scheme. Here, the government's powers, practically speaking, are limited. If Google has significant market power, how should the search engine market be restructured? Or suppose that a firm located in

Korea is dominant in interactive games, what then is the U.S. government's solution? Or, if Skype, the broadband telephony provider, becomes the vastly preferred VoIP or voice telephony choice, how would one deal with that? Or if Apple's iTunes video store maintains its vast market share of broadband users due to its network effects? Or if the Chinese government affirmatively supports a media organization's drive to achieve a global penetration?

And these are merely conceptual questions, to which are added those of politics, litigation resources, trade, intellectual property rights, and international enforcement. The example of Microsoft, which has eluded antitrust action for a very long time, and where the issues are much simpler, should be recalled. Wishing for diversity and achieving it through regulation are very different matters. If creating diversity was so easy there would be no local newspaper monopolies.

Nor is it clear whether media diversification will be a top priority, given conflicting public objectives. Economic stability and growth is another important goal. In information-based societies, the social cost of information sector instability is not acceptable politically. One can see this in the responses to the financial crisis of 2008. Even a conservative Republican Administration moved to considerable activism and intervention.Therefore, governments will get into the business of stabilizing the information economy. The macro-economic instruments of governments are based on the experience of the industrial society and its financial institutions. Classic Keynesian demand stimulation does not seem to address the core problem. That problem is not inadequate demand for information services and media products but oversupply, price deflation, and cost increase. Nor will industrial policy, such as investing or encouraging network upgrades or R&D, work. Here, too, the problem that needs a solution is not inadequate information sector activity.

The main way to address price deflation would therefore be competition policy. This would mean to let industries become more concentrated to reduce competitive pressures. And this may well be what we have been witnessing in the U.S.—the greater willingness of government to permit consolidations in the information sector and in its subsector, mass media.

These are important questions to analyze and discuss, but to do so one must move away from the ideological shouting match.

As pointed out in the beginning of this book, digital networks are at the verge of a historic discontinuity. After over a century of patiently constructing an analog narrowband network that gave individuals in society the equivalent of a kilobit-strength connectivity, we are now upgrading it to individualized megabit strength—broadband—and soon even gigabit bandwidth, ultrabroadband. The transition from a kilobit to gigabit communication system will lead to more fundamental societal and economic impacts than the transition from bicycles to automobiles. We have tried to answer the question of what effect such a move has on media concentration. Our conclusion is that it has raised concentration, over the past decade, and will continue to do so. Technology has not solved the policy question. If anything, technology and the resultant economies of scale are one explanation for the concentration trends.

It is always difficult for laws or regulations to modify fundamental transitions of industries. It is particularly difficult to do so where, as in the case of media, any policy in a free society needs to be one of light touch. Thus, it will be quite difficult, and sometimes impossible, to reduce the concentration trends in many media industries as they become digital and global. This means that the technological and market forces will play a much larger role than in an environment of traditional media, where broadcasting structure could be controlled through spectrum licensing, where the newspaper technology and economics prevented local monopolies from becoming national oligopolies and where telecom networks were price and profit regulated.

Thus, to summarize, we find that the mass media sector has grown in concentration over the past two decades, even as the overall information sector did not. We conclude that the economic and technological dynamics at work for media are increasingly the same as for the information sector generally, and that this leads to an upward concentration trend for media that converges with that of the information sector more generally. The information sector's concentration level is fluctuating, but at a higher level. Thus, the dynamics of digital convergence lead the mass media industries to assume the market structure characteristics of the rest of the information sector. This would mean that concentration trends will continue as they oscillate on the way up and once up.

This situation leads to concentration levels that might be economically efficient but not necessarily favored from a societal perspective. But it will be quite difficult for any set of policies to contain fundamental economic and technological forces that are at play here, even if one ignores the political dimensions. It is also clear that any policy to enhance a media diversity that is not provided for in an open media market needs to be supported by real resources—money and spectrum—beyond structural and access policies. Diversity is valuable, and it cannot be achieved on the cheap.

This conclusion is part media pessimist—media concentration is increasing and will continue to do so. It is part media optimist—media concentration is lower than often feared, and lowered entry barriers lead to periodic deconcentration. But it is mostly media realistic—the structure of media are being transformed by broad forces, and concentration is its symptom, not its cause.

Notes

1. This was also observed in Einstein, Mara. *Program Diversity and the Program Selection Process on Broadcast Network Television* (Federal Communications Commission, Media Ownership Working Group, September 2002).
2. Stewart, James. *Disney Wars*. New York: Simon and Schuster, 2005.
3. Klein, Alec. *Stealing Time: Steve Case, Jerry Levin, and the Collapse of AOL Time Warner*. New York: Simon & Schuster, 2005.
4. Time Warner, after trying unsuccessfully to enter the online world, let itself be merged with AOL and its overvalued stock. Disney never made a go with Go.com; GE and News Corp tried on their own and failed. Viacom played only a minor role. A second wave of acquisitions took place in 2006, with News Corp (MySpace), GE (iVillage), and the New York Times Company (About.com) making big acquisitions.
5. See also Noam, Eli M. "L'impatto economico della conoscenza sull'impresa," in Pilati, Antonio, and Antonio Perucci, eds., *Economia della conoscenza. Profili teorici e evidenze empiriche*. Il Mulino, Bologna, 2005; Arrow, Kenneth J. *The Limits of Organization*. New York: Norton, 1974; Coase, Ronald. "The Nature of the Firm," *Economica*, 4, 1937, pp. 386–405; Hayek, F.A., "The Use of Knowledge in Society." *American Econometric Review*, pp. 519–530, 1945; Simon, Herbert. "Rational Decision-Making in Business Organizations," A.E.R., pp. 493–513, Sept. 1979; Williamson, Oliver. *Markets and Hierarchies*. New York: The Free Press, 1975.

6. The circulation of the *BaltimoreSun* dropped in 2004 by 11.5%; the *Los Angeles Times* by 6.4%; the *Chicago Tribune* by 6.6%; the *San Francisco Chronicle* by 7%; and the *Washington Post* by 2.6%.
7. Since they save paper and distribution cost, one should look at net profits. This would require for total readership to grow maybe by 50% a year to offset the print defections.
8. The so-called "free" generation is also paying uncomplainingly for satellite radio, where their elders were used to free radio; they pay for SMS for downloading music from iTunes, for DVD discs of TV episodes they missed, for TiVo subscriptions to record TV shows, and for ring tones for their phones.
9. Meyer, Philip. *The Vanishing Newspaper: Saving Journalism from the Information Age*. Columbia, Missouri: University of Missouri Press, 2004.
10. The *Washington Post*, for example, already carries several blogs.
11. Actual overhead, not the one listed for accounting purposes to reduce disbursements to profit participants.
12. Kotkin, Joel, and David Friedman. "Why Every Business Will Be Like Show Business," *Inc.*, March 1995; 17, p. 3.
13. There are exceptions, such as New York City, where zoning laws limit floor space, with the explicit goal of protecting small retailers.
14. Noam, Eli. *Interconnecting the Network of Networks*. Oxford University Press, New York, 2001.
15. Noam, Eli M. "Beyond Liberalization: From the Network of Networks to the System of Systems." *Telecommunications Policy*, May/June 1994, pp. 286–294.
16. These could be provided "off-budget" through spectrum allocations, redistributive regulated averaged prices, regulated monopoly prices, or mandated user taxes.
17. *Miami Herald Publishing Co. v. Tornillo*, 418 U.S. 241, 1974.
18. *Red Lion Broadcasting Co. v. FCC*, 395 U.S. 367; 89 S. Ct. 1794; 1969.
19. See *Minneapolis Star & Tribune Co. v. Minnesota Commissioner of Revenues*, 460 U.S. 575 (1983).
20. The divestiture of the studios from theaters, when abolished again, did not result in the studios' long-term return to theater ownership, which suggests that, in time, the studios would have on their own left theater ownership to others.
21. Examples are the interfamily business ties at Sinclair, or the intercompany relations between GE and Paxon Communications.

Bibliography

Abiru, Masahiro. "Vertical Integration, Variable Proportions, and Successive Oligopolies." *Journal of Industrial Economics* 36, no. 3 (1988): 315–325.

Abramson, Bram Dov. "Interpreting Current Statistics: Internet Backbone Market Shares." *TelecomReform* 1, no. 2 (July 2001): 7.

Acs, Zoltan J., & Audretsch, David B. "Innovation in Large and Small Firms: An Empirical Analysis." *American Economic Review* 78 (1988): 678, 686–687.

Adams, John B., & Danielson, Wayne A. "Completeness of Press Coverage of the 1960 Campaign." *Journalism Quarterly* 38 (Autumn 1961): 441–452.

Adelman, M. A. "Concept and Statistical Measurement of Vertical Integration," in Stigler, G. J., ed. *Business Concentration and Price Policy,* Princeton, NJ: Princeton University Press, 1955, pp. 281–322.

Ader, Thorsten, Fueg, Oliver C., Kevin, Deirdre, Pertzinidou, E., & Schoenthal, Max. *Final Report of the Study on the Information of the Citizen in the EU: Obligations for the Media and the Institutions Concerning the Citizen's Right to Be Fully and Objectively Informed.* Düsseldorf: The European Institute for the Media, 2004.

Advisory Panel on Media Diversity, "Transnational Media Concentrations in Europe," Strasbourg, Council of Europe, November 2004.

Ahn, Hoekyun, & Litman, Barry R. "Vertical Integration and Consumer Welfare in the Cable Industry." *Journal of Broadcasting and Electronic Media* 41, no. 3 (1997): 453–477.

Akhavan-Majid, Roya, Gopinath, Sheila, & Rife, Anita. "Chain Ownership and Editorial Independence: A Case Study of Gannet Newspapers." *Journalism Quarterly* 68 (1991): 59–67.

Albarran, Alan B. *Media Economics: Understanding Markets, Industries and Concepts.* 2nd ed. Ames, IA: Iowa State University Press, 2002.

Albarran, Alan B., & Dimmick, J. "Economics of Multiformity and Concentration in the Communication Industries." *Journal of Media Economics* 9 (1996): 41–49.

Albarran, Alan B., & Gormly, Karen. "Strategic Response or Strategic Blunder? An Examination of AOL Time Warner and Vivendi Universal," in Picard, Robert G., ed. *Strategic Responses to Media Market Changes.* Jönköping, Sweden: Jönköping International Business School Research Reports, 2004, pp. 35–46.

Albarran, Alan B., & Mierzejewska, Bozena I. "Media Concentration in the U.S. and European Union: A Comparative Analysis," presented at *6th World Media Economics Conference.* Centre d'Etudes Sure les Médias and Journal of Media Economics, HEC Montreal, Montreal, Canada, May 12–15, 2004. p. 2. Last accessed on January 10, 2008, from http://www.cem.ulaval.ca/6thwmec/ albarran_mierzejewska.pdf.

Alexander, A., Owers J. & Carveth, R. (eds) *Media Economics: Theory and Practice,* 2nd ed, Mahwah, NJ: The Lawrence Erlbaum Associates, 1998.

Alexander, Peter J., & Cunningham, Brendan M. "Diversity and Market Structure: Preliminary Evidence from Broadcast Television News," in *Media Diversity and Localism: Meaning, Metrics, and the Public Interest*. New York: The Donald McGannon Communication Research Center, Fordham University, December 15–16, 2003 pp. 3–4. [conference report]

Alger, Dean E., Cook, Timothy E., Crigler, Ann N., Just, Marion R., Kern, Montague, & West, Darrell M. *Crosstalk: Citizens, Candidates and the Media in a Presidential Campaign*. Chicago: University of Chicago Press, 1996.

Allard, Nicholas W. "Reinventing Rate Regulation." *Federal Communications Law Journal* 46 (December 1993): 63–123.

Alleman, James, & Noam, Eli M. *The New Investment Theory of Real Options and its Implication for Telecommunications Economics*. Dordrecht, The Netherlands: Kluwer Academic Publishers, 1999.

Allen, David S., Blanks, S. Elizabeth, & Glasser, Theodore L. "The Influence of Chain Ownership on New Play: A Case Study." *Journalism Quarterly* 66 (Autumn 1989): 607–615.

Amato, Louis, Ryan, J. Michael, & Wilder, Ronald P. "Market Structure and Dynamic Performance in U.S. Manufacturing." *Southern Economic Journal* 47 (1981): 1105–1110.

Anderson, Chris. "The Long Tail." *WIRED Magazine*, no. 12.10 (October 2004).

Anderson, Simon, & Coate, Steve. "Market Provision of Public Goods: The Case for Broadcasting." NBER Working Paper No. W7513, University of Virginia and Cornell, 2001.

Angelmar, Reinhard. "Market Structure and Research Intensity in High-Technological-Opportunity Industries." *Journal of Industrial Economics* 34, no. 1 (1985): 69–79.

AOL Time Warner Inc. *Dow Jones Interactive Executive Report and Media General/Hoovers Online*. New York: AOL Time Warner Inc., 2001.

Arbitron. "Arbitron America Radio Listening Trends Report." 29 July 2006. Last accessed on 4 May 2007 at http://www.arbitronradio.com/national_radio/arlt.asp.

———. *Arbitron Releases Fall 2001 Radio Network Ratings*. New York: Arbitron, December 17, 2001.

———. *Radio Today, How America Listens to Radio*. New York: Arbitron, 2001.

Archer, Gleason. *Big Business and Radio*. New York: The American Historical Company, 1939, p. 8.

Areeda, Phillip, Edlin, Aaron S., & Kaplow, Louis. *Antitrust Analysis: Problems, Text, and Cases*. 5th ed. New York: Aspen, 1997, pp. 614–15.

Arrow, K. J. "Vertical Integration and Communication." The *Bell Journal of Economics* 6, no. 1 (1975): 173–183.

Associated Press v. United States, 326 U.S. 1, 20 (1945).

Aufderheide, Pat. "After the Fairness Doctrine: Controversial Broadcast Programming and the Public Interest." *Journal of Communication* 40, no. 3 (1990): 47–72.

———. "Too Much Media." *In These Times* 29, no. 12 (May 9, 2005).

Auletta, Ken. *Three Blind Mice: How the TV Networks Lost Their Way*. New York: Random House, 1991.

Ayres, Ian. "Vertical Integration and Overbuying: An Analysis of Foreclosure Via Raised Rivals' Costs." Working Paper No. 8803, American Bar Foundation, 1988, pp. 17–20, 23–24.

Baade, Robert C., Bantz, Charles R., & McCorkle, Suzanne. "The News Factory." *Communications Research* 7, no. 1 (1980): 45–68.

Bachen, Christine, Craft, Stephanie, Hammond, Allen, & Mason, Laurie. "Diversity of Programming in the Broadcast Spectrum: Is There a Link between Owner Race or Ethnicity and News and Public Affairs Programming?" Washington, DC: Federal Communications Commission, 1999.

Bachen, Christine M., Craft, Stephanie L., & Mason, Laurie. "Support for FCC Minority Ownership Policy: How Broadcast Station Owner Race or Ethnicity Affects News and Public Affairs Programming Diversity." *Communication Law and Policy* 6 (2001): 37–73.

Backström, M., & Wahlroos, B. "R&D Intensity with Endogenous Concentration, Evidence for Finland." *Empirical Economics* 7 (1982): 13–22.

Baer, Walter S. *Concentration of Mass Media Ownership: Assessing the State of Current Knowledge*. Santa Monica: Rand, 1974.

Bagdikian, Ben. *The Media Monopoly*. Boston: Beacon, 1983, 1987, 1990, 1992, 1997.

Bailey, Elizabeth E., & Baumol, William J. "Deregulation and the Theory of Contestable Markets." *Yale Journal on Regulation* 1, no. 2 (1984): 111–122.

Bailey, Joseph P. "Economics and Internet Interconnection," presented at *MIT Workshop on Internet Economics*. Massachusetts Institute of Technology, Cambridge, MA, March 1995.

Baker, Edwin C. *Media Concentration and Democracy: Why Ownership Matters*, New York: Cambridge University Press, 2007.

Baker, Jonathan B. "Recent Developments in Economics that Challenge Chicago School Views." *Antitrust Law Journal* 58 (1989): 645–655.

Balio, T. ed. *The American Film Industry.* Madison, WI: University of Wisconsin Press, 1976.

Barnard, J., Broomhead, V., Godwin, L. & Smith, A. "Top Fifty European Media Owners." London: Zenith Media, April 1996.

Barnett, Stephen R., Botein, Michael, & Noam, Eli M., eds. *Law of International Telecommunications in the United States.* Baden-Baden: Nomos, 1988, p. 271.

Bartlett, David. "News Radio: More Than Masters of Disaster," in Pease, Edward C., & Dennis, Everette E., ed. *Radio: The Forgotten Medium.* New Brunswick, Canada: Transaction Press, 1995, pp. 31–41.

Bass, Jack. "Newspaper Monopoly," in Roberts, Gene, Kunkel, Thomas, & Clayton, Charles, eds. *Leaving Readers Behind: The Age of Corporate Newspapering.* Fayetteville: University of Arkansas Press, 2001.

Bates, Benjamin J. "Concentration in Local Television Markets." *Journal of Media Economics* 6 (Fall 1993): 3–22.

———. "Station Trafficking in Radio: The Impact of Deregulation." *Journal of Broadcasting and Electronic Media* 37, no. 1 (1993): 21–30.

Baumgarten, Paul & Farber, Donald. *Producing, Financing and Distributing Film.* New York: Drama Book Specialists/Publishers, 1973.

Baumol, William J., Panzar, John C., & Willig, Robert D. *Contestable Markets and the Theory of Industry Structure.* San Diego, CA: Harcourt Brace, 1982.

Baxter, William F. "Antitrust Policy," in Feldstein, Martin, ed. *American Economic Policy in the 1890s.* Chicago: University of Chicago Press, 1994.

Baynes, Leonard M. "WHITEOUT: The Absence and Stereotyping of People of Color by the Broadcast Networks in Prime Time Entertainment Programming," presented at *Media Diversity and Localism: Meaning, Metrics, and the Public Interest.* The Donald McGannon Communication Research Center, Fordham University, New York, December 15–16, 2003, pp. 9–12.

Beam, Randal A. "What it Means to Be a Market-Oriented Newspaper." *Newspaper Research Journal* 19, no. 3 (summer 1998): 2–20.

———. "Size of Corporate Parent Drives Market Orientation." *Newspaper Research Journal* 23. no. 2/3 (Spring/Summer 2002): 46–63.

Beam, Randy, Becker, Lee B., Russial, John, & Weaver, David H. "Correlates of Daily Newspaper Performance in New England." *Journalism Quarterly* 55 (Spring 1978): 100–108.

Bear Stearns. *"TV's Better Half? Networks More Profitable Non-Primetime Dayparts."* New York: Bear Stearns, June 03, 2004.

Beckerman, Gal. "Tripping Up Big Media." *Columbia Journalism Review* 42, no. 4 (November/December 2003): 15–20.

Beebe, Jack H. "Institutional Structure and Program Choices in Television Markets." The *Quarterly Journal of Economics* 91:1 (1977): 15–37.

Beebe, J. H., Manning, W. G., & Owen, Bruce M. *Television Economics.* Lexington, MA: D. C. Heath, 1974.

"Beeper Madness." *Time Out New York,* September 26, 1996, p. 99.

Benjamin, Stuart Minor, Lichtman, Douglas Gary, & Shelanski, Howard A. *Telecommunications Law and Policy.* Durham, NC: Carolina Academic Press Law Casebook Series, 2001, pp. 293, 301.

Benkler, Yochai. "Free As the Air to Common Use: First Amendment Constraints on Enclosure of the Public Domain." *New York University Law Review* 74 (May 1999): 354–446.

———. "The Wealth of Networks: How Social Production Transforms Markets and Freedom." New Haven: Yale University Press, 2006.

Bensinger, Ari. Industry Surveys: Communications Equipment. Standard & Poor's, February 3, 2005.

Beresteanu, Arie, and Ellickson, Paul B. "FCC Media Ownership Study #7: Minority and Female Ownership in Media Enterprises." *Federal Communications Commission.* FCC. gov, June, 2007. Last accessed on January 6, 2008, from http://hraunfoss.fcc.gov/edocs_public/attachmatch/DA-07-3470A8.pdf.

Berndt, Ernst R., Klein, Lisa R., & Silk, Alvin J. "Intermedia Substitutability and Market Demand by National Advertisers." *Review of Industrial Organization* 20 (June 2002): 323–348.

Bernstein, J. M., & Lacy, S. "Contextual Coverage of Government by Local Television News." *Journalism Quarterly* 69, no. 2 (1992): 329–341.

Bernstein, Peter W. "The Record Business: Rocking to the Big-Money Beat." *Fortune,* April 23, 1979, p. 58.

Berry, Steven, & Waldfogel, Joel. "Do Mergers Increase Product Variety? Evidence from Radio Broadcasting." The *Quarterly Journal of Economics* 116:3 (2001): 1009–10025.

———. "Mergers, Station Entry, and Programming Variety in Radio Broadcasting." Working Paper, National Bureau of Economic Research, April 1999.

———. "Public Radio in the United States: Does it Correct Market Failure or Cannibalize Commercial Stations?" *Journal of Public Economics* 71 (1999): 189–211.

Besen, Stanley M., & Woodbury, John R. "Rate Regulation, Effective Competition, and the 1992 Cable Act." *Hastings Communications and Entertainment Law Journal* 17 (Fall 1994): 203–224.

Bessler, Wolfgang, Norsworthy, John R., & Shusterman, Tatiana G. "Valuation Effects of Telecommunication Mergers: A Comparison of Europe and the United States," presented at the *International Trade and Finance Conference.* Montpellier, Frankreich, June 2000.

"Best Buy Completes Purchase." The *Wall Street Journal,* New York, January 24, 2001, p. B11.

Bezanson, Randall, Cranberg, Gilbert, & Soloski, John. *Taking Stock: Journalism and the Publicly Traded Newspaper.* Ames, IA: Iowa State University Press, 2001.

Bhagwat, Ashutosh. "Unnatural Competition?: Applying the New Antitrust Learning to Foster Competition in the Local Exchange." *Hastings Law Journal* 50 (1999): 1479.

Bigman, Stanley K. "Rivals in Conforminty: A Study of Two Competing Dailies." *Journalism Quarterly* 25 (Spring 1948): 127–131.

Billotti, Richard. "The Case for Moderate Growth in TV Advertising." *Equity Research,* January 3, 2003.

Bishop, Ronal, & Hakanen, Ernest A. "In the Public Interest? The State of Local Television Programming Fifteen Years after Deregulation." *Journal of Communications Inquiry* 26, no. 3 (July 2002): 261–276.

Bittlingmayer, George. "The Antitrust Emperor's Clothes." *Regulation,* Washington, DC, Fall 2002, pp. 46–52.

Bittlingmayer, George, & Hazlett, Thomas W. "DOS Kapital: Has Antitrust Action against Microsoft Created Value in the Computer Industry?" *Journal of Financial Economics* 55, no. 3 (March 2000): 329–359.

———. "The Political Economy of Cable 'Open Access.'" *Stanford Tech. Law Review,* Fall 2001. Available at http://www.manhattaninstitute.org/hazlett/working_01_06.pdf.

Blackstone, Erwin A., & Bowman, Gary W. "Vertical Integration in Motion Pictures." *Journal of Communication,* 49, no. 1 (Winter 1999): 123–139.

Blaiklock, A. Richard M., & Krotoszynski, Ronald J. Jr. "Enhancing the Spectrum: Media Power, Democracy, and the Marketplace of Ideas." *University of Illinois Law Review* 3 (2000): p. 867.

Blair, Roger D., & Kaserman, David L. *Law and Economics of Vertical Integration and Control.* New York: Academic Press, 1983, pp. 20, 82.

Blankenburg, William B. "A Newspaper Chain's Pricing Behavior." *Journalism Quarterly* 60 (Summer 1983): 275–280.

Blankenburg, William B., & Ozanich, Gary W. "The Effects of Public Ownership on the Financial Performance of Newspaper Corporations." *Journalism Quarterly* 70 (Spring 1993): 68–75.

Blaskopf, Lawrence P. "Note, Defining the Relevant Product Market of the New Video Technologies." *Cardozo Arts and Entertainment Law Journal* 4, no.1 (1985): 75.

Blau, Andrew, & Schwartzman, Andrew J. *What's Local About Local Broadcasting?* Washington, DC: Media Access Project and the Benton Foundation, 1998.

Block, Alex Ben. *Outfoxed: Marvin Davis, Barry Diller, Rupert Murdoch, Joan Rivers and the Inside Story of America's Fourth Television Network.* New York: St. Martin's Press, 1990, p. 122.

"Blockbuster Merger with Viacom OK'd." *Chicago Tribune,* September 30, 1994, p. Business 1.

Blommenstein, H. J. "Impact of Institutional Investors on Financial Markets," in Blommenstein, H. J., & Funke, N., eds. *Institutional Investors in the New Financial Landscape.* Paris: OECD, 1998.

Blumer, Jay G., & Spicer, Carolyn Martin. "Prospects for Creativity in the New Television Marketplace: Evidence from Program-Makers." *Journal of Communications* 40 (1990): 78–101.

Boadwee, Harry. "Note, Product Market Definition for Video Programming." *Columbia Law Review* 86 (1986): 1210–1211.

Bogart, Leo. *Press and Public: Who Reads What, When Where, and Why in American Newspapers.* 2nd ed. Hillsdale, NJ: Lawrence Erlbaum Associates, 1989.

Bollinger Jr., Lee C. "Freedom of the Press and Public Access: Toward a Theory of Partial Regulation of the Mass Media." *Michigan Law Review* 75, no. 1 (1976): 30–38.

Bork, Robert. *Antitrust Paradox: A Policy at War with Itself.* New York: Free Press, 1993.

Borland, John. "Broadband Leaps Ahead of AOL." *CNET News.* 13 May 2004. Last accessed on 4 January 2007 at http://news.com.com/2100–1038_3–5212122.html?tag=nefd.top.

Botein, Michael. *Regulation of the Electronic Mass Media: Law and Policy for Radio, Television, Cable and the New Video Technologies.* 3rd ed. St. Paul, MN: West Group, 1998, pp. 267, 285.

Bozeman, Barry, & Link, Albert N. *Investments in Technology: Corporate Strategies and Public Policy Alternatives.* Westport, CT: Praeger Publishers, 1983.

Bradburd, Ralph M., & Caves, Richard E. "The Empirical Determinants of Vertical Integration." *Journal of Economic Behavior and Organization* 9 (1988): 265–279.

Braima, A. M., Mahmoud, Johnson, & Sothirajah, Jayanthi. "Measure for Measure: The Relationship Between Different Broadcast Types, Formats, Measures and Political Behaviors and Cognitions." *Journal of Broadcasting and Electronic Media* 44 (2000): 43–61.

Brancato, Carolyn Kay. "Financial Assets and Equity Holdings. Patterns of Institutional Investment and Control," in the *Institutional Investment Report*. New York: The Conference Board, November 2000.

———. *Institutional Investors and Corporate Governance: Best Practices for Increasing Corporate Value.* Chicago: Irwin Professional Publishing, 1997.

———. "Patterns of Institutional Investment and Control in the United States," in *The Brancato Report on Institutional Investment.* Washington, DC: The Conference Board, 1996, p. 17.

Brancato, Carolyn Kay, & Rabimov, Stephan. *The 2005 Institutional Investment Report: U.S. and International Trends.* New York: The Conference Board, 2005.

Brancato, Carolyn, and Rabimov, Stephan. "The 2007 Institutional Investment Report: U.S. and International Trends." *The Conference Board.* February 2007. Last accessed on January 3, 2008, from http://www.conference-board.org/UTILITIES/pressDetail.cfm?press_ID=3046.

Brendon, Piers. *The Life and Death of the Press Barons.* New York: Athenium, 1983, pp. 100–101.

Bresnahan, Timothy F. "New Modes of Competition and the Future Structure of the Computer Industry," in Eisenach, J. A., & Lenard, T. M., eds. *Competition, Innovation, and the Microsoft Monopoly: Antitrust in the Digital Marketplace.* Washington, DC: The Progress and Freedom Foundation, Kluwer Press, 1999.

Brinkley, Joel. *Defining Vision: The Battle for the Future of Television.* San Diego, CA: Harcourt Brace, 1998.

British Media Industry Group, "The Future of the British Media Industry." A submission to the DNH, London: February 1994.

Broadcasting and Cable Yearbook 1996. New Providence, NJ: R. R. Bowker, 1996.

Broadcasting and Cable Yearbook 1998. New Providence, NJ: R. R. Bowker, 1998.

Broadcasting and Cable Yearbook 2001. New Providence, NJ: R. R. Bowker, 2001.

Broadcasting and Cable Yearbook 2006. New Providence, NJ: R. R. Bowker, 2006.

Brown, Duncan H. "The Academy's Response to the Call for a Marketplace Approach to Broadcast Regulation." *Critical Studies in Mass Communications* 11, no. 3 (September 1994): 257–273.

Brown, Keith, & Williams, George. *Consolidation and Advertising Prices in Local Radio Markets.* Media Bureau Staff Research Paper, Federal Communications Commission, September 2002.

Brown, Richard. "Early American Origins of the Information Age," in Chandler Jr., Alfred D., & Cartada, James W., eds. *A Nation Transformed By Info.: How Information Has Shaped U.S. from Colonial Times to the Present.* New York: Oxford University Press, 2000.

Brush, Michael. "In Music Retailing, Different Drummers." The *New York Times*, July 27, 1997, sec. Money and Business, p. 5.

Burgelman, Robert, & Grove, Andrew. "Strategic Dissonance." *California Management Review* 38 (Winter 1996): 8–9.

Burnett, Richard. "Computer Sales Boots On-Line Market." *Orlando Sentinel Tribune*, February 17, 1993, p. C1.

Burstein, M. L. "A Theory of Full-Line Forcing." *Northwestern University Law Review* 55 (March/April 1960): 62, 68, 76–83.

Burt, Jeffrey. "Gartner: IBM, HP Tops in Server Revenue, Shipments." 22 February 2006. *eWEEK.com.* Last accessed on 24 May 2007 at http://www.eweek.com/article2/0,1895,1930156,00.asp.

Bush, C. Anthony. *On the Substitutability of Local Newspaper, Radio and Television Advertising in Local Business Sales.* Media Bureau Staff Research Paper, Federal Communications Commission, September 2002.

Busterna, John C. "How Managerial Ownership Affects Profit Maximization in Newspaper Firms." *Journalism Quarterly* 66 (Summer 1989): 302–307.

———. "Television Station Ownership Effects of Programming and Idea Diversity: Baseline Data." *Journal of Media Economics* 1, no. 2 (1988): 36–74.

———. "The Cross-Elasticity of Demand for National Newspaper Advertising." *Journalism Quarterly* 64, no. 2/3 (Summer/Fall 1987): 346–351.

———. "Trends in Daily Newspaper Ownership." *Journalism Quarterly* 65 (Winter 1988): 831–838.

Buxton, A. J. "The Process of Technical Change in UK Manufacturing." *Applied Economics, Taylor and Francis Journals* 7, no. 1 (March 1975): 53–71.

Byrne, John, Grover, Ronald, & Melcher, Richard. "The Best and Worst Boards." *Business Week*, December 8, 1997.

"By The Numbers: TVinsite," based on figures from *FCC, Nielsen, and Paul Kagan Associates*, July 17, 2000.

"Cable Developments 2002." *NTCA* 26 (2002): 151–170.

Cabletelevision Advertising Bureau. "The Big Erosion Picture: Ad-Supported Cable vs. All Broadcast." *CAB Research*. 2006. Last accessed on January 9, 2008, from http://www.onetvworld.org/main/cab/research/2006TVFacts/the-big-erosion-picture-a.shtml.

Cabletelevision Advertising Bureau. "Cable Viewership Summary." *2006 TV Facts*.

Onetvworld.org. Last accessed on January 4, 2008, from http://www.onetvworld.org/main/cab/research/2006TVFacts/cable-viewership-summary.shtml.

"Cahners Business Information." *Electronic News* 45 (October 4, 1999): 23.

Cameron, Jim, Johnson, Rolland C., & McLaughlin, Edward F. "Network and Syndicated Radio Programming," in Eastman, Susan T., Head, Sydney W., & Klein, Lewis, eds. *Broadcast/Cable Programming Strategies and Practices*. Third Edition, Belmont, CA: Wadsworth, 1989, pp. 374–393.

Card, David. "Internet Radio: Post-CARP Survival Scenarios." *JupiterResearch*. 4 September 2002. Last accessed on 3 June 2004 at http://www.jup.com/bin/item.pl/research:concept/105/id=85897,keywords1=radio.

———. *Shipments of Portable MP3 Players, 2005 to 2010*. New York: JupiterResearch, 2005.

Card, David, Matiesanu, Corina, McLeary, Roger, Parr, Barry, & Wigder, Zia D. *The Future of News, Capturing a New Audience Online*. Jupiter Research, Vision Report, December 20, 2005.

Carley, Kathleen, Farrow, Scott, & Sheu, Tair-Rong. "Monopoly Power on the Web: A Preliminary Investigation of Search Engines," presented at the 29th *Research Conference on Communication, Information and Internet Policy*. Telecommunications Policy Research Conference, Caret, VA, Alexandria, VA. 27 October 2001.

Carlton, Dennis. "Vertical Integration in Competitive Markets Under Uncertainty." *Journal of Industrial Economics* 27, no. 3 (1979): 189–209.

Carlton, Dennis W., & Perloff, Jeffrey M. *Modern Industrial Organization*. 3rd ed. Reading, MA: Addison Wesley Longman Inc., 2000, pp. 157, 165, 167, 175.

Carroll, Raymond L. "Market Size and TV News Values." *Journalism Quarterly* 66 (1989): pp. 49–56.

Carroll, Raymond L., & Tuggle, C. A. "The World Outside: Local TV News Treatment of Imported News." *Journalism and Mass Communications Quarterly* 74 (Spring 1997): 123–133.

Carstensen, Peter C. "Antitrust Law and the Paradigm of Industrial Organization." *UC Davis Law Review* 16 (1983): 487, 493–501.

Carvajal, M., & Sanchez-Taberno A. *Media Concentration in the European Market: New Trends and Challenges*. Pamplona: EUNSA, 2002.

Cassell, Jonathan. "Seagate Expands Lead in Hard Disk Drive Market." 17 August 2005. *iSuppli Market Watch*. Last accessed on 25 May 2005 at http://www.isuppli.com/marketwatch/default.asp?id=312.

Cavalli, Mario. "HyperTransport Technology Consortium Report." 8 July 2005. HyperTransport Technology Consortium. Last accessed on 31 May 2006 at http://www.hypertransport.org/docs/pres/ISC2005_WebReport.pdf.

Cavallone, Mark. *Computer: Consumer Services and the Internet*. Standard and Poor's Industry Surveys. 15 October 1998. Last accessed on 12 December 2007 at http://www.netadvantage.standardpoor.com.

"CDNow bought by Bertelsmann." *USA Today*, McLean, VA, July 20, 2000.

Cellular Communications Systems, Report and Order, 86 FCC 2d 469, 511 (1981); *modified*, 89 FCC 2d 58 (1982), *further modified*, 90 FCC 2d 571 (1982), *appeal dismissed sub nom.* United States v. FCC, No. 82–1526 (D.C. Cir. Mar. 3, 1983).

Chan-Olmsted, Sylvia M. "A Structural Analysis of Market Competition in the U.S. TV Syndication Industry, 1981–1990." *Journal of Media Economics* 3 (Fall 1991): 9–28.

Chan-Olmsted, Sylvia M., & Frank, Stacy. "How Americans Get Their Political Information: Print versus Broadcast News." *The Annals of the American Academy of Political and Social Science* 546, no. 1 (1996): 48–58.

Chan-Olmsted, Sylvia M., & Litman, B. R. "Antitrust and Horizontal Mergers in the Cable Industry." *Journal of Media Economics* 1 (1988): 63–74.

Chan-Olmsted, Sylvia M., & Park, Jung Suk. "From On-Air to Online World: Examining the Content and Structures of Broadcast TV Stations' Web Sites." *Journalism and Mass Communication Quarterly* 77, no. 2 (2000): 321–339.

Chandler, Jr., Alfred D., & Cortada, James W., eds. *A Nation Transformed by Information: How Information Has Shaped the United*

States from Colonial Times to the Present. New York: Oxford University Press, 2000.

Chandler, David. "Supercalifragilisticexpialidocious." *UNIX Review,* May 1988, p. 38.

Chen, Andy M., & Hylton, Keith N. "Procompetitive Theories of Vertical Control." *Hastings Law Journal* 50 (1999): 573, 583–85, 587, 590–91.

Chen, Jim. "The Last Picture Show (On the Twilight of Federal Mass Communications Regulation)." *Minnesota Law Review* 80 (1996): 1415.

Chen, P. "Who Owns Cable Television? Media Ownership Concentration in Taiwan." *Journal of Media Economics* 15, no. 1 (2002): 41–56.

Chen, Qi, Garcia, D. Linda, & Surles, Ellen. "Fostering a Communication Policy Dialogue: The Need for a Sustainable Communication Interface." Background Paper for the *Social Science Review Center,* 2002.

Children Now. *Big Media, Little Kids: Media Consolidation and Children's Television programming.* Oakland, CA: Children Now, May 21, 2003.

Chipty, Tasneem. "FCC Media Ownership Study #5: Station Ownership and Programming in Radio." *Federal Communications Commission.* FCC.gov. June 24, 2007. Last accessed on January 6, 2008, from http://hraunfoss.fcc.gov/edocs_public/attachmatch/DA-07-3470A6.pdf.

———. "Vertical Integration, Market Foreclosure, and Consumer Welfare in the Cable Television Industry." *American Economics Review* 91, no. 3 (June 2001): 428–453.

Chomsky, Noam, & Herman, Edward S. *Manufacturing Consent: The Political Economy of the Mass Media.* New York: Pantheon, 1988.

Christensen, Clayton M. *The Innovator's Dilemma: When New Technologies Cause Great Firms to Fail.* Boston: Harvard Business School Press, 1997.

Church, Jeffrey, & Ware, Roger. *Industrial Organization: A Strategic Approach.* San Francisco: IRWIN/McGraw-Hill, 2000, pp. 233–240, 247–252, 256–257.

Clark, Jessica, & Van Slyke, Tracy. "Making Connections." *In These Times* 29, no. 12 (May 9, 2005): 17.

Clayton, M. L. "A Condensed Atari History." *HeartBone.* 16 June 2000. Last accessed on 24 May 2007 at http://www.heartbone.com/comphist/Atari.htm.

Cohen, Wesley M., & Levin, Richard C. "Empirical Studies of Innovation and Market Structure," in Schmalensee, Richard, & Willig, Robert, eds. *Handbook of Industrial Organization.* Amsterdam: North-Holland, 1989, pp. 1059, 1074–1078.

Cohen, Wesley M., Levin, Richard C., & Mowery, David C. "R&D Appropriability, Opportunity, and Market Structure: New Evidence on Some Schumpeterian Hypotheses." *American Economic Review* 75, no. 2 (May 1985): 20–24.

Cole, Barry G., ed. *After the Break-Up: Assessing the New Post-AT&T Divestiture Era.* New York: Columbia University Press, 1991.

Cole, George. "More Haste Less Speed." *Financial Times,* London Edition, August 22, 1997, p. Features 9.

Columbia Journalism Review. "CJR: Resources: Who Owns What." CJR.org. June 12, 2007. Last accessed on January 10, 2008, from http://www.cjr.org/resources/.

Collins, Richard. "Enter the Grecian Horse? Regulation of Foreign Ownership of the Media in the UK." *Policy Studies* 24, no. 1 (2003): 17–31.

Comanor, William S. "Market Structure, Product Differentiation, and Industrial Research." *Quarterly Journal of Economics* 81 (1967): 639–657.

Commission of the European Community, "Europe's Way to the Information Society—An Action Plan," Brussels, Document COM (94)347 final, 1994.

Compaine, Benjamin M. "The Impact of Ownership on Content: Does It Matter?" *Cardozo Arts and Entertainment Law Journal* 13 (1995): 755–775.

Compaine, B., & Gomery, D. *Who Owns the Media?: Competition and Concentration in the Mass Media Industry.* 3rd ed. Mahwah, NJ: Lawrence Erlbaum Associates, Inc., 2000.

Compaine, Benjamin, Guback, Thomas, Noble Jr., J. Kendrick, & Sterling, Christopher, eds. *Who Owns the Media?* White Plains, NY: Knowledge Industry, 1979, 1982.

"Consumers Spend a Record $16.8 Billion Buying and Renting Video." *Business Wire,* January 9, 2002.

Cooper, Mark. "Inequality in Digital Society." *Cardozo Journal on Media and the Arts* 73 (2002): 383.

Copps, Michael. "Crunch Time at the FCC." The *Nation,* New York, February 3, 2003.

Coulson, David, Hiromi, Cho, & Lacy, Stephen. "Competition for Readers among U.S. Metropolitan Daily, Non-metropolitan Daily and Weekly Newspapers." *Journal of Media Economics* 15 (January 2002): 21–40.

Council of Europe, "Media Diversity in Europe," Strasbourg, Directorate General of Human Rights, Media Division, 2002.

The Council of the European Communities. "Television Without Frontiers Directive," Brussels, Belgium, CONSLEG System of the Office for Official Publications of the European Communities, March 7, 1997.

Crandall, Robert W. *After the Breakup: U.S. Telecommunications in a More Competitive Era*. Washington, DC: The Brookings Institution, 1991.

Crane, R., Neuman, R., Noam, Eli M., & Sapolsky, H., ed. *The Telecommunications Revolution*. New York: Routledge, 1992.

Crawford, Gregory S. . "FCC Media Ownership Study #3: Television Station Ownership Structure and the Quantity and Quality of TV Programming." *Federal Communications Commission*. FCC.gov, July 23, 2007. Last accessed on January 6, 2008, from http://hraunfoss.fcc.gov/edocs_public/attachmatch/DA-07-3470A4.pdf.

Cricelli, Livio, Gastaldi, Massimo, & Levialdi, Nathan. "Vertical Integration in International Telecommunication System." *Review of Industrial Organization* 14, no. 4 (June 1999): 337–353.

Crocker, Keith J., & Masten, Scott E. "Regulation and Administered Contracts Revisited: Lessons from Transaction-Cost Economics for Public Utility Regulation." *Journal of Regulatory Economics* 9, no. 5 (1996): 14–15.

Cukier, Kenneth Neil, & Hindman, Mathew. "Measuring Media Concentration Online and Offline." 12 February 2004. CUKIER.com. Last accessed on 29 May 2007 http://www.cukier.com/writings/webmedia-jan04.htm.

Culbertson, John D. "Should Antitrust Use the Schumpeterian Model?: The Case of the Food Industries," in Caswell, Julie A., Culbertson, John D., & Wills, Robert L., eds. *Issues after a Century of Federal Competition Policy*. Lexington, MA: Lexington Books, 1987, pp. 103, 106–07.

Curtis, Philip J. *The Fall of the U.S. Consumer Electronics Industry: An American Trade Tragedy*. Westport, CT: Quorum Books, 1994, p. 194.

Dale, Dennis F. "What Subscribers Think of Group Ownership of Newspapers." *Journalism Quarterly* 57 (Summer 1980): 314–316.

Daly, Charles P. "The Business of Magazine Publishing" in Daly, Charles, Henry, Patrick, eds. *The Magazine Publishing Industry*. Boston: Allyn & Bacon, 1996.

Davenport, Lucinda, & Lacy, Stephen. "Daily Newspaper Market Structure, Concentration, and Competition." The *Journal of Media Economics* 7, no. 3 (1994): 33–46.

Davis, D. K., & Robinson, J. P. "Television News and the Informed Public: An Information Process Approach." *Journal of Communication* 40 (1990): 106–119.

Dealerscope. *Dealerscope 80th Annual Statistical Survey and Report*. Dealerscope, August 2002.

——. *Dealerscope 81st Annual Statistical Survey and Report*. Dealerscope, August 2003.

Definition of Radio Markets, Notice of Proposed Rulemaking, MM Docket No. 00–244, 15 FCC Rcd 25077 (2000).

Dejong, A. S., & Bates, B. J. "Channel Diversity in Cable Television." *Journal of Broadcasting and Electronic Media* 35, no. 2 (1991): 159–167.

DeLamarter, Richard Thomas. *Big Blue: IBM's Use and Abuse of Power*. New York: Dodd, Mead, 1986, p. 232.

"Demand for Cable Set-Top Boxes Remains Flat; Scientific-Atlanta is Exception to Trend." *BroadcastEngineering*. 13 Oct. 2003. Last accessed on 24 May 2007 at http://broadcastengineering.com/news/broadcasting_demand_cable_settop/index.html.

Demers, David K. "Structural Pluralism, Corporate Newspaper Structure, and News Source Perceptions: Another Test of the Editorial Vigor Hypothesis." *Journalism and Mass Communication Quarterly* 75 (Autumn 1998): 572–592.

Demers, David P. "Corporate structure and emphasis on profits and product quality at U.S. daily newspapers." *Journalism Quarterly* 68 (1991): 15–26.

——. "Effect of corporate structure on autonomy of top editors at U.S. dailies." *Journalism Quarterly* 70 (1993): 499–508.

——. *The Menace of the Corporate Newspaper: Fact or Fiction?* Ames, IA: Iowa University Press, 1996.

Dempsey, John. "Cable TV Hits Record Numbers." *Variety*: New York. Variety.com. July 31, 2007. Last accessed on January 10, 2008, from http://www.variety.com/article/VR1117969516.html?categoryid=14&cs=1.

Demsetz, Harold, & Lehn, Kenneth. "The Structure of Corporate Ownership: Causes and Consequences." *Journal of Political Economy* 93 (1985): 1155–1177.

Denisoff, R. Serge. *Solid Gold*. New Brunswick, NJ: Transaction, 1975.

——. *Tarnished Gold: The Record Industry Revisited*. New Brunswick, NJ: Transaction, 1986.

Depuy, Chris, & Meeker, Mary. *The Internet Report*. New York: Harper Business, 1996, pp. 5–13.

Dertouzous, J. N., & Trautman, W. B. "Economic Effects of Media Concentration: Estimates from a Model of the Newspaper Firm." The *Journal of Industrial Economics* 39, no. 1 (September 1990): 1–14.

Deutsche Bank Media Research. "Newspapers Unwrapped." Working Paper, Deutsche Bank Media Research Section, March 22, 2002.

DiCola, Peter. "False Premises, False Promises: A Quantitative History of Ownership Consolidation in the Radio Industry." *Future of Music Coalition.* FutureofMusic.org. December, 2006. Pp. 5–6, 36, 41, 43–46, 55, 63. Last accessed on January 10, 2008, from http://www.futureofmusic.org/images/ FMCradiostudy06.pdf2006.

DiCola, Peter, & Thomson, Kristin. *Radio Deregulation: Has It Served Citizens and Musicians?* Washington, DC: Future of Music Coalition, 2002.

Dimmick, J. *Media Competition and Coexistence: The Theory of Niche.* Mahwah, NJ: Erlbaum Associates, 2003.

"Does Ownership Matter in Local Television News: A Five-Year Study of Ownership and Quality." Washington, DC, Project for Excellence in Journalism, February 17, 2003.

Donald, William H. "Advertising." *Standard & Poor's Industry Survey,* 6 December 2001. Last accessed on 3 November 2004 at http:// www.netadvantage.standardpoor.com.

———. *Publishing: Industry Profile.* New York: Standard & Poor's Industry Surveys, May 3, 2001.

Doremus, Mark, Hakanen, Ernest A., & Slattery, Karen L. "The Expression of Localism: Local TV News Coverage in the New Video Marketplace." *Journal of Broadcasting and Electronic Media* 40 (1996): 403–413.

"Dot-com Job Cuts Headed by Consumer, Services Firms." *Silicon Valley/San Jose Business Journal.* 27 August 2002. Last accessed on 8 May 2007 at http://sanjose.bizjournals.com/ sanjose/stories/2002/08/26/daily13.

Downie, Leonard Jr., & Kaiser, Robert. *The News about the News.* New York: Alfred A. Knopf, 2002.

Doyle, Gillian. "Media Ownership—The Economics and Politics of Convergence and Concentration in the U.K. and European Media." *Journal of Cultural Economics* 27 (2003): 290–293.

Doyle, Gillian. "Media Ownership." London: Sage Publications 2002.

———. "Towards a Pan-European Directive? From "Concentrations and Pluralism to Media Ownership." Journal of Communications Law, 3, (1): 11–1527

Duncan's Radio Market Guide. 2002 ed. Kalamazoo, MI: Duncan Media Enterprises, 2002.

Dugger, Ronald. "The Corporate Domination of Journalism," in Seriin, William, ed. *The Business of Journalism.* New York: New Press, 2000, pp. 27–56.

"DVR is Fastest Growing Home Technology." Research Alert 23 (March 18, 2005): m10.

Eco, Umberto. "The Multiplication of Media," in Eco, Umberto, ed. *Travels in Hyperreality: Essays.* San Diego, CA: Harcourt Brace Jovanovich, 2001.

EIM, "Expansion and Concentration of media Companies in Europe." Dusseldorf: European Institute of the Media, 1994.

Ekelund Jr., Robert B., Ford, George S., & Jackson, J. D. "Is Radio Advertising a Distinct Local Market? An Empirical Analysis." *Review of Industrial Organization* 14 (1999): 239–256.

Ekelund Jr., Robert B., Ford, George S., & Koutsky, Thomas. "Market Power in Radio Markets: An Empirical Analysis of Local and National Concentration." *Journal of Law and Economics* 43, no. 1 (April 2000): 157–184.

Electronic Industries Alliance. *Electronic Market Data Book, 1996–2000.* Arlington, VA: Electronic Industries Alliance, 2001, p.14.

Elling, George. *Enterprise Hardware.* New York: Deutsche Bank Alex Brown, 2001.

Ellul, Jacques. *Propaganda: The Formation of Men's Attitudes.* New York: Random House Inc., 1962.

Emery, Edwin, & Emery, Michael. *The Press and America: An Interpretive History of the Mass Media.* Englewood Cliffs, NJ: Prentice Hall, 1984, p. 39.

Emord, Jonathan W. "The First Amendment Invalidity of FCC Ownership Regulations." *Catholic University Law Review* 38 (1989): 401, 449.

Entman, R. M., & Paletz, David L. *Media, Power, Politics.* New York: Free Press, 1981.

Ernst & Young. "Spotlight on Profitable Growth: Media and Entertainment." April, 2006. Last accessed on January 9, 2008, at http:// www.slideshare.net/DaveDuarte/study-on- profitable-new-media-growth/.

Epstein, Mara. *Prime Time Power and Politics: The Financial Interest and Syndication Rules and Their Impact on the Structure and Practices of the Television Industry.* Ph.D. dissertation, Department of Culture and Communications, New York University, 2000.

———. "Program Diversity and the Program Selection Process on Broadcast Network Television." Working Paper, Federal Communications Commission, Media Ownership Working Group, September 2002.

Esarey, Ashley. "Cornering the Market: State Strategies for Controlling China's Commercial Media." *Asian Perspective* 29, no. 4 (2005): 37–83.

European Audiovisual Observatory, "Statistical Yearbook: Cinema, Television, Video and New Media in Europe," Strasbourg, European Audiovisual Observatory, 2003.

———. "Statistical Yearbook: Film, Television, Video and New Media in Europe," Strasbourg, European Audiovisual Observatory, 2002.

European Commission, "Communication from the Commission to the Council and the European Parliament on the application of Articles 4 and 5 of Directive 89/552/EEC as amended by Directive 97/36/EC, for the period 1999–2000," Brussels, August 11, 2002.

European Federation of Journalists. *European Media Ownership: Threats on the Landscape: A Survey of Who Owns What in Europe.* Brussels: European Federation of Journalists, 2003.

European Parliament, "Draft report on the application of Directive 89/552/EEC: Television without Frontiers," Strasbourg, Document 2003/200033 (INI), 2003.

Evans, David S., ed. *Breaking Up Bell.* New York: Elsevier Science Publishing Co. Inc, 1983.

Fairchild, Charles. "Deterritorializing Radio: Deregulation and the Continuing Triumph of the Corporatist Perspective in the USA." *Media, Culture and Society* 21 (1999): 549–561.

Farhi, Paul. "Fear, Loathing and Respect for Cable's Leader; TCI's Size Draws Controversy." The *Washington Post,* January 23, 1992, p. A1.

Farrell, Joseph, & Saloner, Garth. "Installed Base and Compatibility: Innovation, Product Preannouncements, and Predation." The *American Economic Review* 76 (1986): 940, 941.

"FCC: Cable Losing Ground to Satellite TV Services." *Online Reporter.* 26 February 2005. Last accessed on 29 May 2007 at http://www.onlinereporter.com/article.php?article_id=1167.

Federal Communications Commission. 1964 Report and Order, 45 FCC 1476.

———. 1984 Multiple Ownership Report and Order, MM Docket No. 83–46, 100 FCC 2d (1984).

———. 1985 Multiple Ownership of AM, FM and Television Broadcast Stations (MO&O on reconsideration), 100 FCC 2d 74, 94 (1985).

———. 1992 Radio Ownership Report and Order, 7 FCC Rcd. at 2757–2760, pp. 4–10.

———. 1998 Biennial Regulatory Review of the Commission's Broadcast Ownership Rules and Other Rules Adopted Pursuant to Section 202 of the Telecommunications Acts of 1996, MM Docket No. 98–35, FCC 00–191, Biennial Review Report, 15 FCC Rcd 11058, ¶¶ 5–6 (2000).

———. 1998 Biennial Regulatory Review—Streamlining of Mass Media Applications, Rules, and Processes: Policies and Rules Regarding Minority and Female Ownership of Mass Media Facilities, MM Docket Nos. 98–43 and 94–149, 13 FCC Rcd 23056, 23095 (1998).

———. 2000 Biennial Regulatory Review Spectrum Aggregation Limits for Commercial Mobile Radio Services, 16 FCC Rcd. 22668 (2001).

———. 2001 Video Competition Report, 17 FCC Rcd. at 1282, p. 79.

———. 2002 Biennial Regulatory Review—Review of the Commission's Broadcast Ownership Rules and Other Rules adopted Pursuant to Section 202 of the Telecommunications Act of 1996, Cross-Ownership of Broadcast Stations and Newspapers, Rules and Policies Concerning Multiple Ownership of Radio Broadcast Stations in Local Markets, Definition of Radio Markets, 17 FCC Rcd. 18503 (2002).

———. 2002 Biennial Regulatory Review—Review of the Commission's Broadcast Ownership Rules and Other Rules Adopted Pursuant to Section 202 of the Telecommunications Act of 1996, 18 FCC Rcd 13620, 13711–47 (2003) ("2002 Biennial Review Order").

———. "2002 Telecommunications Industry Revenue Report," Washington, DC, Government Printing Office, March 2004.

———. "2006 Review of the Media Ownership Rules." *FCC.gov.* December 29, 2006. Last accessed on January 10, 2008, from http://www.fcc.gov/ownership/.

———. Amendment of Multiple Ownership Rules, 43 FCC 2797, 2801–02 (1954).

———. Amendment of Section 3.636 of the Commission's Rule and Regulations Relating to Multiple Ownership of Television Broadcast Stations, Report and Order, 43 FCC 2797 (1954).

———. Amendment of Section 73.3555 (formerly 73.35, 73.240, and 73.636) of the Commission's Rules Relating to Multiple Ownership of AM, FM, and TV Broadcast Stations, Report and Order, 100 FCC 2d 17 p. 25 (July 26, 1984).

———. Amendment of Section 73.658(g) of the Commission's Rules—The Dual Network Rule, 16 FCC Rcd. 11114 (2001).

———. Annual Assessment of the Status of Competition in Markets for the Delivery of Video Programming, CC Docket No. 00–132, Seventh Report, in BIA Financial. *Television Market Report: 2001.* Chantilly, VA: November 2001.

———. Annual Assessment of the Status of Competition in the Market for the Delivery of Video Programming, Eight Annual Report, CS Docket No. 01–129, FCC 01–389 (January 14, 2002).

———. Annual Assessment of the Status of Competition in the Market for the Delivery of Video Programming, 17 FCC Rcd. 26901, 26975 (2002).

———. Annual Assessment of the Status of Competition in the Market for the Delivery of Video Programming, Tenth Annual Report, MB Docket No. 03–172, FCC 04–5 (January 28, 2004).

———. Attribution of Ownership Interests, 97 FCC 2d 997, 999, 1005 (1984), on recon. granted in part, 58 RR 2d 604 (1985), on further recon. granted in part, 1 FCC Rcd 802 (1986).

———. "Broadcast Station Totals as of September 30, 2001." *FCC.gov.* 30 Oct 2001. Last accessed on 4 May 2007 at http://www.fcc.gov/Bureaus/Mass_Media/News_Releases/2001/nrmm0112.txt.

———. "Broadcast Station Totals." *FCC.gov.* December 31, 2005. Last accessed on January 9, 2008, from http://www.fcc.gov/mb/audio/totals/bt051231.html#START.

———. Cross Ownership of Broadcast Stations and Newspapers, Order and Notice of Proposed Rulemaking, MM Docket No. 01–235 16 FCC Rcd 17283 (2001).

———. Definition of Radio Markets, 15 FCC Rcd. 25077 (2000).

———. "Digital Audio Broadcasting Systems and Their Impact on the Terrestrial Radio Broadcast Service." Washington, DC: Federal Communications Committee, FCC 99–325, May 2004.

———. "FCC Releases Statistics of the Long Distance Telecommunications Industry Report." *FCC.gov.* 14 May 2003. Last accessed on 24 May 2007 at http://hraunfoss.fcc.gov/edocs_public/attachmatch/DOC-234385A1.pdf?date=030514.

———. "Fiber Deployment Update End of Year 1998," Washington, DC, Government Printing Office, September 9, 1999.

———. Implementation of Section 309(J) of the Communications Act—Competitive Bidding for Commercial Broadcast and Instructional Television Fixed Service Licenses: Reexamination of the Policy Statement on Comparative Broadcast Hearings; Proposals to Reform the Commission's Comparative Hearing Process to Expedite the Resolution of Cases, 13 FCC Rcd. 15920, 15994–15995 (1998).

———. Local TV Ownership Report and Order. 14 FCC Rcd. at 12907–08, 8 (1998).

———. "Local Telephone Competition," Industry Analysis and Technology Division, Wireline Competition Bureau, Washington, DC, Government Printing Office, August 1999, p. 11.

———. "Long Distance Market Shares First Quarter 1996," Common Carrier Bureau, Washington, DC, Government Printing Office, Tables 2 and 4, July 12, 1996.

———. "Long Distance Telecommunications Industry," Industry Analysis Division, Common Carrier Bureau, Washington, DC, Government Printing Office, January 2001.

———. In the Matter of Broadcast Ownership Rules, Cross-Ownership of Broadcast Stations and Newspapers, MM Docket 01–235; Rules and Policies Concerning Multiple Ownership of Radio Broadcast Stations in Local Markets, MM Docket 01–317; Definition of Radio Markets, MM Docket 00–244; Definition of Radio Markets for Areas Not Located in an Arbitron Survey Area, MB Docket 03–130 (adopted June 2, 2003, and released July 2, 2003).

———. In the Matter of Broadcast Services, Radio Stations, Television Stations, Rules and Regulations, MM Docket No. 00–108, FCC 01–133 (August 13, 2001).

———. In the Matter of Cross-Ownership of Broadcast Stations and Newspapers, Notice of Proposed Rule Making, MM Docket No. 01–235, FCC 01–262 (September 21, 2001).

———. Multiple Ownership of Standard, FM and Television Broadcasts Stations, Report and Order, 45 FCC 1476, 1476–1477 (1964).

———. Newspaper/Broadcast Cross-Ownership, Notice of Proposed Rulemaking, 16 FCC Rcd. 17292 (2002).

———. Newspaper/Radio Cross-Ownership, Notice of Proposed Rulemaking, 16 FCC Rcd. 17292 (2002).

———. Newspaper/Radio Cross-Ownership NPRM, 16 FCC Rcd. (2001).

———. Policies and Rules Concerning Children's Programming. 11 FCC Rcd 10660, 10676, 34 (1995).

———. Policies and Rules Regarding Minority and Female Ownership of Mass Media Facilities, Notice of Proposed Rulemaking, MM Docket No. 94–149, 10 FCC Rcd 2788 (1995).

———. Prime Time Access Rule, 50 FCC 2nd 829, 32 R.R. 2nd 697 (1975).

———. Review of the Commission's Regulations Governing Attribution of Broadcast and Cable/MDS Interests; Review of the Commission's Regulations and Policies Affecting Investment in the Broadcast Industry, Reexamination of the Commission's Cross-Interest Policy, MM Docket No. 94–150, 92–51, 87–154, 14 FCC Rcd. 12559, 12581–12582. pp. 43–44 (1999) on recon., 16 FCC Rcd. 1097 (2001).

———. Review of the Commission's Regulations Governing Television Broadcasting and in the Matter of Television Satellite Stations

Review of Policy and Rules, MM Docket Nos. 91–221, 87–8, 14 FCC Rcd 12903 (rel. August 6, 1999) ("Local Ownership Report").

———. Review of Commission's Regulations Governing Television Broadcasting, MM Docket No. 91–221 (1992).

———. Revision of Radio Rules and Policies, Memorandum Opinion and Order and Further Notice of Proposed Rule Making, MM Docket No. 91–140, 7 FCC Rcd 6387 (1992).

———. Rules Governing Broadcast Services Other Than Standard Broadcast, 9 Fed. Reg. 5442 (May 23, 1944).

———. Rules and Policies Concerning Multiple Ownership of Radio Broadcast Stations in Local Markets, Noticed of Proposed Rulemaking, MM Docket No. 00–244, 16 FCC Rcd 19861 (2001).

———. Second Further Notice of Proposed Rulemaking, MM Docket No. 92–264, FCC 05–96 (May 17, 2005).

———. Section 257 Proceeding to Identify and Eliminate Market Entry Barriers for Small Businesses, Notice of Inquiry, MM Docket No. 94–149, 11 FCC Rcd. 6280 (May 21, 1996).

———. Statement of Policy on Minority Ownership of Broadcast Facilities. 68 FCC 2d 979 (1978).

———. "Trends in International Telephony Report," Washington, DC, Government Printing Office, Table 3, July 2, 2004.

———. "Trends in Telephone Service," Industry Analysis and Technology Division, Wireline Competition Bureau, Washington, DC, Government Printing Office, Table 9.7, May 2004.

———. "Trends in Telephone Service." *Washington: Federal Communications Commission.*

FCC.gov. February, 2007. pp. 6–3. Last accessed on January 8, 2008, from http://hraunfoss.fcc.gov/edocs_public/attachmatch/DOC-270407A1.pdf.

———. "US Competitive Local Loop Market: 1996," MTA-EMCI, Washington, DC, Government Printing Office, 1996.

Federal Communications Commission v. National Citizens Committee for Broadcasting, 436 U.S. 775, 802 (1978).

Federal Radio Commission, "Second Annual Report of the Federal Radio Commission to the Congress of the United States," Washington, DC, Government Printing Office June 30, 1928.

Ferrall, V. E. "The Impact of Television Deregulation." *Journal of Communications* 26 (1992): 21–30.

Fico, Fredrick, & Lacy, Stephen. "Newspaper Content Quality and Circulation." *Newspaper Research Journal* 12 (Spring 1991): 46–57.

Finn, A., Hoskins, C., & McFayden, S. *Global Television and Film: An Introduction to the Economics of the Business.* Oxford: Clarendon Press, 1997.

Follet, Jennifer Hagendorf. "Avaya, Nortel vie for Cisco Share." *CRN* 1059 (August 25, 2003): 5.

"Forbes 400." *Forbes.com.* 18 September 2003. Last accessed on 10 May 2007 at http://www.forbes.com/2003/09/17/rich4001and.html.

Forkner, David A., Jumps, Brian P., & Soma, John T. "The Essential Facilities Doctrine in the Deregulated Telecommunications Industry." *Berkeley Technology Law Journal* 13, no. 2 (Spring 1998): 565, 594–96.

Foster, R. *Public Broadcasters, Accountability and Efficiency.* Edinburgh, UK: Edinburgh University Press, 1992.

Fox Broadcasting Economic Study. "News and Public Affairs Programming Offered by the Four Top-Tanked Versus Lower-Ranked Television Stations." Fox Top Four Study, comments to FCC, 2002.

Fox, Kraig G. "Paramount Revisited: The Resurgence of Vertical Integration in the Motion Picture Industry." *Hofstra Law Review* 21 (Winter 1992): 505–536.

Fox Television Stations, Inc. v. FCC, 280 F.3d 1027, 1044 (D.C. Cir. 2002).

Froeb, Luke M., & Werden, Gregory J. "The Effects of Mergers in Differentiated Products Industries: Logit Demand and Merger Policy." *Journal of Law, Economics and Organization* 10, no. 2 (October 1994): 407, 423–424.

Fratrik, Mark. "State of the Radio Industry: Ownership and Consolidation 2001." *BIA.com.* 2001 BIA Financial Network.

Frieswick, Kris. "Judgment Calls." *CFO Magazine.* February 2004. Last accessed on 8 June 2004 at http://www.cfo.com/article/1,5309,11902%7C10%7CM%7C806%7C,00.html.

Froeo, Luke M., & Werden, Gregory. "The Effects of Mergers in Differentiated Products Industries: Demand and Merger Policy." The *Journal of Law, Economics, and Organization* 10, no. 2 (1994): 407–416.

Galambos, Louis, & Temin, Peter. *The Fall of the Bell System: A Study in Prices and Politics.* New York: Cambridge University Press, 1987.

Gale, John, Keyte, James, & Overstreet, Thomas, eds. "Understanding Econometric Analysis of the Price Effects of Mergers Involving Differentiated Products." *Antitrust,* Summer 1996, pp. 30–31.

"Gaming Goes to Hollywood." The *Economist,* March 27, 2004.

Gans, Herbert. *Deciding What's News: A Study of CBS Evening News, NBC Nightly News,*

Newsweek and Time. New York: Vintage Books, 1980.

Gans, Joshua. "Concentration-Based Merger Tests and Vertical Market Structure." Discussion Paper, University of Melbourne, June 5, 2006.

Genco, Louis V. *Old-Time Radio: The Golden Years—The Original Old-Time Radio WWW Pages,* 2003. Available at http://www.old-time.com/golden_age/index.html.

George, Lisa. "What's Fit to Print: The Effect of Ownership Concentration on Product Variety in Daily Newspaper Markets." Working Paper, City University of New York, 2001.

George, Lisa, & Waldfogel, Joel. "Who Affects Whom in Daily Newspaper Markets?" *Journal of Political Economy* 11 (2003): 765–785.

———. "Who Benefits Whom in Daily Newspaper Markets?" Working Paper, National Bureau of Economic Research, 2000.

Gerbarg, Darcy, Groebel, Jo, & Noam, Eli M., eds. *Internet Television.* London: Lawrence Erlbaum Associates, 2004.

Gerber, Cheryl. "Prodigy Remakes Itself." *Computerworld,* August 1, 1996, p. t2.

Gher, Leo A., & Amin, Hussein Y. "New and Old Media Access and Ownership in the Arab World." *International Communication Gazette* 61 (1999): 59–88.

Ghiglione, Lauren, ed. *The Buying and Selling of American Newspapers.* Indianapolis: R. J. Berg, 1984.

Gibbons, T. *Regulating the Media.* 2nd ed. London: Sweet & Michael, 1998.

Gilpin, Kenneth N. "Westinghouse Will Spin Off Its Remaining Industrial Businesses." *New York Times,* November 14, 1996, p. D8.

"Global top six handset manufacturers by market share percentages estimated for 2004 and 2005." *Wireless Week* 11 (March 15, 2005).

Goetz, Charles J., & McChesney, Fred S. *Antitrust Law: Interpretation and Implementation.* 2nd ed. Dayton, OH: LexisNexis, 1998, pp. 464–466.

Goldschmid, Harvey, Mann, Michael H., & Weston, Fred, eds. *Industrial Concentration: The New Learning.* New York: Little, Brown, 1974.

Gomery, Douglas. "Interpreting Media Ownership," in Compaine, B., & Gomery, D., eds., *Who Owns the Media?* 3rd ed. Mahwah, NJ: Lawrence Earlbaum Associates, 2000, pp. 507–535.

Goolsbee, Austan, & Petrin, Amil. "The Consumer Gains from Direct Broadcast Satellites and the Competition with Cable Television." Working Paper No. 8317, National Bureau of Economic Research, May 29, 2001, pp. 4, 27–28, 32.

Available at http://gsbwww.uchicago.edu/fac/austan.goolsbee/research/satfin.pdf.

Goolsbee, Austan. "Vertical Integration and the Market for Broadcast and Cable Television Programming." (Federal Communications Commission Study No. 9, April, 2007; MB Docket No. 06–121). FCC.gov, Page 36. Accessed on January 4, 2008, from http://hraunfoss.fcc.gov/edocs_public/attachmatch/DA-07-3470A10.pdf.

———. "Vertical Integration and the Market for Broadcast and Cable Television Programming." *Federal Communications Commission.* FCC.gov, September 5, 2007. Last accessed on January 6, 2008, from http://www.fcc.gov/ownership/studies.html.

Gopbetz, R. H., & Scott, D. K. "Hard News/Soft News Content of the National Broadcast Networks: 1972–1987." *Journalism Quarterly* 69, no. 2 (Summer 1992): 406–412.

Gort, Michael. *Diversification and Integration in American Industry.* Princeton, NJ: Princeton University Press, 1962.

Graber, Doris. *Mass Media and American Politics.* Washington, DC: Congressional Quarterly, 1997.

Graham, Barry. "IBM prepares for 40th anniversary of 360 mainframe with good news." *Rethink IT.* April 2004. Last accessed on 24 May 2007 at http://www.findarticles.com/p/articles/mi_m0PAT/is_2004_April/ai_n6011108.

Graham, Daniel A., & Vernon, John M. "Profitability of Monopolization by Vertical Integration." *Journal of Political Economy* 79, no. 4 (July/August 1971): 924–925.

Graham-Hackett, Megan. *Industry Surveys: Computer Hardware.* Standard & Poor's, June 2, 2005.

Grant, A. E. "The Promise Fulfilled? An Empirical Analysis of Program Diversity on Television." *Journal of Media Economics* 7, no. 1 (1994): 51–64.

Greco, Albert N. "The Impact of Horizontal Mergers and Acquisitions on Corporate Concentration in the U.S. Book Publishing Industry, 1989–1994." *Journal of Media Economics* 12, no. 3 (1999): 165–180.

———. "Market Concentration Levels in the U.S. Consumer Book Industry: 1995–1996." *Journal of Cultural Economics* 24, no. 4 (November 2000): 321–336.

Green, James N. "The Book Trade in the Middle Colonies, 1680–1720," in Hall, David and Amory, Hugh, eds., *The Colonial Book in the Atlantic World,* New York: Cambridge University Press, 2000, p. 218.

Greer, Douglas F., & Rhoades, Stephen A. "Concentration and Productivity Changes in the Long and Short Run." *Southern Economic Journal* 43 (1976): 1031–1044.

Greppi, Michele. "The Insider: ABC's Tale of Too-Different Cities." *Electronic Media*, November 19, 2001.

Groebel, J., Feldmann, V., & Noam, Eli M., eds. *Media Content and Services for Mobile Wireless Communications.* London: Lawrence Erlbaum Associates, 2006, pp. 225–237.

Grunes, Allen P., & Stucke, Maurice E. "Antitrust and the Forum for Democratic Discourse." *Antitrust Law Journal* 69 (2001): 249.

Guback, Thomas. "Theatrical Film," in Compaine, Benjamin, Sterling, Christopher, Guback, Thomas, & Noble Jr., J. Kendrick., eds. *Who Owns the Media?* White Plains, NY: Knowledge Industry Publications, 1982, pp. 199–290.

Guedon, Jean-Claude. *Beyond Core Journals and Licenses: The Paths to Reform Scientific Publishing.* Washington, DC: ARL Bimonthly Report 218, October 2001.

Gustaffson, K. E. "The Circulation Spiral and the Principle of Household Coverage." *Scandinavian Economic History Review* 26, no. 1 (1978): 1–14.

Gwiasda, Gregory W. "Network News Coverage of Campaign Advertisements: Media's Ability to Reinforce Campaign Messages." *American Politics Research* 29, no. 5 (2001): 461–482.

Haddock, David D., & Polsby, Daniel D. "Bright Lines, the Federal Communications Commission's Duopoly Rule, and the Diversity of Voices." *Federal Communications Law Journal* 42 (1990): 331–364.

Hafner, Katie. "Speeding Up Wireless Computing." The *New York Times,* August 26, 1999.

Hahn, Tae-youl, & Nixon, Raymond B. "Concentration of Press Ownership: A Comparison of 32 Countries." *Journalism Quarterly* 47 (Spring 1971): 5–16.

Halimi, Serge. "United States: An Unfree Press." *Le Monde Diplomatique*, Paris, June 8, 2003.

Hamberg, Daniel. *R&D: Essays on the Economics of Research and Development.* New York: Random House, 1966, pp. 64–65.

———. "Size of Firm, Oligopoly, and Research: The Evidence." *Canadian Journal of Economics and Political Science* 30 (1964): 62–75.

Hammond, Allen S., O'Connor, Barbara, and Westin, Tracy. "FCC Media Ownership Study #8: The Impact of the FCC's TV Duopoly Rule Relaxation on Minority and Women Owned Broadcast Stations 1999–2006." *Federal Communications Commission.* FCC.gov. July 31, 2007. Last accessed on January 6, 2008, from http://hraunfoss.fcc.gov/edocs_public/attachmatch/DA-07-3470A9.pdf.

Hand, Chris. "Television Ownership in Britain and the Coming of ITV: What do the statistics show?" *Department of Media Arts, Royal Holloway University of London*, 2002.

"Hand Held Computer Market Growing in Double Digits." *Newsbytes News Network*, May 13, 1997.

Handler, Milton et al. *Cases and Materials on Trade Regulation.* 4th ed. Westbury, NY: Foundation Press, 1997, pp. 582–584.

Hansen, Claus Thustrup, & Kyhl, Soren. "Pay-Per-View Broadcasting of Outstanding Events: Consequences of a Ban." *International Journal of Industrial Organization* 19, no. 3/4 (2001): 598–609.

Hanssen, F. Andrew. "The Block Booking of Films Re-examined." *University of Chicago Journal of Law and Economics* 43, no. 2 (October 2000): 395–426.

Harcourt, Alison. "The Regulation of Media Markets in selected EU Accession States in Central and Eastern Europe." *European Law Journal* 9, no. 3 (2003): 316–340.

Harcourt, Alison. "EU Media Ownership Regulation." *Journal of Common Market Studies* 36, no. 3 (1998): 369–389.

Hargittai, Eszter. *How Wide a Web? Inequalities in Accessing Information Online.* Ph.D. dissertation, Sociology Department, Princeton University, 2003.

Harrigan, Kathryn Rudie. *Strategies for Vertical Integration.* Lexington, MA: Lexington Books, 1983.

Harrison, Jeffrey L., Morgan, Thomas D., & Verkuil, Paul R. *Regulation and Deregulation: Cases and Materials.* St. Paul, Minn.: West Group, 1997, pp. 191–219.

Hart, Oliver, & Jean Tirole, "Vertical Integration and Market Foreclosure," in Brookings Papers on Economic Activity. Washington DC: Brookings Institution Press, 1990, p. 205.

Hartman, Barrie, & Rarick, Galen. "The Effects of Competition on One Daily Newspaper's Content." *Journalism Quarterly* 43 (Autumn 1966): 459–463.

Hausman, Jerry A., & Leonard, Gregory K. "Economic Analysis of Differentiated Products Mergers Using Real World Data." *George Mason University Law Review* 5 (1997): 321, 337–338.

Hay, George A. "An Economic Analysis of Vertical Integration." *Industrial Organization Review* 1 (1973): 188–198.

Heide, Jan, & Rindfleisch, Aric. "Transaction Cost Analysis: Past, Present, and Future Applications." *Journal of Marketing* 61, no. 4 (1997): 432–439.

Hellman, Heikki, & Soramaki, Martii. "Competition and Content in the U.S. Video

Market." *Journal of Media Economics* 7, no. 1 (1994): 29–49.

Helms, Leslie, & Shiver Jr., Jube. "U. S. Faces Uphill Climb in Fight With Microsoft." *Los Angeles Times*, October 19, 1998, p. A1.

Hepp, Erica. "Barking up the Wrong Channel: An Analysis of the Communication Law Problems through the Lens of Media Concentration Rules." *Boston University Law Review* 85 (April 2004): Rev. 553–584.

Herrero, Monica, & Medina, Mercedes. "Concentration and Vertical Integration in the European Television Production Market," presented at 6*th* *World Media Economics Conference*. Centre d'Etudes Sure les Médias and Journal of Media Economics, HEC Montreal, Montreal, Canada, May 12–15, 2004.

Hickey, Neil. "Money Lust: How Pressure for Profits is Perverting Journalism." *Columbia Journalism Review* 37, no. 2 (July/August, 1998): 28–36.

———. "Power Shift: As the FCC Prepares to Alter the Media Map, Battle Lines Are Drawn." *Columbia Journalism Review* 41, no. 6 (March/April 2003): 26–31.

———. "Unshackling Big Media." *Columbia Journalism Review* 40, no. 2 (July/August 2001): 30–33.

Hill, G. Christian. "Bringing it Home." The *Wall Street Journal*, June 16, 1997, p. R1.

Hindman, Matthew, Johnson, Judy A., & Tsioutsiouliklis, Kostas. "Measuring Media Diversity Online and Offline: Evidence from Political Websites," presented at the *Proceedings of the 32nd Annual Telecommunications Policy Research Conference*. Telecommunications Policy Research Conference, Arlington, VA, September 17, 2004.

Hodge, James. "Extending Telecoms Ownership in South Africa: Policy, Performance and Future Options." Working Paper 7, University of Cape Town, 2003.

Holden, Steinar. "Network or Pay-Per-View? A Welfare Analysis." *Economic Letters* 43 (1993).

Holland, Bill. "RIAA Reports Flat '96: Teams with NARM in Industry Study." *Billboard*, February 22, 1997, p. 3.

Holland, Jenny. "XM Radio Announces New Marketing Moves." *Brandweek,* July 13, 2006.

"Horizontal Merger Guidelines." 8 April 1997. US Department of Justice. Last accessed on 24 May 2007 at http://www.usdoj.gov/atr/public/guidelines/horiz_book/hmg1.html.

Horowitz, Ira. "Firm Size and Research Activity." *Southern Economic Journal* 28, n0.3 (1962): 298–301.

Hovenkamp, Herbert. "Antitrust Policy After Chicago." *Michigan Law Review* 84 (1985): 213–284.

———. "Antitrust Policy, Restricted Distribution, and the Market for Exclusionary Rights." *Minnesota Law Review* 71 (1987): 1293, 1301 n.37, 1302, 1310–11.

———. *Federal Antitrust Policy*. 2nd ed. St. Paul, Minn.: West Group, 1999, sec. 1.7, pp. 42–46, sec. 2.2a, p. 60.

———. "Post-Chicago Antitrust: A Review and Critique." *Columbia Business Law Review*, 2001, pp. 257–337.

Hovenkamp, Herbert, & Sullivan, E. Thomas. *Antitrust Law, Policy and Procedure: Cases, Materials, Problems*. 4th ed. Charlottesville, VA: Lexis Law Publishing, 1999, pp. 420–421.

Huber, P., Kellog, M., & Thorne, J. "*The Geodesic Network II: 1993 Report on Competition in the Telephone Industry*." Washington, DC: Geodesic Company, 1992.

Huberty, Kathryn, & Runkle, Rebecca. *June Printer Data Reflects Tough Market, but Overall Supports LXK Trademark*. New York: Morgan Stanley, 21 July 2005.

Hull, Geoffrey. *The Recording Industry*. Boston: Allyn and Bacon, 1998.

Hulten, Olof. "Sweden," in Kelly, Mary, ed. *The Media in Europe*. Sage Publications Inc. 2004, pp. 236–247.

Humphries, P. "Mass Media and Media Policy in Western Europe." *European Policy Research Unit Series*. Manchestor, England: February 27, 1996.

ICE Status 1997. Integrated Circuit Engineering Corporation. 1997. Last accessed on 24 May 2007 http://www.ice-corp.com.

International Trade Administration. "U.S. Industry and Trade Outlook 2000." 18 May 2000. Office of Industry Analysis. Last accessed on 8 May 2007 at http://www.ita.doc.gov/TD/Industry/OTEA/outlook/chapters.html.

Iosifides, Petros. "Methods of measuring media concentration." *Media Culture and Society* 19 (1997): 643–663.

Iosifides, P. "Merger Control and Media Pluralism in the European Union." *Communications Law*. 1 (6): 247–9.

Iyengar, Shanto, & Kinder, Donald R. *News That Matters: Television and American Opinion*. Chicago: University of Illinois Press, 1987.

Jacobs, Michael S. "An Essay on the Normative Foundations of Antitrust Economics." *North Carolina Law Review* 74 (1995): 219–266.

Jones, John. *Server and Enterprise Hardware*. New York: Salomon Smith Barney, 2001.

Jones, Robert L, & Nixon, Raymond B. "The Content of Competitive vs. Non-competitive

Newspapers." *Journalism Quarterly* 33 (Summer 1956): 299–314.

Joskow, Paul L. "Asset Specificity and the Structure of Vertical Relationships: Empirical Evidence." *Journal of Law, Economics and Organization* 4 (1988): 95, 107–11.

———. "Vertical Integration and Long-Term Contracts: The Case of Coal-Burning Electric Generating Plants." *Journal of Law, Economics and Organization* 1 (1985): 33, 37.

Joskow, Paul L., & McLaughlin, Linda. "An Economic Analysis of Subscriber Limits, Comments of the Writers Guild of America Regarding Harmful Vertical and Horizontal Integration in the Television Industry," in FCC Eighth Report. *In the Matter of the Status of Competition in the Market for the Delivery of Video Programming.* January 14, 2002.

"Journal Wars." The *Economist*, London, May 12, 2001. pp. 66–67.

Just, N., & Latzer, M. "EU Competition Policy and Market Power Control in the Mediamatics Era." *Telecommunications Policy* 24, no. 5 (June 2000): 395–441.

Kahn, Kim Fridkin, & Kenny, Patrick J. "The Slant of News: How Editorial Endorsements Influence Campaign Coverage and Citizens' Views of Candidates." *American Political Science Review* 96 (2002): 381–394.

———. *The Spectacle of U.S. Senate Campaign.* Chicago: University of Chicago Press, 1999.

Kakanen, Ernest A., & Slattery, K. L. "Sensationalism Versus Public Affairs Content of Local TV News: Pennsylvania Revisited." *Journal of Broadcasting and Electronic Media* 38 (1994): 205–216.

Kamien, Morton I., & Schwartz, Nancy L. *Market Structure and Innovation.* Cambridge, England: Cambridge University Press, 1982, pp. 86–91.

Kapfer, Jack, Kurpius, David, Shano-Yeon Chern, David, & Voakes, Paul S. "Diversity in the News: A Conceptual and Methodological Framework." *Journalism and Mass Communications Quarterly* 73 (Autumn 1996): 582–593.

Kaplow, Louis. "Extension of Monopoly Power Through Leverage." *Columbia Law Review* 85 (1985): 515, 516–17.

Katz, Michael L. "Old Rules and New Rivals: An Examination of Broadcast Television Regulation and Competition," submitted as an appendix to the Emergency Petition for Relief and Supplemental Comments of Fox Television Stations, Inc., in MM Docket No. 98–35, November 18, 1999.

Katz, Michael L., & Shapiro, Carl. "Systems Competition and Network Effects." *Journal of Economic Perspectives* 8 (1994): 93, 110.

Kauper, Thomas E., & Snyder, Edward A. "Misuse of the Antitrust Laws: The Competitor Plaintiff." *Michigan Law Review* 90 (1991): 551, 564, 566.

Kelly, Thomas Monroe. *The Influences of Firm Size and Market Structure on the Research Efforts of Large Multiple-Product Firms.* Unpublished Ph.D. dissertation, Oklahoma State University, 1970, pp. 85–86.

Kenney, Roy W., & Klein, Benjamin. "How Block Booking Facilitated Self-Enforcing Film Contracts." *Journal of Law and Economics* 43 (2000): 427, 430–432.

———. "The Economics of Block Booking." *Journal of Law and Economics* 26 (1983): 497, 503–504.

Kerner, Sean Michael. "PDA Market Up or Down?" *Internetnews.com.* 18 February 2005. Last accessed on 24 May 2006 at http://www.internetnews.com/stats/article.php/3484291.

Keshen, Richard, & MacAskill, Kent. "I Told You So: Newspaper Ownership in Canada and the Kent Commission Twenty Years Later." *American Review of Canadian Studies* 30, no. 3 (2000): 315–325.

Kessler, Scott H. *"Industry Surveys: Consumer Services and the Internet." Standard & Poor's, March 3, 2005.*

Kharif, Olga, Helm, Burt, & Lacy, Sarah. "The CEO's Tech Toolbox." *Business Week Online.* 26 July 2005. Last accessed on 8 May 2007 at http://www.businessweek.com/technology/content/jul2005/tc20050726_8027.htm.

King, Karen Whitehill, & Reid, Leonard N. "A Demand-side View of Media Substitutability in National Advertising: A Study of Advertisers Opinions about Traditional Media Options." *Journalism and Mass Communication Quarterly* 77 (Summer 2000): 292–307.

Kirkpatrick, David. "Mergers Keep Pushing Up Journal Costs." The *New York Times*, November 3, 2000, p. C1.

Kittross, John, & Sterling, Christopher. *Stay Tuned: A Concise History of American Broadcasting.* 2nd ed. Belmont, CA: Wadsworth, 1990.

Klass, Michael W., & Salinger, Michael A. "Do New Theories of Vertical Foreclosure Provide Sound Guidance for Consent Agreements in Vertical Merger Cases?" *Antitrust Bulletin* 40 (1995): 667.

Klein, Benjamin. "Vertical Integration as Organizational Ownership: The Fisher Body-General Motors Relationship Revisited." *Journal of Law and Economics* 4 (1988): 199, 204–208.

Klein, Peter G., & Shelanski, Howard A. "Empirical Research in Transaction Cost Economics: A Review and Assessment." *Journal of Law, Economics and Organization* 11, no. 2 (October 1995): 334, 349–350.

Klienwachter, W. "Germany." in Goldberg, D., Prosser, T., & Verhulst, S. *Regulating the Changing Media*, Oxford, England: Clarendon Press, 1998. 29–60.

Klieman, H. "Content Diversity and the FCC's Minority and Gender Licensing Policies." *Journal of Broadcasting and Electronic Media* 35 (1991): 411–429.

Knee, Jonathan A. "False Alarm at the FCC?" *Columbia Journalism Review* 42, no. 1 (May/June 2003): 65.

Kohli, Vanita. *The Indian Media Business*. Sage Publications Pvt. Ltd, 2006.

Kolodzy, Janet. "Everything That Rises: Media Convergence is an Opportunity, Not a Curse." *Columbia Journalism Review* 42, no. 2 (July/August 2003): 61.

Kopper, Gerd. *Changing Media Markets in Germany and Strategic Options for the Newspaper Industry*. In Picard, Robert G. *Strategic Responses to Media Market Changes*. Jönköping: Jönköping International Business School Ltd, 2004, pp. 105–120.

Krapf, Eric. "Data Pricing: Ready to Deal?" *Business Communications Review* 32, no. 3 (March 19, 2002): 24–27.

———. "Measuring Internet Backbone Market Shares," presented *Internet Convergence and Self-Governance OECD/OSIPP Workshop*. Osaka University, Osaka, Japan, June 9, 1998.

Krasilovsky, M. William, & Shemel, Sidney. *This Business of Music*. New York: Billboard, 1977.

Krasilovsky, M. William, & Shemel, Sidney. *This Business of Music*. 3rd ed. New York: Billboard, 1995.

Krasilovsky, Peter. "Newspapers Want to Charge for Content, but Will Readers Pay?" *USC Annenberg Online Journalism Review*, 2004.

Krasnow, Erwin G., Stern, Jill A., & Senkowski, R. Michael. "New Video Marketplace and the Search for a Coherent Regulatory Philosophy." *Catholic University Law Review* 32, no. 3 (Spring 1983): 529, 541–543.

Krattenmaker, Thomas G., & Powell Jr., Lucas A. *Regulating Broadcast Programming*. Cambridge, MA: MIT Press; Washington, DC: AEI Press, 1995.

Krugman, Paul. "In Media Res." The *New York Times*, Nov. 29, 2002, p. A39.

Kubey, Robert, Shifflet, Mark, Ukeiley, Stephen, & Weerakkody, Niranjala. "Demographic Diversity on Cable: Have the New Cable Channels Made a Difference in the Representation of Gender, Race, and Age?" *Journal of Broadcasting and Electronic Media* 39, no. 4 (Fall 1995): 459–471.

Kunkel, Thomas, & Roberts, Gene. "Leaving Readers Behind: The Age of Corporate Newspapering." *American Journalism Review* 23 (May 2001): 32–41.

Kwitney, J. "The High Cost of High Profits." *Washington Journalism Review* 12, no. 5 (June 1990): 19–29.

Labaton, Stephen. "Justice Dept. Staff Said to Be Opposing Satellite TV Merger." The *New York Times*, September 24, 2002, sec. A1, p.1.

Lacy, Stephen. "A Model of Demand of News: Understanding the Impact of Competition on Daily Newspaper Content." *Journalism Quarterly* 66, no. 1 (Spring 1989): 40–48, 128.

———. "Effects of Group Ownership on Daily Newspaper Content." *Journal of Media Economics* 4, no. 1 (Spring 1991): 35–47.

———. "The Effects of Intracity Competition on Daily Newspaper Content," *Journalism Quarterly* 64 (Summer/Autumn 1987): 282–290.

———. "The Financial Commitment Model of News Media Competitions." *Journal of Media Economics* 5, vol. 2 (Summer 1992): 5–21.

———. "The Impact of Intercity Competition on Daily Newspaper Content." *Journalism Quarterly* 65 (Summer 1988): 399–406.

Lacy, Stephen, & Blanchard, Alan. "The Impact of Public Ownership, Profits, and Competition on Number of Newsroom Employees and Starting Salaries in Mid-Sized Daily Newspapers." *Journalism and Mass Communication Quarterly* 80, no. 4 (Winter 2003): 949–968.

Lacy, Stephen, & Fico, Fredrick. "Newspaper Content Quality and Circulation." *Newspaper Research Journal* 12 (Spring 1991): 46–57.

———. "Newspaper Quality and Ownership: Rating the Groups." *Newspaper Research Journal* 11 (Spring 1990): 42–56.

Lacy, Stephen, Fico, Frederick, & Simon, Todd F. "The Relationship Among Economic Newsroom and Content Variables: A Path Model." *Journal of Media Economics* 2, no.2 (1989): 51–66.

Lacy, Stephen, & Picard, Robert G. "Interactive Monopoly Power in the Daily Newspaper Industry." *Journal of Media Economics* 3, no. 3 (1990): 27–37.

Lacy, Stephen, & Shaver, Mary Alice. "The Impact of Intermedia and Newspaper Competition on Advertising Linage in Daily Newspapers." *Journalism and Mass Communication Quarterly* 76 (Winter 1999): 729–744.

Lacy, Stephen, Shaver, Mary Alice, & St. Cyr, Charles. "The Effects of Public Ownership and Newspaper Competition on the Financial Performance of Newspaper Corporations: A Replication and Extension." *Journalism and*

Mass Communication Quarterly 73 (Summer 1996): 332–341.

Lacy, Stephen, & Simon, Todd F. "Intercounty Group Ownership of Daily Newspapers and the Decline of Competition for Readers." *Journalism and Mass Communication Quarterly* 74 (Winter 1997): 814–825.

———. *The Economics and Regulation of United States Newspapers.* Norwood, NJ: Ablex, 1993.

Lange, A. & Van Loon, A. "Pluralism, Concentration and Competition in the Media Sector." Montpellier, Amsterdam: Institute of Audiovisual Telecommunication In Europe (IDATE) and Institute for Information Law (IVIR), December 1991.

Lange, David. "The Role of the Access Doctrine in the Regulation of the Mass Media: A Critical Review and Assessment." *North Carolina Law Review* 52 (1973): 1–91.

Larner, Robert J., & Meehan Jr., James W. "The Structural School, Its Critics, and Its Progeny: An Assessment," in Larner, Robert J., & Meehan Jr., James W., eds. *Economics and Antitrust Policy.* New York: Quorum Books, 1989, pp. 179, 180–191.

Learmonth, Michael. "EchoStar Posts Loss, Marketing Costs Rise." *Reuters,* May 6, 2004.

Legg Mason Wood Walker. *Telephone Wars Update.* Baltimore, Maryland: Legg Mason Wood Walker, April 3, 2000.

Leibowitz, Dennis. *Media and Communications Statistics: Industry Viewpoint.* New York: Donaldson, Lufkin & Jenrette, 1996.

Lemley, Mark A., & Lessig, Lawrence. "The End of End-to-End: Preserving the Architecture of the Internet in the Broadband Era." *UCLA Law Review* 48 (2001): 925.

Lenski, Jim, & Rose, Bill. *Internet and Multimedia 2006: On-Demand Media Explodes.* New York: Arbitron/Somerville, NJ: Edison Media Research, 2006.

Lenski, Jim, & Rose, Bill. *The Value of Internet Broadcast Advertising.* New York: Arbitron/Somerville, NJ: Edison Media Research, March 2004.

Lessig, Lawrence. *Code and Other Laws of Cyberspace.* New York: Basic Books, 1999.

Levin, Harvey J., *Broadcast Regulation and Joint Ownership of Media.* New York: New York University Press, 1960.

Levy, Jonathan D., & Setzer, Florence O. *Measurement of Concentration in Home Video Markets.* Washington, DC: Office of Plans and Policy, Federal Communications Commission, December 23, 1982, pp. 51–53.

Lewis, Charles. "Media Money: How Corporate Spending Blocked Political Ad Reform and Other Stories of Influence." *Columbia*

Journalism Review 39, no. 3 (September/October 2000): 20–27.

Lichter, S. Robert, Lichter, Linda S., & Rothman, Stanley. *The Media Elite: America's New Powerbrokers.* New York: Hastings House, 1990.

Lima, Cassio. "All Core Duo Models." *Hardware Secrets.* 13 March 2007. Last accessed on 6 Apr. 2006 at http://www.hardwaresecrets.com/article/311/1.

Lin, C. A. "Diversity of Network Prime-Time Program Formats During the 1980s." *Journal of Media Economics* 8, no. 4 (1995): 17–28.

Link, Albert N. "An Analysis of the Composition of R&D Spending." *Southern Economic Journal* 49 (1982): 342–349.

Litan, Robert E., & Shapiro, Carl. "Antitrust Policy during the Clinton Administration." Paper CPC01–022, Competition Policy Center, Univ. of California at Berkeley, July 1, 2001. Available at http://repositories.cdlib.org/iber/cpc/CPC01–022.

Litman, B. "The Economics of Television Networks: New Dimensions and New Alliances" in Alexander, A., Owers J. & Carveth, R. (eds) *Media Economics: Theory and Practice,* 2nd edn, Mahwah, NJ: The Lawrence Erlbaum Associates, 1998. 131–50.

Litman, B. R. "Economic methods of broadcasting research," in Dominick, J. R., & Fletcher, J. E., eds. *Broadcast Research Methods.* Boston: Allyn & Bacon, 1985, pp. 106–122.

———. "The Television Networks, Competition and Program Diversity." *Journal of Broadcasting* 23, no. 4 (1979): 393–410.

Litman, Barry R., & Bridges, J. "An Economic Analysis of Daily Newspaper Performance." *Newspaper Research Journal* 7, no. 3 (Spring 1986): 9–26.

Litman, Barry R., & Thomas, Laurie. "Fox Broadcasting Company, Why Now? An Economic Study of the Rise of the Fourth Broadcast 'Network.'" *Journal of Broadcasting and Electronic Media* 35, no. 1 (1991): 139–157.

Livesay, Harold C., & Porter, Patrick G. "Vertical Integration in American Manufacturing." *Journal of Economic History* 29 (1969): 494–500.

Lopatka, John E., & Page, William H. "Internet Regulation and Consumer Welfare: Innovation, Speculation, and Cable Bundling." *Hastings Law Journal* 52 (2001): 891.

Lopatka, John E., & Vita, Michael G. "The Must-Carry Decisions: Bad Law, Bad Economics." *Supreme Court Economic Review* 6 (1998): 61–121.

"Low-power TV survey notes progress, goals." *Electronic Media,* April 3, 1989.

Lozano, José-Carlos. "Foreign ownership of the media and telecommunications industries in Mexico." Presented at the Foreign Ownership Seminar. Tecnológico de Monterrey, Monterrey, Montreal, March 1, 2002.

Luening, Erich. "CBS, Viacom in Blockbuster Merger." *CNETNews.com.* September 7, 1999. Last accessed May 3, 2007 at http://news.com.com/2100-1023-230674.html.

Lunn, J., & Martin, S. "Market Structure, Firm Structure, and Research and Development." *Quarterly Review of Economics and Business* 26 (Spring 1986): 31–44.

Machet, E., & Robillard, S. *Television and Culture. Policies and Regulations in Europe.* Düsseldorf: The European Institute for the Media, 1998.

Maddigan, Ruth J. "The Measurement of Vertical Integration." *Review of Economics and Statistics* 63 (1981): 328–335.

Magazine Publishers of America. "Mergers and Acquisitions." 2007. Last accessed on January 7, 2008, at http://www.magazine.org/finance_and_operations/finance_operations_trends_and_magazine_handbook/20923.cfm.

Mallela, Parthasaradhi, & Nahata, Babu. "Theory of Vertical Control with Variable Proportions." *Journal of Political Economy* 88 (1980): 1007, 1014–1015.

Mansfield, Edwin. "Composition of R and D Expenditures: Relationship to Size of Firm Concentration, and Innovative Output." The *Review of Economics and Statistics* 63, no. 4 (1981): 610–615.

———. "Industrial Research and Development Expenditures: Determinants, Prospects, and Relation to Size of Firm and Inventive Output." *Journal of Political Economy* 72, no. 4 (August 1964): 319–340.

———. *Industrial Research and Technological Innovation: An Econometric Analysis.* New York: W. W. Norton, 1968.

Marcuse, Herbert. *One Dimensional Man: Studies in the Ideology of Advanced Industrial Society.* London: Routledge, 1964, p. 8.

Markoff, John. "A 3rd-Quarter Loss at Apple is Smaller Than Expected." The *New York Times,* July 17, 1997. p. D3.

Markoff, John. "Microsoft Acts to Enhance Web Package." The *New York Times,* August 13, 1996.

Martin, Hugh. *A Study of How a Strategy Creating Clusters of Commonly Owned Newspapers Affects Prices, Quality and Profits.* Ph.D. dissertation, Michigan State University, 2003.

Manne, Henry. "Mergers and the Market for Corporate Control." *Journal of Political Economy* 73, no. 2 (April 1965): 110–120.

Martin, Hugh. *A Study of How a Strategy Creating Clusters of Commonly Owned Newspapers Affects Prices, Quality and Profits.* Ph.D. dissertation, Michigan State University, 2003.

Matthews, Martha. "How Public Ownership Affects Publisher Autonomy." *Journalism and Mass Communication Quarterly* 73 (Summer 1996): 342–353.

McChesney, Robert W., & Schiller, Dan. "Foundations for the Emerging Global Debate about Media Ownership and Regulation." Technology, Business and Society Programme Paper 11, United Nations Research Institute for Social Development, 2003.

McClure, R. D., & Patterson, T. E. *The Unseeing Eye: The Myth of Television Power in National Politics.* New York: Putnam Books, 1976.

McCombs, Maxwell, & Shaw, Donald L. "The Agenda-Setting Function of Mass Media." *Public Opinion Quarterly* 36, no. 2 (Summer 1972): 176–187.

McConnel, Bill. "The National Acquirers: Whether Better for News or Fatter Profits, Media Companies Want in on TV/Newspaper Cross-Ownership." *Broadcasting and Cable,* December 10, 2001.

McCormick, Lynde. "What's Happening to Hollywood?" The *Christian Science Monitor,* December 12, 1980, p. B4.

McCormick, Robert E. "The Strategic Use of Regulation: A Review of the Literature," in *The Political Economy of Regulation: Private Interests in the Regulatory Process.* Washington, DC: Federal Trade Commission, March 1984, pp. 13, 18–25.

McCullough, B. D., & Waldon, Tracy. "The Substitutability of Network and National Spot Television Advertising." *Quarterly Journal of Business and Economics* 37, no. 2 (Spring 1998): 3–15.

McGee, John S., & Bassett, Lowell R. "Vertical Integration Revisited." *Journal of Law and Economics* 19, no. 1 (1976): 17–38.

McGowan, David. "Regulating Competition in the Information Age: Computer Software as an Essential Facility Under The Sherman Act." *Hastings Communications and Entertainment Law Journal* 18 (1996): 771, 804–806.

McKean, M. L., & Stone, V. A. "Why Stations Don't Do News." *Communicator,* 1991, pp. 23–24.

McKenzie, L.W. "Ideal Output and the Interdependence of Firms." *Economic Journal* 61 (December 1951): 785–803.

McLeod, Jack M., Moy, Patricia, & Scheufele, Dietram A. "Community, Communications, and Participation: The Role of Mass Media and Interpersonal Discussion in Local Political Participation." *Political Communication* 16, no. 3 (1999): 315–336.

McLaughlin, Linda. "An Economic Analysis of Subscriber Limits, Comments of the Writers

Guild of America Regarding Harmful Vertical and Horizontal Integration in the Television Industry," in FCC, Eight Annual Report, *In the Matter of the Status of Competition in the Market for the Delivery of Video Programming,* CS Docket No. 01–129, FCC 01–389 (adopted on December 27, 2001, released on January 14, 2002).

McManus, John. "A Market-Based Model of News Production." *Communication Theory* 5 (1995): 301–338.

McManus, J. H. "What Kind of a Commodity is News?" *Communications Research* 19 (1992): 787–805.

"MCU/MPU Market Keeps Growing." *EDN.* 5 May 2005. Last accessed on 24 May 2007 at http://www.edn.com/article/CA529824.html.

Meier, W. A., & Trappel, J. "Media Concentration and the Public Interest," in Mcquail, D., & Siune, K., eds. *Media Policy: Convergence, Concentration and Commerce,* London: Sage, 1998, pp. 38–59.

Merrill Lynch. *Data Networking Market Share/ Trends: Review and Outlook.* New York: Merrill Lynch, June 2000.

———. *The Matrix—4Q 01.* New York: Merrill Lynch, March 22, 2002.

Metz, Cade. "Whither Netscape?" *PC Magazine,* January 11, 2003.

Meyer, Philip, & Weardon, Stanley T. "The Effects of Public Ownership on Newspaper Companies: A Preliminary Inquiry." *Public Opinion Quarterly* 48 (1984): 564–577.

Miami Herald Publishing Co. v. Tornillo, 418 U.S. 241 (1974).

Mikkelsen, Kent W, & Stephen, E. *Business Software Alliance Economic Report: U.S. Software Industry Trends, 1987–1994.* Washington, DC: Economists Incorporated, 1995.

Miller, Mark Crispin. "Free the Media." *Nation,* June 3, 1996, p. 9.

———. "The Crushing Power of Big Publishing." *Nation,* March 17, 1997, p. 11.

———. "Who Controls the Music?" *Nation,* August 25, 1997, p. 11.

Milgrom, Paul, & Roberts, John. *Economics, Organization and Management.* Englewood Cliffs, NJ: Prentice Hall, 1992, pp. 552–569.

Milliot, Jim. "From Harcourt to Reed to Thomson." *Publishers Weekly* 248, no. 30 (July 23, 2001): 18.

———. "Sales, Losses Soar at Online Bookstores." *PublishersWeekly.com,* June 28, 1999. Last accessed on 24 May 2007 at http://www.publishersweekly.com/article/CA167043.html.

Millonzi, Joel C., & Noam, Eli M. *The International Market in Film and Television Programs.* Norwood, NJ: Ablex, 1993.

Milyo, Jeffrey. "FCC Media Ownership Study #6: The Effects of Cross-Ownership on the Local Content and Political Slant of Local Television News." *Federal Communications Commission.* FCC.gov, September 17, 2007. Last accessed on January 6, 2008, from http://hraunfoss.fcc.gov/edocs_public/attachmatch/DA-07-3470A7.pdf.

Moksalyuk, Alex. "10.87 mln Cable Set Top Boxes Sold in 2004." *ZDNet.* 23 November 2004. Last accessed on 8 May 2007 at http://blogs.zdnet.com/ITFacts/?p=6565.

———. "24 mln VOIP subscribers in 2008, Vonage, Time Warner, Cablevision Market Leaders." *ZDNet Research.* 15 January 2006. Last accessed on 8 May 2007 at http://blogs.zdnet.com/ITFacts/?p=9925.

More, Greg. "Regulators mold cellular market." *Telephone Engineer and Management,* August 1, 1984, p. 126.

"More People Seeking Wireless for Convenience's Sake." *Wireless Today,* June 28, 1999.

Morgan, Thomas D. *Cases and Materials on Modern Antitrust Law and its Origins.* 2nd ed. St. Paul, Minn.: West Group, 2001, pp. 604–06.

Morgan, Timothy Prickett. "HPC Server Market Explodes to $9.1 Billion in 2005." ITJungle. 4 Apr 2006. Last accessed on 31 May 2006 at http://www.itjungle.com/tlb/tlb040406-story08.html.

Morgan Stanley Dean Witter. *Data Networking/ Internet Infrastructure. The Internet Infrastructure. What Lies Ahead?* New York: Morgan Stanley Dean Witter, December 2000.

Morgensen, Gretchen. "A Pager in Every Pocket." *Forbes,* December 21, 1992, p. 210.

Mortensen, Frands, & Svendsen, Erik N. "Creativity and Control: The Journalist Betwixt His Readers and Editors." *Media, Culture and Society* 2 (1980): 169–177.

Morton, John. "Farewell to More Family Dynasties." *American Journalism Review* 17 (October 1995): 68.

———. "Wall Street Squeeze." *American Journalism Review* 27 (December/January 2006): 7.

Moses, Lucia. "TV or not TV? Few Newspapers are Camera Shy, But Sometimes Two into One Just Doesn't Go." *Editor and Cable,* August 21, 2000, p. 22.

Mott, Frank Luther. *Golden Multitudes: The Story of Best Sellers in the United States.* New York: Macmillan Co., 1947.

Mueller, Dennis C., & Tilton, John E. "Research and Development Costs as a Barrier to Entry." *Canadian Journal of Economics* 2, no. 4 (1969): 570–579.

Mukhopadhyay, Arun K. "Technological Progress and Change in Market Concentration in the U.S., 1963–77." The *Southern Economic Journal* 52, no. 1 (July 1985): 141–149.

Mungwun, A. F. *Video Recording Technology: Its Impact on Media and Home Entertainment.* Hillsdale, NJ: Lawrence Erlbaum Associates, 1989, pp. 152–155.

Murdock, Graham. "Concentration and Ownership in the Era of Privatization," in Marris, Paul, ed. *Media Studies.* 2nd ed. New York: NYU Press, 2000, pp. 142–155.

Napoli, Philip M. "Audience Economics: Media Institutions and the Audience Marketplace." New York: Columbia University Press, 2003.

———. "Audience Valuation and Minority Media: An Analysis of the Determinants of the Value of Radio Audiences." *Journal of Broadcasting and Electronic Media* 46 (2002): 180–181.

———. "Market Competition, Station Ownership, and Local Public Affairs Programming on Broadcast Television." *Journal of Communication,* 2007.

———. *Media Diversity and Localism: Meaning and Metrics.* Rahway: Lawrence Erlbaum Associates, 2007.

———. "Media Ownership Regulations and Local News Programming on Broadcast Television: An Empirical Analysis." *Journal of Broadcasting and Electronic Media,* 2007.

———. "A Principal-Agent Approach to the Study of Media Organizations: Toward a Theory of the Media Firm." *Political Communication* 14 (April 1, 1997): 207–219.

Nasaw, David. *The Chief: The Life of William Randolph Hearst.* Boston: Houghton Mifflin, 2001.

National Telecommunications and Information Administration, "Changes, Challenges, and Charting New Courses: Minority Commercial Broadcast Ownership in the United States," Washington, DC, U.S. Department of Commerce, December 2000.

Navasky, Victor S. *A Matter of Opinion.* New York: Farrar, Straus and Giroux, 2005.

NCTA. *Cable Developments 2002.* Washington, DC: NCTA, Vol. 26, no. 1, 2002.

———. *Cable and Telecommunications Industry Overview 2002,* 2002, p. 10.

Ness, Susan. "Regulation Media Competition: The Development and Implications of the FCC's New Broadcast Ownership Rules." Keynote Address, American University Washington College of Law, November 14, 2003.

Nesvold, Peter. *Communications Breakdown: Developing an Antitrust Model for Multimedia Mergers and Acquisitions.* Last accessed on January 4, 2008, from http://www.vii.org/papers/peter.htm.

Netanal, Neil. "Is the Commercial Mass Media Necessary, or Even Desirable, for Liberal Democracy?" Working paper, TPRC Conference on Information, Communications, and Internet Policy, October 2001, pp. 20–24.

Newspaper Association of America. "Total Paid Circulation." *Naa.org.* 2007. Last accessed on January 4, 2007, from http://www.naa.org/TrendsandNumbers/Total-Paid-Circulation.aspx.

Nicholson, Paul. "Time Warner: A Media Colossus Whose Growth is Driven by Global Ambition." *Television Business International,* October 1992, pp. 32–34.

Nishuilleabhain, Aine, & Noam, Eli M., eds. *Private Networks and Public Objectives.* Amsterdam: Elsevier, 1996.

Nixon, Raymond B. "Trends in U.S. Newspaper Ownership: Concentration with Competition." *Gazette* 14 (March 1968): 181–193.

Noam, Eli M. "Assessing the Impacts of Divestiture and Deregulation in Telecommunications." *Southern Economic Journal* 59, no. 3 (January 1993): 445.

———. "Broadband in America," in Eberspächer, Jörg, & Quadt, Hans-Peter, eds. *Broadband Perspectives,* Berlin: Springer, 2004.

———. "Broadband Networks, Megaband Hype, and Narrowband Research," at *TPRC 2002 Proceedings.*

———. "Cable Productivity Likely to Slow." *Cable TV and New Media,* March 1986, p. 8.

———. "Corporate and regulatory strategy for the new network century," in *International Handbook of Telecommunications Economics.* Cheltenham: Edward Elgar Publishers, 2003, pp. 1–11.

———. "Convergence and the Market Failure of the Information Economy," presented at *Proceedings of the Conference on the Future of Information.* Haifa, Israel, 2004.

———. "The Cyber-communications Revolution," presented at *Telecommunications and Broadcasting Reaching the People.* University of Pretoria, Pretoria, South Africa, 1996.

———. *Cyber-TV. Thesen zur dritten Fernsehrevolution.* Gütersloh: Verl. Bertelsmann Stiftung, 1996, pp. 1–46.

———. "Digital Convergence and the Next Cyber Trade-Wars." *Communications and Strategies,* 2000.

———. "Did AT&T Die In Vain? An Empirical Comparison of AT&T and Bell Canada." *Federal Communications Law Journal* 61, no. 1 (December 2008): 199

———. "A Dim Future for Consumer Electronics?" *Financial Times Online.* 10 March 2005. Last accessed on May 24, 2007 at http://www.ft.com/cms/s/39d1f78a-917e-11d9-8a7a-00000e2511c8.html.

———. "A First Amendment for the internet." *Financial Times*. 15 November 2005. Last accessed on May 10, 2007, at http://search.ft.com/ftArticle?id=051115008975ll.

———. "Eli Noam: How to Measure Media Concentration." *Financial Times Online*, FT.com. August 30, 2004. Last accessed on February 29, 2008, from http://search.ft.com/ftArticle?queryText=media+concentration&y=0&aje=true&x=0&id=040830005743&ct=0&nclick_check=1.

———. "Heroes of the Internet Frontier." *Financial Times*. 16 December 2004. Last accessed on 9 May 2007 at http://search.ft.com/ftArticle?id=051128005813.

———. *Interconnecting the Network of Networks*. Cambridge, MA: MIT Press, 2001.

———. "Internet and Development," in *International Handbook of Telecommunications Economics*. Cheltenham: Edward Elgar Publishers, 2002.

———. "The Internet: Still Wide Open and Competitive?" *Oxford Internet Institute, Internet Issue Brief* 1, August 2003.

———. "The Internet's Third Wave." *Financial Times*. 28 llNovember 2005. Last accessed on 10 May 2007 at http://search.ft.com/ftArticle?id=051128005813.

———. "Moore's Law at risk from industry of delay." *Financial Times*. 19 January 2006. Last accessed on May 9, 2007, at http://www.ft.com/cms/s/c22f7fa4–891b-11da-94a6-0000779e2340.html.

———. "The Next Frontier for Openness: Wireless Communications," in Noam, Eli M., & Steinbock, Dan, eds. *Competition for the Mobile Internet*. New York: Springer-Verlag, 2003, pp. 21–38.

———. "Opening the 'Walled Airwave,'" in Entman, R. ed. *Telecommunications Competition In A Consolidating Marketplace*. Queenstown, MD: The Aspen Institute, 2002, pp. 33–55.

———. *Privacy in Telecommunications: Markets, Rights, and Regulations*. Prospects, Cleveland: United Church of Christ, 1994.

———. "Reconnecting Communications Studies With Communications Policy." *Journal of Communications* 43, no. 3 (Summer 1993): 199–206.

———. "Spectrum Auction: Yesterday's Heresy, Today's Orthodoxy, Tomorrow's Anachronism. Taking the Next Step to Open Spectrum Access." Journal of Law and Economics. Volume 41, Issue S2, October 1998 pp. 765–790.

Noam, Eli M. *Telecommunications in Latin America*. New York: Oxford University Press, 1998.

———. *Telecommunications in Europe*. New York: Oxford University Press, 1992.

———. *Telecommunications Regulation: Today and Tomorrow*. New York: Harcourt Brace Jovanovich, 1983.

———. *Television in Europe*. New York: Oxford University Press, 1991.

———. "An Unfettered Internet? Keep Dreaming." The *New York Times*, CXLVI: 50850, July 11, 1997.

———. "Universal Internet Access: The USA and the European Countries Between Regulation and Deregulation of the Internet," presented at *Academy for the Third Millennium*. Munich, Germany, 1998.

———. "VOIP in America," presented at *German Telecom Regulatory Agency, Annual Conference*. Germany, 2004.

———. "The Web is Bad for Democracy." The *Financial Times*. 28 August 2002. Last accessed on 9 May 2007 at http://search.ft.com/ftArticle?queryText=%E2%80%9CThe+Web+is+Bad+for+Democracy.%E2%80%9D+&y=0&aje=true&x=0&id=020828006319.

———. "Will the Book Become the Dumb Medium." *Educom Review* 33, no. 2 (March/April 1998): 18–24.

———. "Will Internet TV be American?" *Trends in Communications* 11, no. 2 (2003): 101–109.

Noam, Eli M., ed. *Video Media Competition: Regulation, Economy, and Technology*. New York: Columbia University Press, 1985.

Noam, Eli, & Pupillo, Lorenzo, eds. "Peer-to-Peer Video: The Economic, Policy, and Culture of Today's New Mass Medium." New York: Springer, 2008.

Noam, Eli M., & Wolfson, A. J., ed. *Globalism and Localism in Telecommunications*. Oxford: Elsevier Science, 1997.

Noble, J. Kendrick, Jr., "Book Publishing," in Compaine, Benjamin, Guback, Thomas, Noble Jr., J. Kendrick & Sterling, Christopher, eds. *Who Owns the Media?* White Plains, NY: Knowledge Industry Publications, 1982, p. 30.

Nua Internet Surveys. "How many On-Line?" *NUA*. Last accessed on 2 March 2001 at http://www.nua.ie/surveys/how_many_online.

O'Brien, Daniel M., Jewell, R. Todd, & Seldon, Barry J. "Media Substitution and Economies of Scale in Advertising." *International Journal of Industrial Organization* 18 (2000): 1153–1180.

Odlyzko, Andrew. "The Economics of Electronic Journals," in Ekman, R., & Quandt, R., eds. *Technology and Scholarly Communication*, Berkeley, CA: University of California Press, 1998.

Olson, James W., & Spiwak, Lawrence J. "Can Short-Term Limits on Strategic Vertical Restraints Improve Long-Term Cable Industry

Market Performance?" *Cardozo Arts and Entertainment Law Journal* 13, no.2 (1995): 283–315.

"One Against the Other." *Network World*, April 24, 2000.

Ordover, Janusz A., & Saloner, Garth, "Predation, Monopolization, and Antitrust," in Schmalensee, R., & Willig, R. D., eds. *Handbook of Industrial Organization* 1, North Holland, 1989, pp. 538–596.

Ordover, Janusz A., Saloner, Garth, & Salop, Steven C. "Equilibrium Vertical Foreclosure." *American Economic Review* 80, no. 1 (March 1990): 127–142.

Organisation for Economic Co-operation and Development. "Media Mergers." Directorate for Financial, Fiscal, and Enterprise Affairs Competition Committee. JT00149676. OECD.org. 19 September, 2003, p. 52. Last accessed on January 4, 2008, from http://www.oecd.org/dataoecd/15/3/17372985.pdf.

Orwall, Bruce. "Disney's ABC Keeps Ad Hole Mouse-Friendly." The *Wall Street Journal*, New York, July 17, 1997, p. B1.

Osur, Elizabeth. *Sony Reiterates Video Game HW Forecasts; CIR Industry Model Unchanged.* New York: Citigroup, January 26, 2006.

Overholser, Geneva. "What's So Crazy About A Board That Knows Journalism?" *Columbia Journalism Review* 41, no. 2 (July/August 2002): 78–79.

Owen, Bruce M. "Regulatory Reform: The Telecommunications Act of 1996 and the FCC Media Ownership Rules." Prepared by the *Law Review of Michigan State University–Detroit College of Law* for the Fourth Annual James H. Quello Communication Policy and Law Symposium, Washington DC, February 27, 2003.

Owen, Bruce M. et al. *An Economic Analysis of the Broadcast Television National Ownership, Local Ownership and Cross-Ownership Rules.* Washington, DC: Economists Incorporated, 1995, p. 26.

Owen, Bruce M., & Wildman, Steven S. *Video Economics.* Cambridge, MA: Harvard University Press, 1992.

Ownership Concentration of Top Media and IT/Telecom Companies (1988–2001), Compact D—SEC. Bethesda, MD: Compact Disclosure Inc., 2005.

Ozanich, G. W., & Wirth, M. O. "Media Mergers and Acquisitions: A Communications Industry Overview," in Alexander A., Owers, J., & Carveth, R., eds. *Media Economics: Theory and Practice.* 2nd ed. Mahwah, NJ: Lawrence Erlbaum Associates, 1998, pp. 95–107.

Paetsch, Michael. *Mobile Communications in the U.S. and Europe.* Boston, MA: Artech House, 1993.

Page, Benjamin. "The Mass Media as Political Actors." *PS: Political Science and Politics* 29 (March 1996): 20–24.

"Paging and Land Mobile Radio in 1998: What it Was, What it Wasn't." *Land Mobile Radio News*, December 18, 1998.

"Paging Company Set to Declare Bankruptcy." The *New York Times*, April 15, 2002, p. 2.

Paletz, David L. *The Media in American Politics: Contents and Consequences.* New York: Longman, 1999.

Paltridge, Sam. *Internet Infrastructure Indicators.* Paris: OECD, Working Party on Telecommunication and Information Service Policies, Directorate for Science, Technology, and Industry, October 28, 1998.

———. *"Webcasting and Convergence: Policy Implications."* OECD/GD 97, no. 221. OECD. 1 November 1997. Last accessed on 10 May 2007 at http://www.oecd.org/dataoecd/12/13/2091391.pdf.

Paraskevas, Joe. "CanWest Defends Media Ownership." *Times Colonist*, Victoria, Canada, April 14, 2005, p. C13.

Parker, Adam S. *Intel and AMD: Part I—Microprocessor Volumes, Pricing, and Share Trends—AMD Looks Better.* New York: Sanford Bernstein/ Reuters Research-on-Demand, 2006.

"PDA Sales Fall Worldwide." *TWICE* 19, no. 4 (February 9, 2004): 1.

Peck, Drew. *Semiconductor Primer.* New York: SG Cowen Securities, 2001.

Perry, Martin K. "Vertical Integration: Determinants and Effects," in Schmalensee, Richard, & Willig, Robert D., eds. *Handbook of Industrial Organization.* 1st ed. Amsterdam: North Holland, 1989.

Peterson, Iver. "Media." The *New York Times*, September 23, 1996, p. D7.

Petrozello, Donna. "Syndication Faces Boom Times: Radio Syndication." *Broadcasting and Cable,* June 9, 1997, p. 22.

Picard, Robert G. "Economics of the Daily Newspaper Industry," in Alexander, A., Owes, J., & Carveth, R., eds. *Media Economics: Theory and Practice.* New York: Lawrence Erlbaum Association, 1993, pp. 181–204.

———. "Measures of Concentration in the Daily Newspaper Industry." *Journal of Media Economics* 1 (1988): 61–74.

———. *The Economics and Financing of Media Companies.* New York: Fordham University Press, 2002.

Picard, Robert, & Soloski, John. "The New Media Lords: Why Institutional Investors Call The Shots." *Columbia Journalism Review* 35, no. 3 (September/October 1996): 11–12.

Pierce Jr., Richard J. *Economic Regulation.* Cincinnati, OH: Anderson, 1994 Publishing Co., pp. 261–274.

Pike & Fischer. *The Telecommunications Act of 1996: Law and Legislative History.* Bethesda, MD: Pike & Fischer, Inc., 1996.

"The Plumber in Peoria: Justice Inquiry into Motorola's Radio Deal Examines whether Dispatch Customers Will Be Left Behind." *Information Law Alert: A Voorhees Report* 2, no. 12 (July 8, 1994).

Plunkett Research. *Plunkett's Information Technology Almanac.* Houston, TX: Plunkett Research, 2001, p. 26.

Pogrebin, Robin. "Magazines Multiplying as Their Focuses Narrow," The *New York Times,* January 2, 1997, p. C2.

Pollack, Andrew. "ANEC Says Its Computer is Fastest." The *New York Times,* November 8, 1994, p. D7.

Posner, Richard A. "The Chicago School of Antitrust Analysis." *University of Pennsylvania Law Review* 127 (1979): 925.

———. *Antitrust Law: An Economic Perspective.* Chicago, IL: University of Chicago Press, 1976.

Powell, Michael K. "The Public Interest Standard: A New Regulator's Search for Enlightenment," presented at the *17th Annual Legal Forum on Communications Law.* Las Vegas, April 5, 1998.

"The Power of the FCC to Regulate Newspaper-Broadcast Cross-Ownership: The Need for Congressional Clarification." *Michigan Law Review* 25, no. 8 (August 1977): 1708–1731.

Powers, A. "Competition, Conduct, and Ratings in Local Television News: Applying the Industrial Organization Model." *Journal of Media Economics* 6, no. 2 (1993): 37–44.

Powe Jr., Lucas A. "Scholarship and Market." *George Washington Law Review* 56, no. 1 (November 1987): 172–186.

Pozen, Robert. "Institutional Investors: The Reluctant Activists." *Harvard Business Review,* January/February 1994, p. 140.

Pratt, John W., & Zeckhauser, Richard J. "Principals and Agents: An Overview," in Pratt, John W., & Zeckhauser, Richard J., ed. *Principles and Agents: The Structure of Business.* Boston, MA: Harvard Business School Press, 1985, pp. 1–36.

Prehn, Ole, & Jauert, Per. "Ownership and Concentration in Local Radio Broadcasting in Scandinavia." *Nordicom Review* 1 (1996): 81–106.

"Prepared Statement of Senator John McCain Before the Senate Commerce, Science and Transportation Committee." *Federal News Service,* April 10, 1997.

Primeaux, W. J., Rice, E., & Simon, J. "The Price Effects of Monopoly Ownership in Newspapers." *Antitrust Bulletin* 31, no. 1 (Spring 1986): 113–131.

Pritchard, David. "A Tale of Three Cities: 'Diverse and Antagonistic' Information in Situations of Local Newspaper/Broadcast Cross-Ownership." *Federal Communications Law Journal* 54 (December 2001): 31–51.

Radio Advertising Bureau. *2006 RAB Radio Marketing Guide and Factbook.* Texas: Radio Advertising Bureau, 2006.

———. *Radio Advertising Bureau 2006 Marketing Report.* Texas: Radio Advertising Bureau, June 2006.

———. *Radio Marketing Guide and Fact Book for Advertisers 2001–2002 Edition.* New York: Radio Advertising Bureau, 2002.

Raff, Daniel M. G. "Superstores and the Evolution of Firm Capabilities in American Bookselling." *Strategic Management Journal* 21, no. 10/11 (October/November 2000): 1043–1059.

Ravenscraft, David J., & Scherer, F. M. *Mergers, Sell-offs, and Economic Efficiency.* Washington, DC: Brookings Institution Press, 1986.

Ray, W. B. *FCC: The Ups and Downs of Radio-TV Regulation.* Ames, IA: Iowa State University Press, 1990.

Recording Industry of America. "2006 Year-End Shipment Statistics." *RIAA.com.* Last accessed on January 3, 2008, from http://76.74.24.142/6BC7251F-5E09–5359–8EBD-948C37FB6AE8.pdf.

Red Lion Broadcasting v. FCC, 395 U.S. 367 (1969).

Reid, Leonard N., & Whitehill King, Karen. "A Demand-side View of Media Substitutability in National Advertising: A Study of Advertisers Opinions about Traditional Media Options." *Journalism and Mass Communication Quarterly* 77 (Summer 2000): 292–307.

Reiffen, David, & Vita, Michael. "Is There New Thinking on Vertical Mergers?" *Antitrust Law Journal* 63 (1995): 922–924.

Renteria, Maria Elena Gutierrez. "Media Concentration in the Hispanic Market: A Case Study of TV Azteca vs. Televisa." The *International Journal on Media Management* 9, no. 2 (2007): 70–76.

Richard, Jack. "Directory of Internet Service Providers: May/June 1997." *Internet Architecture,* 1997.

Riordan, Michael H. "Anticompetitive Vertical Integration by a Dominant Firm." *American Economic Review* 88, no. 5 (1998): 1232–1248.

Riordan, Michael H., & Salop, Steven C. "Evaluating Vertical Mergers: A Post-Chicago Approach." *Antitrust Law Journal* 63 (1995): 513.

Rosenberg, J. B. "Research and Market Share: A Reappraisal of the Schumpeter Hypothesis." *Journal of Industrial Economics* 25, no. 2 (1976): 101–112.

Rosenfeld, Richard N. *American Aurora: A Democratic-Republican Returns.* New York: St. Martin's Press, 1997.

Rosengren, Karl Erik. "Sweden and its media scene—A bird's-eye view," in Rosengren, Karl Erik, ed. *Media Effects and Beyond.* 1st ed. London: Routledge, 1994, pp. 29–38.

Ross, David, & Scherer, F. M. *Industrial Market Structure and Economic Performance.* 3rd ed. Boston, MA: Houghton Mifflin, 1990.

Ross, Susan Dente. "First Amendment Trump?: The Uncertain Constitutionalization of Structural Regulation Separating Telephone and Video." *Federal Communications Law Journal* 50 (March 1998): 281–308.

Rosse, James N. "The Evolution of One-Newspaper Cities," presented at the *Federal Trade Commission Symposium on Media Concentration.* Federal Trade Commission, Washington, DC, December 14–15, 1978.

Rothenbuhler, Eric W. and John W. Dimmick, "Popular Music: Concentration and Diversity in the Industry, 1974–1980," *Journal of Communication* 33, no. 1 (Winter 1982): 143–149.

Rubinfeld, Daniel L., & Singer, Hal. J. "Open Access to Broadband Networks: A Case Study of the AOL/Time Warner Merger." *Berkeley Technology Law Journal* 16, no.2 (Spring 2001): 631.

Rubinovitz, R. *Market Power and Price Increases for Basic Cable Service Since Deregulation,* Washington, DC: Economic Analysis Regulatory Group, Department of Justice, August 6, 1991 (published in 1993).

———. "Market Power and Price Increases for Basic Cable Service Since Deregulation." *RAND Journal of Economics* 24, no. 1 (1993): 1–18.

Ruggiero, Greg, & Sahulka, Stuart, eds. *The Progressive Guide to Alternative Media and Activism.* New York: Seven Stories Press, 1999.

Rutenberg, Jim. "Fewer Media Owners, More Media Choices." The *New York Times,* December 2, 2002, sec. C, col. 2, p. 1.

Safire, William. "Localism's Last Stand." The *New York Times,* July 17, 2003, p. 27.

Salinger, Michael A. "Vertical Mergers and Market Foreclosure." *Quarterly Journal of Economics* 103, no. 2 (May 1988): 345–356.

———. "Vertical Mergers in Multi-Product Industries and Edgeworth's Paradox of Taxation." *Journal of Industrial Economics* 39, no. 5 (September 1991): 545–556.

Salop, Steven C., & Scheffman, David T. "Raising Rivals' Costs." *American Economic Review* 73, no. 2 (May 1983): 267–271.

Sánchez-Tabernero, Alfonso. "La Concentration des medias en Europe." Dusseldorf: EIM, 1993.

———. "Competition between Public Service and Commercial Television Broadcasting in the European Market," presented at 6th *World Media Economics Conference.* Centre d'Etudes Sure les Médias and Journal of Media Economics, HEC Montreal, Montreal, Canada, 12–15 May 2004.

———. *Media Concentration in Europe: Commercial Enterprise and the Public Interest.* Düsseldorf: European Institute for the Media, 1993.

———. "The Future of Media Companies: Strategies for an Unpredictable World," in Picard, R. G., ed. *Strategic Responses to Media Market Changes.* Jönköping, Sweden: Media Management and Transformation Centre, Jönköping International Business School, 2004, pp. 19–34.

Sarasin Research Group. *Chips Quo Vaditis.* Basel: Sarasin Research Group, November 2000, p. 27.

Schement, Jorge Reina. "Wiring the Castle: Demography, Technology and the Transformation of the American Home." 6 June 2006. Massachusetts Institute of Technology. Last accessed on 24 May 2007 at http://web.mit.edu/comm-forum/forums/Schement%20MIT%202006.pdf.

Scherer, F. M. *Industrial Market Structure and Economic Performance.* Chicago, IL: Rand McNally, 1971.

———. *Innovation and Growth: Schumpeterian Perspectives.* Cambridge, MA: MIT Press, 1984.

———. "Market Structure and the Employment of Scientists and Engineers." *American Economic Review* 57 (1967): 524–553.

Scherer, F. M., & Ross, David. *Industrial Market Structure and Economic Performance.* Boston, MA: Houghton Mifflin, 1990.

Schiffrin, A. *The Business of Books.* New York: Verso, 2000.

Schlesinger, Arthur. *Prelude to Independence: The Newspaper War on Britain, 1764–1776.* New York: Knopf, 1958.

Schmalensee, Richard. "A Note on the Theory of Vertical Integration." *Journal of Political Economy* 81, no. 2 (1973): 442, 448.

Schmalensee, Richard, & Willig, Robert D., eds. *Handbook of Industrial Organization.* New York: North-Holland, 1989.

Schoenherr, Steven E. "History of Television." 15 March 2004. History Department at the

University of San Diego. Last accessed on 4 May 2007 at http://history.sandiego.edu/GEN/recording/television1.html.

Schudson, Michael. *Discovering the News: A Social History of American Newspapers.* New York: Basic Books, 1978.

Schwartzman, Andrew J. "Viacom-CBS Merger: Media Competition and Consolidation in the New Millennium." *Federal Communications Law Journal* 52 (2000): 513, 515–516.

Scott, John T. "Firm Versus Industry Variability in R&D Intensity," in Griliches, Zvi, ed. *R&D, Patents and Productivity.* Chicago, IL: Chicago University Press, 1984, p. 233.

Scoblete, Greg. "Vonage Stays No. 1 In *VoIP* Competition." *TWICE* 8 (May 22, 2006).

"Seagram Time Warner Stake not on Agenda, Allen Says." *Daily Variety,* January 29, 1996, p. 8.

"The Second 50 Years of the Fifth Estate: A Look Back at the Major Communications Events of the Year." *Broadcasting,* December 30, 1985.

Serrin, William, ed. *The Business of Journalism.* New York: New Press, 2000.

Shafer, Jack. "Big Media Octopuses, Cutting Off Tentacles." *Slate Magazine.* November 16, 2007. Last accessed on January 7, 2008, from Lexis Nexis Academic.

Shales, Tom. "Michael Powell and the FCC: Giving Away the Marketplace of Ideas." *Washington Post,* June 2, 2003, p. C01.

Shankland, Stephen. "FAQ: HD-DVD vs. Blu-ray." 1 October 2005. *CNET News.* Last accessed on July 17, 2006 at http://news.com.com/FAQ+HD+DVD+vs.+Blu-ray/2100–1041_3–5886956.html.

Shapiro, Carl. "Exclusivity in Network Industries." *George Mason Law Review* 7, no. 3 (Spring 1999): 673, 678.

———. "Mergers with Differentiated Products." *Antitrust,* Spring 1996, pp. 23, 28–29.

Shapiro, Carl, & Varian, Hal. *Information Rules.* Boston, MA: Harvard Business School Press, 1999.

Shapiro, Sidney A., & Tomain, Joseph P. *Regulatory Law and Policy: Cases and Materials.* 2nd ed. Carlsbad, CA: Lexis Law, 1998, pp. 405–408.

Shaver, Dan, & Shaver, Mary A. "Comparing Merger and Acquisition Activity in the U.S. and the European Union During the 1990s," presented at *5th World Media Conference.* The University of Central Florida, Turku, Finland, 2002.

Shepherd, William G. *The Economics of Industrial Organization.* Englewood Cliffs, NJ: Prentice Hall, 1985.

Shim, Richard. "Palm has the PDA World in Its Hand." *Zdnet UK News.* 29 September 2000. Last accessed 24 May 2007 at http://news.zdnet.co.uk/hardware/0,1000000091,2081686,00.htm.

Shiman, Daniel, Lynch, Kenneth, Stroup, Craig, and Almoguera, Pedro. "FCC Media Ownership Study #4: News Operations." *Federal Communications Commission.* FCC. gov. July 31, 2007. Last accessed on January 6, 2008, from http://hraunfoss.fcc.gov/edocs_public/attachmatch/DA-07-3470A5.pdf.

Shin, Dong-Hee. "Convergence of Telecommunications, Media and Information Technology, and Implications for Regulation." *Journal of Policy, Regulation and Strategy for Telecommunications* 8, no. 1 (2006): 42–56.

Shiver, Jube. "Changes in Industry dim Relevance of Microsoft Trial Technology: Allegation of unfair use of dominance is undermined as AOL-Netscape merger strengthens rivals." *Los Angeles Times,* December 14, 1999.

Shrieves, Ronald E. "Market Structure and Innovation: A New Perspective." *Journal of Industrial Economics* 26, no. 4 (June 1978): 329.

Shughart II, William F. *The Organization of Industry.* Homewood, IL: Richard D. Irwin, 1990, p. 324.

Sidak, J. Gregory, & Spulber, Daniel F. "Deregulation and Managed Competition in Network Industries." *Yale Journal of Regulation* 15, no. 1 (Winter 1998): 117, 122–125.

Sinclair Broadcast Group, Inc. v. FCC, 284 U.S. 148 (2002).

Siwek, Stephen E., & Wildman, Steven S. "The Economics of Trade in Recorded Media Products," in Millonzi, Joel C., & Noam, Eli M., eds. *The International Market in Film and Television Programs.* Norwood, NJ: Ablex, 1993.

Small Entity Compliance Guide. Local Telephone Competition and Broadband Reporting, WC Docket No. 04–141, FCC Form 477, DA 05–1676 (June 16, 2005).

Snider, James H., & Page, Benjamin I. "Does Media Ownership Affect Media Stands? The Case of the Telecommunications Act of 1996," presented at the *55th MPSA Annual National Conference.* Midwest Political Science Association, Chicago, IL, April 1997.

Soderlund, Walter C., & Hildebrandt, Kai. *Canadian Newspaper Ownership in the Era of Convergence.* Edmonton, AB: University of Alberta Press, 2005.

Sonwalker, Prasun. "'Murdochization' of the Indian Press: From By-line to Bottom Line." *Media, Culture and Society* 24, no. 6 (2002): 821–834.

Sparrow, Bartholomew H. *Uncertain Guardian.* Baltimore, MD: Johns Hopkins University Press, 1999.

Speta, James B. "Handicapping the Race for the Last Mile?: A Critique of Open Access Rules for Broadband Platforms." *Yale Journal on Regulation* 17 (2000): 39.

———. "The Vertical Dimension of Cable Open Access." *University of Colorado Law Review* 71 (Fall 2000): 975.

Squire, Jason, ed. *The Movie Business Book.* New York: Fireside, 1992, p. 283.

Standard & Poor's Industry Surveys. *Telecommunications: Wireless.* Standard & Poor's Industry Surveys, December 2000.

Stapleton, Paul. *The 1997 Year End Recap and a 1998 Prognosis.* Walnut Creek, CA: The ISP Market Report. 1998. Available at http://www.boardwatch.Internet.com/mag/98/jan/bwm58.htm.

Starr, Paul. *The Creation of the Media: Political Origins of Modern Communications.* New York: Basic Books, 2004, p. 131.

The State of the News Media 2006: An Annual Report on American Journalism. May 2006. Project for Excellence in Journalism. Last accessed on 8 May 2007 at http://stateofthemedia.org/2006.

Stavitsky, A. G. "The Changing Conception of Localism in U.S. Public Radio." *Journal of Broadcasting and Electronic Media* 38 (1994): 19–34.

Steinbock, Dan. *The Nokia Revolution.* New York: American Management Association, 2001, p. 102.

———. *Triumph and Erosion in the American Media and Entertainment Industries.* Westport, CT: Quorum Books, 1995, pp. iii, 19.

Steiner, Peter. "Program Patterns and Preferences and the Workability of Competition in Radio Broadcasting." The *Quarterly Journal of Economics,* 66 (May 1952): 194–223.

Stets, Dan. "Wintel Threatening to Crush Competition." *Philadelphia Inquirer,* October 27, 1996.

Stewart, David W., & Ward, Scott. "Media Effects on Advertising," in Bryant, Jennings, & Zillman, Dolf, ed. *Media Effects: Advances in Theory and Research.* New Jersey Hove, UK: Lawrence Erlbaum Associates, 1994, p. 328.

Stigler, George J. "A Theory of Oligopoly." *Journal of Political Economy* 72 (1964): 55–59.

———. *The Organization of Industry.* Homewood, IL: Irwin, 1968, pp. 113–122.

Stone, Vernon A. "New Staffs Change little in Radio, Take Cuts in Major Markets TV." *RNDA Communicator,* March 1988, pp. 30–32.

Stoneman, Paul. *The Economic Analysis of Technological Change.* Oxford, England: Oxford University Press, 1983, pp. 46–49.

Streeter, T. "The Cable Fable Revisited: Discourse, Policy, and the Making of Cable Television." *Critical Studies in Mass Communications* 4 (June 1987): 174–200.

Strohmaier, Erich. *20 Years Supercomputer Market Analysis.* Berkeley, CA: Lawrence Berkeley National Laboratory, May 2005.

Sturm, John F. "Time for Change on Media Cross-Ownership Regulation." *Federal Communications Law Journal* 57, no. 2 (March 2005): 201.

Sulkin, Allan. *2004 USA PBX Market Review: IP Telephony Drives PBX Market Resurgence.* Hackensack, NJ: TEQConsult Group, 2004.

Sullivan, Lawrence. "Economics and More Humanistic Disciplines: What Are the Sources of Wisdom for Antitrust?" *University of Pennsylvania Law Review* 1214 (1977): 125.

Sunstein, Cass. *Republic.com.* Princeton, NJ: Princeton University Press, 2001.

Süssenbacher, Daniela. "Foreign Ownership in SEE Region." *deScripto* 2 (2005): p. 11.

Tebbel, John, & Zuckerman, Mary Ellen. *The Magazine in America, 1741–1990.* New York: Oxford University Press, 1991, pp. 140–141.

Tedeschi, Bob. "As Clear Channel Enters the Fray, Online Radio Looks to Be Coming of Age." The *New York Times,* July 18, 2005.

Telecommunications Act of 1996, Pub. L. No., 104–104, 110 Stat. 56 (1996).

Telecommunication Industry Analysis. McGraw Hill: Northern Business Information, 1997.

Telecommunications Industry Association. *Annual Report 2004.* Arlington, VA: Telecommunications Industry Association. Available at http://www.tiaonline.org/business/media/reports/documents/AnRpt04.pdf.

Television and Cable Fact Book. Washington, DC: Warren Publishing, 1987, 1989, 1992, 1996, 2001, 2003, and 2006 editions.

Tewary, Amrit, & Wang, Nelson. *Industry Surveys: Semiconductors.* Standard & Poor's, February 24, 2005.

Thierer, Adam D., "Media Myths: Making Sense of the Debate Over Media Ownership." Washington D.C.: The Progress & Freedom Foundation, 2005.

Thomson Gale Research Reporters. *Market Share Reporter, 2002.* Detroit, MI: Thomson Gale Research Reporters, 2002.

Tılıç, Doğan. "Media Ownership Structure in Turkey." Ankara: Progressive Journalists Association, January 2000.

"The Times Music Index." *Los Angeles Times,* December 31, 1998, p. C5.

Time Warner Entertainment Co. v. United States, 211 F.3d 1313, 1316–1322 (D. C. Cir. 2000).

Time Warner Entertainment Co., L.P. v. FCC, 240 F.3d 1126 (2001).

Tirole, Jean. *The Theory of Industrial Organization*. Cambridge, MA: MIT Press, 1988, pp. 173–181.

Tomaselli, Keyan G. "Ownership and Control in the South African Print Media: Black Empowerment After Apartheid." *Ecquid Novi* 18, no. 1 (1997): 21–68.

Top500 Supercomputer Sites. "TOP500 List—November 2007 (1–100)." *Top500.org.* November, 2007. Last accessed on January 10, 2008, from http://www.top500.org/list/2007/11/100.

Tortorici, Frank. *U.S. Institutional Investors Boost Control of U.S. Equity Market Assets.* New York: The Conference Board, 2005.

"Trans World Entertainment Corp: Net Income Increases 58%, Meeting Analyst's Estimate." The *Wall Street Journal,* New York, August 12, 1999.

Traub, Rie. "CD-ROM Drive Manufacturing." *Emedia Professional* 10, no. 9 (September 1997): 54.

Tucker, Irvin B., & Wilder, Ronald P. "Trends in Vertical Integration in the U.S. Manufacturing Sector." *Journal of Industrial Economics* 26, no. 1 (1977): 81–94.

Tunstall, Jeremy. "A Media Industry Perspective," in Anderson, James A., ed. *Communication Yearbook 14.* Beverly Hills, CA: Sage, 1978, pp. 163–186.

Turner Broadcasting System, Inc. v. FCC, 520 U.S. 180 (1997).

Turner Broadcasting System, Inc. v. FCC, 512 U.S. 622, 129 L.Ed.2d 497, 114 S.Ct. 2445 (1994).

Turnstall, J. & Palmer, M. "Media Moguls." London: Routledge, 1991.

UBS Warburg. *The Cable Sector: A Primer.* New York, analyst report, June 6, 2001.

United States v. Microsoft Corp., 253 F.3d 34, 51, 54 (D. C. Cir. 2001).

United States v. O'Brien, 391 U.S. 367 (1968).

United States v. Prime Star Partners, No. 93-CV-3913 (S.D.N.Y. June 9, 1993).

U.S. Department of Commerce. "1988 U.S. Industrial Outlook." Washington, DC, United States Government Printing, 29:30–31, January 1988.

U.S. Department of Justice. "Opening Markets and Protecting Competition for America's Businesses and Consumers." Washington, DC, Government Printing Office, Parts II and IV, April 7, 1995.

U.S. Department of Justice and the Federal Trade Commission, "Horizontal Merger Guidelines," Washington, DC, Government Printing Office, 57 Fed. Reg. 41552, dated April 2, 1992, revised, April 8, 1997.

U. S. General Accounting Office, "Telecommunications: National Survey of Cable Television Rates and Services," Washington, DC: Government Printing Office, August 4, 1989.

U. S. Government Accounting Office, "Follow-up National Survey of Cable Television Rates and Services," Washington, DC: Government Printing Office, June 13, 1990.

Vance, Ashley. "IBM and HP Monopolize Top 397 Supercomputers List." *The Register,* 28 June 2006. Last accessed on July 13, 2006 at http://www.theregister.co.uk/2006/06/28/top500_june_06/.

Vanhaverbeke, Wim, & Noorderhaven, Niels G. "Competition Between Alliance Blocks: The Case of the RISC Microprocessor Technology." *Organizational Studies.* Vol. 22, no. 1, 1–30 (2001).

Vane, Sharyn. "Taking Care of Business." *American Journalism Review* 24 (March 2002): 60–65.

Veronis Suhler & Associates. *Communications Industry Forecast.* 14th Annual Addition, New York: Veronis Suhler & Associates, July 2000, p. 138.

———. *Communications Industry Reports.* New York: 1995/2001.

Vogel, Harold L. *Entertainment Industry Economics.* 3rd ed. Cambridge: Cambridge University, 1994, p. 34.

———. *Entertainment Industry Economics.* 4th ed. Cambridge, England: Cambridge University, 2001, p. 58.

Von Alven, William H., ed. *The Billboard: A Newsletter for Part 68 Applicants.* February 1992.

Wagner, Jim. "Novell Acquires SUSE and IBM Tosses In." *Internetnews.com.* 4 November 2003. Last accessed on 18 July 2006 at http://www.internetnews.com/dev-news/article.php/3103951.

Waldfogel, Joel. "Consumer Substitution among Media," Media Bureau Staff Research Paper, Media Ownership Working Group, Federal Communications Commission, September 2002.

———. "Who Benefits Whom in Local Television Markets?" *Brookings-Wharton Papers on Urban Affairs* 5 (November 2001): 257–305.

Walett, Francis G. *Massachusetts Newspapers and the Revolutionary Crisis, 1763–1776.* Boston, MA: Massachusetts Bicentennial Commission, 1974.

Wang, Spencer, Blackledge, John, & Chew, Aaron. *Media and Entertainment: Home Video 2005,* JP Morgan, 18 April 2005, via Thomson.

Warren-Boulton, Frederick R. "Vertical Control with Variable Proportions." *Journal of Political Economy* 82 (July 1974): 783, 794–96, 798, 799.

Warshofsky, F. *The Chip War: The Battle for the World of Tomorrow.* New York: Scribner, 1989, p. 12.

Waterman, David, & Weiss, Andrew A. *Vertical Integration in Cable Television.* La Vergne, Tennessee: AEI Press, 1997.

Waterson, Michael. "Vertical Integration, Variable Proportions and Oligopoly." *Economic Journal* 92, no. 365 (1982): 129–144.

Webb, G. Kent. *The Economics of Cable Television.* Lanham, MD: Lexington Books, 1983, pp. 15–16, 181–182.

Weiss, Leonard W. "The Structure-Conduct-Performance Paradigm and Antitrust." *University of Pennsylvania Law Review* 127, no. 4 (April 1979): 1104–1123.

Werbach, Kevin. "A Layered Model for Internet Policy." *Journal of Telecommunications and High Technology Law* 1 (2002): 58–64.

Werden, Gregory J. "Simulating the Effects of Differentiated Products Mergers: A Practical Alternative to Structural Merger Policy." *George Mason Law Review* 5, no. 3 (Spring 1997): 363, 368–69.

Westfield, Fred M. "Vertical Integration: Does Product Price Rise or Fall?" *American Economic Review* 71 (1981): 334, 335–346.

"Where PBX and KTS Markets Are Headed." *Telephone Engineer and Management,* November 1985, p. 67.

White, David M. "The 'Gatekeeper': A Case Study in the Selection of News." *Journalism Quarterly* 27 (1950): 383–390.

Wilkins, Karin Gwinn. "The Role of Media in Public Disengagement from Political Life." *Journal of Broadcasting and Electronic Media* 44, no. 4 (2000): 569–580.

Williams, Dmitri. "Synergy Bias: Conglomerates and Promotion in the News." *Journal of Broadcasting and Electronic Media* 46 (September 2002): 453–472.

Williams, G. "Evidence to Cross Media Ownership Review Submitted by the Campaign for Press and Broadcasting Freedom." London: CPBF, 1994.

Williams, George. "Review of the Radio Industry." *Federal Communications Commission.* FCC. gov, July 31, 2007. Accessed on January 7, 2008, from http://hraunfoss.fcc.gov/edocs_public/attachmatch/DA-07-3470A11.pdf.

Williamson, Oliver E. "Antitrust Enforcement: Where It's Been, Where It's Going." *St. Louis University Law Journal* 27 (1983): 289, 290–292, 312–313.

———. "Assessing Vertical Market Restrictions: Antitrust Ramifications of the Transaction Cost Approach." *University of Pennsylvania Law Review* 127 (April 1979): 953, 965.

———. "Innovation and Market Structure." *Journal of Political Economy* 73, no. 1 (1965): 67–73.

———. *Markets and Hierarchies, Analysis and Antitrust Implications.* New York: Free Press, 1975, pp. 29–30, 35–37.

———. *The Economic Institutions of Capitalism.* New York: Free Press, 1985, pp. 48–49.

———. "The Vertical Integration of Production: Market Failure considerations." *American Economic Review* 61, no. 2 (1975): 112–123.

Willoughby, Wesley F. "Are Two Competing Dailies Better than One?" *Journalism Quarterly* 32 (Spring 1955): 109–204.

Wilson, Robert W. "The Effect of Technological Environment and Product Rivalry on R&D Effort and Licensing of Inventions." *Review of Economics and Statistics* 59, no. 2 (May 1977): 171–178.

Wimmer, Kurt A. "Deregulation and the Future of Pluralism in the Mass Media: The Prospects for Positive Policy Reform." *Mass Communications Review,* 1988.

Winer, Laurence H. "The Signal Cable Sends—Part I: Why Can't Cable Be More Like Broadcasting?" *Maryland Law Review* 46 (Winter 1987): 212, 254–255.

Winsock, Dwayne. "Netscapes of Power: Convergence, Consolidation and Power in the Canadian Mediascape." *Media, Culture and Society* 24, no. 6 (2002): 795–819.

Wirth, Michail O. "Cable's Economic Impact on Over-the-Air Broadcasting." *Journal of Media Economics* (Fall 1990):. 39–53.

———. "The Effects of Market Structure on Television News Pricing." *Journal of Broadcasting* 28 (1984): 215–224.

"With Mergers Behind It, UMG Looks Ahead." *Billboard,* December 25, 1999, p. 78.

Woodhull, Nancy J., & Snyder, Robert W. *Media Mergers.* New Brunswick, NJ: Transaction Publishers, 1998.

Wu, Irene. "Canada, South Korea, Netherlands and Sweden: Regulatory Implications of the Convergence of Telecommunications, Broadcasting and Internet Services." *Telecommunications Policy* 28, no. 1 (2004): 79–96.

Wyly, Brendan. "Competition in Scholarly Publishing? What Publisher Profits Reveal" in *ARL: A Bimonthly Report on Research Library Issues and Actions from ARL, CNI, and SPARC.* Washington, DC: Association of Research Libraries, 1998.

Yoo, Christopher S. "Architectural Censorship and the FCC." *Southern California Law Review* 78 (Spring 2005): 669.

———. "Vertical Integration and Media Regulation in the New Economy." *Yale Journal on Regulation* 19, no.1 (Winter 2002): 171–300.

Young, Doug. "The PCS Auction." *Telecommunications,* July 1995, p. 21.

Zaller, J. R. *The Nature and Origins of Mass Opinion.* New York: Cambridge University Press, 1992.

Zerdick, Axel. *E-Conomics: Strategies for the Digital Marketplace.* New York: Springer Publishing Company, 2000.

Index